ABSOLUTE GENERA

Absolute Generality

Edited by

AGUSTÍN RAYO

and

GABRIEL UZQUIANO

CLARENDON PRESS · OXFORD

OXFORD
UNIVERSITY PRESS

Great Clarendon Street, Oxford OX2 6DP

Oxford University Press is a department of the University of Oxford.
It furthers the University's objective of excellence in research, scholarship,
and education by publishing worldwide in

Oxford New York

Auckland Cape Town Dar es Salaam Hong Kong Karachi
Kuala Lumpur Madrid Melbourne Mexico City Nairobi
New Delhi Shanghai Taipei Toronto

With offices in

Argentina Austria Brazil Chile Czech Republic France Greece
Guatemala Hungary Italy Japan Poland Portugal Singapore
South Korea Switzerland Thailand Turkey Ukraine Vietnam

Published in the United States
by Oxford University Press Inc., New York

First published 2006

British Library Cataloguing in Publication Data

Data available

Library of Congress Cataloging in Publication Data

Data available

Typeset by Laserwords Private Limited, Chennai, India
Printed in Great Britain
on acid-free paper by
Biddles Ltd., King's Lynn, Norfolk

ISBN 0–19–927642–0 978–0–19–927642–4
ISBN 0–19–927643–9 (Pbk.) 978–0–19–927643–1 (Pbk.)

1 3 5 7 9 10 8 6 4 2

Acknowledgements

We are grateful to a number of people for the help they have given us in editing this collection. We would like to thank Peter Momtchiloff for conceiving the project, and for his tireless enthusiasm throughout the process. Thanks are also due to Susan Beer, Catherine Berry, and Sarah Nattrass for their friendly, efficient, and forgiving work during the final stages of publication. We are grateful to an anonymous reader for critiquing the entire typescript, and to Matti Eklund and John MacFarlane for their thoughtful comments on our own contributions. We are also grateful to our authors, who went far beyond the call of duty by reading through the introduction and each other's chapters and sending detailed comments. This substantially improved the volume by smoothing out rough-edges and encouraging a healthy debate amongst contributions (special thanks in this regard are due to Kit Fine). Finally, we would like to thank Salvatore Florio and Alejandro Pérez Carballo for their exceptional work in compiling the index and reading through the proofs, and the Ohio State University and the Massachusetts Institute of Technology for funding Salvatore and Alejandro's work.

Contents

Contributors

Kit Fine is Silver Professor of Philosophy and Mathematics, New York University

Michael Glanzberg is Associate Professor of Philosophy, University of California, Davis

Geoffrey Hellman is Professor of Philosophy and Scholar of the College, University of Minnesota

Shaughan Lavine is Associate Professor of Philosophy, University of Arizona

Øystein Linnebo is Lecturer in Philosophy, University of Bristol

Vann McGee is Professor of Philosophy, Massachusetts Institute of Technology

Charles Parsons is Edgar Pierce Professor of Philosophy, Emeritus, Harvard University

Agustín Rayo is Associate Professor of Philosophy, Massachusetts Institute of Technology

Stewart Shapiro is O'Donnell Professor of Philosophy, The Ohio State University, and Professorial Fellow, the Arché AHRC Research Centre, University of St Andrews

Gabriel Uzquiano is CUF Lecturer in Philosophy and Tutorial Fellow of Pembroke College, University of Oxford

Alan Weir is Professor of Philosophy, University of Glasgow

Timothy Williamson is Wykeham Professor of Logic and Fellow of New College, University of Oxford.

Crispin Wright is Wardlaw Professor of Logic and Metaphysics, at the University of St Andrews, and Global Distinguished Professor of Philosophy and Visiting Professor of Philosophy, New York University

1

Introduction

Agustín Rayo and Gabriel Uzquiano

1.1 THE PROBLEM OF ABSOLUTE GENERALITY

Absolutely general inquiry is inquiry concerning absolutely everything there is. A cursory look at philosophical practice reveals numerous instances of claims that strive for absolute generality. When a philosopher asserts (1), for example, we generally take the domain of her inquiry to comprise absolutely everything there is:

(1) There are no abstract objects.

When presented with a purported counterexample, we do not regard it as open to the philosopher to reply that certain abstract objects are not relevant to her claim because, despite the fact they exist, they lie outside of her domain of inquiry.

Whether or not we achieve absolute generality in philosophical inquiry, most philosophers would agree that ordinary inquiry is rarely, if ever, absolutely general. Even if the quantifiers involved in an ordinary assertion are not explicitly restricted, we generally take the assertion's domain of discourse to be implicitly restricted by context.[1] Suppose someone asserts (2) while waiting for a plane to take off:

(2) Everyone is on board.

We would not wish to attribute her the claim that absolutely everyone in the universe is on board, only the claim that everyone in a group of contextually relevant people is on board.

The topic of this volume is the question whether we are able to engage in absolutely general inquiry, and, more importantly, whether we do as a matter of fact engage in absolutely general inquiry in philosophical and non-philosophical practice. This question breaks down into two related but distinct subquestions:

[1] The question of how this restriction takes place is a delicate and hotly contested issue. According to the standard approach, the phenomenon of quantifier domain restriction is a semantic phenomenon. But Bach (2000) has argued that it is best understood as a pragmatic phenomenon. In what follows, we shall assume the semantic approach for expository purposes. For a characterization of the standard view, and a discussion of the various forms it might take, see Stanley and Szabó (2000).

THE METAPHYSICAL QUESTION
Is there an all-inclusive domain of discourse?

THE AVAILABILITY QUESTION
Could an all-inclusive domain be available to us as a domain of inquiry?

In the special case of linguistic inquiry, it is natural to suppose that the availability question comes down to the question of whether our utterances could ever involve genuinely unrestricted quantifiers—quantifiers unburdened by any (non-trivial) restriction whatever, contextual or otherwise.

It may be of interest to note that the possibility of unrestricted quantification does not immediately presuppose the existence of an all-inclusive domain. One could deny that there is an all-inclusive domain and nevertheless grant that some of our quantifiers are sometimes *unrestricted*.[2] One could claim, for example, that although there is no all-inclusive domain, there are utterances of (1) in which no linguistic or contextual mechanisms impose any restrictions whatever on the quantifier. Such utterances would not be absolutely general since the quantifiers would not range over an all-inclusive domain, but they would nonetheless be unrestricted.[3] (It is an interesting question, however, what the truth-conditions of an unrestricted but non-absolutely general utterance would consist in.)[4] If, on the other hand, one believed both that there is an all-inclusive domain and that our quantifiers are sometimes genuinely unrestricted, then one should presumably believe that our discourse is sometimes absolutely general.

A word on our use of the term 'domain'. We shall be careful not to assume that the existence of an all-inclusive domain requires the existence of a set (or set-like object) of which all objects are members. More generally, when we speak of a domain consisting of certain objects, we shall not assume that there must be a set (or set-like object) of which all and only the objects in question are members; the only requirement we take for granted is that there be such objects. We will return to this point in Section 1.2.2.

1.1.1 A Disclaimer

It would be disingenuous to suggest that we have taken a neutral stance in our characterization of the debate. Notice, for example, that our very statement of the topic

[2] As far as we know this point was first emphasized by Kit Fine. For further discussion, see Fine, Hellman and Parsons' contributions below.

[3] Someone who combines the view that there is no all-inclusive domain with the view that our quantifiers are sometimes absolutely unrestricted might give an affirmative answer to the availability question in the special case of linguistic inquiry. It might be claimed, in particular, that since there are no linguistic or contextual mechanisms restricting the relevant quantifiers, the all-inclusive domain would be available to us as a domain of inquiry, if only it existed. Were the world to cooperate, absolute generality would be achievable.

[4] For relevant discussion, see Lavine's contribution to the volume.

of the volume—'whether there is (or could be) inquiry concerned with absolutely everything'—itself purports to be concerned with absolutely everything.

Notice, moreover, that in characterizing an 'absolutist' as a proponent of (3):

(3) There is (or could be) inquiry concerned with absolutely everything,

one tacitly presupposes that the debate has been settled in favor of the absolutist, since (3) is concerned with absolutely everything on its intended interpretation. Similarly, in characterizing a 'non-absolutist' as a proponent of the negation of (3):

(4) There isn't (or couldn't be) inquiry concerned with absolutely everything.

one tacitly presupposes that the debate has again been settled in favor of the absolutist, since (4), like (3), is concerned with absolutely everything on its intended interpretation.

Of course one might insist that domains of (3) and (4) should be regarded as somehow restricted. But then (3) and (4) would be beside the point. Each of the two claims prejudges the debate in favor of the absolutist when taken at face value and is irrelevant to the debate when not taken at face value. Absolutists might take this to be a point in their favor. They might suggest that whereas they are in a position to give an adequate statement of the debate from their point of view, it dubious whether it is possible to state the view under consideration from the point of view of a non-absolutist.[5]

Even if one is convinced by the absolutist, one should remember that the mere fact that one is not able to characterize a certain state of affairs need not imply that the state of affairs in question fails to obtain. Moreover, non-absolutists might be in a position to gain philosophical ground even if they are not in a position to produce a statement of their view. Conspicuously, they can attempt to derive a *reductio* from the absolutist view, as characterized by the absolutist.[6]

In order to facilitate our exposition in the remainder of this introduction, we will continue to describe the debate from an absolutist perspective, while doing our best to ensure that it does not affect the justice with which non-absolutist arguments are presented.

[5] Non-absolutists might try to articulate their position with the help of a conditional:

(∗) If D is a domain, then there is some individual not in D.

But here it is crucial that (∗) not be read as a universally quantified sentence ranging over all domains. It is to be regarded as 'typically ambiguous' (or 'systematically ambiguous'). But ambiguous between what and what? The obvious response: 'ambiguous between *all* domains', will presumably not do. This has led some philosophers to doubt whether the required kind of ambiguity may be adequately elucidated. For discussion, see Parsons (1974), Parsons (1977), Glanzberg (2004) and Williamson (2003). See also Hellman, Lavine and Parsons' contributions below.

[6] As Williamson emphasizes in his contribution to this volume, the possibility of a *reductio* would appear to be incompatible with the idea that one could find a less-than-all-inclusive domain D such that each of the absolutist's purportedly absolutely general assertions would be true when restricted to D. For further discussion of this sort of idea, see Section 1.2.3 below.

1.2 SKEPTICAL ARGUMENTS

In this section we will discuss some influential arguments against the possibility of absolutely general inquiry. The arguments support a negative answer to the metaphysical question or to the availability question or to both.

1.2.1 Indefinite Extensibility

An influential strategy for casting doubt on the prospects of absolute generality derives from the work of Michael Dummett.[7] It is based on the thought that certain concepts are *indefinitely extensible*. Indefinitely extensible concepts are usually taken to be ones lacking definite extensions. They are instead said to be subject to principles of extendibility which yield a hierarchy of ever more inclusive extensions. The concepts *set* and *ordinal* are often taken to be paradigm cases of indefinite extensibility. Accordingly, should one attempt to specify an extension for *set* or *ordinal*, proponents of indefinite extensibility would claim to be able to find a more inclusive extension by identifying a set or an ordinal that is not in the extension one had specified.[8]

Indefinite extensibility considerations are motivated by a certain view of the set-theoretic antinomies. To appreciate this, it may be helpful to begin by considering and contrasting two different attitudes one might take towards Russell's Paradox.[9] The Paradox arises from the observation that the schema of Naïve Comprehension:

(5) $\exists y \forall x (x \in y \leftrightarrow \phi(x))$, where $\phi(x)$ is any formula not containing 'y' free,

has as an instance:

(6) $\exists y \forall x (x \in y \leftrightarrow x \notin x)$.

But (6) entails each of the following in classical first-order logic:

(7) $\forall x (x \in r \leftrightarrow x \notin x)$,

(8) $r \in r \leftrightarrow r \notin r$.

And (8) is a contradiction.

A common line of response to the Paradox concedes that the argument from Naïve Comprehension to (8) is valid but insists that Naïve Comprehension—and, in particular, its instance (6)—should be rejected: there is no set of all non-self membered sets.

[7] For example, Dummett (1963) and Dummett (1991), pp. 316–19.

[8] Bertrand Russell had identified what appears to be the same pattern in his Russell (1906). See Shapiro and Wright's contribution for a discussion of Russell's thought and for an independent characterization of indefinite extensibility generally. For further discussion of indefinite extensibility, see Fine and Hellman's contributions below. It is worth noting that considerations of indefinite extensibility have played a positive role in the foundations of set theory; see chapter 2 of Hellman (1989).

[9] Our discussion of the paradox closely follows Cartwright (1994).

In contrast, friends of indefinite extensibility would contend that Naïve Comprehension is true, once properly interpreted, on the grounds that the lesson of the paradox is that r should be taken to lie outside the range of 'x'. The inference from (7) to (8) is therefore invalid, and (5)–(7) can all be true even if (8) is false.[10]

This latter attitude towards the paradox plays an important role in a standard argument for the indefinite extensibility of the concept *set*. The argument is based on a challenge: to supply an extension for the concept *set*. Should one respond to the challenge by offering some candidate extension E, one will be asked to consider the set r of all and only sets in E that are not members of themselves:

(9) $\forall x(x \in r \leftrightarrow x \notin x)$, where '$x$' ranges over sets in E.

The next step is to notice that if E contained all sets, r would have to lie within E and (9) would entail:

(10) $r \in r \leftrightarrow r \notin r$,

which is a contradiction. Thus a contradiction has been reached from the assumption that E contains all sets. Most proponents of indefinite extensibility take the lesson to be that supplying a definite extension for the concept *set* is impossible, and that *set* is indefinitely extensible.[11]

Of course, one might protest that the lesson of Russell's Paradox is that there is no such set as r and that it was therefore illegitimate for proponents of indefinite extensibility to insist upon (9). But it is precisely at this point that the attitude that proponents of indefinite extensibility take towards the Paradox comes into play. They will insist instead that when we take the range of 'x' in Naïve Comprehension to range over all and only members of E, a proper interpretation of Naïve Comprehension will still deliver the existence of r as an immediate consequence. But r will lie outside the range of 'x' and will therefore fail to be a member of E. The moral of the Paradox is not, we are invited to suppose, that there is no such set as r, but rather that r is not a member of E.

A variant of this argument, based on the Burali–Forti Paradox, is sometimes used to motivate the conclusion that the concept *ordinal* is indefinitely extensible. And it might be suggested that it follows from either of these arguments that the concept *self-identical* is indefinitely extensible.[12] Admittedly, there is room for doubting whether the concept *self-identical* exemplifies the reproductive pattern illustrated by, e.g. *set*, since it is not obvious that there is an extensibility principle for *self-identical* paralleling the extensibility principle for *set* (i.e. Naïve Comprehension). But perhaps one could argue for the indefinite extensibility of *self-identical* by making use of the observation that all sets are self-identical. From the assumption that a domain D contains all self-identical objects, one might reason that, since all sets are self-identical, D must

[10] See, for example, the discussion of indefinite extensibility in Fine and Lavine's contributions.

[11] Not all, however. Shaughan Lavine suggests, in his contribution, a different route to the view that the concept *set* is indefinitely extensible.

[12] It may be of interest to note that Williamson (1998) supplies an account of indefinite extensibility whereby *set* is indefinitely extensible, but *self-identical* is not.

have the domain E of all sets as a subdomain.[13] One might then use Naïve Comprehension to argue that there must be a set r outside the domain E, and hence a self-identical object outside D, contradicting one's original assumption.

The claim that there are indefinitely extensible concepts is not quite the claim that absolute generality is unattainable. But proponents of indefinite extensibility are typically well-disposed to go from the one to the other. Considerations of indefinite extensibility have been used to question the prospects of absolute generality in at least two different ways. One route is to question the metaphysical presumption that there is an all-inclusive domain of all objects. If the concept *self-identical* lacks a definite extension, what reason could there be for thinking that there is an all-inclusive domain? Of course, absolutists will insist that it is incumbent on proponents of this position to provide some sort of account of what the world is like if there is to be no all-inclusive domain. One kind of answer is inspired by Ernst Zermelo's picture of the universe of set theory as an open-ended but well-ordered sequence of universes, where each universe is strictly more inclusive than its predecessor.[14]

A more modest approach would draw linguistic conclusions but refrain from setting forth any metaphysical theses. The claim would then be simply that considerations of indefinite extensibility show that our quantifiers are systematically restricted to less-than-all-inclusive domains. But, of course, this sort of position must be supplemented with some account of the mechanisms by which the relevant restrictions are supposed to take place.[15]

1.2.2 The All-in-One Principle

A related argument against absolute generality is based on a principle first identified—but never endorsed—by Richard Cartwright:

> **All-in-One Principle** The objects in a domain of discourse make up a set or some set-like object.

With the All-in-One Principle on board, one might argue as follows. Suppose for *reductio* that there is an absolutely general discourse. By the All-in-One Principle, there is a set (or set-like object) with all objects as members. But the lesson of Russell's Paradox is that there is no set (or set-like object) with all objects as members. Contradiction.

There are two main lines of response to this argument. The first is to object that the argument presupposes that Russell's Paradox entails that there is no universal set (or set-like object). But this is only the case in the presence of the Principle of Separation:

[13] While this reasoning may seem plausible, it is not beyond doubt. For one could presumably combine the assumption that D is the domain of all self-identical objects with the further thesis that no subdomain of D is, as a matter of fact, the domain of all self-identical objects that are sets.

[14] This picture of the universe of set theory is developed in Zermelo (1930). For a discussion of the open-endedness of mathematics generally, see Hellman's contribution below.

[15] For suggestions, see Parsons (1974), Parsons (1977), Glanzberg (2004), and Glanzberg and Parsons's contributions below.

(11) $\forall z \exists y \forall x(x \in y \leftrightarrow \phi(x) \wedge x \in z)$, where $\phi(x)$ is any formula of the language not containing 'y' free

And there are set theories that countenance exceptions to the Principle of Separation in exchange for a universal set. (There are also theories of set-like objects that countenance exceptions to an analogue of Separation in exchange for an all-inclusive set-like object.)[16] A problem for this line of response is that the Principle of Separation seems to fall out of what are arguably the two best understood conceptions of set—the Iterative Conception and the Limitation of Size Conception. No set theory motivated by these conceptions allows for a universal set (or set-like object).

The second line of response is to object to the All-in-One Principle. Different motivations for the principle must be undercut by different lines of objection. One might be led to the All-in-One Principle by considerations of indefinite extensibility of the sort discussed in the last section. The obvious objection in that case would be to eschew the Principle of Naïve Comprehension and respond to Russell's Paradox by denying that there is a set of all and only nonselfmembered sets.

There is, however, an alternative motivation for the All-in-One Principle that does not immediately depend on considerations of indefinite extensibility. It begins with the observation that model theory—and, in particular, the model-theoretic characterization of logical consequence—requires quantification over all domains. But on the assumption that (singular) first-order quantification over objects is the only intelligible sort of quantification there is, model theory requires the truth of the All-in-One Principle.[17]

One response at this point, originally due to Richard Cartwright, grants for the sake of argument the claims that model theory requires quantification over domains and that first-order quantification over objects is the only intelligible sort of quantification there is. Instead, it questions the claim that model theory requires quantification over *all* domains. Cartwright's strategy relies on George Kreisel's observation that the material adequacy of the standard model-theoretic characterization of logical truth and logical consequence requires only quantification over *set-sized* domains of discourse.[18] So one might argue that as far as the model-theoretic characterization of first-order logical truth and logical consequence is concerned, the needs of model

[16] For an overview, see Forster (1995). Linnebo and Weir's contributions below both propose mixed theories of sets and properties that allow for properties applying to absolutely all there is. While Linnebo's contribution countenances exceptions to a principle of comprehension for properties, Weir's contribution countenances a revision of classical logic as the underlying logic.

[17] Timothy Williamson has recently articulated the motivation and confronted the argument against absolute generality that ensues in Williamson (2003). For additional discussions of the motivation and its role in arguments against absolute generality, see Linnebo and Parsons' contributions below.

[18] Kreisel's argument is remarkably simple. Suppose that the first-order sentence ϕ is a logical consequence of the set of first-order sentences Γ. Then since every set-sized model corresponds to a legitimate interpretation of the language, ϕ must be true in every set-sized model of Γ. Conversely, suppose that ϕ is true in every set-sized model of Γ. Then, by completeness, ϕ must be a deductive consequence of Γ. But since the axioms of the first-order predicate calculus are valid and its rules are validity-preserving, this means that ϕ must be a logical consequence of Γ. The argument is given in Kreisel (1967).

theory will be met even if the All-in-One Principle fails. Unfortunately, this reply is relatively unstable. It will break down, for instance, if one enriches a first-order language with a quantifier '*Qx*' such that '*Qx Fx*' is true just in case there are more *F*s than there are sets.[19] More generally, Kreisel's argument depends on the existence of a sound and complete deductive system for the language in question, so Cartwright's reply is not guaranteed to be available when one is concerned with languages for which there is no sound and complete deductive system, such as higher-order languages.[20]

An alternative to Cartwright's response is to deny the assumption that first-order quantification is the only intelligible sort of quantification there is.[21] One might contend, in particular, that second-order quantification (and higher-order quantification in general) is just as intelligible as standard first-order quantification, and propose a second-order regimentation of domain-talk.[22]

If one thought of second-order quantification as quantification over first-level Fregean concepts, talk of domains might be regimented as talk of first-level concepts, which are not objects.[23] But, of course, a Fregean interpretation of higher-order quantification is not compulsory. One could instead read higher-order quantification in terms of plural quantification, as in Boolos (1984). Apparently singular talk of domains could then be regimented as plural talk of the objects the domain consists of. For instance, the claim that the domain of Fs exists could be regimented as the claim that the Fs themselves exist. Plural quantifiers can be used to produce an adequate model-theory for first-order languages equipped with absolutely unrestricted quantifiers (and, when conjoined with plural predicates, an adequate model-theory for second-order languages).[24] A feature of this general line of response is that one finds oneself invoking in one's model theory logical resources that go well beyond the logical resources used in one's object language. So one faces a choice between doing without a model-theory for one's metalanguage or embracing an open-ended hierarchy of languages of ever-increasing strengths. Those who embrace a Fregean interpretation of higher-order quantification will presumably embrace such a hierarchy. But an open-ended hierarchy would seem to pose a special challenge for those who prefer a plural interpretation of second-order quantification, since it is doubtful

[19] Vann McGee made this point in McGee (1992).

[20] Kreisel's result can be extended to the case of higher-order languages by assuming suitable reflection principles. But the principles in question are provably independent of the standard axioms of set-theory (if consistent with them). For further discussion, see Rayo and Uzquiano (1999).

[21] This type of response was first explicitly articulated in Williamson (2003).

[22] The intelligibility of higher-order quantification is a hotly contested issue. Proponents of intelligibility include Boolos (1984), Boolos (1985a), Boolos (1985b), Oliver and Smiley (2001), Rayo and Yablo (2001), Rayo (2002) and Rayo's contribution below; skeptical texts include Quine (1986) ch. 5, Resnik (1988), Parsons (1990) and Linnebo (2003). For a different sort of proposal, see Linnebo's contribution below.

[23] By a first-level Fregean concept, we mean a Fregean concept under which only objects fall. Correspondingly, a second-level Fregean concept is one under which only first-level Fregean concepts fall, and, in general, an $n+1$-th level Fregean concept is one under which only n-level Fregean concepts fall.

[24] The details are developed in Rayo and Uzquiano (1999). Rayo and Williamson (2003) employs a similar model theory for the purpose of proving a completeness theorem for first-order logic with absolutely unrestricted quantifiers.

that there is a English reading, e.g. for third-order quantifiers corresponding to the plural reading for second-order quantifiers.[25]

1.2.3 The Argument from Reconceptualization

There is a tradition in philosophy according to which ontological questions are relative to a conceptual scheme, or to a language. It goes back to Rudolf Carnap and includes such recent philosophers as Hilary Putnam and Eli Hirsch.[26] Here is a suggestive example, due to Putnam.[27] We are asked to consider—as a Carnapian might put it—'a world with three individuals': x_1, x_2 and x_3. We are then asked to compare this description of the world with that of a 'Polish logician' who, bound by the principles of classical mereology, believes that the world contains *seven* individuals: x_1, x_2, x_3, $x_1 + x_2$, $x_1 + x_3$, $x_2 + x_3$ and $x_1 + x_2 + x_3$.[28] Putnam suggests that it is nonsensical to ask which of the rival descriptions is correct. Each of them is correct relative to a particular conceptual scheme, but there is no conceptual-scheme-independent fact of the matter as to what individuals there are in the world. And if there is no conceptual-scheme-independent fact of the matter as to what there is, then it is nonsensical to speak of a domain that is objectively all-inclusive. The most one should hope for is a domain which is all-inclusive by the lights of some conceptual scheme or other.[29]

One response to this argument is to note that nothing in Putnam's argument rules out the possibility that the apparent lack of objectivity is merely a matter of linguistic equivocation. For all that has been said, the interlocutors in Putnam's example might have different concepts of existence and objecthood, and therefore mean different things by their quantifiers. On this view, Putnam's scenario poses no obstacle to the *metaphysical* thesis that there is an all-inclusive domain. At most, it would pose an obstacle to the *linguistic* thesis that our use of the quantifiers is univocal.[30] Issues of semantic indeterminacy will be the focus of the next section.

1.2.4 The Argument from Semantic Indeterminacy

Even if one takes for granted that there is such a thing as an all-inclusive domain, one might worry about access. One might worry, in particular, that any use of a quantifier that is compatible with the all-inclusive domain is also compatible with some less-than-all-inclusive domain, and therefore that one could never *determinately* quantify over absolutely everything.

[25] For an attempt to address the issue, see Rayo's contribution below.

[26] A canonical statement of the view is given in Carnap (1950). Hilary Putnam discusses the view in Putnam (1987). A more recent discussion of a similar view occurs in Hirsch (1993).

[27] The example is used in Putnam (1987), pp. 18–19.

[28] The example presupposes that the Polish logician takes each of x_1, x_2 and x_3 to be mereological atoms.

[29] See Hellman and Parsons' contributions for discussions of this general strategy against absolute generality.

[30] Even the argument for equivocation might be resisted. See, for instance, Sider (2006).

W.V. Quine and Hilary Putnam have famously set forth arguments that can be taken to support this sort of indeterminacy.[31] One of the most influential is based on the following technical result:

> Let L be a countable first-order language, and assume that each closed term in L has an intended referent and that each predicate in L has an intended extension. Call an interpretation I of L *apt* if it assigns to each term in L its intended referent and to each predicate in L the restriction of its intended extension to I's domain.[32]
>
> If the intended domain is uncountable, then it is provable that if every sentence of L in a set S is true according to some apt interpretation with an all-inclusive domain, then every sentence in S is also true according to an apt interpretation with a less-than-all-inclusive domain.[33]

The lesson of this result, it might be claimed, is that any use of a first-order quantifier compatible with an all-inclusive (uncountable) domain is also compatible with a less-than-all-inclusive domain, and therefore that first-order quantifiers never determinately range over an all-inclusive domain. But as with most philosophical morals extracted from technical results, the conclusion only follows in the presence of substantive philosophical assumptions. One such assumption might be the thesis that only domains of discourse that are incompatible with the truth of an utterance can be ruled out as unintended.

Even though the formal result is unassailable, there are various ways in which the auxiliary philosophical assumptions might be questioned. One might, in particular, claim that factors other than truth might help determine the domain of quantification of our utterances. One strategy, developed by David Lewis in a broader context, is based on the view that certain collections of individuals are objectively more 'natural' than others: to a larger extent, they 'carve nature at the joints'. The objective naturalness of collections of individuals might be used to argue that some candidate semantic values for an expression are objectively more natural than others. One could then argue that—other things being equal—an assignment of semantic value is to be preferred to the extent that it is objectively more natural than its rivals. This allows one to resist the indeterminacy argument on the grounds that it neglects to take into account the constraint that a semantic interpretation be objectively natural.[34] Ted Sider has explicitly deployed this sort of argument in the context of discussions of absolute generality by claiming that an all-inclusive interpretation of the quantifiers is especially natural.[35]

[31] The arguments are developed in Quine (1968) and Putnam (1980). Field (1998) contains a more recent discussion of the argument.

[32] Since there is no set of all objects, it will not do for present purposes to think of interpretations as set-sized models. For a more appropriate account of interpretation, see the discussion of the All-in-One principle at the end of the last section. The technical result that concerns us carries over without incident on the revised account.

[33] As first noted by Putnam (1980), this result is provable on the basis of a strong version of the Löwenheim–Skolem Theorem.

[34] Lewis outlines the view in Lewis (1983) and Lewis (1984). The second paper is a response to a skeptical argument based on a formal result like the one quoted above.

[35] The suggestion occurs for example in pp. xx–xxiv of Sider (2003).

A different line of resistance has been proposed by Vann McGee. By taking absolutely general quantification for granted in the metalanguage, McGee argues that one's object-language quantifiers are guaranteed to range over absolutely everything on the assumption that they satisfy an *open-ended* version of the standard introduction and elimination rules—that is, a version of the rules that is to remain in place even if the language is enriched with additional vocabulary. As McGee is at pains to insist, it is far from clear that simple standard introduction and elimination rules could exhaust the meaning of the English quantifiers. However, he suggests that open-endedness is a distinctive feature of our quantificational practice, and that this fact alone suffices to cast doubt on the indeterminacy argument, which fails to take considerations of open-endedness into account.[36]

A third strategy for resisting the indeterminacy argument is based on pragmatic considerations. Suppose a resourceful and fully cooperative speaker asserts 'I am speaking of absolutely everything there is' (and nothing else) in a conspicuous effort to clarify what her domain of discourse consists in. Since the sentence asserted can be true relative to any domain of discourse, the speaker was inarticulate. But the speaker is fully cooperative, so if she was inarticulate (and if there is nothing else to explain the inarticulacy), it must have been because she couldn't do any better. And since the speaker is resourceful, it is only plausible that she couldn't do any better if she intended her domain to be absolutely all-inclusive. (Otherwise she would be in a position to say at least that it was not incompatible with her intentions that the original domain was less-than-all-inclusive.) So there is some reason for thinking that the speaker intended her domain to be absolutely all-inclusive. By failing to take pragmatic considerations into account, the argument for indeterminacy is insensitive to this sort of phenomenon.[37]

It is worth emphasizing that the lines of objection we have considered in this section are not aimed at a skeptic of absolute generality. They are best understood as defensive maneuvers, intended to reassure absolutists of the coherence of their own position by explaining *why* it is that the indeterminacy argument fails, given that it does fail.

1.2.5 The Argument from Sortal Restriction

According to an influential account of quantification discussed by Michael Dummett 'each domain for the individual variables will constitute the extension of some substantival general term (or at least the union of the extensions of a number of such substantival terms)'.[38] By a substantival term, Dummett means a term that supplies

[36] See McGee (2000) and McGee's contribution to this volume. For criticism of McGee, see the postscript to Field (1998) in Field (2001) and Lavine and Williamson's contributions to this volume. For additional discussion of open-endedness, see Parsons (1990), Feferman (1991) and Lavine (1994).

[37] This idea is developed in Rayo (2003).

[38] See Dummett (1981), pp. 569 and 570, respectively.

a criterion of identity, and (following Frege) a criterion of identity is taken to be 'a means for recognizing an object as the same again'.[39]

This account of quantification is one step away from the thesis that absolutely general quantification is somehow illicit. All one needs to take the further step is the thesis that purportedly all-inclusive general terms—terms like 'thing', 'object', or 'individual'—do not supply criteria of identity, and are therefore not 'substantival'. This further thesis might perhaps be motivated by appeal to the claim that it is only sensible to ask a question of the form, for example, 'how many *F*s does the room contain' when *F* is a substantival general term. It is nonsense, the suggestion would continue, to ask, without tacit restriction to one substantival term or another, 'how many *things* does the room contain?' (and similarly for other purportedly all-inclusive general terms).[40]

A proper assessment of the thesis that a domain of quantification must be restricted by a substantival general term—and that purportedly all-inclusive general terms are non-substantival—would require discussion of broad issues in the philosophy of language which are beyond the scope of this chapter.[41]

1.3 CONFLICTS

We have considered a number of arguments designed to cast doubt on the prospects of absolutely general inquiry. Absolutists have developed responses, and optimistic absolutists might think that their view has emerged more or less unscathed. But even the optimists must acknowledge that engaging in absolutely general inquiry requires a great deal of caution. For absolutely general theories sometimes place non-trivial constraints on the size of the universe, and different theories might call for inconsistent constraints. Conflicts might also arise among absolutely general theories with different and in fact disjoint vocabularies, as in the case of certain standard formulations of applied set theory and a certain extension of classical extensional mereology. Certain plausible versions of these theories cannot both be true and absolutely general, for whereas the former requires that the universe be of a strongly inaccessible size, the latter requires that the universe be of a successor size.[42]

1.4 SUMMARIES

We conclude with summaries of each of the contributions to the volume in the hope they may allow some readers to identify those most likely to be of interest to them.

[39] See Frege (1884), § 64.

[40] See, for instance, Geach (1962), pp. 38, 153.

[41] Relevant texts in the more recent literature include Lowe (1989), Wiggins (2001) and Linnebo (2002).

[42] The conflict has been discussed in Uzquiano (2006) with a view to questioning the alleged absolute generality of mereology. For a general assessment of the difficulty, see Uzquiano's contribution below.

Kit Fine

In 'Relatively Unrestricted Quantification', Kit Fine reviews the classic argument from indefinite extensibility and suggests that it is unsatisfactory as it stands. While traditional indefinite extensibility considerations challenge the absolutist interpretation of the quantifiers, they have no force in the absence of an absolutist opponent. Fine's contribution develops a modal formulation of indefinite extensibility designed to overcome this defect. On the modal interpretation of indefinite extensibility, the concept of, e.g. *set* is said to be indefinitely extensible on the grounds that whatever interpretation of a quantifier ranging over sets one might come up with, it will be possible to find a more inclusive interpretation. This modal understanding of indefinite extensibility calls for the use of distinctive *postulational* modalities. What is special about postulational modalities is that they concern variation in interpretation rather than variation in circumstances. Since postulational necessities and possibilities are forms of interpretational necessities and possibilities, they are germane to the issue of unrestricted quantification.

Michael Glanzberg

In 'Context and Unrestricted Quantification', Michael Glanzberg offers a development of the view that because of the semantic and set-theoretic paradoxes, seemingly unrestricted quantification is in fact restricted. Glanzberg's focus is not, however, on defending the argument from paradox. The main objective of the chapter is to acquire a better understanding of what the quantificational restrictions required by the argument from paradox consist in. Glanzberg suggests that the argument from paradox results in a shift to a 'reflective context', which in turn leads to an enriched background domain of discourse. He goes on to argue that it is possible to specify a list of general principles governing the construction of the new domain. The process involves the setting of a context-dependent parameter in a sentence, and is said to be fundamentally related to the pragmatic processes governing non-paradoxical contexts. Glanzberg rounds off the proposal by offering some formal models of what the enriched domain might look like.

Geoffrey Hellman

In 'Against "Absolutely Everything"', Geoffrey Hellman distinguishes two general kinds of arguments against absolute generality. One kind of argument is based on considerations of indefinite extensibility and the open-ended character of mathematical concepts and structures; the other is based on the relativity of ontology to a conceptual framework. While the first kind of argument springs from specifically mathematical concerns and relies on a platonist view of mathematical ontology, the second is much more general and threatens the prospects of absolute generality even for theorists with a nominalist view of mathematical ontology. This raises the question of what to make of seemingly absolutely unrestricted generalizations such as 'No donkey talks'. Hellman suggests a contextualist interpretation of such generalizations, according to which they are taken to contain a schematic element.

Shaughan Lavine

In 'Something about Everything: Universal Quantification in the Universal Sense of Universal Quantification', Shaughan Lavine elucidates and defends the notion of a 'full scheme': a scheme whose instances are open-ended and automatically expand as the language in use expands. The notion is then used in support of two main theses. The first is that efforts to counter Putnam-style arguments for the indeterminacy of quantification and the non-existence of an all-inclusive domain through the use of open-endedness are ultimately unsuccessful. Lavine argues that the essential use of open-endedness in these arguments is best understood in terms of full schemes, and that full schemes would not give a proponent of these arguments what she needs. The second thesis is that opponents of absolutely unrestricted quantification do not suffer from crippling expressive limitations: full schemas give them all the expressive power they need. Lavine concludes that we have no positive reason for thinking that either the notion of absolutely unrestricted quantification or the notion of an all-inclusive domain of discourse is a coherent notion.

Øystein Linnebo

In 'Sets, Properties and Unrestricted Quantification', Øystein Linnebo addresses the challenge of embracing absolutely general quantification while avoiding semantic pessimism: the view that there are legitimate languages for which an explicit semantics cannot be given. Linnebo argues that efforts to address the challenge that proceed by postulating an open-ended hierarchy of logical types suffer from important expressive limitations, and lays the foundations for developing a type-free alternative. The alternative supplements standard ZFC set theory with a (first-order) notion of property with the following two features: on the one hand, there are enough properties to do interesting theoretical work; on the other, there are principled reasons for rejecting instances of a comprehension schema for properties that would lead to paradox. Linnebo's philosophical defense of the project is accompanied by a technical discussion of the resulting systems.

Vann McGee

In 'There's a Rule for Everything', Vann McGee is engaged in a defensive project. He aims to explain—from the point of view of a generality absolutist—how it is that the meaning of an absolutely general quantifier might be fixed. The proposal is based on the idea that a rule of inference can be read open-endedly: it can be seen as continuing to hold even if the language expands. By working within a metalanguage in which absolutely general quantification is allowed, McGee uses a Tarski-style model-theoretic semantics to give a rigorous characterization of open-endedness, and argues that only an absolutely general quantifier could satisfy versions of the standard quantifier introduction and elimination rules that are open-ended in the regimented sense. McGee does not claim that English quantifiers should be seen as obeying the rules in question, but he takes his argument to show that considerations of open-endedness can help us understand how English speakers succeed in quantifying over absolutely everything.

Charles Parsons

In 'The Problem of Absolute Universality', Charles Parsons raises the question of whether apparently absolutely unrestricted generalizations such as 'Everything is self-identical' should be taken at face value and argues that they should not. He suggests that the acknowledgment of absolutely unrestricted quantification would commit one to metaphysical realism, understood as the thesis that there is some final answer to the question of what objects there are and how they are to be individuated. This is contrasted with the acknowledgment of merely unrestricted quantification, from which no grand metaphysical conclusion seems to follow. Parsons then presents what he takes to be some of the most important logical obstacles for the viability of absolutely unrestricted quantification. These obstacles emerge when we quantify over interpretations and look at what are now familiar Russellian paradoxes for interpretations. The paper concludes with a discussion of the suggestion that absolutely unrestricted generalizations such as 'Everything is self-identical' should be taken to be systematically ambiguous.

Agustín Rayo

In 'Beyond Plurals', Agustín Rayo has two main objectives. The first is to get a better understanding of what is at issue between friends and foes of higher-order quantification, and of what it would mean to extend a Boolos-style treatment of second-order quantification to third- and higher-order quantification. The second objective is to argue that in the presence of absolutely general quantification, proper semantic theorizing is essentially unstable: it is impossible to provide a suitably general semantics for a given language in a language of the same logical type. Rayo thinks that this leads to a trilemma: one must choose between giving up absolutely general quantification, settling for the view that adequate semantic theorizing about certain languages is essentially beyond our reach, and countenancing an open-ended hierarchy of languages of ever ascending logical type. Rayo concludes by suggesting that the hierarchy may be the least unattractive of the options on the table.

Stewart Shapiro and Crispin Wright

In 'All Things Indefinitely Extensible', Stewart Shapiro and Crispin Wright are primarily concerned with indefinite extensibility. Their departure point is a conjecture they attribute to Bertrand Russell to the effect that a concept is indefinitely extensible only if there is an injection from the concept ordinal into it. After dispensing with apparent exceptions to Russell's conjecture, Shapiro and Wright argue for a more informative characterization of indefinite extendibility from which Russell's conjecture falls out as a consequence. Their characterization promises to cast new light upon the paradoxes of indefinite extensibility and have important ramifications for a variety of issues in the philosophy of mathematics. They suggest, for example, that indefinite extensibility is the key to a proper understanding of the Aristotelian notion of potential infinity. They also consider a restriction of Basic Law V based on indefinite extensibility and its potential for improvement on extant neo-logicist attempts to ground set theory on abstraction principles. Finally, they discuss the question of whether it is ever legitimate to quantify over all of the members of indefinitely extensible totalities, and suggest that no completely satisfactory answer seems to be available.

Gabriel Uzquiano

In 'Unrestricted Unrestricted Quantification: The Cardinal Problem of Absolute Generality', Gabriel Uzquiano raises an internal problem for absolutism. The problem arises when one notices the possibility of conflicts amongst absolutely general theories with different and, in fact, disjoint vocabularies. Uzquiano presents two different examples of such potential conflicts for consideration and casts doubts upon the prospects of a unified and systematic solution for them. Instead, Uzquiano suggests conflicts amongst absolutely general theories should generally be addressed on a case by case basis. Uzquiano argues that in at least some cases such conflicts are best solved by abandoning the claim to absolute generality for some of the theories involved. The paper concludes with a call for caution for the absolutist and a brief discussion of the prospects of an argument against absolute generality based on the possibility of conflicts amongst absolutely general theories with different vocabularies.

Alan Weir

In 'Is it too much to Ask, to Ask for Everything?', Alan Weir argues for a view based on the following three theses: (1) one can quantify over absolutely everything, (2) the domain of discourse of an interpreted language is an individual, and (3) one can characterize a notion of truth-in-an-interpretation for one's object language in one's object language. He proceeds by using a Kripke-style fixed-point construction to characterize a notion of property that satisfies naïve comprehension axioms, and a notion of truth-in-an-interpretation that takes domains to be properties. (Such notions would ordinarily lead to paradox, but Weir addresses the problem by proposing a revision of classical logic.) Weir concludes by arguing that, even though his proposal doesn't deliver everything one might have hoped for, it is nonetheless to be preferred over theories that allow for absolutely general quantification but appeal to an ascending hierarchy of logical types to characterize the notion of truth-in-an-interpretation.

Timothy Williamson

In 'Absolute Identity and Absolute Generality', Timothy Williamson develops an analogy between identity and absolutely general quantification. He argues that just like an open-ended reading of the usual axioms of identity can be used to uniquely characterize the notion of identity, an open-ended reading of the usual introduction and elimination rules for the first-order quantifiers can be used to characterize uniquely the notion of absolutely general quantification. Williamson uses the analogy to to show that certain objections against absolutely general quantification can only succeed if corresponding objections succeed in the case of identity. He concludes by noting that foes of absolutely general quantification cannot coherently maintain both that everything the generality absolutist says can be reinterpreted as something the non-absolutist would accept and that the generality absolutist's position leads to paradox.

REFERENCES

Bach, K. (2000) 'Quantification, Qualification and Context', *Mind and Language* 15:2, 3, 262–83.

Beall, J., ed. (2003) *Liars and Heaps*, Oxford University Press, Oxford.

Benacerraf, P., and H. Putnam, eds. (1983) *Philosophy of Mathematics*, Cambridge University Press, Cambridge, second edition.

Boolos, G. (1984) 'To Be is to Be a Value of a Variable (or to be Some Values of Some Variables)', *The Journal of Philosophy* 81, 430–49. Reprinted in Boolos (1998).

____ (1985a) 'Nominalist Platonism', *Philosophical Review* 94, 327–44. Reprinted in Boolos (1998).

____ (1985b) 'Reading the *Begriffsschrift*', *Mind* 94, 331–4. Reprinted in Boolos (1998).

____ (1998) *Logic, Logic and Logic*, Harvard, Cambridge, MA.

Butts, R. E., and J. Hintikka, eds. (1977) *Logic, Foundations of Mathematics, and Computability Theory*, Reidel, Dordrecht.

Carnap, R. (1950) 'Empiricism, Semantics and Ontology', *Analysis* 4, 20–40. Reprinted in Benacerraf and Putnam (1983), 241–57.

Cartwright, R. (1994) 'Speaking of Everything', *Noûs* 28, 1–20.

Dales, H. G., and G. Oliveri, eds. (1998) *Truth in Mathematics*, Oxford University Press, Oxford.

Dummett, M. (1963) 'The Philosophical Significance of Gödel's Theorem', *Ratio* 5, 140–55. Reprinted in Dummett (1978).

____ (1978) *Truth and other Enigmas*, Duckworth, London.

____ (1981) *Frege: Philosophy of Language*, Harvard, Cambridge, MA, second edition.

____ (1991) *Frege: Philosophy of Mathematics*, Duckworth, London.

Feferman, S. (1991) 'Reflecting on Incompleteness', *Journal of Symbolic Logic* 56, 1–49.

Field, H. (1998) 'Which Undecidable Mathematical Sentences have Determinate Truth Values?' In Dales and Oliveri (1998). Reprinted in Field (2001).

____ (2001) *Truth and the Absence of Fact*, Oxford University Press, Oxford.

Forster, T. E. (1995) *Set Theory with a Universal Set: Exploring an Untyped Universe*, volume 31 of *Oxford Logic Guides*, Oxford Science Publications, Oxford, second edition.

Frege, G. (1884) *Die Grundlagen der Arithmetik*. English Translation by J. L. Austin, *The Foundations of Arithmetic*, Northwestern University Press, Evanston, IL, 1980.

Geach, P. (1962) *Reference and Generality, an Examination of some Medieval and Modern Theories*, Cornell University Press, Ithaca, NY.

Glanzberg, M. (2004) 'Quantification and Realism', *Philosophy and Phenomenological Research* 69, 541–72.

Hellman, G. (1989) *Mathematics Without Numbers*, Clarendon Press, Oxford.

Hirsch, E. (1993) *Dividing Really*, Oxford University Press, New York.

Kreisel, G. (1967) 'Informal Rigour and Completeness Proofs', In Lakatos (1967).

Lakatos, I., ed. (1967) *Problems in the Philosophy of Mathematics*, North Holland, Amsterdam.

Lavine, S. (1994) *Understanding the Infinite*, Harvard University Press, Cambridge, MA.

Lewis, D. (1983) 'New Work for a Theory of Universals', *Australasian Journal of Philosophy* 61, 343–77. Reprinted in Lewis (1999).

—— (1984) 'Putnam's Paradox', *The Australasian Journal of Philosophy* 62, 221–36. Reprinted in Lewis (1999).

—— (1999) *Papers in Metaphysics and Epistemology*, Cambridge University Press.

Linnebo, Ø. (2002) *Science with Numbers: A Naturalistic Defense of Mathematical Platonism*, Doctoral dissertation, Harvard, Cambridge, MA.

—— (2003) 'Plural Quantification Exposed', *Noûs* 37, 71–92.

Lowe, E. (1989) *Kinds of Being: A Study of Individuation, Identity and the Logic of Sortal Terms*, Blackwell, Oxford.

McGee, V. (1992) 'Two Problems With Tarski's Theory of Consequence', *Proceedings of the Aristotelian Society* 92, 273–92.

—— (2000) "Everything". In Sher and Tieszen (2000).

Oliver, A., and T. Smiley (2001) 'Strategies for a Logic of Plurals', *Philosophical Quarterly* 51, 289–306.

Parsons, C. (1974) 'Sets and Classes', *Noûs* 8, 1–12. Reprinted in Parsons (1983).

—— (1977) 'What is the Iterative Conception of Set?'. In Butts and Hintikka (1977). Reprinted in Parsons (1983).

—— (1983) *Mathematics in Philosophy*, Cornell University Press, Ithaca, NY.

—— (1990) 'The Structuralist View of Mathematical Objects', Synthese 84, 303–46.

Putnam, H. (1980) 'Models and Reality', The Journal of Symbolic Logic 45:3, 464–82.

—— (1987) *The Many Faces of Realism*, Open Court, La Salle, IL.

Quine, W. V. (1968) 'Ontological Relativity', *Journal of Philosophy* 65, 185–212. Reprinted in Quine (1969).

—— (1969) *Ontological Relativity and Other Essays*, Columbia University Press, New York.

—— (1986) *Philosophy of Logic, Second Edition*, Harvard, Cambridge, MA.

Rayo, A. (2002) 'Word and Objects', *Noûs* 36, 436–64.

—— (2003) 'When does "Everything" mean *Everything*?' Analysis 63, 100–6.

—— and G. Uzquiano (1999) 'Toward a Theory of Second-Order Consequence', *The Notre Dame Journal of Formal Logic* 40, 315–25.

—— and T. Williamson (2003) 'A Completeness Theorem for Unrestricted First-Order Languages'. In Beall (2003).

—— and S. Yablo (2001) 'Nominalism Through De-Nominalization', *Noûs* 35:1, 74–92.

Resnik, M. (1988) 'Second-Order Logic Still Wild', *Journal of Philosophy* 85:2, 75–87.

Russell, B. (1906) 'On some Difficulties in the Theory of Transfinite Numbers and Order Types', *Proceedings of the London Mathematical Society* 4, 29–53.

Sher, G., and R. Tieszen, eds. (2000) *Between Logic and Intuition*, Cambridge University Press, New York and Cambridge.

Sider, T. (2003) *Four-Dimensionalism: An Ontology of Persistence and Time*, Oxford University Press, Oxford.

—— (2006) 'Quantifiers and Temporal Ontology', *Mind* 115, January 2006, 75–97.

Stanley, J., and Z. G. Szabó (2000) 'On Quantifier Domain Restriction', *Mind and Language* 15:2, 3, 219–61.

Uzquiano, G. (2006) 'The Price of Universality', *Philosophical Studies* 129, May 2006, 137–69.

Wiggins, D. (2001) *Sameness and Substance Renewed*, Cambridge University Press, Cambridge.

Williamson, T. (1998) 'Indefinite Extensibility', *Grazer Philosophische Studien* 55, 1–24.
—— (2003) 'Everything', 415–65. In Hawthorne, J. and D. Zimmerman, eds. *Philosophical Perspectives 17: Language and Philosophical Linguistics*, Blackwell, Oxford.
Zermelo, E. (1930) 'Über Grenzzahlen und Mengenbereiche: Neue Untersuchungen über die Grundlagen der Mengenlehre', *Fundamenta Mathematicae* 16, 29–47.

2

Relatively Unrestricted Quantification

Kit Fine

There are four broad grounds upon which the intelligibility of quantification over absolutely everything has been questioned—one based upon the existence of semantic indeterminacy, another on the relativity of ontology to a conceptual scheme, a third upon the necessity of sortal restriction, and the last upon the possibility of indefinite extendibility. The argument from semantic indeterminacy derives from general philosophical considerations concerning our understanding of language. For the Skolem–Löwenheim Theorem appears to show that an understanding of quantification over absolutely everything (assuming a suitably infinite domain) is semantically indistinguishable from the understanding of quantification over something less than absolutely everything; the same first-order sentences are true and even the same first-order conditions will be satisfied by objects from the narrower domain. From this it is then argued that the two kinds of understanding are indistinguishable tout court and that nothing could *count* as having the one kind of understanding as opposed to the other.

The second two arguments reject the bare idea of an object as unintelligible, one taking it to require supplementation by reference to a conceptual scheme and the other taking it to require supplementation by reference to a sort. Thus we cannot properly make sense of quantification over *mere* objects, but only over objects of such and such a conceptual scheme or of such and such a sort. The final argument, from indefinite extendibility, rejects the idea of a *completed* totality. For if we take ourselves to be quantifying over all objects, or even over all sets, then the reasoning of Russell's paradox can be exploited to demonstrate the possibility of quantifying over a more inclusive domain. The intelligibility of absolutely unrestricted quantification, which should be free from such incompleteness, must therefore be rejected.

The ways in which these arguments attempt to undermine the intelligibility of absolutely unrestricted quantification are very different; and each calls for extensive discussion in its own right. However, my primary concern in the present paper is with the issue of indefinite extendibility; and I shall only touch upon the other arguments in so far as they bear upon this particular issue. I myself am not persuaded by the

The material of the paper was previously presented at a seminar at Harvard in the Spring of 2003, at a colloquium at Cornell in the Fall of 2004, and at a workshop at UCLA in the Fall of 2004. I am very grateful for the comments I received on these occasions; and I am also very grateful to Agustín Rayo, Gabriel Uzquiano, and Alan Weir for their comments on the paper itself.

other arguments and I suspect that, at the end of day, it is only the final argument that will be seen to carry any real force. If there is a case to be made against absolutely unrestricted quantification, then it will rest here, upon logical considerations of extendibility, rather than upon the nature of understanding or the metaphysics of identity.

2.1 THE EXTENDIBILITY ARGUMENT

Let us begin by reviewing the classic argument from indefinite extendibility. I am inclined to think that the argument is cogent and that the intelligibility of absolutely unrestricted quantification should therefore be rejected. However, there are enormous difficulties in coming up with a cogent formulation of the argument; and it is only by going through various more or less defective formulations that we will be in a position to see how a more satisfactory formulation might be given. I shall call the proponent of the intelligibility of absolute quantification a 'universalist' and his opponent a 'limitavist' (my reason for using these unfamiliar labels will later become clear).

The extendibility argument, in the first instance, is best regarded as an ad hominem argument against the universalist. However, I should note that if the argument works at all, then it should also work against someone who claims to have an understanding of the quantifier that is *compatible* with its being absolutely unrestricted. Thus someone who accepted the semantic argument against there being an interpretation of the quantifier that was *determinately* absolutely unrestricted might feel compelled, on the basis of this further argument, to reject the possibility of there even being an interpretation of the quantifier that was *indeterminately* absolutely unrestricted.

Let us use '$\exists$' and '$\forall$' for those uses of the quantifier that the universalist takes to be absolutely unrestricted. The critical step in the argument against him is that, on the basis of his understanding of the quantifier, we can then come to another understanding of the quantifier according to which there will be an object (indeed, a set) whose members will be all those objects, in *his* sense of the quantifier, that are not members of themselves. Let us use $\exists^+$ and $\forall^+$ for the new use of the quantifier. Then the point is that we can so understand the new quantifiers that the claim:

$$\text{(R)}\quad \exists^+ y[\forall x(x \in y \equiv \sim(x \in x))]$$

is true (using $\exists^+ y$ with wide scope and $\forall x$ with narrow scope).

The argument to (R) can, if we like, be divided into two steps. First, it is claimed that on the basis of our opponent's understanding of the quantifier $\exists$, we can come to an understanding of the quantifier $\exists'$ according to which there is an object (indeed, a set) of which every object, in his sense of the quantifier, is a member:

$$\text{(U)}\quad \exists' z \forall x(x \in z).$$

It is then claimed that, on the basis of our understanding of the quantifier $\exists'$, we can come to an understanding of the quantifier $\exists^+$ according to which there is an object whose members, in the sense of $\forall$, are all those objects that belong to some selected object, in the sense of $\forall'$, and that satisfy the condition of not being self-membered:

$$\text{(S)}\quad \forall' z \exists^{+} y \forall x\, [(x \in y \equiv (x \in z \,\&\, \sim(x \in x))].$$

From (U) and (S), (R) can then be derived by standard quantificational reasoning.

(S) is an instance of 'Separation', though the quantifier $\exists^{+}$ cannot necessarily be identified with $\exists'$ since the latter quantifier may not be closed under definable subsets. (S) is relatively unproblematic, at least under the iterative conception of set, since we can simply take $\exists^{+}$ to range over all subsets of objects in the range of $\exists'$. Thus granted the relevant instance of Separation, the existence of a Russell set, as given by (R), will turn upon the existence of a universal set, as given by (U).

There is also no need to assume that the membership-predicate to the left of (R) is the same as the membership-predicate to its right. Thus we may suppose that with the new understanding $\exists^{+}$ of the quantifier comes a new understanding $\in^{+}$ of the membership predicate, so that (R) now takes the form:

$$\text{(R}'\text{)}\quad \exists^{+} y [\forall x (x \in^{+} y \equiv \sim(x \in x))].$$

It is plausible to suppose that $\in^{+}$ 'conservatively' extends $\in$:

$$\text{(CE)}\quad \forall x \forall y (x \in^{+} y \equiv x \in y)).$$[1]

But we may then derive:

$$\text{(R}^{+}\text{)}\quad \exists^{+} y [\forall x (x \in^{+} y \equiv \sim(x \in^{+} x))],$$

which is merely a 'notational variant' of (R), with $\in^{+}$ replacing $\in$.

The rest of the argument is now straightforward. From (R) (or (R^{+})), we can derive the 'extendibility' claim:

$$\text{(E)}\quad \exists^{+} y \forall x (x \neq y).$$

For suppose, for purposes of reductio, that $\forall^{+} y \exists x (x = y)$. Then (R) yields:

$$\text{(R}^{*}\text{)}\quad \exists y [\forall x (x \in y \equiv \sim(x \in x))],$$

which, by the reasoning of Russell's paradox, leads to a contradiction.

But the truth of (E) then shows that the original use of the quantifiers $\exists$ and $\forall$ was not absolutely unrestricted after all.

Even though we have stated the argument for the particular case of sets, a similar line of argument will go through for a wide range of other cases—for ordinal and cardinal numbers, for example, or for properties and propositions. In each of these cases, a variant of the paradoxical reasoning may be used to show that the original quantifier was not absolutely unrestricted. Thus in order to resist this conclusion, it is not sufficient to meet the argument in any particular case; it must be shown how in general it is to be met.

[1] (CE) might be doubted on the grounds that $\in^{+}$ may have the effect of converting urelements according to $\in$ into sets. But even this is not on the cards, if it is insisted that the initial quantifier $\forall$ should only range over sets.

Indeed, even this is not enough. For there are cases in which objects of *two* kinds give rise to paradox (and hence to a paradoxically induced extension) even though each kind of object, when considered on its own, is paradox-free. For example, there would appear to be nothing to prevent the arbitrary formation of singletons or the arbitrary formation of mereological sums, but the arbitrary formation of both gives rise to a form of Russell's paradox (given certain modest assumptions about the mereological structure of singletons).[2] These cases create a special difficulty for the proponent of absolutely unrestricted quantification, even if he is content to block the automatic formation of new objects in those cases in which a single kind of object gives rise to paradox. For it might appear to be unduly restrictive to block the arbitrary formation of both kinds of objects in those cases where two kinds of object are involved and yet invidious to block the formation of one kind in preference to the other. Thus we do not want to block the arbitrary formation of both singletons and mereological sums. And yet why block the formation of one in preference to the other? Rather than have to face this awkward choice, it might be thought preferable to 'give in' to the extendibility argument and allow the arbitrary extension of the domain by objects of either kind.

There are various standard set-theoretic grounds upon which the transition to (R) might be questioned, but none is truly convincing. It has been suggested, for example, that no set can be 'too big', of the same size as the universe, and that it is this that prevents the formation of the universal or the Russell set. Now it may well be that no understanding of the quantifier that is subject to reasonable set-theoretical principles will include sets that are too big within its range. But this has no bearing on the question of whether, given such an understanding of the quantifier, we may come to an understanding of the quantifier that ranges over sets that would have been too big relative to the original understanding of the quantifier. For surely, given any condition whatever, we can so understand the quantifier that it ranges over a set whose members are all those objects (according to the original understanding of the quantifier) that satisfy the condition; and the question of *how many* objects satisfy the condition is entirely irrelevant to our ability to arrive at such an understanding of the quantifier.

Or again, it has been suggested that we should think of sets as being constructed in stages and that what prevents the formation of the universal or the Russell set is there being no stage at which its members are all constructed. We may grant that we should think of sets as being constructed at stages and that, under any reasonable process by which we might take them to be constructed, there will be no stage at which either the universal or the Russell set is constructed. But what is to prevent us from so understanding the quantifier over stages that it includes a stage that lies after all of the stages according to the original understanding of the quantifier ($\exists^{+}\alpha\forall\beta(\alpha > \beta)$)?

[2] The matter is discussed in Lewis (1991), Rosen (1995) and Fine (2005a) and in Uzquiano's paper in the present volume. A similar problem arises within an ontology of properties that allows for the formation both of arbitrary disjunctions (properties of the form: $P \vee Q \;\vee \ldots$) and of arbitrary identity properties (properties of the form: *identical to P*); and a related problem arises within the context of Parsons' theory of objects (Parsons, 1980), in which properties help determine objects and objects help determine properties.

And given such a stage, what is to prevent us from coming to a correlative understanding of a quantifier over sets that will include the 'old' universal or Russell set within its range? The existence of sets and stages may be linked; and in this case, the question of their extendibility will also be linked. But it will then be of no help to presuppose the inextendibility of the quantifier over stages in arguing for the inextendibility of the quantifier over sets.

Or again, it has been supposed that what we get is not a universal or a Russell *set* but a universal or Russell *class*. But I have stated the argument without presupposing that the universal or Russell object is either a set or a class. What then can be the objection to saying that we can so understand the quantifier that there is something that has all of the objects previously quantified over as members? Perhaps this *something* is not a class, if the given objects already includes classes. But surely we can intelligibly suppose that there is something, be what it may, that has all of the previously given objects as its members (in a sense that conservatively extends our previous understanding of membership).

Thus the standard considerations in support of ZF or the like do nothing to undermine the argument from extendibility. Their value lies not in showing how the argument might be resisted but in showing how one might develop a consistent and powerful set theory within a given domain, without regard for whether that domain might reasonably be taken to be unrestricted.

But does not the extendibility argument take the so-called 'all-in-one' principle for granted? And has not Cartwright (1994) shown this principle to be in error? Cartwright states the principle in the following way (p. 7):

> to quantify over certain objects is to presuppose that those objects constitute a 'collection' or a 'completed collection'—some one thing of which those objects are members.

Now one might indeed argue for extendibility on the basis of the all-in-one principle. But this is not how our own argument went. We did not argue that our understanding of the quantifier $\forall$ *presupposes* that there is some one thing of which the objects in the range of $\forall$ are members ($\exists^+ y \forall x(x \in y)$). For this would mean that the quantifier $\forall$ was to be understood in terms of the quantifier $\forall^+$. But for us, it is the other way round; the quantifier $\forall^+$ is to be understood in terms of the quantifier $\forall$. It is through a *prior* understanding of the quantifier $\forall$ that we come to appreciate that there is a sense of the quantifier $\forall^+$ in which it is correct to suppose that some one thing has the objects in the range of $\forall$ as members. Thus far from presupposing that the all-in-one principle is true, we presuppose that it is false!

Of course, there is some mystery as to how we arrive at this new understanding of the quantifier. What is the extraordinary mental feat by which we generate a new object, as it were, merely from an understanding of the quantifier that does not already presuppose that there is such an object? I shall later have something to say on this question. But it seems undeniable that we *can* achieve such an understanding even if there is some difficulty in saying how we bring it off. Indeed, it may plausibly be argued that the way in which we achieve an understanding of the quantifier $\forall^+$ is the same as the way in which we achieve a more ordinary understanding of the set-theoretic quantifier. Why, for example, do we take there to be a set of all natural numbers? Why not simply assume that the relevant portion of the 'universe' is exhausted by the *finite* sets of natural numbers? The obvious response is that we can intelligibly quantify over all the natural numbers and so there is nothing to prevent us from so understanding the set-theoretic quantifier that there is a set whose members are all the natural numbers ($\exists x \forall n(n \in x)$). But then, by parity of reasoning, such an extension in our understanding of the quantifier should always be possible. The great stumbling block for the universalist, from this point of view, is that there would appear to be nothing short of a prejudice against large infinitudes that might prevent us from asserting the existence of a comprehensive set in the one case yet not in the other.[3]

2.2 GENERALIZING THE EXTENDIBILITY ARGUMENT

The extendibility argument is not satisfactory as it stands. If our opponent claims that we may intelligibly understand the quantifier as absolutely unrestricted, then he is under some obligation to specify a particular understanding of the quantifier for which this is so. And once he does this, we may then use the extendibility argument to prove him wrong. But what if no opponent is at hand? Clearly, it will not do to apply the extendibility argument to our *own* interpretation of the quantifier. For what guarantee will we have that our opponent would have regarded it as absolutely unrestricted?

Clearly, what is required is a generalization of the argument. It should not be directed at this or that interpretation of the quantifier but at any interpretation whatever. Now normally there would be no difficulty in generalizing an argument of this sort. We have a particular instance of the argument; and, since nothing special is assumed about the instance, we may generalize the reasoning to an arbitrary instance and thereby infer that the conclusion generally holds. However, since our concern is with the very nature of generality, the attempt to generalize the present argument gives rise to some peculiar difficulties.

The general form of the argument presumably concerns an arbitrary interpretation (or understanding) of the quantifier; and so let us use I, J, ... as variables for interpretations, and I_0 and J_0 and the like as constants for particular interpretations. I make no particular assumptions about what interpretations are and there is no need, in particular, to suppose that an interpretation of a quantifier will require the specification of some 'object' that might figure as its domain. We shall use $\exists_I x\varphi(x)$, with I as a subscript to the quantifier, to indicate that there is some x under the interpretation I for which $\varphi(x)$. Some readers may baulk at this notation. They might think that one should use a meta-linguistic form of expression and say that the sentence '$\exists x\varphi(x)$' is true under the interpretation I rather than that $\exists_I x\varphi(x)$. However, nothing in what follows will turn on such niceties of use-mention and, in the interests of presentation, I have adopted the more straightforward notation.

[3] A somewhat similar line of argument is given by Dummett (1991), pp. 315–16.

Let us begin by reformulating the original argument, making reference to the interpretations explicit. Presumably, our opponent's intended use of the quantifier will conform to a particular interpretation I_0 of the quantifier. We may therefore assume:

(1) $\forall x \exists_{I_0} y(y = x) \& \forall_{I_0} y \exists x(x = y)$.

We now produce an 'extension' J_0 of I_0 subject to the following condition:

(2) $\exists_{J_0} y \forall_{I_0} x(x \in y \equiv {\sim} x \in x)$.

From (2) we may derive:

(3) $\exists_{J_0} y \forall_{I_0} x(x \neq y)$.

Defining $I \subseteq J$ as $\forall_I x \exists_J y(x = y)$, we may write (3) as:

(3)′ $\sim(J_0 \subseteq I_0)$.

Let us use UR(I) for: I is absolutely unrestricted. There is a difficulty for the limitavist in explaining how this predicate is to be understood since, intuitively, an absolutely unrestricted quantifier is one that ranges over absolutely everything. But let us put this difficulty on one side since the present problem will arise even if the predicate is taken to be primitive. Under the intended understanding of the predicate UR, it is clear that:

(4) $UR(I_0) \supset J_0 \subseteq I_0$.

And so, from (3) and (4), we obtain:

(5) $\sim UR(I_0)$.

From this more explicit version of the original argument, it is now evident how it is to be generalized. (2) should now assume the following more general form:

(2G) $\forall I \exists J \exists_J y \forall_I x(x \in y \equiv {\sim} x \in x)$.

This is the general 'Russell jump', taking us from an arbitrary interpretation I to its extension J. (We could also let the interpretation of $\in$ vary with the interpretation of the quantifier; but this is a nicety which we may ignore.) By using the reasoning of Russell's paradox, we can then derive:

(3G) $\forall I \exists J[\sim(J \subseteq I)]$.

Define an interpretation I to be *maximal*, Max(I), if $\forall J\ (J \subseteq I)$. Then (3G) may be rewritten as:

(3G)′ $\forall I {\sim} Max(I)$.

Step (4), when generalized, becomes:

(4G) $\forall I[UR(I) \supset Max(I)]$.

And so from (3G)′ and (4G), we obtain:

(5G) $\forall I \sim UR(I)$,

i.e. no interpretation of the quantifier is absolutely unrestricted, which would appear to be the desired general conclusion.

But unfortunately, things are not so straightforward. For in something like the manner in which our opponent's first-order quantifier over objects was shown not to be absolutely unrestricted, it may also be shown that *our* own second-order quantifier over interpretations is not absolutely unrestricted; and so (5G) cannot be the conclusion we are after. For we may suppose, in analogy with (1) above, that there is an interpretation M_0 to which the current interpretation of the quantifiers over interpretations conforms:

(6) $\forall I \exists_{M_0} J(J = I) \,\&\, \forall_{M_0} J \exists I(I = J)$.[4]

Now associated with any 'second-order' interpretation M is a first-order interpretation I, what we may call the 'sum' interpretation, where our understanding of $\exists_I x\varphi(x)$ is given by $\exists_M J \exists_J x\varphi(x)$. In other words, something is taken to φ (according to the sum of M) if it φ's under some interpretation of the quantifier (according to M). The sum interpretation I is maximal with respect to the interpretations according to M, i.e.$\forall_M J(J \subseteq I)$; and so there will be such an interpretation according to M_0 if M_0 is absolutely unrestricted:

(7) $UR(M_0) \supset \exists_{M_0} I \forall_M J(J \subseteq I)$.

Given (6), (7) implies:

(8) $UR(M_0) \supset \exists I[Max(I)]$.

And so (3G)′ above yields:

(9) $\sim UR(M_0)$.

The second-order interpretation of the first-order quantifier is not absolutely unrestricted.[5]

In this proof, we have helped ourselves to the reasoning by which we showed the universalist's first-order quantifier not to be absolutely unrestricted. But it may be shown, quite regardless of how (5G) might have been established, that its *truth* is not compatible with its quantifier being absolutely unrestricted. For it may plausibly be maintained that if a second-order interpretation M is absolutely unrestricted then so is any first-order interpretation that is maximal with respect to M (or, at least, if the notion is taken in a purely extensional sense). Thus in the special case of M_0, we have:

(10) $UR(M_0) \supset \forall_{M_0} I[\forall_{M_0} J(J \subseteq I) \supset UR(I)]$.

So from (7) and (10), we obtain:

(11) $UR(M_0) \supset \exists_{M_0} I[UR(I)]$.

[4] Instead of appealing to the notion of identity between interpretations in stating this assumption, we could say $\forall I \exists_{M_0} J[\forall_I x \exists_J y(x = y) \& \forall_J y \exists_I x(y = x)]$; and similarly for the second conjunct.

[5] An argument along these lines is also to be found in Lewis (1991), p. 20, McGee (2000), p. 48, and Williamson (2003), and also in Weir's contribution to the present volume.

But given (6), we may drop the subscript M_0. And contraposition then yields:

(12) $\forall I{\sim}UR(I) \supset {\sim}UR(M_0)$.

In other words, if it is true that no interpretation of the quantifier is absolutely unrestricted, then the interpretation of the quantifier 'no interpretation' is itself not absolutely unrestricted.[6]

Of course, it should have been evident from the start that the limitavist has a difficulty in maintaining that all interpretations of the quantifier are not absolutely unrestricted, since it would follow from the truth of the claim that the interpretation of the quantifier in the claim itself was not absolutely unrestricted and hence that it could not have its intended import. What the preceding proof further demonstrates is the impossibility of maintaining a mixed position, one which grants the intelligibility of the absolutely unrestricted 'second-order' quantifier over all interpretations but rejects the intelligibility of the absolutely unrestricted 'first-order' quantifier over all objects. If we have the one then we must have the other.[7]

The resulting dialectical situation is hardly satisfactory. The universalist seems obliged to say something false in defense of his position. For he should say what the absolutely unrestricted interpretation of the quantifier is—or, at least say that there is such an interpretation; and once he does either, then we may show him to be in error. The limitavist, on the other hand, can say nothing to distinguish his position from his opponent's—at least if his opponent does not speak. For his position (at least if true) will be stated by means of a restricted quantifier and hence will be acceptable, in principle, to his opponent. Both the universalist and the limitavist would like to say something true but, where the one ends up saying something indefensible, the other ends up saying nothing at all.

The situation mirrors, in miniature, what some have thought to hold of philosophy at large. There are some propositions that are of interest to assert if true but of no interest to deny if false. Examples are the proposition that there is no external world or the proposition that I alone exist. Thus it is of interest to be told that there is *no* external world, if that indeed is the case, but not that there *is* an external world. Now some philosophers of a Wittgensteinian persuasion have thought that philosophy consists entirely of potentially interesting propositions of this sort and that *none of them is true*. There is therefore nothing for the enlightened philosopher to assert that is both true and of interest. All he can sensibly do is to wait for a less enlightened colleague to say something false, though potentially of interest, and then show him to be wrong. And similarly, it seems, in the present case. The proposition that some particular interpretation of the quantifier is absolutely unrestricted is of interest only if true; and given that it is false, all we can sensibly do, as enlightened limitavists, is to hope that our opponent will claim to be in possession of an absolutely

[6] We should note that, for the purpose of meeting these arguments, it is of no help to draw a grammatical distinction between the quantifiers $\forall I$ and $\forall x$.

[7] It is perhaps worth remarking that there are not the same compelling arguments against a position that tolerates the intelligibility of unrestricted first-order quantification but rejects the intelligibility of unrestricted second-order quantification (see Shapiro, 2003).

unrestricted interpretation of the quantifier and then use the Russell argument to prove him wrong!

2.3 GOING MODAL

The previous difficulties arise from our not being able to articulate what exactly is at issue between the limitavist and the universalist. There seems to be a well-defined issue out there in logical space. But the universalist can only articulate his position on the issue by saying something too strong to be true, while the limitavist can only articulate his position by saying something too weak to be of interest. One gets at his position from above, as it were, the other from below. But what we want to be able to do is to get at the precise position to which each is unsuccessfully attempting to approximate.

Some philosophers have suggested that we get round this difficulty by adopting a schematic approach. Let us use r(I) for the interpretation obtained by applying the Russell device to a given interpretation I. Then what the limitavist wishes to commit himself to, on this view, is the *scheme*:

(ES) $\exists_{r(I)}y\forall_I x \sim (x = y)$ (something under the Russell interpretation is not an object under the given interpretation).

Here 'I' is a schematic variable for interpretations; and in committing oneself to the scheme, one is committing oneself to the truth of each of its instances though not to the claim that each of them is true.[8]

The difficulty with this view is to see how it might be coherently maintained. We have an understanding of what it is to be committed to a scheme; it is to be committed to the truth of each of its instances. But how can one understand what it is to be committed to the truth of each of its instances without being able to understand what it is for an arbitrary one of them to be true? And given that one understands what it is for an arbitrary one of them to be true, how can one be willing to commit oneself to the truth of each of them without also being willing to commit oneself to the claim that each of them is true? But once one has committed oneself to this general claim, then the same old difficulties reappear. For we can use the quantifier 'every instance' (just as we used the quantifier 'every interpretation') to construct an instance that does not fall within its range.

The schematist attempts to drive a wedge between a general commitment to particular claims and a particular commitment to a general claim. But he provides no plausible reason for why one might be willing to make the one commitment and yet not both able and willing to make the other. Indeed, he appears to be as guilty as the universalist in not being willing to face up to the facts of intelligibility. The universalist thinks that there is something special about the generality implicit in our

[8] Lavine and Parsons advocate an approach along these lines in the present volume; and it appears to be implicit in the doctrine of 'systematic ambiguity' that has sometimes been advocated—by Parsons (1974, p. 11) and Putnam (2000, p. 24), for example—as a solution to the paradoxes.

understanding of a certain form of quantification that prevents it from being extended to a broader domain, while the schematist thinks that there is something special about the generality implicit in a certain form of schematic commitment that prevents it from being explicitly rendered in the form of a quantifier. But in neither case can either side provide a plausible explanation of our inability to reach the further stage in understanding and it seems especially difficult to see why one might baulk at the transition in the one case and yet not in the other.

I want in the rest of the chapter to develop an alternative strategy for dealing with the issue. Although my sympathies are with the limitavist, it is not my *principal* concern to argue for that position but to show that there is indeed a position to argue for. The basic idea behind the strategy is to adopt a modal formulation of the theses under consideration. But this idea is merely a starting-point. It is only once the modality is properly understood that we will be able to see how a modal formulation might be of any help; and to achieve this understanding is no small task. It must first be appreciated that the relevant modality is 'interpretational' rather than 'circumstantial'; and it must then be appreciated that the relevant interpretations are not to be understood, in the usual way, as some kind of restriction on the domain but as constituting a genuine form of extension. It has been the failure to appreciate these two points, I believe, that has prevented the modal approach from receiving the recognition that it deserves.[9]

Under the modal formulation of the limitavist position, we take seriously the thought that any given interpretation *can* be extended, i.e. that we can, in principle, come up with an extension. Thus in coming up with an extension we are not confined to the interpretations that fall under the current interpretation of the quantifier over interpretations. Let us use $I \subset J$ for 'J (properly) extends I' (which may be defined as: $I \subseteq J \ \& \sim(J \subseteq I)$). Let us say that I is *extendible*—in symbols, E(I)—if possibly some interpretation extends it, i.e.$\Diamond\exists J(I \subset J)$. Then one formulation of the limitavist position is:

$$\text{(L)} \quad \forall I E(I).$$

But as thorough-going limitavists, we are likely to think that, whatever interpretation our opponent *might* come up with, it will be possible to come up with an interpretation that extends it. Thus a stronger formulation of the limitavist's position is:

$$\text{(L)}^{+} \quad \Box\forall I E(I) (\text{i.e. } \Box\forall I \Diamond\exists J(I \subset J)).$$

It should be noted that there is now no longer any need to use a primitive notion of being absolutely unrestricted (UR) in the formulation of the limitavist's position.

The theses (L) and $(L)^+$ are intended to apply when different delimitations on the range of the quantifier may be in force. Thus the quantifier might be understood, in a generic way, as ranging over *sets*, say, or *ordinals*, but without it being determined which sets or, which ordinals, it ranges over. Thesis (L) must then be construed as saying that any interpretation of the quantifier over sets or over ordinals can be

[9] The approach is briefly, and critically, discussed in §5 of Williamson (2003); and it might be thought to be implicit in the modal approach to set theory and number theory, though it is rarely advocated in its own right.

extended to another interpretation of the quantifier over sets or over ordinals. Thus the extension is understood to be possible within the specified range of the quantifier. We might say that the concept by which the quantifier is delimited is *extendible* if (L) holds and that it is *indefinitely extendible* if $(L)^+$ holds. We thereby give precise expression to these familiar ideas.

It is essential to a proper understanding of the two theses that the interpretations be taken to be modally 'rigid'. Whatever objects an interpretation picks out or fails to pick out, it must necessarily pick out or fail to pick out; its range, in other words, must be constant from world to world.[10] Without this requirement, an interpretation could be extendible through its range contracting or inextendible through its range expanding, which is not what we have in mind. We should therefore distinguish between the concept, such as *set* or *ordinal*, by which the range of the quantifier might be delimited and an interpretation of the quantifier, by which its range is fixed. The latter is constant in the objects it picks out from world to world, even if the former is not.

It will also be helpful to suppose that (necessarily) each interpretation picks out an object within the *current* range of the first-order quantifier ($\Box\forall I\forall_I x\exists y(y = x)$). This is a relatively harmless assumption to make, since it can always be guaranteed by taking the interpretations within the range of '$\forall I$' to include the 'sum' interpretation and then identifying the current interpretation with the sum interpretation. It follows on this approach that there is (necessarily) a maximal interpretation ($\Box\exists I\forall J(J \subseteq I)$) but there is no reason to suppose, of course, that it is necessarily maximal ($\Box\exists I\Box\forall J(J \subseteq I)$). Given this simplifying supposition, the question of whether the current interpretation I_0 is extendible (i.e. of whether $\Diamond\exists J(I_0 \subset J)$) is simply the question of whether it is possible that there is an object that it does not pick out (something we might formalize as $\forall I(\forall x\exists_I y(y = x) \supset \Diamond\exists x{\sim}\exists_I y(y = x))$), where the condition $\forall x\exists_I y(y = x)$ serves to single out the current interpretation I_0).

However, the critical question in the formulation of the theses concerns the use of the modalities. Let us call the notions of possibility and necessity relevant to the formulation 'postulational'. How then are the postulational modalities to be understood? The familiar kinds of modality do not appear to be useful in this regard. Suppose, for example, that '$\Box$' is understood as metaphysical necessity. As limitavists, we would like to say that the domain of pure sets is extendible. This would mean, under the present proposal, that it is a metaphysical possibility that some pure set is not actual. But necessarily, if a pure set exists, then it exists of necessity; and so it is not possible that some pure set is not actual. Thus we fail to get a case of being extendible that we want. We also get cases of being extendible that we do not want. For it is presumably metaphysically possible that there should be more atoms than there actually are. But we do not want to take the domain of atoms to be extendible—or, at least, not for this reason.

[10] I might add that all we care about is which objects are in the range, not how the range is determined, and so, for present purposes, we might as well take '$\forall I$' to be a second-order extensional quantifier.

Suppose, on the other hand, that '$\Box$' is understood as logical necessity (or perhaps as some form of conceptual necessity). There are, of course, familiar Quinean difficulties in making sense of first-order quantification into modal contexts when the modality is logical. Let me here just dogmatically assume that these difficulties may be overcome by allowing the logical modalities to 'recognize' when two objects are or are not the same.[11] Thus $\Box\forall x\,\Box(x = y \supset \Box\, x = y)$ and $\Box\forall x\,\Box(x \neq y \supset \Box\, x \neq y)$ will both be true though, given that the modalities are logical, it will be assumed that they are blind to any features of the objects besides their being the same or distinct.

There is also another, less familiar, difficulty in making sense of *second*-order quantification into modal contexts when the modality is logical. There are perhaps two main accounts of the quantifier '$\forall$I' that might reasonably be adopted in this case. One is substitutional and takes the variable 'I' to range over appropriate substituends (predicates or the like); the other is 'extensional' and takes 'I', in effect, to range over enumerations of objects of the domain.

Under the first of these accounts, it is hard to see why any domain should be extendible, for in the formalization $\forall I(\forall_I x\exists y(y = x) \supset \Diamond\exists x{\sim}\exists_I y(y = x))$ we may let I be the predicate of self-identity. The antecedent $\forall_I x\exists y(y = x)$ will then be true while the consequent $\Diamond\exists x{\sim}\exists_I y(y = x)$, which is equivalent to $\Diamond\exists x{\sim}\exists y(y = x)$, will be false.

The second of the two accounts does not suffer from this difficulty since the interpretation I will be confined to the objects that it enumerates. But it is now hard to see why any domain should be *in*extendible. For let $a_1, a_2, a_3, \ldots$ be an enumeration of all of the objects in the domain. Then it is logically possible that these are not all of the objects ($\Diamond\exists x{\sim}(x = a_1 \vee x = a_2 \vee x = a_3 \vee \ldots)$), since there can be no logical guarantee that any particular objects are all of the objects that there are. This is especially clear if there are infinitely many objects $a_1, a_2, a_3, \ldots$. For if it were logically impossible that some object was not one of $a_1, a_2, a_3, \ldots$, then it would be logically impossible that some object was not one of $a_2, a_3, \ldots$, since the logical form of the existential proposition in the two cases is the same. But there *is* an object that is not one of $a_2, a_3, \ldots$, viz. a_1! Thus just as considerations of empirical vicissitude are irrelevant to the question of extendibility, so are considerations of logical form.

It should also be fairly clear that it will not be possible to define the relevant notion of necessity by somehow relativizing the notion of logical necessity. The question is whether we can find some condition φ such that the necessity of ψ in the relevant sense can be understood as the logical necessity of $\varphi \supset \psi$. But when, intuitively, a domain of quantification is inextendible, we will want φ to include the condition $\forall x(x = a_1 \vee x = a_2 \vee x = a_3 \vee \ldots)$, where $a_1, a_2, a_3, \ldots$ is an enumeration of all the objects in the domain; and when the domain is extendible, we will want φ to exclude any such condition. Thus we must already presuppose whether or not the domain is extendible in determining what the antecedent condition φ should be (and nor are things better with metaphysical necessity, since the condition may then hold of necessity whether we want it to or not).

[11] The issue is discussed in Fine (1990).

2.4 POSTULATIONAL POSSIBILITY

We have seen that the postulational modalities are not to be understood as, or in terms of, the metaphysical or logical modalities. How then are they to be understood? I doubt that one can provide an account of them in essentially different terms—and in this respect, of course, they may be no different from some of the other modalities.[12] However, a great deal can be said about how they are to be understood and in such a way, I believe, as to make clear both how the notion is intelligible and how it may reasonably be applied. Indeed, in this regard it may be much less problematic than the more familiar cases of the metaphysical and natural modalities.

It should be emphasized, in the first place, that it is not what one might call a 'circumstantial' modality. Circumstances could have been different; Bush might never have been President; or many unborn children might have been born. But all such variation in the circumstances is irrelevant to what is or is not postulationally possible. Indeed, suppose that D is a complete description of the world in basic terms. It might state, for example, that there are such and such elementary particles, arranged in such and such a way. Then it is plausible to suppose that any postulational possibility is compatible with D. That is:

$$\Diamond A \supset \Diamond(A \,\&\, D).$$

Or, equivalently, D is a postulational necessity ($\Box$ D); there is not the relevant possibility of extending the domain of quantification so that D is false. Postulational possibilities, in this sense, are possibilities *for* the actual world, and not merely possible alternatives *to* the actual world.

Related considerations suggest that postulational necessity is not a genuine modality at all. For when a proposition is genuinely necessary there will be a broad intuitive sense in which the proposition *must be* the case. Thus epistemic necessity (or knowledge) is not a genuine modality since there is no reason, in general, to suppose that what is known must be the case. Similarly for postulational necessity. That there are swans, for example, is a postulational necessity but it is not something that, intuitively, must be the case. Thus it is entirely compatible with the current 'modal' approach that it is not merely considerations of metaphysical modality, but genuine considerations of modality in general, that are irrelevant to questions of extendibility.

The postulational modalities concern not a possible variation in circumstance but in interpretation. The possibility that there are more sets, for example, depends upon a reinterpretation in what it is for there to be a set. In this respect, postulational possibility is more akin to logical possibility, which may be taken to concern the possibility for reinterpreting the primitive non-logical notions. However, the kind of reinterpretation that is in question in the case of postulational possibility is much more circumscribed

[12] Metaphysical modality is often taken to be primitive and Field (1989, p. 32) has suggested that logical modality is primitive. In Fine (2002), I argued that there are three primitive forms of modality—the metaphysical, the natural, and the normative. Although postulational modality may also be primitive, it is not a genuine modality in the sense I had in mind in that paper.

than in the case of the logical modality, since it primarily concerns possible changes in the interpretation of the domain of quantification and is only concerned with other changes in interpretation in so far as they are dependent upon these.

But if postulational possibility is a form of interpretational possibility, then why does the postulational possibility of a proposition not simply consist in the existence of an interpretation for which the proposition is true? It is here that considerations of extendibility force our hand. For from among the interpretations that there are is one that is maximal. But it is a postulational possibility that there are objects which it does not pick out; and so this possibility cannot consist in there actually being an interpretation (broader than the maximal interpretation) for which there is such an object.[13]

Nor can we plausibly take the postulational possibility of a proposition to consist in the metaphysical possibility of our specifying an interpretation under which the proposition is true. For one thing, there may be all sorts of metaphysical constraints on which interpretations it is possible for us to specify. More significantly, it is not metaphysically possible for a quantifier over pure sets, say, to range over more pure sets than there actually are, since pure sets exist of necessity. So this way of thinking will not give us the postulational possibility of there being more pure sets than there actually are.

The relationship between the relevant form of interpretational possibility and the existence of interpretations is more subtle than either of these proposals lead us to suppose. What we should say is that the existence of an interpretation of the appropriate sort *bears witness* or *realizes* the possibility in question.[14] Thus it is the existence of an interpretation, given by the Russell jump, that bears witness to the possibility that there are objects not picked out by the given interpretation. However, to say that a possibility may be realized by an interpretation is not to say that it consists in the existence of an interpretation or that it cannot obtain without our being able to specify the interpretation.

But still it may be asked: what bearing do these possibilities have on the issue of unrestricted quantification? We have here a form of the 'bad company' objection. Some kinds of possibility—the metaphysical or the logical ones, for example—clearly have no bearing on the issue. So what makes this kind of possibility any better? Admittedly, it differs from the other kinds in various ways—it is interpretational rather than circumstantial and interpretational in a special way. But why should these differences matter?[15]

I do not know if it is possible to answer this question in a principled way, i.e., on the basis of a clear and convincing criterion of relevance to which it can then be shown that the modality will conform. But all the same, it seems clear that there is a notion of the required sort, one which is such that the possible existence of a broader interpretation

[13] We have here a kind of *proof* of the impossibility of providing a possible world's semantics for the relevant notion of interpretational possibility. Any semantics, to be genuinely adequate to the truth-conditions, would have to be homophonic.

[14] What is here in question is the legitimacy of the inference from φ^I to $\Diamond\varphi$, where φ^I is the result of relativizing all the quantifiers in φ to I. This might be compared to the inference from φ-is-true-in-w to $\Diamond\varphi$, with the world w realizing the possibility of φ.

[15] I am grateful to Timothy Williamson for pressing this question upon me.

is indeed sufficient to show that the given narrower interpretation is not absolutely unrestricted. For suppose someone proposes an interpretation of the quantifier and I then attempt to do a 'Russell' on him. Everyone can agree that if I succeed in coming up with a broader interpretation, then this shows the original interpretation not to have been absolutely unrestricted. Suppose now that no one in fact does do a Russell on him. Does that mean that his interpretation was unrestricted after all? Clearly not. All that matters is that the interpretation should be possible. But the relevant notion of possibility is then the one we were after; it bears directly on the issue of unrestricted quantification, without regard for the empirical vicissitudes of actual interpretation.

Of course, this still leaves open the question of what it is for such an interpretation to be possible. My opponent might think it consists in there existing an interpretation in a suitably abstract sense of term or in my being capable of specifying such an interpretation. But we have shown these proposals to be misguided. Thus the present proponent of the modal approach may be regarded as someone who starts out with a notion of possible interpretation that all may agree is relevant to the issue and who then finds good reason not to cash it out in other terms. In this case, the relevance of the notion he has in mind can hardly be doubted.

2.5 RESTRICTIONISM

To better understand the relevant notion of postulational possibility we must understand the notion of interpretation on which it is predicated. Postulational possibilities lie in the possibilities for reinterpreting the domain of quantification. But what is meant here by a reinterpretation, or change in interpretation, of the quantifier?

The only model we currently have of such a change is one in which the interpretation of the quantifier is given by something like a predicate or property which serves to restrict its range. To say that a proposition is postulationally necessary, on this model then, is to say that it is true no matter how the restriction on its quantifiers might be relaxed; to say that an interpretation of the quantifier is extendible is to say that the restriction by which it is defined can be relaxed; and to say that a quantifier is indefinitely extendible is to say that no matter how it might be restricted the restriction can always be relaxed.

Unfortunately, the model, attractive as it may be, is beset with difficulties. Consider the claim that possibly there are more sets than we currently take there to be ($\forall I[\forall x \exists_I y(y = x) \supset \Diamond \exists y \forall_I x(y \neq x)]$). In order for this to be true, the current quantifier '∀x' over sets must not merely be restricted to sets but to sets of a certain sort, since otherwise there would not be the possibility of the set-quantifier '∃y' having a broader range. But it is then difficult to see why the current interpretation of the quantifier '∀x' should not simply be restricted to sets.

For surely we are in possession of an unrestricted concept of a set, not *set of such and such a sort* but *set simpliciter*. When we recognize the possibility, via the Russell jump, of a new set, we do not take ourselves to be forming new concepts of set and membership. The concepts of set and membership, of which we were already in possession, are seen to be applicable to the new object; and there is no question of these concepts embodying some further implicit restriction on the objects to which they might apply.

But given that we are in possession of an unrestricted concept of set, then why is it not legitimate simply to restrict the quantifier to sets so conceived? It might of course be argued that the quantifier should always be restricted to a relevant sort, that we cannot make sense of quantification over objects as such without some conception of which kind of objects are in question. But such considerations, whatever their merits might otherwise be, are irrelevant in the present context. For the quantifier is already restricted to a sort, viz. *set*, and so we have as good a conception as we might hope to have of which kind of objects are in question. To insist upon a further restriction of the quantifier is like thinking that we cannot properly quantify over swans but only over black swans, say, or English swans.

There is another difficulty with the model. Any satisfactory view must account for the act of reinterpretation that is involved in the Russell jump. In making the Russell jump, we go from one interpretation of the quantifier to another; and we need to provide a satisfactory account of how this is done. To simplify the discussion, let us suppose that no set belongs to itself. The Russell set over a given domain is then the same as the universal set; and so the question of the intelligibility of the Russell jump can be posed in terms of the universal rather than the Russell set. Let us now suppose that we have an initial understanding of the quantifier. represented by '$\forall x$' and '$\exists x$'. We then seem capable of achieving a new understanding of the quantifier—which we may represent by '$\forall^+ x$' and '$\exists^+ x$'—in which it also ranges over a universal set. Under this new understanding, it is correct to say that there is a universal set relative to the old understanding ($\exists^+ x \forall y(y \in x)$). The question on which I wish to focus is: how do we come to this new understanding of the quantifier on the basis of the initial understanding?

It is clear that the condition $\forall y(y \in x)$ plays a critical role; since it is by means of this condition that the new understanding is given. But how? The only answer the restrictionist can reasonably give is that the condition is used to relax the condition on the quantifier that is already in play. Thus suppose that the initial quantifier $\forall x$ is implicitly restricted to objects satisfying the condition $\theta(x)$, so that to say $\forall x \varphi(x)$ is tantamount to saying $\forall x[\theta(x): \varphi(x)]$ (every θ-object is a φ-object). The effect of considering the condition $\forall y(y \in x)$ is then to weaken the initial restrictive condition $\theta(x)$ to $\theta(x) \vee \forall y(y \in x)$, so that to say $\forall^+ x \varphi(x)$ is tantamount to saying $\forall x[\theta(x) \vee \forall y(y \in x): \varphi(x)]$.

Unfortunately, this proposal does not deliver the right results. Intuitively, we wanted the quantifier $\forall^+ x$ to include one new object in its domain, the set of all those objects that are in the range of $\forall y$. But the condition $\forall y(y \in x)$ picks out *all* those sets that have all of the objects in the range of $\forall y$ as members, and not just the set that consists solely of these objects. If we had an unrestricted quantifier Πx, then we could pick out the intended set by means of the condition $\Pi y(y \in x \equiv \exists z(z = y))$ but under the present proposal, of course, no such quantifier is at hand.[16]

[16] One might think that the new object should be defined by the condition: $\exists I[\forall x \exists_I y(y = x) \;\&\; \Box \forall y(y \in x \equiv \exists_I z(z = y))]$. But since the condition is modal, it is of little help in understanding the

There is a further difficulty, which is a kind of combination of the other two. As we have seen, the required restriction on the quantifier is not just to sets but to sets of such and such a sort. But how are we to specify the supplementary non-sortal condition? It is clear that in general this will require the use of a complex predicates and not just the use of simple predicates, such as 'set'. But how are the complex predicates to be specified except by the use of lambda-expressions of the form $\lambda x\varphi(x)$? And how is the implicit restriction on the lambda-operator λx in such expressions to be specified except by means of further complex predicates? Thus it is hard to see how the specification of the relevant class of restrictions might get 'off the ground'.[17]

2.6 EXPANSIONISM

The two obvious ways of understanding the postulational modality—the circumstantial and the interpretational—have failed. What remains? I believe that our difficulties stem from adopting an unduly narrow conception of what might constitute an interpretation of the quantifier. To understand better what alternative conceptions there might be, we need to reconsider the Russell jump and how it might be capable of effecting a change in the interpretation of the quantifier.

As I have remarked, the change in the interpretation of the domain of quantification is somehow given by the condition $\forall y(y \in x)$. But rather than thinking of that condition as serving to define a new predicate by which the quantifier is to be restricted, we should think of it as serving to indicate how the range of the quantifier is to be extended. Associated with the condition $\forall y(y \in x)$ will be an instruction or 'procedural postulate', $!x\forall y(y \in x)$, requiring us to introduce an object x whose members are the objects y of the given domain. In itself, the notation $!x\forall y(y \in x)$ is perhaps neutral as to how the required extension is to be achieved. But the intent is that there is no more fundamental understanding of what the new domain should be except as the domain that might be reached from the given domain by adding an object in conformity with the condition. Thus $!x\forall y(y \in x)$ serves as a positive injunction on how the domain is to be extended rather than as a negative constraint on how it is to be restricted.

It might be wondered why the present account of how the domain is to be extended is not subject to a form of the objection that we previously posed against the restrictionist account. For what guarantees that we will obtain the desired extension? What is to prevent the new object from containing members besides those in the range of y?

relevant sense of $\Box$. Also, there would appear to be something viciously circular about specifying an interpretation in this way, since the application of $\Box$ within such conditions must be understood by reference to the very interpretations it is being used to specify. At the very least, it is hard to see how such interpretations could be legitimate unless their application could be grounded in interpretations of an ordinary, nonmodal kind.

[17] Another possibility, under this approach, is to distinguish between free and bound variables. Free variables are absolutely unrestricted, bound variables are not; and conditions with free variables can then be used to specify the relevant restrictions on bound variables. But, as with the schematic approach, it is hard to see what prevents the free variable from being bound.

The answer lies in the nature of the postulational method. For not every object can be postulated into existence. We cannot postulate, for example, that there is to be an object whom everyone admires ($!x\forall y$(y admires x)). And likewise, we cannot postulate an object which stands in the membership relationship to pre-existing objects. But this means that, once a universal set for a given domain has been introduced, no further objects that might be introduced can be among its members. Thus the membership—and hence identity—of the set will be fixed 'for all time', once it has been introduced.

The present account of domain extension should be sharply distinguished from the restrictionist and universalist accounts.[18] Under the universalist account, the old and new domains are to be understood as restrictions; and these restrictions, in turn, are to be understood as restrictions on an absolutely unrestricted domain. Under the restrictionist account, the old and new domains are also to be understood as restrictions; but these restrictions are not themselves to be understood as restrictions of some broader domain. Under the expansionist account, by contrast, the new domain is not to be understood as a restriction at all but as an expansion. What we are provided with is not a new way of seeing how the given domain might have been restricted but with a way of seeing how it might be expanded. We might say that the new domain is understood from 'above' under the universalist and restrictionist accounts, in so far as it is understood as the restriction of a possibly broader domain, but that it is understood from 'below' under the expansionist account, in that it is understood as the expansion of a possibly narrower domain.

Another major difference between the accounts concerns the conditions and consequences of successful reinterpretation. Any attempt to reinterpret the quantifier by means of a restricting predicate will be successful under the universalist account; and it will also be successful under the restrictionist account as long as the predicate does not let in 'too many' objects. However, belief that there is a new object, that the domain has in fact been extended, is not automatically justified under either of these accounts. They do indeed provide us with a new way in which there might be a new object for, given the new understanding of $\exists^+y$, it may now be true that $\exists^+ y\forall x(x \in y)$ even though it was not before true that $\exists y\forall x(x \in y)$. But success in the act of reinterpretation does not in itself guarantee that there *is* such an object. Under the expansionist account, by contrast, success in the act of reinterpretation does guarantee that there is such an object. Thus if the attempt to reinterpret the quantifier $\exists^+y$ by means of the injunction $!x\forall y(y \in x)$ is successful, then the inference to $\exists^+y\forall x(x \in y)$ will be secure.

However, successful reinterpretation, in this case, cannot simply be taken for granted. We do not need to show that there is an object of the required sort in order to be sure of success. Indeed, such a demand would be self-defeating since its satisfaction

[18] It should also be distinguished from a view that takes quantification to be relative to a conceptual scheme. One major difference is this. A procedural postulate presupposes a prior understanding of the quantifier and so it should be possible, under the postulationalist approach, to understand the quantifier in the absence of any postulates. However, it is not usually thought to be possible, under the conceptualist approach, to understand the quantifier apart from any conceptual scheme.

would require the very understanding of the quantifier that we are trying to attain. But in order successfully to postulate an object we do need to demonstrate the legitimacy of the postulate, i.e. the postulational possibility of there being an object of the prescribed sort. Given this possibility, we may then use the condition by which the object is given to secure an interpretation of the quantifier in which there *is* such an object.

It is a remarkable feature of the understanding we achieve through the Russellian jump that the very act of reinterpretation serves to secure the existence of the object in question. It is not as if we can think of ourselves as successfully reinterpreting the quantifier and then go on to ask whether, under this reinterpretation, there is indeed an object of the required sort. The one guarantees the other; and it is a key point in favor of the present approach that it is in conformity with what we take ourselves to be doing in such cases.

There is a third important difference. Both the restrictionist/universalist and the expansionist accounts allow the interpretation of the quantifier to be relative—relative to a restricting predicate in the one case and to a procedural postulate in the other. But the relativity can plausibly regarded as internal to the content in the first case. If I restrict the interpretation of the quantifier to the predicate θ, then what I am in effect saying when I say '$\exists x\varphi(x)$' is that some θ φ's. But the relativity cannot plausibly be regarded as internal to the content in the second case. If I expand the interpretation of the quantifier by means of the postulate α, then what I am in effect saying when I say '$\exists x\varphi(x)$' is simply that something φ's (but in the context of having postulated α), not that something φ's in the domain as enlarged by α. For to say that something φ's in the domain as enlarged by α is to say that something suitably related to α is a φ; and I cannot make proper sense of what this 'something' might be unless I have *already* enlarged the domain by α. We might say that the relativity in the interpretation of the quantifier is understood from the 'inside' under the universalist and restrictionist accounts but from the 'outside' under the expansionist account.[19]

This feature of the postulationism might be thought to be at odds with our previous insistence that a postulate should serve to reinterpret the quantifier. For surely, if I reinterpret the quantifier, then what I say, before laying down a postulate, is different from what I say afterwards. Indeed, it might be thought that the postulationist, as I have characterized him, faces an intolerable dilemma. For a postulate may result in a statement changing its truth-value. But that can be so only because of a change in content or of a change in the circumstances (in what it is for the statement to be true or in what it is that renders the statement true or false). Yet, for different reasons, we have wanted to reject both of these alternatives.

I think that, in the face of this dilemma, we are forced to recognize a quite distinctive way in which a postulate may result in a change of interpretation—one that is

[19] These various differences are discussed in more detail in Fine (2005b); and other forms of external relativism are discussed in Fine (2005c) and Fine (2005d). I should note that there are some similarities between my views on domain expansion and Glanzberg's (this volume). Thus his notion of a 'background domain' corresponds to my notion of an unrestricted domain, as given by a postulational context; and his notion of an 'artifactual object' corresponds to my notion of an object of postulation.

intermediate, as it were, between a change in content and a change in circumstance, as these are normally conceived. We should bear in mind that, on the present view, there is no such thing as *the* ontology, one that is privileged as genuinely being the sum-total of what there is. There are merely many different ontologies, all of which have the same right (or perhaps we should say no right) to be regarded as the sum-total of what there is.[20] But this means that there is now a new way in which a statement may change its truth-value—not through a change in content or circumstance, but through a change in the ontology under consideration. There is another parameter in the picture and hence another possibility for determining how a statement may be true. Postulation then serves to fix the value of this parameter; rather than altering how things are within a given ontology or imposing a different demand on the ontology, it induces a shift in the ontology itself.[21]

The postulational conception of domain extension provide us with two distinct grounds upon which universalism might be challenged. It might be challenged on the ground that any interpretation of the quantifier must be restricted; and it might also be challenged on the ground that any interpretation of the quantifier is subject to expansion. It should be clear that these two grounds are independent of one another. Thus one might adopt a form of restrictionism that is either friendly or hostile to expansionism. In the first case, one will allow the expansion of the domain but the expansion must always be relative to an appropriately restricted domain (to *sets*, say, or *ordinals*); while in the second case, one will not allow an expansion in the domain and perhaps not even accept the intelligibility of the notion. Similarly, one might adopt a form of expansionism that is hostile to restrictionism. On this view, there is nothing to prevent the quantifier from being completely unrestricted; in saying '$\exists x \varphi(x)$', one is saying something φ's, period. However, this is not to rule out the possibility of expanding the unrestricted domain; the resulting quantifier is then unrestricted, but relative to a 'postulate'. Indeed, on this view it is *impossible* to regard expansion as a form of de-restriction, since there is no existing restriction on the quantifier to be relaxed.[22]

I have taken universalism to be the view that there is absolutely unrestricted quantification. Usually, the term 'absolutely' in the formulation of this view is taken to mean 'completely'; there is absolutely no restriction, i.e. no restriction whatever. But if I am right, the view is really a conjunction of two distinct positions, one signified by 'unrestricted' and the other by 'absolutely'. The first is the affirmation of unrestricted (i.e. completely unrestricted) quantification. The second is the rejection of any relativity in the interpretation of the quantifier beyond a restriction on its range; once the range of the quantifier has been specified by means of a suitable predicate, or even by the absence of a predicate, then there is nothing else upon which its interpretation might depend. It is because the view is essentially conjunctive in this way that we have been

[20] Of course, this is not how the postulationist should express himself. What he refuses to privilege is his current ontology as opposed to the various ontologies that might be realized through postulation.

[21] This new form of indexicality is further discussed and developed in Fine (2005c, 2005d).

[22] I might note that there are some intermediate positions. Thus one might suppose that there is an inexpandible domain, but one that can only itself be reached through expansion.

able to find two distinct grounds—restrictionism and expansionism—upon which it might be challenged.

I myself am tempted by the view that embraces expansionism but rejects restrictionism. I am a believer in what one might call 'relatively unrestricted' quantification. However, opposition to universalism—at least, when the issue of extendibility is at stake—has not usually been of this form. The critical question of how an extension in the domain might be achieved has rarely been broached and it has usually been supposed, if only tacitly, that the relevant interpretation of the quantifiers can only be given by means of a restriction, so that it is only through a change in the restriction that the desired change in the domain of quantification might be achieved.

We are therefore left with a radical form of restrictionism, one which requires not only a 'visible' restriction to a sort but also an 'invisible' restriction to some form of nonsortal condition (whose exact identity is never made clear). But, as I have argued, such a form of restrictionism is highly implausible, both in itself and as an account of extendibility. For the need for a non-sortal restriction lacks any independent motivation and a change in the non-sortal restriction is not, in any case, capable of accounting for the desired extension in the domain. The restrictionists have operated within an unduly limited model of how domain extension might be achieved; and I believe that it is only by embracing expansionism that a more adequate account of domain extension and a more viable form of opposition to universalism can be sustained.

2.7 EXPRESSIVITY

I wish, in conclusion, to consider one of the most familiar objections to the limitavist position. It is that it prevents us from saying things that clearly can be said. It seems evident, for example, that we can say that *absolutely everything* is self-identical. But how can such a thing be said, under the limitavist view, if the quantifier by which it is said is either restricted or subject to expansion? Or again, we may wish to assert that no donkey talks (cf. Williamson, 2003). Our intent, in making such a claim, is that it should concern absolutely all donkeys. But then what is to prevent it from being true simply because the domain has been limited—either through restriction or lack of expansion—to objects that are not talking donkeys?

These difficulties can be overcome by using the modal operator to strengthen the universal claims. Instead of saying everything is self-identical ($\forall x(x = x)$), we say necessarily, whatever might be postulated, everything is self identical ($\Box\forall x(x = x)$); and instead of saying no donkey talks ($\forall x(Dx \supset \sim Tx)$), we say necessarily no donkey talks ($\Box\forall x(Dx \supset \sim Tx)$). The claims, if true, will then exclude the possibility of counter-example under any extension of the domain.

If we were to read the 'absolutely' in 'absolutely all' as the postulational box, then we could even preserve some similarity in form between the natural language rendering of the claim and its formalization. However, in many cases we can rely on the unqualified non-modal claim and use suitable 'meaning postulates' to draw out the modal implications. Consider no donkey talks ($\forall x(Dx \supset \sim Tx)$), for example. It is plausibly part of the meaning of 'donkey' that donkeys cannot be introduced into the domain through postulation ($\exists I[\forall x \exists_I y(y = x) \& \Box \forall x(Dx \supset \exists_I y(y = x))]$) and it is plausibly part of the meaning of 'talk' that no non-talking object can be made to talk through postulation ($\forall x(\sim Tx \supset \Box \sim Tx)$).[23] But with the help of these meaning postulates, we can then derive the strengthened modal claim ($\Box \forall x(Dx \supset \sim Tx)$) from the nonmodal claim ($\forall x(Dx \supset \sim Tx)$. We therefore see that in these cases the unqualified nonmodal claims are themselves capable of having the required deductive import.

A similar device can be used, in general, to simulate the effect of absolutely unrestricted quantification. Suppose that Πx is the absolutely unrestricted quantifier of the universalist and that $\varphi(x)$ is a condition whose satisfaction is indifferent to postulational context. Then instead of saying $\Pi x \varphi(x)$, we may say $\Box \forall x \varphi(x)$, where $\forall x$ is the relatively unrestricted quantifier of the expansionist. In general, $\varphi(x)$ may be a condition whose satisfaction is sensitive to postulational context—as with the condition $\exists y(y = x)$ to the effect that x is in the current range of the quantifier. To take care of such cases, we must make use of some device to take us back to the current context (once we are within the scope of $\Box$). To this end, we can appeal to the current interpretation of the quantifier. Thus instead of saying $\Pi x \varphi(x)$, we may say $\exists I(\forall x \exists_I y(y = x) \& \Box \forall x \varphi(x)^I)$, where the embedded condition $\varphi(x)^I$ is the result of relativizing the quantifiers in $\varphi(x)$ to I.[24]

The locution Πx, as understood by the expansionist, behaves like a quantifier: it conforms to all of the right first-order principles; and the universalist can even conceive of it as having a quantificational semantics. But it is not a quantifier. Indeed, contradiction would ensue if the expansionist supposed that there were some genuine quantifier $\forall x$ for which $\Pi x \varphi(x)$ was equivalent to $\forall x \varphi(x)$, for he would then be in no position to perform a Russell jump on $\forall x$ and thereby assert the postulational possibility of some object not in the current domain ($\exists I[\forall x \exists_I y(y = x) \& \Diamond \exists x \sim \exists_I y(y = x)]$).

The curious hybrid status of the quasi-quantifier Πx is able to account for what it right and wrong about Schematism. The schematist takes us to be committed to the schematic truth of $\mathbf{x} = \mathbf{x}$; and he correctly perceives that this is not a matter of being committed to any particular universal truth, i.e. there is no understanding of the universal quantifier $\forall x$ for which the commitment to $\mathbf{x} = \mathbf{x}$ is equivalent to the commitment to $\forall x(x = x)$. But from this he incorrectly infers that to be committed to the schematic truth of $\mathbf{x} = \mathbf{x}$ is not to be committed to any particular truth (something that we previously saw to be implausible); for to be committed to $\mathbf{x} = \mathbf{x}$ is to be committed to $\Pi x(x = x)$ (or $\Box \forall x(x = x)$). Thus it is by appeal to the quasi-quantifier Πx that we may correctly represent the form of generality implicit in a schematic commitment.

[23] I might note, incidentally, that it is unclear how such meaning postulates could have any plausibility under a radical form of restrictionism.

[24] Similar definitions of possibilist quantification in terms of actualist quantification have been proposed in connection with the metaphysical modalities (see Fine (2003) and the accompanying references). When $\varphi(x)$ contains only the unrestricted quantifiers of the universalist, the more complicated form of analysis is not required. A related approach to unrestricted quantification in set theory is discussed at the end of Putnam (1967).

The hybrid status of Πx can also be used to make sense of the obscure distinction between actual and potential infinity. It has been thought that some infinite domains are definite or complete while others are 'always in the making'. But what does this mean? We can take quantification over an actually infinite domain to be represented by a genuine quantifier $\forall x$ and quantification over a potentially infinite domain to be represented by the quasi-quantifier Πx. The domain is then potential in that it is incapable of being exhausted by any actual domain ($\Box\forall I(\forall x\exists_I y(y = x) \supset \Sigma x{\sim}\exists_I y(y = x)$–where Σ is the dual of II); and we can take the peculiar features of quantification over a potential domain, and its inability to sustain domain expansion, to rest upon its underlying modal form.[25]

We see, once the notion of postulational necessity is on the table, that the charge of expressive inadequacy is without merit. The expansionist can, in his own way, say everything that the universalist says. The difficulty over expressive inadequacy lies, if anywhere, in the other direction. For the expansionist can make claims about what is or is not postulationally possible or necessary. But how is the universalist to express these claims? Presumably, for a proposition to be postulationally necessary is for it to be true in all relevant domains. Not all domains whatever, though, since any of the domains should be capable of expansion. But then which ones? It seems to me that, in response to this question, the universalist must either make a substantive assumption about the domains in question, such as that they are all of 'smaller size' than the universe as a whole, or he must work with a primitive notion of the relevant domains. They are ones that in some unexplained sense are 'definite' or 'complete'.

Of course, the universalist will not be happy with the way the expansionist expresses absolutely unrestricted generality. This notion, he wants to say, is quantificational, not modal. But likewise, the expansionist will not be happy with the way the universalist expresses postulational necessity. This notion, he wants to say, is modal in form, not quantificational. It therefore appears as if there is some kind of stale-mate, with neither side enjoying a decided advantage over the other.

I believe, however, that there are some general theoretical considerations that strongly favor the expansionist point of view. For the idea behind expansionism can be used as the basis for a new approach to the philosophy of mathematics and to the philosophy of abstract objects in general. This approach is able to provide answers to some of the most challenging questions concerning the identity of these objects, our understanding of the language by which they are described, and our knowledge of their existence and behavior. Its ability to answer these questions and to throw light over such a wide terrain may well be regarded as a decisive point in favor of the expansionist position.[26]

REFERENCES

Cartwright R. (1994) 'Speaking of Everything', *Nous* 28, vol. 28, no. 1, pp. 1–20.

[25] Dummett's ambivalence between rejecting absolutely unrestricted quantification (1981, pp. 529, 533) and allowing it within the setting of intuitionistic logic (1981, pp. 529–30) can perhaps also be explained in similar terms.

[26] Some details of the expansionist approach are to be found in Fine (2005b) and I hope to give a fuller account elsewhere.

Dummett M. (1981) *Frege: Philosophy of Language*, Duckworth: London.

Dummett M. (1991) *Frege: Philosophy of Mathematics*, Cambridge, MA: Harvard University Press.

Field H. (1989) *Realism, Mathematics and Modality*, Oxford: Blackwell.

Fine K. (1990) 'Quine on Quantifying In', in *Proceedings of the Conference on Propositional Attitudes*, (ed.) Anderson, Owens, CSLI, reprinted in Fine (2005e).

——(2002) 'The Varieties of Necessity', in *Conceivability and Possibility*, (eds.) T. S. Gendler and J. Hawthorne, Oxford: Clarendon Press, 253–82, reprinted in Fine (2005e).

——(2003) 'The Problem of Possibilia', in *The Oxford Handbook of Metaphysics*, (eds.) D. Zimmerman and M. Loux, Oxford: Clarendon Press, 161–79; reprinted in Fine (2005e).

——(2005a) 'Response to Papers on "The Limits of Abstraction" ', *Philosophical Studies*.

——(2005b) 'Our Knowledge of Mathematical Objects', in *Oxford Studies in Epistemology: Volume 1* Oxford: Clarendon Press, 2005, (eds.) T. S. Gendler and J. Hawthorne, pp. 89–110.

——(2005c) 'The Reality of Tense', to appear in *Synthese*, 2006, in a volume dedicated to Arthur Prior.

——(2005d) 'Tense and Reality', in Fine (2005d).

——(2005e) *Modality and Tense: Philosophical Papers*, Oxford: Clarendon Press.

Glanzberg M. (2001) 'The Liar in Context', *Philosophical Studies* 103, 217–51.

——(2004a) 'A Contextual-Hierarchical Approach to Truth and the Liar Paradox', *Journal of Philosophical Logic* 33, 27–88.

——(2004b) 'Quantification and Realism', *Philosophical and Phenomenological Research* 69, 541–72.

Lewis D. (1991) *Parts of Classes*, Oxford: Blackwell.

McGee, V. (2000) 'Everything', in *Between Logic and Intuition* (eds.) G. Sher and T. Tieszen, Cambridge: Cambridge University Press, 54–78.

Parsons C. (1974) 'Sets and Classes', *Nous* 8, 1–12.

Parsons T. (1980) *Non-existent Objects*, New Haven: Yale University Press.

Putnam H. (1967) 'Mathematics without Foundations', *Journal of Philosophy* 64, 5–22; reprinted in 'Philosophy of Mathematics', second edition (eds. P. Benacerraf, H. Putnam), Cambridge: Cambridge University Press.

——(2000) 'Paradox Revisited II: Sets—A Case of All or None', in *Between Logic and Intuition: Essays in Honor of Charles Parsons*, (eds.) G. Sher and R. Tieszen, Cambridge: Cambridge University Press, 16–26.

Rosen G. (1995) 'Armstrong on Classes as States of Affairs', *Australasian Journal of Philosophy* 73 (4), 613–625.

Shapiro S. (2003) 'All Sets Great and Small; and I Do Mean ALL', *Philosophical Perspectives* 17, 467–90.

Williamson T. (2003) 'Everything', *Philosophical Perspectives* 17, 415–65, to be reprinted in *The Philosopher's Annual*, vol. 26, (ed.) P. Grim *et al.*, available online at www.philosophersannual.org.

3

Context and Unrestricted Quantification

Michael Glanzberg

Quantification is haunted by the specter of paradoxes. Since Russell, it has been a persistent idea that the paradoxes show what might have appeared to be absolutely unrestricted quantification to be somehow restricted. In the contemporary literature, this theme is taken up by Dummett (1973, 1993) and Parsons (1974*a*,*b*). Parsons, in particular, argues that both the Liar and Russell's paradoxes are to be resolved by construing apparently absolutely unrestricted quantifiers as appropriately restricted.

Building on Parsons' work, I have advocated a *contextualist* version of the view that there is no absolutely unrestricted quantification (Glanzberg 2001, 2004*a*,*b*). I have argued that all quantifiers must be construed as ranging over contextually provided domains, and that for any context, there is a distinct context which provides a wider domain of quantification. Hence, there is no absolutely unrestricted quantification. Instead, quantification displays a contextual version of what Dummett calls 'indefinite extensibility'. With Parsons, I have argued that this helps us to resolve the Liar as well as Russell's paradoxes.

There remain a great number of issues surrounding the sort of view Parsons and I advocate. Just how to understand the argument from paradox against absolutely unrestricted quantification remains a delicate matter. Questions about how our view might be coherently stated, and whether it is compatible with certain ideas in metaphysics, are often raised. (Many such questions are raised forcefully in Williamson, 2004.) I take these sorts of issues seriously (and have tried to address some of them in my 2004*b*). In this chapter, however, I shall put them aside, in favor of developing important positive aspects of the contextualist proposal.

The rejection of absolutely unrestricted quantification is no doubt an unexpected, if not unwelcome, conclusion. In part, I believe, we have to recognize that any genuine solution to the paradoxes will force some unwelcome conclusion upon us. (We would hardly see a genuine paradox otherwise.) But I have also suggested that the

Versions of this material were presented at a meeting of the Research Group in Logical Methods in Epistemology, Semantics, and Philosophy of Mathematics at the University of Bristol, 2005; at the University of California, Berkeley, Working Group in History and Philosophy of Logic, Mathematics, and Science, 2005; and the Society for Exact Philosophy Meeting in Toronto, 2005. Thanks to the participants there, especially Volker Halbach, Phil Kremer, Jason Stanley, and Philip Welch. Thanks also to Kit Fine, Josh Parsons, Agustín Rayo, and Gabriel Uzquiano for very helpful comments and discussions.

contextualist view mitigates the unwelcome effects, and so offers a better-motivated, less ad hoc approach. It does so by drawing a parallel between the sorts of shifts in quantifier domains required by the paradoxes and the very familiar phenomenon of *contextual quantifier domain restriction*. The more close the parallel, the more we can see what might have looked like an unexpected and unwelcome restriction on what we can say as merely an unusual manifestation of a familiar and wide-spread natural-language phenomenon.

In this chapter, I shall investigate how close this parallel really is. I shall argue for a limited, but still substantial, conclusion. The kind of quantifier behavior we see with the paradoxes is not exactly the same as the more ordinary kind we see in everyday discourse. Even so, I shall argue it is importantly similar. Like ordinary quantifier domain restriction, we can understand it as the setting of a context-dependent parameter in a sentence. The parameters involved in paradoxical and ordinary cases are distinct, but the pragmatic *processes* which set them are fundamentally related. Thus, I shall argue, examining the pragmatics and semantics of quantifier domain restriction does provide us with important insights which may be applied to develop the contextualist response to the paradoxes in detail.

I should make clear at the outset that I shall not be offering a new argument against unrestricted quantification, nor am I claiming that we can resolve the paradoxes simply by observing commonplace linguistic phenomena. Rather, I shall be developing the contextualist view by supplementing familiar arguments derived from the paradoxes by examination of ordinary contextual domain restriction in natural language. Providing these details and establishing where and how they relate to well-established phenomena in natural language will, I hope, show the contextualist view to be plausible and well motivated. This will offer indirect support for the view.

This chapter proceeds as follows. The kind of paradoxical reasoning that the contextualist proposal takes as its starting point is reviewed in Section 3.1, while the basic form of the contextualist response is outlined in Section 3.2. Section 3.3 discusses some ideas about the semantics and pragmatics of quantifier domain restriction, focusing on ordinary cases of contextual domain restriction. Sections 3.4–3.6 apply these ideas towards a systematic development of the contextualist proposal. Some concluding remarks are offered in Section 3.7.

3.1 THE PARADOX REVIEWED

To set the stage, let us rehearse the kind of paradoxical reasoning that will be our main concern. A number of paradoxes will make the point, including forms of the Liar and Russell's paradoxes. I shall present a very elegant and highly general version of Russell's paradox due to Williamson (2004), which will serve as a good illustration of the phenomenon at issue.

Williamson invites us to consider the task of building an interpretation I for some language. As he notes, we need to say little about the formal properties of I, except that for a given predicate term 'P' and collection F, we may build an interpretation $I(F)$ which makes 'P' hold all and only the Fs. We can remain quite neutral on the nature of the *F*s as well. They need not form a set or a class, and it appears we can simply appeal to Boolos-style plural constructions (e.g. Boolos, 1984) to describe them.

The crucial observation is that though interpretations need not be sets or classes, it appears we can talk about them. As Williamson notes, we do so naturally when we investigate logical consequence, for instance. In talking about interpretations, we recognize them as objects of some kind. Once we have this, we have the basics of a Russell-like construction. Let the *R*s be all and only the objects *o* such that *o* is not an interpretation under which '*P*' applies to *o*. Then there is an interpretation $I(R)$. But the object $I(R)$ itself cannot be in the domain of the quantifier *all and only the objects* just used (nor can it be in the domain of any quantifier as interpreted by $I(R)$). If it were, we would have in the case of $o = I(R)$: $I(R)$ is an interpretation under which '*P*' applies to *o* iff $I(R)$ is not an interpretation under which '*P*' applies to *o*. This is a contradiction, just as in the usual version of Russell's paradox.

The response to this and other paradoxes I favor simply says that the object *o* must not have been in the range of the apparently unrestricted quantifier *all objects*. Indeed, it *cannot* be, on pain of logical contradiction. Thus, we must see even quantifiers like *all objects* as in important ways restricted. Of course, Williamson himself disagrees. He holds that we cannot really recognize $I(R)$ as an object, as it is fundamentally predicative or second-order. But as I mentioned above, my goal here is not to engage in this dispute directly, but rather to investigate some of the details of my favored response.

One of the very nice features of Williamson's version of the Russell argument is that it shows that the object we find outside of the domain of an occurrence of *all objects* need not be a set, or class. The argument makes extremely minimal assumptions about the kind of object in question. But if we do help ourselves to some of the basic features of set theory, we can state the problem we face more simply. Relying on some simple set-theoretic reasoning, we can conclude from Williamson's construction that the interpretation of a language in a given stretch of discourse cannot itself be in the domain of any quantifier as used in that stretch of discourse. Some further set-theoretic reasoning allows to reduce this to the fact that the domain of the widest quantifier in a stretch of discourse—the domain of *all objects*—cannot itself be an object in the domain of that quantifier. As usual, we turn the Russell paradox into a proof that there is no universal set.[1]

Though Williamson's argument shows them not to be crucial, I shall make these set-theoretic assumptions for simplicity's sake in what follows. With these assumptions, we can work with the more familiar 'no universal set' form of Russell's paradox. We start with a quantifier *all objects*, recognize its domain as itself an object, and conclude on pain of contradiction that this object cannot be in the domain of the quantifier. We thus find, I maintain, that our apparently absolutely unrestricted quantifier *all objects* is somehow restricted after all.

[1] Of course, the axiom of foundation already tells us no set contains itself. There is a responses to the Liar developed in non-well-founded set theory by Barwise and Etchemendy (1987), but this is already a *contextualist* response. (I discuss the relation of my preferred view to theirs in my 2004*a*.)

3.2 A CONTEXTUALIST PROPOSAL

So far, we have observed that, given any quantifier domain, it is possible to build an object which does not fall under that domain, via directions provided by familiar paradoxes. With some set-theoretic assumptions, we may say that the quantifier domain itself is an object that cannot be among its own members.

Call this the *argument from paradox*. What does this argument really show? Though the issue is contentious, my starting point for this chapter is that the argument shows no quantifier can range over 'absolutely everything'. To fix some terminology, say that an *absolutely unrestricted quantifier* is one that ranges over a fixed domain of 'absolutely everything'. An *absolutist* holds that there are absolutely unrestricted quantifiers. I shall assume the argument from paradox shows that absolutism is untenable.[2]

Rejecting absolutism has appeared implausible to a number of authors (e.g. Cartwright, 1994; McGee, 2000; Williamson, 2004). To many, some form of contextualism has seemed to be the best way to address this worry. The basic contextualist idea is to see the reasoning in the argument from paradox as showing that even quantifiers like *all objects* range over contextually extensible domains. We start with a domain for a quantifier like *all objects*, and via the paradoxes identify an object not in that domain. This causes the context to change, to a new context in which *all objects* ranges over a strictly wider domain including the new object we discovered.

The contextualist holds that this conclusion is not so implausible as it might seem, because in fact contextual restrictions on quantifier domains are the norm in natural language. For instance, consider:

(1) a. Most people came to the party.
    b. Every bottle is empty.

In each, we interpret the quantifier as contextually restricted. Precisely how will depend on the context. Roughly, (1a) says that most people in the contextually salient domain came to the party, e.g. most people among my friends and colleagues. (1b) does not say that every bottle in the world is empty; rather, it is understood as saying that every bottle in the contextually salient domain is empty, e.g. the bottles near the door waiting to be taken outside.

(1a) and (1b) uses the already restricted *most people* and *every bottle*, and provide further contextual restrictions. We see the same thing with *syntactically unrestricted* quantifiers: quantifiers like *everything* or *nothing* which bear no non-trivial overt restricting predicate. For instance:

(2) a. I took everything with me.
    b. Nothing outlasts the energizer.

[2] I hasten to repeat that the assessment of the argument from the paradox is a delicate matter. I have discussed it at greater length in my (2004*b*), and it is pursued with great subtlety by Williamson (2004), and in the chapters by Fine (this volume) and Parsons (this volume).

(2a) says that I took everything in the contextually salient domain, e.g. everything I had brought with me; while (2b) says that nothing of the contextually relevant kind outlasts the energizer, e.g. batteries.

The contextualist seeks to bolster the anti-absolutist position by noting that we already have good reason to see most quantifiers in natural language as ranging over contextually restricted domains, whether they appear overtly restricted or not. The contextualist then argues it is a small step to conclude that all quantifiers are so contextually restricted. There is no way to step outside the normal contextual restrictions on our quantifiers, the contextualist holds, and assuming we can leads to paradox.

It is the task of this chapter to see how far this idea can be pressed. But some initial points about how best to formulate the contextualist proposal should be addressed before we jump into the details of contextually restricted quantifiers. The first is to clarify what we mean by talking about restricted or contextually restricted quantifiers. To regiment some terminology, let us reserve the term *restricted quantifier* for one which contains a *syntactic restrictor*: a predicate either pronounced or unpronounced but present in the underlying syntax, which restricts the domain of a quantifier. It will be convenient to further require that the restrictor be non-vacuous. Restricted quantifiers are thus syntactically restricted, and the restrictor position is filled with a non-vacuous predicate. Each quantifier in (1) is clearly restricted.

By this definition, the quantifiers in (2) are not restricted, as predicates like *thing* are semantically vacuous. But as they occur in their intended contexts, they range over subdomains of objects we can talk about in their contexts, and we can assume that speakers will intend them to range over such restricted domains. Let us say a quantifier is *contextually restricted* if its contextually fixed domain is a subdomain of the objects available for quantification in a given context. All the examples in both (1) and (2) are of contextually restricted quantifiers, though the ones in (2) are unrestricted but contextually restricted, whereas the ones in (1) are both restricted and contextually restricted.

The quantifiers that figure into the argument from paradox, like *all objects* or *everything*, are clearly unrestricted according to this terminology. It is also highly plausible that they are contextually unrestricted. As speakers use them at the beginning of the argument, they do not intend them to range over any proper subdomain of objects they can talk about. When the speaker says *all objects* in such a context, she does not mean 'all objects that are *F*', or 'all objects except those in *Y*', or anything else that would indicate contextual restriction.[3]

To make clear how there might still be room for a contextualist response to the argument from paradox, one more definition is needed. Let us say the *background domain of a context* is the widest domain of quantification available in a given context. This will be the domain of all objects, according to a given context. It is thus the domain over which unrestricted and contextually unrestricted quantifiers range.

[3] Some interesting idea of Rayo (2003) might be used to explain how some unrestricted quantifiers wind up contextually *un*restricted. Of course, by my lights, Rayo's ideas will have to be re-cast in terms of setting quantifiers to range over the background domain of a context, rather than 'absolutely everything', but I think they could serve very nicely in that role.

As far as a single context is concerned, the background domain is simply 'everything', and will not be a proper subset of any other quantifier domain or predicate extension available in that context.

The contextualist response to the paradox is the view that there is contextual relativity of background domains. Whereas the absolutist holds there is one fixed background domain, which is simply 'absolutely everything', the contextualist holds that different contexts can have distinct background domains. The argument from paradox shows us, given a plausible background domain, how to identify an object not in the domain. The contextualist holds that this leads us to a new context with a strictly wider background domain.

The contextualist position on the quantifiers in the argument from paradox is thus that they are both unrestricted and contextually unrestricted. This is just to say that they range over the background domain of a given context. But they are still *contextually relative* unrestricted quantifiers, in that they range over the background domain of a context, and that is a context-relative domain.[4]

I am distinguishing contextual domain restriction, which carves out a subdomain within a background domain, from the contextual relativity of background domains themselves. The contextualist takes the argument from paradox to show that background domains can *expand* in certain changes in context. Clearly this cannot be understood as relaxing some contextual restriction. Indeed, what the paradox does is show us one specific object that was left out of a background domain, and the shift in context must expand the domain to take it in.[5] To understand this, we need to understand how context can re-adjust to take a new object into a background domain, and how this can affect our uses of unrestricted quantifiers. It is to these matters that we now turn.

3.3 THE SEMANTICS AND PRAGMATICS OF RESTRICTED QUANTIFIERS

In this section, I shall investigate how quantifier domains are context-dependent. Much of the focus here will be on the ordinary sort of contextual domain restriction we see in cases like (1) and (2). For cases like these, we may rely on some independently motivated ideas from philosophy of language and linguistics to explain how context interacts with the semantics of quantifiers. With this in hand, I shall identify how context can interact with unrestricted and contextually unrestricted quantifiers

[4] Fine calls these *relatively unrestricted quantifiers*. I am changing the terminology slightly to emphasize the role of context in rejecting absolutism. It is fair enough to say that contextual relativity is a *kind* of contextual restriction, but it would be cheating for the contextualist to let the terminology conflate cases like (1) and (2) with the ones we are confronted with by the paradox. Thus, I shall apply 'contextually restricted' to the former, and 'contextually relative' to the latter.

[5] The contextualism I am proposing here assumes what Fine (this volume) calls *expansionism*, as opposed to *restrictionism*. Fine argues directly against restrictionism, while I am merely noting that the argument from paradox, and the basic contextualist reply, seem to be naturally expansionist and not restrictionist.

as well. I shall also very tentatively explore the pragmatic mechanism by which context sets restricted quantifier domains. Once we have these ideas in hand, I shall go on to apply them to the case of background domains in subsequent sections.

3.3.1 The Semantics of Quantifier Domains

In this section, I shall begin by reviewing some fairly standard points about how ordinary contextually restricted quantifiers like we see in (1) and (2) work. I shall then turn to how the semantics of quantifiers can make room for background domain relativity.

For reference's sake, I shall adopt a standard generalized-quantifier treatment of the semantics of quantification. This is the semantics of *determiners*: expressions like *every, some, most, few*, etc. The standard theory treats these as *relations* between two sets, representing the contents of nominals and verb phrases. Fix a domain M for an interpretation. Assign nominals like *bottle* and verb phrases like *is empty* subsets of M as their semantic values.[6] For a term α, let $[\![\alpha]\!]^c$ be its semantic value in context c, so $[\![\text{bottle}]\!]^c, [\![\text{is empty}]\!]^c \subseteq M$. Then *Every bottle is empty* (1b) expresses the relation $[\![\text{bottle}]\!]^c \subseteq [\![\text{is empty}]\!]^c$. The semantic value of the determiner *every* is thus the generalized quantifier $\mathbf{every}_M$:[7]

(3) For every $A, B \subseteq M$, $\mathbf{every}_M(A, B) \longleftrightarrow A \subseteq B$

Semantically non-trivial nominals, like *bottle*, give us restricted quantifiers.

One of the virtues of generalized quantifier theory is that it provides definitions for many other quantifiers as well. For instance, we can define a value for *most* by:

(4) For every $A, B \subseteq M$, $\mathbf{most}_M(A, B) \longleftrightarrow |A \cap B| > |A \setminus B|$

The theory of generalized quantifiers, and their application to natural-language semantics, is well developed. For surveys, see Keenan and Westerståhl (1997) and Westerståhl (1989).

Definitions like (3) are relative to a fixed M, and give what are called *local* generalized quantifiers. In logic, of course, we can ask about what would happen if we varied M—varied the universe of discourse. To do this, we need what are called *global generalized quantifiers*. These are simply functions from domains M to local generalized quantifiers on M. So we could set:

(5) **Every** is the function from M to $\mathbf{every}_M$.

Global generalized quantifiers capture the most general meanings of determiners.

It is tempting to explain the context-dependence of quantifiers we see in (1) and (2) as the result of context affecting M—the background domain—in a global generalized quantifier. As was argued by Westerståhl (1985*a*), this is not right. Westerståhl offers two important principles:

6 I am assuming an *extensional* semantic framework. As issues of intensionality are not relevant to our concerns here, this can be seen as a mere simplifying assumption.

7 I am denoting the generalized quantifier which interprets an expression like *every* by the corresponding boldface expression $\mathbf{every}_M$.

WP1: Background domains are large. Contextually restricted domains can be small.
WP2: Background domains are (relatively) stable across stretches of discourse. Contextually restricted domains are not.

(Westerståhl makes a stronger claim in place of WP2, but the weaker version will be the relevant one for our discussion here.)

To see how WP1 works, consider:

(6) At the department meeting today, everyone complained about the Governor.

Everyone ranges over members of the department, and excludes the Governor, even though we have to have the Governor in our background domain. Hence, the contextually specified domain of *everyone* is not only quite small, but clearly smaller than the background domain.

To see how WP2 works, consider an example attributed to Peter Ludlow from Stanley and Williamson (1995):

(7) Nobody cared that nobody came.

Here, on many natural readings, we talk about two distinct domains for distinct occurrences of the same quantifier. Hence, neither can be the background domain.

The moral of these arguments is that ordinary quantifier context-dependence is not the result of M being a context-dependent parameter. Rather, we need an additional contextual restriction on quantifier domains, within whatever background domain we have set. There are a number of different ways to do this, and the details of exactly how will not matter here. For argument's sake, I shall adopt the proposal of Stanley (2000) and Stanley and Szabó (2000), which holds that there is a contextual parameter in the *nominal* of a quantifier. Simplifying somewhat, we make *Every bottle is empty* look like:

(8) $\textbf{every}_M(D^c \cap [\![\text{bottle}]\!]^c, [\![\text{is empty}]\!]^c)$

D^c is a contextually fixed set of elements of M, which restricts the quantifier domain by intersection.[8]

Making the semantics of ordinary quantifier domain restriction explicit makes clear that it will not directly explain the context-relativity of *background domains* which the paradoxes seem to show us. It cannot, as it is a mechanism for restriction within background domains. Even so, the semantics of quantification does show us a way to make room for the context-relativity we need. The semantics of each (local) generalized quantifier already depends on M, which is playing the role of the *background* domain.

[8] I am suppressing some further complications in Stanley and Szabó's view. (Incidentally, the specific example (1b) is drawn from their presentation.) Stanley and Szabó (2000) are advancing a particular claim about logical form: that the contextual parameter appears in the nominal position. There are other options. For instance, von Fintel (1994) and Westerståhl (1985*a*) place the parameter on the determiner, though the resulting semantics is still basically that of (8). A more significantly different option is to deny there is any such parameter in logical form at all, and insist that a purely pragmatic process produces quantifier domain restriction. Representatives of this view include Bach (1994) and Carston (2004). Another option is to deny that there is any context-dependence. This route is taken by Cappelen and Lepore (2002).

If, as the argument from paradox seems to show, M can shift with context, then we may see M as introducing context-relativity into the semantic values of determiners as given in definitions like (3) and (4).

To make this explicit, consider an occurrence of *everything is F*, in which *everything* is not contextually restricted. In such a context, we will have $D^c = [\![\text{thing}]\!]^c = M$. Tracing through definition (3), we find the sentence is true iff $M \subseteq [\![\text{F}]\!]^c$. If M is context-relative, so is the interpretation of the contextually unrestricted *everything*.

As the considerations of Section 3.2 already suggested, this sort of contextual relativity is very different from what we see in ordinary cases of contextual domain restriction. First of all, it is a very different sort of mechanism that introduces dependency upon context. In ordinary domain restriction, it is an independent parameter D^c in the underlying logical form of a sentence. In the case of background domain relativity, it is a feature of the semantics of determiners itself that triggers context-dependence. I shall call this M-dependence, but it must be stressed that M in (3) and (4) works very differently than D^c in (8). D^c is a parameter which gets an independent value, and then composes with other semantic values of a sentence, particularly the semantic value of the nominal. M enters into determining the semantic value of a determiner directly.[9]

This is to say, in effect, that determiners function like *indexicals*. As the class of determiners is rather large, one might object that this conclusion posits massive or open-ended indexicality. It certainly does posit indexicality, but the objection is over-stated. First of all, the class of simplex or 'lexical' determiners is not really so large or open-ended, compared to classes like nouns or verbs. (The determiners form what linguists call a 'closed class', whereas nouns and verbs form 'open classes'.) Perhaps more importantly, it is known from work of Keenan and Stavi (1986) that the semantic values of possible human language determiners can be built up from a very small class of basic determiner values, together with some operations not specific to determiners. Indeed, we can built them inductively from $\mathbf{every}_M$ and $\mathbf{some}_M$. So it may well be that we only have to posit indexicality in a very limited class of expressions to get the results we need.[10]

So far, my proposal is that there are two distinct sources of context-dependence in quantifiers. One—D^c dependence—is familiar and commonplace, and responsible for ordinary contextual domain restriction. The other—M dependence—is responsible for the context-relativity of unrestricted and contextually unrestricted quantifiers. If this is right, then the pressing question becomes how context can fix a background domain: how context fixes M. To try to shed some light on this, I shall begin by looking at how context works to set quantifier domains in the more ordinary cases. In doing so, I shall isolate a few general principles. Along with Westerståhl's principles

[9] A global generalized quantifier thus gives the *character* of a determiner, in the sense of Kaplan, (1989). The context-relativity of background domains implies that this character is non-constant.

[10] There are some more ordinary cases where determiners display indexicality. One is the case of *many* discussed by Westerståhl (1985*b*), which appears to have a value sensitive to a contextual input of 'normal frequency' in much the way that I am positing sensitivity to background domain.

about background domains, these will help us understand what context must do in the case of background domains.

3.3.2 The Pragmatics of Quantifier Domains

There are a few general principles about how context sets quantifier domains which we can identify by looking at discourse. One general caveat needs to be mentioned first. There is a significant step between asking how the truth conditions of a sentence vary with context, or what features of a sentence makes it context-dependent, and asking how context itself fixes some context-dependent parameter. By the lights of Stanley and Szabó (2000), the latter is a matter of *foundational* rather than *descriptive* semantics (or pragmatics). Regardless of classification, understanding how context affects content is an important part of our understanding of context-dependence. But foundational issues in pragmatics do tend to get extremely messy, and run into some very hard problems in cognitive science. Explaining what speakers will take to be salient or relevant, for instance, might well involve far-reaching theories of cognition. (To borrow a phrase from Peter Ludlow, foundational problems in pragmatics tend to be 'AI-complete'.)

The best we can do, absent such far-reaching theories, is to stay as close to descriptive matters as we can. Wherever possible, I shall try to isolate relatively clear, well-motivated descriptive constraints, and then try to apply these constraints to shed some light on the foundational issue of what pragmatic processes are at work in domain restriction. The conclusions I shall come to will be limited, but they will be enough, I hope, to further the comparison between ordinary quantifier domain context-dependence, and background domain context-relativity.

3.3.2.1 Quantifier Domains by Anaphora on Predicates

One way context works to set quantifier domains, in the ordinary case of contextual domain restriction, is by anaphora-like processes. The domain-restricting parameter can be mapped to some previous material in a discourse, much like a pronoun can (cf. Geurts and van der Sandt, 1999; Roberts, 1995). We see this in:

(9) There were some passengers on the airplane. Most passengers$_{D^c}$ were killed in the crash.

The domain of *most* is contextually restricted by the predicate *on the airplane*.[11]

Quantifier domain restrictors prefer to find antecedents in predicative material. For instance, we see a contrast in:

(10) John came to the party and Sarah came to the party.

a. They had fun.
b. Everyone had fun.

[11] The example is modified from one of Geurts and van der Sandt (1999), who develop this idea in a DRT-based framework. Gawron (1996) and Roberts (1995) pursue related ideas in the framework of dynamic logic.

They in (10a) picks up the aggregate of John and Sarah, while *everyone* in (10b) ranges over people who came to the party. It picks up its domain from *came to the party*.

Furthermore, it appears that context can construct complex defining properties out of stretches of discourse. For instance:

(11) Susan found most books which Bill needs, but few were important.

The domain of *few* appears to be books which Susan found and Bill needs. Note, this combines relations and terms to form a defining condition.[12]

So far, we have seen that contextually restricted quantifier domains can be set by finding appropriate predicative material in previous discourse. When this happens, it is via predicative material, but that material can be complex, and built out of multiple predicates and singular terms.

3.3.2.2 Accommodation

In many cases, previous discourse does not provide the needed predicates to restrict a quantifier domain. This is the way we interpreted the examples in (1) and (2), for instance. Even when we do have some predicates available in previous discourse, there is no guarantee we will not need more information from context to tell us how to further restrict the domain.

In these cases, speakers will seek to recover from the context enough information to define the right domain restriction. These days, this is often glossed as a process of *accommodation*, in that it makes the continuing discourse as if the new information had been explicitly uttered.[13] There are some very rough-and-ready rules for accommodation we can state for the case of quantifier domain restriction: add information restricting a quantifier domain to make the current utterance coherent and informative, relative to what is common knowledge in the discourse at the point of utterance.[14]

These rules are rough, and leave the task of accommodation drastically underdescribed. I shall not be able to elaborate them much more, but there is one point that will be important. Whatever determines a quantifier domain in accommodation cases—what makes the quantifier domain sustain informative and coherent discourse—is not simply a matter of what objects and properties are salient

[12] This is derived from an example of Kamp and Reyle (1993), who use it in introducing their abstraction operator for plural anaphora (cf. Saebø, 1999).

[13] The notion of accommodation stems from Lewis (1979). It is common to think of accommodation as a kind of *conversational repair strategy*. Something happens in a discourse which would cause it to break down unless some information where present, and we repair the discourse to make it present.

There are a number of distinct ways of understanding how such a process works. Though Lewis proposed that there are distinct rules of accommodation, it can be thought of as flowing from general pragmatic principles, perhaps along Gricean lines. This is the view taken by Stalnaker (1998), and is in keeping with the discussion in Heim (1983) and Roberts (1995). But in theories like that of van der Sandt, (1992), accommodation is understood as a particular kind of operation within a representational theory of discourse like DRT. However, I do not think any of the claims I make here are affected by these distinctions.

[14] These ideas derive from Grice (1975), Stalnaker (1978), and van der Sandt (1992). I have discussed the issue of coherence at length in my (2002).

in the immediate environment. We do not accommodate *merely* by checking what is around us. For instance, consider the familiar:

(12) Everything is packed.

Make the context one in which you are about to step out the door to go on a trip. You have your suitcase, and a bunch of things in your pockets or in hand that you will want for the ride. As we normally interpret it in a case like this, the utterance of (12) is true, in spite of the fact that the things in your pocket are not packed. Accommodation has not set the domain of *everything* to be all the items that are salient in the environment, or even all the salient items that belong to you. Rather, it has made the domain all the salient items *of the kind appropriate for packing for a trip*.

What makes something appropriate in this way is part of what happens on trips, or what normally happens on trips. It is part of what cognitive scientists sometimes describe in terms of frames or scripts, or more often these days, plans. The plan or script or frame of trips is needed to fix the domain of *everything*. Hence, in the accommodation process that gives us the natural reading of (12), we will have to look to some such plan or frame or script. I shall not worry about exactly which of these notions is right for describing accommodation; rather, I shall highlight one general point. A plan or script or frame provides highly situation-specific or activity-specific information, often very complex information. What we need to accommodate in (12) is access to specific and detailed information about what kind of activity a trip is, and what happens on one. This tells us what belongs in a suitcase, which is what we use to set the domain of *everything*.[15]

3.3.2.3 Domains Include Topics

I shall make one more observation about the way contextually restricted quantifier domains are set. This one relies on a general feature of discourse. Discourses have *topics*, roughly, what is under discussion at a given point in a discourse. We can think of discourse topics as given by questions: the topic of a discourse at a given moment is the question that is under discussion. If the question is something like *What did John do?*, we can talk about John being the (current) topic of the discourse. Discourse topics, and how they evolve as discourse progresses, are closely related to the messy issues we encountered when looking at accommodation. Though the facts are sometimes murky here, some helpful generalizations can be made.[16]

[15] A specific proposal on where something script-like fits into domain restriction comes from the analysis of telescoping of Poesio and Zucchi (1992) (they appropriate the term 'script'). Clearly, I am using the term 'plan' very loosely—more loosely than serious work in AI—though I believe this sort of case highlights the 'AI-complete' nature of the problem we face. Some comments relating accommodation to plan recognition more properly construed may be found in Thomason (1990). This paper appears in the collection edited by Cohen, Morgan, and Pollack (1990) which contains a number of other papers discussing the role of plans in discourse.

[16] The literature on the topic is quite large. Some of it is surveyed in my (2002). Important recent developments of the idea of discourse topic include Büring (2003), Roberts (1996), van Kuppevelt (1995), and von Fintel (1994).

Quantifier domains and discourse topics interact in a number of ways.[17] One will be important for our concerns here: Generally, if something is a topic at a given moment in a discourse, we will expect contextually set quantifier domains to include it. Return to the context of (12), and consider:

(13) a. That's a nice watch you are wearing. Tell me about it.
b. ?Everything is packed.

At best, the domain of *everything* can no longer be taken to exclude the watch, as it did in (12). Worse, I am not sure if the pragmatic process of setting a domain even succeeds here, as the second utterance sounds marginal to my ear.

In contrast, we can readily exclude non-topical elements from a quantifier domain by contextual restriction. We saw this with (12). To give one more example, consider:

(14) a. John decided to ship all his belongings to England.
b. Everything is small.

Suppose this discourse is taking place as the movers are loading John's belongings into a giant shipping container. The domain of *everything* still does not include the container, roughly, as it is not what we are talking about, even though it is salient in the environment, and figures into the 'plan' for moving.

If we did bring the container into the discourse as a topic, we would get a different result. Consider:

(15) a. John decided to ship all his belongings to England. So, he went out and started investigating shipping containers. He found some that were about the right size.
b. Everything is small.

Now *everything* definitely contains the shipping containers.

I shall rely on the principle that contextually set quantifier domains include topical items. The principle I need, and think is reasonably well-illustrated by the examples we have seen, is that if an item is a topic, it must be in contextually restricted quantifier domains. I do not think it is generally true that such domains include all and only topical elements.[18]

3.3.3 Setting Quantifier Domains

We now have a few observations about how contextual quantifier domain restriction works. We have assumed that there is a contextual parameter in the nominal of a

[17] The idea that topic and quantifier domain interact has been investigated at length for the case of adverbial quantifiers, by Partee (1991), Roberts (1995), and von Fintel (1994), among others. A somewhat programmatic suggestion along the lines I am indicating here is also found in Beaver (1994).

[18] There are a number of complications to this principle. For instance, the dynamics of topics and subtopics, and interactions with the semantics of nominals, can create apparent violations of the principle. Space limits preclude investigating this, and I shall have to simply assert that attention to details can show these violations to be merely apparent.

quantified noun phrase, which accounts for the 'ordinary' cases of domain restriction. Furthermore, we have isolated some principles which govern how this parameter is set:

(i) When possible, quantifier domains are built out of predicative material. Both predicates and terms appearing in previous discourse can be used to construct complex defining predicates for domains.

(ii) When appropriate predicative material is not available in discourse, a process of accommodation is triggered.

(iii) In constructing domains either anaphorically or by accommodation, domains are constrained to include all topical material.

(iv) Accommodation often makes reference to situation-specific information.

These rules hardly tell us everything we might want to know about setting quantifier domains, but they do tell us something.

A couple of morals for application of these principles to the harder case of background domains are worth highlighting. When possible, contextual domain restriction is a pragmatic way to reproduce what could be done semantically by predicates in restricted quantifiers. We see this in principle (i). But this is not always the way domain restriction works. When the process of accommodation of principle (ii) is triggered, it relies on many other factors than simply finding predicates. Principle (iii) is a clear example of this. No predicate is needed to introduce a topical item into a domain. But the same may be said of the kinds of situation-specific information invoked in principle (iv). The complex information encapsulated in a plan or script need not correspond to anything that speakers can express in the context in question with the language they speak; except insofar as they can use a quantifier whose domain is restricted by that information.

3.4 REFLECTIVE CONTEXTS

In that last section, we enumerated some important features of how contextually restricted quantifier domains are set by context. These applied primarily to ordinary contextual domain restriction, which we identified as setting the parameter D^c in the nominal of a quantified noun phrase. We also saw in the last section that if there is to be contextual relativity of contextually unrestricted quantifiers, it must be from a different source. It flows from the context-dependence of the determiners themselves, which in turn flows from the context-relativity of the background domain M.

My goal now is to apply the lessons of Section 3.3 to the case of background domains, to help us to understand how, in some extreme cases like we see in the paradoxes, background domains vary with context. Indeed, we can now see a little more clearly why focus on the paradox is so important. As we are reminded by principle (iv), any account of the effects of context on quantifier domains will be highly situation-specific. We need to see with what situation the paradoxical reasoning of Section 3.1 confronts us.

3.4.1 Artifacts of Discourse

The argument from paradox of Section 3.1 leads us to identify an object not in the domain of an unrestricted quantifier. To understand how this marks a shift in context, we should begin by asking what the objects we are led to recognize are like.

An important point that is made vivid by the Williamson version of Russell's paradox of Section 3.1 is that the objects in question are semantic in nature. In that version, the object we identify is the *interpretation* $o = I(R)$; in more typical versions, it is the background *domain of quantification* itself. The objects in question are semantic values, or more complicated objects built from semantic values, like an interpretation of an entire language relative to some context. Other forms of the paradoxes can lead us to other related objects, including truth predicates, propositions, contexts, etc. To give this category a label, let us call them *artifacts of discourse*. Semantic values of expressions relative to contexts, including quantifier domains, will be the main artifacts of discourse for our discussion here, but the category is somewhat wider. The characterization of artifacts of discourse is admittedly rough, but at least the main examples are familiar. Rather than refine the definition, I shall move on to examine how artifacts of discourse interact with quantifier domains.

The answer is that usually, they do not. Artifacts of current discourse—the quantifier domains of the context of the current point in the discourse, the interpretation of the language in the context, etc.—are *usually not* part of any contextually restricted quantifier domain given by the context of the current point in the discourse. Here is one example to illustrate the point. At the start of a set theory class, the professor says:

(16) Everything today is finite.

She means, roughly, that everything relevant to the day's class is a finite set. But within this category, the semantic values of her own words are excluded. They are excluded even though they do, in an entirely natural sense, count as relevant to the class. (Apprehending them is crucial to understanding the class's content.) They are also excluded even on the assumption that semantic values are sets. What the professor says remains *true* if the semantic values of her words turn out to be infinite sets.

Though most speakers do not tend to care about semantics (including most set theory professors), that is not the issue here. Artifacts of current discourse tend to be excluded from quantifier domains even if we are generally talking about semantic values, or other artifacts of some discourse or another. Suppose a semantics professor says:

(17) Every semantic value relevant to today's class/in sight/at issue is an individual or a set of individuals.

The domain of the quantifier again does not include the values of her own words, and the claim is not made false by the value of *every* being a relation between sets. To take it as if it did include these objects would not be to stretch the limits of what counts as relevant; rather, it would be to perversely disregard the normal rules of discourse.

The moral is that it is extremely hard to incorporate artifacts of current discourse into contextually restricted quantifier domains. Not impossible (at least, not in all cases), but strongly discouraged by the normal rules governing discourse. It follows from this, together with principle (iii) of Section 3.3.3, that artifacts of current discourse are extremely difficult to make *topics*. This is not simply to say we often do not make them topics, but that it is unusual, and hard, to succeed. At the very least, topicalizing an artifact of current discourse—making it a topic—amounts to a violation of the rules of well-organized and coherent discourse.[19]

Artifacts of current discourse thus have a peculiar status. They are usually non-topical, and cannot even be coherently topicalized in ordinary discourse. But nonetheless, they are clearly active in discourse in another way. They are the semantic values of the very words we are speaking, the context in which we speak, etc. We cannot understand a discourse unless we apprehend them. To fix some more terminology, let us say that artifacts of current discourse are *implicit* in the discourse. They are not explicit, in that they are not normally available to be topics, but they are clearly an important part of the discourse.

3.4.2 Reflection

I have pointed out that it is very difficult to topicalize implicit objects like artifacts of current discourse. The rules of discourse ordinarily tell us not to do it. But in fact, we can do it, if we really want to. At least, for a given point in a discourse, we can step back and start talking about the semantic properties of the discourse as it stood at that point. This introduces what were the current artifacts of discourse as topics. This will be jarring, and outside the normal rules of discourse, but we have the ability to do it.[20]

Doing this will change the context. Generally, what is topical at a given point in the discourse is part of the context. This again is a fact about the way natural language works. Again, I hope it is intuitively clear. It deserves more argument, but I shall leave that to the literature on context.[21] Forcing something implicit like an artifact of current discourse to be a topic is, if anything, a highly marked change of context. It is not a natural evolution of the context as a discourse progresses, but a discontinuous jump in context caused by a change in topic violating the normal rules of discourse.

With this in mind, let us turn to the situation which confronts us in the argument from paradox. The key step in the paradoxical reasoning we rehearsed in Section 3.1 is precisely a step of topicalizing an artifact of current discourse. In the usual forms of the paradox, we topicalize the background domain of the current context (the domain

[19] I am here appealing to what appears to be a fact about natural language, for which (16) and (17) provide a little bit of evidence. I have discussed the relation of topic to discourse coherence extensively in my (2002). Note that in many discussions of the syntax of topic-marking, the term 'topicalization' is used for a particular syntactic construction. I mean making something a discourse topic. It is shorter to say 'topicalize' than 'incorporate as a discourse topic'.

[20] I am taking it for granted that we have the intellectual resources to topicalize artifacts of discourse, even if it is only in unusual contexts where we do so. I suspect this may be the crux of my disagreement with Williamson (2004). Though linguistically speaking we can, it appears to have a nominalizing effect, and so is something I believe he would have to reject.

[21] This is a common theme in most of the pragmatically oriented work on discourse topic, such as those cited in footnote 16.

over which the quantifier *all objects* ranges). In the Williamson version, we topicalize an interpretation of the language, as it is used in some context. We do this when we take the domain or the interpretation and start talking about it, particularly, asking what properties it has. The previous discussion shows that this step in the argument from paradox will amount to a change of context, and indeed, a marked and unusual one.

Paradox also enters the fray here, and tells us something specific about what happens in this change in context. It introduces an object as topical which could not be within the background domain of the initial context of the argument from paradox, upon pain of contradiction. Now, our examination of ordinary cases already gave us some reason to expect this. Artifacts of current discourse are implicit, and so will not normally appear in any restricted quantifier domain, as we saw in Section 3.4.1. Why not? The most natural reason would be that they are not even in the background domain. Considering ordinary discourse can at best lead us to find this natural, but the paradox shows us that it has to be right!

Not every artifact of current discourse leads to paradox. Let us call the ones that do *crucial artifacts of discourse*. The crucial artifacts of discourse include the background domain given by the context of the current point in a discourse, or even the entire interpretation of the language relative to that context. They also include any objects which contain or encode these, or would allow us to extract them by some process of accommodation. With the sorts of set-theoretic assumptions I alluded to in Section 3.1, we can assume that any crucial artifact of discourse will make the background domain of the context available for topicalization. It is a common idea that what makes an artifact of discourse crucial is that it is extremely large or comprehensive relative to a given context, as are the background domain of the context, or the interpretation of the entire language as it is used in that context. A more full account of what makes certain artifacts of discourse crucial would be very useful, but I shall for the moment rest with the usual list of objects which lead to paradox.

To summarize what we have seen, fix a context c_0 for a discourse. Say a *reflective context* for c_0 is one in which we have topicalized any crucial artifact of the discourse at c_0. I am assuming that this will at least implicitly introduce the background domain M_0 of context c_0 as a topic. Call the reflective context for c_0 by c_0^R. A reflective context has the feature of taking something that was only *implicit* in c_0 and making it topical—making it explicit—in c_0^R.[22]

We have noted that we have solid reason, coming from observations about ordinary discourse, to expect that c_0^R is really a new context, and at least some reason to expect that it should have a strictly wider background domain than c_0. Furthermore, we have seen that the argument from paradox shows that c_0^R *must* have a strictly wider background domain, and so must certainly be a distinct context. In particular, the background domain M_0^R of c_0^R must contain M_0. Indeed, as M_0 is a topic in c_0^R, we may expect even contextually restricted domains in c_0^R to contain M_0. The paradox

[22] The idea of reflection making what was implicit to be explicit appears in other forms as well. In a proof-theoretic setting, a similar idea is discussed in Kreisel (1970). I tried to apply this to the Liar in my (2004*c*). A related point is made in Parsons, (1974*a*).

hardens our expectation that c_0^R is a new context with a strictly wider background domain into a requirement of logic.

We now have one major piece of the contextualist response to the paradoxes in place. There is, I have argued, a context shift in the course of the argument from paradox. It is of a particular sort: a step to a reflective context, which makes topical something which was merely implicit in the initial context.

3.5 DOMAINS FOR REFLECTIVE CONTEXTS

If we take the step to a reflective context—the step from c_0 to c_0^R—we face a problem. We have topicalized an item which cannot be in the background domain of our initial context c_0, so a new, strictly wider background domain M_0^R for c_0^R is needed.

So far, I have argued that we should have expected this, and that the paradox shows it must be the case. But that just presses the issue of what M_0^R looks like. If there is a change in context from c_0 to c_0^R, it is not enough to simply say that M_0^R must be strictly bigger than M_0. We want to know how the change in context expands the domain.

It is here that our investigation of quantifier domains in Section 3.3.2 will pay off. Building a new background domain is not the same as setting the contextual parameter D^c for restricted domains, but it is still setting a domain of quantification. If so, it should be governed by the principles of Section 3.3.3. In this section, I shall show how these principles, supplemented by some of the observations about why background domains are different from Section 3.3.1, help us to see how M_0^R might be constructed. They will tell us how context can set a new background domain as we move to a reflective context.

3.5.1 Triggering Accommodation

My first observation is that principles (i)–(iii) from Section 3.3.3 trigger an accommodation process. Of course, the paradox already forces c_0^R to have a strictly wider background domain. But once we take the step to the reflective context c_0^R, this is not merely a recondite fact of logic. Once we topicalize the domain M_0, principle (iii) requires this object to appear in *restricted* quantifier domains relative to c_0^R. We will have to talk about it and quantify over it. Thus, we will really have to make use of the expanded domain M_0^R. So, the pragmatics of domain-setting will require us to work out what the new domain is.

If the same domain-setting processes at work in ordinary cases are at work here, then we would expect the construction of c_0^R to first try to recover a new domain M_0^R from previous discourse. But of course, this is impossible. By principle (i), it would have to do so by finding appropriate predicative material. But predicative material from previous discourse will not be able to describe any domain containing M_0 as an object. At best, it will describe the objects in M_0. Hence, by principle (ii), we must accommodate.

3.5.2 Towards a 'Plan' for Accommodation

How should this accommodation proceed? As we are reminded by principle (iv), we will need to make use of highly specific information about the particular situation involved: the situation of shifting to a reflective context. This information should provide us with guidelines for building the new domain—something like a plan or script or frame from which we can extract an accommodation process. I shall thus loosely talk about a 'plan' for accommodation. (I shall usually put 'plan' in scare quotes, to remind us how loose the talk of plans is.)

They key feature of a reflective context is the topicalizing of a crucial artifact of the discourse as it stood at c_0. To build any kind of coherent plan in this situation, we should have at our disposal vocabulary for describing such artifacts and their basic properties. So as a first step, we should add this if it is not already present:

Step 1: Add vocabulary that describes in c_0^R the semantics of the language as it was used in c_0. (Even if the relevant vocabulary was present, we may need to adjust extensions for the new context.)

As with any case of accommodation, speakers may have trouble finding words to make explicit exactly what information they have accommodated. So, when saying we should add 'vocabulary', we should say more fully to add information that could appear in a fully articulated discourse even if speakers only tacitly grasp this information.

Step 1 is really only a set-up move. It puts us in a situation to make some sort of coherent plan appropriate for a reflective context. So far, we have from the prior context the elements of M_0, from the transition to c_0^R we have M_0 as an object itself, and we have vocabulary for describing the semantic properties of the language as it was used in c_0 (for shorthand, let us say the *semantics of* c_0).

To add the next step to the 'plan', we need to remember that we are not simply trying to build any old set containing M_0. We need to construct a viable background domain. One of the crucial roles of background domains is to be the source of restricted quantifier domains. As principle (i) of Section 3.3.3 tells us, the basic way restricted quantifier domains subsequent to c_0^R will be built is by forming possibly complex predicates out of material available in the context. These predicates then define restricted domains as subsets of the background domain. A viable background domain must be rich enough to allow for the formation of restricted domains by this process. In particular, once we have taken step 1, we need to build a domain which will include any restricted quantifier domain we can define using the extended vocabulary provided by step 1.

Assuming that the extended vocabulary provided by step 1 is rich enough, this will require including subsets of M_0 as elements of our new domain M_0^R. For instance, if we have predicates like *x is a semantic value of a verb phrase in* c_0, we will have to make sure M_0^R contains each subset of M_0 definable in the extended vocabulary. Thus, we should at least take as our next step:

Step 2: Close under definable subsets of M_0 in the extended vocabulary.

This begins to get us a suitable background domain for providing contextually restricted domains of quantification in c_0^R and subsequent contexts.

Actually, we need a little more than step 2. As stated, step 2 only provides subsets of M_0. But if we are thinking of having vocabulary for the semantics of something like a natural language, we will have higher-type objects as well. Determiners will have relations between sets as their values, for instance. At the very least, we will have to iterate step 2 several times. We should re-formulate step 2 as:

Step 2′ Close under definable subsets of M_0 in the extended vocabulary. Iterate as many times as needed by the semantics of c_0.

As we iterate, the extended vocabulary will get used more and more, to describe the behavior of more and more complicated artifacts of discourse from c_0.

3.5.3 Westerståhl's Principles Revisited

So far, we have begun to describe a process of accommodating a new background domain M_0^R for the reflective context c_0^R. Step 2 tries to take into account the fact that we are not just constructing any old quantifier domain; rather, we are constructing a *background domain*. Once we have the extended vocabulary we need to accommodate the new domain, it ensures that we can also provide for additional contextually restricted domains that we could define using that vocabulary.

But step 2 does not go far enough. It does not, I suggest, precisely because it does not yet pay attention to the two principles we discussed while considering Westerståhl's argument in Section 3.3.1. Westerståhl's principles show that background domains behave very differently than contextually restricted quantifier domains. To build an acceptable background domain, we need to write into our 'plan' rules that ensure we satisfy these principles.

We satisfy both if we do as much as we can to satisfy WP1, which reminds us that background domains are large. The result of step 2 appears unduly small. It includes a few new elements from M_0, but then just stops. Using step 2′ instead iterated this process a few times, but then it still just stops. We can certainly iterate much further than is required by step 2′. To build a large domain, as WP1 requires, we should do just that. We should iterate step 2 as far as we can.

The more we iterate step 2, the more we satisfy WP2 as well. This principle tells us that background domains should be stable. Westerståhl had in mind that they never change. I have rejected that, but I have argued that shifting to a reflective context is a fairly unusual step. We should still build a domain which minimizes the need for such transitions. The larger the domain, the less need we will ever have to expand it.

For instance, what happens if we succeed in topicalizing *the domain of semantic values from* c_0? This object will not be in the domain resulting from step 2, or step 2′. Would topicalizing it amount to a step to a new reflective context? I am inclined to think not. Topicalizing it is introducing a metasemantic object—a meta-artifact of discourse—as a topic. But the object is one we get simply by collecting together the semantic values from the original context c_0. It results from the metasemantics of the semantics of c_0. Topicalizing it does not seem to be a new instance of reflection, but rather continuing the reflection we had already started. A new reflective context would be one which reflects on the semantics of c_0^R itself. To avoid counting this kind of continued reflection as leading to a new reflective context, we need to make sure objects like *the domain of semantic values from* c_0 are already in the background domain M_0^R provided by c_0^R. To do so, we need to iterate step 2 past what step $2'$ itself requires.

The more we iterate step 2, the more we satisfy both Westerståhl's principles. The more we iterate, the bigger the background domain of c_0^R is. Likewise, the more we iterate, the less we see occasions for shifting to a new reflective context with a bigger background domain. The more we iterate, the more stable background domains are. Thus, it appears that to satisfy Westerståhl's principles for background domains, we need one more step in our 'plan':

Step 3: Iterate step 2 as far as possible.

What is as far as possible? Presumably until some appropriate closure condition is reached, or until the resources for iteration are exhausted. I shall discuss this further in Section 3.6.

3.5.4 Tarski and Kripke

It is worth pausing to note that the issue of how far to iterate, and where we see new reflective contexts, essentially reprises the contrast between Tarskian and Kripkean approaches to the Liar.

If we were to stop at step $2'$, we would have an essentially Tarskian view (Tarski, 1935). Though we have replaced talk of languages with talk of what is expressed in contexts, we would essentially have in c_0^R resources for describing the semantics of a language as used in c_0, but nothing more. Any further metasemantic reflection would require ascending to a new reflective context, which we can count as for all intents and purposes ascending one level in a hierarchy.

On the other hand, just as in the Liar case, iteration helps to minimize the number of distinct levels. Just as with Kripkean iteration of the Tarskian truth predicate (Kripke, 1975), iterating step 2 allows for some modest amounts of metasemantic discourse within c_0^R itself.

I have suggested that Westerståhl's principles give us reason to pursue this more Kripkean strategy. Even so, it is still possible to reflect on the semantics of c_0^R itself, and that will induce a new reflective context. If $c_0^R = c_1$, then we can always move to c_1^R by topicalizing a crucial artifact of the discourse at c_1.[23] Though the proposal I am making is more Kripkean than Tarskian, it is still in effect a hierarchical proposal.[24]

[23] Kripke notes something like this in talking about "the ghost of the Tarski hierarchy" (1975, 80).

[24] It may be that from c_1^R, the next reflective context up, we might be able to find a predicate which defines M_0^R as a subdomain of M_1^R. Indeed, the 'plan', and the considerations of Section 3.6

3.6 ITERATION

So far, we have taken a number of steps towards articulating the contextualist response to the paradox. Semantically, we have identified two different sources of context-dependence in Section 3.3.1. Contextual domain restriction sets a parameter D^c, which combines with the semantic values of nominals. The context-relativity of unrestricted quantifiers flows from the context-relativity of the background domain M, which affects the semantic values of determiners. In effect, the context-relativity of M gives determiners an indexical character.

Pragmatically, we saw in Section 3.4 how the step to a reflective context counts as a genuine change in context, and how it induces a change in the background domain. Unlike cases of contextual domain restriction, these context shifts are highly unusual, and violate some general guidelines for keeping discourse orderly and coherent.

When it comes to setting domains of quantification, we isolated some general principles in Section 3.3.2–3.3.3, by studying ordinary contextual restriction. We applied these, together with Westerståhl's principles from Section 3.3.1, to the case of background domains in Section 3.5. The plan we developed in Section 3.5 differed from the process of setting restricted quantifier domains in some important ways. But where it does, it is because of the specific features of reflective contexts and background domains. The rules for setting quantifier domains already require us to take into account such specific features of contexts. Thus, it is fair to say that the pragmatic processes that set background domains and contextually restricted domains are in fundamental respects the same.

The 'plan' I sketched in Section 3.5 instructed us in step 3 to iterate step 2. How far such iteration will go remains an open question. In this section, I shall examine this question, by bringing to bear some tools from mathematical logic. This will also enable me to offer a somewhat idealized mathematical model of what the background domains described in Section 3.5 might look like. My discussion here will, by necessity, be somewhat more technical than what has come before. For those readers wishing to skip the technicalities, the principal claim of this section can be summarized as follows: logic provides some plausible stopping points for the iteration required by step 3.

3.6.1 Reflective Contexts and Constructible Sets

The 'plan' I sketched in Section 3.5 will have a very familiar ring to logicians. It is essentially the instructions for building levels of the constructible hierarchy with urelements. In this section, I shall spell out the basic idea of this connection. I shall give a more technically precise account in Section 3.6.2.

to follow, make this seem likely. But the process of building M_0^R as part of the step to a reflective context is not that process at all. Rather, it is the process of from the 'bottom up', or as I shall suggest in a moment, inductively, generating a new domain which can serve as a background domain. Hence, the basic outlook is still, in the terms of Fine (this volume), expansionist.

The 'plan' of Section 3.5 told us to take our initial background domain M_0 and start a process of adding elements to it. The elements we are to add are those subsets that are definable in an appropriately extended vocabulary. Adding definable subsets as members is just the process of building the constructible sets. Starting with M_0 in effect would be to build the constructible sets with urelements from M_0. Thus, the plan tells us to build the constructible sets with urelements up to some appropriate level in the constructible hierarchy.

Why just the constructible sets? Why not build up all the sets, up to some appropriate level in the rank hierarchy? The quick answer is because the plan does not tell us to. The plan has us expand our initial domain M_0 for specific reasons: to make an acceptable background domain for our reflective context c_0^R. None of those reasons indicated going beyond the constructible sets, as they do not ask us to include anything beyond the definable. This plan came from considering what happens in the step to a reflective context, and asking how the general guidelines for fixing quantifier domains should be applied to it. Thus, what the plan tells us to do really does seem to be all that we should do. As the plan tells us only to add constructible sets, that is all that should be added.

There is also good reason to keep the process of building a new context as constrained as we can. Establishing a new context is something that speakers do. In passing to a reflective context c_0^R, speakers will at least implicitly have to carry out the task of building the new background domain M_0^R. The general principle 'do no more than required' seems to be a good one to invoke for what is already a massive task. Thus, though speakers may be able to understand what it would be to build a larger domain than the plan calls for, it is not required, and so they will not build it.

What of the rest of set theory? The most natural proposal, I think, is that an initial background domain M_0 had better include the usual objects of mathematics and science. Shifting to talk about mathematics or science is not shifting to a reflective context, and we have no particular reason to think it requires a shift of background domain of any kind. Hence, if we are concerned about sets, we should think of them as included in M_0.[25]

If this is right, the question of how far to iterate in step 3 of the plan comes down to what level of the constructible sets with urelements to stop at. The considerations we just raised point to a strategy for answering this question as well. The process of building a new domain for c_0^R must be something speakers can at least implicitly make sense of. Thus, the iteration should proceed as far as speakers can likewise make sense of.[26]

[25] Kit Fine suggested to me that the sorts of domain completion found often in mathematics, like passing from the real numbers to the complex numbers, might count as cases of background domain expansion. The proposal I am floating here would be to treat them as a cases of passing from one restricted domain to another, all within M_0. This would leave the cases of genuine background domain expansion limited to passing to reflective contexts. Both options are consistent with the general outlook of contextualism. If we accept Fine's option, we no longer need to assume that all, or even most, of the objects of mathematics are in a given initial background domain.

[26] If we really do assume that the initial background domain M_0 contains all the sets, we will encounter some technical complications I shall ignore for current purposes. Rather than

How far is that? The plan describes a kind of inductive process for generating a new domain by adding elements in stages. Thus, it is natural to suggest that the right stopping place is the limit of the lengths of inductive processes that are available relative to the expressive resources of c_0. I shall spell this out a little more formally in the next section.

3.6.2 A Little More Formally

Let us now try to spell out the basic idea of Section 3.6.1. To begin, suppose we describe c_0 by fixing a language $\mathcal{L}$ and a structure $\mathcal{M}_0$ for $\mathcal{L}$. $\mathcal{M}_0$ provides the semantics of c_0, and so interprets $\mathcal{L}$ as it is being used in context c_0. To facilitate doing a little logic, let us suppose $\mathcal{L}$ is a first-order language. This is certainly an idealization, but it will prove useful. (I shall use M_0 for the universe of $\mathcal{M}_0$, which preserves its role as the background domain of c_0.)

As c_0 is supposed to be an initial context, where we have not engaged in any reflection, we could either suppose that $\mathcal{L}$ contains no semantic vocabulary, or that all the semantic vocabulary has empty interpretations in $\mathcal{M}_0$. It will simplify matters slightly, and allow us to invoke some standard notation, to take the former route. When we move from c_0 to c_0^R, step 1 of the 'plan' of Section 3.5 instructs us to add all the vocabulary we might use to describe the semantic properties of the language as used in c_0. We thus extend $\mathcal{L}$ to a language $\mathcal{L}^*$ having the needed semantic vocabulary.

I shall continue in my practice of treating semantic values as sets, and generally, of identifying semantic talk with set-theoretic talk. Relative to this simplifying assumption, we should suppose $\mathcal{L}^*$ supplements $\mathcal{L}$ by adding set-theoretic vocabulary: a membership relation $\in$, and quantifiers and variables over sets. $\mathcal{L}^*$ is a two-sorted language, with one sort of variables ranging over elements of M_0, the other ranging over sets. We will enforce this strictly, by having set variables not range over urelements.

We are thinking of $\mathcal{L}^*$ as being used in context c_0^R. Relative to this context, it must be interpreted by an appropriate structure. A structure for $\mathcal{L}^*$ is a structure $\langle \mathcal{M}, A, E \rangle$, where A is a universe of sets with urelements drawn from M, and E interprets $\in$. Conventionally, we insist that A contains only sets and no urelements, to keep the two sorts of quantification in $\mathcal{L}^*$ separate.

As step 1 tells us to move from $\mathcal{L}$ to $\mathcal{L}^*$, step 2 tell us to add to our domain the subsets of M_0 definable in $\mathcal{L}^*$. Step 3 tells us to iterate this process. Iterating up to an ordinal α is essentially building $L(M_0, \alpha)$: the constructible sets with urelements from M_0 up to level α. We can then use $L(M_0, \alpha)$ to form the $\mathcal{L}^*$-structure $L(\alpha)_{\mathcal{M}_0} = \langle \mathcal{M}_0, L(M_0, \alpha) \cap V_{M_0}, \in \rangle$.[27]

constructible sets, for instance, we should perhaps be talking about iterated predicative classes. For thinking about the matter more technically, I shall assume that M_0 is a set.

[27] V_{M_0} is the universe of *sets* with urelements from M_0. The intersection with V_{M_0} is needed to make sure the second universe is strictly a universe of sets, and not of both sets and urelements. Clearly, the details of working with $\mathcal{L}^*$ and urelements here can be somewhat fussy. For a full exposition, see Barwise (1975), whose notation and conventions I am following. The basic idea is

Carrying out the 'plan' for building a background domain sketched in Section 3.5 can thus be modeled by the process of constructing $L(\alpha)_{\mathcal{M}_0}$ for an appropriate α. As step 3 of the plan leaves open how far to iterate step 2, we have so far left open which ordinal α will be appropriate. But setting that aside, $L(\alpha)_{\mathcal{M}_0}$ provides an interpretation of $\mathcal{L}^*$, the enriched language being used in the reflective context c_0^R. This in turn gives us an expanded background domain for c_0^R, which we get by combining M_0 with the domain A of sets we have added. In fact, this simply gives us $L(M_0, \alpha)$.

Step 3 tells us to iterate 'as far as possible'. How far is that? A moment ago I suggested that we think about 'as far as possible' in terms of the limits of processes speakers could at least implicitly make sense of, given the expressive resources they start with in c_0. The slightly picky definitions we have just given will allow us to flesh this out formally. As we are assuming speakers can pass to a reflective context, they are able to reason about the semantics of $\mathcal{L}$ as used in c_0, which is given by $\mathcal{M}_0$. Moreover, in following the 'plan' of Section 3.5, they must be able to make sense of a kind of 'bootstrapping process' which uses $\mathcal{M}_0$ to build up the new domain in stages. Formally, this is an inductive definitions on $\mathcal{M}_0$. Insofar as they understand these inductive processes, they should be able to make sense of iterating 'as far as such processes go'. This suggests the limit of the lengths of inductive definitions on $\mathcal{M}_0$ as a way to capture the amount of iteration needed in the step from c_0 to c_0^R.

The formal model of iterating to exactly this limit is the well-studied structure known as $HYP_{\mathcal{M}_0}$. In the case where $\mathcal{M}_0 = \mathbb{N}$, the natural numbers, $HYP_{\mathcal{M}_0}$ is simply $L(\omega_1^{CK})_{\mathbb{N}}$, where ω_1^{CK} is the first non-recursive ordinal. For $\mathbb{N}$, we build $HYP_{\mathbb{N}}$ by iterating through all the recursive ordinals. More generally, for structures $\mathcal{M}_0$ which share enough properties with the natural numbers, $HYP_{\mathcal{M}_0} = L(\alpha)_{\mathcal{M}_0}$ for α the limit of the closure ordinals of (first-order positive) inductive operators on $\mathcal{M}_0$.[28]

One of the very nice features of the *HYP* construction is that it is iterable. The problem of building background domains is not restricted to c_0^R. As we observed in Section 3.5.4, the process of stepping to new reflective contexts continues. From $c_0^R = c_1$, we can pass to c_1^R, which will need a new background domain. *HYP* allows for a uniform account of these steps. From $HYP_{\mathcal{M}_0}$ we can form $HYP(HYP_{\mathcal{M}_0})$, which can provide the background domain for c_1^R.[29]

So, one appealing option for how far to iterate is given by $HYP_{\mathcal{M}_0}$. There are other options as well. For instance, we might take the idea of iterating 'as far as

still just that of building the constructible sets as is done in any set theory textbook, or more closely, building $L_\alpha[M_0]$ while taking definability in $\mathcal{L}$ into account.

[28] These results are surveyed in Barwise (1975), among other places. As I mentioned above, we might have to think of our starting structure $\mathcal{M}_0$ as looking different from the natural numbers. We might encounter contexts in which our background domain already looks like a model of set theory, for instance. On the other hand, thinking about the issue from the perspective of linguistics or cognitive scientist, we might see things very differently. From those perspectives, a natural working hypothesis might be that the background domain we start with is *finite*.

[29] There is also a nice match-up between $HYP_{\mathcal{M}}$ and Kripke constructions on $\mathcal{M}$, as has been thoroughly investigated by McGee (1991), and by my (2004*a*).

possible' to be that of iterating until you get nothing new. Insofar as this might mean nothing *recognizably* new, this might mean iterating until $L(\alpha)_{\mathcal{M}_0}$ is an elementary substructure of $L(\alpha + 1)_{\mathcal{M}_0}$. An ever stronger option, taking into account the role of inductive definitions I just alluded to, would be to iterate until $L(\alpha)_{\mathcal{M}_0} \prec_1 HYP(L(\alpha)_{\mathcal{M}_0})$. Ordinals satisfying these properties can be found.[30]

We thus have a number of viable options for how far iteration must go to build an appropriate background domain for c_0^R. As a working hypothesis, I am inclined to opt for $HYP_{\mathcal{M}_0}$. It provides a workable picture of the semantics of $\mathcal{L}^*$ in c_0^R, and a plausible picture of what background domain this context might give us. Furthermore, it is fairly well-understood mathematically. All the same, the little exercise in mathematical modeling we have just been through does not conclusively tell us which option to choose (and as an exercise in mathematical modeling, it builds in some incidental features of the mathematics used, as well as the features we are trying to capture with the model). In considering multiple options, I do not want to suggest that there is nothing to distinguish among them, which would induce rampant indeterminacy in the notion of background domain. Rather, I think the moral to be drawn is that we do not yet know enough to be certain just how far iteration really does go.

Let me close this section by briefly mentioning one important feature of the formal model. It respects the distinction between artifacts of the discourse and other objects in a thoroughgoing way. Non-artifacts of the discourse correspond to urelements. These do not change as we move to reflective contexts. Indeed, the predicates *x is an urelement* and *x is a set* are Δ, and so are *absolute* in the logician's sense of not changing as models expand. Furthermore, the same holds for any 'ordinary' non-semantic expression. In the model, these will be expressions of $\mathcal{L}$, and their interpretations all remain constant. For instance, for a predicate P of $\mathcal{L}$, the set $\{m \mid P(m)\}$ does not change at all as we move from c_0 to c_0^R, etc. P in $\mathcal{M}$ is the same as P in $HYP_{\mathcal{M}}$ is the same as P in $HYP(HYP_{\mathcal{M}})$. The absoluteness of the set/urelement distinction ensures this, mathematically trivially.

This holds for all formulas of $\mathcal{L}$. Quantification in $\mathcal{L}$ is not a problem, as quantification over urelements is bounded quantification in $HYP_{\mathcal{M}_0}$. Nor is negation a problem, in the formal treatment using a two-sorted language I have offered here. However, the two-sorted language may appear somewhat artificial. If instead, for instance, we think of an expression like P as having its extension in $M_0 \cup A$, the combined domain urelements and sets, we have to a little more careful. $\neg P$ would then change its extension as A expands. But even so, the absoluteness of the set/urelement distinction will allow us to form an absolute predicate $U(x) \wedge \neg P(x)$, where $U(x)$ is *x is an urelement*. The extension of this predicate will not change as the domain of sets expands. (As usual, this observation really applies to Σ-formulas of $\mathcal{L}^*$.)

[30] The former is what is known as an $\alpha + 1$-stable ordinal, the latter an α^+-stable ordinal (where α^+ is the next admissible ordinal greater than α). These were extensively investigated by Richter and Aczel (1974), who show that they are analogs in generalized recursion theory of indescribable cardinals. They also show that the least α^+-stable ordinal is the limit of the closure ordinals of non-monotone Π_1^1-inductive operators.

The moral of this observation is that changing to a reflective context does change the background domain of quantification, and the interpretation of the language of artifacts of discourse, but it leaves the interpretations of other aspects of the language as we speak it in c_0 unchanged.[31]

3.7 CONCLUSION

I have now presented the core features of the contextualist approach to the paradoxes, and so made my basic case. I have argued that quantifiers which are both unrestricted and contextually unrestricted show relativity to a contextually determined background domain. They do so because of the way the background domain M figures into the semantics of determiners. I noted that this is a distinct phenomenon from the usual quantifier context-dependence, as it is relativity to the background domain M, over and above the context-dependence of the parameter D^c in the nominal of a noun phrase. But I also argued that the pragmatic mechanisms that set M are fundamentally related to those that set contextually restricted quantifier domains. First of all, I argued that there really is a context shift in the argument from paradox, as it involves a step to a reflective context. Furthermore, I showed how the same general principles which govern the setting of contextually restricted domains govern the setting of a new expanded background domain for a reflective context. Where setting M for a reflective context differs from setting a contextually restricted domain, it is because setting M relies on the specific nature of reflective contexts. Yet it is a general feature of domain-setting to rely on such specific features. Finally, to flesh out my proposal, I offered some formal models of what an expanded background domain might look like.

To close, let me mention some issues that remain open (over and above the larger issues I put aside at the beginning of this chapter). Two seem to me most important. First, this chapter has concentrated on how domains expand, particularly, how they expand in the step to a reflective context, which I see as the crucial step in the argument from paradox. Very little has been said here about how an *initial* background domain is set, and understanding this is important for a full account of the context-relativity of background domains. Second, a great deal of weight has been placed on the distinction between artifacts of discourse and other objects. I gave a rough-and-ready version of this distinction, and more needs to be done to understand it in its full generality.

I hope that developing the positive aspects of the contextualist approach systematically, as I have tried to do here, will serve to dispel some the air of mystery which seems to attach to it. Answering these questions would do so all the more.

[31] In a longer version of this chapter, I used this moral to counter an objection from Williamson (2004) that non-absolutist views of quantification, including the contextualist view I have been pursuing here, cannot even capture *restricted* quantification properly. However, a full discussion of this interesting challenge will have to wait for another occasion.

REFERENCES

Bach, K. (1994) 'Conversational Impliciture', *Mind and Language*, 9: 124–62.

Barwise, J. (1975) *Admissible Sets and Structures* (Berlin: Springer-Verlag).

—— and Etchemendy, J. (1987) *The Liar* (Oxford: Oxford University Press).

Beaver, D. (1994) 'Accommodating Topics', in P. Bosch (ed.), *Proceedings of the IBM/Journal of Semantics Conference on Focus*, vol. 3 (Heidelberg: IBM), 439–48.

Boolos, G. (1984) 'To Be is to Be the Value of a Variable (or to Be Some Values of Some Variables)', *Journal of Philosophy*, 81: 430–49.

Büring, D. (2003) 'On D-Trees, Beans, and B-Accents', *Linguistics and Philosophy*, 26: 511–45.

Cappelen, H. and Lepore, E. (2002) 'Insensitive Quantifiers', in J. Keim Campbell, M. O'Rourke, and D. Shier (eds.), *Meaning and Truth: Investigations in Philosophical Semantics* (New York: Seven Bridges Press), 197–213.

Carston, R. (2004) 'Explicature and Semantics', in S. Davis and B. Gillon (eds.), *Semantics: A Reader* (Oxford: Oxford University Press), 817–45.

Cartwright, R. L.(1994) 'Speaking of Everything', *Nous*, 28: 1–20.

Cohen, P. R., Morgan, J., and Pollack, M. E. (eds.) (1990) *Intentions in Communication* (Cambridge: MIT Press).

Davis, S. (1991) *Pragmatics* (Oxford: Oxford University Press).

Dummett, M. (1973) *Frege: Philosophy of Language* (Cambridge: Harvard University Press).

—— (1993) 'What is Mathematics About?', in *The Seas of Language* (Oxford: Oxford University Press), 429–45.

Fine, K. (this volume) 'Relatively Unrestricted Quantification', in A. Rayo and G. Uzquiano (eds.), *Absolute Generality* (Oxford: Oxford University Press).

Gawron, J. M. (1996) 'Quantificational Domains', in S. Lappin (ed.), *Handbook of Contemporary Semantic Theory* (Oxford: Blackwell), 247–67.

Geurts, B. and van der Sandt, R. (1999) 'Domain Restriction', in P. Bosch and R. van der Sandt (eds.), *Focus: Linguistic, Cognitive, and Computational Perspectives* (Cambridge: Cambridge University Press), 268–92.

Glanzberg, M. (2001) 'The Liar in Context', *Philosophical Studies*, 103: 217–51.

—— (2002) 'Context and Discourse', *Mind and Language*, 17: 333–75.

—— (2004*a*) 'A Contextual-Hierarchical Approach to Truth and the Liar Paradox', *Journal of Philosophical Logic*, 33: 27–88.

—— (2004*b*) 'Quantification and Realism', *Philosophy and Phenomenological Research*, 69: 541–72.

—— (2004*c*) 'Truth, Reflection, and Hierarchies', *Synthese*, 142: 289–315.

Grice, P. (1975) 'Logic and Conversation', in P. Cole and J. L. Morgan (eds.), *Speech Acts*, vol. 3 of *Syntax and Semantics* (New York: Academic Press), 41–58. Reprinted in Grice (1989).

—— (1989) *Studies in the Way of Words* (Cambridge: Harvard University Press).

Heim, I. (1983) 'On the Projection Problem for Presupposition', *Proceedings of the West Coast Conference on Formal Linguistics*, 2: 114–125. Reprinted in Davis (1991).

Kamp, H. and Reyle, U. (1993) *From Discourse to Logic* (Dordrecht: Kluwer).

Kaplan, D. (1989) 'Demonstratives', in J. Almog, J. Perry, and H. Wettstein (eds.), *Themes From Kaplan* (Oxford: Oxford University Press), 481–563. First publication of a widely circulated manuscript dated 1977.

Keenan, E. L. and Stavi, J. (1986) 'A Semantic Characterization of Natural Language Determiners', *Linguistics and Philosophy*, 9: 253–326. Versions of this paper were circulated in the early 1980s.

____ and Westerståhl, D. (1997) 'Generalized Quantifiers in Linguistics and Logic', in J. van Benthem and A. ter Meulen (eds.), *Handbook of Logic and Language* (Cambridge: MIT Press), 837–93.

Kreisel, G. (1970) 'Principles of Proof and Ordinals Implicit in Given Concepts', in A. Kino, J. Myhill, and R. E. Vesley (eds.), *Intuitionism and Proof Theory* (Amsterdam: North-Holland), 489–516.

Kripke, S. (1975) 'Outline of a Theory of Truth', *Journal of Philosophy*, 72: 690–716. Reprinted in Martin (1984).

Lewis, D. (1979) 'Scorekeeping in a Language Game', *Journal of Philosophical Logic*, 8: 339–59. Reprinted in Lewis (1983).

____ (1983) *Philosophical Papers*, vol. 1 (Oxford: Oxford University Press).

Martin, R. L. (ed.) (1984) *Recent Essays on Truth and the Liar Paradox* (Oxford: Oxford University Press).

McGee, V. (1991) *Truth, Vagueness, and Paradox* (Indianapolis: Hackett).

____ (2000) 'Everything', in G. Sher and R. Tieszen (eds.), *Between Logic and Intuition* (Cambridge: Cambridge University Press), 54–78.

Parsons, C. (1974*a*) 'The Liar Paradox', *Journal of Philosophical Logic*, 3: 381–412. Reprinted in Parsons (1983).

____ (1974*b*) 'Sets and Classes', *Nous*, 8: 1–12. Reprinted in Parsons (1983).

____ (1983) *Mathematics in Philosophy* (Ithaca: Cornell University Press).

____ (this volume) 'The Problem of Absolute Generality', in A. Rayo and G. Uzquiano (eds.), *Absolute Generality* (Oxford: Oxford University Press).

Partee, B. H. (1991) 'Topic, Focus and Quantification', *Semantics and Linguistic Theory*, 1: 257–80.

Poesio, M. and Zucchi, A. (1992) 'On Telescoping', *Semantics and Linguistic Theory*, 2: 347–66.

Rayo, A. (2003) 'When Does 'Everything' Mean Everything?', *Analysis*, 63: 100–6.

Richter, W. and Aczel, P. (1974) 'Inductive Definitions and Reflecting Properties of Admissible Ordinals', in J. E. Fenstad and P. G. Hinman (eds.), *Generalized Recursion Theory* (Amsterdam: North-Holland), 301–81.

Roberts, C. (1995) 'Domain Restriction in Dynamic Semantics', in E. Bach, E. Jelinek, A. Kratzer, and B. H. Partee (eds.), *Quantification in Natural Languages* (Dordrecht: Kluwer), 661–700.

____ (1996) 'Information Structure in Discourse: Towards an Integrated Formal Theory of Pragmatics', *Ohio State University Working Papers in Linguistics*, 49: 91–136.

Sæbø, K. J. (1999) 'Discourse Linking and Discourse Subordination', in P. Bosch and R. van der Sandt (eds.), *Focus: Linguistic, Cognitive, and Computational Perspectives* (Cambridge: Cambridge University Press), 322–35.

Stalnaker, R. C. (1978) 'Assertion', in P. Cole (ed.), *Pragmatics*, vol. 9 of *Syntax and Semantics* (New York: Academic Press), 315–22. Reprinted in Stalnaker (1999).

____ (1998) 'On the Representation of Context', *Journal of Logic, Language, and Information*, 7: 3–19. Reprinted in Stalnaker (1999).

____ (1999) *Context and Content* (Oxford: Oxford University Press).

Stanley, J. (2000) 'Context and Logical Form', *Linguistics and Philosophy*, 23: 391–434.

____ and Szabó, Z. G. (2000) 'On Quantifier Domain Restriction', *Mind and Language*, 15: 219–61.

Stanley, J. and Williamson, T. (1995) 'Quantifiers and Context-Dependence', *Analysis*, 55: 291–5.

Tarski, A. (1935) 'Der Wahrheitsbegriff in den formalizierten Sprachen', *Studia Philosophica*, 1: 261–405. References are to the translation by J. H. Woodger as 'The Concept of Truth in Formalized Languages', Tarski (1983).

—— (1983) *Logic, Semantics, Metamathematics* (Indianapolis: Hackett), 2nd edn. Edited by J. Corcoran with translations by J. H. Woodger.

Thomason, R. H. (1990) 'Accommodation, Meaning, and Implicature', in P. R. Cohen, J. Morgan, and M. E. Pollack (eds.), *Intentions in Communication* (Cambridge: MIT Press), 325–63.

van der Sandt, R. A. (1992) 'Presupposition Projection as Anaphora Resolution', *Journal of Semantics*, 9: 333–77.

van Kuppevelt, J. (1995) 'Discourse Structure, Topicality and Questioning', *Journal of Linguistics*, 31: 109–47.

von Fintel, K. (1994) *Restrictions on Quantifier Domains*, Ph.D. dissertation, University of Massachusetts at Amherst.

Westerståhl, D. (1985*a*) 'Determiners and Context Sets', in J. van Benthem and A. ter Meulen (eds.), *Generalized Quantifiers in Natural Language* (Dordrecht: Foris), 45–71.

—— (1985*b*) 'Logical Constants in Quantifier Languages', *Linguistics and Philosophy*, 8: 387–413.

—— (1989) 'Quantifiers in Formal and Natural Languages', in D. Gabbay and F. Guenthner (eds.), *Handbook of Philosophical Logic*, vol. IV (Dordrecht: Kluwer), 1–131.

Williamson, T. (2004) 'Everything', *Philosophical Perspectives*, 17: 415–65.

4

Against 'Absolutely Everything'!

Geoffrey Hellman

4.1 INTRODUCTION

Please note the quotes. (We are not (absolute) nihilists!)

Does absolutely general quantification, totally unrestricted in domain or by context, even make sense? How could one possibly doubt it? According to Lewis (1991, 68), the skeptical position is undermined in its very voicing (i.e., in saying, 'You cannot quantify over absolutely everything', you are implying there is something you can't quantify over!). Even posing the question as we just have seems to presuppose a positive answer, since, if called upon to explain what is meant by 'absolutely general quantification', will we not have to say, 'It is quantification purporting to be over absolutely everything' (where here, despite the cautious 'purporting', the dreaded phrase has been *used,* not mentioned)? Or is this somehow a fatuous play on words? But even it if is (and that must be argued), don't we presuppose the sensibility of absolutely general quantification in denying (at least with overwhelming probability), say, the existence of ghosts or gods? Truth of the matter apart, surely atheism is a *meaningful* position, and equally surely it does not merely deny deities with respect to some restricted domain. Indeed, Williamson (2003) has argued that the presupposition pervades even the most mundane denials of existence, e.g. of talking donkeys or flying pigs.

Nevertheless, *pace* Lewis *et al.*, there are powerful arguments against the intelligibility or coherence of absolutely general quantification, and the central Sections, 4.3 and 4.4, of this chapter will be devoted to spelling these out. As will emerge, platonistic and nominalistic positions *vis-à-vis* mathematics are affected rather differently by these arguments; indeed platonism faces the greater liability. Nevertheless, nominalistic frameworks face problems of their own with regard to absolutely general quantification. This will leave us squarely confronting the challenges to the skeptic: how *can* one meaningfully deny (and non-constructively affirm) existence, and can

Support of the National Science Foundation, Award SES-0349804, is gratefully acknowledged. I owe thanks also to Stewart Shapiro, Timothy Williamson, and the editors of this volume for comments on an earlier draft, and to Richard Grandy, Tim McCarthy, and others at the Fifth Annual Midwest Philosophy of Mathematics Workshop, held at the University of Notre Dame, 10 November 2004.

one ultimately avoid falling back on absolutely unrestricted quantification? A partial resolution, at least, will be proposed. Finally, we will touch (lightly) on the (heavy) question of what lessons there are concerning 'metaphysics' and whether it is viable at all.

But *wait*, you may already say: how can you proceed to present arguments for a 'conclusion' that you cannot even express without implicitly supposing the denial of that very conclusion? Our first task must be to attempt to dismantle this roadblock. Then we will take up two main lines of argument against the coherence of 'absolutely everything', the first applicable to platonist mathematical frameworks, the second to nominalistic frameworks as well. Finally, we will suggest what needs to be done in order to get by without 'absolutely everything'.[1]

4.2 FRAMING SKEPTICISM

The first point to be made here is that there is, at the least, a minimal fallback position for the skeptic which avoids self-destruction. As hinted at the outset, one must sharply distinguish between *use* and mere *mention* of suspect quantifier phrases or occurrences thereof, such as 'absolutely everything, without any domain or context restrictions'. One is always free to *mention* such phrases or particular uses or utterances of them and claim not to be able to make sense of them. Further, one can present arguments that, at least given certain background assumptions, they involve hidden contradictions or incoherence and cannot be made sense of. This avoids the trap of saying, 'You cannot quantify over absolutely everything.' Of course, there is still a burden to be met, that of showing that various things we regard as perfectly intelligible and which seem to depend on such unrestricted quantifier phrases are either not really intelligible or else do not really so depend. But at least incoherence in enunciating a skeptical view will have been avoided.

Can one do better? Is there a coherent, defensible, positive thesis that the skeptic, or 'generality-relativist', can articulate? A seemingly promising suggestion begins by recognizing that quantifiers are always used in contexts, and that contexts matter to their meaning and truth conditions. Following Williamson, let us speak of contexts, C, C', etc., in which quantifiers ('q's' for short) are or can be used. Then it is tempting, at least for a mathematical realist focusing on the open-endedness of mathematics, to assert,

(*GR*1) $\forall C \exists C'$('the range, R', of q's in C' exceeds that, R, of q's in C').

But if we spell out 'exceeds' in the standard way, we expose another quantifier: $\exists x$('x is in R' & x is not in R (but not vice versa)'). Taking into account that (GR1) has a

[1] One should distinguish 'absolute generality' from 'unrestrictedness', as Parsons has suggested (in his contribution to this volume). In this chapter, we argue mainly that the former is not coherent. While absolutely general quantification is naturally taken as implying lack of restriction, the converse is questionable. As will emerge, room will be left for a kind of open-ended, unrestricted quantification, despite the critique of absolute generality.

context, C^*, we infer that a quantifier in C^* ranges over something asserted not to be in its range, i.e. (GR1) is self-defeating. In his (2003), Williamson exposes this problem and goes on to find similar ones with related strategies that might be pursued, ultimately finding no suitably general positive thesis that the generality-relativist can assert. Something more subtle is needed.

It seems that as long as the relativist is confined to extensional, factual claims about ranges of quantifiers, problems such as this will arise. A better approach is to recognize intensional aspects of ontological *commitments*. Instead of futilely saying that there are ('in fact') always more things than can ever be recognized on any given occasion of use or in any context, one can say that, for any context, there is (or can be) another in which the objects *recognized* or *countenanced* go beyond what are recognized or countenanced in the former. What are compared are not asserted in the thesis actually to exist but only to be claimed or taken to exist. (We need not take a stand on just how one wants to analyze such comparisons; all we need suppose is their meaningfulness and freedom from direct ontological commitment in the context of assertion of the general thesis itself.) As it stands, however, the thesis is clearly inadequate: *so what* if more things can always be dreamt up? What must be added is that the more far-reaching, intended quantifier ranges in the new contexts are well motivated 'candidates for truth' in relation to the original. One may even come to jettison the notion of 'truth' for certain ontological claims; but what matters is that new, more extensive contexts are always forthcoming such that it would be *arbitrary* to stop at any one, identifying its ontology with 'Reality'. This, it seems to me, is a good way to meet Williamson's challenge. The general form of such a thesis would thus be,

(*GR2*) $\forall C \exists C'$ ('the range, R', of q's *countenanced* in C' exceeds that, R, *countenanced* in C & commitments in C' are well-motivated relative to those in C').

Here 'exceeds' means that C' countenances things which C does not, but not vice versa, however this is spelled out precisely. Crucially, 'existential commitment' here is merely *attributed* to C', not actually *made* in the context in which GR2 is maintained. The absolutist can retort that all this is logically compatible with there being a unique, absolutely maximal ontology, the range (plurally speaking) of totally unrestricted quantifiers. Indeed, as will emerge, the skeptic here is aiming for less than strict logical refutation on premises the absolutist will accept. In fundamental matters of this sort, that is hardly to be expected. It is sufficient if the skeptic can make the absolutist nervous, and even better if it's *very* nervous.[2]

Essentially the same idea can be got at in the form of a *reductio* of the absolutist position: assuming an absolutely maximal range of quantifiers, one appeals to some principle that leads to recognition of further objects which could not have been in the given putatively maximal range. The need for such a principle means that the refutation is not purely logical. But the principle may be well-motivated, and the better motivated it is, the more nervous the absolutist should become. Such principles can

[2] In Mel Brooks' film, 'High Anxiety', a sign is displayed over the entrance driveway of a mental institution reading, 'Institute for the Very, VERY Nervous'.

indeed be found in the sphere of pure mathematics, the *locus* of the first line of argument, to which we now turn.

4.3 ARGUMENT FROM THE OPEN-ENDEDNESS OF MATHEMATICS

Modern set theory embodies an iterative conception according to which 'the (transfinite) ordinals go on and on', hence levels of 'the cumulative hierarchy' go on and on without end. But the very statement of this illustrates the tension that Zermelo (1930) highlighted, between two opposing tendencies of human thought, that of 'creative progress' on the one hand, and that of 'all embracing completeness' on the other. For the phrases 'the ordinals' and 'the cumulative hierarchy' suggest ultimate totalities after all, contrary to the idea of 'going on and on without end'. It is not merely that there are infinitely many ordinals with no maximal one. That is also true of the natural numbers; and yet there is nothing in the concept of 'natural number' that provides an operation or operations that lead beyond any domain of them to 'new natural numbers', i.e. speaking of all the natural numbers is unproblematic in this way. But in the case of ordinals, that is precisely what the concept provides: given any totality of ordinals, if there is a maximal one in the totality, a successor is provided for (simply by extending the given well-ordering by one item, the totality itself if need be), and if there is not, one can pass to a new limit by considering the order-type of the totality itself. Michael Dummett (1978) marked this distinction nicely, calling 'ordinal' an 'indefinitely extensible' concept. The passage is worth quoting (almost) in full:

> A concept is indefinitely extensible if, for any definite characterization of it, there is a natural extension of this characterisation which yields a more inclusive concept; this extension will be made according to some general principle for generating such extensions, and, typically the extended characterisation will be formulated by reference to the previous unextended characterisation. We are much less tempted to misinterpret a concept possessing this variety of inherent vagueness as a completely determinate concept which we can descry clearly from afar, but a complete description of which we can never attain, although we can approach indefinitely close, than in the general case. An example is the concept of 'ordinal number'. Given any precise specification of a totality of ordinal numbers, we can always form a conception of an ordinal number which is the upper bound of that totality, and hence of a more extensive totality... it remains an essential feature of the intuitive concept of 'ordinal number' that any [such] definite specification can always be extended. This situation we are *not* tempted to interpret as if, in thus recognising the possibility of indefinitely extending any characterisation of the ordinals so as to include new ordinals, we were approaching ever closer to *a perfectly definite ('completed') totality of all possible ordinal numbers,* which we can never describe but of which nevertheless we can form a clear intuitive conception. We are content in this case to acknowledge that part of what it is to have the intuitive concept of 'ordinal number' is just to understand the general principle according to which any precise characterisation of the ordinals can be extended.' (p. 196, my emphasis)

Of course, the concept of 'set' itself is also indefinitely extensible in this sense: given any (precisely specified?) totality of sets, that totality itself behaves intuitively like a set: it is identified by its members, and it can be subject to further set-theoretic operations, e.g. forming its singleton, taking its power set, etc. (Similarly, general notions of 'collection', 'totality', and also of 'function', 'relation', and, presumably, their intensional counterparts, 'property', 'attribute', provide further examples. Significantly, we would argue, the mathematical notion of 'category' also qualifies.) Even if we appeal to *plural quantification* (recognized by Boolos (1985) well after Dummett wrote this), the situation is not essentially changed. Even if we begin, 'given any (precisely specified?) sets', rather than 'totality of sets', the reasoning will then invoke the *possibility* (not the necessity) of intelligibly speaking of a totality of them as built into the intuitive concept of 'collection', a possibility that leads to set theory in the first place, and which must be respected if the 'creative progress' side of mathematical thought is to be given its due. We will return to this point below.

But, before going further, the question arises, why is there the restriction in Dummett's description to 'precisely specified' or 'definitely characterized' totalities (or to 'precise specifications' or 'definite characterizations'), and what does it mean? First, it seems odd (and counterintuitive) to impute to 'the intuitive concept of ordinal' an implicit reference to precise specifications. More important, what counts here, and why does it matter? Does, for instance, the definition von Neumann gave of 'ordinal' in set theory qualify as 'a precise specification'? Whether it does or not, the conclusion should be the same, namely that 'set ordinal' is indeed an indefinitely extensible notion. The indefinite extensibility arises, it seems, not by appeal to a standard of 'precision', but rather through our capacity to entertain new totalities, 'collecting in thought' as it were everything already presupposed or given, and then, in the manner of set theory itself, reifying 'the result' of this thought process, speaking in objective terms of *a collection of those things* (taking care to avoid paradox, about which more momentarily). Thus, it seems quite counter to the italicized portion of the quote to infer that space is being allowed for a 'totality of all possible ordinals', or 'all possible sets', as 'not definite' and therefore (?) perhaps not extensible. So long as such a totality is recognized at all, whether 'precisely specified' or not, ordinal-theoretic operations can still be applied to obtain yet further 'ordinals' according to the intuitive concept. Thus, I have tended to speak directly of 'extendability of structures or models' of various theories (of sets, functions, categories, etc.), as has Putnam (1967) and, implicitly, Zermelo (1930). But the essential point is the same: as Mac Lane puts it:

> Understanding Mathematical operations leads repeatedly to the formation of totalities... There are no upper limits; it is useful to consider the 'universe' of all sets (as a class) or the category *Cat* of all small categories as well as CAT, the category of all big categories. After each careful delimitation, bigger totalities appear. No set theory and no category theory can encompass them all—and they are needed to grasp what Mathematics does. (Mac Lane, 1986, 290)

Of course, in considering new totalities and operations on them, we must avoid paradox—in the case of ordinals, the Burali-Forti paradox. Thus the order-type of the putatively all-embracing totality of 'all ordinals' cannot qualify as an ordinal belonging to the totality (e.g. a 'set ordinal'); but it still qualifies as marking or giving rise to an ordinal in the intuitive sense ('type of well-ordering, as a binary relation'), and formally we could introduce hyper-ordinals 'going on and on' beyond it, in just the way the ordinary ordinals 'go on and on' (i.e. via the same intuitive operations). (Cf. Shapiro, 2003.) Indeed, set theorists label this 'it' with 'Ω' whenever it is convenient to do so. (And you know what can then happen: hyper-hyper, ..., α-hyper, for ordinary ordinals α, and why not draw from hyper-ordinals to index the order of 'hypers', obtaining hyper-α-hyper, ..., β-hyper-α-hyper, and so on.) This, of course, while logically consistent in itself, is an embarrassment to set theory conceived as already a fully general theory of collections. There seems to be, after all, no mathematical substance to speaking of hyper-ordinals and hyper-sets that isn't captured by recognizing instead a new inaccessible level of 'the cumulative hierarchy' and identifying the hyper-objects as occurring at and beyond that level. Moreover, introducing talk of hyper-objects merely shifts the focus from the question of intelligibility of 'absolutely all (or all possible) sets (or ordinals)' to that of the intelligibility of 'absolutely all (or all possible) collections (or order types) (of any level whatsoever)'. (And note that, by hypothesis of a *reductio* of the absolutist's position, in which we are currently engaged, this latter reference to 'any level whatsoever' should also make perfect sense.)

The point should now be clear: however precisely we choose to slice it, we have general mathematical concepts Φ, indefinitely extensible in roughly Dummett's sense, which we take as spelling out that the notion 'absolutely all (or all possible) Φ's' fails to be 'absolutely maximal'. Whatever such a quantifier phrase is supposed to encompass can be subject to (informal or formal) mathematical operations leading to new totalities, in accordance with extensibility, and this conflicts with the idea—espoused by the believers—that we (they) were really referring to 'absolutely all of the Φ's'. But—to reconnect us with the over-arching topic—if one recognizes Φ's as genuine objects, 'part of Reality', and if 'absolutely all Φ's' is illegitimate, then so must be 'absolutely everything', i.e. the illegitimacy—failure of purported absolute maximality—is transmitted 'upward' to more inclusive (putative) totalities. Put in the terms of Dummett's discussion, if the quantifier 'absolutely every' were legitimate, then we could use it to specify just 'absolutely all' those things which are Φ (a general form of 'Separation'), and this could not be regarded as extensible. Let us consider some objections and ways out.

Looking back, there are essentially only two premises to the argument: (1) the indefinite extensibility of certain general mathematical concepts (or extendability of structures of theories utilizing them); and (2) a platonist ontological view of mathematical objects as part of a 'unique Reality'. Included under (2), we assume, are (i) the view that the very possibility of mathematical objects suffices for their actuality; and (ii) the general Separation principle just appealed to. The subscriber of (2) is thus faced with denying (1).

There seem to be only two places to try to break the (sub)argument for indefinite extensibility of the relevant concepts: first, at the step where a collection or totality of 'absolutely all the Φ's' is appealed to; and second, at the further step where mathematical operations on that collection (or related object, e.g. ordinal) are invoked. Challenging the first corresponds to the forswearing of proper classes (in the context of ZF set theory); challenging the second (but not the first) corresponds to allowing proper classes but treating them in the manner of NBG (von Neumann, Bernays,

Gödel) set theory, not allowing them to be members. The most promising approach to mounting the first challenge is to appeal to plural quantification, resisting the move passing from, say, 'all the sets' to a *totality* them, of any type whatever. As in first-order ZF set theory, no such totality is recognized First-order languages, however, are limited in expressive power in well-known ways; moreover they open the challenger to the charge of imposing *arbitrary* limitations on what can be said about the intended (face-value, absolutist, platonist) interpretation of set theory. (Indeed, Boolos' original motivation in introducing plural quantification (1985) was to take advantage of the greater expressive power of second-order languages, in particular the power to express satisfaction and truth with respect to 'all sets', without presupposing any extravagant 'new totalities', proper classes.) While this move does demonstrate that indeed we (or the platonist) *can* gain certain advantages of proper classes while avoiding them as objects, this of itself is insufficient as a strategy to counter the implications of indefinite extensibility in the present context. The point here, as already broached above, is that the argument from indefinite extensibility appeals not to any alleged *impossibility* of avoiding proper classes but rather to a positive *possibility* of cogently entertaining higher totalities, as is routinely done (and, it might be said from the standpoint of ordinary mathematical practice, with utter abandon,) in set theory itself. *It is this possibility, the coherence of introducing (talk of) higher totalities, that a philosophy of mathematics must make sense of, and to cut it off at a certain stage, saying that it would be inconsistent with the hypothesis that we were speaking already of 'absolutely all totalities', appears arbitrary and question-begging.* Of course, the absolutist can dig in the heels and consistently impose such a limitation.[3] But the price is high. Since part and parcel of the platonist view is that, for purely mathematical objects, 'possibility' implies 'actuality', the stance has to be that the higher totalities are not even possible, in spite of their relative consistency with ordinary set theory (+ inaccessibles), and in spite of the fact that we are only continuing processes already assumed coherent at earlier stages.

These considerations apply even more clearly to the second way of trying to break the argument, acknowledging the higher totalities but withholding mathematical operations on them. This, we would submit, simply conflicts with rules implicit in our ordinary understanding of mathematical operations, such as applying (more accurately, extending) a function to a newly recognized object, or taking it as the value of a function, taking its singleton, forming products with the totality, taking

[3] It is this appeal to arbitrary restrictions on 'forming totalities' and/or applying operations that blocks a derivation of generalized versions of the paradoxes such as Russell's or Cantor's. Suppose one considers 'all totalities' (or 'totality-like objects' to emphasize the unrestricted scope) as 'part of Reality'. A version of the Russell paradox looms by then applying Separation to infer a totality of all totalities not belonging to themselves (the 'Total Russell paradox', we can call it). But if the absolutist insists on limiting Separation somehow, e.g. by understanding it as giving only 'the non-self-membered totalities' in the sense of plural logic, refusing to admit a *totality* of these, then paradox is blocked. Similar considerations can block a Total-Cantor's paradox (the sub-totalities of 'Reality' being at once *objects in* Reality *and* more numerous than all the objects). Thus, as announced at the outset, we are not claiming that the absolutist position necessarily leads to inconsistencies. But the need for arbitrary restrictions on mathematical operations should indeed make the absolutist nervous.

functional exponentiation (passing to a class of functions from the totality to a given value-set, delivering the 'power-totality', as a special case), etc. Again, the absolutist can consistently refuse to recognize these (extended) operations or their results, even while recognizing the higher totality (e.g. of 'absolutely all sets') as an object. But again *this appears as an arbitrary limitation on mathematical thought processes*, all the more arbitrary in that, unlike in the former case, we are not introducing any new limits but merely operating on a single 'thing' (like applying 'successor' to ω to obtain $\omega + 1$, in contrast to recognizing ω or the totality of natural numbers in the first place).

In the context of a debate Lewis (1991) constructed between a 'singularist' and himself, as a proponent of plural quantification, Lewis derided skepticism about 'absolutely everything', writing, 'Maybe the singularist replies that some mystical censor stops us from quantifying over absolutely everything without restriction' (p. 68). The present context is very different: We fully agree with Boolos, Lewis, Yi, *et al.*'s view that plurals are intelligible on their own and not to be reduced to singulars. And, in framing the current challenges to 'absolutely everything' we have been careful to avoid the trap of illicit *uses* of such phrases. What has emerged is that the skeptic turns the table: it is the absolutist who seems to invoke a mystical censor that stops us from applying mathematical operations by fiat, with nothing to fall back on but the absolutist, platonist view of mathematics and ontology.

But suppose the absolutist grants all this concerning the indefinite extensibility of the key mathematical concepts we have been discussing. There is yet a further move that has been suggested on the absolutist's behalf, namely balking at the inference from the application of Separation used in the above (*reductio*) argument, i.e. to infer from the *inextendability* of the range of 'absolutely everything' that, e.g. 'absolutely all sets' or 'absolutely all ordinals' must also be inextendable. It has been suggested that the absolutist might hold out for the intelligibility of unrestricted quantification while at the same time conceding the indefinite extensibility of concepts such as 'set', 'ordinal', 'set-like entity', etc., maintaining that these—along with even 'absolutely all sets', 'absolutely all ordinals', 'absolutely all set-like entities', etc.—subtly shift their meaning as we consider wider and wider contexts, while 'absolutely everything' remains fixed throughout.[4] On this view, Separation itself is not really being challenged, for a predicate such as 'set-like entity' is being assigned a unique extension, but it is one that gives way to another more comprehensive one as soon as we reflect on extensibility and recognize new, higher totalities, etc. This is analyzed as shifting to a new language, with new meanings and extensions assigned to 'set', 'set-like entity', etc. (These predicates could be indexed to reflect this language relativity.) But how it is that 'entity' itself manages to remain fixed and maximal throughout all such changes remains an utter mystery. Surely our common understanding would have it that, in recognizing new, higher totalities, we are also recognizing new entities, not merely relabelling some old ones![5] In any case, the relativist can argue that all this

[4] See Shapiro's helpful discussion (2003).

[5] Williamson has suggested in correspondence that in 'recognizing new types' we may be newly 'singling them out' but without newly 'quantifying over them'. I take it that this is equivalent

maneuvering is for nought: the mathematical operations appealed to in connection with pure *mathematicalia,* as in the argument we have concentrated on above, can also be *applied* to *mathematicalia-cum-non-mathematicalia*: once given 'absolutely all entities', one can entertain a totality of *these*, and pass to all (absolutely all!) *subtotalities*, generating essentially Cantor's paradox (for such subtotalities count as entities, by hypothesis that this term is indeed maximal and fixed), or one can generate a 'Total–Russell paradox' (applying Separation to infer a totality of all non-self-membered totalities, cf. n. 3 above).[6] Indeed, as already granted, the absolutist can consistently refuse to recognize the application of such mathematical operations; but again we will repeat the conclusion above that such restrictions are arbitrary and face-saving (better: metaphysics-saving) devices, that the tables have indeed been turned regarding 'mystical censorship'.

Without claiming to have exhausted absolutely every absolutist manoeuvre, let us now shift frameworks and consider what becomes of 'absolutely everything' when we move beyond mathematical platonism.

4.4 ARGUMENT FROM MULTIPLICITY OF 'FACTUALLY EQUIVALENT' ONTOLOGIES

Although this line of argument affects all known frameworks, it is useful to think of it in the first instance as applying to nominalistic ones in order to help separate out the special features of mathematical concepts and structures that have occupied us so far.[7]

In a nutshell, the argument runs as follows: one begins with the point (adapted from Kant) that, to think or say practically anything interesting about material reality, a conceptual apparatus must be brought to bear. One then reflects that any such apparatus involves a 'parsing' of experience and of what we take to be the objective subject matter of our inquiry, involving notions of 'object', 'property', 'relation' or 'attribute', correlated with linguistic distinctions, e.g. 'singular term', 'general term', etc. Further, one notices that, even with these familiar categories, we can contemplate two or more (equally) accurate and adequate ways of describing a situation or given subject matter, and, in particular, the items recognized as values of our quantified variables differ under the different parsings. In some sense, the alternative descriptions are 'factually equivalent', despite the fact that when we try to describe the relevant 'facts' of the situation, of course we have to use a language to do so,

to saying that 'entity' is remaining fixed throughout. Perhaps our different stances at this point reflect different linguistic intuitions; but I would be inclined to describe the 'new recognition' to an expanded meaning of 'all entities', not to what qualifies as 'set-like'. If anything, it seems to be the latter that remains fixed, contra this whole strategy of the absolutist's.

[6] As Roy Cook has pointed out to me, this Total–Russell paradox relies on less than the Total–Cantor paradox with its presupposition of 'absolutely all subtotalities'. Parsimony has its virtues, I suppose, even when discussing 'absolutely everything'!

[7] For discussion of an interesting case of the argument from multiplicity which turns on mathematical ontology, see Uzquiano's contribution to this volume.

and this will seem to prejudice the case in favor of a particular parsing associated with that language. But we can reflect on this and discount for it, clinging to our insight about multiplicity rather than opting for a parochial, unrelativized monism. The upshot, then is a kind of 'ontological relativity' (perhaps closer to Carnap's or Goodman's than Quine's): multiple universes of discourse are equally 'correct'; taking their 'union' is ill defined (what are 'all frameworks' over which the union is to be taken?), unwieldy ('satisfying no one'), and arbitrary. Conclusion: 'absolutely everything' must be relativised to a parsing; it cannot really be 'absolute'.

As an illustrative example from the sciences, consider standard Newtonian gravitation theory (in differential form, based on Poisson's equation), with its quantification over gravitational forces, as compared with the 'neo-Newtonian', geometrized, curved-spacetime theory (Trautman, *et al.*), in which such forces are displaced in favor of spacetime (geodesic) curvature, much as in general relativity.[8] Now, as such, these theories are not 'fully factually equivalent', at least according to a fairly robust standard, namely Glymour's 'theoretical equivalence' (1971), which requires translations (in both directions) built up from explicit definitions of primitives (not just observational) preserving theoremhood. The problem is that, as Malament (1995) pointed out, recovery of gravitational forces from the curved spacetime framework is not unique, but depends on a 'gauge' choice of how to divide up the (physically significant) sum of 'purely gravitational' and 'inertial' forces, which taken separately lack physical significance. Uniqueness, however, does obtain if reasonable boundary conditions on curvature or the gravitational potential are imposed. It suffices, for example, to require asymptotic approach to flatness or zero gravitational potential at spatial infinity, a reasonable condition if one is dealing with a bounded system (e.g. a solar system or a cluster of galaxies). Of course, we suppose that our world is not really Newtonian in any case, but the example is suggestive: many situations we can imagine and describe fulfill both theories and the boundary conditions. The same underlying factual situation, we would like to say, is described accurately and adequately in ontologically diverse ways. It would be arbitrary and unwarranted to say that just one is 'really correct'.

Cataloguing and describing such examples from the sciences would be a major and worthy undertaking, clearly beyond the scope of this chapter.[9] But the phenomenon of ontological multiplicity can also be illustrated in less esoteric terms.

[8] I am indebted to Paul Teller for calling my attention to this example, and to David Malament for helpful correspondence. For details on these theories and discussion of their interrelationship, including the question of 'factual equivalence', see Malament (1995). Cf. also Jones (1991) and Musgrave (1992) for discussion of related examples.
While these theories and their ontological commitments are, of course, couched in abstract mathematical terms, this should not be a distraction in the present context for at least two reasons. First, one can think of the mathematical objects (vector or tensor fields, derivative operators, etc.) as corresponding to or 'representing' various physical phenomena, reasonably taken as within the purview of nominalism; and second, in any case, the mathematics in question can be nominalized in various ways (à la Chihara (1990), or Hellman (1989, 1996), and perhaps also Field (1980)).

[9] Of particular interest in this connection would be a thoroughgoing quantum field theoretic view of physical reality, and its effect on 'particle' concepts, let alone macroscopic ones. (It seems that we confront even more than Eddington's famous 'two tables'.)

Familiar examples cited long ago by Goodman (1977, 1978) and others come from geometry (pure or applied), e.g. a framework with points and lines (say, in the two-dimensional case) vs. a framework with just lines, points being definable as (suitably selected) pairs of intersecting lines. Or one may consider a system with points and regions vs. a system with just regions, points defined as (suitable) nested regions.[10] Now one might dismiss such examples as 'ontologically benign' by pointing out that, due to the various ways of introducing 'points' by explicit definition, all the systems agree on the assertion, 'Points exist'. However, such a facile separation of ontology from 'status' of objects is misguided. All the systems indeed agree on the existence of points, disagreeing over 'what they are'. But, the point is, *this* can be put as a question of ontology: Are there *sui generis* points, i.e. points which are distinct from pairs of lines or nested volumes, etc., not constructed out of anything else? The absolutist must claim that there is one correct answer: we may not ever know it, but it shows up one way or another in the range of 'absolutely everything'![11] (An analogy from pure mathematics comes to mind: Dedekind (1872) thought of real numbers as really distinct from the famous 'cuts' in the rationals which he introduced to 'define them', despite the isomorphism (hence 'structural identity') between them.[12] This is ('heavy duty') ontology, if anything is!)

Even more problematic are examples of a second sort, where certain objects recognized in one system are completely omitted by another, not being reconstructed by any mode of composition from other recognized objects at all. Let one system be our familiar one recognizing ordinary material objects and their material properties (including relations, if you like). Let an alternative system recognize instead spatio-temporal regions together with novel 'occupation' properties of these which get at the ordinary material objects. (Occurrences of such properties might be called (possibly extended) 'events'. The beginnings of such a system as we are contemplating are commonly encountered in representing ordinary phenomena in space-time theories. Cf. e.g. Geroch (1978)) Instead of saying 'there are books over there', we can say 'that region is "booked"'. Instead of saying, 'There are more books over there than over here', we can say, 'That region is 'more booked' than this one'; instead of, 'No more books can be fit into that region', we can say, 'That region is 'fully booked'', and so forth. Yet one does not identify books in this framework with the space-time regions they occupy. Apart from the problems of vagueness—problems in saying

[10] It should be noted that plural quantification (over regions, for example) can supplant applied set theory, which might distract us from our focus on nominalistic frameworks. With some effort, various of these can recover standard analytic mathematics over spaces (for geometry and physics), whether or not points of the space are taken as primitive or defined. Cf. Hellman (1989, 1996), Chihara (1990), Burgess and Rosen (1997).

[11] Nothing we are saying here should be construed as prejudging the question whether it might not be better to reconceive physics as dealing with 'gunky ('pointless') spacetime' rather than standard, 'pointy' spacetime. (This is being explored by Arntzenius MS.) While it is true that 'points' could be reintroduced by definition (e.g. as sets or pluralities of suitable nested gunky regions), the mathematical treatment of pointless spacetime would still differ from that of pointy spacetime, and such differences could matter physically, as well as mathematically. The theories would not then be 'factually equivalent'.

[12] Cf. Shapiro's discussion (1997), 170–5.

which region should serve—one can insist that material objects such as books, on the one hand, and space-time regions, on the other, are categorically different kinds of things. For limited purposes (e.g. in representing certain structural space-time relations, e.g. causal accessibility in Minkowski space-time), it may be convenient to think of a book as just a certain region, but that is only for limited purposes. Radical differences show up in modal discourse, which we may seek to preserve, as in 'This book might have occupied a different space-time region', which becomes nonsense under substitution of 'the region actually occupied by this book' for 'this book'. We can, in a sense, respect such a statement by saying of various individual *properties*, normally associated with the book, that they might have been manifested elsewhere. But we still may resist literally *identifying* the book with a cluster of properties. For one thing, the occupation properties recognized in the contemplated framework are literally *of* space-time regions, not *of* ordinary material objects. (Thus, a book may 'have 450 pp.' or be 'of cloth', but neither of these properties is possessed by the region; and a *haecceity* such as 'being this book' is not recognized; rather it is the occurrence or manifestation, the 'being at', of such a property that, at best, is recognized.) For another, what is the 'clustering' relation? It shouldn't be set-membership, as material objects are not sets (by ordinary lights), and other modes of composition, e.g. part/whole only seem to apply by stipulation. For particular purposes, that may be fine, but do we want to say that various such 'wholes' of properties 'really are' the material objects we're looking for?

Thus, we have various piecemeal strategies for respecting ordinary truths about books, etc., inside a framework which speaks, intuitively, only of space-time regions and a sufficiently rich variety of properties that can be instantiated at regions, but we literally recognize no books, etc., as objects inside that framework. One is treating 'book', etc., *contextually*, or *syncategorematically*. But what about 'Books exist' itself? Well, that too is respected, but not fully literally. In the envisioned framework of regions and occupation properties, we certainly can have 'booked regions exist', although the whole point of this example is that—as we would put it from the outside—no entity recognized in the ontology of this theory is literally a book.

While it may seem radical to 'dispense with' ordinary material objects such as books, etc., there are many cases of apparent reference to objects, and quantification 'over them', in ordinary discourse for which we may deem it quite reasonable to think that a contextual or syncategorematic treatment ought at least to be possible in principle, even if we are in no position to supply such a treatment in full detail. Consider an example such as, 'There is a social convention of handshaking (in many places, especially between males) on being introduced to someone in public.' Do we think that we *must* take literally quantification over social conventions as objects, or do we rather envision that, in principle, at least, it ought to be possible to explain this away by making reference instead to how people are disposed to behave, and feel they should behave, in the given circumstances? Similarly, could not reference to 'things' such as 'diseases' be eliminated in principle in favor of particular events and processes in organisms? Similarly many cases of reference to social and institutional 'objects' are candidates for contextual analyses in favor of individual people, their dispositions, states, interrelations, etc. Similarly in many cases on a mundane material level, e.g. reference to 'ripples' on a pond, to 'holes' in swiss cheese, etc.[13] Rather than trying to define literally such terms in more basic ones (which, as has been learned from the record of failed attempts, confronts enormous obstacles and may not even be possible in principle if the demands on 'good definition' are strong enough to include respect for counterfactuals, and if the language of the *definentia* is finitary), we may more reasonably suppose that, on a case by case basis, the relevant aspects of the underlying factual situation can be got at in a language which dispenses with quantification into such higher-order contexts (i.e. 'over such higher-order entities').[14] So long as such analyses or replacements are possible, we will have examples of ontologically diverse frameworks of the sort we are considering. The absolutist must insist that, in every such case, at most one of the frameworks is correct, the one (if any) that quantifies over only those objects in the range of the absolute quantifiers, the objects that 'really exist' ('*REALLY EXIST*'?). A moderate relativist, on the other hand, will make no sense of this, allowing that a certain degree of multiplicity is unavoidable, that there simply is no non-arbitrary, absolutely correct choice among such alternatives.

To be sure, unlike the case cited above from spacetime physics, these cases from everyday discourse are not spelled out in anything like full detail, which is understandable given the complexity and scope of ordinary usage. Nevertheless, considering the resources of specially tailored predicates, such as the occupation predicates of spacetime regions of the example described, we regard the claim of multiplicity of frameworks as very plausible, correlatively the contrary claim of uniqueness of the absolutist as highly implausible. It must also be acknowledged, however, that spelling out the argument from multiplicity with greater rigor would require saying more than has yet been said here about 'factual equivalence' of alternatives. In cases of contextual or syncategorematic analyses or replacements, we may not be able to fall back on the sort of translational equivalence cited above in connection with Newtonian gravitation, for there may be no suitable translations between the languages of the theoretical alternatives. Instead, one may appeal to a weaker standard, such as 'co-determination' or mutual supervenience: roughly put, fixing the factual situation as described in the language of one of the frameworks uniquely fixes the situation as described in the language of the other, and vice-versa.[15] In cases in which an overarching theory can be framed, incorporating two or more theories or frameworks in question, including 'bridge laws' among them (which may fall short of term by term biconditionals as required by definability criteria), such co-determination corresponds to 'implicit definability' of the predicates of one theory in terms of the other, over a class of models representing mutually recognized natural possibilities.[16] Thus, a plurality of frameworks, irreducible by translatability criteria, may still be regarded

[13] See e.g. Lewis and Lewis (1970).

[14] Here 'higher-order' refers to the familiar hierarchical picture of the empirical sciences, with fundamental microphysics at the bottom, the biological sciences in the middle somewhere, and perhaps 'geo-politics' at the top. This should not be confused with the logician's sense of 'higher-order' entities such as classes and properties.

[15] Such a standard was proposed in Hellman and Thompson (1977).

[16] As pointed out in Hellman and Thompson (1975, 1977), when such a class of models is not so broad as to include all the models of a first-order theory, the 'implicit definability' standard does

as 'factually equivalent', without our having to presuppose some entirely theory-free vantage point from which to judge this, something we regard as quite impossible.

A final point in this section is in order: having just invoked, in effect, (extensions of) unions of theories, it might be suggested, on behalf of 'absolutely everything', that this can be understood—even by the critic—in terms of one grand union. But what is this union to be? One might say, over '(absolutely) all true theories', or at least 'theories true in existential commitments'. But, even setting to one side the terrible indefiniteness of this—presumably it must encompass 'possible theories in possible languages'—surely the critic will regard this as question-begging, even if 'true in existential commitments' is taken as primitive, rather than introduced in Tarskian fashion with reference to ... well, 'absolutely everything'. Alternatively, it may be suggested that the grand union be over all 'acceptable theories', where this refers to some standards that we lay down. While this avoids the circularity just noted, it does so, however, at the price of having 'absolutely everything' refer to what exists relative to our own standards, which surely contravenes the spirit, and presumably the letter, of absolutism. Why should what exists absolutely, 'in Reality', depend on any subjects' standards? Furthermore, while (extensions of) unions of particular theories may be a useful tool for spelling out standards of 'factual equivalence', that does not mean that any particular such union, much less some huge, vaguely specified grand union, would itself meet suitable standards of acceptability. For one thing, its ontology is apt to seem excessively bloated (satisfying no one), since, by hypothesis, it would be encompassing multiple, individually adequate bases. And it may be otherwise unwieldy, poorly systematized, and so forth. In any case, the critic is not committed to letting in 'absolutely everything' through the back door, as it were, merely by invoking some (limited) unions as a logical tool, as above.

4.5 MAKING DO WITH 'LESS'

If I cannot make sense of 'absolutely everything', then how can I get across the intended force of even so simple a denial of existence as that of 'no donkey talks', 'no cocker spaniel runs for US president', etc? If this must be understood relative to a restricted domain, how do we insure that we haven't left out of account a counterinstance to our intended denial? Williamson (2003) discusses this problem at length, examining a number of approaches, finding in every case that unwanted restrictions can find their way back in ... unless, he suggests, we simply appeal to 'absolutely everything' in a completely unrestricted, unrelativized sense. Clearly, if the above arguments against the cogency of this have merit, as I think they have, then we have a problem.

Here is a partial solution. One of the options Williamson considers is the 'sortal approach'. Avoiding the absolutist's assumption of a fixed, 'all-embracing' real-world domain from which sequences of objects come in the usual Tarski semantics for satisfaction and truth, quantification is understood as contextually bound with a sortal

not necessarily collapse to 'explicit definability' of the vocabulary of one theory in terms of that of the other, as the well-known Beth definability theorem for first-order theories need not apply.

term carrying a non-trivial principle of individuation that defeats attempts at absolute generality. In his mundane example, the sortal would be 'donkey', and one then just says that what this sortal *applies to*, or what *complies with* the sortal, fails to talk. The problem, Williamson suggests, comes in trying to provide a fully *general* semantics for such constructions. For example, he considers a truth-conditional clause for the determiner 'every' given in the metalanguage:

[Every] 'Every F, x, is φ' is true under assignment A iff any *compliant* of F under A, d, is such that φ is true under A $[x/d]$.

Here, 'F' is a variable over sortal terms and 'φ' a variable over grammatically suitable predicates (e.g. verb phrases). (Reference to contexts is also allowed, but suppressed for simplicity.) However, Williamson points out, '*compliant of F*' itself is in sortal position, but *it* is not associated with any non-trivial principle of individuation in the context of this general, semantical principle, which is supposed to govern all sortal constructions of this general form available in the language. As he puts it, 'compliant' must be applicable in the context of [*Every*] to the compliants of all [available] noun [phrases]. If a single non-trivial principle of individuation individuated them all, the supposed obstacle to absolute generality would dissolve, for sortalism is not intended to imply any restriction on what can be a compliant of some noun or other in the language (2003). Thus, there seems to be no good general sortalist semantics which doesn't collapse to absolutism. But such a semantics is needed, for we grasp uses of 'every' in new contexts without having to master instances of the above clause, one by one (which themselves can use the relevant sortal noun itself or a translation of such in the metalanguage, i.e. avoiding the semantic term, 'compliant').

Now we have no wish to defend 'sortalism' as a general semantical doctrine; indeed, Williamson is quite correct when he points out that many general terms in our own language lack anything that could be called a 'non-trivial principle of individuation', terms such as 'entity', 'object', 'instance', 'compliant', etc., as well as complements such as 'non-donkey', 'non-stone', etc., but which enter quite meaningfully into quantifier phrases. However, in light of the special problems that we have seen with indefinitely extensible predicates, we may reasonably resist the demand that a single semantical principle govern all constructions (even in our own language) of the same overt syntactic form at once. Indeed, the skeptic or generality-relativist will balk at the suggestion that we really do understand absolutely general uses of 'every' in cases of problematic, indefinitely extensible predicates such as 'ordinal', 'collection', etc. The fact that we reason logically perfectly well with such terms must indeed be explained, but that does not require the intelligibility of phrases such as 'absolutely all ordinals', 'absolutely all collections', etc. Moreover, the explanation need not involve the same principles that enter into an account of our understanding of 'no donkey talks', 'no broomstick flies', etc. Without our taking a stand on whether ultimately a sortalist approach is viable even in these mundane cases, it does seem to contain a kernel of truth and is instructively pursued just a bit further in the present context.

Let us acknowledge, then, a marked difference between the 'indefinitely extensible' predicates on which the argument of Section 4.3 turned and the more 'concrete', ordinary ones relevant in the argument of Section 4.4. The latter we may call '*limited*' predicates. '*Unlimited*' predicates F can be described inductively by the conditions:

(i) F is indefinitely extensible;
(ii) If E is *unlimited* and 'All E are F' is taken as true (or analytic), then F is *unlimited.*

That is, the unlimited predicates are 'closed upwards' in the sense of inclusion: intuitively, any condition at least as encompassing (by standards of usage, not necessarily 'in fact') as an unlimited predicate is itself unlimited. '*Limited*' is then defined as 'not unlimited'.

Now, if F is limited, and if we set problems of borderline vagueness to one side, the notion 'compliant of F' is relatively unproblematic. Any dog is a compliant of 'dog'; the compliants of 'dog' are just *the dogs*, to invoke this plural usage (thereby avoiding postulating new objects in our metalanguage, *extensions* of predicates, associated with unlimited concepts). What the sortalist clause [*Every*] comes to in such a particular case is,

'No dog talks' is true under A iff among the dogs, d,
'x doesn't talk' is true under A$[x/d]$.

If this is generalized as a *scheme for limited predicates,* we even eliminate the need for the semantic relation 'compliant of':

'Every F, x, is φ' is true under A iff among the $F's$, d, $\varphi[x]$ is true under A$[x/d]$.

While this provides a recipe for finding truth conditions of sentences of the relevant form on a case by case basis, it would not serve as a clause in a proper inductive definition of truth (under an assignment). But even if we stick with Williamson's formulation (that could serve), notice that the condition or sortal term, 'compliant of some sortal or other' is itself *not* a limited predicate, at least not on the usual platonist conception of mathematics, according to which terms like 'set', 'ordinal', etc. are sortals that accompany quantifiers, together with truisms such as that any set is a compliant of 'set', etc. Thus, we do not expect the principle [*Every*] to apply to 'compliant' itself in an unrestricted sense, and the collapse to absolutism is blocked.

Closer to home, how can the above help with 'flat-out' or 'categorical' denials of existence, such as 'There are no such things as ghosts', or an atheistic position? We cannot work these into the above scheme by a reformulation such as, 'No thing is a ghost', for 'thing', like 'object', 'entity', 'existent', etc. is an unlimited term *par excellence*, in light of condition (ii) above (assuming that here we are not confined to nominalistic frameworks). A better strategy is to find some limited term to replace 'thing' or 'entity', i.e. a term that, while limited, is not *too* limited. For example, the predicate 'occurs in space-time', while broad, is still limited. So we can assert, 'Everything occurring (anywhere) in space-time fails to be a ghost', or 'Nothing in space-time is a ghost'. If ghosts are conceived as (ever) occurring in space-time, this intuitively rules out such things. Similarly, if deities are conceived as causes (at least on occasion), then the limited term 'cause' can serve to express, 'Every cause fails to be a deity'. This effectively rules them out too. (Perhaps completely inert 'deities' (under some novel usage of 'deity') can be ruled out by other means.) Thus ordinary denials of existence—asserting emptiness of sortal predicates extended by limited ones—are well-handled by this 'modest sortalist' approach, which explicitly limits itself to limited concepts.[17] Here are some remarks concerning the 'limited/unlimited' distinction:

Remark 1 Basic Boolean relations of limited and unlimited predicates should correspond to those of sets and proper classes in set theory:

If F and G are both limited, so is $F \vee G$ as well as $F \wedge G$. If F is unlimited, so is $F \vee G$, for any G. If F is unlimited and G is limited, then $F - G$ is unlimited. But if F is limited, unrestricted $\neg F$ is unlimited. And if F and G are unlimited, $F \wedge G$ may be either unlimited or limited (even empty).

Remark 2 If one has domain relativity (as in model theory), then all predicates are in effect treated as limited, and a uniform semantical treatment is straightforward (along Tarskian lines, although it need not be carried out in set theory; a background logic of plurals would also suffice).

Remark 3 If an unlimited predicate G is employed such that 'Set' $\wedge$ G is empty—e.g. if G is 'Property' or 'Proposition' or 'sui generis World', etc.—then we have a counterexample to the 'Urelement-Set Axiom', that the non-sets are in one–one correspondence with a set, invoked by McGee (1997) for purposes of a kind of categoricity for full set theory. (Cf. Shapiro (2003).)

Remark 4 Taking indefinitely extensible predicates as actually having ranges of application is essentially platonistic, i.e. nominalism is marked by treating such predicates as not actually applying. (The nominalist can still say that, in a platonist framework, various predicates are treated as unlimited.)

This is clear for notions such as 'set', 'ordinal', 'function', and 'category'. What about 'property'? Here caution is necessary: only in a very general sense involving mathematics and/or higher-order logic is this unlimited. 'Physical property' for example is limited, leading to no unending hierarchy. Similarly for sensory *qualia* or other mentalist properties, if such things are countenanced. It seems to us that more attention should be given to this contrast between platonism and nominalism, which is sharper than the traditional one between 'abstract' and 'concrete'. Indeed,

[17] Another suggestion, due to Tim McCarthy, is to apply the sortalist scheme directly to a limited predicate such as 'ghost' as the sortal, and assert, e.g. that 'Among ghosts, none is self-identical'.

Remark 5 General 'ontological terms' such as 'object', 'entity', etc. count as unlimited in a framework employing indefinitely extensible predicates, but in a nominalistic framework they count as limited. Thus the boundary of the distinction is relative to framework.

Remark 6 (Historical) There is a connection between unlimited predicates and Carnap's 'Allwörter' (1937), but it is complex. Many of our unlimited predicates, especially 'thing', 'entity', etc. (in the context of mathematical platonism) are 'Allwörter' for Carnap, but he also included many notions associated with large-scale theoretical frameworks, notions such as 'process', 'event', 'action', 'spatial relation', etc., which count as limited for us.

While the modest sortalist approach seems promising in the sorts of cases considered, it needs to be supplemented in at least two respects. First, even in the case of limited predicates, the relativity to 'parsings' encountered in Section 4.4 above needs somehow to be taken into account. And, second, of course, we still need an account of (especially, negative) existential claims pertaining to *un*limited predicates. A full examination of either of these topics cannot be undertaken here. But let us conclude with some indications of the direction in which reasonable answers may lie.

Concerning the first topic, taking account of relativity to 'parsings' of a domain of facts, two types of cases should be distinguished. The first concerns ontological categories, such as 'location property', '(ordinary) material thing', etc.—the very source of relativity encountered in Section 4.4. In such cases, relativity is indeed called for, its counterintuitive consequences mitigated by contextual translation. (Recall, e.g., 'There's a book on the desk' can be respected without recognition of books or desks as objects.) But what of the second type of problematic cases in which a denial of existence (of ghosts or gods, etc.) is intended to be 'absolute'? Here a possible solution lies in the observation that certain general notions or sortals are common to many, perhaps all acceptable, frameworks. Examples may include: 'cause' or 'causal factor'; 'spatio-temporal entity'; 'agent' or 'agency'; and so forth. While *limited* in our sense, we expect these notions to make sense in multiple frameworks or 'parsings'. Thus, instances of (negative) existential claims with such terms occurring as the sortal tied to the initial quantifier already go beyond any single framework, as desired: in effect, we can express, e.g., 'In *any* framework recognizing causal factors, the causal factors include no ghosts', or 'In *any* framework recognizing agents, none created the cosmos'; and so forth. What about 'any framework'? Well, that must be suitably circumscribed so that it too is clearly limited, although it may have to be left rather vague, as in 'any humanly intelligible framework', or 'any rationally acceptable framework by such-and such standards', etc.

When it comes to unlimited predicates, either of two contrasting approaches can be pursued, one Quinean, the other Carnapian. The Quinean approach takes metaphysics seriously, or, at any rate, insists on a blurring of the distinction between metaphysical and ordinary/scientific existence questions. 'Do sets (really) exist?' is not different in kind from 'Do ghosts (really) exist?', or 'Do gravity waves (really) exist?', and so forth. Of course, the absolutist view that we've been challenging is Quinean in this sense, and agrees with Quine's own (eventual, reluctant, 'Ah, if only it were not so') version of mathematical platonism.[18] But now we are considering options available to the generality relativist who takes seriously the critique of mathematical platonism based on indefinite extensibility. This suggests pursuing a nominalist or nominalist-structuralist reconstruction of mathematics and simply denying that indefinitely extensible predicates actually apply. For example, one may treat them as only applying in a hypothetical or possible structure, recognizing their indefinitely extensible character in the possibility of further, more extensive structures. Indeed, modal-structuralist interpretations of mathematical theories were designed to handle indefinitely extensible mathematical concepts: general extendability principles are explicitly adopted as axioms to the effect that, for example, any possible model, or ordinal sequence of models, of ZF set theory can be embedded in a more extensive model, while the second-order modal logical comprehension axioms are restricted so as not to allow the possibility of any 'grand union' of all possible models.[19] But now notice, as announced in *Remark 5* above, that on this or other nominalistic reconstructions of mathematics, universal predicates, such as '(actual) entity', '(actual) existent', etc., no longer need be regarded as unlimited, for they may be regarded as coextensive with '(actual) spatio-temporal entity', which we have already classed as limited. Indeed, if it weren't for the implied uniqueness of ontology that, as we have argued, even the nominalist must renounce, there would be no objection from nominalist quarters to 'absolutely everything' in the first place. Still, the nominalist can say, e.g., 'Among actual existents, none are sets, or higher-order properties, or propositions, etc.', i.e. the modest sortalist approach is adequate here after all. Of course, there is a built in limitation to a framework in the background language (or metalanguage, if truth conditions are being offered) in which such things are expressed; but, if we are right, there is nothing to be done about that.

The Carnapian position (1950), in contrast, tries to draw a sharp line between 'internal questions' of existence, such as 'Is there really telepathic communication?', 'Is there really a life force, over and above known physical forces?', 'Are there really gravitons?', etc., and 'external questions', such as 'Are there (really) sets, or (higher-order) properties, propositions, etc.?', 'Are there (really) material objects?', 'Are there (really) mental objects, e.g. thoughts, percepts, after-images, etc.?', questions which, according to Carnap, make no sense except as misleadingly worded questions about the utility of adopting the framework in question, which typically takes for granted the corresponding objects and provides standards and rules for discourse 'about them'. (These 'external questions' can also be construed as internal to the respective framework, in which case they receive a trivial, affirmative answer.) Now the problems with this effort to dispose of metaphysics are well known. Even more serious,

[18] Cf. Burgess' entertaining discussion (2004), which takes issue with Boolos' pronouncement that Carnap's line of argument against ontological absolutism is 'rubbish' and attempts to rehabilitate that line.

[19] See Hellman (1989), (1996). Note that the phrasing in terms of 'models' and 'elements' just given is informal; officially, such talk is eliminated in favor of direct, modal-mathematical language (in the preferred (1996) version, combining plural quantification, mereology, and ordinary predication).

in our estimation, than the appeals to an empirical verifiability criterion of meaningfulness that are commonly associated with Carnap's argument (cf. Burgess, 2004), is the failure to mark a principled distinction between what counts as a 'framework' and what counts as simply a theory or classification 'within a framework'. (Quine's critique (1966) in effect makes this point.) Presumably, Carnap would not recognize Nordic mythology, for example, as a 'framework', and would regard the claim that, really, there are no such things as Nordic gods, as 'factual' and not merely a misleadingly worded claim about the disutility of a framework. Presumably this would not change even if Nordic mythology were embedded in something qualifying as a 'global system of the world'. But no satisfactory general criterion for the distinction has, to our knowledge, ever been put forward.

Short of that, one may pursue Carnap's idea in connection with the specific, indefinitely extensible concepts that have occupied us in this paper. For, it may be argued, it is precisely their indefinitely extensible character that undermines meaningfulness of phrases such as, 'All the sets', 'All the ordinals', 'All the categories', 'All the properties', 'All the propositions', and so forth. This, however, does not at all prevent one from doing set theory or general category theory (or from *trying* to do property theory or proposition theory, cf. e.g. Rouilhan, 2004). Such theories take for granted a 'world' or 'universe' of sets, ordinals, categories, etc. (which may, of course, include *Urelemente*, hence various applications), and all kinds of advantages can be claimed for them. As for semantical and logical principles internal to such theories or frameworks, the background assumption of a 'world' or 'universe' functions as a domain restriction (a 'universe of discourse'), so that the usual Tarskian semantics can be carried out—relative to such a universe. If one then complains that the 'universe' can itself be treated as a member of a more extensive one, one can accommodate this and then relativize discourse to a proper extension. But there is no pretense to treat 'absolutely all' ordinals, sets, etc., in a fixed, ultimate universe. Thus, the Carnapian can recognize indefinite extensibility in a fairly straightforward way. This is of a piece with the Carnapian view that a question such as, 'Do sets exist?', stripped of all context and relativity to framework, is deviant. (Contrast this with the child's question, 'Do fairies really exist?') From within set theory or category theory, one says, 'Of course, we're presupposing such things', but no sense is attached to the question beyond this 'Let us assume . . .' mode.[20] What can our erstwhile nominalist say? Not 'There are no sets, ordinals, abstract categories', etc., stripped of any relativity to framework, for that is just as deviant as as the blanket, context-free (pseudo) assertions of existence. Rather one can say (and try to defend) that no such things *need be recognized*, except as a convenience, and that that is a good thing for various reasons, e.g. permitting a thoroughgoing structuralist treatment of set theory while blocking bad questions about 'them' and 'how we come to know them', etc.

But didn't we come to essentially the same conclusion about books, etc., above? Their status as objects was also found to be framework relative. Moreover, although

[20] That is the normal mode of mathematical discourse. By way of contrast: Paul Ehrlich recounts somewhere a fishing trip with a theoretical economist who, unable to find a can opener for their lunch, quipped, 'Assume a can opener!'

we slid by this, alternative frameworks, say, based on fundamental physical objects (fields or fields + particles, along with combinations or wholes of these), could also be said to have certain advantages, including blocking bad questions, quite different from those confronting mathematical *abstracta* but still worth blocking, e.g. pertaining to vagueness: 'just *which* whole of fundamental physical objects is this book?'[21] Many choices are equally good so that no single one can be claimed 'correct'; but then how can we claim that this book *is* (=) in fact a whole of basic physical parts? And if it isn't that, what is it? Such considerations suggest that the Carnapian approach may well extend beyond the mathematical and other abstract examples cited. Although we lack a suitably general criterion for what counts as a 'framework', that approach seems still to have life left in it and should not yet be taken out to the alley.

Finally, while we have concentrated on a multifaceted critique of absoluteness and the need for some relativity to frameworks, nothing we have said rules out a kind of *unrestricted* quantification in the sense of 'indefinite, schematic, and open-ended' (as foretold in n. 1). Our most general ontological terms, 'object', 'entity', and 'thing' as in 'everything', provide examples, especially in connection with the law of identity, 'Everything is self-identical', or other logical laws. It is not necessary to insist that, all appearances to the contrary notwithstanding, there is really some hidden restriction in such cases. Instead, we can take such a law as saying, in a Carnapian spirit, 'Anything that we ever recognize as an entity at all will be assumed to obey this', i.e. as stipulative of how 'thing', 'entity', etc., and '=' are to be understood in our language. While there is no sense in speaking of 'absolutely all objects', or even 'absolutely all the objects in this room',[22] we still allow, 'Whatever may be recognized as an object (in this room or otherwise) will count as self-identical'. In this way, relativity and unrestrictedness actually go hand in hand.

REFERENCES

Boolos, G. (1985) 'Nominalist Platonism', *Philosophical Review* **94**: 327–44.

Burgess, J. P. (2004) 'Mathematics and *Bleak House*', *Philosophia Mathematica* (3) 12: 18–36.

——and Rosen, G. (1997) *A Subject with No Object* (Oxford: Oxford University Press).

Byeong-UK, Y. (2005) 'The Logic and Meaning of Plurals. Part I', *Journal of Philosophical Logic* **34**(5–6): 459–506.

——(2006) 'The Logic and Meaning of Plurals. Part II', *Journal of Philosophical Logic* 35(3): 239–88.

Carnap, R. (1937) *The Logical Syntax of Language* (London: Routledge and Kegan Paul).

—— (1950) 'Empiricism, Semantics, and Ontology', *Revue Internationale de Philosophie* 4: 20–40 (reprinted as Supplement A in *Meaning and Necessity* (Chicago: University of Chicago Press, 1956), pp. 205–21).

Chihara, C. (1990) *Constructibility and Mathematical Existence* (New York: Oxford University Press).

21 Cf. McGee and McLaughlin's nice discussion (2000) of an example involving Mt. Kiliminjaro + a pebble near its base. See also McGee (2004).

22 We thus arrive at the same place as Hilpenen (1996) on this. Cf. Musgrave (2001), 41–43.

Dummett, M. (1963, 1978) 'The Philosophical Significance of Gödel's Theorem', in *Truth and Other Enigmas* (Cambridge, MA: Harvard University Press, 1978), pp. 186–201.
Dedekind, R. (1872) *Stetigkeit und irrationale Zahlen* (Brunswick: Vieweg), trans. *Continuity and Irrational Numbers* in W.W. Beman (ed.) *Essays on the Theory of Numbers* (New York: Dover, 1963), pp. 1–27.
Field, H. H. (1980) *Science Without Numbers: A Defence of Nominalism* (Oxford: Blackwell).
Geroch, R. (1978) *General Relativity from A to B* (Chicago: University of Chicago Press).
Glymour, C. (1971) 'Theoretical Realism and Theoretical Equivalence' in R. C. Buck and R. S. Cohen, Editors, *Boston Studies in the Philosophy of Science,* Vol. 8 (Dordrecht: Reidel), pp. 275–88.
Goodman, N. (1977) *The Structure of Appearance*, 3rd edn. (Dordrecht: Reidel).
—— (1978) *Ways of Worldmaking* (Indianapolis: Hackett).
Hellman, G. (1989) *Mathematics without Numbers: Towards a Modal-Structuralist Interpretation* (Oxford: Oxford University Press).
—— (1996) 'Structuralism without Structures', *Philosophia Mathematica* (3) 4: 100–23.
Hellman, G. and Thompson, F. W. (1975) 'Physicalism: Ontology, Determination, and Reduction,' *Journal of Philosophy*, 71, 17: 551–64.
—— (1977) 'Physicalist Materialism,' *Noûs*, 11, 4: 309–45.
Hilpenen, R. (1996) 'On Some Formulations of Realism, or How Many Objects Are There in the World?' in R. S. Cohen *et al.*, Editors, *Realism and Antirealism in the Philosophy of Science* (Dordrecht: Kluwer, 1996), pp. 1–10.
Jones, R. (1991) 'Realism About What?' *Philosophy of Science* 58: 185–202.
Lewis, D. (1991) *Parts of Classes* (Oxford: Blackwell).
—— and Lewis, S. (1970) 'Holes', *Australasian Journal of Philosophy* 48: 206–12.
McGee, V. (2004) 'The Many Lives of Ebenezer Wilkes Smith', in G. Link, Editor, *One Hundred Years of Russell's Paradox* (Berlin: de Gruyter), pp. 611–24.
—— and McLaughlin, B. (2000) 'The Lessons of the Many', *Philosophical Topics* 28: 128–51.
Mac Lane, S. (1986) *Mathematics: Form and Function* (New York: Springer-Verlag).
Malament, D. (1995) 'Is Newtonian Cosmology Really Inconsistent?' *Philosophy of Science* 62, 4: 489–510.
Musgrave, A. (1992) 'Discussion: Realism About What?' *Philosophy of Science* 59: 691–7.
—— (2001) 'Metaphysical Realism *versus* Word-Magic', in D. Aleksandrowicz and H. G. Ruß (eds.), *Realismus Disziplin Interdisziplinarität* (Amsterdam: Rodopi), pp. 29–54.
Putnam, H. (1967) 'Mathematics without Foundations', *Journal of Philosophy* 64: 5–22 (reprinted in P. Benacerraf and H. Putnam (eds.) *Philosophy of Mathematics: Selected Readings*, 2nd edn. (Cambridge: Cambridge University Press, 1983), pp. 295–311).
Quine, W. V. (1976) 'On Carnap's Views on Ontology', in *Ways of Paradox and Other Essays*, revd. edn. (Cambridge, MA: Harvard University Press), pp. 203–11.
Rouilhan, P. de (2004) 'The Basic Problem of the Logic of Meaning (I)', *Revue Internationale de Philosophie* 58: 329–72.
Shapiro, S. (1997) *Philosophy of Mathematics: Structure and Ontology* (New York: Oxford University Press).
—— (2003) 'All Sets Great and Small: and I Do Mean ALL', *Philosophical Perspectives* 17: 467–90.
Uzquiano, G. [2006] 'Unrestricted Unrestricted Quantification: The Cardinal Problem of Absolute Generality'. This volume.

Williamson, T. (2003) 'Everything', *Philosophical Perspectives* 17: 415–65.

Zermelo, E. (1930) 'Über Grenzzahlen und Mengenbereiche: Neue Untersuchungen über die Grundlangen der Mengenlehre", *Fundamenta Mathematicae* 16: 29–47; trans. by M. Hallett in W. Ewald (ed.) *From Kant to Hilbert: Readings in the Foundations of Mathematics* (Oxford: Clarendon Press), pp. 1208–33.

5

Something About Everything: Universal Quantification in the Universal Sense of Universal Quantification

Shaughan Lavine

Some simple metaphysical truths apparently cannot be expressed without the notion of everything, a notion that therefore seems indispensable. It is often argued that the notion inevitably leads to paradox and must therefore be avoided. McGee has highlighted arguments by Quine and Putnam that are fruitfully understood as arguments that there is no coherent notion of everything, arguments not based on the claim of paradoxicality, a claim he does not take to be central. He argues against Quine and Putnam and affirmatively in favor of everything. I shall try to up the ante by showing that Putnam's argument withstands McGee's criticism so that the notion of everything faces serious problems even if it avoids outright paradox. I then demonstrate that we can live comfortably without everything by making use of full schematic generality, a form of generality not reducible to quantification, and showing that full schematic generality is not subject to the criticisms by Williamson of the use of schemes in the absence of quantification over everything.

5.1 EVERYTHING AND UNRESTRICTED QUANTIFICATION

'All' is usually used with an explicit or, often, implicit limitation. When a waitress informs me that 'All the oysters are gone', she is not announcing an ecological catastrophe. The quantification is implicitly limited to the restaurant for the evening.

Philosophers, in contrast, often attempt to make perfectly general claims. Consider a simple, widely accepted, example: 'everything is self-identical'. Were I to say that to the waitress, the intended domain would not be the restaurant, Earth, or even just the physical world.

The preparation of this chapter was supported in part by a Research Professorship of the School of Social and Behavioral Sciences at the University of Arizona, and by a Sabbatical Fellowship from the American Philosophical Society. The present version has benefited greatly from correspondence with Vann McGee and from comments by the editors of this volume.

Everything is apparently the domain of the quantifiers (if it can be called a domain) when they are used without contextual restrictions, and we seem to need, if not everything, such unrestricted quantifiers for metaphysical and other philosophical purposes. Frege and Russell endorsed everything, and Quine expressed an allied view when he opined that there is only one notion of existence (1960, 131; 1969*a*, 100) and that there is a single identity relation (1976, 860n).

How did I get from everything to unrestricted quantifiers? I shall assimilate the complexities of natural language, my real target, to the comparative simplicity of formal logic because formal logic shares enough features with natural language to make the resulting analyses suggestive and often reasonably certain to extend to at least a significant part of natural language. The use of formal logic is nothing more than taking the simplest case first. As McGee (2000, 56) puts it, formal logic is the philosopher's equivalent of a frictionless plane.

5.2 OBJECTIONS TO UNRESTRICTED QUANTIFICATION

My main purpose here is to object to everything. I shall argue that, first, whether or not there is a consistent notion of unrestricted quantification, we could never, even in principle, know whether the quantifiers we use are in fact unrestricted—commitment to unrestricted quantification saddles us with an irreducible mystery; and, second, that taking all of our quantifiers to be, if not explicitly, then implicitly restricted has no disadvantages and some advantages—we can live comfortably without postulating unrestricted quantification. I distinguish between unrestricted quantification, which may be unrestricted only with respect to something like a Carnapian linguistic framework, and absolutely unrestricted quantification, which ranges over absolutely everything, in some final, assumption-free sense. That will be discussed below. I shall motivate my view primarily by defending certain objections to everything against McGee's ingenious attempts to defeat them.[1]

I begin with a sketch of the four most substantial and influential objections to everything of which I am aware.[2]

[1] McGee's contribution to this volume may be taken to be primarily devoted to arguing that there is an internally coherent notion of absolutely unrestricted quantification. The only form of skepticism McGee discusses here is skepticism about whether usage suffices to establish that absolutely unrestricted quantification is absolutely unrestricted, given the presumption that we do employ absolutely unrestricted quantification. I deny the presumption. The position that there is an internally coherent notion of absolutely unrestricted quantification is not my target, though it will follow, if I am correct, that, even if there is an internally coherent notion of absolutely unrestricted quantification, there can be no good reason to adopt it. McGee (2000, 59, 62) suggested that one can 'fend off' or 'forestall' certain 'antirealist' or 'skeptical' arguments due to Skolem (1923) and Putnam (1980) against the possibility of determining whether quantification is unrestricted by making use of techniques based on arguments of Harris (1982). I have argued elsewhere that related techniques do successfully block closely related arguments. Such techniques do not succeed in the present case. In this case, the arguments of Skolem and Putnam go through. I do not take that conclusion to have skeptical or antirealist consequences.

[2] The objections, while they are familiar arguments, are not usually framed as objections to everything. In presenting the objections, I have by no means followed McGee, though my presentation has certainly been influenced by his in important respects.

5.2.1 Head-on Objections

5.2.1.1 Paradox

First, there is the objection on which Frege and Russell foundered: given any class, including everything, there is a class not in it. In the case of the class of everything, that is impossible: there can be nothing that is not a part of everything. The proof that there is a class not in any given class is a well-known modification of the argument that yields Russell's paradox: Given a class C, let R be the class of all members of C that are not members of themselves. The assumption that R is in C yields the familiar contradiction: R is in itself if and only if R is not in itself. Thus, R is not in C, and we have shown that for every class C there is a class R not in it—there is no C that can serve as everything. Informally, the upshot is that 'for any discussion, there are things that lie outside the universe of discourse of that discussion' (McGee, 2000, 55). (That formulation is self-defeating (Lewis, 1991, 68), and it is not obvious how to repair it, as Williamson (2003, 427–35) has noted in some detail, but for now I am discussing problems for unrestricted quantification, not for alternatives to it. I shall return to the point below.) I shall call this objection to everything the objection from paradox.

There are many variant forms of the objection from paradox. If there is a class of everything, there will be a class of all ordinals, and the order type of that class would have to be the largest ordinal, contradicting that there is no largest ordinal—a modified form of the argument that leads to the Burali–Forti paradox. Shapiro (2003, 471) takes this form of the objection to be the most basic. If there is a class of everything, it has the largest possible cardinality, which contradicts that the class of all sub-classes of everything has a larger cardinality—a modified form of the argument that leads to Cantor's paradox. Dummett (1963, 195–7; 1991, 316–19; 1993, 441), following Russell (1905*b*), assimilates all such arguments to a common phenomenon: indefinitely extensible concepts, Russell's self-reproductive classes. Finally, if one can quantify over everything, one can quantify over a universe of discourse[3] that includes among its members all interpretations of formal languages (including those that have everything as the range of their quantifiers) and hence that includes, for any property P, an interpretation $\mathfrak{I}$ such that $\mathfrak{I}(A) = P$, where A is an arbitrarily fixed symbol of a formal language. But there cannot be such an interpretation when P is the property that an interpretation $\mathfrak{I}$ has just if $\mathfrak{I}$ does not have the property $\mathfrak{I}(A)$. That final variant, which is due to Williamson (2003, 426), avoids any special assumptions about classes or properties, assuming instead that it is possible to give a semantic theory of a certain sort.

I view all the variant forms as essentially a single objection to everything, a head-on objection: The objection is supposed to show that quantification must always be relative to a restricted domain since the very idea of an absolutely unrestricted domain,

[3] Extending the terminology of Cartwright (1994, 3), I shall take the term 'universe of discourse' to be absolutely neutral, free of the implications that the members of the universe of discourse are entities in any full-blooded sense and that there is any class, property, or anything else that may be taken to be in any sense comprised of or characteristic of what is in the universe of discourse.

or even an unrestricted domain within a suitably powerful framework, leads to contradictions. The objection from paradox is generally regarded as the most important objection to unrestricted quantification. Cartwright (1994, 2), though he acknowledges that there are a variety of objections to unrestricted quantification, concerns himself with responding only to the objection from paradox. Shapiro (2003, 469) takes it that it is agreed that the objection from paradox provides the basic motivation for holding that it is not possible for a quantifier to have everything in its domain.[4] Williamson (2003, 424), a supporter of absolute generality, says of absolute generality that 'by far the strongest grounds for scepticism are associated with the paradoxes of set theory'. He expresses a similar sentiment in this volume. In addition, in this volume, Linnebo, Rayo, and Weir, all supporters of some form or other of unrestricted quantification, also take the objection from paradox to be, in varying senses, primary, as do Fine, Glanzberg, and Parsons, all opponents in one sense or another of unrestricted quantification. In sharp contrast, McGee (2000) does not even directly mention the objection from paradox, and in his contribution to this volume he outlines a version of it and says that it 'strikes [him] as a bit naive'. The reason that I have concentrated in this piece on McGee's defense of unrestricted quantification is that he and I agree on what the important arguments against unrestricted quantification are, though my reasons do not seem to be the same as his—I would certainly not characterize the argument from paradox as naive, and I am not sure I have understood his reasons.

There are a number of standard responses to the argument from paradox. One is to try to block it by denying that there is a class of all members of C that are not members of themselves by restricting class-formation principles in some way or other, at least for problematic C, in particular, for C the class of things over which one is quantifying. Russell's vicious-circle principle is one example. Another response is to deny that there is anything like a class of things over which one is quantifying, and hence remove any reason to suspect that one can form problematic sub-classes. That is Cartwright's (1994) strategy. Nothing I say directly argues against such moves, but they become much less attractive when one sees that there are alternatives available.

The reason I do not take the objection from paradox to be central to our question is not that the paradoxes raise no important issues. They do. Rather, it is that the considerations that arise from the paradoxes cannot be of any use in settling the dispute at hand.

Attempts to rescue unrestricted quantification from the paradoxes all involve imposing limitations on what seem to be intuitively evident principles, or at least extremely plausible ones, in itself a substantial cost, and, worse, the limitations typically are such that they make it impossible to give a semantic theory of the language used to talk about everything save by introducing quantifiers with a universe of discourse over and above that of the quantifiers that are supposed to have ranged over everything. Weir,

[4] Shapiro and Wright's contribution to this volume discusses, not quantification over everything, but whether it is coherent to quantify over all 'pure set-like totalities'. As the title, 'All things indefinitely extensible', suggests, they focus entirely on considerations that I would characterize as related to the objection from paradox.

in his contribution to this volume, gives the beginnings of a theory that allows unrestricted quantification and permits giving the semantics of the theory within the theory, but, as he acknowledges, the attempt is not completely successful, and it comes at the price of abandoning two-valued logic and of introducing non-extensional attributes into the domain of discourse.

The prices paid for the maneuvers employed to avoid paradox, while they do not rule out the proposed theories, are substantial. Indeed, it seems to me that a theory of unrestricted quantification loses its point when it allows quantification over a universe of discourse outside the universe of discourse that was supposed to include everything. Moreover, such maneuvers do nothing to protect the theories against the objections discussed below.

On the other side, the claim that no universe of discourse is unrestricted seems to lead inevitably to the self-defeating claim that in an unrestricted sense absolutely every universe of discourse has something outside of it. Avoiding that result, it would seem, will also require abandoning apparently intuitively evident principles, and, in any case, absent unrestricted quantification, it will apparently again be impossible to provide a semantic theory for the language in use.

There is a stand-off between the two sides: each finds the other paradoxical, and the question which theory retains the most important intuitively evident principles winds up resting on nothing more than one's personal intuitions, a matter of nothing more than taste. Weir, in his contribution to this volume, goes so far as to term the stand-off a Kantian antinomy. While I would be the last one to deny the importance of intuitions and taste in good philosophy, if we are to settle the issue of the possibility of unrestricted quantification, it will have to be on grounds other than those that arise from the objection from paradox, which is not to deny that any finally acceptable theory will have to find some way to exist within the constraints imposed by the paradoxes and allied issues.

5.2.1.2 Frameworks

The second objection, call it the frameworks objection, arises because differing metaphysical frameworks differ on what there is. Is the physical world made up of continuant physical objects, or point events, or congeries of sense data? Are there mental entities (sensations, ideas) or third-realm entities (meanings, propositions) over and above physical objects? Is the empty physical space between physical objects itself a thing, or nothing, or composed, say, of points? Are there any mathematical entities? If so, are there any other than sets? Is there a single, univocal notion of identity, or is identity only with respect to a sort?

If the answers to any of the above or similar questions are not matters of fact, but of choice of framework or the like, or if identity is only with respect to a sort, then there cannot be a well-defined notion of absolutely everything, since there would, in such a case, be no framework-independent or sort-independent fact of the matter about what there is. Within each framework (or sort), one can still raise the question whether there is unrestricted quantification, quantification over everything there is according to the framework, and so the objection is not against unrestricted quantification, only absolutely unrestricted quantification. Since I shall conclude that (at least for sufficiently comprehensive frameworks) there is no unrestricted quantification, it will follow *a fortiori* that there is no absolutely unrestricted quantification. Thus, the view defended here handles, but does not presume, the objection.

Hellman, in his contribution to this volume, makes the nice point that some of the apparent problems with unrestricted quantification may go away in nominalistic frameworks. To give a quick example, mine, not Hellman's, the set of all sets would pose no special problem in a framework in which there are no sets. He discusses the objection in detail, especially in Section 4.4 of his contribution to this volume. Like the objection from paradox, the frameworks objection attacks its target, in this case absolutely unrestricted quantificational generality, head-on, by arguing that no absolutely universal universe of discourse is possible.

5.2.2 Inexpressibility

The remaining two objections are of a more subtle type. The idea is that what the universe of discourse is, when we attempt quantification that is unrestricted—that is, for brevity, everything—turns out to be hopelessly ambiguous. So far, that is not a difficulty for unrestricted quantification *per se,* but an epistemological difficulty about the universe of discourse when unrestricted quantification is employed. However, the epistemological difficulty is not that further work would need to be done to determine the universe of discourse when quantification is unrestricted, it is a difficulty in principle: no one could ever be in a position to know what the universe of discourse of unrestricted quantification is. It follows that there is no way to communicate what is meant by everything. If the notion of everything cannot be communicated, it cannot be instituted or learned. As a result, there simply is no such thing as unrestricted quantification.[5] The final claim here may be taken to be self-defeating in much the

[5] I have heard it remarked that objections of this type are weaker than the ones above, because even if they succeed, it could still turn out to be the case that, for example, there is a domain comprising absolutely everything even though we could not determinately quantify over it. In fact, McGee (2000) can plausibly be taken to assume that there is a universe of discourse comprising absolutely everything and argue that we can determinately quantify over it—the assumption is certainly employed at some points, but it is not completely clear whether it is just intended as a mathematical convenience or as a central assumption of the paper. But the objections are not compatible with the existence of an unrestricted universe of discourse: if an objection of the present type succeeds, then whatever universes of discourse there may in fact be, there cannot be one answering to the description 'comprising absolutely everything' in the sense of that phrase intended by the remark—contrary to appearances, there simply is no such sense, for that is what follows from our inability to establish one. According to the objection from paradox, the putatively referring term 'the domain comprising absolutely everything' can be proved not to refer—it is no better than 'the largest number'. According to the frameworks objection, the putatively referring term 'the domain comprising absolutely everything' cannot refer because it is incomplete—to fix a reference, one would need something more like 'the domain comprising absolutely everything there is according to framework *F*'. According to the objections that follow, the putatively referring term 'the domain comprising absolutely everything' simply does not, indeed cannot, mean what the advocate of unrestricted quantification has apparently taken it to mean. What it should be taken to mean does not follow from the objections, but I shall take it to be just one more restricted term: the domain

manner discussed earlier for the claim that every domain of quantification has something outside. Bear with me. I shall address that complaint below.

5.2.2.1 *Substitutional Quantification*

The third objection to everything is technical and a bit difficult to state, and in addition it is relatively easily countered, and so I shall be brief and perhaps not absolutely clear to anyone without sufficient background. The objection is due to Quine (1968, 63–7). I shall call it the objection from substitutional quantification.

There will be, in plausible attempts to formalize everything, subject areas[6] in which, for every true existential sentence $(\exists x)\phi(x)$ about that subject area,[7] there is a name, say c, such that $\phi(c)$. The most straightforward case to describe is one in which we take the subject area to be concerned with objects and to be such that every object has a name—for example, that is true of the natural numbers or the class of people over the age of one month. (Neither example is above criticism, but they serve to illustrate the point, which only requires that such a subject area *could* exist.) In such a subject area, quantification can be understood either referentially:

$(\exists x)\phi(x)$ is true if and only if there is an object of which ϕ holds

(no name for the object is invoked) or substitutionally:

$(\exists x)\phi(x)$ is true if and only if there is a name c such that $\phi(c)$ is true.

Since there are enough names, the same sentences come out true either way. Since, Quine argues, the only way to determine the meaning or use of words (and, in particular, the quantifiers) is to see what sentences they make true, there simply is no fact of the matter about whether the quantifiers concerning such a subject area are used referentially or substitutionally. But, if they are used referentially, the subject area concerns things that exist, while, if used substitutionally, no such things are claimed to exist, since no reference to the world, but only to words, is made in the truths concerning the subject area. Thus, even given all the relevant facts, there is no way to determine whether or not the subject area concerns things that exist. The universe of discourse of the quantifiers, the supposed everything, is therefore inherently

of absolutely everything countenanced in the present context (compare Williamson's (2003, 416) example, 'Of course I'm late—you left me to pack ABSOLUTELY EVERYTHING!'), and I shall then read the theories of the advocates of "unrestricted quantification" as just more contextualism. I am not sure which is really the stronger objection to a view—that it is logically impossible, or that it cannot even be formulated—but the latter sort of objection, the sort discussed below in the text, is certainly not weak in the sense suggested by the remarks mentioned at the beginning of this note.

One can make largely parallel remarks about 'the maximal universe of discourse'. I have chosen 'the domain comprising absolutely everything' because it can be used to get the central point across in a grammatically simpler fashion—nominalization, whatever else one may think about it, is certainly a *grammatical* convenience!

[6] I have adopted the unfamiliar term 'subject area' in an attempt to be neutral between referential and substitutional quantification.

[7] When I say that a sentence is 'about' a subject area, what I mean is that all of its quantifiers are restricted to a predicate characterizing that subject area. I have not made the quantifier restrictions explicit in the text.

ill defined, and this time, no additional parameter—no framework—can be of any help, since the ambiguity concerning what is claimed to be in the universe of discourse is inherent in the entire language and framework in use.

In giving the above argument, I assumed only simple names. If one allows other resources—definite descriptions or the like—variant forms of the argument arise. I omit discussion, since the objection is, in any event, easily answered, but I should note that such other resources and, in particular, Hilbert's ϵ-operator, do obviate one objection to the argument: one might argue that quantification over the subject area is referential, not substitutional, on the grounds that quantification is referential elsewhere, where there are not enough names, and the use of quantification must be uniform throughout: the substitutional interpretation is *ad hoc,* and therefore does not come into use. That counter to the objection from substitutional quantification is reasonable so far as it goes, but it is not of much use, because the general mechanism of reference provided by the ϵ-operator guarantees that there are enough names. Quantification can be interpreted as either referential or substitutional.

5.2.2.2 Special Effects

I shall argue below that the objection to everything from substitutional quantification can be defeated, but, first, I introduce the fourth and final objection to everything. I shall call it the Hollywood objection, for reasons that will become clear shortly. The objection was first raised, not for quantification over everything, but for quantification over the mathematical universe of all sets by Skolem (1923), and it was applied to everything, in essentially the same sense employed here, by Putnam (1980). It is pretty much Skolem's argument for skepticism about axiomatic mathematics or the version of Putnam's so-called model-theoretic argument that relies on Skolem's work.

Here is how the objection goes, though neither Putnam nor Skolem put it this way. Hollywood routinely produces the appearance of large cities, huge crowds, entire alien worlds, and so forth, in movies, but, of course, they don't actually build large cities and entire alien worlds or necessarily employ huge crowds—the trick is to only produce exactly those portions of the cities, crowds, and worlds at which the camera points, and even to produce only those parts the camera can see—not barns, but barn façades (Goldman, 1976, 772–4). One can produce appearances indistinguishable from those of cities, crowds, and worlds using only a miniscule part of those cities, crowds, and worlds.

Skolem (1920, 259), using pretty much the Hollywood technique, essentially showed that for every structure for a formal language—that is, for every interpreted formal language—with an infinite domain, there is a small (countable) infinite substructure in which exactly the same sentences are true.[8] Here, instead of just producing what the camera sees, one just keeps what the language 'sees', or asserts to exist: one takes out of the original structure one witness to every true existential sentence, however many witnesses there may have been in the original, and proceeds in like

[8] The result as stated in the text only applies to countable languages, but, since for present purposes formal languages are a proxy for natural languages, that condition can be silently assumed.

manner from that point in the construction. Löwenheim had obtained a similar result by a different method (and indeed Skolem gave at least one other proof as well) and so the result is known as the Löwenheim–Skolem theorem.

Skolem (1923, 296) applied his result to the language of set theory, and used it to argue that the axiomatic specification of set theory is hopelessly inadequate: nothing in the theory, including all of its assertions concerning the existence of large infinite sizes, prevents the theory from having a small model in which all of the supposedly large infinite sizes are in fact small.[9]

Putnam (1980, 423) employed the Löwenheim–Skolem theorem for a purpose directly related to present concerns: he applied the theorem not to the language of set theory, but to our total language. The result is a countable subset of our universe of discourse, call it *S*, such that if we bound all of the quantifiers in all we say to *S*, exactly the same sentences will come out true as if we let them range over what they did before. The set *S* is the Hollywood, façade-only, version of everything. It is not everything, since there are uncountably many things—uncountably many sets, uncountably many space-time points. The point is not—and here, though I believe I am following Putnam, that may not be absolutely uncontroversial[10]—the point is not that nothing in our language (and hence nothing in our language and behavior, since the behavior would be describable in language) determines exactly which of everything and *S* is intended, but rather that, since there isn't anything beyond our language and behavior that determines which of everything and *S* is intended,[11] there simply cannot be any fact of the matter concerning which is intended. The universe of discourse of quantification is intrinsically and essentially ambiguous when there is an attempt to quantify in an unrestricted fashion. Thus, according to the Hollywood objection, it is not merely impossible to communicate the intention to quantify over everything, it is impossible to form such an intention.

We have four objections to the possibility of quantifying over everything: the objection from paradox, the frameworks objection, the objection from substitutional quantification, and the Hollywood objection. The first two, I have argued, will be of no use in resolving the question whether there can be unrestricted quantification.

5.3 REPLIES

I shall now run through how one staunch advocate of everything, Vann McGee, attempts to deflect the last two objections. I choose him because he is the one who

[9] I believe Skolem's argument can in that case be thwarted by using an axiomatization of a suitable type, and I am at present engaged in writing a book in which I discuss that extensively, but it is not our present topic. The view is sketched in Lavine (1994, 235–9). Note, however, that I do not take the Skolem argument against set theory or related arguments against other parts of mathematics to, in the end, succeed, but I am arguing here that the related argument against unrestricted quantification does in fact succeed. My main interest in the topic of unrestricted quantification is in bringing out the difference between the two kinds of cases.

[10] I *am* following McGee (2000, 58–9).

[11] Adding intensions to languages and behavior won't help because we could add mentalese to the language to which the Löwenheim–Skolem theorem is applied.

has most clearly framed the objections at issue, and because I think his attempts have the form of the best attempts to deflect them.[12]

The objection from substitutional quantification is based on the thesis that there is no way to distinguish substitutional from referential quantification when enough objects have names. The two forms of quantification are supposed to be indistinguishable since the same sentences come out true using either one.

The argument apparently works if the only data that can be used to distinguish substitutional from referential quantification are the truth values of sentences about the subject matter at issue. But, as McGee (2000, 57–8) points out, that is not the only data: The existential quantifier over a subject area is referential if, were there to be an object in the universe of discourse that is in the subject area at issue (note that there is no consideration of any names here) with a property P, $(\exists x)P(x)$ would be true and it would not be true were there no such object. The existential quantifier over a subject area is substitutional if, were there to be a name c in the language we use to speak of the subject area such that $P(c)$ is true, $(\exists x)P(x)$ would be true and it would not be true were there no such name. Those counterfactual conditions go beyond a consideration of what is true of the subject area, and yet they are clearly decisive. Quine, who proposed the objection from substitutional quantification, ignored such considerations because he had independent doubts about counterfactuals, but the use of counterfactuals here seems unexceptionable.

I think McGee's refutation of the objection from substitutional quantification is decisive, but there is a variant of the argument that requires separate discussion: I mentioned above that one can argue that all quantification is referential on the grounds that it is sometimes used referentially and that it is used univocally, but that the argument fails in the case in which there are enough names in every part of the language, since then quantification can be taken to be entirely substitutional. But now we are in the case in which the universe of discourse under discussion is supposed to be everything, and we, to keep the argument going, have allowed a mechanism of naming so powerful that there are enough names. It is now at least not clear that the above counterargument will make sense, because the counterfactual envisions objects outside the unrestricted universe of discourse, everything. But the argument is, in this context, moot in any event, since the only way to get into the situation was to allow a mechanism of naming so powerful as to make our putative substitutional quantification in fact merely a notational variant of referential quantification—the distinction rests on the possibility that a sentence could have different truth values when read referentially and substitutionally, a possibility we have just ruled out of consideration.

The Hollywood objection depends upon the existence of two universes of discourse, E (everything) and S, in which exactly the same sentences are true. That sounds like the situation in the case of the objection from substitutional quantification, but introducing counterfactuals doesn't counter the Hollywood objection. Since the objection depends on the Löwenheim–Skolem theorem, it depends upon using formalized languages with their associated structures as a proxy for ordinary

[12] I say 'form of the best attempts' because I have made what I take to be improvements in the details.

language. We therefore discuss how the objection confronts a formal counterpart of the introduction of counterfactuals, namely, the introduction of possible worlds and an associated semantics for modal operators. 'Were it that ϕ, then ψ' is formalized, following Lewis (1973), roughly as 'ψ is true in every world in which ϕ is true that is otherwise as much like the actual world as can be'. Once we have the new formal model, we can get up to our old tricks—an application of the Löwenheim–Skolem theorem yields a countable subset of the set of possible worlds and countable subdomains of the domains of those possible worlds in which the same sentences are true as in the originally envisioned counterfactual situation. The counterfactuals are now of no help in determining whether the universe of discourse of the quantifiers is S or E, for the new choice of S.

The point about counterfactuals is actually far broader: the Löwenheim–Skolem theorem can be given an extremely general form that applies, so far as I know, to every formal language that has ever been proposed as an analysis of an ordinary language, including all the formal languages discussed in this collection, with a single exception: languages that employ full schemes, discussed below. The Löwenheim–Skolem result does not apply to such languages, but another theorem can be employed to the same ends, as is also discussed below, and so the Hollywood objection applies even to them. No strengthening of the language will help to overcome the Hollywood objection. In particular, note that moving to second-order logic is of no help: only "full" or "standard" second-order logic blocks the Hollywood objection, and it does so only by building in as an assumption that the second-order quantifiers range over every subcollection of the first-order universe of discourse, that is, that the second-order quantifiers are unrestricted. That may, for some purposes, be a reasonable assumption, but when the possibility of unrestricted first-order quantification is what is at issue, the assumption of unrestricted second-order quantification clearly begs the question.

5.4 LEARNABILITY

McGee runs an objection from learnability against the Hollywood objection: he attempts to show that quantification over S is not learnable, while quantification over E is. If he succeeded, that would serve to distinguish E from S and to rule out S, showing that the two are distinguishable despite the Löwenheim–Skolem theorem. Learnability considerations move beyond the formal languages here discussed as mathematical structures to the rules and practices that constitute natural languages, and so it is certainly not implausible that they could defeat the type of indistinguishability that results from the Löwenheim–Skolem theorem. I shall, however, argue that neither leg of the argument stands. The techniques of the second part of the argument will show how we can live without everything.

To discuss the first part of the argument, I shall quote the relevant passage from McGee in full, since I am not sure that I have completely understood it.

> ... S-quantification is not learnable. To quantify over S, we would have to be able to distinguish the Ss from the non-Ss. Either the rule of universal specification would have to be

restricted so that we could only infer $\phi(\tau)$ from $(\forall x)\phi(x)$ in the special case in which τ denotes a member of S or the grammatical rules would have to include a special provision that forbade closed terms that designated non-Ss. In either case, it would be necessary to distinguish the Ss from the non-Ss before we could learn and employ the rules.

(2000, 59)

It seems clear from the 'in either case' in the final sentence that McGee thinks the reason we would have to be able to distinguish the Ss from the non-Ss is to introduce one of the rules. The formal rules of a formal language are intended to be the formalized, simplified counterparts of the actually relevant rules of a natural language. McGee makes a closely related argument in this volume. He adds that there is no comparable problem for unrestricted quantification. In that case, we can trivially distinguish what is in the domain from what is outside, since there isn't anything outside.

McGee is wrong about the need for special rules: in the first case, S has carefully been chosen so that the inference from $(\forall x)\phi(x)$ to $\phi(\tau)$ is valid for every τ of the original language. That is a direct consequence of the fact that the same sentences are true whether the domain is E or S. It was S that had to be carefully chosen, not the rule that had to be carefully restricted.

In the second case ('the grammatical rules would have to include a special provision that forbade closed terms that designated non-Ss'), once again, it isn't so: the domain S is to be chosen only after the original interpreted language has been fixed. Since it is known when choosing S what the closed terms are, it is just part of the proof of the existence of S that every object denoted by a closed term will be put in S.

If the issue were learning S-quantification as a form of restricted quantification within the larger universe of discourse of unrestricted quantification, so that the universal S-quantification over ϕ that binds the variable x was, essentially by definition, $(\forall x)(S(x) \rightarrow \phi)$, where I have somewhat sloppily used 'S' in the formula as a predicate symbol with extension S, then McGee would be perfectly correct, save for some necessary minor adjustments in terminology. The actual challenge is, however, rather different. We are to envision twin users of two languages who differ in only one respect: One takes the quantifiers to range over universe of discourse S, the other takes them to range over universe of discourse T. We may suppose that one of S and T is everything, and that the other is not, but it is better for present purposes not to specify which is which, to ensure that no external information is smuggled into the discussion. The twins take 'the same' sentences to be true, and they have had the same experiences—in particular, they acquired their current linguistic usage in virtue of those experiences. We can't even tell which of the twins has the larger universe of discourse, since neither has encountered, or will encounter, or could encounter, anything that the other has not. Even supposing, as I have, that we could make sense of the claim that one of the twins has a larger universe of discourse than the other—how could one possibly tell?—and further supposing we knew which of the two had the larger universe of discourse, we still could not determine which twin was quantifying over everything: there are two possibilities. First, the twin with the smaller universe of discourse has left some things out, and the one with the larger universe of discourse is the one quantifying over everything. Second, the twin with the smaller universe of discourse is quantifying over everything, and the one with the larger universe of discourse has mistakenly taken the universe of discourse to include at least one thing that does not, in fact, exist—I do not see how that possibility can be excluded so long as one grants that people have sometimes taken things to exist that in fact do not.

The claim that it is somehow easier, or more natural, to get from our experiences and language to everything, E, than it is to get from that same starting point to some comparatively accessible proper subset S of everything seems to require assuming some mysterious faculty of directly grasping existents. Let me emphasize once again that the moral is not that we cannot tell when quantification is unrestricted, but that we do not have a concept of such metaphysically unrestricted quantification and hence that the claim that we sometimes employ it is vacuous. I need not deny that there are perfectly good distinctions between grammatically or contextually restricted quantification—syntactically restricted quantification—and quantification that is not so restricted, that is, for example, between quantification over everyone and everything and between 'everything is packed' and 'everything is self-identical'. In addition, I need not deny that the word 'everything' can be used to declare that a given use of a quantifier is grammatically or contextually unrestricted. What I do deny is that any such syntactically unrestricted quantification is metaphysically unrestricted, since I deny that the claim of metaphysical unrestrictedness is meaningful. I shall continue to refer to metaphysically unrestricted quantification simply as unrestricted quantification; I shall always refer to syntactically unrestricted quantification using that term.

My counterargument seems too easy, and so I wonder whether I am missing something. Going beyond McGee's argument, I don't know of any additional reason for which it would be necessary to distinguish the Ss from the non-Ss, and I don't even know what it would mean to distinguish Ss from non-Ss—the ability to, given an object, tell whether or not it is in S won't do, since any object that we can in any sense be given will be in S just because that is part of how we choose S. I suppose what McGee's talk of learnability suggests is that the language is changing, and so there might be a problem about adding new closed terms τ that denote things not in S. But that won't work any more than the move to counterfactuals did, and it won't work for the same reason: we can move to a language that includes all the closed terms that will be added, or even all the terms that could be added, in any possible modal sense of could, and produce an S tailored for it. Even the maximalist demand that the language include terms for everything in the domain of quantification, a demand that would be hard to justify in the context of natural languages or of formal languages going proxy for them, can easily be met using the Hollywood technique.[13] It is not quite clear how to combine the modal and the maximalist demands, since it is not quite clear how to handle constant symbols for objects that could exist but do not, but whatever formalism is proposed to handle that will be subject to a form of the Löwenheim–Skolem theorem. The upshot will be a domain S that includes every

[13] One proof of the Löwenheim–Skolem theorem proceeds by iterating the operation of closing a set under a set of Skolem functions ω times. To prove the result mentioned in the text, one just modifies the proof by adding constant symbols for every object added at each stage of the iteration.

object for which a term can be added, in any suitable modal sense of 'can'. Putnam offers arguments along these kinds of lines. In sum, the rules and practices governing quantification over S are exactly the same as those governing quantification over E, and so the rules and practices concerning quantification over S are exactly as learnable as those concerning quantification over E—there is no difference between the two systems of rules and practices. The first leg of McGee's argument fails.

Now for the second leg: quantification over E is learnable. The question is one of principle, not of how quantification is actually learned. That pretty much goes with the territory once we have agreed to consider quantification instead of the complex systems of reference of natural language.

The rules governing formal inference are certainly learnable if any syntactic rules at all are, since they are more straightforward than most. McGee, pretty much along lines laid out by Harris (1982), argues that the formal rules of inference alone jointly completely determine what all the logical constants mean, and hence, in particular, the nature of quantification. McGee then claims that since the rules place no restriction on quantification, the quantification so determined is, for that very reason, over everything, and, thus, that quantification over E is learnable.

5.5 CHARACTERIZING THE LOGICAL CONSTANTS

To make the argument, one must first know what it would be to have completely determined the meanings of the logical constants. Here, I agree completely with McGee, who extends a criterion devised by Belnap (1962) to the present case: Belnap proposed that the addition of a new connective is acceptable if it is *conservative* (a sufficient but not necessary condition) in the sense that adding it to the language adds no new truths that can be expressed without its use—it doesn't add any new logical principles concerning the original portion of the language—and *unique* in the following, slightly complicated sense: if one adds two copies of the new connective with parallel rules (say, connectives $\circ_1$ and $\circ_2$) then any formula ϕ_1 involving only $\circ_1$ should be interderivable with the analogous formula ϕ_2 obtained by replacing each occurrence of $\circ_1$ by $\circ_2$. That is, ϕ_2 should be a consequence of ϕ_1 in the joint system, and conversely. If two such formulas are always interderivable, then the two connectives always play the same logical role—the rules of usage allow no alternative interpretations.

Belnap essentially extended the usual conditions of existence and uniqueness required for introducing a new symbol via a definite description, the conditions discussed by Russell in 'On Denoting' (1905*a*) and analyzed formally by Hilbert in his textbooks, to the introduction of logical symbols. Conservativeness is just the requirement that the introduction of the new connective be compatible with earlier work, which suffices to guarantee existence, and uniqueness guarantees that the connective is well defined, that is, that there are no variant interpretations that lead to differing truth values.

The Belnap criterion raises many questions of principle concerning, for example, what constitutes a notion of logical consequence and how to put connectives from different languages together, but the answers will seem hopelessly abstract until they have an application. Thus, I shall first prove conservativeness and give essentially the proof of uniqueness proposed by Harris, and then discuss what principles have actually been employed.

Fix a formal language $\mathcal{L}_1$ with logical symbols $\forall_1, \wedge_1, \neg_1, =_1$ and a formal language $\mathcal{L}_2$ with logical symbols $\forall_2, \wedge_2, \neg_2, =_2$.

Theorem 1 (Conservativeness). *The logic $\mathcal{L}_1 \cup \mathcal{L}_2$ is a conservative extension of $\mathcal{L}_1$.*

Proof. Suppose $\Gamma_1 \vdash \phi_1$ by a proof $\mathcal{P}$ in $\mathcal{L}_1 \cup \mathcal{L}_2$. Let $\mathcal{P}_1$ be the sequence of formulas obtained from $\mathcal{P}$ by replacing each subscript 2 by a subscript 1. Then it is routine to check that $\mathcal{P}_1$ is a proof of ϕ_1 from Γ_1 in $\mathcal{L}_1$, as required.

Theorem 2 (Uniqueness—Harris (1982)). *For any sentence ϕ of $\mathcal{L}_1$ or $\mathcal{L}_2$, $\phi_1 \vdash \phi_2$ and $\phi_2 \vdash \phi_1$ in the logic $\mathcal{L}_1 \cup \mathcal{L}_2$, if $\mathcal{L}_1$ and $\mathcal{L}_2$ have the same set of predicate symbols, function symbols, and of infinitely many constant symbols.*

Proof. By symmetry, it suffices to prove for any sentence ϕ_1 of $\mathcal{L}_1$ that $\phi_1 \vdash \phi_2$ and $\phi_2 \vdash \phi_1$ by induction on the formation of ϕ_1. Again by symmetry, it is enough to show that $\phi_1 \vdash \phi_2$.

Nonlogical atomic: $P(\tau_1, \ldots, \tau_n) \vdash P(\tau_1, \ldots, \tau_n)$, where $\tau_1, \ldots, \tau_n$ are closed terms.

$=$: $\tau =_1 \tau', \tau =_2 \tau \vdash \tau =_2 \tau'$ and $\tau =_2 \tau$, so $\tau =_1 \tau' \vdash \tau =_2 \tau'$,
where τ and τ' are closed terms.

$\wedge$: $\phi_1 \wedge_1 \psi_1 \vdash \phi_1$, $\phi_1 \vdash \phi_2$, (inductive hypothesis) so $\phi_1 \wedge_1 \psi_1 \vdash \phi_2$.
Similarly, $\phi_1 \wedge_1 \psi_1 \vdash \psi_2$.
But $\phi_2, \psi_2 \vdash \phi_2 \wedge_2 \psi_2$, and so $\phi_1 \wedge_1 \psi_1 \vdash \phi_2 \wedge_2 \psi_2$.

$\neg$: $\phi_2 \vdash \phi_1$, (inductive hypothesis) so $\neg_1 \phi_1, \phi_2 \vdash \phi_1$.
But $\neg_1 \phi_1, \phi_2 \vdash \neg_1 \phi_1$ and $\phi_1, \neg_1 \phi_1 \vdash \neg_2 \phi_2$, so $\neg_1 \phi_1, \phi_2 \vdash \neg_2 \phi_2$.
Thus, $\neg_1 \phi_1 \vdash \neg_2 \phi_2$.

$\forall$: $(\forall_1 x)\phi_1(x) \vdash \phi_1(c)$, where c is a constant symbol that does not appear in $(\forall_1 x)\phi_1(x)$.
$\phi_1(c) \vdash \phi_2(c)$, (inductive hypothesis) so $(\forall_1 x)\phi_1(x) \vdash \phi_2(c)$.
Thus, $(\forall_1 x)\phi_1(x) \vdash (\forall_2 x)\phi_2(x)$, since c does not occur on the left-hand side.

A similar proof would go through for second-order logic. The added step for the second-order quantifier is "the same" as the one for the first-order quantifier. The proof is intuitionistically valid. No mixed formulas are used.

Now to a discussion of the theorems. First, the assumption that there are infinitely many constant symbols may seem implausible for a use of formal logic that is intended to stand in for natural language, but what is in fact used is that for any sentence there is a constant symbol not in it, and that seems a quite natural assumption.

The consequence relation $\vdash$ is taken to be a part of the shared background of $\mathcal{L}_1$ and $\mathcal{L}_2$, but that is not a substantial assumption.[14] All that $\Gamma \vdash \phi$ means is that one can obtain the formula ϕ from the formulas in Γ by following the rules, and so acceptance, truth, or commitment to the formulas in Γ leads, if one accepts that the rules preserve acceptance, truth, or commitment, to acceptance, truth, or commitment to ϕ. If I am looking to see if my logical commitments unambiguously determine a notion of unrestricted quantification, it will be enough to see that they do based on an antecedently assumed notion of a truth and commitment preserving rule. Such a notion is part and parcel of my having commitments to holding sentences true at all. But that is just part of speaking a language.

5.6 OPEN-ENDEDNESS

The truly novel feature of the Harris proof is the way in which the rules of two logics are combined: for example, from the rule $\phi_1, \neg_1\phi_1 \vdash \psi$ of $\mathcal{L}_1$, we concluded $\phi_1, \neg_1\phi_1 \vdash \neg_2\phi_2$—the ψ of an $\mathcal{L}_1$ rule is taken to be a formula of $\mathcal{L}_2$. Note for future reference that the Harris proof uses only a conventional universal instantiation rule, not an open-ended one.[15]

Harris—and, following him, McGee—says that the rules of logic must be taken to be open ended—to apply not just in the present logical language but in any extension of it, whether that extension has been envisioned or not. Such open-endedness does what the proof requires, and we surely do take our logical rules to be open ended in some such sense: Consider, for example, the rule $\phi, \neg\phi \vdash \psi$ mentioned above. We do not stop to reevaluate it when moving to an expanded vocabulary, or from first- to second-order logic, or even when moving to modal logic—all the new formulas are automatically to be allowed into the rule. As McGee puts it for the case of *reductio ad absurdum,*

> We do not accept *reductio ad absurdum* because we have surveyed the forms of expression found in English and found that its expressive power is circumscribed in such a way as as to validate the rule.
>
> (2000, 66)

[14] McGee (2000, 65) takes the common consequence relation to be full model-theoretic logical consequence, which *is* a substantial assumption, as he duly notes. In this volume, he does something similar, but restricts consideration to 'models' with 'domain' absolutely everything, which, for example, has the strange result that 'there are at least seven things' is a *logical* truth if and only if there are at least seven things.

[15] The open-ended rules employed in the proof of the Harris theorem given here are substitution, cut, thinning, reiteration, *ex falso quodlibet,* negation introduction, and universal generalization. It is interesting to note that no open-ended rule is required for conjunction.

Thus, the rule $\phi, \neg\phi \vdash \psi$ of $\mathcal{L}$ is not

> if ϕ, $\neg\phi$, and ψ are formulas of $\mathcal{L}$, then from ϕ and $\neg\phi$ infer ψ,

but rather,

> if ϕ, $\neg\phi$, and ψ are any formulas whatsoever, then from ϕ and $\neg\phi$ infer ψ.[16]

The notion of 'any formula whatsoever' is hopelessly vague. One important way in which my presentation differs from that of McGee (2000, 62, 66–8, 69–71 and in his contribution to this volume), is that he commits himself to a model-theoretic account of consequence and formulahood in order to be able to provide a precise definition of 'any formula whatsoever': he (2000) assimilates each sentence of a language to the class of structures in which it is true.[17] The notion 'any sentence whatsoever' now becomes that of 'any (isomorphism-closed) class of models whatsoever'. Let $\mathcal{E}$ be a class of models, or, equivalently in the present setting, a sentence ϕ, and let $\mathcal{F}$ be a class of models or sentence, ψ, disjoint from $\mathcal{E}$. Then the intersection of $\mathcal{E}$ and $\mathcal{F}$ is empty, or, to put that another way, every member of both $\mathcal{E}$ and $\mathcal{F}$ is a member of $\bot$, which, in accordance with the 'open-ended' rule $\bot \vdash \phi$, must be the empty class of structures, at least if we assume there is no model in which every sentence is true. Thus, $\phi, \psi \vdash \bot$ and so, by our 'open-ended' rules, $\psi \vdash \neg\phi$, that is, $\mathcal{F}$ is contained in $\neg\phi$. We have shown that the negation of a sentence considered as a class of models is its complement, and the open-ended rule above now becomes,

> For any classes of models $\mathcal{E}$, or ϕ, and $\mathcal{F}$, or ψ, the models in both $\mathcal{E}$ (ϕ) and its complement ($\neg\phi$) are in $\mathcal{F}$ (ψ).

McGee's rigorous characterization of open-endedness, while it is mathematically useful and permits him to derive suggestive results that are of interest in their own right,[18] builds in a lot of assumptions that, for the purpose of assessing objections to unrestricted quantification, would best be avoided when possible and made explicit when used. For example, the use of arbitrary classes of structures commits McGee (2000) to the class of all structures, and hence, presumably, to the class of their domains and its union, the class of absolutely everything, and in this volume McGee outright assumes a domain of absolutely everything. But then, it would seem, the spirit of open-endedness would also require a commitment to the class of all classes that are not members of themselves, or at least some argument that whatever principle was used to exclude that class did not also omit some classes, and hence some sentences, required in order that the proposed definition capture the spirit of open-endedness.

[16] I have included $\neg\phi$ in the antecedent to duck the subtle but irrelevant question whether $\neg\phi$ is a formula when ϕ is not in $\mathcal{L}$—we have no present need for mixed formulas, and so I intend to avoid them.

[17] Since one can employ a formalism in which no open formulas appear, it is enough to consider only sentences. In the present volume, he gives analogous model-theoretic counterparts of formulas. Nothing turns on that but technical convenience.

[18] For example, McGee (2000 and in his contribution to this volume), derives Tarski's definition of truth from essentially the assumptions I have outlined in the previous paragraph of the text, using the techniques illustrated there.

McGee's (2000, 73) own way of avoiding commitment to the class of all classes that are not members of themselves is to presume that second-order logic is truly logic, which I take to mean taking the classes to be the universe of discourse of the second-order quantifiers without thereby being committed to classes as first-order objects. In this volume, he uses plural quantification in place of second-order logic. Such moves in themselves raise difficulties for the claim that the first-order universe of discourse includes everything. Parsons discusses that issue in some detail in his contribution to this volume. McGee remarks that the semantics of his theory appears to require introducing third-order logic, a step he is reluctant to endorse, saying only that what to do is a difficult question. Williamson (2003, 458–9) proposes an account of unrestricted quantification along related lines that does endorse a hierarchy of quantifiers of increasing order. Rayo works out another proposal of that type in his contribution to this volume. I have doubts whether any such account can be given in an internally coherent form, since that would require introducing infinitely many orders of quantification in a framework that must block generalization across all the orders in order to maintain that the second-order classes are not part of everything. Linnebo's contribution to this volume discusses the issue in detail in Sections 3 and 4, coming to a similar conclusion. Rayo acknowledges the problem and bites the bullet.

McGee (2000, 62) certainly does not disagree with the conclusion that he has built in a lot of assumptions. He notes explicitly that he is making nontrivial assumptions that subsequent investigation could undermine. His contribution to this volume assumes outright that there is a domain of absolutely everything and that English includes quantification over it. Insofar as McGee's project is not to argue for the existence of such a domain or such quantification, the assumptions might not be inappropriate. Since I am interested in assessing the possibility of unrestricted quantification, I reinterpret McGee's arguments as applying to a notion of open-endedness more suitable for that purpose than his model-theoretic one.

I see no reason to provide a precise account of open-endedness here, and indeed some reason not to: since our formalism is going proxy for natural language, we should surely avoid unnecessary commitment to a particular semantics. That is all very well, but how can we live with rules as vague as 'if ϕ, $\neg\phi$, and ψ are any formulas whatsoever, then from ϕ and $\neg\phi$ infer ψ'? Well, even vague rules have clear cases of application, and we only need the rules in clear cases: the envisioned addition of $\mathcal{L}_2$ to the logic $\mathcal{L}_1$ looks "just like" $\mathcal{L}_1$ and so surely constitutes an acceptable addition if anything does—what is in doubt is not the coherence of $\mathcal{L}_2$ but whether $\mathcal{L}_1$ is ambiguous. A symmetric remark applies to the addition of sentences of $\mathcal{L}_1$ to $\mathcal{L}_2$. Given that we are only interested in a clear case, we have no present reason to worry about the ambiguity of the formulation.

The 'open ended' rules of logic are clearly in a certain sense very general, but what is the nature of that generality? We surely do not, if at all possible, wish to understand $\phi, \neg\phi \vdash \psi$ along the lines of

$$(\forall\phi)(\forall\psi)(\phi, \neg\phi \vdash \psi).$$

It is not even clear that the "formula" is well formed: the turnstile '$\vdash$' is not a part of the language, but a symbol that is used to specify a rule—from the antecedent, infer the consequent. If it is not well formed, it is surely not an appropriate way in which to understand the relevant generality. But even if we brush such niceties aside, using such a formalism to introduce the rule would be to employ the formalism of logic in introducing that very formalism—a circularity that is best avoided if we wish to take account of issues of learnability. To make the circularity more stark, consider how we would apply the rule universal universal specification[19]

$$(\forall\phi)(\forall x)(\forall\tau)((\forall x)\phi \vdash \phi(\tau)) \tag{UUS}$$

to show that

$$(\forall x)P(x) \vdash P(c)$$

is a valid inference. We would first apply UUS to UUS (circularity!) with $\phi = (\forall x)(\forall\tau)((\forall x)\phi \vdash \phi(\tau))$, $x = \phi$, and $\tau = P(x)$ to obtain

$$(\forall\phi)(\forall x)(\forall\tau)((\forall x)\phi \vdash \phi(\tau)) \vdash (\forall x)(\forall\tau)((\forall x)P(x) \vdash P(\tau)).$$

We would then apply MP[20] to UUS and the formula immediately above to yield

$$(\forall x)(\forall\tau)\ (\forall x)\phi \vdash \phi(\tau),$$

knocking off the first quantifier ($(\forall\phi)$), and then apply UUS twice more. This accomplishes nothing toward establishing learnability: we would have to understand UUS to use UUS. The point is entirely parallel to one made by Quine in 'Truth by Convention' (1936, 351–2). McGee's (2000) account of how we learn unrestricted universal first-order quantification is faced with a similar problem, though the circle is considerably larger: His account of the rules of inference that play the central role in his rational reconstruction of how we learn such quantification takes them to employ unrestricted second-order quantification over classes of structures. That is a part of why he (2000, 60, 70) takes his scenario to be a preliminary starting point for developing an internally coherent account of the acquisition of the logical terms of classical mathematics.

If I have understood McGee's article in this volume correctly, he here argues for the much less qualified claim that 'the semantic values of the quantifiers [and the

[19] The first three quantifiers are substitutional, the last may be either referential or substitutional. If you think the two possibilities should not be combined into a single rule, fine. I have combined them only for brevity of exposition. The variable 'x' is of the sort bound by the leftmost '$(\forall x)$'. It has a substitution class consisting of the variables suitable to be bound by the quantifier of the second '$(\forall x)$' Thus, for example, if the variables bound by the quantifier of the second '$(\forall x)$' include 'u' and 'v', then both will be in the substitution class of the leftmost '$(\forall x)$' and the rightmost one will instantiate to '$(\forall u)$', '$(\forall v)$', and the like. If you don't think that is coherent, so much the worse for expressing the generality of (US) using quantification. I have put the problem into the category of niceties to be passed over.

[20] Actually, MMP—meta-modus ponens, since '$\vdash$' is not in the language. But we have already agreed to put such considerations aside.

other logical constants] are fixed by the rules of inference'. That claim is supposed to be argued for without assuming any particular semantic theory. The idea is, at least roughly, that once one has fixed a semantic theory of the nonlogical parts of a language, that plus the rules of inference will determine the semantic values of the logical constants. I think, by and large, that the claim is correct,[21] subject to some disagreements about what constitutes a semantic theory. The one aspect about which we clearly disagree is that I do not think that the universes of discourse of the quantifiers are fixed by the rules of inference.[22] If, as McGee claims here, the semantic values of the logical constants are fixed by the rules of inference, it is a natural step to conclude once more that the way in which we learn the logical constants is in some sense through learning the rules of inference.

There is no reason why learning has to be neat and tidy, and it seems entirely likely that there are circles of things that depend each on the next that we somehow manage to pick up. Nonetheless, the circle itself does not show how we manage to pick them up. We learn more about a concept or practice when we see how it could be acquired on the basis of something independent of it, and, all else being equal, such foundational explanations are to be preferred. One use for foundational explanations that has often been emphasized is that of defeating skepticism, but foundational explanations have advantages and employments quite independent of allaying skeptical worries. In general, foundational explanations are, when we can get them, to be preferred even by those, like myself, who are not foundationalists, and the fact that a view facilitates providing them is a powerful argument for that view.

5.7 FULL SCHEMES

5.7.1 Full Schemes Defined

It would be desirable to have an account of how the open-ended rules of inference are to be understood that does not depend on the use of logic, especially on the use of controversial putative portions of logic like unrestricted quantification, because that will make it possible to give a foundational explanation of how the logical constants might be learned. Fortunately, there is another form of generality more primitive than quantificational generality that will do the job: we can take the logical rules, for example, $\phi, \neg\phi \vdash \psi$, to be schemes used to declare that any instance is valid, where 'any' is to be sharply distinguished from 'every': the statement of a rule, though it does involve generality, does not involve quantification. In our example, ϕ and ψ are schematic letters, and to say that the scheme is open ended is to declare that the letters are what I (1994, 230–2) have elsewhere called full schematic variables:

[21] I argue for the allied claim that the rules of inference can be used to determine what we take to be the logical terms of a foreign language in some detail in a not-yet-completed manuscript.

[22] Given certain sorts of semantic theories, including the ones favored by McGee, the universe of discourse of the quantifiers does end up getting fixed. But it is not the rules of inference that do the fixing: it is the metalinguistic specification of the permissible instances of open-ended rules, a specification made using unrestricted quantification.

'full' is added to indicate that what counts as an acceptable substitution instance is open ended and automatically expands as the language in use expands. There will, of course, generally be some restrictions on what can replace a full schematic letter in any given scheme. The restrictions will be different for different schemes. In our example, ϕ and ψ may be replaced by arbitrary truth-bearing sentences. The restriction is two-fold: it has a syntactic component ('sentence') and a semantic one ('truth-bearing'). That is typical. The need for semantic restrictions will bar certain kinds of skeptics about semantics from making use of full schemes.[23] The position for which I am arguing has nothing to do with semantic skepticism, and is therefore unaffected by that point.

The free schematic letter in a schematic formula, like an ordinary free variable, prevents the formula from being a truth bearer. To assert that a formula involving a schematic letter is an axiom scheme does not commit us to any true axioms involving a schematic letter or a free variable: it commits us to accepting any sentence that we recognize to be a closed instance of the scheme as an axiom. A parallel remark applies to schematic rules. Acceptance of a full scheme is certainly not neutral with respect to truth: it commits us to truths, namely its instances, and it blocks us from taking to be true sentences inconsistent with its instances and from commitment to full schemes that have instances inconsistent with its instances. I therefore take full schemes to be, in an extended sense, assertible.

The way I have just proposed to construe schemes is very different from the usual one, and the proposed construal is critical for what follows. Schemes are usually introduced in terms of an antecedently given notion of quantificational generality: the commitment to a scheme is taken to be commitment to *all* of its instances. That understanding requires that there be a universe of discourse already given to which the instances of the scheme belong[24] or, if the universal quantifier is taken to be substitutional, that there be a substitution class to which all the items that can be substituted into the scheme belong.

For a scheme interpreted according a standard quantificational reading to yield the same consequences as a full scheme as the term is used here, it would be necessary that its universe of discourse or substitution class include not only all appropriate items (that is, instances or substituends) from the present language, but also, as the language expands, those from the expansion. Since a scheme can hardly have instances that are not a part of the actual language, the universe of discourse or substitution class would, on the standard quantificational readings of schemes, have to change as the language changed, which is hardly standard. Thus, the standard quantificational readings of schemes are not adequate for full schemes,[25] and a full schematic letter has neither an

[23] My remarks about semantic skepticism are prompted by McGee's remarks in a draft of his contribution to this volume.

[24] Fine, in his contribution to this volume, takes me to understand commitment to a scheme as commitment to all of its instances, and he criticizes the resulting position as incoherent. I pretty much agree with his criticisms. But the position is not mine. Because of his comments, I now emphasize that much more clearly than I did in the draft he read.

[25] If one is determined to describe full schemes in terms of other logical devices, the considerations just noted in the text suggest a modal account in which the possible worlds do not represent possible

associated universe of discourse nor an associated substitution class—it is not relative to any domain, universe, or context.[26] Full schematic letters cannot be regarded as referential or substitutional variables that have not been quantified.

I have not defined schematic generality, merely described it in its own terms. There is little alternative, since full schematic generality cannot be defined in familiar quantificational, or even modal, terms. One can, of course, formally specify the semantics of full schemes in a suitable metalanguage, but that isn't terribly helpful, since the metalanguage will also employ full schemes. Since the usual semantics for the quantifiers makes use of quantifiers in the metalanguage, I do not view the—fully parallel—situation for full schemes as in any way problematic. The addition of full schemes to our conceptual framework for introducing formalisms is worthwhile because it will permit us to give a foundational explanation of the familiar logical constants. Perhaps the single most characteristic use of full schemes is their use to express the intention to uphold certain principles however the language is refined and expanded—the rules of logic are an important example.[27]

Full schemes, though they are not a familiar part of our formal apparatus, are in fact familiar in other contexts. When, early on in an introductory logic course, before a formal language has been introduced, one says that NOT(*P* AND NOT *P*) is valid, and gives natural language examples, the letter '*P*' is being used as a full schematic letter: The students are not supposed to take it as having any particular domain—there has as yet been no discussion of what the appropriate domain might be—and it is, in the setting described, usually the case that it is not 'NOT(*P* AND NOT *P*)' that is being described as valid, but the natural-language examples that are instances of it.

Even Quine (1945, 1961), who was so chary of admitting logical devices other than those of first-order predicate logic with equality, granted that schemes are a mechanism for expressing generality distinct from quantification, one with some pedagogical and ontological advantages, though he never, to the best of my knowledge, mentioned considerations relevant to full schemes as opposed to ordinary ones. Schemes are arguably employed by Russell (his typical ambiguity—see Lavine (1994, 74–6) for a discussion) and Hilbert (in finitary mathematics—see

states of affairs, but possible languages. If it is always possible to expand a language by a new term that denotes an object not in the universe of discourse of the original language, then the relevant modality will not be explicatable in the familiar terms of possible-world semantics. One will wind up having to take the modality, or at least something closely allied to it, as basic. It seems to me that it is considerably simpler and more direct to take full schematic generality to be basic than it is to take such an unusual type of modality to be basic, but Fine, in his contribution to this volume, develops just such a modality—his 'postulational possibility'.

[26] Anyone who denies that a quantifier needs a domain of quantification (following Cartwright, 1994, 1), will be hard pressed for grounds on which to maintain that a scheme must have a universe of discourse or a substitution class.

[27] Parsons, in his contribution to this volume, argues, though on grounds related to the indefinite extensibility of the notion of set, that there is a non-quantificational type of generality associated with statements of schematic type that is at least in part concerned with the ways our conceptions could develop. Hellmann, in his contribution to this volume, notes that there is a kind of unrestricted, indefinite, schematic, open-ended generality that is stipulative of how certain terms in our language are to be used.

Lavine (1994, 192–3) for a discussion). Full schemes are used by Feferman (who introduced them as early as 1977, see Feferman (1991)) in discussing Gödel-type independence phenomena, by Burge (1984) in his theory of truth, by McGee (1997) in his theory of 'How we learn mathematical language', and by Field (1994, 406), Parsons (1990, 324), and me (1994, 231n)—we have all taken mathematical induction to be a full schematic principle.

5.7.2 Schemes Are Not Reducible to Quantification

There is nothing inconsistent about denying that schemes are in any sense assertible and concluding that schematic generality must collapse into quantificational generality,[28] but it is *ad hoc* for at least two reasons. First, it denies the existence of a non-quantificational mechanism for expressing generality that has commonly been thought to exist and to play a genuine role in our reasoning without motivation for doing so. Second, it blocks the introduction of full schemes without providing an alternative mechanism for expressing generalizations that survive expansions of our language. The position amounts to little more than a dogmatic denial of the possibility of any mechanism for expressing generality other than quantification.

A schematic letter, full or not, cannot be viewed as a free variable, substitutional or referential, one that could be bound by a quantifier, for reasons besides the one given above for full schematic letters.

Schematic letters and quantifiable variables have different inferential roles. If n is a schematic letter, one can infer $S0 \neq 0$ from $Sn \neq 0$, but that is not so if n is a quantifiable variable—in that case the inference is valid only if n did not occur free in any of the premises of the argument. No such proviso is required in the case of the schematic letter. Full schemes do not obey an analog of universal generalization: Just because everything in the present universe of discourse demonstrably shares a property need not guarantee that that will remain true as the language changes. For example, if we introduce a predicate letter 'D' for the present universe of discourse, then we will accept $(\forall x)D(x)$ and hence $D(c)$ for a 'new' constant symbol c, but $D(s)$ does not follow for a full schematic letter s.

There are schemes other than full schemes that cannot be represented using quantification. One can, of course, infer $S0 \neq 0$ from $(\forall n)Sn \neq 0$, and so perhaps one might wish to argue that the schematic version of $Sn \neq 0$ is really just an alternative notation for the more familiar universally quantified sentence. But the analogous argument does not go through for the following example: The scheme $Sn \neq 0$ with n a schematic letter ranging over some standard set of numerals for the natural numbers is not a full scheme and, it is straightforward to see, is not equivalent to the corresponding universally quantified formula, since it yields claims only about objects denoted by numerals, without giving any reason to presume that everything in the universe of discourse is denoted by a numeral, or that every member of the substitution class appears in a provable identity statement with a numeral, or that either the

[28] As Weir, in his contribution to this volume, seems to do.

class of objects denoted by a numeral or of terms that appear in a provable identity statement with a numeral is definable. Because there is a syntactic restriction on what may replace the schematic letter, the scheme does not obey the straightforward analog of universal instantiation,[29] and it is clear that the scheme is quite distinct from any quantificational generalization.

Schemes provide a general method of obtaining particular assertions without any need to have a clear notion in advance of all the suitable instances. One can directly infer $(\forall x)\phi(x)$ from $\phi(0)$ and the universally quantified formula $(\forall x)(\phi(x) \rightarrow \phi(Sx))$, but not from $\phi(0)$ and the scheme $\phi(n) \rightarrow \phi(Sn)$, since the latter, rather than making an assertion about all numbers, which is what would be required to reach the conclusion, provides a mechanism for making assertions about particular numbers. That is not to deny that in certain cases, indeed, the cases that will be of primary interest to us here, the reasons for endorsing the instances of the scheme may not also be reasons for endorsing the single universally quantified statement that all of the instances are true. Indeed, in the present case, in a suitable formalism one can infer the open formula $\phi(x) \rightarrow \phi(Sx)$, with quantifiable variable x, from the scheme $\phi(n) \rightarrow \phi(Sn)$, and then form the universal closure, which is exactly the universally quantified formula we need to conclude $(\forall x)\phi(x)$. As Fine puts it in his contribution to this volume, the particular commitment to a general claim follows from the general commitment to particular claims. But, *pace* Fine, that need not always be the case: one who doubts that the natural numbers form an actually infinite class will not take the scheme $\phi(n) \rightarrow \phi(Sn)$ to have a well-circumscribed class of instances, and hence will not be willing to infer $\phi(x) \rightarrow \phi(Sx)$ from it: the latter formula involves a quantifiable variable with the actually infinite class of all numbers as its domain or the actually infinite class of all numerals included in its substitution class. Given such a doubt, while the scheme $\phi(n)$, with its potentially infinite class of instances, will follow from $\phi(0)$ and $\phi(n) \rightarrow \phi(Sn)$, the universally quantified $(\forall x)\phi(x)$, with its commitment to an actually infinite class of numbers, will not.[30]

Whether or not one has doubts about the actually infinite class of numbers, the example of the previous paragraph shows that the general commitment to particular claims represented by $\phi(n) \rightarrow \phi(Sn)$ does not by itself entail the particular commitment to a general claim expressed by $(\forall x)(\phi(x) \rightarrow \phi(Sx))$ and, in general, that a scheme does *not* entail the formula obtained from it by replacing the schematic letters in it by quantifiable variables, whether referential or substitutional, and then universally quantifying them (Lavine, 1994, 193, 196, 208, 259). In that respect, a scheme is weaker than any universally quantified counterpart even when there is no restriction on the closed terms that may replace the schematic letters.

[29] 'Straightforward' because it does obey an analog with a suitable restriction on what may be substituted.

[30] I (1994) use the schematic methodology described in the text to avoid commitment to the actual infinite in the finitist portions of my work. Fine, in his contribution to this volume, proposes handling potential infinity in a very similar way. Indefinitely extensible properties can also be handled. I sketch that for sets below. That is relevant to the problems raised by general claims about indefinitely extensible properties discussed by Shapiro and Wright in their contribution to this volume.

There is a different respect in which a full scheme is stronger than any universally quantified counterpart: a universally quantified sentence only makes a claim about all the members of its universe of discourse or claims using all the members of its substitution class. As we have seen, in a suitable setting, those claims will follow from the corresponding scheme. However, those claims concern only the members of the substitution class or universe of discourse, while a full scheme will have additional consequences outside any given substitution class or universe of discourse. If there is an unrestricted universe of discourse,[31] it might seem that a full scheme is only stronger in a vacuous sense, but that is not completely clear: if it is possible that something could have existed (that is, been a number of the unrestricted universe of discourse) that in fact does not, then the full scheme expresses commitments we would have had had such things existed that are not expressed by the universally quantified form. Such commitments might follow from the claim that the universally quantified form is not only true, but necessarily true. That would tend to demonstrate that, as claimed, the full schematic form is in the relevant sense stronger than the universally quantified one even in the presence of unrestricted quantification, since it has not only the universally quantified form but also its necessitation as a consequence.

The use of necessitation in combination with unrestricted quantification poses a problem for the advocate of unrestricted quantification. The universe of discourse is supposed to be unrestricted, and so it should include all states of affairs, possible worlds, or whatever else one might think a robust notion of necessity requires. It ought therefore to be possible to express necessity without any modal apparatus that goes beyond what can be expressed using unrestricted quantification. The apparent need for a necessitation operator already casts doubt on the claim that the nominally unrestricted quantification is unrestricted in a sufficiently robust sense.

I grant that it is likely that there will be various ways to argue that there is a modality that cannot be expressed using unrestricted quantification, for example, simply by taking the modality to be basic, that is, not reducible to facts about anything like states of affairs or possible worlds, and so, while there is a problem here that must be solved by the advocate of unrestricted quantification, it is hardly an insuperable one. However, if it is possible that something could have been possible that is not in fact possible,[32] the position of the advocate of unrestricted quantification becomes considerably more difficult: in that case, a full scheme captures commitments we would have had there been such possibilities that are not even expressed by the necessitation of a universally quantified form. One might attempt to use some form of meta-necessity either to express such commitments or to deny that there are any such second-order possibilities. In either case, the advocate of unrestricted quantification who is unwilling to accept that full schematic generality is in the relevant

[31] I am ignoring the possibility of an unrestricted substitution class in the text. I have some doubts about whether there could be such a thing—cardinality considerations seem to pose an obstacle. However, if there is, what I say in the text about an unrestricted universe of discourse probably would, *mutatis mutandis,* also apply to it.

[32] The formulation in the text is only adequate for an S5 modality. A more general formulation would have to involve a notion of unrestricted possibility or the like: a state of affairs is possible if it is accessible from the present state of affairs; every state of affairs is possible in the unrestricted sense.

sense stronger than unrestricted quantification is faced with an infinite modal hierarchy above the unrestricted quantifiers and the attendant problem of expressing generalizations across the levels of the hierarchy.

Ordinary schemes are in some respects weaker than the corresponding universally quantified formulas, which has played a role in my argument that schematic generality is not reducible to quantificational generality. It is equally true that full schemes are in some respects weaker than the corresponding universally quantified formulas, but full schemes are also, in other respects, stronger than the corresponding universally quantified formulas. For the purposes of this chapter, it is the respects in which full schematic generalization is stronger than quantificational generalization that are of primary importance. To avoid getting mired in side issues, for the rest of the chapter I shall consider only settings in which we may take schemes to have their universally quantified counterparts as consequences, that is, settings in which schemes are at least as strong as their universally quantified counterparts.

To summarize, schematic letters are neither referential nor substitutional variables. Full schematic generality is different from, and not directly comparable to, the generality of universal quantification, whether substitutional or referential. Finally, no universally quantified sentence can have the same consequences as does a suitable corresponding full scheme.[33]

5.7.3 Restricted Schemes

Let us now look in more detail at schematic letters intended to be restricted to terms that refer to objects in a particular domain of discourse—like the *n* in the induction scheme discussed above, which was implicitly restricted to terms that refer to natural numbers. Just as in the case of referential variables, we usually leave such restrictions implicit. If a referential quantification over x, $(\forall x)\phi$ or $(\exists x)\phi$, is restricted to a domain **D**, we can make that explicit by using $(\forall x)(D(x) \rightarrow \phi)$ and $(\exists x)(D(x) \wedge \phi)$ in place of the original formulations, where I have used 'D' as a predicate symbol with extension **D**. Similarly, a scheme ϕ may include a schematic letter that we intend to restrict to terms that denote objects in **D**. We can then write $D(s) \rightarrow \phi$ to make the restriction explicit. When a referential variable x is restricted to a domain **D** and a schematic

[33] Williamson (2003, 429) in effect argues in some detail that the force of full schematic generality (he doesn't use the term) cannot be captured using quantification except by using unrestricted quantification or at least comparably strong mechanisms from which unrestricted quantification is definable. I take that to be the point of his extended discussion of the condition '*SECOND*'. He takes that to count against the possibility of employing full schemes in the absence of unrestricted quantification. I fully agree with Williamson that the force of full schematic generality cannot be captured using quantification except by using unrestricted quantification and for the most part I endorse his arguments to that effect except in matters of minor detail. I add, however, that the force of full schematic generality cannot be captured even using unrestricted quantification, or, more precisely, that doing so raises substantial difficulty for giving a coherent account of unrestricted quantification. But my conclusion is quite different from that of Williamson: I conclude that full schematic generality is a distinct type of generality not reducible to quantification. That conclusion is supported by the fact that quantification *can* be introduced using full schematic generality and, moreover, by the fact that standard pedagogical methods of introducing quantification do in fact, in effect, employ full schematic generality.

letter s is restricted to terms that denote objects in **D**, we obtain

$$(\exists x)x = s,$$

or, when we make the restrictions explicit,

$$D(s) \rightarrow (\exists x)(D(x) \wedge x = s).$$

5.8 THE EVERYTHING AXIOM

5.8.1 McGee's Argument

Now that I have introduced the notion of a full scheme, we can return to the idea that the axioms and rules of logic provide a complete characterization of *the* logical operators. We take the open-ended axioms and rules of logic to be full schemes. Since the use of full schemes does not presuppose an understanding of the logical operators, we can take Harris to have proved that the full schematic axioms and rules of logic provide a complete characterization of the logical operators in a form that is suitable for introducing those operators on the basis of antecedently understood notions. That is more than enough to enable us to conclude that the logical operators are in principle learnable in a sense far stronger than has generally been thought possible. Let us see how McGee might use that to conclude that absolutely unrestricted quantification is unambiguously specified.

McGee (2000, 68) says that, given any object whatsoever, say, a, we can let c be a constant symbol referring to a and then infer $(\forall x)P(x) \vdash P(c)$ for any predicate P using the open-ended rule of universal instantiation. Then, if P is a predicate that applies to all and only those things that lie in the range of our quantifiers, $(\forall x)P(x)$ will be true, and hence so will $P(c)$. We have shown that a is in the domain of the quantifiers. Since a was arbitrary, that shows that quantification is absolutely unrestricted. The argument relies on the open-ended rule of universal instantiation, a rule not used in the Harris proof.

There is in fact a commonplace predicate that applies to exactly the things in the universe of discourse of the quantifiers (cf. Quine, 1969*a*, 94): $P(x) =_{\text{def}} (\exists y)y = x$. Thus, we can apply the above proof to start with $(\forall x)(\exists y)y = x$ and derive $(\exists y)y = c$.[34] Since we are already allowing the use of full schematic letters, we can express the open-ended character of our choice of c by giving the proof schematically, with conclusion

$$(\exists y)y = s,$$

where s is a full schematic letter. I shall call the formula immediately above, which we have shown to be a logical truth, the *everything axiom.*

Here is a formal version of the argument for the uniqueness of everything using the everything axiom: Let $\mathcal{L}_1^E$ be the usual axioms of logic for some arbitrarily chosen

[34] McGee adopts the suggested version of the argument in the present volume.

language explicitly relativized to a domain D_1, plus the relativized everything axiom

$$(\exists x \in D_1)x = s.$$

The relativized universal specification rule is

$$(\forall x \in D_1)\phi(x) \vdash \phi(\tau)$$

provided that $D_1(\tau)$ holds.

The relativization to D_1 does not impose any restriction on the universe of discourse. We can in what follows always assume $(\forall x)D_1(x)$ in theories in the language $\mathcal{L}_1^E$, though I do not, since no use is made of that assumption. The advantage of the relativization is purely expository: it provides us with a name in the language for the universe of discourse, which, since it is the universe of discourse that is at issue, is convenient.

Let $\mathcal{L}_2^E$ be defined in the obvious parallel way, relativized to D_2. To show that the universe of discourse is uniquely determined, we must show that $D_1^{\mathcal{L}_1^E} = D_2^{\mathcal{L}_2^E}$. By symmetry, it is enough to prove that $D_2^{\mathcal{L}_2^E} \subseteq D_1^{\mathcal{L}_1^E}$.[35] To do so, let a be an arbitrary object in $D_2^{\mathcal{L}_2^E}$ and let c be a new constant symbol used to denote a. Since s is a full schematic letter, the everything axiom includes the new symbol as a possible substituend for s, and so we have as a theorem of $\mathcal{L}_1^E$,

$$(\exists x \in D_1)(x = c).$$

Thus, a is in $D_1^{\mathcal{L}_1^E}$, as required. We seem to have shown that any two implementations of logic with the everything axiom have the same domain of quantification, as required.

McGee's argument amounts to claiming—though this is not at all how he puts it, since he doesn't make use of full schemes or of the everything axiom—that the uniqueness of the logical connectives in combination with the everything axiom gives us a learnable, unambiguously specified absolutely unrestricted quantifier.

Williamson (2003, 444) also argues that the everything axiom can be used to convey that the universe of discourse includes absolutely everything. He concludes that anyone who is unwilling to accept unrestricted quantification must take the everything axiom to be illegitimate. I do not—the axiom is perfectly legitimate. I

[35] There is a problem with the way I am putting things in the text: I am acting as if $D_1^{\mathcal{L}_1^E}$ and $D_2^{\mathcal{L}_2^E}$ are subsets of a common universe of discourse on which D_1 and D_2 have extensions in the usual way. Since $D_1^{\mathcal{L}_1^E}$ and $D_2^{\mathcal{L}_2^E}$ are the unrestricted universes of discourse of the users of languages $\mathcal{L}_1^E$ and $\mathcal{L}_2^E$ in the intended application, I am not entitled to assume that there is such a common universe of discourse. But without such a common universe of discourse, what could, for example, $D_2^{\mathcal{L}_2^E} \subseteq D_1^{\mathcal{L}_1^E}$ possibly mean? I take it to mean that every object countenanced by the user of language $\mathcal{L}_2^E$ as a member of $D_2^{\mathcal{L}_2^E}$ is also countenanced by the speaker of language $\mathcal{L}_1^E$ as a member of $D_1^{\mathcal{L}_1^E}$. All of what I say below using $D_1^{\mathcal{L}_1^E}$ and $D_2^{\mathcal{L}_2^E}$ can and should be similarly translated. I have sacrificed complete accuracy in the text for the sake of readability.

reject the argument that purports to show that it follows from the everything axiom that the universe of discourse is unrestricted.

The Harris proof *does* show that the two logics $\mathcal{L}_1$ and $\mathcal{L}_2$ are fully equivalent, and thus that the logical operators can unambiguously be added to an antecedently given language. Though I am not sure I have understood him correctly, that seems to be all Harris claims. It is a quite impressive result, but it is useless for McGee's intended purpose except in concert with the everything axiom, since it does not require open-ended universal instantiation and makes no mention of adding new constant symbols to a language.[36] Does the use of a unique logic that incorporates the everything axiom constrain the universe of discourse of the quantifiers to be everything, showing that unrestricted quantification is learnable? It does not.

5.8.2 The Everything Axiom is Not What it Seems

The everything axiom has been taken to commit us to having everything in the universe of discourse because for each thing there is or could be an instance of the axiom that guarantees that that thing is in the universe of discourse. (The 'could be' clause is necessary to handle objects that do not have names in the original language.) It is supposed to follow that everything must be in the universe of discourse of the quantifiers because to satisfy the everything axiom is to satisfy all of the potential instances of the axiom.

The problem with the argument is that it employs quantification over all the potential instances of the axiom to make sense of the idea of satisfying them all, and it is that quantification, not the everything axiom or the notion of a full scheme, that does the work. It is standard practice to identify a scheme with the set or class of all of its instances, and it does not seem unreasonable to consider extending that practice to identifying a full scheme with the universe of all of its potential instances, whether or not they form a set or class. McGee (2000, 62, 66–8, 69–71) in effect makes that extension when he assimilates the open-ended possibilities for sentences to arbitrary classes of structures, which ensures that every element of the domain of every structure is denoted by the term in some instance of the everything axiom, and it is also in effect what Williamson (2003, 439–40) does when he takes an instance of a scheme open-ended with respect to a free variable to involve an assignment to the variable and takes the permissible assignments to include the assignment of every member of every domain to the variable. But to interpret a full scheme in such a manner here is to beg the relevant question: that interpretation of the scheme employs quantification over all the potential instances of the scheme, a form of quantification from which, under reasonably weak assumptions, unrestricted quantification is definable. The argument

[36] The Harris result and the everything axiom together provide a powerful new argument for the claim that to be is to be nameable—that a theory is committed to the existence of an object if and only if the language of that theory includes or can be expanded to include a constant symbol that denotes the object. I think that that is correct, and I (2000) have argued for that as a criterion of ontological commitment. The criterion, since it makes no mention of quantification, has the effect of completely separating issues of ontological commitment from both quantification and notions of truth concerning any but atomic sentences.

that the everything axiom can be used to show that the quantifiers are unrestricted, since it is based on understanding full schemes in terms of the quantificational notion of all—in an unrestricted sense of all—of their potential instances, amounts to little more than noting that if we allow unrestricted quantification over all the potential instances of a scheme, we may as well allow unrestricted quantification over the universe of discourse. Since what is at issue is the claim that unrestricted quantification is learnable, such an argument is of no probative value. What would be required instead would be an analysis of open-endedness independent of the acceptance of unrestricted quantification that would allow non-trivial use of the (open-ended) everything axiom. No one has provided such an analysis.

If we track the use of the everything axiom in formal detail without assuming that all its instances are given in advance, we can see what goes wrong. The problem is to determine whether $D_1^{\mathcal{L}_1^E}$ and $D_2^{\mathcal{L}_2^E}$ are the same. Each is supposed to play the role of a universe of discourse. That is, to be in $D_1^{\mathcal{L}_1^E}$ is to exist$_1$ (or, in other words, $D_1^{\mathcal{L}_1^E}$ is everything$_1$), and to be in $D_2^{\mathcal{L}_2^E}$ is to exist$_2$, and we want to know if we can prove that existence$_1$ and existence$_2$ coincide, that is, that there is a well-defined unrestricted sense of 'everything.' If an arbitrary element a of $D_2^{\mathcal{L}_2^E}$ should happen *not* to be in $D_1^{\mathcal{L}_1^E}$, that is, if a should happen not to exist$_1$, then from the perspective established by $\mathcal{L}_1^E$ it is not possible to let c denote a—a constant symbol must denote$_1$ an object$_1$, and this c does not.[37] In fact, the addition of c to the language of the logic $\mathcal{L}_1^E$ will only be acceptable if a is in $D_1^{\mathcal{L}_1^E}$. To simply assume that a is in $D_1^{\mathcal{L}_1^E}$ is to beg the question at issue—whether there could be a universe of discourse $D_2^{\mathcal{L}_2^E}$ not contained in $D_1^{\mathcal{L}_1^E}$. The "proof" given above that unrestricted quantification has a unique universe of discourse is worthless: the assumption that the addition of c to $\mathcal{L}_1^E$ is acceptable amounts to assuming that the everything axiom has a predetermined, unique set of instances, which is pretty nearly what was to have been proved.

The flaw in the argument becomes starkly apparent if we make the relativization of the schematic letters explicit, not just the relativization of the quantified variables. (Just as in the case of the quantified variables, the relativization in and of itself is just an expository convenience, which need not restrict the application of the scheme.) Then we have

$$(\forall x \in D_1)\phi(x) \vdash D_1(\tau) \to \phi(\tau)$$

and

$$D_1(s) \to (\exists x \in D_1)x = s,$$

the rule of universal instantiation and the everything axiom, respectively, and similar formulas for $\mathcal{L}_2^E$. The assumption that the schematic letters are to be restricted to the

37 It is possible to have constant symbols that do not denote in various so-called free logics, and so one could uphold the everything rule. But such logics have a way of expressing which constant symbols are denoting symbols, and the problem will reappear at that point. A detailed discussion would be far too long because there are so many variants of free logic.

same predicate letter, D_1, as the quantificational variables might be taken to be an unwarranted restriction. I do not think that it is, but I shall note only that it follows from McGee's analysis of open-endedness that that assumption is appropriate when the predicate D_1 holds of the entire universe of discourse and the quantifiers are unrestricted. Now, if we let a be an arbitrary object in $D_2^{\mathcal{L}_2^E}$ and c a new constant symbol used to denote a, we can substitute c into the everything$_1$ axiom to obtain

$$D_1(c) \rightarrow (\exists x \in D_1)x = c,$$

which is correct, but is no help in showing that a is in $D_1^{\mathcal{L}_1^E}$—we need to verify the antecedent $D_1(c)$ in order to detach the conclusion, and the antecedent is precisely what we are trying to show. The circularity is evident.

McGee's argument for the learnability of unrestricted quantification turns out to be at best a self-consistency argument—it, at best, could hope to show that, assuming that there is such a thing as unrestricted quantification, unrestricted quantification is learnable. In fact, it does not show even that, because one would have to show somehow that the notion of all of the potential instances of the everything axiom is learnable independently of the general notion of unrestricted quantification in order for the argument to play any role in an account of how it is possible to learn unrestricted quantification, and it is not possible to do so. Note that the argument is of absolutely no use in showing that the notion of unrestricted quantification is well defined.

I suspect that the initial appeal of the idea that the open-ended everything axiom guarantees that quantification is unrestricted is that unrestricted quantification is often thought of as quantification over a maximal universe of discourse and open-endedness is taken to be a way of ensuring maximality. But neither maximality claim is as useful as it may at first seem.

The universe of discourse of an unrestricted quantifier is not in fact fruitfully conceived of as a maximal universe. It is not maximal in some absolute sense, since it excludes nonexistent objects. Supposing for the moment that there is a well-defined universe of discourse for unrestricted quantifiers, a universe that included Sherlock Holmes would be larger. Naturally, we do in fact exclude Sherlock Holmes from the universe of discourse of the unrestricted quantifiers because he does not exist, and that is the appropriate thing to do,[38] but it is not maximality that drives the choice.

The most obvious way to implement formally a maximality requirement would be to require that the everything axiom take every term in the language or any future expansion of it as a legitimate substituend, a purely syntactic criterion. But that semantically unrestricted axiom is so strong that no one subscribes to it. For example, it has as an instance

$$(\exists x)x = \text{God},$$

but no one will accept that as a sound argument for the existence of God, which shows that the suggested version cannot be correct.

[38] Dieveney (2006) argues that even unrestricted quantification is insufficiently general for metaphysics, and advocates a form of radically unrestricted quantification that can be used to draw consequences in which non-referring terms occur.

It is obvious, in outline, how to fix the unrestricted everything axiom: one must restrict the terms that can replace the schematic letter to terms that actually denote. I suppose one could do that via a property of terms directly introduced as a property of terms, but I see no advantage to be gained. The usual procedure is to say that a term 'τ' denotes if τ exists.[39] But what is it to exist? It is just to be in the universe of unrestricted discourse, and so, for a user of language $\mathcal{L}_1^E$, a term 'τ' denotes if $D_1(\tau)$. But that is exactly the restriction on the everything$_1$ axiom imposed by the relativization introduced above, and so the discussion above applies unchanged.

If there were unrestricted quantifiers, and they had a determinate universe of discourse, it might be the case that that universe of discourse would be the maximum universe of discourse all of whose members exist—I have my doubts about the claim since it seems to involve quantification over universes of discourse including the maximum one, which, if not handled carefully, could lead to the necessity of accepting that every universe of discourse, including the maximum one, is a member of the maximum universe of discourse. Even putting such problems concerning the coherence of the claim to one side, the claim is completely uninformative: the notion of existence with respect to which the universe of discourse is taken to be maximal is just the same notion as that of the universe of discourse of an absolutely unrestricted quantifier. After all, it is quite plausible to just take '$(\exists y) y = x$' with an unrestricted quantifier to define existence.

The maximality condition is as uninformative about the intended universe of discourse as is describing the universe of discourse of quantification over the numbers as the maximum universe of discourse all of whose members are numbers. Of course, one can give a nontrivial maximality condition that yields the natural numbers. That will suggest that the universe of discourse of the unrestricted quantifiers might be obtained from some independent characterization of existence. That is perfectly correct, but I know of no attempt to provide such a characterization, and it seems to me very unlikely one can be provided, especially given the paucity of logical resources available for the purpose.

One might object that by giving the two language users two different, supposedly unrestricted universes of discourse, I have failed to respect a presupposition of McGee's argument, namely that there is a determinate universe of absolutely everything, or, what amounts to the same thing, a determinate extensional predicate 'Exists'. On McGee's account, given that interpretation of it, there is no issue of whether there is such a universe, that is simply assumed, and the issue is only whether we can learn to use quantifiers that range over it.

The appropriate setting in which to explore the utility of the everything axiom under the assumption that there is a determinate universe of absolutely everything, it seems, is one in which our language user (there will be no point to having two) is using quantifiers relativized to D (we drop the subscript, since there is only one language user) and the background universe of discourse is absolutely everything. Our question has become, how can the language user ensure that everything is in the universe of discourse D, that is, that it be true that $(\forall x)D(x)$?

[39] The quotes are Quine quotes.

It is not possible for the language user to simply state that $(\forall x)D(x)$ is true, because the sentence uses an unrestricted quantifier, and the restricted version to which the language user is entitled, $(\forall x)(D(x) \rightarrow D(x))$, says the wrong thing. The thought must be that commitment on the part of the language user to the unrestricted everything axiom will do what is required. But what does the requisite version of the everything axiom say? As we have seen, the semantically unrestricted everything axiom is too strong. So, what will the appropriate semantic restriction be? It will be that the schematic letter can be replaced by every term in the language or any expansion of it that denotes an object that Exists. In order for the language user to apply the restriction, the language user will have to, prior to any use of the everything axiom, possess the ability to tell whether or not something Exists. The everything axiom then states that

$$E(s) \rightarrow (\exists x \in D)x = s,$$

which is logically equivalent to

$$E(s) \rightarrow D(s).$$

In using that formula to show that the language user's quantifiers are unrestricted, all the work will be done by the ability to add new terms. The requisite ability is that for every object that Exists, the language user can expand the language by a term that denotes that object—that is what is required to ensure that if the everything axiom holds, then so does $(\forall x)D(x)$. It is necessary to assume that even once it has been granted that the language user has the concept of Existence. The assumption cannot be formulated by the language user, since it involves unrestricted quantification. Thus, the argument does nothing to counter the central claim of the Hollywood objection that nothing the language user can do can evince a commitment to using quantifiers that are unrestricted. What the argument *does* appear to show is that one can come to believe that a language user who endorses the everything axiom also employs unrestricted quantification by attributing two abilities to the speaker without evidence: first, the ability to tell whether a term refers to something that Exists, and, second, the ability to name each object that Exists. Whether or not that is the case, it does nothing to show that unrestricted quantification is learnable given only that there is a determinate universe of absolutely everything. The imputed abilities beg the question.

To forestall misunderstanding, let me emphasize that I am not objecting to simply taking existence, in some unrestricted sense, to be basic—my complaint is not that of the skeptic. My point is rather that once the advocate of unrestricted quantification has done so the everything axiom, a maximality principle, or open-endedness can be of no additional use in defending unrestricted quantification from the Hollywood objection.[40]

Suppose two users of the same vocabulary, Gottlob and Thoralf, have different universes of discourse but that their usage agrees on all names and that on the overlap between their universes of discourse they agree on the extensions of all relations and functions. Suppose further that the two speakers agree completely about which

[40] I take Williamson's use of open-endedness in his contribution to this volume to be otiose for the reason outlined, since he presumes a univocal notion of whether a term has a reference.

sentences of the language are true. It will follow that the overlap between the two universes will include all definable objects. It is not implausible to suppose that such a situation can arise, for it occurs if we let the vocabulary be that of a formal language and the universes be the E and S of the Hollywood objection. The two language users will each be able to claim that their syntactically unrestricted quantifiers range over everything, and each will be able to endorse the open-ended everything axiom. Using the everything axiom, maximality, and open-endedness, let us attempt to adjudicate which universe of discourse (if either) is "really" everything.

If one of the two language users could, employing only the common vocabulary, name or describe something that is not in the universe of discourse of the other, life would be easy. Since the name or description is in the common vocabulary, the one who had omitted its referent would be forced to admit that the universe of discourse from which it had been omitted is not everything, since it is not maximal and does not satisfy the obvious instance of the everything axiom.

In the setting under discussion, however, by hypothesis, everything that can be named or described in the common vocabulary lies in the overlap between the universes of discourse, and so an object that is in one of the two universes but not the other can only be named or described in an expanded vocabulary. Once an object has been described, it can be named, and so we may, without loss of generality, assume that if one of the users of the language, say, Gottlob, wishes to call attention to an object in his universe of discourse that is not in the universe of discourse of the other, Thoralf, he will expand his vocabulary by adding a name for the object. For expository convenience, let us suppose that he names the object 'North'. Nothing will prevent Thoralf from conceding that Gottlob has named an object not in his, Thoralf's, universe of discourse, and that his universe of discourse was *ipso facto*, not everything, though Thoralf will have to move to an extended universe of discourse in order to do so. But, and this is the key point, Thoralf is by no means obligated to do so: he can always coherently maintain that 'North' does not denote and consequently that it is not a defect of his universe of discourse that 'North' does not denote anything in it.[41] Thoralf and Gottlob, since they agree on which sentences are true, agree on the principles that constrain adding new names to the language. They may, then, reasonably agree on the following principles, which I believe are implicit in McGee's "Everything" (2000) and in his contribution to this volume, and which therefore beg no questions against him: something can be named if and only if it exists, and something exists if and only if it is in the universe of discourse of the unrestricted quantifiers. Naturally, each language user will interpret the principles within the language used, and, in particular, within the universe of discourse

[41] Quine (1948) has shown how to replace a language in which there are names by an equally expressive language without them. Such a language is not affected by the possibility of non-denoting 'names'. I have ignored such a possibility in the text, since the line of argument is not affected. Quine shows how to translate from the language with names to the language without them, and the resulting translation of the argument presented here is just as persuasive as the original and for the (translations of) the same reasons. A similar remark applies to other variants of the language discussed in the text, including those in which the quantifiers are introduced on the basis of Hilbert's ϵ operator.

used. Thoralf's options—conceding that his original universe of discourse was not everything or denying that 'North' exists—follow from those principles.

Since the maximality of the universe of discourse of unrestricted quantifiers is only with respect to what exists and the open-endedness of the everything axiom is only with respect to what instances exist, language users who differ about what exists will not find either of any use in settling their differences, even if they accept the notion of unrestricted quantification. No method has been provided for settling such disputes, for learning a univocal notion of everything, even if one allows the use of an unrestricted notion of existence, maximality, and the everything axiom.

Your notion of everything, presuming for the moment that you have one, and my notion of everything, presuming for the moment that I have one, can be different even while we subscribe to a common logic and to the everything axiom. A weaker possibility remains: Might the everything axiom be used to establish that each of us has an individual notion of everything, even if we have not reached a common agreement on what everything is? In particular, does my everything axiom establish a unique universe of discourse for my unrestricted quantification? It does not.

When it is only my own interpretation of the everything axiom that is at issue, there is no room for ambiguity, or at least so I am prepared to grant. When an object exists, I can designate it by a constant symbol, and that constant symbol can be substituted for the schematic letter of the everything axiom to form an instance. That shows that anything that I take to exist can be in the universe of discourse of one of my quantifiers. Once again, were there a definite universe of all the instances or potential instances of the everything axiom, it would also suffice to prove that I have a well-defined individual sense of unrestricted quantification. But, once again, to assume the existence of such a universe is to assume that which we were supposed to be using the everything axiom to verify, and so the everything axiom turns out not to have been of any help.

At this point, we have seen that the argument for the characterizability or learnability of unrestricted quantification fails in every form. It fails for absolutely unrestricted quantification. It fails for unrestricted quantification for an individual or, for the same reason, unrestricted quantification within a framework or with respect to a sort. It fails whether or not one allows the presupposition of a universe of unrestricted or even absolutely unrestricted discourse. It fails whether cast in terms of open-endedness, maximality, or full schemes. The Hollywood objection survives the attempted refutation unscathed.

Our defence of the Hollywood objection is still not done: Other uses of full schemes, including the Harris result, succeed, and they block the application of the Löwenheim–Skolem theorem on which the Hollywood objection has been based. The Hollywood objection still goes through, but only on the basis of a different result. To tell that story, I now turn to an analysis of how typical correct uses of full schemes differ from the applications of the everything axiom that we have been discussing.

5.8.3 Proper Use of Full Schemes

The attempt to employ the everything axiom to characterize the universe of discourse of unrestricted quantification makes use of the idea that a full scheme commits us to every one of its instances. It is important to note that the strategy employed in standard applications of open-endedness, including the Harris proof of the uniqueness of the logical operators,[42] the use of an open-ended induction principle to uniquely characterize the natural numbers, and the use of an open-ended replacement scheme in set theory does not have comparable defects.[43]

In typical uses of open-endedness only a single, completely specified instance of a full scheme is employed. Consider, for example, the Harris proof of the uniqueness of negation: in the fourth line, $\phi_1, \neg_1\phi_1 \vdash \neg_2\phi_2$, the *ex falso quodlibet* rule of $\mathcal{L}_1$ is applied in an open-ended way—it is used to infer the sentence $\neg_2\phi_2$ of $\mathcal{L}_2$. In the transition from the fifth line to the sixth, the negation introduction rule of $\mathcal{L}_2$ is used in an open-ended way—it is applied even though the sentence $\neg_1\phi_1$ of $\mathcal{L}_1$ is in the antecedent. To see whether a full scheme is applicable in such cases, in sharp contrast to the case of the everything axiom, there is no need to have a rigorous characterization of what instances the scheme yields, and indeed there is no reason to even be committed to the possibility of such a characterization. It is only necessary to check a single case. In the cases of interest for the Harris proof of the uniqueness of negation, one need not look far for reason to accept the necessary instances: as was noted above in the discussion following the Harris proof the envisioned addition to the logic $\mathcal{L}_1$ looks 'just like' $\mathcal{L}_1$ and so surely constitutes an acceptable addition to the language. Analogous considerations suffice for virtually every proposed application of open-endedness of which I am aware—except for the application of the everything axiom now being criticized—but I know of no reason why other types of considerations could not turn out to be relevant.

The argument that open-endedness cannot be employed to show that there is a legitimate context-independent notion of everything or, more precisely, that open-endedness cannot be employed to defeat a certain objection to that claim, is not a general objection to, and does not stem from skepticism about, the coherence and utility of open-endedness. It is based on the unusual way in which open-endedness is

[42] The fact that the Harris proof of the uniqueness of identity goes through but that no comparable argument works for unrestricted quantification serves to substantially weaken the analogy Williamson claims in his contribution to this volume between identity and unrestricted quantification.

[43] I accept the use of open-endedness in the non-defective cases, and that includes the Harris proof of the uniqueness of the quantifiers. I discuss negation at this point in the text instead of the quantifiers only because it is more convenient for expository purposes. The Harris proof ensures only that everything that can be named in a quantificational context is in the universe of discourse of the quantifiers of that context. (Compare McGee's (2000, 69) similar assessment, which is repeated in his contribution to this volume.) The further conclusion that when the quantifiers in a context are not explicitly restricted, they range over everything, in some well-defined, context-independent sense of everything, which is the conclusion I dispute, requires more, including the acceptance of an open-ended version of universal instantiation not employed in the Harris proof. McGee (2000, 69) says, for example, '[The rules of inference] ensure . . . that the domain of quantification in a given context includes everything that can be named within that context. In [contexts in which there are no restrictions on what can be named], the quantifiers range over everything.' There is, on my analysis, an unwarranted jump in that passage from the absence of restrictions on what can be named to the conclusion that everything can be named, a jump that begs the question against the Hollywood argument. As I have formalized the argument, it uses the everything axiom, and the jump is from the open-endedness of the axiom to the use of all of its instances.

employed in the argument. Moreover, I do not even object, in general, against such a use of open-endedness. The objection is rather that such a use is question-begging in the case at hand.

For the everything axiom to be of any use in picking out the universe of discourse of unrestricted quantification, it would have to pick it out using some particular instances, not by presuming a well-defined notion of all instances. So far as I am aware, however, any plausible characterization of a class of instances that does not illicitly rely on the notion of all (all things, all ordinal numbers, all sets, . . .) results in a set $\mathfrak{I}$ of instances, not a proper class. But then we are in a position to form a Hollywood set S that includes $\mathfrak{I}$. Since S is not a proper class, it is not E, and the everything axiom fails to pick out a unique universe of everything that there is.

5.8.4 Hollywood Survives Propriety

I have argued above that the Harris argument shows, making proper use of full schemes, that logic can be uniquely characterized. I have argued (1999) that, *pace* Skolem, we can, by making use of a full schematic replacement axiom for set theory, characterize the following properties up to isomorphism: the property of being an ordinal, that of being a regular class of ordinals, and the function $V(U)$ on the ordinals defined by

$$V_0(U) = U,$$

$$V_{\alpha+1}(U) = \mathrm{Pow}(V_\alpha(U)),$$

$$V_\lambda(U) = \bigcup_{\alpha\in\lambda} V_\alpha(U), \qquad \text{when } \lambda \text{ is a limit ordinal,}$$

where U is the set of all urelements (that is, non-sets) and Pow is the genuine power-set operation.[44]

If we take the formal language that is going proxy for natural language to include full schemes, then the Löwenheim–Skolem theorem will not apply, since it does not guarantee the existence of a model in which the power-set operation is standard as is required by full schematic replacement. Thus, to apply a Hollywood argument as above to show that no set of instances of the everything axiom characterizes everything, I must show that for any set $\mathfrak{I}$ there is a set S including $\mathfrak{I}$ that is a proper elementary substructure of E such that its ordinals and $V_\alpha(U)$s are all standard, and, moreover, such that the set of ordinals in S is regular. I shall, for this purpose, view E as a model of set theory with a set of urelements, possibly with new relations (that is, other than set membership) on the pure sets. (It is possible to avoid treating E as

[44] The notion of a regular class of ordinals is not a usual one. It is defined as follows: a class of ordinals is *regular* if it is an initial segment of the ordinals and if it has no cofinal subset that can be put into one-to-one correspondence with a proper initial segment of the class. If a regular class is a set, then it is a regular ordinal in the usual sense, and an ordinal is a regular class if and only if it is a regular ordinal in the usual sense. Any class of ordinals is a regular class if and only if it is an initial segment of the ordinals and the class of all sets that are in the $V_\alpha(U)$s for the αs in the class satisfies the full second-order replacement axiom.

a model, but it significantly complicates the formulation.) New relations might be definable, for example, as part of mathematical physics—the urelements constituting the physical universe with their physical relations might, for example, pick out some dimensionless constants, say, real numbers, which are pure sets. The restriction that the urelements form a set can be relaxed, but the special case serves to make the general point without getting tangled in technicalities concerning urelements. The result we need is that for every relation R on E, there is a strongly inaccessible cardinal α such that

$$\langle V_\alpha(U), \in, R \cap V_\alpha(U)\rangle \prec \langle E, \in, R\rangle,$$

or at least that result for the particular R of interest.[45] When that obtains, for suitable R, $V_\alpha(U)$ will be our Hollywood set. But the required result is precisely that the ordinals form a strongly Mahlo cardinal (Lévy, 1960, compare Kanamori, 1994, Proposition 6.2, 57) or, more formally, that the following axiom holds:

Every normal function has a strongly inaccessible fixed point.

(Compare Axiom F (Drake, 1974, 115), and see (Drake, 1974) for definitions.) That axiom has been widely regarded as quite plausible as, indeed has the stronger axiom that there is a proper class of strongly Mahlo cardinals.[46]

Thus, even given the controversial assumption that there are ways to axiomatize substantial portions of mathematics that circumvent Skolem's argument, unrestricted quantification is still subject to the Hollywood objection. The attempt at characterizing an unrestricted notion of everything has not succeeded, and it cannot possibly be patched up to succeed except in the unlikely event that one can defeat widely accepted hypotheses concerning Mahloness. Of course, the upshot is not that E quantification is indistinguishable from S quantification, but rather that no one has succeeded in characterizing or describing or showing that there is a coherent notion of E quantification.[47] It is therefore reasonable to conclude, on pragmatic rather than skeptical grounds, that, absent some compelling need for it in our conceptual economy, the notion of a fundamental, unrestricted universe of discourse is one it would be better to do without. I shall canvass reasons that the notion has been thought to be necessary below, in order to show that it can in fact readily be replaced.

5.9 UNRESTRICTED QUANTIFICATION IS DISPENSABLE

Now that we have seen that McGee's arguments against the Hollywood objection fail, where does that leave us? First of all, of course, the Hollywood objection to

[45] Shapiro and Wright, in their contribution to this volume, discuss a closely related principle.

[46] Gödel (1947, 476–7n), for example, said that the existence of Mahlo cardinals is 'implied by the general concept of set.' See (Maddy, 1988, 502, 504n) for discussion and additional references.

[47] The conclusion is very much like the one Williamson dubs 'generality absolutism is inarticulate' in his contribution to this volume. I argue not that there is no consistent theory that purports to incorporate unrestricted quantification but that there is no informative theory *of* unrestricted quantification, that is no theory that does better than simply taking unrestricted quantification as basic, no theory of how unrestricted quantification could be characterized or learned, or the like.

everything succeeds. At the outset, I granted that we seem to need the notion of everything to make general claims like 'everything is self-identical', and other more interesting general philosophical claims. Were that true, we would have to postulate everything even though we have found that the notion cannot be unambiguously characterized. Alonzo Church and Quine have adopted an analogous position about second-order logic or set theory (Shapiro, 1991, Ch. 8). We would just have to take everything (that is, more precisely, the possibility of using unrestricted quantification) to be basic, given, not learnable or subject to further explanation.

Fortunately, the same conceptual clarifications that showed that everything has not been unambiguously defined show how to live without everything. For example, given that identity is uniquely characterized by the Harris result, we can express what 'everything is self-identical' is intended to express by saying that $s = s$, where s is a full schematic letter.[48] Full schematic generality is the appropriate sort of generality for many logical, metaphysical, and other philosophical claims, which claims can be reformulated without loss. We don't need everything, and so there is no need to adopt desperate measures to rescue it.

Williamson (2003), has catalogued many truths that he claims cannot be expressed without using 'absolutely universal quantification'. I shall run through his list to show how they can be handled using the generality of full schemes instead of that of universal quantification. To understand my analysis, it is important to recall that I take the generality of schemes, including full schemes, to be *sui generis,* not to be regarded as defined using quantifiers and that full schemes are stronger than their universally quantified counterparts, since full schemes express truths encompassing objects that need not be in the current universe of discourse. The full schemes I shall be considering will have their universally quantified counterparts over any universe of discourse as consequences.

The first class of examples Williamson (2003, 423) mentions is that of universal generalizations falsified by counterexamples. From 'this page is rectangular', $R(t)$, it follows that $\neg(\forall x)\neg R(x)$, where the quantifier is absolutely unrestricted. (The example is Williamson's with the contextual reference of 'this' shifted.) I would agree, were there any reason to think absolutely unrestricted quantification possible. But the full schematic rules of logic guarantee that $\neg(\forall x)\neg R(x)$ is true in any universe of discourse, given Williamson's assumption that $R(t)$ is. The word 'any' in the preceding sentence is to be understood as indicating schematic, not quantificational generality. The guaranteed conclusion is $\neg(\forall x \in D)\neg R(x)$, where D is a full schematic letter that is to be replaced by universes of discourse. The scheme $\neg(\forall x \in D)\neg R(x)$ is the proposed full schematic replacement for Williamson's $\neg(\forall x)\neg R(x)$. Since quantifiers have a universe of discourse in any context, we may conclude $\neg(\forall x)\neg R(x)$ in any context, and I take that to explain the basis of the intuition that underlies Williamson's

[48] Readers familiar with Parsons's (1974*a*, 240, 246–8, 250–1; 1974*b*, 219–20) proposal, which he briefly mentions in his contribution to this volume, that statements like 'everything is self-identical' are systematically ambiguous will recognize how strong the affinities are between the present proposal and his. His reasons, however, which are related to various paradoxes, are very different from the ones considered here.

claim. Note that

$$(\forall D)(D \text{ is a universe of discourse} \rightarrow R(t) \rightarrow \neg(\forall x \in D)\neg R(x)),$$

which is the quantified counterpart of the full schematic claim, doesn't do the same job: it is nowhere near general enough, since it only encompasses universes of discourse that are in the present universe of discourse.[49] My version looks odd because of the explicitly restricted quantifier, but it is in fact a rather normal kind of claim: we ordinarily use sentences of a system of formal logic in (at least) two ways. One, we use them to state truths in a particular interpretation. That is how Williamson is claiming to use the sentence $\neg(\forall x)\neg R(x)$, in an interpretation with absolutely unrestricted quantification. By my lights, he fails, since there is no such interpretation. Two, we use sentences of formal logic to express something about interpretations of some kind. The claim '$\neg(\forall x)\neg R(x)$ is true in any universe of discourse, given that $R(t)$ is', made just above is an example, as is the claim that '$P \vee \neg P$ is true', when used as a way of expressing a general fact, absent any particular characterization of P. My proposed replacement of Williamson's absolutely unrestricted $\neg(\forall x)\neg R(x)$, expressed in that ordinary way, would be '$\neg(\forall x)\neg R(x)$, given that $R(t)$', which looks natural, not at all odd. Of course, in the present setting it is also potentially ambiguous in a most undesirable way. The device of full schemes with a schematic letter that is to be replaced by universes of discourse provides an unambiguous and explicit notation for such uses of sentences of formal languages.

Williamson's (2003, 423–4) second class of examples is that of logical truths and logical consequences of singular premises. His examples include $(\forall x)\neg(R(x) \wedge \neg R(x))$ and $(\forall x)(\neg R(x) \vee R(t))$ given $R(t)$, and I add $(\forall x)x = x$, all to be understood as employing absolutely unrestricted universal quantification. Those claims can be understood, given what was said in the previous paragraph, as attempts to express facts more appropriately rendered $(\forall x \in D)\neg(R(x) \wedge \neg R(x))$, $(\forall x \in D)(\neg R(x) \vee R(t))$ given $R(t)$, and $(\forall x \in D)x = x$, respectively, where D is in each case a full schematic letter to be replaced by universes of discourse. That is not unreasonable, but it is unnecessarily complicated, unless one wishes to insist that the generality being expressed is quantificational: full schemes can be used to express generality directly, unmediated by quantification. The general facts supposedly expressed using unrestricted universal quantification are better rendered $\neg(R(s) \wedge \neg R(s))$, $\neg R(s) \vee R(t)$ given $R(t)$, and $s = s$, respectively, where s is, in each case, a full schematic letter to be replaced by a term, either closed or open. Universally quantified counterparts of each of the schemes follow directly from them: in any context in which a universe of discourse has been fixed, one replaces the schematic letter by a variable and forms the universal closure. I believe that the full schematic forms come closer to expressing our pre-theoretic intentions than do the quantified versions, either Williamson's or mine. That seems particularly clear in the case of logical truths, since even advocates of everything have already wanted to take the basic logical truths to be open ended,

[49] Fine, in his contribution to this volume, seems to conclude that 'the restrictionist' cannot do better than the unsatisfactory quantificational formulation under discussion, and thus that the restrictionist view is inexpressible. The full schematic formulation expresses what is required.

that is, to be full schematic. For example, I take $\neg(R(s) \wedge \neg R(s))$, now generalized by taking R to be a full schematic letter to be replaced by predicates instead of as having the fixed interpretation 'rectangular', and $s = s$, interpreted as before, to be logical truths not because they hold of absolutely all objects and predicates but rather because we use them to declare our intention to continue to apply them to whatever we may ever come to take to be objects and predicates.

Williamson (2003, 424) also considers what he takes to be universal generalizations we endorse from which we may draw universal consequences, for example, the transitivity of the longer-than relation, which he renders $(\forall x)(\forall y)(\forall z)(L(xy) \wedge L(yz) \rightarrow L(xz))$, where, as usual, he takes the quantifiers to be absolutely unrestricted. He notes that from $L(ab)$ we can infer $(\forall x)(L(xa) \rightarrow L(xb))$, whatever a and b are, and where, once again, the quantifier is absolutely unrestricted. He is right that taking the quantifiers in such claims to be restricted to some universe of discourse or other that is not comprised of absolutely everything does not do justice to what we are claiming, but the full schematic formulations $L(st) \wedge L(tu) \rightarrow L(su)$ and $L(sa) \rightarrow L(sb)$ do, where s, t, and u are full schematic letters to be replaced by closed or open terms.

The full schematic versions not only serve as adequate replacements, but have advantages for other purposes: If 'longer than' is vague, then it may not be determined whether $L(ca)$ is true. In that setting, one can still draw the conclusion $L(ca) \rightarrow L(cb)$ from $L(sa) \rightarrow L(sb)$, and $L(st) \wedge L(tu) \rightarrow L(su)$ is naturally interpreted as expressing our determination to uphold the transitivity of the longer-than relation as we continue to refine it. The interpretation of full schemes as expressing the intention to uphold certain principles as the language is refined and expanded thus extends without modification to their use in expressing the principles by which we constrain the use of vague predicates. While I do not doubt that it may be possible to use Williamson's unrestricted quantificational principle of the transitivity of 'longer-than' to the same end, the application will hardly be routine: it will require providing a theory of how quantification interacts with vagueness.

Next, Williamson (2003, 436) considers what he calls 'kind-generalizations', with examples 'Every electron moves at less than the speed of light', and 'No donkey talks'. He takes them to deserve special consideration because it may seem possible to handle them using only restricted quantification. After all, it is quite reasonable to think that there is a restricted universe of discourse that includes all donkeys, and $(\forall x)(D(x) \rightarrow \neg T(x))$, with quantifiers restricted to such a universe of discourse, expresses 'No donkey talks'. His criticism of that maneuver is of no concern here, since kind-generalizations can be expressed using full schemes without any use of quantification, restricted or unrestricted, and hence without any need for an appropriate restricted universe of discourse for any particular kind, however problematic: the full schemes $E(s) \rightarrow L(s)$ and $D(s) \rightarrow \neg T(s)$, interpreted in the obvious way, handle the examples without quantification.

Williamson (2003, 438) objects to the use of schemes to represent kind generalizations on the grounds that schemes cannot occur unasserted, for example, negated or in the antecedent of a conditional. It seems to me that that understates the force of his objection, which, after all, will apply to every use of schemes to represent what Williamson contends should be represented using universal quantification:

the quantified versions can be negated and can appear in the antecedents of conditionals; the schemes cannot. He is perfectly correct. For example, the negation of $(\forall x)(D(x) \rightarrow \neg T(x))$ is $\neg(\forall x)(D(x) \rightarrow \neg T(x))$, 'there is a talking donkey', but the negation of $D(s) \rightarrow \neg T(s)$ is $\neg(D(s) \rightarrow \neg T(s))$, 'anything is a talking donkey'. There is apparently no way to say that there is a talking donkey, or anything to the same effect, without quantifiers.

If '$\neg(\forall x)(D(x) \rightarrow \neg T(x))$' is true, then it is possible to expand the language by a new constant symbol, say 'c', so that '$D(c) \wedge T(c)$' is true. The sentence '$D(c) \wedge T(c)$' expresses what is required without unrestricted quantification, which is what we need, provided we can state a condition to the effect that if anything is a talking donkey, then c is. Here is the condition: $(D(s) \rightarrow \neg T(s)) \vee (D(c) \wedge T(c))$. We *can* express the negation of a full scheme, though not simply by placing a negation sign in front.

The method exemplified suffices to answer the objection. For any full scheme $\phi(s)$, we introduce a new constant symbol c with axiom $\phi(s) \vee \neg\phi(c)$ and use $\neg\phi(c)$ to serve as the negation of $\phi(s)$. Indirect occurrences other than simple negations are all reducible to negations. For example, $\phi \rightarrow \psi$ is equivalent to $\neg\phi \vee \psi$, and so one can make the appropriate substitution for $\neg\phi$.

The trick sketched suffices to handle the unasserted occurrences Williamson claimed could only be expressed using unrestricted quantification. There is therefore no need to postulate unrestricted quantification.

Finally, Williamson (2003, 444–9) argues that one cannot give the semantics for the universal quantifier without unrestricted quantification, an objection that presumes that something like the Tarskian semantics are appropriate. I shall, in replying, adopt that presumption. I have no objection to it, indeed I am inclined to think it correct for present purposes. I am noting it as a special assumption only because I make no use of it outside of the present discussion.

In addition to my actual reply, I have available the following brief, unsatisfying reply: as McGee (2000, 69–71) has shown (see also his contribution to this volume), the Tarskian semantics for the connectives and quantifiers is derivable from Tarskian semantics for the nonlogical part of a language (denotations for terms, extensions for predicates, and a universe of discourse), the assumption that a variable can be assigned any object in the universe of discourse (or, if one wishes to avoid assumptions concerning formulas with free variables, the assumption that the language and its expansions can be expanded by a constant symbol denoting any object in the universe of discourse), and the open-ended axioms and rules of logic. As I am entitled to the hypotheses of McGee's result, it follows that, not only *can* I give the Tarskian semantics for the universal quantifier, I *must* do so. The reply is fully adequate; it is only unsatisfying since I haven't provided the complete derivation. I shall not do so, since it is far simpler to directly provide the semantics for the universal quantifier than it would be to derive them on the basis of other assumptions.

Since I take all quantification to be restricted, the universe of discourse will be determined by a context of use. I can therefore, following Williamson, keep things simple by taking the context also to determine the interpretations of any constant, function, and relation symbols.

The semantics for the universal quantifier are then given by the following clause in the definition of satisfaction:

The universally quantified formula $(\forall x)\phi$ is satisfied by assignment a in context C if a is an assignment for C and, for every member u of the universe of discourse in context C, the formula ϕ is satisfied by the assignment $a\left[\begin{smallmatrix}x\\u\end{smallmatrix}\right]$, the assignment that assigns u to x and agrees with a on all other variables.

The letters x, ϕ, a, and C may as well all be taken to be full schematic letters, though I shall only use the fact that C is a full schematic letter in replying to Williamson. The language in which the definition of satisfaction is given must be one in which there is a sufficiently strong background theory available to make sense of the notions of universally quantified formula, assignment, context, member of the universe of discourse of a context, formula, variant assignment, and so forth required to make sense of the definition of satisfaction. On standard ways of formalizing, a weak theory of sets will suffice. Note that the only quantifier in the clause is 'for every member u of the universe of discourse in context C', which has an explicitly specified universe of discourse.

Williamson (2003, 445) has two related worries about giving the semantics for the universal quantifier without unrestricted quantification, both of which stem from from his assumption that the only form of generality available in the absence of unrestricted quantification will be restricted quantification. He takes that assumption to have the consequence that the definition of satisfaction will have to be given in a fixed context, with a fixed, restricted universe of discourse, which I shall refer to as the overarching universe of discourse. The first worry is that the semantics will not work for universes of discourse that are not included in the overarching universe of discourse. To fix that, one would presumably somehow require that the overarching universe of discourse include the universe of discourse of the quantifier for which the semantics are to be given. That leads to the second worry. The overarching universe of discourse must include everything that can, in any context, be in the universe of discourse for the quantifier for which the semantics are being presented. That leaves us with the following dilemma: either the overarching universe of discourse must include everything, in violation of our stipulation that there is no unrestricted quantification, or there must be something that is not in the universe of discourse for the quantifier for which the semantics are being presented in any context, what Williamson calls a 'semantic pariah'. Of course, neither alternative is acceptable.

Williamson (2003, 448–9) considers the use of schemes to give the semantics for the universal quantifier. He takes a scheme to represent a commitment to *all* of its instances so that the universe of discourse for the use of 'all' implicit in the proposed semantics for the universal quantifier will have to be an overarching universe of discourse in almost exactly the sense of the discussion just above with all of the attendant problems. The semantics for the universal quantifier I have proposed, however, avoid Williamson's worries by falsifying his assumption: the full scheme that gives the semantics for the universal quantifier is not restricted to a single context or universe of discourse, and so the first worry never arises—different instances of the scheme occur in different contexts, and the very occurrence of an instance in a context guarantees that the requisite universe of discourse is included in the universe of discourse of the context in which that instance occurs.

In empirical semantics, Williamson claims, one may propose a definition of satisfaction for a language as an empirical hypothesis, and it is therefore necessary to consider denials and other unasserted occurrences of clauses in a definition of satisfaction as well as assertions of them.[50] But unasserted occurrences of clauses in a definition of satisfaction can be handled in the same way as unasserted occurrences of kind generalizations, discussed above.

Williamson (2003, 424) concludes that 'unrestricted generality is inescapable'. He is right. It is. But that provides no reason to think that unrestricted *quantificational* generality is inescapable: full schematic generality will suffice, and has a variety of advantages ranging from simplicity and metaphysical parsimony to the ability to provide a unified account of a variety of phenomena. Moreover, if the advocate of unrestricted quantificational generality also employs the notion of open-endedness, for example to express principles of logic, then the use of full schematic generality will have no disadvantages, since it will have already in effect been employed for at least some purposes.

If metaphysics is the study of the general properties shared by all things than metaphysics is impossible if there is no unrestricted quantification. (Compare McGee, 2000, 54; Williamson, 2003, 415.) But it is entirely reasonable to suspect that metaphysics in that sense is, in fact, impossible. Most metaphysical claims can be expressed perfectly well using full schematic generality. One can even express a version of Aristotle's conception of ontology as the most general of sciences (*Metaphysics* Γ): 'The subject-matter of ontology includes *s*'. That interpretation, though I am certainly not putting it forward as a serious contribution to Aristotle scholarship, avoids a problem with the version that involves unrestricted quantification: the universe of discourse of the unrestricted quantifiers is actually infinite, a possibility Aristotle rejected. For example, the universe of discourse will include, for each line, an actually infinite set of points on it, which violates Aristotle's conception that there are potentially, not actually, infinitely many points on a line. The full schematic version can be used to avoid a commitment to the actually infinite, which is more in the spirit of what Aristotle intended.

5.10 LIVING WITHOUT EVERYTHING

What final position do the considerations here suggest? They suggest denying that there is any such thing as everything, not merely accepting that there is such a thing

[50] Though nothing in the text relies on it, I am not so sure that the clauses for the logical operators in a definition of satisfaction *do* play a role in empirical semantics. The clauses for atomic sentences and formulas, since they are intimately associated with the denotations of terms and extensions of predicates, may well play a role in empirical semantics, and the full schematic rules of logic, since they impose constraints on the use of what have been taken to be logical words, may well play a role in empirical syntax or, even, perhaps semantics, depending on precisely how things are carved up. But, granted all that, there is no further role for the clauses in a definition of satisfaction that are concerned with logical words to play in empirical semantics, since those clauses will, as McGee has shown, be derivable from the other data.

but that it is mysterious—not describable or learnable. The denial of everything apparently has as a consequence

for any discussion there are things that lie outside the universe of discourse of that discussion,
(McGee, 2000, 55) (*)

which can be formalized $(\forall D)(\exists x)\neg D(x)$, a consequence that leads to a contradiction. Such a contradiction would be, to say the least, a severe problem for the position I am advocating. However, the consequence is merely

there are things that lie outside D, (**)

where D is a full schematic letter that ranges over universes of discourse, formalizable as $(\exists x)\neg D(x)$. Once again, a universal quantification has been replaced by a full scheme. The contradiction evaporates: let A be the present universe of discourse. We obtain the claim that something lies outside A, $(\exists x)\neg A(x)$, a claim that evidently must belong to a new universe of discourse, broader than A.[51]

The denial of everything must not commit us to semantic pariahs. That is, we must apparently be ready to endorse

for each thing o, it is possible to include o in the range of the quantifiers
(Shapiro, 2003, 467),

which employs unrestricted quantification. But it is enough to endorse $(\exists y)y = s$, where s is a full schematic letter. That is just the everything axiom.

The coherence of the analysis rests on the fact that we have taken full schematic generality to be basic, not dependent upon any form of quantification, and not dependent upon any universe of discourse. A universe of discourse serves as a universe for the quantifiers, but places no restrictions on the instances of a scheme. McGee has made the universe of discourse in his discussion a member of itself by quantifying over discourses in a discourse that discusses itself, and that leads to the contradiction: the fact that the present universe of discourse, A, must be in the universe of discourse of the quantification $(\forall D)$ in (*) causes the trouble, since it prevents us from concluding that certain kinds of discussion of a universe of discourse break out of that universe: if A were not in the universe of discourse of $(\forall D)$, then (*) would not apply to A, and would thus not be sufficiently general, but if A is in that universe of discourse, then there is a contradiction. In contrast, the full schematic statement (**), by not mentioning its universe of discourse in a context, leaves it coherent to mention that that universe of discourse is not a member of itself, though doing so inevitably shifts the context.[52]

[51] Glanzberg's contribution to this volume discusses the process of 'accommodation' by which shifts in the universe of discourse are accomplished. His goal is handling examples much like the one discussed here.

[52] Williamson (2003, 427–8) argues that anyone like myself who does not accept the possibility of unrestricted quantification must accept that 'I am not quantifying over everything', and argues that that is self-defeating. But I do *not* accept that I am not quantifying over everything: Such acceptance presupposes that there is a coherent, unrestricted notion of everything. Since I deny the presupposition, I deny the coherence of what Williamson presumes I must accept. He infers

The context-shifting nature of the full scheme (**) has as a consequence that there is no single context in which one can assert every one of its instances. Williamson (2003, 429) complains that that means that the limitation is not 'fully expressible' in any context. Williamson's notion of 'fully expressible' makes implicit use of unrestricted quantification, and his complaint is therefore one with which anyone who does not endorse unrestricted quantification will have no sympathy. But it seems to me that in a less tendentious sense of the term, the scheme (**) succeeds in fully expressing the fact that any universe of discourse is restricted: any instance of that fact is expressed by an instance of the scheme, where 'any' is to be read as expressing full schematic, not quantificational, generality. As this example and the analysis of Williamson's examples above shows, absolutely general thought is perfectly possible in the absence of unrestricted quantification—the generality of full schemes does all that is required (contrast Williamson, 2003, 440). Absolute generality need not invoke the notion of absolutely everything or the allied notion of unrestricted quantification: absolutely general statements are those that are preserved across changes in the universe of discourse.[53]

5.11 PARADOXES

The point of view adopted here suggests an approach to paradoxes. For brevity, I only discuss Russell's paradox: properties are always properties of the elements of a given universe of discourse. Every property determines a set. But that set need not be in the original universe of discourse, even when the property is definable in quantificational terms on it. We can, from that perspective, actually prove that there are things that lie outside universe of discourse D:

$$\{x \in D : x \notin x\} \notin D$$

by Russell's familiar argument. Hence, $(\exists x)(x \notin D)$.[54] It is part of the approach that any universe of discourse and any universe of set theory is, in another universe of

that anyone who does not accept the possibility of unrestricted quantification must accept, as a consequence of 'I am not quantifying over everything', 'something is not being quantified over by me'. I don't accept that either. It doesn't even sound plausible unless one takes the 'something' to be a natural-language form of unrestricted quantification, which, of course, I reject. By my lights, 'something' can only mean what 'something in my present universe of discourse' does, on which reading the sentence is obviously false. I *am* prepared to accept, for a suitable term τ, '$\tau(D)$ is not in universe of discourse D', as discussed below. I take that to express one aspect of the incoherence of unrestricted quantification, one that Williamson is, with his proposals, groping toward, but it does so in a way that is not self-defeating.

[53] I hope that by this point it is clear that I mean across *any* change in the universe of discourse in the full schematic sense of 'any', *not* every change in the universe of discourse in a quantificational sense.

[54] The approach itself does not lead to paradox because there is no notion of all universes of discourse: we cannot anticipate our future universes of discourse, since they may be defined in languages, and over universes of discourse, not expressible in our present language. Compare Williamson's (1998) analogous remarks concerning the liar's paradox.

We can use absolute schematic generality to generate a contradiction comparable to the one that plagues the advocate of unrestricted quantification, but it does not pose a problem: suppose we try to introduce a set r into the language via the full scheme '$s \in r$ if and only if $\neg s \in s$', where s is a discourse, a set. No illicit quantification over universes of discourse is involved in that claim, since a suitable new universe of discourse can be defined from the old one. I do not claim that the approach to the paradoxes is superior, considered solely as an approach to paradoxes, to one that involves stopping the unfolding of universes of discourse at some maximum, final, unrestricted universe of discourse. As I said earlier, I think the two sorts of approaches have, on internal grounds alone, comparable virtues. The present approach, of course, avoids commitment to unrestricted quantification, and I take the tie between the approaches to be broken by the undesirable features of unrestricted quantification discussed in the bulk of this paper, features associated with the Hollywood objection, which are external to the debate about the consequences of the paradoxes.

I shall discuss two examples of the standoff between the two sorts of approaches to the paradoxes, the first only briefly. Here it is: Williamson (2003, 434–5) proposes a 'crucial test' in the dispute between advocates of unrestricted quantification and opponents. The advocates are to propose a context that is congenial to unrestricted quantification and defend the claim that quantification in that context is in fact unrestricted. The opponents are to shift from that context to a new one and demonstrate that there is something in the new universe of discourse that was not in the old one. If the dispute is engaged on the grounds provided by the paradoxes, the test gets us nowhere. The opponent uses some paradox to generate an object not in the universe of discourse of the original context—in the particular version I have been exemplifying I would use the collection of all objects in the original universe of discourse that are not members of themselves. The advocate then claims that definition of the object in question employs some principle that begs the question against unrestricted quantification—in this case, the principle that one can collect all the objects in the universe of discourse that are not members of themselves. I then, for example, take the claim that one cannot collect the objects to be an *ad hoc* maneuver in defense of unrestricted quantification. The dance is now complete. It has gotten us nowhere.

The argument against the acceptance of unrestricted quantification that I have actually employed, based on the Hollywood objection—in contrast to considerations involving paradox—does not take the form of the proposed test. Given a context congenial to the advocate of unrestricted quantification, the response is not to shift to a new context at all, let alone to continue from there by specifying an object in the new context. It is rather to inquire into the sense in which the context is congenial, what reason there could be for taking the context to be one in which quantification is unrestricted. After all, the purpose of language is communication, and so if the context were indeed one in which quantification is to be unrestricted, there would have to be some feature of the communicative situation in the context, or perhaps of the communicative situation in establishing the context, that showed it to be one in which

full schematic letter. We are faced with the familiar contradiction. Fortunately, in contrast with the paradoxical result for unrestricted quantification, there is no plausible reason or intuition to support the idea that introducing such an r is legitimate. Though we characterize parts of our language using full schemes, we do so only as seems useful and well motivated. There do not seem to be any principles requiring us to allow the use of any particular full schemes, let alone the one for r under discussion.

quantification is to be unrestricted. I have, of course, concluded that there can be no such feature.

Here is the second example of the standoff between the two sorts of approaches to the paradoxes: Cartwright (1994, 1), a defender of first-order quantification over everything there is, argues, in my view quite correctly, that to quantify over certain objects is not to presuppose that they form a collection, and so the fact that certain objects are all and only the objects in the universe of discourse of some quantifier is not a reason to conclude that they constitute a set, class, or any other kind of collection (1994, 8–9). On that basis, he concludes that there is no collection of everything, though there is a perfectly good universe of discourse that includes everything. That blocks my assumption that every universe of discourse and every universe of set theory is, in another universe of discourse, a set, and hence the Russellian proof that something is outside the universe of discourse comprised of everything (Cartwright, 1994, 12).

While I agree with Cartwright that the fact that certain objects can be quantified over is not itself a reason to conclude that they constitute a collection, I believe we have other reasons to take them to constitute a collection. My basic reason is 'why not?' We understand perfectly well what it would be to form a collection of them, and so, in the absence of a clear reason why our general ability to collect is thwarted when we try to collect the objects in a universe of discourse, it is *ad hoc* to deny that they can be collected just to save unrestricted quantification. Fine, who, like me, rejects unrestricted quantification—he takes it to be self-defeating—but who, also like me, takes there to be a rather different sort of absolutely unrestricted generality, expresses similar sentiments in his contribution to this volume. Shapiro (2003, 469), who 'allows unrestricted, absolute first-order quantification', says that what I say is what the opponent of unrestricted quantification should say, but that the supporter of unrestricted quantification will claim that it is question begging (2003, 477), and he and Wright express similar sentiments in their contribution to this volume. I can cheerfully accept that the principle that every universe of discourse is a set in another universe of discourse is question-begging, since it plays no role in my reasons for rejecting unrestricted quantification. I employ it only after I have already rejected unrestricted quantification on quite independent grounds connected with the Hollywood objection.

My second reason for accepting that every universe of discourse is a set in another universe of discourse is mathematical: an important part of the historical motivation for and present utility of set theory is the desire to provide maximally general notions of function and collection, so that the domains of applicability of theorems concerning functions and collections can be specified as subcollections of the functions and collections of set theory. (See Lavine (1994, 7, 28, 30, 35–6, 77) for a brief discussion and references.) On the type of account I have suggested, any collection and any universe of discourse is a set in some universe of discourse, which gives set theory the desired absolute generality. Although quantified statements will always have some set or other as a universe of discourse, there will be no restrictions on what may be a member of a universe of discourse—we shall in any circumstances be free to extend the present universe of discourse—and full schemes can be used to make absolutely general claims. The indefinite extensibility of the notion of 'set' can be taken to show that quantified replacements for such full schemes are inadequate. (Other indefinitely extensible notions can be handled within set theory so formulated or treated directly in an analogous manner.)

For 'proper classes', the approach is a familiar one: it is more or less that of Zermelo (for a description and references, see Shapiro and Wright's contribution to this volume), though expressed in a way less directly tied to a particular theory of sets. It provides a comparatively straightforward way to understand, for example, proofs of theorems about 'all sets', that is, all sets in a universe of discourse, that are proved using collections outside that universe of discourse, for instance, proofs by recursion on ordinals up to twice the length of the class of all the ordinals in the universe of discourse. (See Shapiro's (2003, 471–3) or Shapiro and Wright's contribution to this volume for examples of such proofs actually utilized by mathematicians and for discussion.)

The approach is less familiar for universes of discourse, but it has comparable advantages: second-order logic on a universe of discourse becomes nothing more than a fragment of the first-order logic on a universe of discourse in which the first one is a set. Every interpreted extensional language has, in some universe of discourse, an ordinary set-theoretic model with a set as its domain of quantification. That means that many model-theoretic results, including the completeness theorem, apply in complete generality, which removes the need to provide special versions of them, proved by essentially the original proofs, for a few supposedly special cases. There is no need for models with a proper class for the universe of discourse (presented, for example, by Lévy (1979, 33)) and no need for a separate version of the completeness theorem for any collection of such models. (Williamson (1999, 135–7) proves such a completeness theorem, one which he, as an advocate of unrestricted quantification, must prove separately, imitating the usual proof, but which follows from the usual proof on the present account.)

Everything is not a communicable or learnable notion, as is shown by the Hollywood argument. There is no affirmative reason to believe that everything is a coherent notion. Moreover, even metaphysicians can do without everything, and so there is just no need to introduce it as a mysterious but necessary idea. When we add that denying that there is such a thing as quantification over everything suggests the beginnings of an attractive approach to the paradoxes, we see that there is every reason to believe that there is no such thing as everything.

REFERENCES

Belnap, N. D. (1962) 'Tonk, Plonk and Plink', *Analysis* **22**, 130–4.

Benacerraf, P. and Putnam, H., (eds.) (1983) *Philosophy of Mathematics*, 2nd edn., Cambridge University Press, Cambridge.

Burge, T. (1984) 'Semantical Paradox', in R. L. Martin, (ed.), *Recent Essays on Truth and the Liar Paradox*, Oxford University Press, New York, 85–117.

Cartwright, R. L. (1994) 'Speaking of Everything', *Nôus* **28**, 1–20.

Dieveney, P. (2006) 'Quantification and Indispensable Ontology', PhD thesis, University of Arizona.

Drake, F. R. (1974) *Set Theory*, North-Holland, Amsterdam.
Dummett, M. A. E. (1963) 'The Philosophical Significance of Gödel's Theorem', *Ratio* 5, 140–55. Page references are to the reprinting as Dummett, 1978, 186–201.
____(1978) *Truth and Other Enigmas*, Harvard University Press, Cambridge, Massachusetts.
____(1991) *Frege: Philosophy of Mathematics*, Harvard University Press, Cambridge, Massachusetts.
____(1993) *The Seas of Language*, Clarendon Press, Oxford.
Feferman, S. (1991) 'Reflecting on Incompleteness', *Journal of Symbolic Logic* **56**, 1–49.
Field, H. (1994) 'Are our Logical and Mathematical Concepts Highly Indeterminate?', in P. A. French, T. E. Uehling, Jr. and H. K. Wettstein, (eds.), *'Philosophical Naturalism'*, number 19 in *Midwest Studies in Philosophy*, University of Notre Dame Press, Notre Dame, Indiana, 391–429.
Gödel, K. (1947) 'What Is Cantor's Continuum Problem?', *American Mathematical Monthly* **54**, 515–25. Errata, vol. 55, 151. Revised and expanded for the first (1964) edition of Benacerraf and Putnam, 1983. Page references are to the revised and expanded version (Benacerraf and Putnam, 1983, 470–85).
Goldman, A. I. (1976) 'Discrimination and Perceptual Knowledge', *Journal of Philosophy* **73**, 771–91.
Harris, J. H. (1982) 'What's so Logical about the 'Logical' Axioms?', *Studia Logica* **41**, 159–71.
Kanamori, A. (1994) *The Higher Infinite: Large Cardinals in Set Theory from Their Beginnings*, Perspectives in Mathematical Logic, Springer-Verlag, Berlin.
Lavine, S. (1994) *Understanding the Infinite*, Harvard University Press, Cambridge, Massachusetts.
____(1999) 'Skolem Was Wrong', Widely circulated but unpublished manuscript.
____(2000) 'Quantification and Ontology', *Synthese* **124**, 1–43.
Lévy, A. (1960) 'Axiom Schemata of Strong Infinity in Axiomatic Set Theory', *Pacific Journal of Mathematics* **10**, 223–38.
____(1979) *Basic Set Theory*, Perspectives in Mathematical Logic, Springer-Verlag, New York.
Lewis, D. K. (1973) *Counterfactuals*, Blackwell Publishers, Oxford.
____(1991) *Parts of Classes*, Basil Blackwell Publishers, Oxford. With Appendix by John P. Burgess, A. P. Hazen, and David K. Lewis.
Maddy, P. (1988) 'Believing the Axioms. I', *Journal of Symbolic Logic* **53**, 481–511.
McGee, V. (1997) 'How We Learn Mathematical Language', *Philosophical Review* **106**, 35–68.
____(2000) "Everything", in G. Sher and R. Tieszen, (eds.), *Between Logic and Intuition: Essays in Honor of Charles Parsons*, Cambridge University Press, New York, 54–78.
Parsons, C. (1974*a*) 'The Liar Paradox', *Journal of Philosophical Logic* **3**, 381–412. Page references are to the reprinting as Parsons 1983, 221–51, which has an added postscript, 251–67.
____(1974*b*) 'Sets and Classes', *Noûs* **8**, 1–12. Page references are to the reprinting as Parsons, 1983, 209–220.
____(1983) *Mathematics in Philosophy; Selected Essays*, Cornell University Press, Ithaca, New York.
____(1990) 'The Structuralist View of Mathematical Objects', *Synthese* **84**, 303–46.
Putnam, H. (1980) 'Models and Reality', *Journal of Symbolic Logic* **45**, 464–82. Presidential Address to the annual meeting of the Association for Symbolic Logic, December, 1977. Page references are to the reprinting as Benacerraf and Putnam, 1983, 421–44.

Quine, W. V. O. (1936) Truth by Convention, in O. H. Lee, (ed.), *Philosophical Essays for Alfred North Whitehead*, Longmans, Green, New York, 90–124. Page references are to the corrected reprinting as Benacerraf and Putnam, 1983, 329–54.

—— (1945) 'On the Logic of Quantification', *Journal of Symbolic Logic* **10**, 1–12.

—— (1948) 'On What There Is', *Review of Metaphysics* **2**, 21–38. Reprinted with minor changes as Quine, 1961, 1–19.

—— (1960) *Word and Object*, MIT Press, Cambridge, Massachusetts.

—— (1961) 'Logic and the Reification of Universals', in *From a Logical Point of View: Logico-Philosophical Essays*, (2nd, revised edn.), Harvard University Press, Cambridge, Massachusetts, 102–29.

—— (1968) 'Ontological Relativity', *Journal of Philosophy* **65**, 185–212. Page references are to the reprinting as Quine, 1969*b*, 26–68.

—— (1969*a*) 'Existence and Quantification', in *Ontological Relativity and Other Essays*, number 1 in *John Dewey Essays in Philosophy*, Columbia University Press, New York, 91–113.

—— (1969*b*) *Ontological Relativity and Other Essays*, number 1 in *John Dewey Essays in Philosophy*, Columbia University Press, New York.

—— (1976) 'Worlds Away', *Journal of Philosophy* **73**, 859–63.

Russell, B. (1905*a*) 'On Denoting', *Mind* **14**, 479–93.

—— (1905*b*), 'On Some Difficulties in the Theory of Transfinite Numbers and Order Types', *Proceedings of the London Mathematical Society* 2nd series, 4, 29–53. Reprinted as Russell 1973, 135–64.

—— (1973) *Essays in Analysis*, George Braziller, New York. Edited by Douglas Lackey.

Shapiro, S. (1991) *Foundations without Foundationalism*, Clarendon Press, Oxford.

—— (2003) 'All Sets Great and Small: And I do Mean All', *Philosophical Perspectives* **17**, 467–89.

Skolem, T. (1920) 'Logische-kombinatorische Untersuchungen über die Erfüllbarkeit und Beweisbarkeit mathematischen Sätze nebst einem Theoreme über dichte Mengen' ('Logico-Combinatorial Investigations in the Satisfiability or Provability of Mathematical Propositions: A Simplified Proof of a Theorem by L. Löwenheim and Generalizations of the Theorem'), *Skrifter, Videnskabsakademiet i Kristiania, I* (4), 1–36. Page references are to the translation of section 1 by Stefan Bauer-Mengelberg (van Heijenoort, 1967, 254–63).

—— (1923) 'Einige Bemerkungen zur axiomatischen Begründung der Mengenlehre' ('Some remarks on axiomatised set theory'), in *Matematikerkongressen i Helsingfors den 4–7 Juli 1922, Den femte skandinaviska matematikerkongressen, Redogörelse*, Akademiska Bokhandeln, Helsinki, 217–32. Page references are to the translation by Stefan Bauer-Mengelberg (van Heijenoort, 1967, 291–301).

van Heijenoort, J., (ed.) (1967) *From Frege to Gödel: A Source Book in Mathematical Logic, 1879–1931*, Harvard University Press, Cambridge, Massachusetts.

Williamson, T. (1998) 'Indefinite Extensibility', in J. L. Brandl and P. Sullivan, (eds.), *New Essays on the Philosophy of Michael Dummett*, Vol. 55 of *Grazer Philosophische Studien*, Rodopi, Atlanta, Georgia, 1–24.

—— (1999) 'Existence and Contingency', *Proceedings of the Aristotelian Society* n.s. 100, 117–39.

—— (2003) 'Everything', *Philosophical Perspectives* **17**, 415–65.

6

Sets, Properties, and Unrestricted Quantification

Øystein Linnebo

6.1 INTRODUCTION

Call a quantifier *unrestricted* if it ranges over absolutely all things: not just over all physical things or all things relevant to some particular utterance or discourse but over absolutely everything there is. *Prima facie*, unrestricted quantification seems to be perfectly coherent. For such quantification appears to be involved in a variety of claims that all normal human beings are capable of understanding. For instance, some basic logical and mathematical truths appear to involve unrestricted quantification, such as the truth that absolutely everything is self-identical and the truth that the empty set has absolutely no members. Various metaphysical views too appear to involve unrestricted quantification, such as the physicalist view that absolutely everything is physical.

However, the set-theoretic and semantic paradoxes have been used to challenge the coherence of unrestricted quantification. It has been argued that, whenever we form a conception of a certain range of quantification, this conception can be used to define further objects not in this range, thus establishing that the quantification wasn't unrestricted after all.[1]

This chapter has two main goals. My first goal is to point out some problems with the most promising defense of unrestricted quantification developed to date. My second goal is to develop a better defense. The most promising defense of unrestricted quantification developed to date makes use of a hierarchy of types (Section 6.3). I show that there are some important semantic insights that type-theorists cannot express in full generality (Section 6.4). I argue that this problem is analogous to those faced by philosophers who deny the coherence of unrestricted quantification. My alternative defense of unrestricted quantification is based on a sharp

I am grateful to Agustín Rayo, Gabriel Uzquiano, Bruno Whittle, and Tim Williamson for valuable comments on earlier versions of this chapter. Thanks also to audiences at the Universities of Bristol, Oslo and Oxford and at the Fifth European Congress for Analytic Philosophy in Lisbon, August 2005, for discussion.

[1] See for instance Dummett (1981) ch. 16, Parsons (1974 and 1997), and Glanzberg (2004).

distinction between sets and properties (Section 6.5). Sets are combinatorial entities, individuated by reference to their elements. Properties are intensional entities, individuated by reference to their membership criteria. I propose that predicates be assigned properties as their semantic values rather than sets. This allows us to express the semantic insights that the type-theorists failed to express. Instead the paradoxes threaten to re-emerge. I deal with this by imposing a restriction on the property comprehension scheme—a restriction which I argue flows naturally from the nature of properties (Section 6.7) and which I prove to be consistent relative to set theory (Appendix), but which still yields enough properties to allow the desired kind of semantic theorizing (Sections 6.6 and 6.8).

6.2 THE SEMANTIC ARGUMENT

I begin by outlining what I take to be the strongest argument against the coherence of unrestricted quantification. Since this argument is based on a demand for semantic explicitness, I will refer to it as the *Semantic Argument.*[2]

Given any legitimate first-order language $\mathcal{L}$, it must be possible to develop the semantics of $\mathcal{L}$ in a systematic and scientifically respectable way, without imposing any arbitrary restrictions on the ranges of its quantifiers. I will refer to such a semantic theory as a *general semantics*. The requirement that any legitimate language should admit a general semantics is *prima facie* perfectly reasonable. Granted, it is perhaps conceivable that *Semantic Pessimism* should be true: that is, that there should be legitimate languages whose semantics for some reason cannot be made explicit. But Semantic Pessimism should be a last resort. In semantics, as well as in any other area of inquiry, a sound scientific attitude demands that we seek general and informative explanations until the impossibility thereof has been firmly established.

Assume for contradiction that it is possible to quantify over absolutely everything. In order to develop a general semantics for $\mathcal{L}$, we need to generalize over interpretations of $\mathcal{L}$'s primitive non-logical expressions. Let 'P' be a monadic predicate of $\mathcal{L}$. Let F be any contentful predicate of our meta-language, which for present purposes we may assume to be English. Then it must be possible to interpret 'P' as meaning F. Or, to state this claim more precisely, let an *interpretation* be an assignment of suitable semantic values to the primitive non-logical expressions of $\mathcal{L}$. Then there must exist an interpretation I_F such that

(1) $\forall x$ (I_F is an interpretation under which 'P' applies to $x \leftrightarrow Fx$)

where the universal quantifier '$\forall x$' ranges over absolutely everything.

Now come two more controversial steps, which I label for future reference.

Sem1 An interpretation is an object.

By this is meant simply that interpretations are the kinds of entities that first-order variables can range over. This seems reasonable, at least at the outset. Given **Sem1**, it also seems reasonable to go on and make the following step.

[2] My formulation of this argument draws heavily on Williamson (2003).

Sem2 We can define a contentful predicate 'R' as follows:

(2) $\forall x\,(Rx \leftrightarrow x$ is not an interpretation under which 'P' applies to $x)$

Having made the steps **Sem1** and **Sem2**, the rest of the argument is uncontroversial. First we put 'R' for 'F' in (1) and apply the definition of 'R' from (2) to get

(3) $\forall x\,(I_R$ is an interpretation under which 'P' applies to $x \leftrightarrow$
x is not an interpretation under which 'P' applies to $x)$.

Since the quantifier '$\forall x$' in (3) is assumed to range over absolutely everything, we can instantiate it with respect to I_R to get

(4) I_R is an interpretation under which 'P' applies to $I_R \leftrightarrow$
I_R is not an interpretation under which 'P' applies to I_R.

Since this is a contradiction, we must reject the assumption that we can quantify over absolutely everything.

Suppose that the Semantic Argument works.[3] What would this establish? The answer seems simple enough: it would establish that we cannot quantify over absolutely everything. But let's attempt to be a bit more precise. When I is an interpretation of our language, let $\forall_I$ and $\exists_I$ be the resulting interpretations of the quantifiers. Let $I \subseteq J$ abbreviate $\forall_I x \exists_J y(x = y)$, that is, the claim that all the objects that exist according to I also exist according to J. Then if unrestricted quantification is possible, there must be an interpretation that is maximal in this ordering. But what the Semantic Argument would establish, if successful, is that there is no such maximal interpretation but on the contrary, that every interpretation has a proper extension:

(5) $\forall I\, \exists J\, (I \subset J)$

where $I \subset J$ is defined as $I \subseteq J \wedge \neg (J \subseteq I)$

However, things are not as simple as they seem. If the thesis that unrestricted quantification is impossible is true, then this thesis must apply to its own statement as well. This means that the quantifier '$\forall I$' cannot be unrestricted but must range over some limited domain D. But then all (5) says is that every interpretation *in the domain* D can be properly extended. But this is compatible with the existence of a maximal interpretation *outside of* D. Thus, if we limit ourselves to restricted quantification, we cannot even properly state the thesis that unrestricted quantification is impossible. In order to properly state the thesis, we appear to need precisely what the thesis disallows.

We thus appear to be in an unacceptable situation. On the one hand we have an argument that absolutely unrestricted quantification is incoherent. On the other hand we appear unable to properly state the conclusion of this argument. Something has got to give. In what follows I discuss two strategies for defending the coherence of unrestricted quantification, each based on rejecting one of the premises of the Semantic Argument.[4]

[3] My discussion in this paragraph and the next draws on Fine (2006), Section 2.

[4] Another strategy, which will not be discussed here, is to look for a way in which the conclusion of the Semantic Argument can be properly stated after all. For some attempts to carry out this strategy, see Fine (2006), Glanzberg (2004), and Glanzberg (2006).

6.3 TYPE-THEORETIC DEFENSES OF UNRESTRICTED QUANTIFICATION

Can the coherence of unrestricted quantification be defended against the Semantic Argument? The most promising class of defenses developed to date attempt to use higher-order logic to undermine the argument's first premise, **Sem1**.[5] This premise, which says that interpretations are *objects*, records the fact that we used first-order variables to range over interpretations. So if we instead use second-order variables to talk about interpretations, this premise will no longer be true. It has therefore been suggested that an interpretation be represented by means of a second-order variable I with the convention that under I, an object-language predicate 'P' applies to an object x just in case $I\langle 'P', x\rangle$.[6] The definition of the Russell predicate 'R' in **Sem2** must then be rejected on the ground that it confuses first- and second-order variables. This blocks the rest of the Semantic Argument.

But it would be premature for a defender of unrestricted quantification to declare victory.[7] For a simple modification of the Semantic Argument shows that it isn't sufficient to admit second-order quantification but that quantification of arbitrarily high (finite) orders is needed. We see this as follows. The Semantic Argument challenges us to develop a general semantics for some first-order language $\mathcal{L}_1$, say that of ZFC set theory. The response just outlined develops a general semantics for $\mathcal{L}_1$ in a second-order language $\mathcal{L}_2$. However, the Semantic Argument was based on the requirement that it be possible to develop a general semantics for *any* legitimate language. Now clearly, if the above response to the Semantic Argument is to succeed, the language $\mathcal{L}_2$ must itself be legitimate. But then the Semantic Argument will require that a general semantics be developed for $\mathcal{L}_2$ as well.

In order to do this, we need to adopt a language that is more expressive than $\mathcal{L}_2$. For in order to develop a general semantics for $\mathcal{L}_2$, we would among other things have to give a theory of truth for the language $\mathcal{L}_2$ of second-order ZFC when its first-order quantifiers range over absolutely all sets. But by Tarski's theorem on the undefinability of truth, this cannot be done within $\mathcal{L}_2$ itself. The most natural thing to do at this point is to adopt an extended language $\mathcal{L}_3$ that includes *third*-order quantification as well. The argument just given can then be applied to $\mathcal{L}_3$. Advocates of the response

[5] This kind of defense of unrestricted quantification was given a clear and powerful statement in Boolos (1985), has since been endorsed in Cartwright (1994) and Lewis (1991), and has recently been developed with quite a lot of technical and philosophical detail in Rayo and Uzquiano (1999), Williamson (2003), Rayo and Williamson (2003), and Rayo (2006).

[6] As shown in Rayo and Uzquiano (1999), we can also define a satisfaction predicate which holds of an interpretation I and the Gödel number of a formula ϕ just in case I satisfies ϕ. But this will require not only second-order quantification but *second-order predicates* (that is, predicates that apply to second-order variables in the same way as first-order predicates apply to first-order variables).

[7] This is openly acknowledged by at least some of the defenders of this response. See for instance the papers by Rayo, Uzquiano, and Williamson cited in footnote 5.

based on second-order logic will in this way be forced up through the hierarchy of higher and higher levels of quantification.[8]

This response will thus need at least what is known as *simple type theory* (or ST for short). In the language $\mathcal{L}_{\text{ST}}$ of this theory, each variable and each argument place of every predicate has a natural number as an upper index. These indices are called *types*. A formula is well-formed only if its types mesh, in the sense that only variables of type n occur at argument places of type n, and that only variables of type $n + 1$ are predicated of variables of type n.[9] The theory ST contains the usual rules for the connectives and quantifiers, as well as a full impredicative comprehension scheme for each type.

How should advocates of this response (or *type-theorists* as I will henceforth call them) interpret the formal theory ST? There are two main alternatives, one based on plural quantifiers, and another based on quantification into concept position. I will refer to the former as *pluralism* and the latter as *conceptualism*.

Pluralism uses as its point of departure George Boolos's interpretation of second-order quantifiers in terms of natural language plural quantifiers: '$\forall v^2 \ldots$' is rendered as 'whenever there are some things vv then…', '$\exists v^2 \ldots$' as 'there are some things vv such that…', and predication $v^2(v^1)$ as the claim that v is one of vv (in symbols $v \prec vv$). But what about quantifiers of orders higher than two? For instance, in order to extend Boolos's idea to third-order quantifiers we would need quantifiers that stand to ordinary plural quantifiers as ordinary plural quantifiers stand to singular quantifiers. Let's call such quantifiers *second-level* plural quantifiers. Do such quantifiers exist? The answer may be negative if by 'existence' we here mean *existence in natural language*. However, existence in natural language is at best a *sufficient* criterion for something to be a legitimate device in semantic theorizing; it is certainly not a *necessary* condition. This opens the possibility of independent arguments for the legitimacy of higher-level plural quantifiers.[10]

Conceptualism interprets the formal theory ST in a much more Fregean way: the second-order quantifiers range over ordinary concepts taking objects as their arguments, third-order quantifiers over concepts of such concepts, and so on. But when glossing this interpretation, the conceptualist has to be stricter than Frege himself was.

[8] Strictly speaking, the situation is a bit more complicated. A language with n-th order quantification may or may not contain predicates taking n-th order variables as arguments. If it does (doesn't), let's say that it is a *full* (*basic*) n-th order language. We can then prove that one cannot develop a general semantics for a basic (full) n-th order language in any basic (full) n-language, but that one can develop a general semantics for a basic n-th order language in a full n-th order language and for a full n-th order language in a basic $(n + 1)$-th order language. For discussion, see Rayo (2006). But my claim remains valid: The requirement that it be possible to develop a general semantics for any permissible language forces advocates of the second-order response up through the hierarchy of types.

[9] That is, whenever we have an expression of the form $\ulcorner \mathbf{v}_1(\mathbf{v}_2) \urcorner$, where $\mathbf{v}_1$ and $\mathbf{v}_2$ are variables, then the type of $\mathbf{v}_1$ is one higher than that of $\mathbf{v}_2$. (Throughout this chapter, meta-linguistic variables will be indicated by means of boldface.)

[10] Such arguments are given in Hazen (1997), Linnebo (2004), and (at greater length) Rayo (2006).

For instance, the conceptualist cannot say that the second-order quantifiers range over concepts; for both argument places of the predicate 'ranges over' are first-order and hence apply only to *objects*. It therefore seems that the conceptualist interpretation of the language of higher-order logic can be adequately explained only using $\mathcal{L}_{ST}$ *interpreted in precisely the way at issue*. One prominent conceptualist, Timothy Williamson, therefore suggests that '[w]e may have to learn [higher-order] languages by the direct method, not by translating them into a language with which we are already familiar'.[11]

6.4 A PROBLEM WITH THE TYPE-THEORETIC DEFENSES

I will now argue that all type-theorists face a serious problem: On their view, there are certain deep and interesting semantic insights that cannot properly be expressed.[12]

These insights all involve the notion of a *semantic value*, which plays a fundamental role in modern semantics and philosophy of language. Very briefly, this notion can be explained as follows. Each component of a sentence appears to make some definite contribution to the truth or falsity of the sentence. This contribution is its *semantic value*. It further appears that the truth or falsity of the sentence is determined as a function of the semantic values of its constituents. This is the *Principle of Compositionality*. In classical semantics, the semantic value of a sentence is taken to be its truth-value, and the semantic value of a proper name is taken to be its referent. Once we have fixed the kinds of semantic values assigned to sentences and proper names, it is easy to determine what kinds of semantic values to assign to expressions of other syntactic categories. For instance, the semantic value of a monadic first-order predicate will have to be a function from objects to truth-values.

We have seen that the type-theorists respond to the Semantic Argument by denying **Sem1**, which says that interpretations are objects. We have also seen that this forces the type-theorists up the hierarchy of higher and higher levels of quantification. This commits the type-theorists to a deep and interesting semantic view. On this view, proper names make a distinctive kind of semantic contribution to sentences in which they occur, namely the objects to which they refer. Likewise, monadic first-order predicates make a distinctive kind of semantic contribution: loosely speaking, a function from objects to truth-values, but, according to the type-theorists, properly represented only by means of second-order variables. And so it continues up through the types: for each natural number n, monadic n'th-order predicates make a distinctive kind of semantic contribution, properly represented only by means of $(n + 1)$'th-order variables. The type-theorist is therefore committed to generalizations of the following sorts.

- *Infinity*. There are infinitely many different kinds of semantic value.
- *Unique Existence*. Every expression of every syntactic category has a semantic value which is unique, not just within a particular type, but across all types.

[11] See Williamson (2003), p. 459, where this claim is made about *second-order* languages. But his 'fifth point' on p. 457 makes it clear the same has to hold of higher-order languages more generally.

[12] Similar arguments are familiar from the literature. For a nice example, see Gödel (1944), p. 466.

- *Compositionality.* The semantic value of a complex expression is determined as a function of the semantic values of the expression's simpler constituents.

However, type-theorists are prevented from properly expressing any of these insights. For according to type-theory itself, no variable can range over more than one level of the type-theoretic hierarchy. But the above insights essentially involve generalizations across types. Type-theorists thus face expressive limitations embarrassingly similar to those that they set out to avoid in the first place.[13]

Can the type-theorists express the relevant insights in a more devious way? One suggestion is that, although these insights cannot be said straight out, they can nevertheless be *shown*, say by the logical forms of the things that can be properly said. (A similar view is often attributed to Wittgenstein's *Tractatus*.) Another suggestion is that the relevant insights can be expressed in what Carnap calls 'the formal mode,' that is, by talking about the type-theoretic distinctions only at the level of syntax, never at the level of semantic values. However, it seems doubtful that the former suggestion can be developed without resorting to unpalatable mysticism, and the latter, without denying the possibility of semantics in any sense worthy of the term. Moreover, both suggestions run completely counter to the spirit of the Semantic Argument. By giving up on semantic explicitness, these suggestions have much more in common with the view that I called Semantic Pessimism.

A third and more promising suggestion is that the generalizations in question can be expressed by some sort of *schematic generality*. This was the idea behind Russell's notion of *typical ambiguity*. But this suggestion too is problematic. Firstly, a notion of schematic generality would have to be developed which doesn't collapse to ordinary universal quantification. Given that the two sorts of generality are subject to the same introduction and elimination rules, it is unclear whether this can be done. Secondly, since schematic generalities involve free variables but not quantifiers, they yield the expressive power of universal quantification but not of existential.[14] But each of the above three generalizations about the type-theorists' hierarchy make essential use of existential quantifiers in addition to universal ones. Moreover, this expressive limitation means that claims involving schematic generality cannot properly be negated or figure in the antecedents of conditionals. This sits very poorly with the spirit of semantic explicitness associated with the Semantic Argument.

It seems to me that the problem is best dealt with head on by avoiding all type-theoretic restrictions. The simplest option is obviously to avoid going type-theoretic in the first place. But it is not unreasonable to hold that natural language and the refinements thereof that are used in mathematics have a type-theoretic structure. Even if this is granted, however, we still have the option of lifting all type-restrictions

[13] For instance, Williamson (2003) argues that theorists who deny the coherence of absolutely unrestricted quantification cannot properly express the claim that absolutely no electron moves faster than the speed of light. But it can likewise be argued that theorists who deny the coherence of quantification across types cannot properly express Unique Existence, as this would require expressing the claim that, one exception apart, absolutely nothing (regardless of type) is a semantic value of some given expression.

[14] More precisely, schematic generalities can formalize Π^1_1-statements but not Σ^1_1 or anything more complex.

associated with our object-language when we describe its semantics in some meta-language. We do this by allowing the first-order variables of the meta-language to range over *all* semantic values assigned to expressions of the object-language, regardless of the expressions' type. I will refer to this move as a *nominalization.* (The phenomenon of nominalization is familiar from the syntax of natural language, where it is often permissible to convert an expression that isn't a singular term (for instance '... is red') into one that is (in this case 'redness').)

But the suggestion that we carry out a thoroughgoing nominalization when developing the semantics of our object-language comes at a cost. The cost is the reinstatement of the first premise **Sem1** of the Semantic Argument; for the first-order variables of the meta-language will then be allowed to range over interpretations. This will remove the type-theorists' defense against paradox. To avoid paradox, by far the most natural move will then be to reject the second premise **Sem2**, which allows the formation of the Russell-entity. But this rejection must not be some *ad hoc* trick invented merely to avoid paradox. Ideally, the rejection should be based on restrictions that are natural given a proper understanding of the entities in question. This is obviously a tall order. In what follows I will attempt to find and defend such a natural way of rejecting **Sem2**. Although this undertaking is fraught with difficulties, it can hardly be denied that it deserves to be explored. For as we have seen, the main alternatives all involve some degree of Semantic Pessimism. And although we have no *a priori* guarantee that the kind of semantic explicitness that we desire is possible, this is no excuse for not exploring potentially attractive ways in which it may be achieved.

6.5 SETS AND PROPERTIES

Given that we have rejected the type-theoretic responses, we have no choice but to take the semantic value of a predicate to be an *object* of some sort. Moreover, given that we want to allow quantification over absolutely everything, we have no choice but to accept that a predicate can be true of absolutely everything. Such a predicate must thus have as its semantic value an object that somehow collects or represents absolutely all objects, including itself.

Existing attempts to allow such objects have, as far as I know, always suggested that we trade traditional ZFC set theory for some alternative set-theory that allows universal sets. Such suggestions have been very unpopular, and rightly so. Traditional ZFC set theory is an extremely successful theory, which rests on a powerful conception of what sets are, namely the iterative conception.[15] By contrast, all known set theories with a universal set, such as Quine's New Foundations,[16] are not only technically unappealing but have lacked any satisfactory intuitive model or conception of

[15] It has been argued that the iterative conception of sets favors a set-theory somewhat different from ZFC. For instance Boolos (1971) argues that it favors Zermelo set-theory Z. But nothing in what follows turns on precisely ZFC being the theory that is most naturally motivated by the iterative conception.

[16] See Quine (1953) and Forster (1995).

the entities in question. It would therefore be folly to trade traditional ZFC for one of these alternative set theories.

But recall that what is needed is an object that 'somehow collects or represents absolutely all objects.' *Why does this object have to be a set?* After all, this object is needed as the semantic value of a certain predicate, and predicates are more plausibly taken to stand for concepts or properties than to stand for sets. For a predicate is associated with a condition that an object may or may not satisfy, and such conditions are more like concepts or properties than like sets. For instance, such conditions can be negated. Since concepts and properties have complements whereas (ordinary) sets don't, this means that conditions are more like the former than the latter. In fact, since (ordinary) sets don't have complements, they are extremely poorly suited to serve as the semantic values of predicates. So rather than *replacing* standard ZFC set theory with a non-standard set theory with a universal set, perhaps it is better to *supplement* it with a theory of properties, which can then include a property that is absolutely universal? We can then take interpretations to be countable sets that map well-formed expressions to their semantic values, and we can insist that predicates be mapped to properties rather than to sets. The challenge confronting us is then to articulate a conception of properties which (just like that of sets) is independently appealing, and which justifies enough properties to serve the semantic needs that we have delineated.

I will now argue that sets and properties relate to objects in very different ways, each of which is independently legitimate and interesting.[17] A set relates to objects in a *combinatorial* way by combining or collecting many objects into one. Each object among the many objects that are collected into a set is said to be *an element* of this set. It is essential to a set that it has precisely the elements that it in fact has: this set could not be the object it is had it not had precisely these elements. A property relates to objects in an *intensional* way by specifying a universally defined condition that an object must satisfy in order to possess the property. It is not essential to this property that it applies to precisely those objects to which it in fact applies. Rather, it is essential to the property that it applies to all and only such objects as satisfy the condition associated with the property: this property could not have been the property it is had it not applied to all and only such objects.

My defense of these claims will make use of a theory of *individuation*. This theory will be stated in a way that is sufficiently abstract to be shared by most philosophers who believe in a theoretically interesting notion of individuation. To produce a fully satisfactory account of individuation, this account would obviously have to be fleshed out and defended. But since the present article can afford to remain neutral on these difficult issues, I will not attempt to do so here.[18]

According to our abstract theory, individuation is based on two elements. Firstly, for every sort of object that can be individuated, there is a class of *fundamental specifications* of such objects. To use Frege's classic example, directions are most

[17] My distinction between sets and properties is inspired by a similar distinction that Charles Parsons draws between sets and classes. See especially Parsons (1974) and Parsons (1977).

[18] For one attempt to flesh out and defend the abstract theory of individuation described below, see my Linnebo (forthcoming).

fundamentally specified by means of lines or other directed items. Secondly, for every sort of object that can be individuated, there is an equivalence relation on the fundamental specifications of such objects which states when two such specifications determine the same object. Continuing with Frege's example, the equivalence relation associated with directions is that of parallelism: two lines or other directed items determine the same direction just in case they are parallel. I will refer to such equivalence relations as *unity relations*. I will say that a specification and a unity relation *individuates* the object that the former determines in accordance with the latter.

Let's apply this theory to sets. A set is most fundamentally specified by means of a plurality of objects. Such pluralities can be represented by plural variables (as in Section 6.4).[19] Let's write $\textsc{Form}(uu, x)$ for the claim that uu form a set x; that is, that there is a set x whose elements are precisely the objects uu. It is standardly thought that some pluralities are 'too large' to form sets. But when two pluralities do form sets, the extensionality of sets requires that these sets be identical just in case the pluralities from which they are formed encompass precisely the same objects. I therefore claim that sets are individuated in accordance with the following principle:

(Id-Sets) $\textsc{Form}(uu, x) \wedge \textsc{Form}(vv, y) \rightarrow [x = y \leftrightarrow \forall z(z \prec uu \leftrightarrow z \prec vv)]$[20]

Since sets are bona fide objects, they may themselves be among the objects that make up a plurality. This means that the process of forming sets can be iterated. Moreover, since any object can be among the objects that make up a plurality, we must modify standard ZFC set theory so as to allow urelements. Let *ZFCU* be like ZFC except that the axiom of Extensionality is restricted so as to apply only to sets.[21]

A property F is said to be *essential* to an object x just in case x must possess F in order to be the object it is.[22] The above account of how sets are individuated explains why it is essential to a set that it have the elements that it in fact has, and why any characteristics by means of which these elements are specified need not be essential to the set. To see this, let x be a set, and let uu be some objects that jointly form this set. Then an object y cannot be identical with x unless y is a set formed by some objects vv such that $\forall z(z \prec uu \leftrightarrow z \prec vv)$. This means that y cannot be identical with x unless y has precisely the same elements as x. But since vv can be specified by means of characteristics completely different from those used to specify uu, it need not be essential to x what characteristics its elements have.[23]

[19] For an elegant use of plural logic to motivate the axioms of ZFC, see Burgess (2004). Like Burgess, I allow 'degenerate' pluralities consisting of only one or zero objects.

[20] In my Linnebo (unpublished) I defend the heretical view that *every* plurality forms a set. I avoid paradox by formulating and defending a restriction on the naive plural comprehension scheme (which says that for every condition, there are some things which are all and only the things that satisfy this condition). Let $\sigma(uu)$ be the set formed by uu. Sets are then individuated in accordance with the following, simpler principle: $\sigma(uu) = \sigma(vv) \leftrightarrow \forall z(z \prec uu \leftrightarrow z \prec vv)$.

[21] Unlike some axiomatization of ZFCU, ours will not have an axiom postulating the existence of a *set* of all urelements. The reason is that we want to allow there to be as many properties as there are sets.

[22] See Fine (1994).

[23] However, if it is essential to one of x's elements that it possess some characteristic, it will be essential to x that it has an element with this characteristic. (Fine calls such properties *mediately* essential.)

Turning now to properties, we begin by observing that it suffices for present purposes to consider *monadic* properties. For we will always be working in theories that allow the formation of sets, which means that an n-adic property can be represented as a monadic property of (set-theoretic) n-tuples. So officially I will henceforth only operate with monadic properties. But unofficially I will still often talk about polyadic properties or relations, with the understanding that these are represented in the way just described.

It is useful to approach properties by way of *concepts*, roughly in the sense of Frege (or of the conceptualist of Section 6.3). A concept is most fundamentally specified by means of some completely general condition. By 'condition' I mean any meaningful one-place predicate, possibly with parameters. An account of what it is for a condition to be completely general will be given in Section 6.7. Next, two completely general conditions $\phi(u)$ and $\psi(u)$ determine the same concept just in case they stand in some suitable equivalence relation, which I will write as $Eqv_u(\phi(u), \psi(u))$. For present purposes, all we need to assume about this equivalence relation is that it cannot be coarser than co-extensionality; that is, if $Eqv_u(\phi(u), \psi(u))$, then $\forall u(\phi(u) \leftrightarrow \psi(u))$. (Why this requirement suffices will become clear shortly.) Concepts are then individuated as follows:

$$(\Lambda) \quad \Lambda u.\phi(u) = \Lambda u.\psi(u) \leftrightarrow Eqv_u(\phi(u), \psi(u))$$

It is important to bear in mind that the Λ-terms are second-order terms.[24] An object x is said to *fall under* a concept $\Lambda u.\phi(u)$ just in case $\phi(x)$.

This account of how concepts are individuated shows their essential properties to be very different from those of sets. For the identity of a concept $\Lambda u.\phi(u)$ is essentially tied to its condition of application $\phi(u)$. Had there been other objects satisfying the condition $\phi(u)$ than there actually are, then these objects too would have fallen under the concept $\Lambda u.\phi(u)$. And had some of the objects that actually satisfy the condition $\phi(u)$ not done so, then they would not have fallen under this concept $\Lambda u.\phi(u)$. So the essential properties of a concept have to do with the condition that an object must satisfy in order to fall under the concept, not with those particular objects that happen to satisfy this condition. For instance, it is essential to the universal concept $\Lambda u.\ (u = u)$ that absolutely every object fall under it.

Next, observe that basic logical operations such as negation, conjunction, and existential generalization preserve the complete generality of conditions to which they are applied; for instance, the negation of a completely general condition will in turn be a completely general condition. This means that the realm of concepts is closed under the algebraic counterparts of these logical operations. (These algebraic operations will be described in more detail in the next section.) This in turn means that concepts, unlike sets, are well suited to serve as the semantic values of predicates.

24 It may therefore be objected to (Λ) that identity is a relation that can only hold between objects, not between concepts. I have no quarrel with this view provided it be conceded that there is a (second-order) relation on (first-order) concepts which is *analogous to identity* in that it is an equivalence relation which supports the analogue of Leibniz's Law. I will henceforth ignore this complication and talk as if concepts can be identical.

Let's now attempt to nominalize concepts, that is, to bring concepts into the range of the first-order variables. We must then replace the second-order Λ-terms with analogous first-order λ-terms. I will refer to the resulting entities as *properties*. I use this label solely because in English the nominalization of a concept is often called a property. For instance, the nominalization of the concept involved in 'Fido is a dog' is the property of being a dog. It is important to leave aside other philosophical connotations of the word 'property'. In what follows the word will be used exclusively in the sense of a nominalization of a concept. Properties are then individuated by the following first-order counterpart of (Λ)

$$(\lambda)\ \lambda u.\phi(u) = \lambda u.\psi(u) \leftrightarrow Eqv_u(\phi(u), \psi(u))$$

with some suitable restriction on the conditions $\phi(u)$ and $\psi(u)$ to avoid paradox.

Next we introduce a predicate P to be true of all and only properties by laying down the following axiom scheme:

$$(P)\ P(\lambda u.\phi(u))$$

We also define the relation η of property possession by laying down:

$$(\eta)\ v\,\eta\,\lambda u.\phi(u) \leftrightarrow \phi(v)$$

Note that the predicates P and η aren't explicitly defined but that their meanings will depend on what properties there are. This will become important towards the end of this chapter.

Because properties are just nominalized concepts, they inherit from concepts their essential properties, namely their conditions of application. This means that properties and sets have completely different essential properties, which in turn means that no property can be a set and that the two relations $\in$ and η are fundamentally different.

Since my concern in this paper is chiefly with pure mathematics and its semantics, a simplification is possible. In pure mathematics there appears to be no difference between truth and necessary truth. It is therefore customary to regard all mathematical concepts as extensional. I will therefore assume that the equivalence relation $Eqv_u(\phi(u), \psi(u))$ is simply that of co-extensionality. Although the ensuing properties will behave slightly oddly on objects whose existence is contingent, this is irrelevant to our present concerns.[25] With this simplification, properties are individuated as follows:

$$(V)\ \lambda u.\phi(u) = \lambda u.\psi(u) \leftrightarrow \forall u(\phi(u) \leftrightarrow \psi(u))$$

Since this is just Frege's famous Basic Law V, some restriction will have to be imposed on the conditions $\phi(u)$ and $\psi(u)$ so as to avoid paradox. The task of finding and defending some such restriction will be our concern in Section 6.7.

[25] My commitment to calling the resulting entities 'properties' is not very deep anyway. Perhaps it would be better to call them 'extensions.' But this too is potentially confusing, as there is a long tradition of taking extensions to be sets.

It is often advantageous to adopt an axiomatization of our theory of properties different from the one based on (P), (η), and (V). We can do this by 'factoring' (V) into two components, one representing its existential import, the other representing its criterion of identity for properties. The first component consists of a property comprehension scheme that specifies what properties the theory is committed to. That is, for every suitable condition $\phi(u)$ we include an axiom stating that it defines a property:

$$(V\exists)\quad \exists x[Px \wedge \forall u(u \, \eta \, x \leftrightarrow \phi(u))]$$

The second component consists of the following axiom that provides a criterion of identity for properties:

$$(V =)\quad Px \wedge Py \rightarrow [x = y \leftrightarrow \forall u(u \, \eta \, x \leftrightarrow u \, \eta \, y)]$$

This axiomatization uses the predicates P and η as primitives but does away with λ. We may still use the λ-notation, however, subject to the contextual definition that $\psi[\lambda u.\phi(u)]$ be understood as short for $\exists x[\forall u(u \, \eta \, x \leftrightarrow \phi(u)) \wedge \psi(x)]$.

6.6 A GENERAL SEMANTICS FOR FIRST-ORDER LANGUAGES

I will now show how a theory of both sets and properties allows us to develop a general semantics for first-order languages. I will define the notion of an interpretation of a first-order language and outline some simple applications of it. As will become clear shortly, I will take an interpretation to be a set-theoretic function that maps well-formed expressions to their semantic values, some of which are properties. The resulting semantics illustrates how beautifully sets and properties can interact.

A *first-order language with identity* is a language $\mathcal{L}$ of the following form. The simple expressions of $\mathcal{L}$ divide into *logical constants*, *non-logical constants*, and *variables*. The logical constant are the connectives $\neg$, $\wedge$, and $\exists$, as well as the predicate $=$. These expressions have a fixed interpretation (as respectively negation, conjunction, existence, and identity). The non-logical constants of $\mathcal{L}$ divide into names a_i and n-ary predicates F_i^n (where $i < \omega$ and $0 < n < \omega$). Being non-logical, these expressions are assigned different values by different interpretations. Finally, $\mathcal{L}$ has first-order variables x_i for $i < \omega$. On the semantics to be developed, a variable is a mere place-holder and will as such not be assigned any semantic value on its own. A *singular term* is either a name or a variable. An *atomic formula* is an n-ary predicate applied to n singular terms. Something is a *formula* just in case it is either an atomic formula or can be obtained from formulas in the usual way by means of negation, conjunction, or existential generalization.

A *lexicon* for a first-order language $\mathcal{L}$ is a set-theoretic function that assigns to each of $\mathcal{L}$'s non-logical constants (but not to the variables) an appropriate semantic value: to each name an object, and to each predicate a property (which is just a special kind of object). An *interpretation of a language* $\mathcal{L}$ is a set-theoretic function that maps *any* well-formed expression of $\mathcal{L}$ to an appropriate semantic value in a way that respects the expression's logical structure (of which more shortly).[26] An interpretation of a language $\mathcal{L}$ *satisfies* an $\mathcal{L}$-theory T just in case all the axioms of T come out true under this interpretation.

Our first goal is to extend a given lexicon I^- to an interpretation I. The obvious way to proceed is by recursion on the formation rules of $\mathcal{L}$. We begin by interpreting an atomic formula ϕ of the form $\mathbf{P}(\mathbf{t_0}, \ldots, \mathbf{t_n})$. Assume the variables among the singular terms $\mathbf{t_i}$ are $x_{i_0}, \ldots, x_{i_k}$ for some $k \leq n$. Assume also that these variables are *naturally ordered*, in the sense that $i_p < i_{p+1}$ for each $p < k$. Where J is a lexicon or an interpretation, let $[\![E]\!]_J$ abbreviate $J(E)$; where there is no danger of confusion, the subscript will be dropped. For such J, we also define the following translation of terms into the meta-language (which we assume to have the same variables as the object-language $\mathcal{L}$):

$$\mathbf{t_i}^J = \begin{cases} \mathbf{t_i} & \text{if } \mathbf{t_i} \text{ is a variable} \\ [\![\mathbf{t_i}]\!]_J & \text{if } \mathbf{t_i} \text{ is a name} \end{cases}$$

The interpretation $[\![\phi]\!]_I$ of the atomic formula ϕ is then defined by the universal generalization of the following formula:

$$(I_{At}) \quad \langle x_{i_0}, \ldots, x_{i_k} \rangle \ \eta \ [\![\phi]\!]_I \leftrightarrow \langle \mathbf{t_0}^{I^-}, \ldots, \mathbf{t_n}^{I^-} \rangle \ \eta \ [\![\mathbf{P}]\!]_{I^-}$$

If on the other hand the singular terms $\mathbf{t_i}$ are *all names*, then $[\![\phi]\!]_I$ won't be a property but a truth-value. Assume the truth-values are represented by the numbers 1 and 0 (which may in turn be represented by sets). In this special case, the left-hand side of (I_{At}) must be replaced by '$[\![\phi]\!]_I = 1$'. To see that (I_{At}) and the special case just mentioned are reasonable definitions, it helps to consider some simple examples. For instance, according to (I_{At}) the semantic values of the atomic formulas $F_0^2(x_1, x_0)$ and $F_0^2(a_0, x_0)$ are given by the universal closures of the following formulas:

$$\langle x_0, x_1 \rangle \ \eta \ [\![F_0^2(x_1, x_0)]\!] \leftrightarrow \langle x_1, x_0 \rangle \ \eta \ [\![F_0^2]\!]$$

$$x_0 \ \eta \ [\![F_0^2(a_0, x_0)]\!] \leftrightarrow \langle [\![a_0]\!], x_0 \rangle \ \eta \ [\![F_0^2]\!]$$

This is as one would expect: $[\![F_0^2(x_1, x_0)]\!]$ is the converse of $[\![F_0^2(x_0, x_1)]\!]$ (= $[\![F_0^2]\!]$), and $[\![F_0^2(a_0, x_0)]\!]$ is the property obtained by assigning $[\![a_0]\!]$ to the first argument place of the relation $[\![F_0^2]\!]$.

To describe the recursion clauses for formulas in general, it is useful to let $\vec{x}$ abbreviate strings of variables of the form $\langle x_{i_0}, \ldots, x_{i_k} \rangle$. The semantic values of formulas in general are then given recursively by the universal closures of the following formulas

$$(I_\neg) \quad \vec{x} \ \eta \ [\![\neg\phi]\!] \leftrightarrow \neg(\vec{x} \ \eta \ [\![\phi]\!])$$

$$(I_\wedge) \quad \vec{z} \ \eta \ [\![\phi \wedge \psi]\!] \leftrightarrow (\vec{x} \ \eta \ [\![\phi]\!]) \wedge (\vec{y} \ \eta \ [\![\psi]\!])$$

$$(I_\exists) \quad \vec{x}_0 \ \eta \ [\![\exists \mathbf{v}\phi]\!] \leftrightarrow \exists \mathbf{v}(\vec{x} \ \eta \ [\![\phi]\!])$$

[26] To keep things simple, I will not consider interpretations that restrict the ranges of the quantifiers to a property x. But this would be a straightforward modification.

where $\vec{x}$ is the tuple of variables occurring in ϕ, $\vec{y}$ is the corresponding tuple for ψ, $\vec{z}$ is the tuple of variables occurring in the conjunction $\phi \wedge \psi$, and finally $\vec{x}_0$ is as $\vec{x}$ except with **v** removed. We must also add special clauses for the cases where the formulas are sentences, ensuring that these sentences are assigned the right truth-values.

We would now like to formalize semantic theorizing about the object-language $\mathcal{L}$. The following two formal languages will be particularly important in this undertaking.

Definition 1

(a) Let $\mathcal{L}_0$ be the language of ZFCU, that is, the first-order language with identity whose only non-logical constant is the set membership predicate $\in$.

(b) Let $\mathcal{L}_1$ be as $\mathcal{L}_0$ except for containing an additional non-logical predicate constant η for property possession. We will also use the λ-notation, subject to the contextual definition that $\psi[\lambda u.\phi(u)]$ be understood as short for $\exists x[\forall u(u\ \eta\ x \leftrightarrow \phi(u)) \wedge \psi(x)]$.

Given that our semantic theorizing involves both sets and properties, it is natural to base our meta-theory T on $\mathcal{L}_1$.

Our first task will be to convert the above implicit definition of an interpretation (relative to some given lexicon) into an explicit definition. Assume our meta-theory T contains enough set theory to handle n-tuples and to carry out set-theoretic recursion on syntax. Then, on the assumption that T contains enough axioms to ensure the existence of the requisite properties, we can simply use set-theoretic recursion on syntax to provide an explicit definition of the interpretation I. This is an example of how nicely sets and properties interact. Note in particular that this construction would have been impossible had concepts not been nominalized to properties. For the elements of a set are always in the range of *first-order* variables.

Precisely what axioms concerning properties must T contain? In general terms the answer is that T must contain enough axioms to ensure the existence of all the properties invoked in the above recursion clauses. But let's be more specific. First we need the existence of a property i to interpret the identity predicate, that is, a property had by all and only ordered pairs of the form $\langle u, u\rangle$. Then we need a series of axioms that ensure that the realm of properties is closed under some simple algebraic operations corresponding to the logical operations that are used in the recursion clauses. These will be operations such as permuting the argument places of a property, evaluating a property of n-tuples at some particular object in one of its argument places (both of which are crucial for the clause governing atomic formulas), taking the complement of a property (which is crucial for negation), taking the intersection of two properties (which is crucial for conjunction), projecting a property of n-tuples onto all but one of its axes (which is crucial for the existential quantifiers), and taking the inverse of a projection (which is needed for the conjunction of two formulas with different variables). Let's call these *the basic operations*. The previous section explained why it is reasonable to assume that the realm of properties is closed under these operations. An appendix will provide a proper consistency proof.

Definition 2

(a) Let *the minimal theory of properties*, V^-, be the $\mathcal{L}_1$-theory whose non-logical axioms are (V=), a comprehension axiom ensuring the existence of the identity property i, and axioms ensuring that the basic operations are always defined on properties.

(b) Where X is some class of property comprehension axioms, let V^X be the $\mathcal{L}_1$-theory which in addition to the axioms of V^- also has the property comprehension axioms in X. In particular, let $V^{\in}$ be the theory that extends V^- by a comprehension axiom ensuring the existence of a property ϵ had by all and only ordered pairs $\langle u, v\rangle$ such that $u \in v$.

(c) Let $ZFCU_0$ be the $\mathcal{L}_1$-theory that contains all the usual axioms of ZFCU except that the Replacement and Separation schemes are replaced by single axioms quantifying over properties. Separation is thus formalized as

$$\text{(Sep)} \quad \forall x \forall p \exists y \forall u (u \in y \leftrightarrow u \in x \wedge u \,\eta\, p),$$

and likewise for Replacement.

(d) Let $ZFCU_0 + V^X$ be the $\mathcal{L}_1$-theory whose set-theoretic axioms are those in $ZFCU_0$ and whose property-theoretic axioms are those in V^X.

Say that a meta-theory T is *minimally adequate* if it contains the minimal theory of properties and enough set-theory to handle n-tuples and set-theoretic recursion on syntax. A great amount of general semantic theorizing can be formalized in any minimally adequate meta-theory. We have already seen how such theories allows us to extend any lexicon to an interpretation. This also ensures that such theories can do justice to the claims that eluded the type-theorists in Section 6.4. The first claim, *Infinity*, is no longer relevant, as we now have only one kind of semantic values, namely objects. *Unique Existence* says that an interpretation assigns a unique semantic value to each expression. This is established by an easy induction on syntax. *Compositionality* too can be stated and proved. For instance, one easily shows that the truth-value of a simple subject-predicate sentence depends only on the semantic values assigned to the subject and the predicate.

Moreover, the usual method of Gödelization enables us to code various syntactic and proof-theoretic properties in T. For instance, let $Int(I)$ and $Thm(x)$ formalize respectively the claim that I is an interpretation of $\mathcal{L}$ and the claim that x is the Gödel number of a logical theorem. Then T proves the formalizations of a number of semantic truths. The first fundamental result of this sort concerns how the interpretation of an $\mathcal{L}$-formula ϕ relates to a very natural translation of ϕ into the meta-language $\mathcal{L}_1$, which I will now describe. Given an $\mathcal{L}$-lexical J (or an $\mathcal{L}$-interpretation J which is based on some lexicon) I have already defined a translation $t \mapsto t^J$ of singular terms of $\mathcal{L}$ into $\mathcal{L}_1$. This translation can be extended to $\mathcal{L}$-formulas as follows. Where ϕ is an atomic formula $\mathbf{P}(\mathbf{t_0}, \ldots, \mathbf{t_n})$, let ϕ^J be $\langle \mathbf{t_0}^J, \ldots, \mathbf{t_n}^J \rangle \,\eta\, [\![\mathbf{P}]\!]_J$. Let the translation commute with the logical connectives. Then we get the following lemma, which will be very useful in semantic theorizing about $\mathcal{L}$.

Lemma 1 (Interpretation Lemma)

Let T be a minimally adequate meta-theory. If the $\mathcal{L}$-formula ϕ has free variables, let $\vec{x}$ be based on its free variables taken in their natural order. Then

$$\vdash_T Int(I) \to \forall \vec{x}\,(\vec{x}\,\eta\,[\![\phi]\!]_I \leftrightarrow \phi^I).$$

If on the other hand ϕ is a sentence, the consequent of the above conditional must be replaced by $[\![\phi]\!]_I = 1 \leftrightarrow \phi^I$. This special case becomes clearer if we introduce a predicate $Tr_I(x)$ defined as $[\![x]\!]_I = 1$. Then T proves that, whenever I is an interpretation, $Tr_I(x)$ expresses the property of truth on the interpretation I.

Proof. By induction in T on the complexity of ϕ.

Theorem 1 (Soundness Theorem)

Let T be a minimally adequate meta-theory. Then T proves the soundness of first-order logic with respect to our semantics. More precisely, if we let $C(x)$ be a function that maps the Gödel number of a formula to the Gödel number of its universal closure, then

$$\vdash_T Thm(x) \wedge Int(I) \to Tr_I(C(x)).$$

Proof. Assume a Frege-Hilbert style axiomatization of first-order logic with identity. Since the translation $\phi \mapsto \phi^I$ commutes with the logical constants, it maps each axiom of the object theory to an axiom of the meta-theory T. By the Interpretation Lemma, T proves $Tr_I(C(x))$ for each axiom x and each interpretation I. It remains to show that satisfaction of $Tr_I(C(x))$ is preserved under applications of the inference rules. The Interpretation Lemma allows us to translate this question to the question whether the corresponding inferences are truth-preserving in the meta-language, which they clearly are. Hence the corollary follows by induction in T.

We can in a similar way define the usual notion of logical consequence and prove basic truths about it.

Our definitions and results thus far have only involved universal generalizations over interpretations but no claims about the existence of specific interpretations. We have therefore been able to make do with a minimally adequate meta-theory. But claims about the existence of specific interpretations will be needed in order to develop the intended semantics of a given theory and to give a formal proof of its consistency. For the former purpose, we need a meta-theory that proves the existence of an intended interpretation. For the latter purpose, it is extremely useful to be able to prove the existence of an interpretation that satisfies the object theory. For these purposes we typically need more than a minimally adequate meta-theory. The following theorem provides an example of such reasoning.

Theorem 2 (General Semantics of ZFCU)

In $\mathrm{ZFCU}_0 + \mathrm{V}^{\in}$ we can prove the existence of the intended interpretation of ZFCU. This means in particular that $\mathrm{ZFCU}_0 + \mathrm{V}^{\in}$ proves the consistency of ZFCU.

Proof. The only non-logical constant of the language $\mathcal{L}_0$ of ZFCU is the membership predicate '∈'. In $\text{ZFCU}_0 + \text{V}^{\in}$ we can define the intended lexicon I^- for $\mathcal{L}_0$ that assigns to '∈' the membership property ϵ. We can also define an interpretation I based on this lexicon. By the Interpretation Lemma, $\text{ZFCU}_0 + \text{V}^{\in}$ proves $Tr_I(\phi) \leftrightarrow \phi^I$ for every $\mathcal{L}_0$-sentence ϕ. But since I is the intended interpretation, ϕ^I can be simplified. Recall that $(u \in v)^I$ is $\langle u, v\rangle \; \eta \; [\![\in]\!]_I$, and that $[\![\in]\!]_I = \epsilon$. From the definition of ϵ it thus follows that $(u \in v)^I \leftrightarrow u \in v$. Since all of this is provable in $\text{ZFCU}_0 + \text{V}^{\in}$, this theory proves $Tr_I(\phi) \leftrightarrow \phi$ for every $\mathcal{L}_0$-sentence ϕ.

Next, observe that $\text{ZFCU}_0 + \text{V}^{\in}$ licences property comprehension on any $\mathcal{L}_0$-formula. Such property comprehension enables us to derive all the comprehension and separation axioms of ZFCU. Since $\text{ZFCU}_0 + \text{V}^{\in}$ thus proves every axiom of ZFCU, it follows from (a formalization of) the result of the previous paragraph that $\text{ZFCU}_0 + \text{V}^{\in}$ also proves that every axiom of ZFCU is true on the intended interpretation. By the Soundness Theorem, $\text{ZFCU}_0 + \text{V}^{\in}$ proves that every theorem of ZFCU is true on the intended interpretation. But if ZFCU was inconsistent, not all of its theorems could be true on one and the same interpretation.

A natural question at this point is whether we can go on and prove the existence of an interpretation that satisfies what we just used as our meta-theory, namely $\text{ZFCU}_0 + \text{V}^{\in}$. This question is answered affirmatively in Section 6.8, which describes an infinite sequence of theories of sets and properties, each strong enough to prove the existence of an interpretation satisfying all of the preceding theories.

Another natural question is what property comprehension axioms are true, or can at least consistently be added to ZFC set theory. The next two sections address the issue of truth, relying on a mixture of philosophical and mathematical considerations. An appendix gives a mathematical proof of consistency relative to ZFC plus the existence of an inaccessible cardinal.

6.7 WHAT PROPERTIES ARE THERE?

To be acceptable, a proposed restriction on the property comprehension scheme must satisfy two potentially conflicting requirements. Firstly, the restriction must be liberal enough to allow the properties we need in order to carry out the desired kind of semantic theorizing. Secondly, the restriction must be well motivated. As an absolute minimum, the restriction must give rise to a consistent theory. But ideally, the restriction should be a natural one, given an adequate understanding of properties. The restriction should be one it would have been natural to impose anyway, even disregarding the fact that paradox would otherwise ensue. I will now develop an account of properties that attempts to walk this fine line between admitting too few properties (such that the desired kind of semantic theorizing cannot be carried out) and admitting too many (such that contradiction ensues).[27]

[27] It should be noted that nothing claimed in the paper so far commits me to the particular account of properties that follows. All that is required is an account of properties that satisfies the two requirements just described.

My account of what properties there are is based on the requirement that individuation be well-founded. According to this requirement, the individuation of some range of entities can only presuppose such objects as have already been individuated. A requirement of this sort is *prima facie* very plausible. To individuate is to give an account of what the identity of some range of entities consists in. If this account is to be informative, it cannot presuppose the very entities in question, since doing so would amount to presupposing precisely what we are trying to explain. I will now investigate how such a well-foundedness requirement is best formulated and understood.[28]

The well-foundedness requirement applies to both kinds of elements on which individuation is based: specifications and unity relations. The requirement that specifications not involve or presuppose the object to be individuated is fairly straightforward. Sets provide a nice example. I argued in Section 6.5 that sets are specified by means of pluralities of objects. The well-foundedness requirement then says that no such plurality can contain the very set that it is supposed to specify. This means that no set can be an element of itself. More generally, it gives rise to the familiar set-theoretic axiom of Foundation. Concepts and properties provide another example. Here it is required that a condition that is supposed to specify some concept or property not contain parameters referring to the very concept or property that we are attempting to individuate.

It is somewhat harder to tell what the well-foundedness requirement amounts to in the case of unity relations. The presence of any parameters in the characterization of these relations causes no problems: this will be handled as just discussed. The problem comes from the fact that the characterization of a unity relation often makes use of quantifiers. It is natural to think that, in order to determine the truth-value of a quantified statement, we need to consider all the corresponding instances. And clearly each instance involves or presupposes the entity with respect to which it is an instance. So from this natural thought it follows that a unity relation presupposes all entities in the ranges of its quantifiers. When this analysis of the presuppositions of a quantified statement is plugged into the well-foundedness requirement, we get the familiar Vicious Circle Principle, according to which the concept or property defined by a condition $\phi(u)$ cannot itself belong to the totality over which the variable u is allowed to range. This result would be disastrous for our project of developing a semantics for languages with genuinely universal quantification. For if a concept or property can never belong to the totality on which it is defined, then this totality cannot be completely universal. It would therefore be impossible to define a concept or a property that is genuinely universal.

Fortunately, this analysis of the presuppositions of a quantified statement is excessively strict. For although natural, the thought that the truth-value of a quantified statement requires consideration of all of its instances is incorrect. The most extreme example of this is the statement that absolutely everything is self-identical. The truth of this statement can be determined without consideration of a single instance. This

[28] I won't here attempt any systematic defense of the resulting requirement. This would require fleshing out the abstract and minimal account offered in Section 6.5. For some ideas towards a defense, see Linnebo (forthcoming).

means that we need a better analysis of what objects a quantified statement presupposes. I will here focus on the presuppositions carried by the conditions that define concepts and properties. Such conditions must be capable of occurring within the scope of absolutely universal quantifiers. What objects do such conditions presuppose?

The answer I would like to propose distinguishes between two kinds of presuppositions carried by a condition: An entity can be presupposed either for its mere *existence* or for its *identity*, that is, for being the thing it is. For an example of the former, consider the two conditions $u = u$ and $u \neq u$. Whether these two conditions are co-extensive depends on whether there is anything in the domain on which they are defined. Now, the domain we are interested in is the absolutely universal one. Since this domain contains all sets, this sort of presupposition will not be a problem, as there will always be enough sets available. I will also assume that the universal domain contains as many objects not yet individuated as there are sets. This is a very plausible assumption. We may always go on to individuate new mathematical objects. This assumption will prove to be important below.

What is it for a condition to presuppose an entity for its identity? Since what a condition does is distinguish between objects—those of which it holds and those of which it doesn't—this notion of presupposition should be spelled out in terms of what distinctions the condition makes. Now, a condition can only presuppose an object if it is able to distinguish this object from other known objects. I therefore propose that we analyze what it is for a condition to presuppose only entities that are already individuated in terms of the condition's not distinguishing between entities not yet individuated. This proposal can be made mathematically precise as follows. Consider permutations π that fix all objects already individuated and that respect all relations already individuated in the sense that for each such relation R we have

$$(\forall x_0 \ldots \forall x_n (Rx_0 \ldots x_n \rightarrow R\pi x_0 \ldots \pi x_n))$$

My proposal is then that a condition $\phi(u)$ presupposes only entities that are already individuated just in case $\phi(u)$ is invariant under all such permutations.

When a formula presupposes only entities that have already been individuated, there is no obvious philosophical reason why it should not define a property. For we have specified in a non-circular way what this property would be. Nor is there any mathematical reason why such a formula should not define a property. To see this, begin by observing that such a condition clearly defines a *concept*. Next I claim that any concept individuated in accordance with the well-foundedness requirement can be nominalized. For each such concept can be represented by means of one of the objects not yet individuated. Since these concepts don't distinguish between objects not yet individuated, it doesn't matter which representative we choose. Moreover, since we have assumed that there are as many objects not yet individuated as there are sets, there will be enough objects to represent all the concepts definable by conditions in any reasonable language. And we can carry out this process as many times as there are sets. I therefore conclude that the independently motivated well-foundedness requirement on the definition of concepts gives us nominalization of concepts for free.

Let's apply the above analysis of the well-foundedness requirement to the task of justifying such properties as were needed for the semantic theory developed in the previous section. Assume we have individuated all sets and that we want to go on and individuate concepts and properties. Say that a permutation π of the universe is $\in$*-preserving* just in case $\forall x \forall y(x \in y \rightarrow \pi x \in \pi y)$. By transfinite induction one easily proves that $\in$-preserving permutations leave pure sets untouched. There are also objects that are partially individuated, such as the singleton of an object u that is not yet individuated. But $\in$-preserving permutations preserve precisely the relation between this object u and its singleton. To fix everything already individuated, it is therefore sufficient to require that a permutation be $\in$-preserving. The well-foundedness requirement, as analyzed above, therefore demands that the condition used to define a concept or a property be invariant under $\in$-permutations.

The following lemma says that a large class of conditions satisfy this requirement.

Lemma 2 (Indiscernibility Lemma)

Let $\phi(v_0, \ldots, v_n)$ be an $\mathcal{L}_0$-formula, possibly with parameters referring to pure sets. Let π be a $\in$-preserving permutation. Then $\langle x_0, \ldots, x_n \rangle$ satisfies ϕ just in case $\langle \pi x_0, \ldots, \pi x_n \rangle$ satisfies ϕ.

The proof is an easy induction on the logical complexity of ϕ. (Note that when π is $\in$-preserving, we have $\pi \langle x_0, \ldots, x_n \rangle = \langle \pi x_0, \ldots, \pi x_n \rangle$.)

Say that x and y are *set-theoretically indiscernible* (in symbols: $x \approx y$) just in case there is a $\in$-preserving permutation π such that $\pi x = y$. This is easily seen to be an equivalence relation. Note that any two urelements are set-theoretically indiscernible. Say that a property x is *set-theoretic* just in case it doesn't distinguish between objects that are set-theoretically indiscernible (that is, just in case $u \; \eta \; x \wedge u \approx u' \rightarrow u' \; \eta \; x$). Set-theoretic properties make maximally coarse distinctions among non-sets: if such a property applies to one non-set, it applies to all. The Indiscernibility Lemma thus says that any property defined by a $\mathcal{L}_0$-formula with parameters referring to pure sets must be set-theoretic.

We can give a particularly nice explanation of how set-theoretic properties are individuated if we avail ourselves of second-order logic. The second-order theory I will use is von Neumann-Bernays-Gödel set theory with urelements (henceforth, *NBGU*).[29] The intended interpretation of this second-order language will have the first-order variables range over absolute everything. Thus, when I speak below about 'the whole universe,' I mean *the whole thing*. I use capital letters as second-order variables and refer to their values as *classes*.

I begin by characterizing what is required for a formula to be universally defined, not just on objects individuated thus far, but on all such as are yet to be individuated.

Definition 3

M is a *mock universe* for a formula ϕ iff M is indistinguishable from the whole universe from the point of view of ϕ. More precisely, M is a mock universe for ϕ iff there

[29] *NBGU* is the (conservative) extension of ZFCU that allows second-order variables and quantifiers, contains a predicative second-order comprehension scheme, but allows no bound second-order variables in instances of the Separation or Replacement schemes.

is an equivalence relation $\approx$ on the whole universe such that ϕ cannot distinguish between objects that are thus equivalent and such that $\forall x \exists y(My \wedge x \approx y)$.

Definition 4

M is an *individuating domain* for a formula ϕ iff
(a) M is a mock universe for ϕ;
(b) M does not involve any property defined by ϕ;
(c) ϕ is defined on all of M.

Thus, to ensure that a formula is defined on the whole universe, including objects yet to be individuated, it suffices to show that it has an individuating domain.

Let $V[I]$ be the standard model of ZFCU based on a proper class I of as many urelements as there are sets. Then we have the following lemma.

Lemma 3

$V[I]$ is an individuating domain for $\mathcal{L}_0$-formulas with parameters referring to pure sets.

Proof. By the Indiscernibility Lemma, such formulas cannot distinguish between objects that are set-theoretically indiscernible. Since every object is set-theoretically indiscernible from some object in $V[I]$, this is a mock universe for $\mathcal{L}_0$-formulas. Next, $V[I]$ can be described without in any way presupposing properties. ($V[I]$ can for instance be simulated in the standard model V of ZFC by letting some of the pure sets serve as urelements). Finally, all $\mathcal{L}_0$-formulas are defined on $V[I]$.

Next I state a corollary that ensures that any property defined by a formula of the kind in question is individuated by its behavior on $V[I]$.

Corollary 1

Let $\phi(u)$ and $\psi(u)$ be two $\mathcal{L}_0$-formulas, possibly with parameters referring to pure sets. Then the two properties $\hat{u}.\phi(u)$ and $\hat{u}.\psi(u)$ defined by these formulas are identical iff $\forall u(\phi(u) \leftrightarrow \psi(u))$ holds in $V[I]$.

Proof. The only non-trivial direction is right-to-left. Assume $\hat{u}.\phi(u) \neq \hat{u}.\psi(u)$. Then by (V=) there is an object x on which $\phi(u)$ and $\psi(u)$ disagreed. But then, by the above lemma, these formulas also disagree on some object y in $V[I]$ such that $x \approx y$.

This strategy can easily be adapted to show that other classes of formulas have individuating domains. We may for instance allow the formulas to contain parameters referring to other kinds of objects already individuated or to contain predicates that are true only of such objects. Let X be the class consisting of all referents of such parameters and all objects of the sort that these predicates can be true of. Consider the class of permutations that not only preserve the $\in$-relation but that also fix all the objects in X. Let $\approx$ be defined as above except in terms of this more restrictive class of permutations. We can then prove a modified Indiscernibility Lemma to the effect that the relevant formulas cannot distinguish between $\approx$-equivalent objects. We can also prove that, when I is a proper class of new urelements, $V[X \cup I]$ is an individuating domain for these formulas.

I now turn to the second of the two requirement on a theory of properties that were described at the beginning of this section. According to this requirement, the theory of properties must in a natural and well-motivated way rule out such properties as would give rise to paradox. Since the most obvious threat of paradox stems from the Semantic Argument, I will examine what this argument looks like in our present setting. Recall that we are taking interpretations to be countable sets that map expressions to objects. This means that the premise **Sem1**, which says that interpretations are objects, is incontrovertible. But we have also stipulated that interpretations are to map predicates to properties. Our hope is that this will provide a principled reason for rejecting the other premise **Sem2**, which permits the definition of a Russell-like property.

Assume the predicate letter 'P' is first in the series of non-logical expressions to which an interpretation must assign values. Then **Sem2** permits the following definition of a Russell-like property r_0:

$$(\text{Def} - r_0)] \ \ \forall x(x \ \eta \ r_0 \leftrightarrow \neg x \ \eta \ x(0))$$

How plausible is it to reject this attempted definition? With some minimal assumptions, we can show that this definition is permissible just in case the following definition of a more traditional Russell property r is permissible:

$$(\text{Def} - r) \ \ \forall x(x \ \eta \ r \leftrightarrow \neg x \ \eta \ x)$$

Our question is thus how plausible it is to reject (Def-r).

I claim that we have good reason to reject this attempted definition. Let's begin by considering the predicate η in its intended sense, as true of two objects u and x just in case x is a property possessed by u. I claim that, if this intended sense can be made out at all, the well-foundedness requirement disallows the predicate η from defining any concept or property. For η will then represent the relation of property possession for all properties whatsoever. But two properties x and y are identical just in case they are borne η by precisely the same objects, that is, just in case $\forall u(u \ \eta \ x \leftrightarrow u \ \eta \ y)$. This means that η in its intended sense would distinguish every property from every other, thus maximally violating the well-foundedness constraint.

Although this gives us reason to be suspicious, the official verdict on the legitimacy of comprehension on formulas containing η must be based on the whatever meaning has *officially* been assigned to this predicate. The only such meaning comes from (V=) and the property comprehension axioms, which implicitly define η and the other primitive P (for being a property). I claim that already this official meaning makes η problematic from the point of view of the well-foundedness requirement. Assume we have individuated certain entities and now want to go on and individuate a property defined by '$u \ \eta \ x$'. The requirement is then that the condition '$u \ \eta \ x$' be invariant under all permutations that fix all objects and respect all relations individuated thus far. But this requirement isn't satisfied. For the second argument place of '$u \ \eta \ x$' distinguishes between objects yet to be individuated as non-properties (on which the condition will always be false) and objects yet to be individuated as non-empty properties (on which the condition will be true for suitable values of u).

Even so, we have not yet excluded the possibility that the Russell condition '$\neg u \eta u$' is less problematic than the more general condition '$u \eta x$'. To examine this possibility, assume we attempt to individuate the Russell property after having individuated certain other entities. The well-foundedness requirement then says that the Russell condition must be invariant under all permutations that fix all objects and respect all relations individuated thus far. But just as above, this requirement isn't satisfied, since the Russell condition distinguishes between objects yet to be individuated as non-properties (on which the condition will be true) and objects yet to be individuated as properties that possess themselves (on which the condition will be false). The well-foundedness requirement therefore disallows property and concept comprehension on the Russell condition as well.

6.8 A HIERARCHY OF SEMANTIC THEORIES

I have just argued that the well-foundedness requirement disallows property and concept comprehension on the condition '$u \eta x$'. But in order to avoid Semantic Pessimism, we will have to develop a general semantics for languages such as $\mathcal{L}_1$ that contain the predicate η. This means that some property will have to be assigned to this predicate as its semantic value. What could this semantic value be?

I begin with an informal description of my answer.[30] The problem we have encountered is that η—whether in its intuitive sense or its official sense fixed by the axioms—is concerned with objects yet to be individuated and therefore violates the well-foundedness requirement. But this problem can be avoided by adding to the condition '$u \eta x$' the restriction that x must be a property *already individuated*. The resulting condition does not distinguish between objects not yet individuated, and the well-foundedness requirement therefore allows it to define a property, which I will call e_0. When this new property e_0 is assigned to 'η' as its semantic value, we get an interpretation that satisfies $\text{ZFCU}_0 + \text{V}^{\in}$. Next, we can apply the basic operations to e_0 to define a whole range of new properties, which will thereby have been individuated. These new properties allow us to relax the restriction on the condition '$u \eta x$', now requiring only that x belong to the larger range of properties that have now been individuated. The resulting condition can again be shown to satisfy the well-foundedness requirement. It therefore defines a new property, which I will call e_1. When e_1 is assigned to 'η' as its semantic value, we get an interpretation that satisfies not only $\text{ZFCU}_0 + \text{V}^{\in}$ but also the property comprehension axiom by which

[30] In August 2005, two months after having completed this chapter, I learnt from a talk by Kit Fine at the European Congress of Analytic Philosophy in Lisbon that he has carried out a construction very similar to the one I am about to describe; see his Fine (2005). Fine has also proved a number of technical results about his construction that go far beyond anything anticipated in this chapter. He informs me that most of this work dates back to the academic year 1996-7; the construction is also alluded to in Fine (1998), pp. 602 and 623.

e_0 was introduced. Continuing in this way, we get an infinite sequence of theories of sets and properties, each of which can be shown to be strong enough to prove the consistency of the preceding ones.

I now describe this construction in more detail. We begin by individuating some class of set-theoretic properties. For concreteness, assume we individuate those set-theoretic properties definable by formulas of $\mathcal{L}_0$ but allowing for parameters referring to pure sets. Now we want to use the set-theoretic properties we have just individuated to individuate more properties. We therefore look at permutations that not only respect the elementhood relation $\in$ but that fix the set-theoretic properties we have just individuated. By the argument of the previous section, any condition that is invariant under all such permutations defines a property. We would therefore like to characterize the conditions that are invariant in this way.

These conditions can clearly contain the predicate $\in$. But more interestingly, I will now show that they can also contain a two-place predicate ψ, which we get by adding to the condition '$u\ \eta\ x$' the restriction that x is one of the set-theoretic properties just individuated. I begin by observing that this predicate ψ is definable in $\text{ZFCU}_0 + \text{V}^{\in}$. For x is one of the set-theoretic properties just individuated if and only if x is definable from i and ϵ by basic operations (where any parameters must again refer to pure sets). We can therefore use set-theoretic recursion to define what it is for a property x to be definable from i and ϵ. This allows us to formulate the desired predicate $\psi(u, x)$. I next prove that $\psi(u, x)$ is invariant under the permutations just described. Let π be any such permutation. If x isn't one of the properties just individuated, then nor is πx. Hence it follows that both $\psi(u, x)$ and $\psi(\pi u, \pi x)$ are false. If, on the other hand, x is such a property, then $\pi x = x$. But since x is then a set-theoretic property, we have $\psi(u, x) \leftrightarrow \psi(\pi u, x)$. Combining these observations, we get $\psi(\pi u, \pi x) \leftrightarrow \psi(u, x)$, as desired.

Since $\psi(u, x)$ is invariant under the relevant class of permutations, it defines a property, which I will call e_0. We therefore adopt the following property comprehension axiom:

$$(V^0)\ \ \exists e_0 \forall u \forall v[\langle u, v\rangle\ \eta\ e_0 \leftrightarrow \psi_0(u, v)]$$

I claim that, when e_0 is assigned to 'η' as its semantic value, we get an $\mathcal{L}_1$-interpretation that satisfies $\text{ZFCU}_0 + \text{V}^{\in}$. We begin by observing that since i and ϵ are definable from e_0, we can in $\text{ZFCU}_0 + \text{V}^0$ define an $\mathcal{L}_1$-lexicon that assigns to '$\in$' and 'η' respectively ϵ and e_0. We have also seen how to extend this lexicon to an interpretation. This interpretation clearly satisfies ZFCU_0. Moreover, by our choice of ψ_0, this interpretation also satisfies the property-theoretic axioms in $\text{V}^{\in}$.[31] This means that every axiom of $\text{ZFCU}_0 + \text{V}^{\in}$ is true under our interpretation. In fact, this claim itself is provable in $\text{ZFCU}_0 + \text{V}^0$, using the Interpretation Lemma. This means that $\text{ZFCU}_0 + \text{V}^0$ proves the consistency of $\text{ZFCU}_0 + \text{V}^{\in}$.

Our next task is to define an interpretation that satisfies our new theory $\text{ZFCU}_0 + \text{V}^0$. The minimal way of doing this is by introducing a property comprehension

[31] In fact, e_0 is the smallest property which, when interpreted as the relation of property application, satisfies the property-theoretic axioms in $\text{V}^{\in}$.

axiom (V^1) that ensures the existence of a property e_1 under which fall all and only ordered pairs $\langle u, x\rangle$ such that x is definable by basic operations from i, ϵ, and e_0 and such that u possesses this property x. As above, we can write down a comprehension axiom for e_1 and prove that this comprehension axiom satisfies the well-foundedness requirement. We can also prove that the resulting theory of sets and properties allows us to define an interpretation that satisfies $\mathrm{ZFCU}_0 + \mathrm{V}^0$.

I end by outlining how this process can be continued up through the ordinals. The process is carried out by set-theoretic recursion in a meta-theory containing ZFC. Assume the process has been carried out for all ordinals $\gamma < \alpha$. Then there is a (set-theoretic) sequence $\langle i, \epsilon, e_0, \ldots, e_\gamma, \ldots\rangle_{\gamma<\alpha}$ listing the properties explicitly licensed by comprehension axioms so far, each e_γ being defined as the property under which falls all and only ordered pairs $\langle u, x\rangle$ such that x is a property definable by basic operations from the preceding elements of the sequence and such that u possesses this property. Call such sequences *eta-sequences*. Let *EtaSeq*(x) be a formalization in $\mathcal{L}_1$ of the claim that x is an eta-sequence. One easily proves that, given any two eta-sequences, they are either identical or one is an initial segment of the other. Let *Length*(x, α) be a formalization of the claim that x is a sequence of length α. Property comprehension axioms can then be stated as axioms asserting the existence of eta-sequences of various ordinal lengths:

$$(V^\alpha)\exists x(\mathit{EtaSeq}(x) \wedge \mathit{Length}(x, \alpha + 2))$$

$$(V^{<\infty})\forall\alpha(\mathit{Ord}(\alpha) \rightarrow \exists x(\mathit{EtaSeq}(x) \wedge \mathit{Length}(x, \alpha + 2)))$$

I now state a fundamental theorem about theories based on such comprehension axioms.

Theorem 3

(a) $\mathrm{ZFCU}_0 + \mathrm{V}^\alpha$ proves that, for any ordinal $\gamma < \alpha$, $\mathrm{ZFCU}_0 + \mathrm{V}^\gamma$ is consistent.
(b) $\mathrm{ZFCU}_0 + \mathrm{V}^{<\infty}$ proves that, for any ordinal α, $\mathrm{ZFCU}_0 + \mathrm{V}^\alpha$ is consistent.

Proof sketch. For (a), observe that $\mathrm{ZFCU}_0 + \mathrm{V}^\alpha$ proves the existence of an interpretation that maps 'η' to the $(\alpha + 2)$'th element of an eta-sequence, which we may refer to as e_α. This interpretation is easily seen to satisfy $\mathrm{ZFCU}_0 + \mathrm{V}^\gamma$ for each $\gamma < \alpha$. For (b), observe that $\mathrm{ZFCU}_0 + \mathrm{V}^{<\infty}$ proves that for each α there is an interpretation of the form just described.

I show in an Appendix how to develop purely set-theoretic consistency proofs for all these theories of sets and properties.

6.9 CONCLUSION

I will end by taking stock of what has been accomplished. I began by explaining what I take to be the strongest argument against the coherence of unrestricted quantification, namely the Semantic Argument (Section 6.2). Then I outlined the type-theoretic response to this argument (Section 6.3). Although I believe this to be the strongest response developed to date, I argued that the type-theorists are unable to properly express certain important semantic generalizations about their view, and that in order to do better, we need a type-free theory where some sort of *object* can serve as the semantic values of predicates (Section 6.4).

Next I introduced a distinction between sets and properties, which I argued is natural and well motivated, and according to which properties are very well suited to serve as the semantic values of predicates (Section 6.5). I also showed how a theory of sets and properties can be used to develop a very explicit semantics for first-order theories whose quantifiers range over absolutely everything (Section 6.6).

The main challenge that remained at the end of Section 6.6 was to give an account of what properties there are. This account must satisfy two potentially conflicting requirements. On the one hand, the theory must allow enough properties to enable the desired sort of semantic theorizing. On the other hand, the theory must in a natural and well motivated way disallow such properties as would lead to paradox. I attempted to meet this challenge in Section 6.7 by means of the plausible requirement that individuation be well-founded. I showed that the resulting account allows all the properties needed for the semantic theory of Section 6.6, while simultaneously disallowing paradoxical properties such as the Russell-property postulated by the second premise **Sem2** of the Semantic Argument.

The most serious worry remaining at the end of Section 6.7 concerns the fact that the predicate η, in its intended sense, fails to define a property. Many people will no doubt feel this as a loss. But it should be kept in mind that the rejection of such a property is not an *ad hoc* trick to avoid paradox but follows from the independently motivated well-foundedness requirement. So perhaps we must give up as illusory our apparent grasp of an absolutely general relation of property application. What we do have, however, are relations of property application restricted to whatever properties have been individuated. And as we saw in Section 6.8, these restricted relations suffice to develop general semantics for all of our theories containing the predicate η.

No doubt, further investigations will be needed, especially of how unnatural it is to do without an absolutely general relation of property application. But I firmly believe that my arguments and results represent progress. I hope in particular to have shown that a first-order theory of sets and properties offers an approach to the problem of unrestricted quantification that is at least as promising as the popular type-theoretic responses of Section 6.3.

APPENDIX. SET-THEORETIC CONSISTENCY PROOFS

I will now describe a method for proving the consistency of various theories of sets and properties relative to ZFC plus the existence of an inaccessible cardinal. I will therefore only be concerned with *set-theoretic* models of our object theories. Although this means that second-order variables of the meta-language can be interpreted set-theoretically, I will continue to speak of the values of these variables as 'concepts' and 'relations.' Recall also our convention from Section 6.7 of using lower- and upper-case letters as respectively first- and second-order constants and variables.

Definition 5

Let $\mathcal{M}$ be a model of ZFCU. Let E be a dyadic relation on its domain M. Let F be a concept on M. Say that E *nominalizes* a concept F iff there is an x such that $\forall u(Fu \leftrightarrow E\langle u, x\rangle)$. This x will then be said to *nominalize F under E* or to be *the nominalization of F under E*. Finally, say that E is *nominalizing* iff E nominalizes the identity relation and the concepts that E nominalizes are closed under the basic operations.

Note that for a model $\mathcal{M}$ of ZFCU to satisfy the minimal theory of properties V^-, there must be a nominalizing relation E on M that can interpret 'η'. Our goal will therefore be to construct models of ZFCU with suitable nominalizing relations. Unfortunately, our next lemma shows that we cannot have the sort of nominalizing relation that we most would have wanted.

Lemma 4

Let $\mathcal{M}$ be a model of ZFCU. Then no nominalizing relation E on M can nominalize itself.

Proof. Assume for *reductio* that some nominalizing relation E nominalizes itself. Then there is some x such that $E\langle u, v\rangle \leftrightarrow E\langle\langle u, v\rangle, x\rangle$. Since E is nominalizing, one of its nominalizations is the Russell property r, which is definable from x and the nominalization i of identity as $(\pi_0(x \cap i))^c$ by the basic operations of projection, intersection, and complementation. This definition of r ensures that $E\langle u, r\rangle \leftrightarrow \neg E\langle\langle u, u\rangle, x\rangle$. By substituting r for u we thus get $E\langle r, r\rangle \leftrightarrow \neg E\langle\langle r, r\rangle, x\rangle$. But from our choice of x we also have $E\langle r, r\rangle \leftrightarrow E\langle\langle r, r\rangle, x\rangle$. This produces a contradiction.

This lemma leaves us with two main options. Either we can give up our insistence that all properties be total and assign to 'η' a partial property. Or we can maintain our view that all properties are total and instead make use of nominalizing relations that don't nominalize themselves. These relations will serve as lower approximations to the desired partial property. Although I have no principled objection to the former option, I will here pursue the latter.

Definition 6

Where κ is a cardinal, let $V^{<\kappa}[U]$ be the iterative hierarchy based on the class U of urelements but with the requirement that at every stage of the iterative construction of sets all sets be of cardinality $< \kappa$.

It is easily seen that, when κ is a regular cardinal, the construction of $V^{<\kappa}[U]$ terminates after κ steps. It is also easily seen that κ is inaccessible just in case $V^{<\kappa}[U] \models$ ZFCU.

Lemma 5 (Nominalization Lemma)

Let κ be an infinite cardinal and U a collection of κ urelements. Assume there is a nominalizing relation E on $V^{<\kappa}[U]$. Assume there is a subclass $I \subseteq U$ containing κ

urelements that don't nominalize any concepts under E. Let Q be a class of at most κ concepts on $V^{<\kappa}[U]$. Then it is possible to extend E to a nominalizing relation E^+ that nominalizes all the concepts in Q. Moreover, E^+ can be chosen such that there are still κ urelements that don't nominalize any concepts under E^+.

Proof. We begin by making some simplifying assumptions. We may assume that Q contains all the concepts nominalized by E. For upon addition of these concepts, the cardinality of Q will still be $\leq \kappa$. We may also assume that Q is closed under the basic operations. To see this, note first that the cardinality of $V^{<\kappa}[U]$ is κ. Using this, a simple cardinality argument shows that the cardinality of the closure of Q is still $\leq \kappa$.

Next we identify each member of Q that is not already nominalized by E with a unique member of I. We can do this in such as a way that $J = I \setminus Q$ is of cardinality κ. Then we let E^+ be such that $E^+\langle u, x\rangle$ iff either $E\langle u, x\rangle$ or x has been identified with some concept $F \in Q$ such that Fu. By our assumptions regarding Q it follows that E^+ is a nominalizing relation that nominalizes all the desired concepts. By our choice of J, there are still κ urelements that don't nominalize any concepts under E^+.

Theorem 4

$\mathrm{ZFCU}_0 + \mathrm{V}^{\in}$ is consistent.

Proof. Let κ be an inaccessible cardinal. Then $V^{<\kappa}[U]$ is a model of ZFCU. Let E be the empty relation. Use the Nominalization Lemma to produce an extended nominalizing relation E^+ that nominalizes the concepts defined by $u = v$ and $u \in v$. Interpreting 'η' as E^+ produces a model of $\mathrm{ZFCU}_0 + \mathrm{V}^{\in}$.

Theorem 5

$\mathrm{ZFCU}_0 + \mathrm{V}^{<\infty}$ is consistent.

Proof sketch. Let $\mathcal{M}$ be the model of $\mathrm{ZFCU}_0 + \mathrm{V}^{\in}$ resulting from the proof of Theorem 4. Our task is to construct, for every ordinal $\alpha < \kappa$, an eta-sequence of length α. We proceed by induction on α. Let E_0 be the nominalizing relation on M emerging from the proof of Theorem 4 (where this relation was called E^+). Recall that E_0 can be chosen such that there is a collection I of κ urelements of M that don't nominalize concepts under E_0. So by the Nominalization Lemma, there is a larger nominalizing relation E_1 that nominalizes E_0 while still preserving a collection of κ urelements that don't nominalize concepts. Let e_0 be the nominalization of E_0 under E_1. For $\alpha = \beta + 1$, let E_β be the nominalizing relation that emerges from stage β. We then proceed as above to define an extended nominalizing relation E_α that nominalizes E_β, say as e_β. For α a limit ordinal, we let the new nominalizing relation E_α be the union of the nominalizing relations at the preceding stages. Our construction can be carried out such that at every step there are still κ urelements that don't nominalize any concepts under this new nominalizing relation.

REFERENCES

Benacerraf, P. and Putnam, H., (eds.) (1983) *Philosophy of Mathematics: Selected Readings*, Cambridge. Cambridge University Press. Second edition.

Boolos, G. (1971) 'The Iterative Conception of Set', *Journal of Philosophy*, 68: 215–32. Reprinted in Boolos (1998).

——(1985) 'Nominalist Platonism', *Philosophical Review*, 94(3): 327–44. Reprinted in Boolos (1998).

——(1998) *Logic, Logic, and Logic*. Harvard University Press, Cambridge, MA.

Burgess, J. P. (2004) *E Pluribus Unum*: Plural Logic and Set Theory, *Philosophia Mathematica*, 12(3): 193–221.

Cartwright, R. L. (1994) 'Speaking of Everything', *Noûs*, 28: 1–20.

Dummett, M. (1981) *Frege: Philosophy of Language*. Harvard University Press, Cambridge, MA, 2nd ed.

Fine, K. (2005) *Journal of Philosophy*, 102. 11: 547–72.

——(1994) 'Essence and Modality', In Tomberlin, J., (ed.), *Language and Logic*, volume 8 of *Philosophical Perspectives*, pp. 1–16. Ridgeview, Atascadero.

——(1998) 'Cantorian Abstraction: A Reconstruction and Defense', *Journal of Philosophy*, 115(12): 599–634.

——(2006) 'Relatively Unrestricted Quantification', in Rayo and Uzquiano (2006).

Forster, M. (1995) *Set Theory With a Universal Set: Exploring an Untyped Universe*. Oxford University Press, Oxford, 2nd ed.

Glanzberg, M. (2004) 'Quantification and Realism', *Philosophy and Phenomenological Report*, 69: 541–72.

——(2006) 'Context and Unrestricted Quantification', in Rayo and Uzquiano (2006).

Gödel, K. (1944) 'Russell's Mathematical Logic', in Benacerraf and Putnam (1983).

Hazen, A. (1997) 'Relations in Lewis's Framework without Atoms', *Analysis*, 57(4): 243–8.

Lewis, D. (1991) *Parts of Classes*. Blackwell, Oxford.

Linnebo, Ø. (2004) 'Plural Quantification', in *Stanford Encyclopedia of Philosophy*, (ed.) E. Zalta. Available at http://plato.stanford.edu/entries/plural-quant/.

——(forthcoming) 'Frege's Context Principle and Reference to Natural Numbers', forthcoming in *Logicism, Formalism, Intuitionism: What Has Become of Them?*, ed. S. Lindström, Springer.

——(2000y) 'Why Size Doesn't Matter', Unpublished manuscript.

Parsons, C. (1974) 'Sets and Classes', *Noûs*, 8: 1–12. Reprinted in Parsons (1983).

——(1977) 'What is the Iterative Conception of Set?' in Butts, R. and Hintikka, J., (eds.), *Logic, Foundations of Mathematics, and Computability Theory*. Reidel, Dordrecht. Reprinted in Benacerraf and Putnam (1983) and Parsons (1983).

——(1983) *Mathematics in Philosophy*. Cornell University Press, Ithaca, NY.

Quine, W. (1953) 'New Foundations for Mathematical Logic,' in his *From a Logical Point of View*.

Rayo, A. (2006) 'Beyond Plurals', in Rayo and Uzquiano (2006).

——and Uzquiano, G. (1999) 'Toward a Theory of Second-Order Consequence', *Notre Dame Journal of Formal Logic*, 40(3): 315–25.

——and Uzquiano, G., (eds.) (2006). *Absolute Generality*. Oxford, Oxford University Press.

——and Williamson, T. (2003) 'A Completeness Theory for Unrestricted First-Order Languages', in Beall, J., (ed.), *Liars and Heaps: New Essays on Paradox*, pp. 331–56. Oxford University Press, Oxford.

Williamson, T. (2003) 'Everything', in Hawthorne, J. and Zimmerman, D., (eds.), *Philosophical Perspectives 17: Language and Philosophical Linguistics*. Blackwell, Boston and Oxford.

7

There's a Rule for Everything

Vann McGee

7.1 SEMANTICAL SKEPTICISM IN GENERAL

Nothing in sociology is certain, but a sociological thesis that is about as sure as anything we'll find is that human beings use language to communicate, and one of the ways they accomplish this is by expressing judgments that are capable of being true or false. To understand how communication is possible, we have to understand what makes true statements true.

The first duty of a theory of truth is to provide truth conditions that appropriately reflect speakers' dispositions to assertion and denial and to assent and dissent. What exactly is required here is a matter of some delicacy, since the proposal that comes first to mind—speakers assent to things they regard as true—overlooks the possibilities of irony and deceit. However it's understood, the requirement that truth conditions reflect conditions of assertion and assent leaves truth conditions drastically underdetermined, because it doesn't give us any guidance in determining the semantic status of sentences sincere speakers aren't prepared either to assert or deny. Are they true but unknown, false but unrefuted, or so semantically deformed as to count as neither true nor false?

There are some further constraints on a theory of truth, in addition to getting the right matchup between truth conditions and assertibility conditions, of which I'll mention two. The first is that the language has to be learnable by human beings. One consequence of this requirement is that the semantics has to be, in some sense, compositional, to take account of speakers' ability to understand sentences they've never heard before, and of the astonishing facility with which a child, upon learning a new word, is able to figure out the meanings of sentences that contain it. This requirement is less informative than one might have hoped, however, because the possibilities for what aspects of an expression's use are counted as its meaning and for the

I would like to thank Gabriel Uzquiano and Agustín Rayo for their help.

manner in which the meanings of the parts determine the meaning of the whole are so multifarious.[1] Certainly the requirement gives us no assurance that anything like the account of the simplest sentences that we find in the *Sophist* (261d–263d)—nouns name individuals and verbs name properties and actions, and the sentence obtained by combining a name with a verb is true if and only if the individual has the property or performs the action—has to hold. Indeed, there are a number of potent arguments, centered mainly around chapter 2 of Quine's *Word and Object*, that purport to show that a name doesn't have a uniquely determined referent.

The other constraint is that semantic theories need to reflect the fact that whatever semantic values an expression has are given to it by the activities of the community of speakers. This condition makes the linguist's task harder, because it limits her options. The linguist is not permitted to fill in the gaps arbitrarily, choosing, from among the assignments of truth values that reflect community patterns of assent and assertion, whichever is most convenient for the linguist, for such a fiat would yield semantic values that are imposed by the linguist, rather than being discovered, indigenous in the community's practices.

Skepticism is apt to creep in through the smallest crack, and the gap between semantic theory and the totality of actual and potential data is less a crack than a chasm. I don't intend to address the general problem of semantic skepticism here, but only to discuss a small corner of the problem, namely, skepticism about logical terms, the quantifiers in particular. Against skepticism, I want to uphold the view that the meaning of the logical terms is fixed by rules of inference.

Semantical skepticism takes a peculiar form. Scarcely anyone wants to deny that people say things that are true. The prevalent skeptical view, which is sometimes called *deflationism*[2] or *minimalism*,[3] allows that a speaker can say things that are true, but denies that her ability to do so depends on the linguistic practices of herself and her community.

Deflationism, as I understand it, comprises two theses. An oversimplified version of *disquotationalism*,[4] which is the first thesis, tells us that the (T)-sentences—sentences that follow the paradigm, '"Snow is white" is true if and only if snow is white'—are analytic, and that there is nothing more to the notion of truth than the (T)-sentences provide. This way of putting things is conveniently simple, but it runs the risk of seriously misleading. Sentences aren't either true or false. When we say 'It is snowing' at a time and a place it is snowing, we say something true, whereas when we say the same sentence at a time and place it is not snowing, we say something false; the sentence itself is neither true nor false. A sentence can only be said to be true in a language in a context. Such attributions are widely thought to be derivative, on the grounds that the primary bearers of truth values are propositions, so that a sentence is said to be true in a language in a context because, in that language and context, the sentence expresses a true proposition. Derivative or not, ascribing truth to a

[1] See Schiffer (1987). [2] See Leeds (1978) and Field (1986 and 1994).

[3] Paul Horwich's (1990) minimalism is primarily a doctrine about propositions, rather than sentences.

[4] See Quine (1970), p. 12.

sentence in a language in a context is perfectly intelligible. So-called *eternal sentences* of a language,[5] whose truth conditions in the language don't vary by context, can be said to be true in the language, and which language is relevant can often be reasonably presumed to be tacitly understood. With these reservations in mind, it makes sense to speak of a sentence as true, but the reservations should not be forgotten.

However many codicils and caveats we lay down, we'll not save all the (T)-sentences, on account of the Liar paradox. The Liar paradox is a deeply important problem, but not our problem here, so we'll not be talking about sentences that have significant self-reference.

According to disquotationalism, as I understand it, to say that snow is white and to say that 'Snow is white' is true are, for normal speakers of English, two ways of saying the same thing. In particular, whatever is required to cause it to be the case that snow is white will be necessary and sufficient to cause it to be the case that 'Snow is white' is true. The requirement that the two assertions are alike in meaning isn't automatically entailed by the thesis that the (T)-sentences are analytic. One could, for example, use the (T)-sentences as a reference-fixing device for establishing a framework upon which to hang a substantial theory of truth.[6] But the thesis that the two assertions say the same thing is part of disquotationalism, as I understand it.

Disquotationalism is a surprising doctrine. One would have thought that what makes it the case that snow is white are facts about crystallography and optics, whereas to make it the case that 'Snow is white' is true requires both the facts about crystallography and optics that make snow white and the facts about English usage that make the sentence mean what it does. But according to disquotationalism, the truth of 'Snow is white' doesn't have any implications at all about how the sentence is used in English.

Because disquotationalism doesn't connect truth conditions with patterns of usage, there is a gap between what we would have naively expected a semantic theory to give us and what disquotationalism provides. Deflationism's second thesis is that there aren't any other, more robust semantic notions that fill the gap. One popular way of thinking about vagueness provides an example of a position that is disquotational but not deflationary. If Clare is a border case of 'poor', so that our customs in using the word 'poor', together with the facts about Clare's financial situation, leave it unsettled whether the word 'poor' properly applies to Clare, then one naturally wants to say that 'Clare is poor' is neither true nor false. One wants to say this but cannot, on a disquotational conception of truth and falsity (treating falsity as the truth of the negation), since ' "Clare is poor" is either true or false' is logically entailed by:

'Clare is poor' is true if and only if Clare is poor.
'Clare is poor' is false if and only if Clare is not poor.

The solution is to introduce an operator 'determinately', so that, if linguistic and financial factors conspire to put Clare in the extension of 'poor', Clare is determinately poor and 'Clare is poor' is determinately true, whereas if Clare is a borderline case, she

[5] See Quine (1960), p. 193f.
[6] This possibility was suggested to me by Stephen Yablo. Cf. Evans, (1982), ch. 2.

is neither determinately poor nor determinately not poor, and the sentence is neither determinately true nor determinately false. Because correct attributions of determinate truth are grounded in linguistic usage, this version of disquotationalism counts as inflationary.

To count as an inflationist, one needn't believe that the connections between usage and meaning are regular enough to submit themselves to a useful theoretical understanding. It may well be that for each word there is an etymological history that connects the word to its meaning, but that when you bundle the different histories together you get a ragtag assemblage of capricious accidents, with too few common features to allow significant generalizations.[7] If that's the way you think things are, you still won't count as a deflationist, because you are willing to admit that there are paths that lead to meaning from usage, even if the pathways are too ragged to permit a tractable theory.

Disquotationalism gives us a notion of truth for our own language, and we can extend the notion of truth to other languages by translating those languages into our own. Correct translation is guided by the aim of preserving an appropriate combination of causal connections and conceptual roles. The result is a theory that can describe communication by saying what a speaker means by the words she uses, but, unless it is supplemented by further semantical notions not permitted to the deflationist, it cannot explain communication, because it has nothing at all to say about why our words mean what they do. Deflationism can help itself to a notion of sameness of meaning, according to which our neighbor's sentence that we translate 'Snow is white' means the same thing as our own sentence 'Snow is white', but the deflationist can't explain why either of us mean what we do by the words we use, because the (T)-sentences for our own language are, for the deflationist, an inexplicable brute fact. Sentences don't get their truth conditions by magic. They are given them by the activities of a community of speakers, but how this is done is, for the deflationist, a complete mystery.

7.2 SKEPTICISM ABOUT THE QUANTIFIERS, IN PARTICULAR

Deflationism suffers from blatant explanatory deficiencies. Even so, the disparity between what an inflationary semantic theory requires and what the totality of possible data supplies is so great that deflationism has sometimes seemed inescapable. Here I would not like us to talk about the general problems faced by inflationary semantics, but rather to talk specifically about the prospects for an inflationist account of the logical operators. If we intend to construct an inflationist theory, the logical operators are a good place to start, because of the central role of the logical words in the construction of complex sentences, and of the fundamental role of logical inferences in successful communication. One has the feeling that, if we can't even put

[7] See Leeds (1995).

together a more-than-disquotational account of the logical words, then inflationist semantics is a lost cause.

We are going to be restricting our attention to formal languages formulated using the first-order predicate calculus, and to fragments of English that can be aptly formalized within such formal languages. Our methodological strategy is to investigate a complex phenomenon by examining its simplest manifestations first, then to work our way up to the more complicated manifestations that we really care about. It's a good general strategy, but in this case the differences between the first-order languages and the natural language are so vast that it may well turn out that, even if we are fully successful at getting a satisfactory semantic theory for the formal languages, nothing of what we learn is applicable to the semantics of English, so that we have made no progress at all toward our real goal. That's OK, because our intention here is less ambitious than to try to develop the beginning of a semantics of English. Our intention here is to soothe a skeptical itch, by showing that an inflationary semantics for the basic logical connectives is, in principle, possible, and for that success with the toy languages will be enough.

The formal-language quantifiers '$(\forall x)$' and '$(\exists x)$' are used in different ways in different contexts, as are the English phrases 'for all', 'everything', 'for some', and 'something'. Sometimes they are used in such a way that the domain of quantification is tacitly or explicitly restricted, but other times no such restriction is apparent. If we take this appearance at face value, then, following the generally sound strategy of beginning an inquiry by investigating relatively simple phenomena and working our way up toward greater complexity, we would be wise to start with unrestricted quantification, since Frege taught us how to reduce restricted quantification to unrestricted. If our domain of quantification has hitherto been restricted to *A*s, we can make the restriction explicit by writing '$(\forall x)(Ax \supset Bx)$' and '$(\exists x)(Ax \wedge Bx)$' in place of '$(\forall x)Bx$' and '$(\exists x)Bx$', with the quantifiers now understood as unrestricted. (We cannot do this for other English quantifiers like 'for most' and 'for many'; that is one reason why only paying attention to first-order logical devices is such a severe restriction.)[8] A semantic theory that encompasses restricted quantification is sure to be a lot more complicated that one that only takes account of unrestricted quantification because the domain of quantification, whether it's given explicitly or tacitly, is almost certain to be vaguely defined. A theory of restricted quantification will have to confront all the old problems about vague predication, which have bedeviled philosophers since Eubulides, as well as whatever new problems the quantifiers may bring. If we are following the maxim, 'Simple things first', unrestricted quantification is the place to start.

Vagueness is omnipresent in human language. Our most rigorous efforts at scientific exactitude reduce, but do not eliminate, imprecision. Unrestricted quantification offers us something quite extraordinary: a sharp boundary. Vagueness appears when there are actual or potential borderline cases, and something that's alleged to be on the border between being and nonbeing is still something, and hence not on

[8] Barwise and Cooper (1981) have initiated the search for a more comprehensive theory.

the border. A painting that's sketched by Valázquez and completed by his pupil may occupy an intermediate position between 'Valázquez' and 'counterfeit Valázquez', but whoever its author is, the painting unmistakably exists. The idea of a thing occupying a position intermediate between being and nonbeing is nonsensical.

In regarding unrestricted quantification as simple and restricted quantification as complex, I am presuming that the default value of the quantifiers, the value they take when they aren't subject to any restriction, public or private, spoken or silent, is quantification over absolutely everything. One could try to tell an alternative story, in which one starts out with variables ranging over middle-sized objects in one's immediate neighborhood and expands the domain by acknowledging new objects as conceptually or conversationally required, but it's hard to see how such an account would go. When we expand the domain by recognizing new objects, we'll need to specify the new objects, and it's hard to see how we could specify the new objects when the logical devices at our disposal are limited to quantifiers that range over the old objects. One can imagine a mental representational faculty, entirely unlike anything we find in public language, that picks out the varying domains, but such imaginings are purely speculative.

The realist doctrine is that unambiguously unrestricted quantification is possible. Skeptics have challenged both aspects. Some have argued that our usage never picks out a uniquely determined infinite domain of quantification, while others have contended that, even when our quantified variables do have a specific domain, that domain is never all-inclusive.

The doctrine that quantification can never be fully comprehensive originates in *Principia Mathematica*'s analysis of the paradoxes. To have a single, unified domain of quantification would be illegitimate, we are told, since if we attempt to define a set employing quantifiers that range over all sets, we violate the vicious circle principle, which is our bulwark against antinomy.

This objection strikes me as a bit naive, since it takes at face value what Whitehead and Russell said they were doing in *Principia Mathematica*, without taking account of the disparity between what they said they were doing and what they actually did. What they actually did was something truly marvelous: they provided a uniform foundation for all of classical mathematics, including classical analysis. What they said they did was to accomplish this while holding themselves strictly within the confines of the vicious circle principle. However, to get analysis in its classical form, you need the principle that every nonempty collection of real numbers that's bounded above has a least upper bound. The least upper bound is defined in terms of the totality of upper bounds, and hence it's defined in terms of a totality that includes itself, in violation of the vicious circle principle. Whitehead and Russell talk as if they were rigorously constrained, at every step, by the vicious circle principle, but the Least Upper Bound Principle puts them in a tight place. To escape, they adopt the Axiom of Reducibility, but accepting the Axiom of Reducibility means abandoning the vicious circle principle. As Ramsey (1925) noted clearly, after we adopt Reducibility, we still have a hierarchy of sets—a set has to be at a higher level than its elements—but the basis of the hierarchy is consideration of how sets are built up out of their elements, rather than restrictions on what things we are allowed to talk about when we are doing set theory. With the acceptance of the axiom, the earlier requirement that a propositional function has to lie above, not only all its arguments, but all the things you talk about in defining the function, is neutralized. This line of reasoning was completed by Gödel (1944), who noted that it was possible to consolidate the entire labyrinth of type theory into a straightforward and uniform first-order theory. Indeed, if we modify the *Principia Mathematica* framework by allowing cumulative types, a modification that doesn't transgress the vicious circle principle, we find that the axioms we need were already provided by Zermelo (1908).

The thesis that genuinely universal quantification is not possible, so that, whenever we use quantifiers, even if it looks as if we are using them unrestrictedly, there will always be things that lie outside our universe of discourse, is not an easy doctrine to maintain. Indeed, it is not a doctrine that can be propounded coherently. To uphold it, you would have to maintain that, for every discussion, there are things that lie outside the domain of that discussion. This, you will have to say, holds for all discussions, including the discussion we are having right now. So there are things that lie outside the domain of our current discussion. But in saying, 'There are things that lie outside the domain of our present discussion', you can't be saying something true, because any witness to its truth would have to lie outside the domain of our current discussion.

The doctrine that quantifiers are always restricted is not easy to maintain, but it has been thought to be forced upon us by the relentless logic of Russell's paradox. But a look at the post-*Principia* history of set theory shows that Russell's paradox is not as merciless as it first appears. The bothersome worry, it seems to me, is not that our domain of quantification is always assuredly restricted but that the domain is never assuredly unrestricted. The origin of this worry is Skolem's paradox, and it finds its sharpest expression in Hilary Putnam's 'Models and Reality'. Suppose, for *reductio ad absurdum*, that our usage picks out a unique intended model for our language, and that this model has an all-inclusive domain. The Löwenheim–Skolem theorem tells us that there is a countable set S such that we get an elementary submodel of the intended model when we restrict the domain to S. There isn't anything in our thoughts and practices in virtue of which the so-called intended model fits our intentions in using the language better than the countable submodel, so that there isn't anything that makes unrestricted quantification, rather than quantification over S, the intended meaning of the quantifiers.

The Löwenheim–Skolem theorem applies to languages for the first-order predicate calculus, but not to logically more robust languages, and one might dismiss the problems aroused by Skolem's paradox as an artifact of an overly simplified model. They are serious difficulties for creatures who speak first-order languages, but we aren't such creatures. This response is correct as far as it goes, but I'm not sure it goes far enough. The worry is that, when we move to logically more expressive languages, the difficulties will reassert themselves in a slightly different form. If we go to second-order logic, we find that there are so-called Henkin models,[9] countable models in which

[9] From Henkin (1950).

a nonstandard interpretation of the second-order quantifiers makes all the right sentences true even though the second-order variables range over a countable collection of collections. A similar treatment can be applied to modal operators and counterfactuals. If we describe the possible-world semantics by a first-order model, taking a countable elementary submodel gives us a model of the modal language in which all the expected modal and counterfactual statements are true, albeit with a notion of possibility more restrictive than expected. Of course, even these more robust formal languages don't come close to the logical complexity of English, but one lacks confidence that the Löwenheim–Skolem theorem won't follow us, in one form or another, even as we move to languages that are logically highly complex.

Applied to first-order languages, the Löwenheim–Skolem construction takes the purported intended model of the language, and provides a countable submodel in which the same sentences are true. A righteous complaint against the philosophical application of the construction, which claims that the countable submodel has as good a claim to count as 'intended' as the original, is that it requires too little of the intended model. In supposing that sentences are either true or false, one implicitly restricts one's attention to sentences that are used to make assertions, as opposed to such activities as making promises and issuing commands, and among those, one only looks at sentences for which the truth value of what one says in uttering the sentence does not vary by context of utterance. Surely an adequate interpretation of the language has to account for occasion sentences, as well as eternal sentences, and it has to say correctly when promises are fulfilled and when commands are obeyed.

The problem about not accounting for speech acts other than assertions isn't so serious, since questions about the conditions of satisfaction of other speech acts are reducible to questions about the truth conditions of assertions. The situations in which the request, 'Please lend me $10 until payday' is fulfilled are the ones in which the assertion 'You will lend me $10 until payday' is true. The problem about not taking account of occasion sentences is more serious, but Putnam (1980, pp. 431–3) has an ingenious answer to it. The Skolem construction allows us to hold denumerably infinitely many individuals fixed in place as we move from original model to elementary submodel. In effect, we can introduce names for $\aleph_0$ individuals, chosen however we wish, and we can use those names to pin down the correct truth values for utterances of occasion sentences.

A related complaint is that, to account for speakers' dispositions to verbal behavior, it is not enough to find an interpretation that gets the right truth *values*; it needs to get the right truth *conditions*. To understand what speakers assert and accept, we have to know what sentences they regard as true, which we figure out by discerning what the truth conditions for a sentence are and whether their situation is one in which they are likely to believe that those conditions are met. The sentences they regard as true will coincide with the sentences that are, in fact, true only for speakers who are omniscient.

This is a serious complaint, but our earlier discussion of the status of modal statements provides a ready answer. Taking a countable elementary submodel of the possible-worlds model enables us to associate an intension with each term in such a way that every sentence gets the right truth value in every identifiable counterfactual situation. One can reply that identifying possible-world truth conditions isn't enough to determine conditions for assertion and acceptance. 'The Red Sox won the pennant in 2004' has different assertion conditions from its conjunction with Fermat's Last Theorem, even though they're true in the same possible worlds. But one would like some assurance that, once these more refined assertion and acceptance conditions are discerned, the Skolemite skeptic won't still be a position to make mischief.

Another objection, one I don't know how the Skolemite can answer, concerns learnability. To learn to employ quantification over the countable set S, we would have had to distinguish the Ss from the non-Ss somehow, but the construction has been artfully contrived to ensure that we can't make the distinction. If, in fact, we can make the distinction, then we can introduce a new predicate true of only the Ss, and we can differentiate the two modes of quantification by asking whether '$(\forall x)Sx$' is true. If, on the other hand, we can't distinguish the things inside and outside the domain, then we can't learn S-quantification. There isn't a comparable problem for learning unrestricted quantification, because there aren't any things outside.

A further realist rebuttal to Skolemite skepticism appeals again to the disparity between natural languages and the various formal languages we use to represent them. The formal languages always have a fixed vocabulary, whereas natural languages change continually. Whenever we adopt and name a stray dog or we introduce a new scientific theory with concomitant vocabulary, we expand the language. Fundamental principles of inference, like the principle of mathematical induction, are upheld even with the enlarged vocabulary. We don't have to reassess the validity of mathematical induction when we expand our inventory of theoretical concepts, for our current understanding of the natural numbers ensures that, no matter how we expand our language in the future, induction axioms formulated with the enlarged vocabulary will still be true. That's one reason for the remarkable stability of mathematics; scientific paradigms may come and go, but the principles of number theory, pure and applied, remain the same.

The recognition that the rules of logical inference need to be *open-ended*, in the sense that they will continue to be upheld even if we add new constants and predicates to the language, frustrates Skolemite skepticism. The Löwenheim–Skolem construction requires that every individual that's named in the language be an element of the countable subdomain S. If the individual constant c named something outside the domain S, then if '$(\forall x)$' were taken to mean 'For every member x of S', the principle of universal instantiation, which permits us to infer $\varphi(c)$ from $(\forall x)\varphi(x)$, would not be truth preserving. A counterexample would be the inference from '$(\forall x)(\exists y)y = x$' to '$(\exists y)y = c$'. Following Skolem's recipe gets us a countable set S with the property that interpreting the quantifiers as ranging over S makes the classical modes of inference truth-preserving, but when we expand the language by adding new constants, truth preservation is not maintained. The hypothesis that the quantified variables range over S cannot explain the inferential practices of people whose acceptance of universal instantiation is open-ended. As long as we restrict our attention to the original language, S-quantification and unrestricted quantification act alike, but expanding the language puts S-quantification under stresses it cannot endure.

The appeal to open-endedness taps into a standard strategy for responding to semantic skepticism. For example, we want to say that the nonstandard models of arithmetic are not the 'intended' models, but what is there about our intentions that selects the standard models? Not our theory. Even if we were somehow able to discern all the arithmetical truths, the Compactness Theorem assures us that our theory would have a nonstandard model. Not our practices in using numbers in applications. For counting out apples, it makes no difference whether the system of 'numbers' we employ has nonstandard elements. But apart from theory and practice, what else is there? The reply is to appeal to the open-endedness of our theoretical commitments. Standard models support the open-ended application of the principle of mathematical induction.[10]

Another source of skepticism about unequivocally unrestricted quantification is the thought that in order to have a fully precise domain of quantification, one would have to have definite answers to all the major ontological questions. But not all the major ontological questions have definite answers. Most ontological questions can be less glamorously rephrased as questions about the choice of a system of symbolic notation, and such choices are, to a certain extent, arbitrary. Moreover, even if the ontological questions have definite answers, there is little likelihood that we, the people who are supposed to use these unambiguously unrestricted quantifiers, are going to know them.

Let me illustrate this worry with an example. I find the arguments Davidson (1967) presents for including events among the basic constituents of reality to be persuasive but not quite compelling. One cannot help but admire the power and elegance of the theory Davidson advances, but one also feels the attraction of a more Spartan ontology that makes room for bodies of various shapes and sizes that move about and from time to time collide, but doesn't allow that, in addition to the bodies, there are some further things, their occasional collisions. There is quite a lot to be said, one way or the other, but it's not implausible to imagine that, at the end of the day, rational inquiry will fail to resolve the issue. In fact, it seems to me not too implausible to imagine that, in the end, we'll want to say that you can have it either way you like. If you find it useful to talk about events, you are free to talk that way, whereas if you are more comfortable with the sparer ontology, that's OK too. There is, I want to suggest, no fact of the matter whether there are events. (This example works for me. It won't work for you, if you are persuaded either that there are events or that there aren't any, in which case you should change the example. There is surely some ontological question about which your views are so unsettled that you are inclined to allow that there may be no fact of the matter.)

How can this be? How can there be indeterminate ontological questions when there is a fully exact domain of quantification? If we had the luxury of a variable universe of discourse, we might find ourselves in a position where we could include or exclude events at our convenience. But if we are decisively quantifying over everything, then if we are permitted to allow events into our ontology, we are

[10] For an illuminating further discussion of Skolemite skepticism, see Lavine (forthcoming), which is, however, focused on quantification in mathematics, rather than quantification in general.

obligated to do so. To say that there is no fact of the matter is to relegate events to the impossible border between being and nonbeing.

The answer to this problem, I want to suggest, is to allow that there is no fact of the matter whether there are events, but to explain this imprecision by the indeterminate reference of the word 'event', rather than by any slackness in the reach of the quantifiers. We embrace the ontological thesis that there are events by adopting a theory that entails their existence. If it isn't possible to find any things to play the theoretical role of events while upholding the underlying facts about bodies in motion, then we can say definitively that there are no such things as events. But things that are able to play the theoretical role of events are not necessarily events, and showing that there are things able to play the role only shows that event theory is consistent with the facts about bodies in motion; it doesn't show that the theory is true.

Ramsey's 'Theories' develops the radical empiricist thesis that only statements that describe observable things express genuine propositions, so that theoretical statements are useful merely as intermediaries to help us in describing and predicting the results of observations. Even people who aren't radical empiricists have found the logical machinery he develops valuable, as a way of accommodating modes of speech that are metaphysically dubious but practically useful. For our purposes here, we'll think of statements about bodies in motion as playing the role of Ramsey's 'observational' sentences, and we'll treat terms like 'event' and 'happens at' as 'theoretical'. Ramsey regards a theory as true if the existential closure of the open sentence you get by taking the conjunction of the theory's axioms and replacing all the theoretical terms by variables of appropriate type is true. This way of putting things has the peculiar consequence that logically incompatible theories are sometimes both counted as true,[11] but this verbal oddity shouldn't detract from the account's value in helping us understand a theory's dual role in describing and predicting the results of observations and in fixing the meanings of theoretical terms. If the existential closure is true, then the theory has done all it's required to do by way of conforming to the observable facts. That it has met this obligation is, as I understand it, what Ramsey has in mind by declaring such a theory true. If the theory is 'true' in Ramsey's sense, then it is possible, while keeping the meanings of the observation terms fixed, to assign semantic values to the theoretical terms in such a way as to make the theory 'true' as judged by a Tarski-style theory of truth,[12] but the fact that we are able to use the theoretical terms in such a way as to make the theory true by no means obligates us to do so. We might use the terms in some other way, or not use them at all. What we choose to do is a pragmatic matter. Once we have ascertained that the theory is Ramsey-true, we are free to use it; that is, we are free to employ the theoretical terms in such a way as to make the theory true. We'll choose to use the theory if we find it useful.

Ramsey's analysis explains why ontological questions, like the question whether there are events, can remain unsettled even if the domain of quantification is made fully precise. If event theory is Ramsey-false, we must reject it as false. If, however, the theory is Ramsey-true, we are free to accept or to reject it, deciding on pragmatic

[11] See McGee (2004). [12] See Tarski (1935).

grounds. If pragmatic considerations are completely indecisive, so that the issue cannot be settled except by arbitrary fiat, then we say that there's no fact of the matter. If so, then we get to choose whether to use the word 'event' in such a way that the sentence, 'There are events', is true. The indefiniteness arises from limitations we face in pinning down the meanings of theoretical terms, and it will persist even if our domain of quantification is unambiguously unrestricted.

7.3 A RULE FOR 'EVERYTHING'

The bifurcation of our naive notion of truth into two notions, disquotational truth and correspondence truth, is an unwelcome development.[13] It is a theoretical misfortune, since the dialectical tension between opposing tendencies within a single complex notion is a source of cognitive power, lost when the notion snaps in two; and it is a misfortune intuitively, inasmuch as there is nothing in ordinary usage to suggest that the word 'true', as we presently use it, is ambiguous. It is an unhappy development, but it is forced upon us by our inability to reconcile two nearly irresistible theses—that the correct usage of 'true' is governed by the (T)-sentences, and that sentences have the truth conditions they have as an effect of the activities of a community of speakers—with the fact that there are meaningful assertions, such things as borderline attributions of vague terms, for which speakers' usage fails to establish precise, exclusive, and exhaustive truth and falsity conditions. A 'fact' I call it, that there is indeterminacy at the boundaries of vague terms, but to establish it conclusively, I would need something no one now has, a comprehensive theory of meaning fixation for English. Timothy Williamson (1994) has thrown himself into the argumentative gap, arguing that subtle nuances of the verbal behavior of English speakers establish an exact, down-to-the-last-penny boundary where the applicability of 'poor' leaves off and that of 'not poor' begins. Williamson's argument is straightforward: The conclusion that speakers' usage somehow delineates sharp boundaries whenever a vague term is meaningfully used is forced upon us by the two theses. The force of Williamson's argument is undeniable, but I nonetheless want to resist its conclusion, because it seems to me so *prima facie* implausible that our usage of such woolly phrases as 'a little on the heavy side' and 'sounds sort of like a polka' establishes precisely delimited boundaries, and because Williamson, while insisting that our usage fixes exact boundaries, doesn't provide even a hint of an account of how this is done.

The reason I am rehashing the debate with Williamson[14] here is the worry that I am making myself vulnerable to the same complaint I am lodging against him. We haven't found any compelling reason to deny that there is a causal mechanism by which speakers of English are able to effect unambiguously unrestricted quantification, and, other things being equal, we would like to avoid theories that postulate widespread semantic indeterminacy, since such theories make it hard to understand

[13] See McGee (2005).

[14] It was hashed in an exchange in *Linguistics and Philosophy* between Williamson (2004) and Brian McLaughlin and me (1998 and 2004).

the ease with which people are able to communicate. So we'd like to hope that there is a causal mechanism for bringing it about that our quantifiers have limitless range, but to suppose our hopes are realized without at least the beginning of an account of what that mechanism might be is little more than wishful thinking. It would be too much to demand to see the mechanism in virtue of which the English word 'everything' means what it does; such a demand would require an extensive investigation into the sociology of English speakers and the psychology of its members. In the same way, it would be too much to require that Williamson explain in detail how vague terms get sharp boundaries. But without at least the crude beginnings of a sketch of how the causal mechanisms we postulate might operate, one can't help suspecting that he and I are bluffing.

The positive account I would like to develop is the simplest one you can think of: the semantic values of the quantifiers are fixed by the rules of inference. I don't for a moment suppose that this is a correct account of quantification in English. The story is only supposed to apply to a suitable class of formalized languages, but this will be enough to assuage the skeptical worry that unambiguously unlimited quantification isn't available at all.

The worry about the quantifiers isn't that they are meaningless, like the braying of cattle. People are too successful at using quantified sentences to convey information for the thesis that quantifiers are meaningless to be even remotely plausible. The worrisome hypothesis is that, while our usage partially determines the semantic values of the quantifiers, it's not incisive enough to uniquely pin the values down.

Where there is indeterminacy, there are multiple candidates. Where there are several candidates for what the semantic value of a word might be, each conforming to our practices in using the word and none emerging as superior to the others, then we have good reason to suppose that there is no fact of the matter which candidate the word refers to. That this is not the situation of the quantifiers is a remarkable theorem of J. H. Harris (1982). Specifically, Harris showed that, if '$\forall_1$' and '$\forall_2$' are operators that play the syntactic and inferential roles of the universal quantifier, so that each of them is governed by the rules Universal Specification (US)[15] (From $\{(\forall x)\varphi(x)\}$, you may infer $\varphi(c)$, for any individual constant c) and Universal Generalization (UG) (If you are able to infer $\varphi(c)$ from Γ, where c is an individual constant that doesn't appear in $\varphi(x)$ or in Γ, then you can infer $(\forall x)\ \varphi(x)$ from Γ), then from each of $(\forall_1 x)\ \varphi(x)$ and $(\forall_2 x)\ \varphi(x)$ you can derive the other. The proof is easy. From $\{(\forall_1)\ \varphi(x)\}$ you can infer $\varphi(c)$ by US, where c is a constant that doesn't appear in $\varphi(x)$,[16] and then you can use UG to strengthen the conclusion to $(\forall_2 x)\ \varphi(x)$. The other direction is symmetrical, showing that, assuming that interderivability is a sign of logical equivalence, '$\forall_1$' and '$\forall_2$' are logically equivalent. Similar arguments apply to '$\exists$', and also to the standard sentential connectives and '$=$', showing that these operators satisfy *uniqueness*, one of two criteria Nuel Belnap (1962) proposed for successful introduction of a logical operator by rules of inference. Belnap's other criterion, *conservativeness* (if you can use the new rules to derive a conclusion that doesn't contain the

[15] Our formulation of the rules follows Mates (1972).

[16] I am taking it for granted that we have an unlimited supply of individual constants.

new operator from premises that don't contain the new operator, then it was already possible to derive the conclusion from the premises without the new rules), is also satisfied.

The Harris theorem doesn't show that there aren't other legitimate uses of '$\forall$' and '$\exists$', apart from unrestricted universal and existential quantification. It does show that different ways of using the symbols cannot peacefully coexist within a single context. Thus if '$\forall_1$' is universal quantification over the objects in the Milky Way, '$(\forall_1 x)x$ is within one million light years of the earth' will be true, and so, in order for Universal Instantiation to be truth preserving, individual constants that denote stars in the Andromeda galaxy must be forbidden. If '$\forall_2$' designates unrestricted quantification, then, in order for us to be assured of the truth of a sentence of the form $(\forall_2 x)\ \varphi(x)$ on the basis of having inferred $\varphi(c)$ (where φ doesn't contain c) from premisses that don't contain c, any objects at all, including stars in Andromeda, must be allowed as possible referents of 'c'. We can't use both rules for both quantifiers within a single context.

We can, if we like, use '$\exists_3$' in such a way that '$(\exists_3 x)\ \varphi(x)$' means that, according to *Lord of the Rings* there exists a φ. Within contexts in which we are interested in truth within the story, rather than truth, we can use 'Frodo' and 'Gandalf' as legitimate names, suitable for application of Existential Generalization (EG) (the rule that permits you to derive $(\exists x)\ \varphi(x)$ from $\{\varphi(c)\}$). 'Frodo' and 'Gandalf' are not, of course, names that denote nonexistent things, for there are no nonexistent things, but we can describe the names' use by defining a *Lord of the Rings* model to be a model in which the story, together with whatever innocent background truths we are willing to import into the story, is true (such models have to exist if the story is consistent, by the Completeness Theorem), and regarding a sentence as true within *Lord of the Rings* if it is true in all *Lord of the Rings* models. This semantics legitimates both EG and Existential Specification (ES) (the rule that tell you that, if you are able to infer ψ from $\Gamma \cup \{\varphi(c)\}$, where the individual constant c doesn't appear in $\Gamma, \varphi(x)$, or ψ, you may infer ψ from $\Gamma \cup \{(\exists x)\varphi(x)\}$), since the rules preserve truth within *Lord of the Rings* models. We cannot, however, use EG and ES for '$\exists_3$' within a context within which we are also using '$\exists_2$' to denote ordinary existential quantification over actually existing things. If we could, we could use EG for '$\exists_2$' to derive '$(\exists_2 x)x$ is a Nazgul' from {'c is a Nazgul'}, then employ ES for '$\exists_3$' to upgrade our premiss set to {'$(\exists_3 x)x$ is a Nazgul'}, and finally use Conditional Proof to conclude that, if there are Nazguls in the story, then there are Nazguls in real life.

The Harris theorem doesn't tell us what the semantic values of the quantifiers are, or even what sort of thing we ought to look for as the 'semantic value' of a logical operator. Nevertheless, the theorem gives us reason to anticipate that, when we do develop a semantic theory, it will favor unambiguously unrestricted quantification. The theorem tells us that, in any context within which we are willing to give the quantifier rules free rein, either the rules misfire completely, so that there is no candidate for the semantic value of the quantifier that is compatible with our usage, or else there is a uniquely determined optimal candidate.

I'm not sure what it would take for the first alternative to obtain, but possibilities that come to mind are that the attempt to use the quantifier according to the rules somehow lapses into incoherence, and that the pattern of use we get by following the rules consistently is so erratic that the quantifier doesn't contribute to the truth conditions of sentences in any systematic way. But if there were an incoherence it would surely have shown up before now, and the quantifiers figure so prominently in successful communication and demonstration that it's hard to believe that they don't make a reliable contribution to truth conditions.

Accepting the second Harris alternative, so that the quantifier has a uniquely determined semantic value, doesn't tell us what that value is, but it does limit the range of choices. Quantification over the things in the Milky Way is excluded, as is *Lord of the Rings* quantification, because they are imprecise. We could perhaps, with enough effort and ingenuity, devise fully precise quantifiers that had more-or-less the same effect as quantification over the inhabitants of the Milky Way or of the Tolkien trilogy.[17] We could do so, but is there any reason to imagine that we actually have done so? To suppose that we are employing a precisified variant of Milk Way quantification is to adopt an hypothesis that is wildly speculative and extravagantly complicated when a simple and straightforward alternative is ready to hand. The name of the game, in semantics as in the other sciences, is inference to the best explanation, not inference to the only possible explanation, and in that game the smart money is on the unrestricted quantifiers.

The Harris theorem tells us that the quantifiers and the other logical operators each assume at most one semantic value, but it doesn't tell us anything about what that semantic value might be. This is hardly surprising. The principal task of semantic theory is to identify features of the world that make true sentences true and false sentences false, and Harris's theorem restricts its concern to logical connections that are sure to hold no matter what the world is like. Only after we already have a fundamental understanding of the notions of truth and consequence as those notions apply to logically simple expressions does it make sense to look to inferential roles to help extend these notions to logically complex expressions.

The simplest semantic theory that will suit our purposes is that of Tarski (1936), who defines a *model* of a language as a function assigning a value of appropriate type to each nonlogical constant.[18] For us, the nonlogical constants will be individual constants, each of which is assigned an individual, and n-place predicates other than the 2-place logically constant predicate '=', each of which is assigned a collection of n-tuples. (In supposing that the things assigned to a 1-place predicate invariably form

[17] The simplest method for trying to get Milky Way quantification would be an *ad hoc* restriction on the category of individual constant, so that, for the purposes of the rules of inference, an ordinary name that denotes a star in Andromeda doesn't count as an individual constant; it plays the right syntactic role, but it doesn't pass a further semantic test. This effort stumbles at the galaxy's vague border, where we can have names in the ordinary sense whose status as names for the purpose of the rules is dubious. In order to make sure that US is truth preserving, we'll want to be stingy about allowing disputed terms, whereas a liberal policy is required to ensure that UG preserves truth in every Milky Way model. To get the two rules to act in harmony, we'll need to make the border precise.

[18] Actually, Tarski defines a model of a theory Γ to be a variable assignment that satisfies the formulas you get from Γ by uniformly substituting variables of appropriate types for the nonlogical constants, but it's simpler to avoid the detour through the substituted variables.

a collection, I am oversimplifying, but bear with me for the moment.) A *variable assignment* is a function that assigns an individual to every variable. The conditions under which a variable assignment satisfies an atomic formula in a model and under which an atomic sentence (atomic formula with no free variables) is true in a model are defined in the standard way.

The notion of satisfaction in a model provides us with an natural notion of logical consequence. A formula φ is a *logical consequence* of a set of formulas Γ if and only if φ is satisfied in every model by every variable assignment that satisfies all the members of Γ. Because the semantics is extensional, we can trace the descendance of this notion of logical consequence as a relation among open sentences[19] from the, perhaps more basic, notion of logical consequence as truth preservation. A formula φ is a logical consequence of Γ if and only if the sentence we get from φ by uniformly substituting new constants for variables is true in every model in which sentences we obtain by making the same substitutions into the formulas of Γ are true. Thus we may harmlessly extend whatever rules of inference we adopt by allowing open as well as closed sentences to appear, confident that, provided we are careful to avoid unintentionally bound variables, the extended rules will preserve satisfaction in a model if the original rules preserved truth in a model.

The notion of logical consequence is eminently clear, but, so long as we are only talking about atomic formulas, one can't resist sniping that, of course it's clear, because we're peering through empty space. Atomic formulas are mutually logically independent, so that an atomic formula φ is a logical consequence of a set of atomic formulas Γ if and only if φ is a element of Γ. A useful notion of logical consequence will need to take account of formulas that are logically complex. The standard way to proceed is, first, to introduce the logical connectives syntactically, then to give truth and satisfaction conditions for the new operators, next to see which patterns of inference preserve truth and satisfaction, and finally to provide rules that generate the approved inferences. Here we would like to proceed in opposite direction, starting with rules of inference and seeing what we can learn about truth and satisfaction conditions by enforcing the constraint that the rules have to be truth and satisfaction preserving.

Arnold Koslow (1992) initiated what he calls a 'structuralist' approach to logic, which identifies logical operators in terms of their inferential role. The conjunction of two sentences is, for Koslow, whatever sentence plays the appropriate role in inferences, whether or not that role is marked by the syntax. Specifically, the conjunction of two sentences is the weakest sentence that entails them both, so that we have the rules:

From $\{(\varphi \wedge \psi)\}$, you may infer φ.
From $\{(\varphi \wedge \psi)\}$, you may infer ψ.
If you can infer φ from $\{\eta\}$ and you can also infer ψ from $\{\eta\}$, then you may infer $(\varphi \wedge \psi)$ from $\{\eta\}$.

[19] A sentence (or 'closed sentence' for emphasis) is an open sentence with no free variables.

These rules suffice for the proof of Harris's theorem, so they pin down a unique semantic value for the operator. This is a surprising result, since the rules leave the rudimentary logical properties of the conjunction operator—notably, the principle that $(\varphi \wedge \psi)$ is a logical consequence of $\{\varphi, \psi\}$—unproved.[20] The explanation, I think, is that the weakest sentence within a given language that entails both φ and ψ might or might not play the semantic role of their conjunction, depending on the expressive power of the language. A sentence χ might be the weakest sentence that entails both φ and ψ merely because the language is impoverished, and it might be dislodged from this position, without any change in the meanings of φ, ψ, or χ, just by introducing into the language a new sentence of intermediate logical strength. To truly count as the conjunction of φ and ψ, it must entail both φ and ψ, and it must be weaker than any other sentence that does this, not only within the current language, but within any possible extension of the current language.

Absent a semantic theory, the notion of a possible extension of a language is hopelessly murky, but a good semantic theory clears things up nicely. Within a model, an individual constant names an individual, and one way to extend the language is to add new constants to designate heretofore unnamed individuals. An n-place predicate is satisfied by a collection of n-tuples, and one way to extend the language is by introducing a new predicate for a new collection of n-tuples. A formula with free variables $v_1, \ldots, v_n$ is satisfied by a collection of variable assignments with the property that, whenever two variable assignments assign the same values to each of the v_is, then both are in the collection if either is. If $\mathfrak{C}$ is such a collection of variable assignments, we can produce an atomic formula satisfied by $\mathfrak{C}$ by introducing an appropriate n-place predicate.

Given formulas φ and ψ and a model $\mathfrak{A}$, we can produce a formula θ that is satisfied, in $\mathfrak{A}$, by precisely the variable assignments that satisfy both φ and ψ. The formula we use doesn't depend on the model $\mathfrak{A}$, though its interpretation does, so we can think of θ as a formula that, within each model $\mathfrak{A}$ of the original language, is satisfied by precisely those variable assignments that satisfy both φ and ψ in $\mathfrak{A}$. Whether a variable assignment satisfies θ is determined, as we go from one model to another, by which variable assignments satisfy φ and ψ; so we should think of θ as logically complex, since the three formulas don't manifest the mutual logical independence we would expect if they were all atomic.[21] Any variable assignment that satisfies θ in a model also satisfies φ in that model, and so $\{\theta\}$ entails φ. $\{\theta\}$ likewise entails ψ, and so, since the third of the three rules for '$\wedge$' preserves entailment, $\{\theta\}$ entails $(\varphi \wedge \psi)$. Consequently, since any variable assignment that satisfies both φ and ψ in a model satisfies θ in that model, any such variable assignment also satisfies $(\varphi \wedge \psi)$. Since $\{(\varphi \wedge \psi)\}$ entails φ, any variable assignment that satisfies $(\varphi \wedge \psi)$ satisfies φ; similarly for ψ. Thus we get the expected satisfaction condition for conjunction: A variable assignment satisfies $(\varphi \wedge \psi)$ in a model if and only if it satisfies both φ and ψ.

[20] For a proof, see Koslow (1992), p. 129.

[21] Note that the implicational structure does not uniquely determine which formulas are to count as atomic.

The semantic value of a binary connective is a binary function that takes collections of model/variable-assignment pairs as inputs and yields a collection of model/variable-assignment pairs as outputs.[22] The first two rules for '$\wedge$' assure us that the output is included in each of the two inputs. The third rule, understood as open-ended, so that every collection of model/variable-assignment pairs is a possible semantic value of η, tells us that the output includes every collection that is included in both inputs. In other words, the output is the intersection of the two inputs, which is just what the classical semantics tells us. Given, in the background, the standard Tarskian semantics for the atomic formulas, the standard semantics for '$\wedge$' is forced upon us by the rules of inference.

Similar connections between semantics and rules can be found for the other standard sentential connectives, for '$=$', and for the quantifiers.[23] For '$\forall$', the validity of US ensures that, if a variable assignment σ satisfies $(\forall x)\varphi$ in $\mathfrak{A}$, then every variable assignment that agrees with σ except possible at x satisfies φ in $\mathfrak{A}$. The validity of UG establishes the converse.

The crucial step was at the very beginning, where we followed Tarski (1936) in defining a model to be what we get by assigning values of appropriate type to nonlogical constants. The usual definition of model begins by discerning a universe of discourse and then assigning values from within the universe of discourse (in ways appropriate to their types) as values of the nonlogical constants. In employing Tarski's simpler definition of 'model', the construction presupposed a fixed domain of discourse.[24] What it aimed to show was how observance of the rules establishes the same domain for the object language as for the metalanguage.

I am not, I want to insist, cheating. If I were proposing that our examination of the rules refuted skepticism, I would be blatantly assuming what I was trying to prove, but that's not the proposal. The argument against skepticism, to the extent there is one (I don't suppose it will convince the confirmed skeptic), is that our success in using the quantifiers to communicate creates a presumption in favor of deterministic hypotheses. The rule-based semantics is intended, not to repel skepticism, but to fill in part of a realist story, told from a realist point of view. For those who already are inclined to suppose that unabashedly unrestricted quantification is something we sometimes do, the narrative about the rules is intended to provide an idealized and stylized account of how we do it.

Tarski obtained his theory of truth in a model by generalizing methods he developed in (1935) for devising theories of truth *simpliciter*. His techniques provide truth theories for languages that are fully precise, so they are not directly applicable to our concerns here, where we are especially interested in languages that are imprecise. They are, it turns out, indirectly relevant. Bas van Fraassen (1966) and Kit

[22] There are constraints that reflect the requirement that whether a variable assignment satisfies a formula in a model only depends on the values it assigns to the variables that occur free in the formula.

[23] See McGee (2000) and (2002).

[24] Tarski's simpler-than-usual notion of model causes substantial difficulties for his analysis of logical truth and logical consequence. These difficulties are examined by Etchemendy (1990).

Fine (1975) made the remarkable discovery that Tarski's methods could be straightforwardly adapted to provide semantic theories for imprecise languages. Instead of providing a unique intended model for the language, usage provides a family of *acceptable* models, and a sentence counts as true, false, or unsettled according as it is true in all, none, or some but not all of them. Their methods allow indefiniteness in quantification as well as in naming and predication, there being no logical impediment to having the universe of discourse vary from one acceptable model to another. For situations in which our discourse is restricted to some imprecisely delimited domain—Milky Way quantification, for instance—this is the sensible procedure. Where we haven't done anything to restrict the domain, however, it would, I think, be a mistake to allow the domain to vary. The difference is that picking an extension of 'poor' is a matter of choosing, more or less arbitrarily, one undistinguished candidate from a vast array of equally plausible possibilities, whereas one candidate for the semantic value of '∀' stands apart from all the others.

An overdue correction: the realist thesis we've been developing upholds the possibility of fully comprehensive quantification that holds all things, of whatever sort, within its domain. Among the things we want to be able to talk about are collections. We would like, for example, to be able to discuss the merits of von Neumann's (1925) limitation-of-size principle, according to which things form a collection unless they can be put in one-one correspondence with the universe. However, the semantic theory we've been investigating tells us that the semantic value of a n-place predicate is a collection of n-tuples. But when we ask about the collection assigned to a binary predicate true of the pairs $< x, y >$, where y is a collection and x is not a element of y, we run headlong into Russell's paradox. Happily, George Boolos ((1984) and (1985)) has provided us a way to say the things we want to say without succumbing to paradox, by using plural noun phrases to take the place of talk about collections. For example, we shall say that things form a model if they meet these three conditions:[25]

Each of them is an ordered pair whose first component is a nonlogical term.
For any individual constant c, there is exactly one of them whose first component is c.
Each of them that has an n-place predicate as its first component has an n-tuple as its second component.

Unfortunately, the plural constructions, while lovely metaphysically, are quite cumbersome, so the practice I've followed here—first approximating what one wants to say while pretending that there aren't any things that don't form a collection, then indicating how the approximation can be cashed out in the official plural idiom—will, I hope, be forgiven.

We've been talking about first-order languages, but giving the semantics required us to employ plural quantification,[26] which is tantamount to second-order logic.[27] Typically, in fact, when we develop the semantic theory of a language, we require logical resources beyond what are available within the language itself. This is a deeply

[25] See Rayo and Uzquiano (1999).
[26] See Rayo and Williamson (2004).
[27] See Boolos (1985).

troubling phenomenon, but when we set the Liar paradox aside, we agreed not to worry about it here.

We've been working with first-order languages, but the languages we really care about are natural languages. Our hope was that the first-order languages, while obviously much, much simpler than natural languages, would nonetheless be rich enough in logical structure to provide some useful lessons when we turn to the more important project of trying to understand natural-language quantification. The thought was that everything we can do in the first-order language, we can do in a natural language, so, in particular, if one of the things we can achieve in the artificial language is unambiguously unrestricted quantification, then that's something we should expect to be able to accomplish in natural languages as well. There is, however, a sticking point: the role in the first-order theories of individual constants. Individual constants play in the formal language a role directly analogous to that of proper names in English, but individual constants always denote something—that's what validates US and EG—whereas proper names are often associated with fictional or mythological characters. EG isn't valid in English, since 'Frodo is a hobbit' does not entail 'There are hobbits'. The story is supposed to go that human beings are capable of learning and employing the artificial language, and that they can employ it in such a way that their quantifiers range over everything. If that story depends on the assumption that hypothetical speakers of the artificial language learn and use individual constants the same way that actual speakers of the natural language use proper names, then it breaks down at a crucial stage. We need a version of the story that doesn't depend of the analogy between individual constants and proper names.

Frege faced a similar problem in §11 of the *Grundgesetze.* He wanted to introduce a mechanism into his concept-writing that served the purposes definite description serves in German or English, but he wanted his *Begriffschrift* to be a logically perfect language, unblemished by nondenoting terms. Frege's solution was the simplest possible. In situations where the definite description is well-behaved, that is, situations in which there is one and only one φ, $(\iota x)\ \varphi(x)$ denotes that uniquely selected individual, whereas if the φs are none or many, the symbol designates an arbitrarily selected default value.

Following Frege's lead, we want to utilize definite descriptions, used in such a way that they are automatically guaranteed referents, to play the roles that have hitherto been played by proper names. To do this, it is not necessary that we identify a Fregean sense for each proper name. Following a suggestion of Quine (1948), we can introduce a new atomic predicate for each proper name, stipulating that the new predicate is to be true of exactly one thing, either the referent of the name, if it has one, or else the default value. To implement our plan, we need to do two things. First, we need to settle upon a default value or default values for the different descriptions. Second, we need to adopt appropriate rules to fix the inferential roles of the quantifiers and the definite description operators. We keep the familiar rules, US and EG, modified to allow other singular terms—in particular, definite descriptions—in addition to individual constants, and we modify UG and ES, as follows:

If you can derive $\psi((\iota x)\ \varphi(x))$ from Γ, and if the atomic predicate $\varphi(x)$ does not appear either in Γ or in ψ, then you may derive $(\forall x)\psi(x)$ from Γ.

If you can derive χ from $\Gamma \cup \{\psi((\iota x)\ \varphi(x))\}$, and if the atomic predicate $\varphi(x)$ does not appear in Γ, in $\psi(x)$, or in χ, then you may derive χ from $\Gamma \cup \{(\exists x)\psi(x)\}$.

In addition, we adopt rules for '(ιx)':

You may derive $(\psi((\iota x)\ \varphi(x)) \leftrightarrow (\forall x)(\varphi(x) \rightarrow \psi(x)))$ from $\{(\exists y)(\forall x)(\varphi(x) \leftrightarrow x = y)\}$.
You may derive $(\psi((\iota x)\varphi(x)) \leftrightarrow \psi(\text{Default Value}))$ from $\{\sim (\exists y)(\forall x)(\varphi(x) \leftrightarrow x = y)\}$.

Harris's argument shows that these rules, taken together, determine unique values for both quantifiers and for the definite description operator.

A cause of dissatisfaction here is that it presumes a uniquely determined referent for 'Default Value', and the inscrutability of reference arguments make us less than fully confident in this presumption. Moreover, even if we are able to pick out a unique referent, in order for this determination to count as logical, the chosen referent will have to be a logical object. Frege believed that there were such things as logical objects, but few have followed him here.

We don't really need the uniquely determined default value to accomplish the aim of affixing a unique semantic value to each quantifier. If we remove the rule involving the default value, we shall still have the following:

From $\{(\forall_1 x)\varphi(x)\}$, you may derive $(\forall_2 x)\varphi(x)$, and conversely.
From $\{(\exists_1 x)\varphi(x)\}$, you may derive $(\exists_2 x)\varphi(x)$, and conversely.
From $\{(\exists_i y)(\forall_i x)(\varphi(x) \leftrightarrow x = y)\}$, for $i = 1$ or 2, you may derive $(\iota_1 x)\varphi(x) = (\iota_2 x)\varphi(x)$.

In this more relaxed system, 'the present king of France' plays a similar role to 'the shortest tall man'. Assuming, for simplicity, that there are no exact ties in height, we can be sure of the truth of 'There is a tall man who is shorter than every other tall man'. We can be assured of its truth because it follows logically from 'There is at least one tall man', 'There are fewer than (say) fifty billion tall men', and the assumption that the men are ordered by height. It is determined that there is a shortest tall man because, on any way of drawing the border between men who satisfy 'tall' and those who satisfy 'not tall', there will be a shortest man of the tall side of the partition, but there isn't any individual of whom it is determined that he is the shortest tall man, because different ways of drawing the border select different candidates for 'the shortest tall man'. Similarly, 'E!$(\iota x)x$ is now king of France' is determinated to be true, because '$(\iota x)x$ is now king of France' is assigned a unique value by any plan for assigning default values to defective definite descriptions, but different plans pick out different default values, so there isn't any individual of whom it is determined that '$(\iota x)x$ is now king of France' refers to him.

Let me end this paper on a defensive note. I have been sketching a crude account of how rules of inference fix the meanings of the logical terms. I hope that you find it attractive. But if you don't, I would urge you respond by looking about for a better story, perhaps one closer to natural language and less dependent on formalistic toy models. What I hope you will not do is succumb to the skeptical doctrine that the fact that 'everything' means everything is an inexplicable brute fact that can't be accounted for by the way speakers use the word. Communication by language is too central a feature of the human experience for us willingly to relegate its causes to a realm of mystery.

REFERENCES

Barwise, Jon, and Robin Cooper (1981) 'Generalized Quantifiers and Natural Language', *Linguistics and Philosophy* 4: 159–218.

Belnap, Nuel, Jr. (1962) 'Tonk, Plonk and Plink', *Analysis* 22: 130–4.

Benacerraf, Paul, and Hilary Putnam (1983) *Philosophy of Mathematics*, 2nd edn. Cambridge: Cambridge University Press.

Boolos, George S. (1984) 'To Be is to Be a Value of a Variable (or to Be Some Values of Some Variables)', *Journal of Philosophy* 81: 430–39. Reprinted in Boolos (1998), pp. 54–72.

——(1985) 'Nominalist Platonism', *Philosophical Review* 94: 327–44. Reprinted in Boolos (1998), pp. 73–87.

——(1998) *Logic, Logic, and Logic*. Cambridge, MA, and London: Harvard University Press.

Davidson, Donald (1967) 'The Logical Form of Action Sentences', in Nicholas Rescher, (ed.), *The Logic of Decision and Action*. Pittsburgh: University of Pittsburgh Press, pp. 81–95. Reprinted in Davidson (2001), pp. 105–21.

——(2001) *Essays on Actions and Events*, 2nd edn. Oxford: Oxford University Press.

Etchemendy, John (1990) *The Concept of Logical Consequence*. Cambridge, MA: Harvard University Press.

Evans, Gareth (1982) *The Varieties of Reference*. Oxford: Clarendon Press.

Field, Hartry (1986) 'The Deflationary Conception of Truth', in Graham MacDonald and Crispin Wright, (eds.), *Fact, Science, and Value*. Oxford: Blackwell, pp. 55–117.

——1994 'Deflationary Views of Meaning and Content', *Mind* 103: 249–85. Reprinted in Field (2001), pp. 104–40.

——2001 *Truth and the Absence of Fact*. Oxford: Clarendon Press.

Fine, Kit. (1975) 'Vagueness, Truth, and Logic', *Synthese* 30: 265–300. Reprinted in Keefe and Smith (1996), pp. 119–50.

Frege, Gottlob (1892) *Grundgesetze der Arithmetik*, vol. 1. Olms: Hildesheim. Partially reprinted in Frege (1964).

——(1964) *The Basic Laws of Arithmetic*, trans. by Montgomery Furth. Berkeley and Los Angeles: University of California Press.

Gödel, Kurt (1944) 'Russell's Mathematical Logic', in P. A. Schilpp, (ed.), *The Philosophy of Bertrand Russell*. Evanston and Chicago: Northwestern University Press, pp. 123–53. Reprinted in Benacerraf and Putnam (1983), pp. 447–69, and in Gödel (1990), pp. 102–43.

——(1990) *Collected Works*, vol. 2. Oxford and New York: Oxford University Press.

Harris, J. H. (1982) 'What's So Logical About the Logical Axioms?' *Studia Logica* 41: 159–71.

Henkin, Leon (1950) 'Completeness in the Theory of Types', *Journal of Symbolic Logic* 15: 81–91.

Horwich, Paul (1990) *Truth*. Oxford: Blackwell.

Keefe, Rosanna, and Peter Smith, (eds.) (1996) *Vagueness: A Reader*. Cambridge, MA, and London: MIT Press.

Koslow, Arnold (1992) *A Structuralist Theory of Logic*. Cambridge and New York: Cambridge University Press.

Lavine, Shaughan. (Forthcoming.) *Skolem Was Wrong*.

Leeds, Stephen (1978) 'Theories of Truth and Reference', *Erkenntnis* 13: 111–129.

____(1995) 'Truth, Correspondence, and Success', *Philosophical Studies* 79: 1–36.

Mates, Benson (1972) *Elementary Logic*, 2nd edn. Oxford and New York: Oxford University Press.

McGee, Vann (2000) 'Everything', in Gila Sher and Richard Tieszen, (eds.), *Between Logic and Intuition*. New York and Cambridge: Cambridge University Press, 2000, pp. 54–78.

____(2002) 'Ramsey and the Correspondence Theory', in Volker Halbach and Leon Horstein, (eds.), *Principles of Truth*. Frankfurt: Hänsel-Hohenhausen, pp. 153–67.

____(2004) 'Ramsey's Dialetheism', in Graham Priest, J. C. Beall, and Bradley Armour-Garb, (eds.) *The Law of Non-Contradiction*. Oxford: Oxford University Press, pp. 276–91.

____(2005) 'Two Conceptions of Truth?' *Philosophical Studies* 124: 71–104.

McGee, Vann, and Brian P. McLaughlin (1998) Review of Timothy Williamson's *Vagueness*. *Linguistics and Philosophy* 21: 221–35.

____(2004) 'Logical Commitment: A Reply to Williamson', *Linguistics and Philosophy* 27: 123–36.

Putnam, Hilary (1980) 'Models and Reality', *Journal of Symbolic Logic* 45: 464–82. Reprinted in Benacerraf and Putnam (1983), pp. 421–44. Page references are to the reprint.

Quine, Willard van Orman (1948) 'On What There Is', *Review of Metaphysics* 2: 21–8. Reprinted in Quine (1980), pp. 1–19.

____(1960) *Word and Object*. Cambridge, MA: MIT Press.

____(1970) *Philosophy of Logic*, 2nd edn. Cambridge, MA, and London: Harvard University Press.

____(1980) *From a Logical Point of View*, 2nd edn. Cambridge, MA: Harvard University Press.

Ramsey, Frank Plumpton (1925) 'The Foundations of Mathematics', *Proceedings of the London Mathematical Society* 25: 338–84. Reprinted in Ramsey (1931), pp. 1–61.

____(1929) 'Theories', in Ramsey (1931), pp. 212–36, and in Ramsey (1990), pp. 112–39.

____(1931) *The Foundations of Mathematics and Other Logical Essays*. London: Routledge and Kegan Paul.

____(1990) *Philosophical Papers*. Cambridge: Cambridge University Press.

Rayo, Agustín, and Gabriel Uzquiano (1999) 'Toward a Theory of Second-Order Consequence,' *Notre Dame Journal of Formal Logic* 40: 315–25.

____and Timothy Williamson (2004) 'A Completeness Theorem for Unrestricted First-Order Languages', in J. C. Beall, (ed.), *Liars and Heaps*. Oxford: Oxford University Press, pp. 331–56.

Schiffer, Stephen (1987) *Remnants of Meaning*. Cambridge, MA: MIT Press.

Tarski, Alfred (1935) 'Der Wahrheitsbegriff in den formalisierten Sprachen', *Studia Philosophica* 1: 261–405. English translation by J. H. Woodger in Tarski (1983), pp. 152–278.

____(1936) 'Über den Begriff der logischen Folgerung', *Actes du Congrès International de Philosophie Scientifique* 7: 1–11. English trans. by J. H. Woodger in Tarski (1983), pp. 409–20.

____(1983) *Logic, Semantics, Metamathematics*, 2nd edn. Indianapolis: Hackett.

Tolkien, J. R. R. (1993) *The Lord of the Rings*, 2nd edn. 3 vols. Boston: Houghton Mifflin.

van Fraassen, Bas C. (1966) 'Singular Terms, Truth-Value Gaps, and Free Logic', *Journal of Philosophy* 63: 481–95.

van Heijenoort, Jean (1967) *From Frege to Gödel.* Cambridge, MA, and London: Harvard University Press.

Von Neumann, John (1925) 'Eine Axiomatisierung der Megelehre', *Journal für die reine und angewandte Mathematik* 154: 219–40. English trans. by Stefan Bauer-Mengelberg in van Heijenoort (1967), pp. 393–413.

Whitehead, Alfred North, and Bertrand Russell (1927) *Principia Mathematica,* 2nd edn. 3 vols. Cambridge and New York: Cambridge University Press.

Williamson, Timothy (1994) *Vagueness.* New York: Routledge.

—— (2004) 'Reply to McGee and McLaughlin', *Linguistics and Philosophy* 27: 113–22.

Zermelo, Ernst (1908) 'Untersuchungen über die Grundlagen der Mengenlehre', *Mathematische Annalen* 65: 261–81. English trans. by Stefan Bauer-Mengelberg in van Heijenoort (1967), pp. 199–215.

8

The Problem of Absolute Universality[1]

Charles Parsons

8.1

Very often, when we make general statements, there is an explicit or contextually understood restriction. 'All ravens are black' is a generalization about ravens. It is now standardly understood as applying a quantifier restricted to ravens to the predicate 'is black'. We can read it as not saying anything about objects other than ravens. When leaving an airplane with my wife, she might ask, 'Were you sure to take everything?' Clearly that refers to the possessions I brought onto the plane (and perhaps such of hers as she took me to be responsible for). So a negative answer would not be implied by my not having taken the in-flight magazine or the airsickness bag from the pocket in front of my seat.

It is probable that most generalizations made in everyday life and even in scientific inquiry can be understood as restricted in this way. In logic, mathematics, and philosophy things are not so simple. Timothy Williamson quotes F. H. Bradley as describing metaphysics as 'the effort to comprehend the universe, not simply piecemeal or by fragments, but somehow as a whole'.[1] Williamson reasonably asks how we could comprehend the universe as a whole, if a contextual restriction made some parts irrelevant.[2] The universe of such a metaphysician's purview surely includes everything, with no restriction tacit or otherwise. Logic might at first sight seem to envision only restricted generalizations. We interpret the language of quantificational logic with respect to a domain or 'universe of discourse' (in the case of higher-order logic, a domain of individuals and then further domains for the higher-order variables). Typically, the domain is a set, and set theory tells us how, given a set, to describe a set containing elements not in the first set.[3] In a sense, the received way

1 Earlier versions of this chapter were presented as a paper as the Reichenbach Lecture at UCLA on June 4, 2004, and at the conference on Mathematical Knowledge at Fitzwilliam College, Cambridge, on July 2. Later versions were presented at the Hebrew University of Jerusalem, and the University of California, Riverside and Irvine. I am grateful to the members of the audiences and to the editors for their comments. Individuals are acknowledged in footnotes below. I am also much indebted to Michael Glanzberg, who presents a view congenial to my own in his (2004).

2 (1893), p. 1. 3 (2003), p. 415.

4 Of course there are variant set theories allowing a universal set. I will leave them out of account for the moment. The relevance, or lack of it, of taking the domain to be a proper class will emerge as we proceed.

of interpreting quantificational logic takes all the quantifiers to be restricted. It is significant, however, that the restriction arises at the meta-level, with the interpretation, and is not explicitly given in the sentences themselves.

However, logic seems to give us some outright statements, of which we want to say they are simply true. In first-order logic, only identity could occur essentially in such a statement, but that still leaves examples, such as 'Everything is self-identical', $\forall x(x = x)$. Quine offered this as an example of an especially obvious logical truth. But then surely it is supposed to mean that *everything* is self-identical. If there is a contextually understood restriction, it is hard to imagine what it could be. Similarly, identity is symmetric, $\forall x \forall y(x = y \rightarrow y = x)$. No matter what x and y may be, if $x = y$ then $y = x$.

It seems that more humdrum examples can be cited of statements whose quantifiers are unrestricted and might be presumed to range over absolutely everything. One type would be statements of nonexistence. There are no unicorns. Suppose 'there are' ranges over some domain D. Then it seems that the statement might be true even though somehow there is a unicorn outside D. But it will be protested that the statement says there are no unicorns *period*, and thus the hypothesized unicorn would be a counterexample. That would imply that either we were wrong in supposing that the domain is D, or D includes the counterexample. Can we exclude this outcome short of admitting a D that is absolutely everything?

Mathematics is at first sight a domain where quantification is more or less restricted. Generalizations are over number systems, spaces, algebraic structures, sets, categories, and the like. A situation where quantification purporting to be over absolutely everything arises in mathematics would be somewhat artificial. But suppose for the moment that all mathematical objects are sets and furthermore (apparently trivially) that sets are mathematical objects. Then non-mathematical objects are not sets and so must be urelements in the technical sense of set theory. Now it seems that we might understand the quantifiers of the usual language of set theory as ranging over absolutely everything. On our hypothesis, whatever is true in set theory with urelements that does not depend on the number of the latter will be true on this interpretation.[4]

A second way in which mathematics touches on our question is the universal applicability of mathematics, or at least of some branches such as arithmetic. Frege famously insisted that it should be a constraint on any analysis of number that objects of any kind should be countable. The domain of what is countable is 'the most comprehensive of all; for it is not only what is actual, not only what is intuitable, that belongs to it, but everything thinkable'.[5] If Frege's thesis is correct, then mathematics is brought into relation with everything there is. It seems that reference to absolutely everything is needed even to state the thesis.

[5] If there is a definite number (presumably infinite) of non-mathematical objects, then of course it will also be true that there is that number of urelements.

[6] *Grundlagen* §14; cf. §24 and (1885), p. 94. In the latter text he makes the qualification that 'a certain sharpness of circumscription' is required; he evidently means that concepts to which number is attributed must have sharp boundaries.

It also turns out that the logical problems that have been raised about generalizations covering absolutely everything already arise in mathematics before the issues about application that underlie the above remarks, since if quantification over everything is problematic on logical grounds, then so is quantification over all sets, or possibly even talk of 'the universe of sets', which set theorists engage in rather freely.

How can one characterize the statements an inquiry about absolute generality is about? Try the following: call a statement an absolute generalization if it is of the form $(Qx)Fx$ where the variables range over absolutely everything. However, normally when we talk of what variables range over, we are describing a domain that they range over. One might object that there is no domain comprising absolutely everything, on roughly the grounds on which standard set theory rejects a universal set. Although replies to this objection can be made, it may be that it is not possible to give a characterization of the statements that concern us that is neutral on questions about absolute generality that will be contested.

Natural language gives us conflicting signals about whether generalization covering absolutely everything is a normal part of the expressive resources of a language. On the one hand the determiners that express quantifiers call for a noun phrase that typically gives rise to a restriction. On the other hand, this syntactic condition can be fulfilled by the 'thing' in 'everything' or 'something' or by a word like 'object' or 'entity'. Although there may still be a contextually indicated restriction, as in the example with which I began, it is not obvious that such is required. The word 'thing' is often used so that much is excluded from the realm of things, but it is doubtful that such an exclusion is intended in the context 'everything'; for example, logicians, in saying that everything is self-identical, don't intend to leave out such non-things as persons. One could express this by saying that 'everything' doesn't mean 'every thing'.[6] 'Object' is in most usage more general than 'thing', but conceptions of 'entities' that are not objects have had defenders, notably Frege.

8.2

One might ask how one could possibly doubt that we make meaningful statements about absolutely everything. The principal reasons are logical, and we will come to them shortly. First, however, I want to deal with a problem of a more metaphysical character. Metaphysicians differ about what there is. That is neither news nor especially interesting. What seems to me a potential problem is that if our quantifiers can really capture everything in some absolute sense, then some form of what Hilary Putnam calls 'metaphysical realism' seems to follow.[7] As I understand it that is that there is some final answer to the question what objects there are and how they are individuated.

7 Working in other languages, we might not even be tempted to think that it does; for example, 'everything' and 'every thing' would be rendered in German as 'alles' and 'jedes Ding'.

8 The kind of view I have in mind may not be incompatible with some forms of idealism, because the question is whether there is an absolute reality accessible to the human mind, not whether this reality is in the end independent of the mind in whatever sense is relevant to realism. I have

Doubts about this are suggested by simple metaphysical examples. We might describe objects and their properties in the straightforward way, so that to monadic predicates correspond properties, and an object's having a property is a sort of brute fact. Alternatively, we might view an object as consisting of parts some of which are abstract and, we might say, property-like. Among the parts of my shirt, for example, is its particular color, which would differ from the color-part of another shirt that was, in ordinary parlance, of exactly the same color. Then for objects *a* and *b* to have exactly the same color is for *a* and *b* to have color-parts that are exactly similar. Parts of this kind are, following Donald Williams, now usually called tropes.[8] It is at least plausible that we could describe the world in the language of objects and properties and instantiation of the latter by the former, and equally in the language of objects, tropes, and their resemblance. Now consider the statement 'There are tropes.' On the first scheme it appears to be false, on the second a trivial truth.

To be sure 'Are there tropes?' is just what Carnap called an external question. We could avoid this by using as our example a particular situation described differently in the two schemes. But we might consider the implications of invoking Carnap's distinction. It certainly implies a rejection of metaphysical realism, since external questions are addressed by choosing a linguistic framework, and different frameworks will postulate different kinds of objects. According to the property framework, tropes don't exist, and according to the trope framework, properties don't exist. Does that mean that the quantifiers of a particular framework cannot really capture everything? To do this seems to require an overarching framework that encompasses the ontology of all. But in the absence of such a framework, the Carnapian perspective shows something nonabsolute about the quantifiers in a given framework, since by going to another we can envisage objects of which the first framework knows nothing.

Our problem is that for statements of an absolutely general kind to have a definite truth-value, it appears that there has to be a final answer to the question what objects there are, when they are identical and different, and what their properties and relations are. That is metaphysical realism. I don't want to enter into the arguments against such a view advanced by Putnam and others.[9]

There is, however, a reason why this conclusion might be questioned. In our example there seemed to be an equivalence between the language of properties and the language of tropes. What we could say in one, we could find a way of saying in the other. It follows that given sufficient logical resources, each way of talking could

little knowledge of British idealism, but it seems to me that Bradley and probably McTaggart were metaphysical realists in the sense that concerns me.

I do assume in the discussion in this section that our logic is classical, as Crispin Wright pointed out. I have trouble understanding what metaphysical realism would be in the context of intuitionistic logic, but the issue would require further discussion.

[9] Williams (1953). Williams borrowed the word from Santayana while changing its meaning; see p. 115. The concept is much older, going back to Edmund Husserl and G. F. Stout; it probably descends from the traditional notion of accident.

[10] Glanzberg (2004) argues that a view of absolute quantification of the general kind advanced in this paper is not incompatible with metaphysical realism. What he denies is that metaphysical realism implies that quantifiers have a straightforward absolute reading, i.e. the converse of the claim made in this section.

reconstruct the other. A trope, for example, could be a pair of an object and a property (possibly a very refined property). Even if such constructions are highly artificial, they do give a framework a claim to embrace everything without making claims of nonexistence that are certain to be contested. But would a view that allowed alternative equivalent descriptions, each of which is able to construct the entities postulated by the other, really be a metaphysical realism in the sense that concerns us? That is less important than the question whether such equivalent comprehensive descriptions actually exist. The mere fact of the possibility of construction is not sufficient, since constructions that may be offered will not necessarily satisfy the metaphysical intuitions that drive the alternative framework. That's a reason for thinking that even if this possibility gives us a way of talking about everything in the world that does not commit us to metaphysical realism, even making sense of it gets us into heavy-duty metaphysics.

The Carnapian point of view suggests a distinction that will turn out to be important. Within a Carnapian framework, there is nothing to prevent our having quantifiers of maximal range, i.e. such that anything that can be recognized as a term with reference can be instantiated for them and is a potential counterexample to a universal statement or witness for an existential one. Together with our observation that natural language contains quantifier expressions where there is no noun phrase that restricts them, and at least some cases where there is on the surface at least no restriction given by the context, it suggests that we do encounter quantifiers that are *unrestricted.* That a quantifier is unrestricted, however, is not the same as its being absolute.[10] Just what the relativity might be remains to be explored. On the Carnapian view, an alternative framework can recognize potential values of variables that a given framework does not, and it may be a pragmatic question which framework to adopt. In general there will be alternatives. Some might be extensions of the given one, in the sense that there will be a natural interpretation of the first in the second, so that the entities of the first are a proper subclass of those of the second. When I talk of interpretations or purported interpretations that treat the quantifiers as ranging over absolutely everything, I will call them absolute or absolutely unrestricted.

8.3

I have suggested that the discussion of our question has been driven not by the sort of consideration suggested in the last section but by logical difficulties. Although reasons of this kind are not difficult to articulate, it is not so easy to say what they are supposed to show. But they arise from considering how sentences or discourses containing quantifiers are interpreted. This apparently innocent talk of interpretation turns out to have considerable weight.

We might first consider the strongest conclusion, that contrary to appearances there is simply no such thing as quantification over absolutely everything, that in

[11] The importance of this distinction was urged by Kit Fine in a seminar at Harvard University in the fall of 2003.

order to make sense of any generalization we would have to understand its reach as falling short of that, so that even unrestricted quantifiers have a relative character, as the Carnapian view just canvassed suggests. This conclusion seems to differ from the ostensibly weaker one that absolute quantification is in some way illegitimate or logically mistaken. But if it is genuinely possible to speak about absolutely everything, how could it be illegitimate or mistaken to do so? It can't be that any such statement is false, because if so its negation is true and still contains quantifiers ranging over absolutely everything.[11]

A more natural reading of the weaker view is that statements that purport or attempt to quantify over absolutely everything miss their mark; either they are meaningless or sense can be made of them only by interpreting their quantifiers as covertly restricted, contrary perhaps to the intentions of the speakers who make them. Then there is no real difference between the strong conclusion and its apparent weakening.

Something like the strong conclusion was affirmed by Michael Dummett in *Frege: Philosophy of Language*. In another place Dummett went so far as to say that this was the consensus view among modern logicians:

> The overwhelming majority of logicians . . . do not think it possible to quantify over all objects whatever.[12]

However, Dummett's affirmation of the strong conclusion is not quite so unqualified as that statement suggests, as we shall see later.

We can see how one might be driven in that direction by considering the usual semantics for first-order logic. Quantifiers are interpreted as ranging over some domain, and predicates by subsets of the domain or its Cartesian product with itself some finite number of times. The domain is understood to be a set. But then, as we have pointed out already, in standard set theory it cannot be universal. If we were to use instead a variant set theory with a universal set, then we would have to restrict the axiom of separation, which is what insures that we have an interpretation for every predicate of objects in the domain.

The semantic definitions of logical validity and consequence have often been thought to lack generality because of this feature of the usual semantics. A natural remedy would be to allow that the domain might be a proper class. The usual theories of classes allow them to be closed under first-order definability, so that classes will be available to interpret predicates, but with more restrictions since we cannot freely postulate arbitrary subclasses of the domain. If the domain is to include absolutely everything, moreover, we will have a problem in designing a theory so that these classes will also fall into the domain.

[12] It may still be held that there are no true absolutely universal statements, but there are true absolute existential statements. That is highly implausible; if we can really understand 'Everything is self-identical' as about absolutely everything, how can we reject it? That example also makes it implausible to hold that we cannot know absolutely universal statements although we can know absolute existential statements.

[13] Dummett (1981a), p. 229. As we shall see, this is not Dummett's most careful formulation. For calling such passages of Dummett to my attention, I am indebted to Cartwright (1994), p. 2.

However, the difficulty does not come specifically from the notion of set or class. Semantic interpretation typically works by assigning objects to the parts of a sentence; the domain is an object so assigned to the quantifiers. Any such assignment runs into a limitation dramatized by Russell's paradox. Suppose that to one-place predicates are assigned objects $(\mathrm{O}x)Fx$. In application there will be some copula-like expression η so that 'Fa' is equivalent to '$a\ \eta\ (\mathrm{O}x)Fx$'. (I will call this the basic equivalence.) The familiar form of this schema is where $(\mathrm{O}x)Fx$ is the (alleged) set or class of x's such that Fx, and η means 'is an element of'. But $(\mathrm{O}x)Fx$ could be the property of being an F, and we could read η simply as 'has'. Or $(\mathrm{O}x)Fx$ could be what Frege calls the concept F (which of course is by his lights an object), and η would be read 'falls under'. But if we suppose that the predicate η is in the language, then we obtain Russell's paradox by considering $(\mathrm{O}x)\neg(x\ \eta\ x)$, since if t is that term, we have

$$t\ \eta\ (\mathrm{O}x)\neg(x\ \eta\ x) \text{ iff} \neg(t\ \eta\ t), \text{ i.e. } t\ \eta\ t \text{ iff} \neg(t\ \eta\ t).$$

Of course the paradox admits of a number of ways out. If $(\mathrm{O}x)Fx$ is what is assigned to F by the standard set-theoretic semantics, then $(\mathrm{O}x)\neg(x\eta x)$ does not belong to the domain of the interpretation, so that the quantifiers are not absolutely unrestricted. An alternative would be to say that there is no such object as $(\mathrm{O}x)Fx$ or to say that in some cases the equivalence of 'Fa' and '$a\ \eta\ (\mathrm{O}x)Fx$' fails. Suppose, for example, that the only relevant objects are sets and classes. Then there is no set of all objects that are not elements of themselves or even a set of all such sets, but we can admit a class of all sets that are not elements of themselves. But if we admit a class of all objects, sets, classes, or otherwise, that are not elements of themselves, then it must either fail to satisfy the basic equivalence (which seems contrary to the specification) or not be in the range of our variables. But then it is not the class of absolutely all such objects.

One can object to drawing the strong conclusion from even the full generality of the Russellian paradox on the ground that our notion of interpretation is ontologically loaded in a way that it seems possible to avoid. We have assumed that interpretation proceeds by assigning *objects* to linguistic structures. One discussion of our question challenges forcefully the assumption that in understanding quantification we must understand the domain as an object that in some way comprehends the objects in it. Commenting on a remark of Frank Drake, Richard Cartwright writes:

> The general principle appears to be that to quantify over certain objects is to presuppose that these objects constitute a 'collection' or a 'completed collection'—some one thing of which those objects are members. I call this the All-in-One Principle.[13]

The principle is not just the assumption that if we quantify over certain objects we can identify a single object of which they can be said to be *in some sense* members. That might be done in a trivial way. Evidently what Cartwright has in mind is that the object should be set-like in that the relation of membership satisfies principles close

[14] (1994), p. 7.

to those of set theory.[14] In fact he canvasses some assumptions, mostly from set theory, by which the all-in-one principle leads to the rejection of absolute quantification. The further assumption the argument from Russell's paradox made was that there is a general assignment of objects to linguistic expressions, predicates included, from which truth-conditions could be constructed.

Cartwright himself seems sometimes to permit himself such an object as the all-in-one principle would call for, as when he talks of 'the universe of discourse' over which one is quantifying. I think, however, that he sees a way out of recognizing reference to an object here, since more often he uses the plural, as when he writes:

> It is generally agreed that *the members of any non-empty set* can simultaneously be the values of the variables of a first-order language. But the disputed proposition extends to the case in which *the objects in question* do not constitute a set.[15]

He also uses other non-singular phrases, such as 'any objects there are' (p. 2). The relevance of the plural to our question will be considered in Section 8.4.

In an earlier paper, I interpreted the generality of Russell's paradox just pointed to as an intrinsic limitation on the 'method of nominalization' for generalizing over the places in language occupied by predicates.[16] In the present context, where the problem arises from ontologically loaded notions of interpretation, it is natural to look for less loaded notions of interpretation along the lines of what I there called the method of semantic ascent (obviously following Quine). That is, we would characterize truth-conditions directly in an inductive manner. Sticking to a first-order language for simplicity, the domain is given by a predicate in the language in which the interpretation is formulated, and predicates are interpreted by translation (which of course may be homophonic). Such a paradigm of interpretation is familiar from the writings of Donald Davidson. For our purposes we need not concern ourselves with the epistemological problems that drive his notion of 'radical interpretation'. But you will recall that in early papers motivating his program he argued that meanings as objects were not helpful for his theoretical purposes. Though the issues were quite different, that should remind us that there might be reasons independent of our present problem for preferring less ontologically loaded notions of interpretation.

On such a conception, there seems to be no obstacle to choosing as a domain predicate something trivial like '$x = x$', so that we don't allow ourselves to introduce objects that we don't attribute to the ontology of the language we are interpreting. We may need to have some mathematical objects such as at least finite sequences, but if the question is whether the domain of the object language includes absolutely everything, we can freely assume it includes what we need. But we have a predicate that does the work of η, namely 'true of', or, if we need to deal with predicates of arbitrary numbers of places, Tarski's 'satisfies'.

[15] The mention of a 'completed collection' is misleading, since it seems to rule out the intended sense of quantification in intuitionistic mathematics. But Cartwright's arguments do not turn on that.

[16] Ibid., pp. 2–3, emphasis mine. [17] (1982), §5.

We then find, apparently miraculously, that there is no obstacle to correlating an object with each predicate of the language. For a one-place predicate F, $(\mathrm{O}x)Fx$ might as well be F itself, so that 'a η $(\mathrm{O}x)Fx$' is just 'F is true of a', and the basic equivalence is a case of Tarski's truth schema (more properly, satisfaction schema). Evidently nothing requires us to take the domain as less than absolutely everything, unless the quantifiers used in our own interpretation fall short of absoluteness. Although the all-in-one principle as Cartwright intended it is not satisfied, the more trivial variant is, where the object is just the open sentence '$x = x$'.

In this case our version of 'Russell's paradox' reduces to a familiar semantic paradox, in effect the 'heterological' paradox. But in a classical interpretation 'satisfies' and therefore 'true of' are not in the language interpreted. That was one of the options regarding η mentioned above. So the interpretation does require 'ideology' not present in the language interpreted, but it does not require an expansion of ontology. So far so good for the idea that the domain of the variables includes absolutely everything.

Matters may become more difficult, however, if one tries to generalize about interpretation.[17] Suppose we consider only interpretations of the form just mentioned, where we introduce a predicate for the domain and translate the expressions of the language interpreted by expressions of the same syntactic type. Experience in other areas, such as understanding schemata in mathematics such as induction and separation, tells us that what counts as a 'predicate' is open-ended and sensitive to our ontology.[18] The familiar examples of the latter come from mathematics; what counts as an instance of the schemata of separation and replacement in set theory depends on what values are admitted for parameters, and also what the quantifiers in an instance range over. If we assume that we understand quantification over absolutely all sets, then of course we will understand what an instance of (first-order) separation or replacement is. Any set (and any of whatever urelements are admitted) can be a value of a parameter.

If we consider interpretations themselves to be objects, then we will face the difficulties that we faced with the ontologically loaded notion of interpretation, as both Williamson and Michael Glanzberg have pointed out. Can actual paradox be generated when one has the notion of truth under an interpretation? Evidently so if the interpretation assigns objects to predicates so that the usual satisfaction condition holds; that was one of the versions of Russell's paradox mentioned above. Can we weaken this assumption? An attempt to do so in earlier versions of this chapter was unsuccessful.[19] I am not sure whether the assumption can be weakened in a decisive

[18] This may be needed to define notions of semantic validity and consequence, as the editors point out. I do not propose any particular treatment, because what is appropriate will depend on further particulars about the language. If it is first-order and contains arithmetic, then (following Bolzano and Quine) we can define a sentence as valid if it remains true on every uniform substitution of nonlogical terms. In this case, we do not really have to generalize about interpretations.

[19] The first-order separation scheme might seem quite adequate for all the purposes of set theory. Even if so, what counts as an instance depends on the values that can be taken by parameters. These can be arbitrary sets, so that the same problem arises as with the notion of 'all sets'.

[20] This was the so-called 'superliar paradox' of my (1974), p. 251. The example is a sentence that says of itself that it is not true under any interpretation. If we model the notion of truth under

way, completely cutting loose from the idea of assigning objects to predicates. The different versions of the liar paradox do so, but it is not obvious how they bear on our present problem.

However, a version of the Russellian paradox due to Williamson is instructive.[20] Recall that even the Davidsonian paradigm of interpretation led to an assignment of objects to predicates, although in that case the assignment seemed to bear no logical weight. Imagine that our language contains a schematic one-place predicate P, which can be interpreted freely. In English 'Px' might be expressed as 'x is one of them'. Then if F is any predicate we can formulate, it seems we can form an interpretation I, call it $I(F)$, so that for any x

(1) P is true of x according to $I(F) \leftrightarrow Fx$.

But we can define a predicate R by the condition

(2) $Rx \leftrightarrow \neg(P$ is true of x according to $x)$.

But then by (1) and (2)

(3) P is true of x according to $I(R) \leftrightarrow \neg(P$ is true of x according to $x)$.

Taking $I(R)$ as the value of x

(4) P is true of $I(R)$ according to $I(R) \leftrightarrow \neg(P$ is true of $I(R)$ according to $I(R))$.

This is a contradiction.[21]

In the application of the simple Russell paradox to Davidsonian interpretation, the natural conclusion was the Tarskian one, that 'true of' is not in the language interpreted. There one could go on to interpret the metalanguage, with a new predicate 'true of'. In Williamson's setting, this response can be resisted, since now we are taking interpretations themselves to be objects in the range of the variables. If we really capture all interpretations in an absolute sense, why should we not have a perfectly general notion of truth under an interpretation? But it is those two assumptions that lead to a contradiction in Williamson's argument.

In the usual Liar paradox we can pass to a more comprehensive scheme of interpretation and say that, although what I said was not true under the scheme underlying its

an interpretation by the set-theoretic notion of truth in a model, then the formal sentence that says of itself that it is true in no model can be refuted by a simple argument using the reflection principle. But the turning of the tables leading to a derivation of the sentence that is characteristic of Strengthened Liar examples would be possible on this modeling only in an inconsistent extension of ZF. These considerations suggest that the original informal example is simply false. I think the transmission back to the informal example of the formal refutation has some plausibility, but I do not insist on it. (I am indebted to Byeong-Uk Yi and especially Hartley Slater for pointing out difficulties in my presentation of this example in the UCLA and Cambridge lectures.)

[21] (2003), p. 426. In presenting his paradox, I have adjusted the terminology to fit my own.

[22] It is natural to take 'P is true of x according to y' to imply that y is an interpretation. However, we might not assume this and replace (1) by the conditional whose antecedent is '$I(F)$ is an interpretation' and whose consequent is (1). Then the conclusion of the argument is that $I(R)$ is not an interpretation.

use of 'true', it is true (or, depending on the example, false) under a more comprehensive scheme. One way we might do this in the face of Williamson's paradox is to admit that the interpretation $I(R)$ was not in the range of the quantifiers, so that their range falls short of absoluteness. Resisting this conclusion forces us to take the Tarskian view now about the predicate 'P is true of x according to I'. That amounts again to saying that we have determinate quantification over absolutely all interpretations but do not have an equally general notion of truth under an interpretation. One way of making sense of this is not congenial to the friends of absolute quantification: the objects playing the role of 'interpretations' are proxies in some model of interpretation, possibly even chosen from a clearly restricted domain.

It is instructive to consider what happens with interpretations of the sort usually considered in formal semantics, which we have called ontologically loaded. Suppose, to begin with, that interpretations are models in the usual set-theoretic sense, and 'P is true of x according to M' is just a case of satisfaction in a model and is definable in set theory. However, (1) holds only for x in the domain of M, and since it is easy to see that $I(R)$ cannot be in the domain, no paradox ensues. That illustrates what we already know, that the set-theoretic notion of model will not satisfy the demand for interpretations with domain absolutely everything, or even all sets. One could expect a similar result if interpretations are objects of another kind such that the theory of them allows definition of the notions of truth and satisfaction under an interpretation.

A more natural reading has the result that 'all interpretations' behaves in many ways like 'all sets'. The interpretation function yielding $I(R)$ will not be a set, since its domain comprehends all sets, so that it does not fall under the original set-theoretic concept of interpretation. Thus even given absolute quantification over sets, the informal concept of interpretation extends beyond the one that is modeled set-theoretically. This situation is familiar from G. Kreisel's well-known remarks about the intuitive notion of logical validity and the completeness of first-order logic.[22]

The friends of absolute quantification owe us a resolution of the tension between quantification over all interpretations and the absence of a determinate notion of truth under an interpretation. One way of putting the point is that the position seems to be that 'interpretation' is not an indefinitely extensible concept while 'truth under an interpretation' is.

8.4

Surely, you will protest, when we say that everything is identical to itself, we don't intend any restriction, and we would fault any interpreter who would take our statement to be restricted in any way. This seems clearly to be the case for many existential statements, already invoked above, and even for some logically more complex statements. 'Every ordinal has a successor' is not a strictly unrestricted quantification, but as we have indicated 'all ordinals' is problematic in many of the ways that 'all objects whatsoever' is.

[23] (1967), pp. 152–55.

At this point I would like to return to Dummett. His remarks suggest a nuance that he does not emphasize himself and that Cartwright does not pick up on. In particular, this concerns his conception of the consensus among modern logicians:

All modern logicians are agreed that, in order to specify an *interpretation* of any sentence or formula containing bound variables, it is necessary expressly to stipulate what the range of the variables is to be.[23]

This, of course, does not say that the range cannot comprehend absolutely everything, but apparently he takes that to be a lesson of the set-theoretic paradoxes. But we should note that this is a condition on *interpretation*. After introducing some examples like those I have just cited, he goes on to interpret his own position:

What is meant, rather, is that it is not possible to suppose that, by specifying a range of some style of individual variables as being over 'all objects', or 'all sets', or 'all ordinals', we have thereby conferred a *determinate truth-value* on all statements containing quantifiers binding such variables (even given that the other symbols occurring in these statements have been assigned a determinate *sense*). Any attempt to stipulate *senses* for the predicates, relational expressions and functional operators that we shall want to use relative to such a domain will either lead to contradiction or will prompt us to concede that we are not, after all, using the bound variables to range over absolutely everything that we could intuitively acknowledge as being an object, a set, or an ordinal number.[24]

Earlier, he formulates the lesson of the set-theoretical paradoxes as being

that quantification over that domain [all objects whatsoever] cannot be regarded as yielding, in all cases, a sentence with a determinate truth-value.[25]

Thus, his problem is with the interpretation of a language where the domain is to be all objects whatsoever and with the idea that such interpretation confers determinate truth-values on all sentences of the language. In the longer of the above quotations, it appears that interpretation attributes senses to expressions, precisely the type of interpretation that assigns objects to the expressions that we considered in Section 8.3. So it may be that Dummett does not adhere to the all-in-one principle absolutely but rather that he takes it to be implicit in a certain very natural and persuasive conception of interpretation.

With Dummett, we all want to say that such statements as 'Everything is identical with itself' can be understood without any implicit restriction. The first observation to be made is that the quantifier is unrestricted, and we can suppose that there is nothing in the context that would lead to such a restriction; indeed a speaker's telling us that he means *everything* or to include *anything whatsoever* would be a rejection of any such restriction. We might interpret a larger part of what he has to say so as to take his quantifiers to range over a domain that is not absolute. On any paradigm of interpretation that is exact enough to be formulated mathematically, such interpretations will be available at least of finite discourses because of set-theoretic reflection principles. It may be, however, that our speaker will persist in protesting against any interpretation

[24] (1981), p. 567, emphasis mine.
[25] Ibid., pp. 568–69, emphasis mine.
[26] Ibid., p. 516.

of that kind that is offered, for example by embracing the stronger axioms that the interpreter must be assuming.

Persisting in this policy would allow the speaker to reject any interpretation that restricts the range of his variables. The interpreter may be skeptical; he may reply that the speaker is shifting his conceptual ground; the very meaning of 'object' or 'entity' is changing as he goes along and is confronted with more comprehensive interpretations. But let's suppose we let the speaker have his way. The interpreter may give up and say that he doesn't any longer have the resources to interpret the speaker so that his variables have a restricted range.

Unrestricted quantifiers are a part of language, and their use is not what posed our problem. Rather, the problem arose because interpretation gave rise to admitting objects not in their range, so that they fall short of being absolute. But is it clear that in order to understand the speaker we have to interpret him in this sense? We might bite the bullet thoroughly and say that we can understand our absolutist speaker's language, without engaging in any form of semantic reflection on it. Such a renunciation of semantic reflection is a very high price to pay. The considerations at the end of the last section suggest that we don't have to go quite that far, but if we maintain that our quantifiers comprehend all interpretations in an absolute sense one has to admit, by the absence of a full notion of truth under an interpretation, that the interpretations quantified over do not contain all the information that we usually think of an interpretation as embodying.

In recent literature other attempts have been made to have one's cake and eat it too, to understand the variables of a first-order language as absolutely unrestricted and at the same time construct a semantics for the language. That would be a response to the difficulty we are raising. The idea is to use second-order logic. Agustín Rayo and Timothy Williamson prove a completeness theorem for first-order logic with the variables ranging over absolutely everything.[26] (If one is skeptical of that understanding, the theorem certainly shows completeness for models whose domain of individuals is the same as that of the metalanguage.) One might ask how one could even state such a theorem. The models or interpretations are in the range of the second-order variables. This would pose no difficulty for the Fregean point of view: models are concepts or relations, and the completeness theorem concerns first-order logic with the variables ranging over all objects. But of course on Frege's view, concepts and relations are not objects, so that on this suggested reading the first-order variables fall short of ranging over absolutely everything.[27] However, so long as there are only a small number of types, as is the case in Frege's published writings, the effect of absolute quantification is achieved by quantifying over all objects, all concepts, all relations, and so on.

Rayo and Williamson, following other friends of absolute quantification, accept the claim of George Boolos that the appeal to the natural language plural to interpret

[27] Rayo and Williamson (2004).

[28] Thus up to now I have interpreted the problem of absolute universality rather narrowly, so that quantification over all *objects* is not absolute if other styles of quantifiers are allowed that are still ontologically committing. Richard Heck reminded me that some discussion of the Fregean option was needed. I am indebted here also to the editors.

monadic second-order quantifiers makes such quantification ontologically innocent. (That view may well have been behind Cartwright's use of plural formulations to describe his 'universe of discourse'.) They obtain polyadic quantification for free, since they naturally assume that the objects there are are closed under the usual operations of set theory, so that a pairing function is easily defined. But the appeal to Boolos's claim is not needed for the immediate purpose, since they could have taken the position I just offered to the Fregean view.

I have been skeptical of Boolos's claim and have criticized it in an earlier paper.[28] It implies, for example, that there is no ontological difference between a second-order theory with full comprehension and one with only first-order comprehension, even though that difference can give rise to great differences in proof-theoretic strength. Furthermore, Boolos's own suggestion for a semantics for second-order logic as he interprets it introduces a primitive second-level predicate. It seems to be another matter when second-order variables take the place of arguments; can it really be that that does not commit us to pluralities or, in Russell's phrase, classes as many? However, with the help of a suggestion of Vann McGee, Rayo and Williamson are able to avoid such second-level predicates in their completeness proof.[29]

However, it seems to me that even accepting Boolos's thesis only postpones the day of reckoning.[30] As a language in use, Rayo and Williamson have a second-order language with variables ranging over all objects, claiming that they embrace absolutely everything. But it appears that even by their own lights interpretation and metatheory have to end there, since the next steps will go into third-order logic, and they have no suggestion of how to formulate a semantics for that without abandoning the claim that the range of the individual variables is absolutely everything.

In his chapter in this volume, Rayo does make a proposal. That is to extend plural logic to the higher levels. The thesis of the ontological innocence of traditional plural logic already has its difficulties, and Rayo's extension loses one of its main props, the appeal to the linguistic intuitions that Boolos and others rely on, since Rayo admits that 'superplural' and higher levels are not found in natural languages. Furthermore,

[29] (1990), end of Section 6. Of course I was even then not alone in criticizing Boolos' claim. Linnebo (2004) contains a judicious summary of the issues in the debate surrounding Boolos' thesis.

[30] They cannot avoid using the global axiom of choice, which on their reading implies that there is a well-ordering of absolutely everything. More carefully put: some pairs well-order everything. A result of Harvey Friedman implies that with some restrictions on the language, their completeness theorem is equivalent to the weaker principle that the universe has a linear ordering. (See Friedman, 'A complete theory of everything,' posted at www.math.ohio-state.edu/~friedman.) Friedman is skeptical about the truth of this, while Rayo and Williamson seem willing to accept the stronger global choice principle. It should be remembered that, as usually deployed in set theory, global choice implies a well-ordering of the *pure sets*. Rayo and Williamson's principle is stronger than that. However, the issue arises because absolute quantifiers would have to take in all *non-mathematical* objects, and on such a view there is some plausibility in supposing that they constitute a set. Someone doubtful about Rayo and Williamson's assumption might already be disposed to question the axiom of choice in some applications of set theory with urelements, independent of the question of absolute universality. Thus a friend of absolute quantification might question the global choice principle and renounce the Rayo-Williamson completeness theorem.

[31] The same will be true of the Fregean interpretation of the second-order variables as ranging over concepts and relations, where one stops the ascent to higher levels.

he faces the problem how to understand semantic reflection on the full language with all finite levels.[31]

8.5

A suggestion made in earlier writings of my own, embraced by some recent skeptics about absolute quantification, is that statements like 'Everything is identical to itself' be understood as systematically ambiguous, akin to Russell's typical ambiguity. I have always felt some discomfort at not having more of a theory about systematic ambiguity. I'm not in a position to offer much more now than I did earlier, and I think there is some reason to think there are limits to what one can expect. A precise theory will behave like theories in formal semantics and will run into the problems about generalizing about interpretation that we have considered.

In the particular case at hand, we are confident that no matter how our conception of 'object' or 'entity' might be expanded, the truth of '$\forall x(x = x)$' will be preserved. It is, one might say, a constraint on possible expansions of these conceptions. In this particular case, it also cuts across the different ways in which even the objects of the familiar world are conceived in science and metaphysics; in particular whatever 'criteria of identity' we deploy, the law of self-identity will hold.

The 'ambiguity' in this case is broader than that that statements about sets or propositions might have, where it is expansion of the domain while leaving the individuation of the objects we already have alone that is at issue. That would be the situation with 'Every ordinal has a successor' (Dummett's example) and even about many of the axioms of set theory, possibly all of those that are firmly accepted.[32] The idea is that we don't have a definite conception of 'all sets' according to which these axioms are true when the variables are taken to range over all sets. The fact, pointed out by Gödel already in 1933 and underlying Zermelo's famous paper of 1930, that any means of specifying how sets might be 'generated' gives rise to new means that will generate more, and according to which what the means available generate will be a set, discourages the idea that we have such a conception. One could say that statements about all sets, even quite simple and unproblematic ones, have a schematic

32 Rayo's generalization of plural logic has full comprehension at all levels (see Section 4.1). This is not necessary in order to define truth and satisfaction at lower levels. A weaker version of Rayo's logic, with full second-order comprehension but only predicative comprehension from there up, would allow the definitions of truth and satisfaction at each level. Full second-order comprehension seems to be needed for the completeness theorem. The higher than second-level quantifiers could be given a relative substitutional interpretation (relative to the values of the first- and second-order variables). That might vindicate the claim that beyond the second level, the ascent is one of ideology and not ontology, and for the second level only Boolos's original thesis would be needed. On this reading, at higher levels the motivation from the plural would play only a heuristic role. (I have benefited here from discussion with Rayo.)

33 With the exception of purely existential axioms, in particular the axiom of infinity. Once the domain is large enough to contain a witness for that, it remains true under expansion of the domain, even many expansions insensitive to the principles of set theory.

character.[33] That suggests that there is an implicit dimension of generalization, not captured by the quantifiers. That is correct, but the generalization is only partly over mind-independent objects, since it concerns the possible development of our own conceptions. Attempting to capture it by an additional style of quantifier will run into all sorts of difficulties.

A view like ours faces a challenge posed by Williamson, according to which the usual understanding even of statements with restricted quantifiers presupposes absolute quantification.[34] An ordinary restricted statement, such as 'No donkey talks' (Williamson's example), is understood as containing a quantifier restricted to donkeys. But in order for it to have the right truth-conditions, we need to be sure that its range at least takes in all *donkeys*. And surely that means all the donkeys that there are. Now we describe this situation with unrestricted quantifiers. But if an interpretation of our discourse makes them range over less than absolutely everything, don't we face a problem mentioned at the beginning, that our statement 'No donkey talks' may be true even though (from the point of view of the metalanguage) there is a talking donkey out there?

In some cases such as simple existential statements like 'There are donkeys', we can rely on logical properties such as the persistence of such statements under expansion of the domain, as Michael Glanzberg emphasizes. In the case of universal statements, we need something else, assurance that if our domain is expanded it won't change the class of donkeys.[35] But that seems pretty clear from the considerations that in fact drive such expansion. Why should donkeys be worse off than, say, pure sets of finite rank? We know where counterexamples to 'No donkey talks' are to be found if they exist, in the relatively recent history of our planet, a highly circumscribed region of space. Certainly the least unlikely way in which 'No donkey talks' might come to be rejected is through finding a talking donkey approximately where we now think donkeys are to be found, in such a way that the statement is falsified according to our present understanding.

However, there might be an analogy between the logically driven expansion we have emphasized and conceptual changes in the development of science. Then it might be imaginable that in some at present unconceived part of the universe, there might be or have been more donkeys. It is not obvious how to understand the bearing of such possibilities on 'manifest image' facts such as that donkeys do not talk.

[34] An idea I have entertained is that one might reason with such statements by taking on restrictions like what Hilbert proposed for finitary mathematics: generality would be expressed by free variables, so that universal statements would not enter into logical combinations, and an existential statement could be made only by presenting a witness, in this case a limited domain in which a witness is to be found. But I have not developed a formal language that would model this idea.

However, in a lecture at UCLA in June 2005, Saul Kripke presented an axiomatization of set theory based on just this conception, where bounded quantification behaves in the usual way, but unbounded generalizations are expressed using free variables. That requires adding to the language terms for certain basic operations, such as power set.

[35] (2003), Section 8.4.

[36] In fact it would do if it didn't change some essentials of the nature of donkeys which distinguish them from humans and even, perhaps, parrots.

And it can be argued, on Kripkean grounds, that if the future development of science turns up a possibility like that, the entities involved will not be donkeys, because they have no evolutionary connection with the donkeys we know. However that may be, I don't think the statement 'No donkey talks' as we actually use it has to deal with possibilities like that, of which we have at present no conception. One could discern metaphysical realist prejudice in the expectation that it should. It seems that what we can now understand as 'the objects that there are' (even on rather different ontological schemes) doesn't have a provision for expansion that would allow more donkeys. But when we think of the ways our views of things in science and philosophy have changed over time, are we really 100 percent sure that future generations won't show us wrong in that?

REFERENCES

Bradley, F. H. (1893) *Appearance and Reality.* London: S. Sonnenschein. 2nd ed., (1897), reprints from 1930. Oxford: Clarendon Press.

Cartwright, Richard L. (1994) '*Speaking of Everything*', *Noûs* 28: 1–21.

Dummett, Michael (1981) *Frege: Philosophy of Language.* 2nd ed. London: Duckworth, and Cambridge, MA: Harvard University Press. (First published 1973)

____ (1981a) *The Interpretation of Frege's Philosophy.* London: Duckworth.

Frege, Gottlob (1884) *Grundlagen der Arithmetik.* Breslau: Koebner.

____ (1885) 'Über formale Theorien der Arithmetik.' *Sitzungsberichte der Jenaischen Gesellschaft für Medicin und Naturwissenschaft für das Jahr 1885*, 94–104. Reprinted in Kleine Schriften, (ed.) Ignacio Angelelli (Hildesheim: Olms, 1967). Trans. in *Collected Papers on Mathematics, Logic, and Philosophy*, (ed.) Brian McGuinness. Oxford: Blackwell, 1984.

Glanzberg, Michael (2004) 'Quantification and Realism.' *Philosophy and Phenomenological Research* 69, 541–72.

Kreisel, G. (1967) 'Informal Rigour and Completeness Proofs.' In Imre Lakatos (ed.), *Problems in the Philosophy of Mathematics*, pp. 138–86. Amsterdam: North-Holland.

Linnebo, Øystein (2004) Plural Quantification. *Stanford Encyclopedia of Philosophy*, http://plato.stanford.edu.

Parsons, Charles (1974) 'The Liar Paradox.' *Journal of Philosophical Logic* 3 (1974), 381–412. Cited according to reprint in *Mathematics in Philosophy.* Ithaca, NY: Cornell University Press, 1983.

____ (1982) 'Objects and Logic.' *The Monist* 65, 491–516.

____ (1990) 'The Structuralist View of Mathematical Objects.' *Synthese* 84, 303–46.

Rayo, Agustín, and Timothy Williamson (2004) 'A Completeness Theorem for Unrestricted First-Order Languages,' in J. C. Beall (ed.), *Liars and Heaps: New Essays on Paradox*, pp. 331–56. Oxford: Clarendon Press.

Williams, Donald C. (1953) 'On the Elements of Being I.' *Review of Metaphysics* 7, 3–18. Cited according to reprint in D. H. Mellor and Alex Oliver (eds.), *Properties.* Oxford University Press, 1997.

Williamson, Timothy (2003) 'Everything', in John Hawthorne and Dean Zimmerman (eds.) *Philosophical Perspectives* 17: *Language and Philosophical Linguistics*, pp. 415–65. Oxford: Blackwell.

9

Beyond Plurals

Agustín Rayo

I have two main objectives. The first is to get a better understanding of what is at issue between friends and foes of higher-order quantification, and of what it would mean to extend a Boolos-style treatment of second-order quantification to third- and higher-order quantification. The second objective is to argue that in the presence of absolutely general quantification, proper semantic theorizing is essentially unstable: it is impossible to provide a suitably general semantics for a given language in a language of the same logical type. I claim that this leads to a trilemma: one must choose between giving up absolutely general quantification, settling for the view that adequate semantic theorizing about certain languages is essentially beyond our reach, and countenancing an open-ended hierarchy of languages of ever ascending logical type. I conclude by suggesting that the hierarchy may be the least unattractive of the options on the table.

9.1 PRELIMINARIES

9.1.1 Categorial Semantics

Throughout this chapter I shall assume the following:

CATEGORIAL SEMANTICS
Every meaningful sentence has a semantic structure,[1] which may be represented as a certain kind of tree.[2] Each node in the tree falls under a particular semantic category (e.g. 'sentence',

Many thanks to Kit Fine, Øystein Linnebo, John MacFarlane, Tom McKay, Charles Parsons, Marcus Rossberg, Barry Schein, Gabriel Uzquiano, Tim Williamson, Crispin Wright, and audiences at MIT's MATTI Reading Group, La Universidade de Santiago de Compostela and *Arché* the AHRC Research Centre for the Philosophy of Logic, Language, Mathematics and Mind.

[1] If a sentence is ambiguous, it might have more than one semantic structure. I will henceforth ignore ambiguity of this kind to simplify my presentation. For present purposes, ambiguity may be thought of as a matter of homophonic but distinct expressions.

[2] More precisely, as a *finite tree with ordered nodes*. A *finite tree* is an ordered-pair $\langle N, \leq \rangle$, where N is a finite set of 'nodes' and $\leq$ is a binary relation on N with the following properties: (i) $\leq$ is reflexive, transitive and antisymmetric; (ii) N has a $\leq$-minimal element, which we call 'base node'; (iii) every node x in N other than the base node has an immediate $\leq$-predecessor (i.e. there is a y in N such that $y \leq x$ and there is no z in N such that $y \leq z \leq x$); and (iv) for any x in N there is

'quantifier', 'sentential connective'), and has an intension that is appropriate for that category. The semantic category and intension of each non-terminal node in the tree is determined by the semantic categories and intensions of nodes below it.

Although I won't attempt to defend CATEGORIAL SEMANTICS here,[3] two points are worth emphasizing. First, the claim that meaningful sentences are endowed with some sort of semantic structure is not optional. It is forced upon us by considerations of compositionality. (It is hard to understand how a sentence could have different semantic 'constituents' in the absence of some kind of semantic structure.) Second, the notions of semantic structure and semantic category should be distinguished from the notions of *grammatical* structure and *grammatical* category. Whereas the former are chiefly constrained by a theory that assigns *truth-conditions* to sentences, the latter are chiefly constrained by a theory that delivers a criterion of *grammaticality* for strings of symbols. (The two sets of notions are nonetheless interrelated, since we would like to have a transformational grammar that specifies a class of legitimate transformations linking the two.)

9.1.2 An Example

Let L_0 be an (interpreted) propositional language. It consists of the following symbols: the sentential-letters 'p', 'q', and 'r'; the one-place connective-symbol '$\neg$'; the two-place connective-symbols '$\vee$' and '$\wedge$'; and the auxiliary symbols '(' and ')'. Well-formed formulas are defined in the usual way.

Here is an example of a categorial semantics for L_0. There are three semantic categories: 'sentence', 'one-place connective' and 'two-place connective'. To each of these categories corresponds a different kind of intension: the intension of a sentence is a set of possible worlds, the intension of a one-place connective is a function that takes each set of possible worlds to a set of possible worlds, and the intension of a two-place predicate is a function that takes each pair of sets of possible worlds to a set of possible worlds. We let the basic semantic lexicon of L_0 consist of 'p', 'q', 'r', '$\neg$', '$\vee$' and '$\wedge$'. The lexical items 'p', 'q' and 'r' fall under the 'sentence' category and have the following intensions:

$$I(`p\text{'}) = \{w : \text{snow is white according to } w\}$$

$$I(`q\text{'}) = \{w : \text{roses are red according to } w\}$$

$$I(`r\text{'}) = \{w : \text{violets are blue according to } w\}$$

a unique path back to the base node (i.e. for any y and z, if $y \leq x$ and $z \leq x$ then either $y \leq z$ or $z \leq y$). We say that x is a *terminal node* if, for every y, $x \leq y$ only if $x = y$. If $x \leq y$ and $x \neq y$ we say that y is *below* x in the tree. If y is below x and no z is such that z is below x and y is below z, then we say that y is *immediately* below x. Finally, a finite tree *with ordered nodes* is a pair $\langle T, F\rangle$ where T is a finite tree and F is a one–one function from nodes in T to natural numbers. If y and z are both immediately below x, we say that y is *to the left* of z just in case $F(y) < F(z)$.

[3] For a defence, see Lewis (1970) and Montague (1970).

The lexical item '¬' falls under the 'one-place connective' category and has the following intension:

$$I(\text{'}\neg\text{'}) = \text{the function taking } W \text{ to its set-theoretic complement } \overline{W}$$

The lexical items '∨' and '∧' fall under the 'two-place connective' category and have the following intensions:

$$I(\text{'}\vee\text{'}) = \text{the function taking each pair } \langle W, V \rangle \text{ to } W \cup V$$

$$I(\text{'}\wedge\text{'}) = \text{the function taking each pair } \langle W, V \rangle \text{ to } W \cap V$$

The semantic structure of a formula of L_0 mirrors its syntax. For instance, the semantic structure of '$(p \wedge q) \vee \neg r$' (or, in Polish notation, '$\vee \wedge p\, q \neg r$') is given by the following tree:

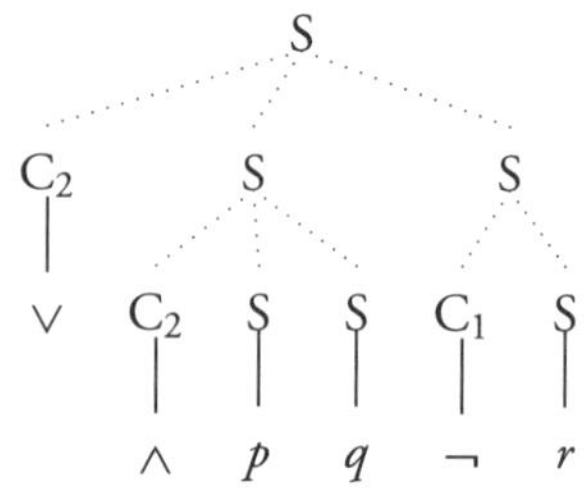

('S', 'C_1' and 'C_2' stand for 'sentence', 'one-place connective' and 'two-place connective', respectively.) Each terminal node in the tree is assigned the intension and semantic category of the lexical item displayed underneath. The intensions and semantic categories of non-terminal nodes are determined by the intensions and semantic categories of nodes below them, in the obvious way (e.g. the intension of base node is $(I(\text{'}p\text{'}) \cap I(\text{'}q\text{'})) \cup \overline{I(\text{'}r\text{'})}$).

Since the intensions of sentences are taken to be sets of possible worlds, the semantics immediately delivers a characterization of truth for sentences in L_0: sentence S is true in world w if and only if w is a member of the intension assigned to the base node of S's semantic structure.

9.1.3 Legitimacy

I shall say that a semantic category $\mathcal{C}$ is *legitimate* just in case it is in principle possible to make sense of a language whose semantic properties are accurately described by a categorial semantics employing $\mathcal{C}$.

One can certainly make sense of a propositional language. So 'sentence', '1-place connective' and '2-place connective' are all legitimate semantic categories. One can also make sense of a first-order language. So 'name', 'n-place predicate' and 'first-order quantifier' (with suitable intensions), are also legitimate semantic categories. But where do the limits lie? Might a purported semantic category be ruled out by the very nature of language?

An example might bring the matter into sharper focus. Let L_1 be an (interpreted) first-order language, and suppose it is agreed on all sides that the individual constant 'c' of L_1 falls under the semantic category 'name', and that the predicate '$P(\ldots)$' of L_1 falls under the semantic category 'one-place predicate'.[4] To fix ideas, think of the intension of a name as a function that takes each world to an individual in that world, and of the intension of a one-place predicate as a function that takes each world to a set of individuals in that world. Now suppose we tried to enrich L_1 with the new item 'ξ', in such a way that '$\xi(c)$' and '$P(\xi)$' are both sentences. It is tempting to think that there is no way of carrying out the extension without lapsing into nonsense. If this is right, then there is reason for thinking that 'ξ' could not fall under a legitimate semantic category.

This is something of an extreme case, since the possibility of a semantic category corresponding to 'ξ' is ruled out by the category-formation rules of standard implementations of categorial semantics.[5] But the philosophy of logic is peppered with cases that are more difficult to adjudicate. Consider, for example, the debate that is sometimes labeled 'Is second-order logic really logic?'[6] Quine has famously argued that the only way of making sense of second-order quantifiers is by understanding them as first-order quantifiers ranging over set-like entities. If this is right, second-order quantifiers cannot fall under a legitimate semantic category, at least not insofar as it is insisted that they not be thought of as first-order quantifiers.

Contrary claims are made by Quine's rivals. Boolos (1984) argues that it is possible to make sense of the Geach-Kaplan Sentence:

[Some critics admire only one another.]

even though it is 'a sentence whose quantificational structure cannot be captured by first order logic.' If this is right, plural quantifiers fall under a semantic category that is both legitimate and distinct from 'first-order quantifier'.

Boolos's work on plural quantification is an important contribution to the debate on second-order logic *not* because it shows that second-order quantifiers are plausibly understood as plural quantifiers. (Although plural quantifiers can be used to play the same role as second-order quantifiers for certain purposes, they should not be identified with second-order quantifiers because plural terms such as 'they' and 'them' do not take predicate positions.)[7] Rather, it is important because it makes a convincing

[4] Strictly, one should distinguish between the expressions of a first-order language, and the members of the language's semantic lexicon. Only the latter can be properly said to fall under semantic categories. I shall fudge this distinction—here and throughout the remainder of the chapter—for presentational purposes.

[5] According to Lewis (1970), for example, the semantic category of a predicate is $\langle S/N \rangle$ and the semantic category of a name is N (or, alternatively, $\langle S/(S/N) \rangle$). So, in order for '$\xi(c)$' to be a sentence, the semantic category of 'ξ' would have to be $\langle S/N \rangle$ (or, alternatively, either $\langle S/N \rangle$ or $\langle S/(S/(S/N)) \rangle$), and in order for '$P(\xi)$' to be a sentence, the semantic category of 'ξ' would have to be either N or $\langle S/(S/N) \rangle$. And it is impossible to fulfill both of these conditions at once.

[6] For the Quinean side of the debate see Quine (1986) ch. 5, Resnik (1988), Parsons (1990) and Linnebo (2003) (among others). For the Boolosian side of the debate see Boolos (1984), Boolos (1985a), Boolos (1985b), McGee (1997), Hossack (2000), McGee (2000), Oliver and Smiley (2001), Rayo and Yablo (2001), Rayo (2002) and Williamson (2003) (among others).

[7] See Simons (1997), Rayo and Yablo (2001) and Williamson (2003).

case for the view that quantifiers other than the standard (singular) first-order quantifiers can fall under a legitimate semantic category, and this opens the door for thinking that it might be possible to understand second-order quantifiers in such a way that they too belong to a semantic category that is both legitimate and distinct from 'first-order quantifier'.

Needless to say, the concession that second-order quantifiers fall under a semantic category that is both legitimate and distinct from 'first-order quantifier' would leave a number of important issues unresolved. The *logicality* of second-order quantifiers would not automatically be settled, since a single semantic category might include both logical and non-logical items (e.g. ' ... = ... ' and ' ... is a parent of ... '). The *ontological commitments* of second-order quantifiers would not automatically be settled, since the standard criterion of ontological commitment—Quine's criterion—applies only to first-order languages.[8] And the *determinacy* of second-order quantifiers would not automatically be settled, since an expression can be indeterminate even if its semantic category is fixed.[9]

9.2 BEYOND PLURALS

In this section I will introduce an infinite hierarchy of predicates, terms and quantifiers. I will claim without argument that each element in the hierarchy falls under a legitimate semantic category. Later in the chapter I will try to motivate this claim.

9.2.1 First-Level Predicates

A first-level predicate is a predicate that takes a singular term in each of its argument places. It is tempting to think that the semantic value of the monadic first-level predicate ' ... is an elephant' is the set of elephants. More generally, it is tempting to think that the semantic value of the monadic first-level predicate '$P^1(\ldots)$' is the set of individuals '$P^1(\ldots)$' is true of. But now assume—as I will throughout the remainder of the paper—that it is possible to quantify over absolutely everything.[10] Then the thought is unsustainable. For it leads to the unwelcome conclusion that predicates such as ' ... is self-identical' or ' ... is a set' lack a semantic value.

(The problem cannot be solved by appealing to a non-standard set theory, or by employing entities other than sets. Suppose, for example, that one takes the semantic value of a monadic first-level predicate to be a set* rather than a set. It follows from a generalization of Cantor's Theorem that at least one of the following must be the case:[11] either (*a*) there are some things—the Fs—such that there is no set* consisting of all and only the Fs, or (*b*) there are some things—the Fs—and some things—the

[8] For an expanded criterion of ontological commitment, see Rayo (2002).

[9] For discussion of determinacy, see Jané (2005).

[10] For more on absolutely unrestricted quantification see Parsons (1974b), Dummett (1981) chs. 14-16, Cartwright (1994), Boolos (1998b), Williamson (1999), McGee (2000), the postscript to Field (1998) in Field (2001), Rayo (2003), Rayo and Williamson (2003), Glanzberg (2004), and Williamson (2003).

[11] See Rayo (2002).

Gs—such that the Fs are not the Gs but the set* of the Fs is identical to the set* of the Gs. So we are left with the unsettling conclusion that either there are some things such that a predicate true of just those things would lack a semantic value, or there might be two predicates that share a semantic value but are not true of the same things.)

Rather than taking '... is an elephant' to stand for the set of elephants, I would like to suggest that one should take it to stand for the elephants themselves. It is grammatically infelicitous to say that the semantic value of '... is an elephant' is the elephants. So I shall say state the view by saying that '... is an elephant' *refers* to the elephants. Formally,

$$\exists xx(\forall y(y \prec^{1,2} xx \leftrightarrow \text{Elephant}^1(y)) \wedge \text{Ref}^{1,2}(\text{`}\ldots \text{ is an elephant'}, xx))$$

which is read:

There are some things—the *xxs*—such that: (*a*) for every *y*, *y* is one of the *xxs* if and only if *y* is an elephant, and (*b*) '... is an elephant' refers to the *xxs*.

Double variables are used for plural terms and quantifiers,[12] and superscripts indicate the type of variable that the relevant predicate takes in each of its argument places. Predicates are interpreted in the obvious way: '$y \prec^{1,2} xx$' means '*y* is one of the *xxs*' (or 'it$_y$ is one of them$_{xx}$'), '$\text{ELEPHANT}^1(y)$' means '*y* is an elephant' and '$\text{REF}^{1,2}(y, xx)$' means '*y* refers to the *xxs*' (or 'it$_y$ refers to them$_{xx}$'). The proposal therefore makes use of *second-level predicates*. (A second-level predicate is a predicate that takes a plural term in one of its argument places, and either a singular term or a plural term in the rest; more will be said about second-level predicates below.)

A snappy way of stating my claim is by saying that the reference of a monadic first-level predicate is a *plurality*. (One could say, for instance, that the reference of '... is an elephant' is the plurality of elephants.) But it is important to be clear that apparently singular quantification over 'pluralities' is a syntactic abbreviation for plural quantification over individuals; and that plural quantification is not the standard sort of (first-order) quantification over a new kind of 'item' ('plurality'); it is a new kind of quantification over individuals, which are the only kind of 'item' there is.

9.2.2 First-Level Terms

Let us now turn our attention to plural terms (or *first-level terms*, as I shall call them).[13] I argued above that it implausible to think that the first-level predicate '... is an elephant' refers to the set of elephants. It is similarly implausible to think that the first-level term 'the elephants' refers to the set of elephants, since the general view that 'the Fs' refers to the set of Fs leads to the unwelcome result that first-level terms such as 'the self-identical things' or 'the sets' are without reference. (And, for the same reasons as before, the problem cannot be avoided by appealing to a non-standard set-theory, or by employing entities other than sets.)

12 In using this notation I follow Burgess and Rosen (1997).

13 Although a cleaner example of an English first-level term would be 'they' in 'Some elephants passed by; they were generally nice to each other', I treat expressions like 'the elephants' as if they were uncontroversially first-level terms for ease of exposition.

I would like to suggest that first-level terms—like monadic first-level predicates—refer to pluralities. Thus, 'the elephants' refers, not to the set of elephants, but to the elephants themselves. Formally,

$$\exists xx(\forall y(y \prec^{1,2} xx \leftrightarrow \textsc{elephant}^{1}(y)) \wedge \textsc{ref}^{1,2}(\text{'the elephants'}, xx))$$

which is read:

There are some things—the *xxs*—such that: (*a*) for every *y*, *y* is one of the *xxs* if and only if *y* is an elephant, and (*b*) 'the elephants' refers to the *xxs*.

9.2.3 The Saturation Operator

Let the *saturation operator* 'σ' be such that, given any monadic first-level predicate '$P^1(\ldots)$', '$\sigma[P^1(\ldots)]$' is a first-level term for which the following holds:

$$\forall xx(\textsc{Ref}^{1,2}(\text{'}P^1(\ldots)\text{'}, xx) \leftrightarrow \textsc{Ref}^{1,2}(\text{'}\sigma[P^1(\ldots)]\text{'}, xx))$$

The term '$\sigma[P^1(\ldots)]$' may therefore be thought of as something along the lines of the plural definite description 'the P^1s'. (See, however, Section 9.3.4.)

There are interesting similarities between our saturation operator and the abstraction operator 'λ'. But, of course, they are distinct. Whereas the saturation operator transforms predicates into terms, the abstraction operator transforms sentences into predicates.

One may wish to insist that it is inappropriate to use a single reference relation for predicates and terms. One might think that, strictly speaking, there are two different kinds of reference: predicate-reference and term-reference. Nothing I shall say is incompatible with such a view. If one wanted, one could characterize the saturation-operator as follows:

$$\forall xx(\text{P-}\textsc{Ref}^{1,2}(\text{'}P^1(\ldots)\text{'}, xx) \leftrightarrow \text{T-}\textsc{Ref}^{1,2}(\text{'}\sigma[P^1(\ldots)]\text{'}, xx))$$

But the real difference between ' ... is an elephant' and 'the elephants' is that they fall under distinct semantic categories. And, since that is a difference that is already reflected in the syntax, I won't bother distinguishing between predicate-reference and term-reference.

9.2.4 Second-Level Predicates

There is a case to be made for the view that English predicates such as ' ... are scattered on the table' in 'The seashells are scattered on the table' or ' ... are surrounding the building' in 'the students are surrounding the building' are best understood as genuine second-level predicates.[14] Suppose such a view is correct. One might then be tempted to think that the reference of ' ... are scattered on the table' is the set of all and only sets whose members are scattered on the table (or, alternatively, the plurality consisting of all and only sets whose members are scattered on the table).

[14] See Rayo (2002).

More generally, one might be tempted to think that the second-level predicate '... are P' refers to the set of all and only sets whose members are collectively P (or, alternatively, to the plurality consisting of all and only sets whose members are collectively P). But one would then be forced to withhold reference from, e.g. a second-level predicate true of all and only pluralities whose members are too many to form a set. (And, as before, the problem cannot be avoided by appealing to a non-standard set-theory, or by employing entities other than sets.)

I propose instead that the reference of ' ... are scattered on the table' should be characterized as follows:

$$\exists xxx(\forall yy(yy \prec^{2,3} xxx \leftrightarrow \text{S}\textsc{cattered}^2(yy)) \wedge \text{R}\textsc{ef}^{1,3}(\text{`... are scattered'}, xxx))$$

where treble variables are used for *super-plural* terms and quantifiers. There are, of course, no super-plural terms or quantifiers in English, but I would like to suggest the relevant semantic category is nonetheless legitimate: super-plural quantifiers are to third-order quantifiers what plural quantifiers are to second-order quantifiers.

Since I cannot use English to state my proposal, I shall state it by saying that the reference of a monadic second-level predicate is a *super-plurality*. The reference of '... are scattered on the table', for example, is the super-plurality to which all and only pluralities scattered on the table belong. But it is important to be clear that apparently singular quantification over 'super-pluralities' is a syntactic abbreviation for super-plural quantification over individuals. Super-plural quantification is not singular (first-order) quantification over a new kind of 'item' ('super-plurality'), nor is it plural quantification over a new kind of 'item' ('plurality'). Super-plural quantification is a new kind of quantification altogether. And like its singular and plural counterparts, it is quantification over individuals, which are the only kind of 'item' there is.

I would like to insist that thinking of super-plural quantification as an iterated form of plural quantification—plural quantification over pluralities—would be a serious mistake. Plural quantification over pluralities can only make sense if pluralities are taken to be 'items' of some kind or other. And a plurality is not an 'item': apparently singular quantification over pluralities is a syntactic abbreviation for plural quantification over individuals.

It is one thing to have a general understanding of the sort of role super-plural quantifiers are supposed to play. But acquiring a genuine *grasp* of super-plural quantification—making sense of a language containing super-plural quantifiers—is a very different matter. The remarks in this section are intended to help with the former, but certainly not the latter. The best way of attaining a genuine grasp of super-plural quantification is presumably by mastering the use of super-plural quantifiers. (A suitable deductive system is discussed in Section 9.4.2.)

9.2.5 Second-Level Terms

Debatable examples such as 'the couples' or 'the collections' aside, English appears to contain no second-level terms. But I submit that the relevant semantic category is nonetheless legitimate.[15] One can use the saturation operator, 'σ', to form second-level terms by stipulating that, for any monadic second-level predicate '$P^2(\ldots)$', '$\sigma[P^2(\ldots)]$' is a second-level term for which the following holds:

$$\forall xxx(\text{Ref}^{1,3}(\text{`}P^2(\ldots)\text{'}, xxx) \leftrightarrow \text{Ref}^{1,3}(\text{`}\sigma[P^2(\ldots)]\text{'}, xxx))$$

Thus, '$\sigma[\text{Scattered}^2(\ldots)]$' is to '... are scattered' what '$\sigma[\text{Elephant}^1(\ldots)]$' is to '... is an elephant'. In each case, there is a difference in semantic category without a difference in reference.

9.2.6 Beyond

A third-level predicate is a predicate that takes a second-level term in one of its argument places, and either a second-level term, a first-level term or singular term in the rest. It seems clear that English contains no third-level predicates. But I submit that the relevant semantic category is nonetheless legitimate. In analogy with the above, the reference of a monadic third-level predicate '$P^3(\ldots)$' may be characterized as follows:

$$\exists xxxx(\forall yyy(yyy \prec^{3,4} xxxx \leftrightarrow \text{P}^3(yyy)) \wedge \text{Ref}^{1,4}(\text{`}P^3(\ldots)\text{'}, xxxx))$$

where quadruple variables are used for *super-duper-plural* terms and quantifiers. There are, of course, no super-duper-plural terms or quantifiers in English, but, again, I submit that the relevant semantic category is nonetheless legitimate: super-duper-plural quantifiers are to fourth-order quantifiers what super-plural quantifiers are to third-order quantifiers and plural quantifiers are to second-order quantifiers.

And, of course, one can use the saturation operator, 'σ', to form third-level terms by stipulating that, for any monadic third-level predicate '$P^3(\ldots)$', '$\sigma[P^3(\ldots)]$' is a third-level term for which the following holds:

$$\forall xxxx(\text{Ref}^{1,4}(\text{`}P^3(\ldots)\text{'}, xxxx) \leftrightarrow \text{Ref}^{1,4}(\text{`}\sigma[P^3(\ldots)]\text{'}, xxxx))$$

A similar story can be told about n-th level terms and predicates for any finite n.

9.3 FINE-TUNING

9.3.1 Improving the Notation

Consider the first-level predicate '... is an ancestor of Clyde'. The first-level term

σ[... is an ancestor of Clyde]

might be read 'the ancestors of Clyde' (or, more idiomatically, 'Clyde's ancestors'). We can therefore write

[15] In this connection, see Black (1970) and Hazen (1997).

(1) VERYNUMEROUS^2(σ[... is an ancestor of Clyde]),

(read: 'Clyde's ancestors are very numerous').

Now consider the result of deleting 'Clyde' from (1). Since 'Clyde' is a singular term and (1) is a sentence, what we should get is a first-level predicate, true of all and only individuals whose ancestors are very numerous. But it is be infelicitous to write

VERYNUMEROUS^2(σ[... is an ancestor of ...]),

because it is unclear which of the two empty argument places in ' ... is an ancestor of ... ' the saturation operator is germane to. We need to improve our notation. One possibility is to add indices to 'σ' and each of the empty argument places in ' ... is an ancestor of ... '. This allows us to distinguish between

VERYNUMEROUS^2(σ_1[... $_1$ is an ancestor of ... $_2$])

and

VERYNUMEROUS^2(σ_2[... $_1$ is an ancestor of ... $_2$]).

Both are first-level predicates. The first is true of all and only individuals whose ancestors are very numerous; the second is true of all and only individuals whose descendants are very numerous. Accordingly, one can construct the following sentences:

(2) FORMCLUB^2(σ_2[VERYNUMEROUS^2(σ_1[... $_1$ is an ancestor of ... $_2$])]),
(roughly: the individuals whose ancestors are very numerous form a club);

and

(3) FORMCLUB^2(σ_1[VERYNUMEROUS^2(σ_2[...$_1$ is an ancestor of ...$_2$])]),
(roughly: the individuals whose descendants are very numerous form a club).

Maintaining the dotted-line notation turns out to be somewhat inconvenient, however. I shall therefore forego the use of '...$_i$' in favor of 'v_i^n' (where n is the level of terms taking the place of '...$_i$'). Thus, (2) and (3) become (2′) and (3′), respectively:

(2′) FORMCLUB^2(σ_2^0[VERYNUMEROUS^2(σ_1^0[v_1^0 is an ancestor of v_2^0])])

(3′) FORMCLUB^2(σ_1^0[VERYNUMEROUS^2(σ_2^0[v_1^0 is an ancestor of v_2^0])])

9.3.2 The Reference of Polyadic Predicates

I offered a proposal about the reference of monadic *n*th level predicates in Section 9.2. But nothing has been said so far about the reference of polyadic predicates, such as 'ANCESTOR^{1,1}(..., ...)', or '... $\prec^{1,2}$ ...'.

One possibility is to take the reference of 'ANCESTOR^{1,1}(..., ...)' to be a plurality of ordered-pairs. Alternatively, one can take it to be a super-duper-plurality. (Specifically: the super-duper-plurality consisting of all and only super-pluralities that consist of two pluralities, one of them consisting of an individual and her ancestor and the other consisting of the ancestor alone.[16]) Such proposals generalize naturally to polyadic predicates of any arity and any finite level. A generalization of the first proposal is supplied in the appendix.

9.3.3 Intensions

Section 9.2 focused on the notion of reference. But the proposal can easily be generalized to provide a characterization of the *intensions* of *n*th-level predicates and terms.

Consider the monadic first-level predicate '$\textsc{Elephant}^1(\ldots)$' as an example. One possibility is to take its intension to be the plurality of ordered-pairs $\langle w, x\rangle$ such that w is a possible world and x is an elephant in w. Alternatively, one can take the intension of '$\textsc{Elephant}^1(\ldots)$' to be a super-duper-plurality. (Specifically: the super-duper plurality consisting of all and only super-pluralities that consist of two pluralities, one of them consisting of a possible world and an elephant in that world and the other consisting of the world alone.)[17] Such proposals generalize naturally to polyadic predicates of any arity and any finite level.

To keep things simple, I will focus on reference rather than intension throughout the remainder of the paper. But the view can be extended to accommodate intensions if need be.

9.3.4 Empty Predicates

The second-order sentence

(4) $\exists X \forall y \neg(Xy)$

is true, since it can be derived from the true sentence '$\forall y \neg(\textsc{Unicorn}^1(y))$' by existential generalization. By contrast, the structurally analogous plural sentence

(5) $\exists xx \forall y \neg(y \prec^{1,2} xx)$

[16] Formally,

$$\exists xxxx \forall yyy[yyy \prec^{3,4} xxxx \leftrightarrow \forall zz(zz \prec^{2,3} yyy \leftrightarrow \exists w \exists u(\textsc{Ancestor}^{1,1}(w,u) \wedge (\forall t(t \prec^{1,2} zz \leftrightarrow (t = w \vee t = u)) \vee \forall t(t \prec^{1,2} zz \leftrightarrow (t = w)))))\wedge \textsc{Ref}^{1,4}(\text{`}\textsc{Ancestor}^{1,1}(v_i^0, v_j^0)\text{'}, xxxx)].$$

[17] Formally,

$$\exists xxxx \forall yyy[yyy \prec^{3,4} xxxx \leftrightarrow \forall zz(zz \prec^{2,3} yyy \leftrightarrow \exists w \exists u(\textsc{World}^1(w) \wedge \textsc{Elephant-in}^{1,1}(w,u) \wedge (\forall t(t \prec^{1,2} zz \leftrightarrow (t = w \vee t = u)) \vee \forall t(t \prec^{1,2} zz \leftrightarrow (t = w)))))\wedge \textsc{Int}^{1,4}(\text{`}\textsc{Elephant}^1(v_i^0)\text{'}, xxxx)].$$

is false, since it is to be interpreted as 'there are some things such that nothing is one of them'.[18] In some respects, the difference in truth-value between (4) and (5) is of little importance: Boolos (1984) has shown that there is a systematic way of paraphrasing second-order sentences as sentences of a first-level language enriched with plural quantifiers (and no second-level predicates other than '$\prec^{1,2}$'). We will see, however, that the falsity of (5) is not without implications in the present context.

One cannot say of the predicate 'UNICORN^1(...)', which is satisfied by no object, that it has a reference—not if the reference of a monadic first-level predicate is to be a plurality. For saying of 'UNICORN^1(...)' that it refers to an 'empty' plurality amounts to saying:

(6) $\exists xx(\text{REF}^{1,2}(\text{`UNICORN}^1(\ldots)\text{'}, xx) \wedge \forall y \neg(y \prec^{1,2} xx))$;

and the falsity of (6) is an immediate consequence of the falsity of (5). Happily, the claim that 'UNICORN^1(...)' has no reference is distinct from the claim that it is meaningless.[19]

To characterize the compositional behavior of empty predicates, let us begin by stipulating that an atomic predication based on an empty predicate is always false. Thus, for the case of 'UNICORN^1(...)', we have:

(7) $\neg\text{TRUE}^1(\ulcorner\text{UNICORN}^1(t^0)\urcorner)$,

for $\ulcorner t^0 \urcorner$ an arbitrary singular term. This does not, however, settle the question of how to deal with 'UNICORN^1(...)' when it occurs within the scope of the saturation operator, as in 'σ_1^0[UNICORN$^1(v_1^0)$]'. We know from Section 9.2.3 that:

$$\forall xx(\text{REF}^{1,2}(\text{`UNICORN}^1(\ldots)\text{'}, xx) \leftrightarrow \text{REF}^{1,2}(\text{`}\sigma_1^0[\text{UNICORN}(v_1^0)]\text{'}, xx)).$$

Since 'UNICORN^1(...)' is referenceless, it follows that 'σ_1^0[UNICORN$^1(v_1^0)$]' must be referenceless as well. So the question we face is that of characterizing the compositional behavior of empty terms. For instance, under what circumstances should one say that the following sentence is true?

$$\text{P}^2(\sigma_1^0[\text{UNICORN}^1(v_1^0)]).$$

Think of the matter like this. An atomic *first*-level predicate $\ulcorner \text{P}^1(\ldots)\urcorner$ is used to say of an individual that it is thus-and-so. Thus, when $\ulcorner t^0 \urcorner$ is an empty singular term, such as 'Zeus', $\ulcorner \text{P}^1(t^0)\urcorner$ is false; for one cannot truthfully say of *nothing* that it is thus-and-so. Similarly, an atomic *second*-level predicate $\ulcorner \text{P}^2(\ldots)\urcorner$ is used to say of some individuals that they are thus-and-so. Thus, when $\ulcorner t^1 \urcorner$ is an empty singular term,

18 See, however, Schein (forthcoming).

19 This way of thinking of empty predicates yields the result that a predicate not-F might be referenceless even though F is not, and that a predicate F-and-G might be referenceless even though F and G are not. One must also take special care in dealing with generalized quantifiers (see Rayo (2002)). Empty predicates may not be the only case of meaningful but referenceless predicates. Predicates such as 'is taller than him' in a context in which 'him' hasn't been assigned a reference might constitute another example. (Thanks here to Tim Williamson.)

such as '$\sigma_1^0[\textsc{Unicorn}^1(v_1^0)]$', '$\ulcorner \mathrm{P}^2(t^1)\urcorner$' is false; for one cannot truthfully say of *no things* that they are thus-and-so.[20]

Let us therefore stipulate that an atomic predication that applies to an empty term is always false. For the case of '$\sigma_1^0[\textsc{Unicorn}^1(v_1^0)]$', we have:

(8) $\neg\textsc{True}(\ulcorner P^2(\sigma_1^0[\textsc{Unicorn}^1(v_1^0)])\urcorner)$,

for $\ulcorner P^2(\ldots)\urcorner$ an arbitrary atomic monadic second-level predicate. (The polyadic case is analogous). A semantics based on (7) and (8) is developed in the appendix.

9.3.5 Collapse

Say that Socrates is the one and only Socratizer. It would still be incorrect to say the following:

(∗) Socrates is the same individual as the Socratizers

But this is not because (∗) is false. The problem with (∗) is that it is *ungrammatical.* It is ungrammatical in just the way that each of the following is ungrammatical:

*The Socratizers is the same individual as Socrates
*Socrates are the same individuals as the Socratizers

It is important to be clear, however, that this is a point about grammar, not metaphysics. Just because mixed identity statements are ungrammatical, it doesn't follow that the world contains additional items—the 'pluralities'—over and above individuals. Individuals are the only 'items' there are.

One could, if one wished, extend the formation rules of one's language so as to admit mixed identities as well-formed, and extend the semantics for one's language to assign mixed identities suitable truth conditions. More generally, one could, if one wanted, allow *n*th-level predicates to take *m*th-level terms as arguments for any $m < n$. The most natural way of doing so is by identifying the truth-conditions of $\ulcorner \mathrm{P}^n(v_l^k)\urcorner$ $(k + 1 < n)$ with those of

$$\exists v_i^{k+1}\forall v_j^k((v_j^k \prec^{k+1,k+2} v_i^{k+1} \leftrightarrow v_j^k =^{k+1,k+1} v_l^k) \wedge P^n(v_i^{k+1}));$$

where $\ulcorner v_i^n =^{n+1,n+1} v_j^n\urcorner$ $(0 < n)$ is a syntactic abbreviation of

$$\forall v_s^{n-1}(v_s^{n-1} \prec^{n,n+1} v_i^n \leftrightarrow v_s^{n-1} \prec^{n,n+1} v_j^n);$$

(and similarly for polyadic predicates). With the extended conception of grammaticality in place, (∗) can be formalized as something which is both well-formed and true.

This revised conception of grammaticality will be ignored in what follows. But as long as one is prepared to resist the temptation of drawing metaphysical conclusions from terminological maneuvering, I can see no objections to adopting it.

[20] Compare with the treatment of empty names in Oliver and Smiley (typescript).

9.3.6 Higher-*Order* Predicates

A monadic $(n + 1)$th-*level* predicate should be distinguished from a monadic $(n + 1)$th-*order* predicate: whereas the former takes an nth-level *term* in its argument-place, the latter takes a nth-level *predicate* in its argument-place.

On its most natural interpretation, the hierarchy of higher-order predicates is not structurally analogous to the hierarchy of higher-level predicates we have considered here. One important difference was emphasized in the preceding section. If '$E^1(\ldots)$' is a first-order predicate satisfied by nothing, the standard semantics for higher-order languages allows for the atomic second-order predication '$P^2_x(E^1(x))$' to be either true or false. But, on the semantics sketched above, the atomic second-level predication '$\mathrm{P}^2(\sigma^0_i[E^1(v^0_i)])$' is always false.

In this paper I give no reason for favoring a hierarchy of higher and higher level predicates over a hierarchy of higher and higher order predicates. I have chosen to focus on the former because it seems to me that second-level predicates deliver a more natural regimentation of English predicates with collective readings than their second-order counterparts. But either hierarchy will do, as far as the purposes of this paper are concerned.[21]

9.4 HIGHER-LEVEL LANGUAGES

9.4.1 Limit$_\omega$ Languages

Let a limit$_\omega$ language consist of the following symbols:

1. The logical connectives '$\wedge$' and '$\neg$';
   ('$\vee$', '$\supset$' and '$\leftrightarrow$' are characterized in terms of '$\neg$' and '$\wedge$' in the usual way);
2. for $n \geq 0$ and $i \geq 1$, the placeholder $\ulcorner v^n_i \urcorner$;
3. for $i \geq 1$, the individual constant symbol $\ulcorner c^0_i \urcorner$;
   (in practice, we will sometimes write, e.g. 'Clyde' or 'c' in place of $\ulcorner c^0_i \urcorner$);
4. for s a finite sequence of positive integers and $i \geq 1$, the non-logical predicate-letter $\ulcorner P^s_i \urcorner$;
   (in practice, we will sometimes write, e.g. '$\text{ANCESTOR}^{1,1}$' and 'SCATTERED^2' in place of $\ulcorner P^{1,1}_i \urcorner$ and $\ulcorner P^2_j \urcorner$);
5. for $n \geq 2$, the logical predicate-letters '$=^{1,1}$', $\ulcorner \prec^{n-1,n} \urcorner$ and $\ulcorner \mathrm{Ex}^n \urcorner$;
   (in practice, we will sometimes write '=' in place of '$=^{1,1}$', and '$\prec$' in place of $\ulcorner \prec^{n-1,n} \urcorner$);
6. for $n \geq 0$ and $i \geq 1$, the saturation-symbol $\ulcorner \sigma^n_i \urcorner$;
7. the auxiliaries '(', ')', '[' and ']'.

21 This subsection and the last have benefited greatly from discussion with Øystein Linnebo.

Terms and formulas are characterized simultaneously, as follows:

1. $\ulcorner c_i^0 \urcorner$ is a term of level 0;
2. $\ulcorner v_i^n \urcorner$ is a term of level n;
3. if s is the sequence $n_1, \ldots, n_m$ and $\ulcorner t_1 \urcorner, \ldots, \ulcorner t_m \urcorner$ are terms of level $n_1 - 1, \ldots, n_m - 1$ (respectively), then $\ulcorner P_i^s(t_1, \ldots, t_m) \urcorner$ is a formula;
4. if $\ulcorner t_1 \urcorner$ and $\ulcorner t_2 \urcorner$ are terms of level 0, then $\ulcorner t_1 = t_2 \urcorner$ is a formula;
5. if, for $n \geq 2$, $\ulcorner t_1 \urcorner$ and $\ulcorner t_2 \urcorner$ are terms of level $n-2$ and $n-1$ (respectively), then $\ulcorner t_1 \prec^{n-1,n} t_2 \urcorner$ is a formula;
6. if, for $n \geq 2$, $\ulcorner t \urcorner$ is a term of level $n-1$, then $\ulcorner \mathrm{Ex}^n(t) \urcorner$ is a formula;
7. if φ is a formula, then $\ulcorner \sigma_i^n[\varphi] \urcorner$ is a term of level n+1;
8. if φ and ψ are formulas, $\ulcorner \neg\varphi \urcorner$ and $\ulcorner (\varphi \wedge \psi) \urcorner$ are formulas;
9. nothing else is a term or a formula.

Finally, we say that formula φ is a *sentence* if every occurrence of a placeholder $\ulcorner v_i^n \urcorner$ in φ is within a subformula of the form $\ulcorner \sigma_i^n[\psi] \urcorner$.

It is worth emphasizing that limit$_\omega$ languages contain no primitive quantifier-symbols. Instead, we introduce the following syntactic abbreviations:

$$\exists v_i^n(\varphi) \equiv_{df} \mathrm{Ex}^{n+2}(\sigma_i^n[\varphi])$$

$$\forall v_i^n(\varphi) \equiv_{df} \neg\exists v_i^n(\neg\varphi)$$

On the intended interpretation of $\ulcorner \mathrm{Ex}^n \urcorner$, this has the result that '$\exists v_i^0$' may be used to play the role of singular quantifiers, '$\exists v_i^1$' may be used to play the role of plural quantifiers, '$\exists v_i^2$' may be used to play the role of super-plural quantifiers, and so forth. Thus, '$\exists v_1^0(\text{ELEPHANT}^1(v_1^0))$', which abbreviates

> $\mathrm{Ex}^2(\sigma_1^0[\text{ELEPHANT}^1(v_1^0)])$
> (roughly: the plurality of elephants exists),

may be paraphrased as

> $\exists x(\text{ELEPHANT}^1(x))$
> (there is something that is an elephant);

and '$\exists v_1^1 \exists v_1^0(v_1^0 \prec v_1^1)$', which abbreviates

> $\mathrm{Ex}^3(\sigma_1^1[\mathrm{Ex}^2(\sigma_1^0[v_1^0 \prec v_1^1])])$
> (roughly: the super-plurality *xxx* exists, where *xxx* consists of all and only pluralities *xx* such that the plurality *yy* exists, where *yy* consists of all and only individuals *y* such that *y* is one of the *xx*),

may be paraphrased as

> $\exists xx \exists y(y \prec xx)$
> (there are some things such that something is one of them).

To improve readability, I shall sometimes write, e.g. $\ulcorner \exists x^n \urcorner$ and $\ulcorner \exists y^m \urcorner$ in place of $\ulcorner \exists v_i^n \urcorner$ and $\ulcorner \exists v_j^m \urcorner$.

9.4.2 A Deductive System

In this section I will specify a deductive system for limit$_\omega$ languages.[22] It is sound with respect to the semantics supplied in the appendix. But Gödel's Incompleteness Theorem implies that one cannot hope for completeness.

We begin with a standard deductive system for the propositional calculus:

(P1) $\varphi \supset (\psi \supset \varphi)$
(P2) $(\varphi \supset (\psi \supset \chi)) \supset ((\varphi \supset \psi) \supset (\varphi \supset \chi))$
(P3) $(\neg\varphi \supset \neg\psi) \supset (\psi \supset \varphi)$
(MP) *Modus Ponens*

$$\frac{\varphi, \varphi \supset \psi}{\psi}$$

Next, we introduce an axiom-schema governing the identity-sign:

(I) $t_i^0 = t_j^0 \supset (\varphi(t_i^0) \supset \varphi(t_j^0))$
(where t_j^0 is free for t_i^0 in φ)[23]

A universally quantified version of reflexivity, '$\forall v_1^0(v_1^0 = v_1^0)$', is an immediate consequence of (UI^1) below. But our deductive system does not include the reflexivity axiom-schema '$t^0 = t^0$'. This is because we wish to allow for empty singular terms. When 't^0' is empty, the semantics sketched in Section 9.3.4 makes any sentence of the form $\ulcorner P^1(t^0)\urcorner$ false (and its negation true), for $\ulcorner P^1\urcorner$ atomic. It makes, for instance, 'Zeus = Zeus' false (and its negation true)—though, of course, if the language includes an atomic non-identity-symbol '$\neq$', then 'Zeus $\neq$ Zeus' will be false (and its negation true).

The next step is to introduce axioms and rules governing quantification. But care must be taken. For, whereas a limit$_\omega$ language may involve empty terms of any level, there is no such thing as an 'empty' individual, or an 'empty' plurality, or an 'empty' super-plurality (and so forth). So each of the axioms and rules includes a provision disallowing empty terms:

(EI^1) *Existential Introduction—first-level version*

$$t^0 = t^0 \supset (\varphi(t^0) \supset \exists v_i^0(\varphi(v_i^0)))$$

(where t^0 is free for v_i^0 in φ)

(EE^1) *Existential Elimination—first-level version*

$$\frac{\Gamma}{c = c \supset (\varphi(c) \supset \psi)} \rightarrow \frac{\Gamma}{\exists v_i^0(\varphi(v_i^0)) \supset \psi}$$

(where c does not occur in Γ or ψ)

22 With some modifications, I follow the presentation in Shapiro (1991), §3.2.

23 The required notion of freedom-for is an exact analogue of the notion of freedom-for in a standard first-order language: t_j is free for t_i in φ just in case no occurrence of t_i in φ lies within a formula of the form $\ulcorner \sigma_j^m[\psi]\urcorner$, where $\ulcorner v_j^m\urcorner$ is a placeholder occurring in t_j. Thus, 'v_0^0' is free for 'v_1^0' in '$G^2(\sigma_1^0[\mathrm{F}^1(v_1^0)])$' or '$G^2(\sigma_2^0[\mathrm{F}^1(v_1^0)])$' but not in '$G^2(\sigma_0^0[\mathrm{F}^1(v_1^0)])$'.

(EI^H) *Existential Introduction—higher-level version*

$$\exists v_j^n(\psi(v_j^n)) \supset (\varphi(\sigma_j^n[\psi(v_j^n)]) \supset \exists v_i^{n+1}(\varphi(v_i^{n+1})))$$

(where $\sigma_j^n[\psi(v_j^n)]$ is free for v_i^{n+1} in φ)

(EE^H) *Existential Elimination—higher-level version*

$$\frac{\Gamma}{\exists v_j^n(P_k^{n+1}(v_j^n)) \supset (\varphi(\sigma_j^n[P_k^{n+1}(v_j^n)]) \supset \psi)} \rightarrow \frac{\Gamma}{\exists v_i^{n+1}(\varphi(v_i^{n+1})) \supset \psi}$$

(where P_k^{n+1} does not occur in Γ or ψ)

Finally, we include an axiom-schema that simultaneously governs the behavior of '$\prec$' and the behavior of the saturation-operator:

(S) $\forall v_i^n(v_i^n \prec \sigma_j^n[\varphi(v_j^n)] \leftrightarrow \varphi(v_i^n))$

And one could, if one wished, add some version or other of the Axiom of Choice.

On the basis of these axioms and rules, it is straightforward to prove a suitable version of the Deduction Theorem. One can also derive an axiom-schema of comprehension and principles governing universal quantification:

(C) *Comprehension*

$$\exists v_i^n(\varphi(v_i^n)) \supset \exists v_i^{n+1}\forall v_j^n(v_j^n \prec v_i^{n+1} \leftrightarrow \varphi(v_j^n))$$

(where v_i^{n+1} does not occur in φ)

(UE^1) *Universal Elimination—first-level version*

$$t^0 = t^0 \supset (\forall v_i^0(\varphi(v_i^0)) \supset \varphi(t^0))$$

(where t^0 is free for v_i^0 in φ)

(UI^1) *Universal Introduction—first-level version*

$$\frac{\Gamma}{c = c \supset (\psi \supset \varphi(c))} \rightarrow \frac{\Gamma}{\psi \supset \forall v_i^0(\varphi(v_i^0))}$$

(where c does not occur in Γ or ψ)

(UE^H) *Universal Elimination—higher-level version*

$$\exists v_j^n(\psi(v_j^n)) \supset (\forall v_i^{n+1}(\varphi(v_i^{n+1})) \supset \varphi(\sigma_j^n[\psi(v_j^n)]))$$

(where $\sigma_j^n[\psi(v_j^n)]$ is free for v_i^{n+1} in φ)

(UI^H) *Universal Introduction—higher-level version*

$$\frac{\Gamma}{\exists v_j^n(P_k^{n+1}(v_j^n)) \supset (\psi \supset \varphi(\sigma_j^n[P_k^{n+1}(v_j^n)]))} \rightarrow \frac{\Gamma}{\psi \supset \forall v_i^{n+1}(\varphi(v_i^{n+1}))}$$

(where P_k^{n+1} does not occur in Γ or ψ)

9.4.3 *n*th-Level Languages

Some additional notation will be useful in what follows:

- A *basic first-level* language is what one might recognize as a first-order language with no non-logical vocabulary. It is the fragment of a limit$_\omega$ language containing no placeholders other than those of the form $\ulcorner v_i^0 \urcorner$, no non-logical predicates, no logical predicates other than '$=$' and 'Ex^2', and no occurrences of the saturation-symbol other than those of the form $\ulcorner \sigma_i^0 \urcorner$.
- A *full first-level language* is the result of enriching a basic first-level language with non-logical first-level predicates.
- A *first-level language* is a full or basic first-level language.

And correspondingly for finite levels greater than 1:

- A *basic* $(n+1)$*th-level language* is the result of enriching a full *n*th-level language with placeholders of the form $\ulcorner v_i^n \urcorner$, the logical predicates '$\prec^{n,n+1}$' and 'Ex^{n+2}', and occurrences of the saturation-symbol of the form $\ulcorner \sigma_i^n \urcorner$.
- A *full* $(n+1)$*th-level language* is the result of enriching a basic $(n+1)$th-level language with non-logical $(n+1)$th-level predicates.
- An $(n+1)$*th-level language* is a full or basic $(n+1)$th-level language.

9.5 MOTIVATING THE HIERARCHY

9.5.1 Preliminaries

Let me begin with a warm-up case. Consider a skeptic who doubts that the standard first-level quantifiers fall under a legitimate semantic category. How might one respond to such skepticism?

The first thing to note is that the skeptic's doubts might take two different forms. A radical skeptic would deny that there is any sense to be made of sentences involving quantifier-symbols (as used by logicians). A moderate skeptic, on the other hand, would concede that the sentences make sense but contend that their semantic properties are best described by semantic categories other than 'first-level quantifier' (or, more generally, 'second-level predicate'). Each type of skepticism calls for a different kind of response.

Let us consider the more radical position first. In responding to the radical skeptic, appeals to introspection are unlikely to be very effective. One might claim, for instance, that one gets a certain 'feeling of understanding' when one considers, e.g. '$\exists x$ ELEPHANT(x)'. But it is open to the skeptic to counter by arguing that speakers are not always reliable judges of what they do and do not understand.

An alternative approach is to set forth a theory of what linguistic understanding consists in, and respond to the skeptic by arguing that the relevant speakers satisfy the constraints of the theory when it comes to the relevant sentences. But even this more sophisticated strategy is likely to be of limited effectiveness. Suppose one held the view that to understand a sentence is, at least in part, to know its truth conditions. It would be useless to respond to the skeptic by claiming that speakers know that '$\exists x$ ELEPHANT(x)' is true just in case there is an individual such that it is an elephant. For rather than conceding that there is sense to be made of '$\exists x$ ELEPHANT(x)', the skeptic would protest that one has begged the question by attributing to speakers knowledge whose intelligibility is under dispute.

A more promising strategy would be to bracket the question of what linguistic understanding consists in and attempt to come to an agreement with the skeptic about the sorts of things that would count as *evidence* of linguistic understanding. Here are some natural candidates:

1. that speakers have the ability to use assertions of sentences containing the disputed vocabulary to update their beliefs about the world;
2. that speakers have the ability to use their beliefs about the world to regulate their assertions of sentences containing the disputed vocabulary;
3. that speakers have the ability to use sentences involving the disputed vocabulary as part of a robust and consistent inferential practice.

One can then go on to produce a non-question-begging argument for the intelligibility of sentences involving quantifier-symbols by showing that the relevant constraints are met.

As long as something along the lines of 1–3 is admitted as evidence of linguistic understanding, there will be a route for silencing the radical skeptic. But nothing has been done so far to address the moderate skeptic's concerns. The moderate skeptic can agree that 1–3 provide evidence for the view that speakers understand '$\exists x$ ELEPHANT(x)', and go on to insist that the semantic properties of such sentences are best described by appeal to semantic categories other than 'first-level quantifier'. She might insist, for example, that the semantic structure of '$\exists x$ ELEPHANT(x)' is best described as the infinite disjunction

$$\text{ELEPHANT}(n_1) \vee \text{ELEPHANT}(n_2) \vee \text{ELEPHANT}(n_3) \vee \ldots$$

where the $\ulcorner n_i \urcorner$ are the singular terms in the language. How might the issue be resolved?

As before, linguistic introspection is unlikely to help. For in response to the claim that one's intuitions suggest that 'first-level quantifier' is the right semantic category, the skeptic can claim that her intuitions suggest otherwise (and add that she is as competent a logician and English speaker as you). And, as before, one shouldn't expect much progress from the suggestion that a speaker's understanding of '$\exists x$ ELEPHANT(x)' consists, at least in part, of knowing that that '$\exists x$ ELEPHANT(x)' is true just in case there is an individual such that it is an elephant. For the skeptic will immediately grant the point, and go on to claim that the semantic properties of 'there is an individual such that ... ' are best described by appeal to semantic categories other than 'first-level quantifier'.

It seems to me that the best way of addressing the moderate skeptic's concern is to argue that relevant mental and linguistic phenomena are best explained by a semantic theory that makes use of 'first-level quantifier' (or 'second-level predicate') as a semantic category. Here are some examples of considerations that might be set forth on behalf of the standard semantics:

- on the skeptical semantics, but not the standard semantics, the semantic structure of quantified sentences has infinitely many semantic constituents;
- on the skeptical semantics, but not the standard semantics, the meaning of '$\exists x\, F(x)$' is in constant flux, as some singular terms are introduced to the language and others are dropped;
- on the skeptical semantics, but not the standard semantics, there is a risk of being left with the result that speakers cannot fully grasp '$\exists x\, F(x)$' until they learn every singular term in the language.

If, as one might expect, it turns out that the best semantic theory (all things considered) is the standard semantic theory, one will be in a position to answer the moderate skeptic. It is worth noting, in particular, that there is a certain kind of argument that it would be illegitimate for the skeptic to employ. She should not defend her position by arguing that until one has *independent* evidence for the view that first-level quantifiers fall under a legitimate semantic category, the relevant linguistic practice cannot be accounted for by a categorial semantics that mentions first-level quantifiers. That would be to put the cart before the course. The best evidence one could have for the legitimacy of a semantic category is its presence in our best—simplest, most fruitful, best integrated—semantic theorizing.

9.5.2 The Argument

In preceding sections I claimed without argument that, for any finite n, nth-level predicates and terms belong to legitimate semantic categories. (I also claimed that plural quantifiers, super-plural quantifiers and beyond fall under legitimate semantic categories, but we saw in Section 9.4.1 that the such quantifiers needn't be taken as primitive once one has higher-level predicates and terms.) In this section I will try to supply the missing justification. My argument will be similar in form to that of the warm-up example, but this time proponents of the view that nth-level predicates and terms do not fall under legitimate semantic categories will take the place of the skeptic. The argument will not be conclusive, but I hope it is enough to show that the legitimacy of higher-level predicates and terms can be taken seriously.

I begin with the following observation:

No Paraphrase
When an all-encompassing domain of discourse is allowed, it is not generally possible to paraphrase a basic second-level language as a first-order language.

(We say that a basic second-level language $\mathcal{L}^2$ can be *paraphrased* as a first-order language just in case there is a range of individuals—the 'classes', say—such that, for any sentence in $\mathcal{L}^2$, the following transformation preserves truth-value:

- $(\exists v_i^0(\varphi))^{Tr} \rightarrowtail \exists x_i(\varphi^{Tr})$
- $(\exists v_i^1(\varphi))^{Tr} \rightarrowtail \exists \alpha_i(\varphi^{Tr})$

- $(v_i^0 \prec v_j^1)^{Tr} \rightarrowtail x_i \in \alpha_j$
- $(v_i^0 = v_j^0)^{Tr} \rightarrowtail x_i = x_j$
- $(P(v_{i_1}^0, \ldots, v_{i_n}^0))^{Tr} \rightarrowtail P(x_{i_1}, \ldots, x_{i_n})$
- $(\varphi \wedge \psi)^{Tr} \rightarrowtail \varphi^{Tr} \wedge \psi^{Tr}$
- $(\neg\varphi)^{Tr} \rightarrowtail \neg(\varphi^{Tr})$

where $\ulcorner x_i \urcorner$ ranges over the individuals in the domain of discourse of $\mathfrak{L}^2$, $\ulcorner \alpha_i \urcorner$ ranges over (non-empty) 'classes' of these individuals, and '$\in$' expresses a membership relation appropriate for 'classes'.)

To see that No Paraphrase holds, assume for *reductio* that it is generally possible to paraphrase a second-level language as a first-order language. Let the domain of discourse of $\mathfrak{L}^2$ consist of absolutely everything, and let $\mathfrak{L}^2$ contain a predicate, 'Member', which is true of x and y just in case x is a member of 'class' y. Then the following must be true:

(9) $\forall v_1^1 \exists v_1^0 \forall v_2^0 (v_2^0 \prec v_1^1 \leftrightarrow \text{Member}(v_2^0, v_1^0))$,

since the result of applying Tr to (9) is:

(10) $\forall \alpha_1 \exists x_1 \forall x_2 (x_2 \in \alpha_1 \leftrightarrow \text{Member}(x_2, x_1))$,

(which is true because 'Member' and '$\in$' must be coextensive in light of the fact that the domain of discourse of $\mathfrak{L}^2$ is absolutely unrestricted). But, on the assumption that there are at least two objects, (9) entails a contradiction. To see this, note that one can derive the following from (9) by applying (UE^H) and (S):

(11) $\exists v_2^0 (\neg\text{Member}(v_2^0, v_2^0)) \supset \exists v_1^0 \forall v_2^0 (\neg\text{Member}(v_2^0, v_2^0) \leftrightarrow \text{Member}(v_2^0, v_1^0))$.

A tedious but straightforward proof shows that the antecedent of (11) can be derived from (9) (together with the assumption that there are at least two objects). So we are left with:

$$\exists v_1^0 \forall v_2^0 (\neg\text{Member}(v_2^0, v_2^0) \leftrightarrow \text{Member}(v_2^0, v_1^0)),$$

from which one can derive a contradiction by applying (EE^1) and (UE^1). This concludes the *reductio*.

I would like to suggest that No Paraphrase provides some evidence for the view that second-level predicates and first-level terms fall under legitimate semantic categories. The argument runs as follows.

Consider a community of speakers that sets out to speak a second-level language. They let their syntax be governed by (suitable restrictions of) the rules in Section 9.4.1, and let their deductions be constrained by (suitable restrictions of) the axioms and rules in Section 9.4.2. The new conventions eventually take hold, and speakers come to engage in a successful linguistic practice. In particular, conditions 1–3 from Section 9.5.1 are all satisfied.

As long as it is conceded that such a scenario is possible, one will be in a position to counter radical skepticism: one will be in a position to argue that members of the community succeed in speaking some language or other and, accordingly, that there is sense to be made of the relevant sentences. But this is not yet to concede that second-level predicates and first-level terms fall under legitimate semantic categories. A moderate skeptic would concede that there is sense to be made of the relevant sentences but doubt that the language is best described by a semantic theory employing the semantic categories 'second-level predicate' and 'first-level term'. In particular, the moderate skeptic might endorse a *firstorderist* view whereby members of the community speak the first-order language induced by *Tr*, and supply a semantics accordingly.

The lesson of No Paraphrase is that when an all-encompassing domain of discourse is allowed, proponents of the firstorderist position must make a concession. They must concede that some of the rules and axioms that speakers take their inferences to be constrained by are not, in fact, logically valid. For the proof of No Paraphrase entails that the following is a *theorem* of the deductive system in Section 9.4.2:

(12) $\exists v_1^0 \exists v_2^0 (\neg(v_1^0 = v_2^0)) \supset \neg\forall v_1^1 \exists v_1^0 \forall v_2^0 (v_2^0 \prec v_1^1 \leftrightarrow \mathrm{P}_1^{1,1}(v_2^0, v_1^0))$

But from the perspective of a firstorderist, (12) must be false when '$\mathrm{P}_1^{1,1}$' expresses the membership relation appropriate for 'classes' and the domain of discourse is absolutely unrestricted.

This puts the firstorderist position under some pressure. Suppose, for example, that speakers resolve to enrich their language with the first level predicate 'Member', which, as before, is to be true of *x* and *y* just in case *x* is a member of 'class' *y* (and that speakers continue to take their syntax to be governed by the rules in Section 9.4.1, and their deductions be constrained by the axioms and rules in Section 9.4.2). Firstorderists will then face an awkward decision. On the one hand, they might concede that some of the community's fundamental axioms are not merely not logically valid but outright false (or that some of the community's fundamental rules are not merely not logically valid but have a true premise and a false conclusion). For firstorderists must regard the result of replacing '$\mathrm{P}_1^{1,1}$' with 'Member' in (12) as false, even though it is a deductive consequence of the community's fundamental rules and axioms. Alternatively, firstorderists might claim that enriching the language with 'Member' leads to a change in the way quantification works: whereas in the original language the $\ulcorner \alpha_i \urcorner$ range over 'classes', in the enriched language they range over 'classes*', which are such that (12) is true. This would certainly forestall any breaches in charity, but at the cost of complicating one's semantic theory, since the semantic behavior of the quantifiers will have to depend on what predicates the language happens to contain. And there would appear to be little independent motivation for the additional complexity.

Of course, the firstorderist position might still be vindicated at the end of the day. For all I have argued here, it might be possible to make a case for the view that, e.g. the gain in parsimony that is achieved by limiting one's stock of legitimate semantic categories is significant enough to outweigh firstorderism's less palatable consequences. But, as in the warm up case considered earlier, it is important to keep in mind that the there is a certain kind of argument that it is important to resist. One should not argue for the firstorderist position by claiming that, unless one has *independent* evidence for the view that higher-level predicates and terms fall under legitimate semantic categories, the relevant linguistic practice cannot be accounted for by a categorial semantics that mentions higher-level predicates and terms. The best evidence one could have for the legitimacy of a semantic category is its presence in our best—simplest, most fruitful, best integrated—semantic theorizing. By insisting that higher-level predicates and terms remain unavailable to semantic theorizing until the relevant semantic categories have been shown to be legitimate on independent grounds, firstorderists would be begging the question against their opponents.

In sum, my argument is this. Should it turn out that a community's linguistic practice is best accounted for by a semantic theory that makes use of the categories 'second-level predicate' and 'first-level term', we would be justified in thinking that second-level predicates and first-level terms fall under legitimate semantic categories. But when an all-encompassing domain of discourse is allowed, No Paraphrase suggests that firstorderism—the most salient alternative—will be subject to certain kinds of difficulties. So, when an all-encompassing domain of discourse is allowed, we have some preliminary evidence for the view that second-level predicates and first-level terms fall under legitimate semantic categories.

I have focused on second-level languages for expository purposes, but the argument is quite general. For each finite n, one can prove a version of No Paraphrase for $(n+1)$th-level languages:[24]

> When an all-encompassing domain of discourse is allowed, it is not generally possible to paraphrase a basic $(n+1)$th-level language as an nth-level language.

[24] In analogy with the above, we say that a basic $(n+1)$th-level language $\mathcal{L}^{n+1}$ $(n \geq 2)$ can be *paraphrased* as an nth-level $\mathcal{L}^n$ language just in case there is a range of individuals—the 'classes'—such that, for any sentence in $\mathcal{L}^{n+1}$, the following transformation into $\mathcal{L}^n$ preserves truth-value (certain clauses are omitted for the sake of brevity):

- for $m < (n-1)$, $(\exists v_i^m(\varphi))^{Tr} \rightarrowtail \exists v_i^m(D^{m+1}(v_i^m) \wedge \varphi^{Tr})$
- $(\exists v_i^{n-1}(\varphi))^{Tr} \rightarrowtail \exists v_{2i-1}^{n-1}(D^n(v_{2i-1}^{n-1}) \wedge \varphi^{Tr})$
- $(\exists v_i^n(\varphi))^{Tr} \rightarrowtail \exists v_{2i}^{n-1}(C^n(v_{2i}^{n-1}) \wedge \varphi^{Tr})$
- $(v_i^{n-1} \prec v_j^n)^{Tr} \rightarrowtail v_{2i-1}^{n-1} \ll v_{2j}^{n-1}$
  where 'D^m', 'C^m' and $v_i^m \ll v_j^m$ are characterized as follows:

  — 'D^1' is true of all and only individuals in the domain of discourse of $\mathcal{L}^{n+1}$
  — $\mathrm{D}^{k+2}(v_s^{k+1}) \leftrightarrow \forall v_t^k(v_t^k \prec v_s^{k+1} \supset \mathrm{D}^{k+1}(v_t^k))$
  — 'C^1' is true of all and only (non-empty) 'classes' of individuals in the domain of discourse of $\mathcal{L}^{n+1}$
  — $\mathrm{C}^{k+2}(v_s^{k+1}) \leftrightarrow \forall v_t^k(v_t^k \prec v_s^{k+1} \supset \mathrm{C}^{k+1}(v_t^k))$
  — $v_i^0 \ll v_j^0 \leftrightarrow v_i^0 \in v_j^0$
  — $v_i^{k+1} \ll v_j^{k+1} \leftrightarrow \exists v_s^k(v_s^k \prec v_j^{k+1} \wedge \forall v_t^k(v_t^k \prec v_i^{k+1} \leftrightarrow v_t^k \ll v_s^k))$,

  and '$\in$' expresses a membership relation appropriate for 'classes'.

The higher-level version of No Paraphrase can then be established by focusing on the following sentence of $\mathcal{L}^{n+1}$:

$$\forall v_1^n \exists v_1^{n-1} \forall v_2^{n-1}(v_2^{n-1} \prec v_1^n \leftrightarrow \mathrm{MEMBER}(v_2^{n-1}, v_1^{n-1}))$$

where 'Member' is characterized just like '$\ll$'.

If one then considers a community of speakers who have set out to speak an $(n+1)$th-level language, one can replicate the argument above to make a preliminary case for the view that the relevant linguistic practice is best accounted for by a semantic theory that mentions $(n+2)$th level predicates and $(n+1)$th level terms, and therefore a preliminary case for the view that $(n+2)$th-level predicates and $(n+1)$-level terms fall under legitimate semantic categories. All of this on the assumption that an all-encompassing domain of discourse is allowed.[25]

9.6 MODEL-THEORY

A model-theory for a language L is *strictly adequate* just in case it agrees with one's categorial semantics for L in the following sense: any reference a (non-logical) predicate might take by the lights of one's categorial semantics corresponds to the semantic value the predicate gets assigned by some model of one's model-theory. Thus, given a categorial semantics whereby the reference of a first-level predicate is a plurality, a model-theory for the relevant language can only be strictly adequate if, for any plurality, there is a model on which a given first-level predicate is assigned a semantic value corresponding to that plurality.

When quantification over absolutely everything is allowed, it is easy to show that there must be 'more' pluralities than there are individuals.[26] So, on the assumption that the reference of a monadic first-level predicate is a plurality, there must be 'more' ways of assigning reference to a monadic first-level predicate than there are individuals. It follows that a model-theory for a full first-level language can only be strictly adequate if it appeals to 'more' models than there are individuals.

An immediate consequence of this result is that no model-theory according to which a model is a *set* can be strictly adequate. More generally, one cannot give a strictly adequate model-theory for a full first-level language in a first-level language, since a model-theory requires quantification over models, and the only kind of quantification available in a first-level language is singular quantification over individuals. Fortunately, this does not mean that it is impossible to give a strictly adequate model-theory for full first-level languages. By taking a model to be a *plurality*, one can give a strictly adequate model-theory for first-level languages in a basic second-level language.[27] (To fix ideas, think of a model m^1 as a plurality consisting of ordered-pairs of the form $\langle `\forall', x^0\rangle$ and ordered-pairs of the form $\langle `P_i^1', x^0\rangle$, for '$P_i^1$' a predicate in the language. Intuitively, $\langle `\forall', x^0\rangle \prec m^1$ just in case $x^0$ is in the 'domain' of $m^1$, and $\langle `P_i^1', x^0\rangle \prec m^1$ just in case x^0 is in the reference of 'P_i^1' according to m^1.) For reasons relating to Tarski's Theorem, it is impossible to give a strictly adequate model-theory

25 This section benefited greatly from discussion with Gabriel Uzquiano and Crispin Wright.

26 The basic idea is due to Bernays (1942); for a formal statement of the result see Rayo (2002). The proof is analogous to that of theorem 5.3 of Shapiro (1991).

27 See McGee (forthcoming). For present purposes, it is best to think of the dyadic second-order quantifier in McGee's construction as a monadic quantifier ranging over ordered-pairs.

for a basic second-level language in another basic second-level language.[28] But one can give a strictly adequate model-theory for a basic second-level language in a full second-level language.[29]

These results can be generalized for $n \geq 1$.[30] Thus:

SEMANTIC ASCENT

(*a*) It is impossible to give a strictly adequate model-theory for a full *n*th-level language in an *n*th level language.

(*b*) It is possible to give a strictly adequate model-theory for full *n*th-level languages in a basic $(n+1)$th-level language.

(*c*) It is impossible to give a strictly adequate model-theory for a basic $(n+1)$th-level language in a basic $(n+1)$th level language.

(*d*) It is possible to give a strictly adequate model-theory for basic $(n+1)$th-level languages in a full $(n+1)$-th level language.

(A strictly adequate model-theory for *n*th-level languages is developed in the appendix.)

A famous argument of Kreisel's can be used to show that any first-level sentence that is true according to some model of a strictly adequate model-theory is also true according to some model of a standard model-theory (in which models are *sets* rather than pluralities).[31] This result—which I shall refer to as *Kreisel's Principle*—guarantees that an extensionally adequate characterization of logical consequence for a first-level language can be given within another first-level language. In light of Kreisel's Principle, it is tempting to conclude that a thorough understanding of first-level languages can be attained by appeal to a model-theory that is not strictly adequate, and hence that the requirement of strict adequacy is unnecessarily strong.

The temptation should be resisted. For there is more to model-theory than a characterization of logical consequence. Conspicuously, model-theory might be thought to deliver a generalized notion of reference, which is concerned not just with the assignment of reference an expression actually takes, but with any possible assignment of reference the expression might take. Suppose, for example, that one wished to record the fact that, by the lights of one's categorial semantics, a monadic first-level predicate could be assigned a reference that consists of too many objects to form a set. A strictly adequate model-theory immediately delivers the resources to do so:

$$\exists mm \exists xx[\textsc{Model}^2(mm) \wedge \textsc{Ref}^{2,1,2}(mm, `P^1(\ldots)', xx) \wedge \neg\exists y \forall z(z \in y \leftrightarrow z \prec^{1,2} xx)]$$

[28] See Rayo and Williamson (2003), footnote 7.

[29] See Rayo and Uzquiano (1999).

[30] One might worry that my arguments for SEMANTIC ASCENT rely on unwarranted assumptions about predicate-reference. For I used the assumption that, e.g. the reference of a monadic first-level predicate is a plurality. But what if one held a view such as the following?

$$\forall x(\textsc{Ref}^{1,1}(`\ldots \text{ is an elephant'}, x) \leftrightarrow \textsc{Elephant}^1(x))$$

In fact, it makes no difference whether one chooses to say that something is a referent of '. . . is an elephant' just in case it is an elephant, rather than saying that the reference of '. . . is an elephant' is the plurality of elephants. The arguments for SEMANTIC ASCENT go through just the same.

[31] See Kreisel (1967).

(where '$\text{MODEL}^2(mm)$' is a second-level formula stating that the *mm*s form a model, and '$\text{REF}^{2,1,2}(mm, `P^1(\ldots)\text{'}, xx)$' is a second-level formula stating that the reference assigned by the *mm*s to '$P^1(\ldots)$' is the plurality consisting of all and only the *xx*s). But it is hard to see how one could make a similar statement within the confines of a standard model-theory.

This limitation of standard model-theory also affects its ability to produce extensionally adequate characterizations of logical consequence in certain special cases. Consider, for instance, the result of enriching a first-level language with a quantifier '$\exists^{AI}$', as in McGee (1992). The sentence '$\exists^{AI}x(\phi(x))$' is to be true just in case the individuals satisfying '$\phi(x)$' are too many to form a set. So '$\exists^{AI}x(x = x)$' is true (and therefore consistent). But it would be deemed false by any model of a standard model-theory. The lesson is clear. Kreisel's Principle shows that strictly adequate model-theories can be supplanted by standard model theories for the purposes of one particular application, but not that they can be supplanted in general.

Two further points are worth emphasizing. First, the benefits of Kreisel's Principle can only be claimed by those who have already ventured beyond first-level languages. For although the principle is often stated informally, it cannot be formulated properly within a first-level language. Within a second-level language, on the other hand, it has a straightforward formulation.

Second, the status of higher-level versions of Kreisel's Principle is increasingly problematic. A version of Kreisel's Principle for a basic second-level language, for instance, is provably independent of the standard axioms of set theory (if consistent with them).[32] So friends of plural quantification cannot make use of Kreisel's Principle to avoid giving a strictly adequate model-theory without making substantial set-theoretic presuppositions.

9.7 AN OPEN-ENDED HIERARCHY

Since a limit$_\omega$ language contains an *n*th-level language as a part for each finite *n*, the following is a consequence of SEMANTIC ASCENT (*a*) and (*c*):[33]

SEMANTIC ASCENT

(*e*) It is impossible to give a strictly-adequate model-theory for a limit$_\omega$ language in a limit$_\omega$ language.

I would like to consider two different ways of dealing with this result. The first strategy is to settle for what I shall call *semantic pessimism*: the view that it is impossible to provide a strictly adequate model-theory for some language built up from legitimate semantic categories. Philosophers have grown accustomed to the fact that any

32 It implies, for example, the existence of inaccessible cardinals. See Shapiro (1991), §6.3.

33 *Proof:* Suppose for *reductio* that some formula φ in a limit$_\omega$ language captures the notion of truth-in-a-model. Since φ contains finitely many symbols, it is also a formula in some *n*th-level language. And this contradicts the conjunction of (*a*) and (*c*), since a limit$_\omega$ language includes *n*th-level languages as proper parts for any finite *n*.

given language must suffer from important expressive limitations. The Liar Paradox, for instance, has taught us that (on appropriate assumptions) the truth predicate for a given language cannot be expressed in the language itself, even though it can be expressed in a different language of the same logical type. But semantic pessimism is pessimism of a much more radical kind. For one is forced to countenance the view that a language might have features whose investigation is ruled out by the nature of language itself.[34]

The second strategy is to try to avoid semantic pessimism by claiming that the *legitimate* languages—the languages it is in principle possible to make sense of—form an open-ended hierarchy such that any language in the hierarchy can be given a strictly adequate model-theory in some other language higher-up in the hierarchy. So there is no legitimate language with respect to which semantic pessimism would threaten. The simplest way of setting forth such a hierarchy is by claiming that nth-level languages are legitimate for any finite n but denying that languages of transfinite level (including limit$_\omega$ languages) are legitimate. An alternative is to take the hierarchy into the transfinite by treating limit$_\omega$ languages as legitimate and postulating the legitimacy of a language $L^\star$ of transfinite-level in which a strictly adequate model-theory for limit$_\omega$ languages can be given, postulating the legitimacy of a language $L^{\star\star}$ in which a strictly adequate model-theory for $L^\star$ can be given, and so forth.[35] Whatever the details of the hierarchy, what is crucial is that there be no such thing as an *absolute*-level language: a language combining the resources of all legitimate languages. For a suitable generalization of Semantic Ascent would imply that it is impossible to give a strictly adequate model-theory for an absolute-level language. So the result of making room for an absolute-level language is that one would be left with semantic pessimism after all.

A potential difficulty for the postulation of such hierarchies emerges from the observation that the legitimacy of absolute-level languages follows from two seemingly plausible principles: the first is a Principle of Union according to which the result of combining the resources of legitimate languages is itself a legitimate language; the second is a principle to the effect that it make sense to talk about all languages in the hierarchy. For, by the first principle, the hierarchy must be closed under unions, and, by the second, one of the unions must be maximal.

Denying the second of these principles seems especially problematic in the present context. For we began our investigation by assuming that one can quantify over absolutely everything and used this assumption to argue for the view that higher-level predicates and terms fall under legitimate semantic categories. But now, in an attempt to study the semantic properties of higher-level resources, we are under pressure to countenance the idea that one cannot talk about all legitimate languages. Is this not a *reductio* of the original assumption? If it is possible to quantify over absolutely

[34] See Williamson (2003).

[35] The matter of giving a strictly adequate model-theory for languages of transfinite-level is non-trivial. Andrews (1965) develops a strictly adequate model-theory for limit$_\omega$ languages by allowing quantification over types.

everything, and if 'F(...)' is a predicate in good standing, shouldn't it be possible to quantify over all Fs?

It is not clear, however, that ' ... is a language' is a predicate in good standing in the relevant respect. To see the problem, observe that there are at least as many (interpreted) first-level languages as there are assignments of reference to a first-level predicate. Since the reference of a first-level predicate is a plurality, and since there are 'more' pluralities than there are objects, this means that there are 'more' first-level languages than individuals, and therefore that a first-level language cannot, in general, be an individual. It is best to think of a first-level language as a certain kind of *plurality*. For analogous reasons, it is best to think of a second-level language as a certain kind of super-plurality, and best to think of a third-level language as a super-duper-plurality, and so forth. Accordingly, the predicate ' ... is an nth-level language' must be (at least) of level $n + 1$. And one can expect a similar result to hold for languages of infinite level: the predicate ' ... is an αth-level language' must be (at least) of level $\alpha + 1$. So what type of predicate could ' ... is a language' be? Any predicate falling under a legitimate semantic category must be of some level or other. But ' ... is a language' cannot be an αth-level predicate, lest one be left with the unintended result that α-level languages are not languages. The lesson, I would like to suggest, is that ' ... is a language' is best understood as ambiguous between various legitimate predicates of the form ' ... is a language of at most level α'. And if this is right, one cannot go from quantification over absolutely everything to quantification over all languages.

(*Parenthetical remark:* The preceding remarks suggest a novel way of making sense of the idea that the classes form an *indefinitely extensible* totality.[36] For if one thinks of a class, not as an *individual* of a certain kind, but as the reference of a predicate in some language, then the predicate ' ... is a class' will have a status similar to that of ' ... is a language'. The reference of a first-level predicate is a plurality; the reference of a second-level predicate is a super-plurality; the reference of a third-level predicate is a super-duper-plurality; and so forth. So what type of predicate could ' ... is a class' be? Any predicate falling under a legitimate semantic category must be of some level or other. But ' ... is a class' cannot be an αth-level predicate, lest one be left with the unintended result that the reference of an α-level predicate is not a class. Accordingly, ' ... is a class' is best understood as ambiguous between various legitimate predicates of the form ' ... is a class of at most level α'.)

The postulation of an open-ended hierarchy of languages faces a familiar difficulty: it leads to the result that statements of the form 'the hierarchy is so-and-so' are, strictly speaking, nonsense.[37] (This does not, of course, imply that the state of affairs under discussion fails to obtain; what it shows is that there are important limits in the sorts of statements that can be made about it.)

In spite of its problems, the postulation of an open-ended hierarchy of languages may turn out to be the least unattractive of the options on the table. It may very well be part of the nature of language and thought that matters cannot be improved upon.

[36] For more on indefinite extensibility, see Russell (1906), Dummett (1963), Parsons (1974a), Parsons (1974b), Dummett (1991) pp. 316-19, Dummett (1993b), Hazen (1993), Williamson (1998), Glanzberg (2004), Shapiro ((2003a) and (2003b)).

[37] For a detailed discussion of these matters, see Priest (2003).

Note, for example, that there is a striking parallel between the open-ended hierarchy of *ideology* that we have considered here and the open-ended hierarchy of *ontology* that defenders of the view that it is impossible to quantify over absolutely everything have sometimes set forth.[38] (This is not to say, of course, that the two pictures are equivalent: whereas proponents of the ideological hierarchy consider only a fragment of their logical resources at a time, and are thereby able to supply a strictly adequate model-theory for the language under consideration, proponents of the ontological hierarchy consider only a fragment of their ontology at a time, and are thereby *unable* to supply a strictly adequate model-theory for any language complex enough to be interesting.) From the present perspective, one might think of the ontological hierarchy as the first-order 'projection' of the ideological hierarchy that results from objectifying pluralities, super-pluralities and beyond.

APPENDIX

I provide a model-theory for a full *n*th-level language $\mathcal{L}$ ($n > 1$) in a basic $(n+1)$th-level language.

The first step is to characterize a generalized notion of *n*-tuple membership:

- $z^0 \ll^{1,1}_{i,n} x^0 \equiv_{df} \exists y^0_1 \ldots \exists y^0_i \ldots \exists^0_n (x^0 = \langle y^0_1, \ldots, y^0_i, \ldots, y^0_n \rangle \wedge z^0 = y^0_i)$
  (z^0 is the *i*th member of zeroth-level *n*-tuple x^0)
- $z^1 \ll^{2,2}_{i,n} x^1 \equiv_{df} \forall w^0 (w^0 \prec z^1 \leftrightarrow \exists y^0 (y^0 \prec x^1 \wedge w^0 \ll^{1,1}_{i,n} y^0))$
  (z^1 is the *i*th member of first-level *n*-tuple x^1)

  ⋮
- $z^m \ll^{m+1,m+1}_{i,n} x^m \equiv_{df} \forall w^{m-1} (w^{m-1} \prec z^m \leftrightarrow \exists y^{m-1} (y^{m-1} \prec x^m \wedge w^{m-1} \ll^{m,m}_{i,n} y^{m-1}))$
  (z^m is the *i*th member of *m*th-level *n*-tuple x^m)

  ⋮

Next, we characterize a same-level pseudo-identity relation:

- $x^0 \approx y^0 \equiv_{df} x^0 = y^0$
- $x^{n+1} \approx y^{n+1} \equiv_{df} \forall z^n (z^n \prec x^{n+1} \leftrightarrow z^n \prec y^{n+1})$

and a cross-level pseudo-identity relation:

- $x^n \approx y^{n+1} \equiv_{df} \forall z^n (z^n \prec y^{n+1} \supset x^n \approx z^n)$
- $x^n \approx y^{n+k+1} \equiv_{df} \exists z^{n+1} \ldots \exists z^{n+k} (x^n \approx z^{n+1} \wedge \ldots \wedge z^{n+k} \approx y^{n+k+1})$

By using the pseudo-identity relation we can extend our characterization of generalized *n*-tuple membership as follows:

[38] See, for instance, Parsons's contribution to this volume. For further discussion of this point, see Linnebo and Weir's contributions.

$z^r \ll_{i,n}^{r+1,m+1} x^m \equiv_{df} \exists z^m(z^r \approx z^m \wedge z^m \ll_{i,n}^{m+1,m+1} x^m)$
(where $r < m$)

Some additional pieces of preliminary notation:

$x^m \approx \langle y_1^{r_1}, \ldots, y_k^{r_k} \rangle \equiv_{df} (y_1^{r_1} \ll_{1,k}^{r_1+1,m+1} x^m \wedge \ldots \wedge y_k^{r_k} \ll_{k,k}^{r_k+1,m+1} x^m)$
(where $r_i \leq m$)

$\langle y_1^{r_1}, \ldots, y_k^{r_k} \rangle \prec x^{m+1} \equiv_{df} \exists z^m(z^m \approx \langle y_1^{r_1}, \ldots, y_k^{r_k} \rangle \wedge z^m \prec x^{m+1})$
(where $r_i \leq m$ and 'z^m' is an unused variable)

$y^r \prec x^{m+1} \equiv_{df} \exists z^m(y^r \approx z^m \wedge z^m \prec x^{m+1})$
(where $r \leq m$)

We may now characterize the notion of an assignment function. Intuitively, an assignment function maps an object to each zeroth-level placeholder, a plurality to each first-level placeholder, a super-plurality to each second-level placeholder, and so forth, for every place-holder in $\mathfrak{L}$. Formally, an nth-level predicate '$A(x^{n-1})$' (read 'x^{n-1} is an assignment') may be characterized as follows:

$$
\begin{aligned}
A(x^{n-1}) \equiv_{df} \{&\forall y^{n-2}(y^{n-2} \prec x^{n-1} \supset \\
&[\exists w^0 \exists z^0(w^0 \text{ is a zeroth-level place-holder} \wedge y^{n-2} \approx \langle w^0, z^0 \rangle) \vee \\
&\exists w^0 \exists z^0(w^0 \text{ is a first-level place-holder} \wedge y^{n-2} \approx \langle w^0, z^0 \rangle) \vee \\
&\exists w^0 \exists z^1(w^0 \text{ is a second-level place-holder} \wedge y^{n-2} \approx \langle w^0, z^1 \rangle) \vee \\
&\vdots \\
&\exists w^0 \exists z^{n-2}(w^0 \text{ is an } (n-1)\text{th-level place-holder} \wedge y^{n-2} \approx \langle w^0, z^{n-2} \rangle)]) \wedge \\
&\forall w^0(w^0 \text{ is a place-holder} \supset \exists z^{n-2}(\langle w^0, z^{n-2} \rangle \prec x^{n-1})) \wedge \\
&\forall w^0(w^0 \text{ is a zeroth-level place-holder} \supset \\
&\exists z^0(\langle w^0, z^0 \rangle \prec x^{n-1} \wedge \forall t^{n-2}(\langle w^0, t^{n-2} \rangle \prec x^{n-1} \supset z^0 \approx t^{n-2})))\}
\end{aligned}
$$

When $A(x^{n-1})$ and v is a place-holder of $\mathfrak{L}$, it will sometimes be useful to employ the following notational abbreviation:

$\Phi(\alpha_{x^{n-1}}(v)) \equiv_{df} \exists y^{n-1} \forall z^{n-2}(((\langle v, z^{n-2} \rangle \prec x^{n-1} \leftrightarrow z^{n-2} \prec y^{n-1}) \wedge \Phi(y^{n-1}))$
where 'y^{n-1}' is an unused variable.

(Intuitively, '$\Phi(\alpha_{x^{n-1}}(v))$' says that the value that placeholder v is assigned by assignment x^{n-1} is Φ.)

We shall also use the following notation:

- $x^0 \prec_{trans}^{1,2} y^1 \equiv_{df} x^0 \prec y^1$
- $x^0 \prec_{trans}^{1,3} y^2 \equiv_{df} \exists z^1(x^0 \prec_{trans}^{1,2} z^1 \wedge z^1 \prec y^2)$

⋮

- $x^0 \prec^{1,k+1}_{trans} y^k \equiv_{df} \exists z^{k-1}(x^0 \prec^{1,k}_{trans} z^{k-1} \wedge z^{k-1} \prec y^k)$

⋮

The next step is to characterize the notion of a model. Intuitively, a model might be thought of as codifying four distinct things. Firstly, it codifies information about a domain (in the form of a plurality of ordered-pairs $\langle \text{`}\forall\text{'}, x\rangle$); secondly, it a codifies a function mapping an object (or nothing at all) to each individual constant symbol, a plurality (or nothing at all) to each non-logical monadic first-level predicate-letter, a super-plurality (or nothing at all) to each non-logical monadic second-level predicate-letter, and so forth for every non-logical monadic predicate-letter in $\mathcal{L}$ (and similarly for non-logical polyadic predicate-letters); thirdly, it codifies information about the denotations of terms of $\mathcal{L}$ (relative to an assignment function a^{n-1}); finally it codifies information about the satisfaction of formulas of $\mathcal{L}$ (relative to an assignment function a^{n-1}). Formally, the notion of a model can be characterized as follows. (In each clause, I omit initial universal quantifiers for the sake of readability.)

$\mathrm{M}(x^n) \equiv_{df}$

$\{[c$ is an individual constant $\supset (\langle c, a^{n-1}, z^{n-1}\rangle \prec x^n \leftrightarrow$

$$\exists w^0(w^0 \approx z^{n-1} \wedge \langle c, w^0\rangle \prec x^n \wedge \forall y^{n-1}(\langle c, y^{n-1}\rangle \prec x^n \supset w^0 \approx y^{n-1})))] \ \wedge$$

(*Intuitive gloss: the reference assigned to individual constant c by the model relative to assignment a^{n-1} is the reference assigned to c by the model.*)

$[v$ is a place-holder $\supset (\langle v, a^{n-1}, z^{n-1}\rangle \prec x^n \leftrightarrow$

$$\exists y^{n-2}(y^{n-2} \approx z^{n-1} \wedge y^{n-2} \prec \alpha_{a^{n-1}}(v)))] \ \wedge$$

(*Intuitive gloss: the reference assigned to placeholder v by the model relative to assignment a^{n-1} is the reference assigned to v by a^{n-1}.*)

$[\ulcorner t_1 = t_2 \urcorner$ is a formula $\supset (\langle \ulcorner t_1 = t_2 \urcorner, a^{n-1}\rangle \prec x^n \leftrightarrow$

$$\exists z^0(\langle t_1, a^{n-1}, z^0\rangle \prec x^n \wedge \langle t_2, a^{n-1}, z^0\rangle \prec x^n))] \ \wedge$$

(*Intuitive gloss: $\ulcorner t_1 = t_2 \urcorner$ is true in the model relative to assignment a^{n-1} just in case $\ulcorner t_1 \urcorner$ and $\ulcorner t_2 \urcorner$ are assigned the same reference by the model relative to a^{n-1}*)

$[\ulcorner t_1 \prec^{k-1,k} t_2 \urcorner$ is a formula $\rightarrow (\langle \ulcorner t_1 \prec^{k-1,k} t_2 \urcorner, a^{n-1}\rangle \prec x^n \leftrightarrow$

$$\exists z^{n-1}(\forall w^{n-2}(w^{n-2} \prec z^{n-1} \leftrightarrow \langle t_1, a^{n-1}, w^{n-2}\rangle \prec x^n) \wedge \langle t_2, a^{n-1}, z^{n-1}\rangle \prec x^n))] \ \wedge$$

(*Intuitive gloss: $\ulcorner t_1 \prec^{k-1,k} t_2 \urcorner$ is true in the model relative to assignment a^{n-1} just in case the reference assigned by the model to $\ulcorner t_1 \urcorner$ relative to a^{n-1} is 'among' the reference assigned by the model to $\ulcorner t_2 \urcorner$ relative to a^{n-1}.*)

$[\ulcorner P_j^{r_1,\ldots,r_k}(t_1,\ldots,t_k)\urcorner$ is a formula $\supset ((\ulcorner P_j^{r_1,\ldots,r_k}(t_1,\ldots,t_k)\urcorner, a^{n-1}\rangle \prec x^n \leftrightarrow$

$(\exists y^{n-1}[\langle\ulcorner P_j^{r_1,\ldots,r_k}\urcorner, y^{n-1}\rangle \prec x^n \wedge$ for each $\ulcorner t_i\urcorner$ $(1 \leq i \leq k)\ \exists z^{n-1}$

$(\forall w^{n-2}(w^{n-2} \prec z^{n-1} \leftrightarrow \langle t_i, a^{n-1}, w^{n-2}\rangle \prec x^n) \wedge$

$\exists r^{n-1}(\langle i, k, z^{n-1}, r^{n-1}, y^{n-1}\rangle \prec x^n))] \wedge$

$\forall z^{n-1}\forall r^{n-1}\forall y^{n-1}(\langle 1, k, z^{n-1}, r^{n-1}, y^{n-1}\rangle \prec x^n \leftrightarrow$

$(z^{n-1} \ll_{1,2}^{n,n} y^{n-1} \wedge r^{n-1} \ll_{2,2}^{n,n} y^{n-1})) \wedge$

$\forall i(1 \leq i \leq k)\forall z^{n-1}\forall r^{n-1}\forall y^{n-1}(\langle i+1, k, z^{n-1}, r^{n-1}, y^{n-1}\rangle \prec x^n \leftrightarrow \forall w^{n-1}\forall u^{n-1}$

$(\langle i, k, w^{n-1}, u^{n-1}, y^{n-1}\rangle \prec x^n \supset (z^{n-1} \ll_{1,2}^{n,n} u^{n-1} \wedge r^{n-1} \ll_{2,2}^{n,n} u^{n-1}))))))] \wedge$

(*Intuitive gloss:* $\ulcorner P_j^{r_1,\ldots,r_k}(t_1,\ldots,t_k)\urcorner$ *is true in the model relative to assignment* a^{n-1} *just in case the (generalized) k-tuple consisting of the references assigned by the model to each of the* $\ulcorner t_i\urcorner$ *relative to assignment* a^{n-1} *is 'among' the reference assigned by the model to* $\ulcorner P^{r_1,\ldots,r_k}\urcorner$ *relative to* a^{n-1}*. The clause is cumbersome because it makes use of an encoding system to attain the effect of quantifying over k-tuple positions: '*$\langle i, k, z^{n-1}, r^{n-1}, y^{n-1}\rangle \prec x^n$*' might be thought of as enconding the information that according to the model,* z^{n-1} *(which is the reference assigned by the model to* $\ulcorner t_i\urcorner$ *relative to* a^{n-1}*) is the ith component of* y^{n-1} *(which is 'among' the reference assigned by the model to* $\ulcorner P^{r_1,\ldots,r_k}\urcorner$ *relative to* a^{n-1}*). The last three lines of the clause are a specification of how the coding is to work.*)

$[\phi$ is a formula $\supset (\langle\ulcorner \sigma_i^k[\phi]\urcorner, a^{n-1}, z^{n-1}\rangle \prec x^n \leftrightarrow$

$(\forall s^0(s^0 \prec_{trans}^{1,n} z^{n-1} \supset \langle\text{'}\forall\text{'}, s^0\rangle \prec x^n) \wedge$ the assignment $\hat{a}^{n-1}$ (which is just like a^{n-1} except that $\alpha_{\hat{a}^{n-1}}(\ulcorner v_i^k\urcorner) \approx z^{n-1}$)is such that $\langle \phi, \hat{a}^{n-1}\rangle \prec x^n)] \wedge$

(*Intuitive gloss: 'among' the reference assigned by the model to* $\ulcorner\sigma_i^k[\phi]\urcorner$ *relative to assignment* a^{n-1} *are all and only those* z^{n-1} *such that: (a) the 'transitive closure' of* z^{n-1} *consists entirely of individuals in the domain, and (b)* ϕ *is true in the model relative to the* a^{n-1}*-variant assigning* z^{n-1} *to* $\ulcorner v_j^k\urcorner$.)

$[\ulcorner \mathrm{Ex}^k(t)\urcorner$ is a formula $\supset (\langle\ulcorner \mathrm{Ex}^k(t)\urcorner, a^{n-1}\rangle \prec x^n \leftrightarrow \exists z^{n-1}(\langle t, a^{n-1}, z^{n-1}\rangle \prec x^n))] \wedge$

(*Intuitive gloss:* $\ulcorner \mathrm{Ex}^k(t)\urcorner$ *is true in the model relative to assignment* a^{n-1} *just in case the model assigns a reference to t relative to* a^{n-1}.)

$[\phi$ is a formula $\rightarrow (\langle\ulcorner\neg\phi\urcorner, a^{n-1}\rangle \prec x^n \leftrightarrow \neg(\langle\ulcorner\phi\urcorner, a^{n-1}\rangle \prec x^n))] \wedge$

(*Intuitive gloss:* $\ulcorner\neg\phi\urcorner$ *is true in the model relative to assignment* a^{n-1} *just in case* ϕ *is not.*)

$$[\phi \text{ and } \psi \text{ are formulas} \rightarrow (\langle \ulcorner \phi \wedge \psi \urcorner, a^{n-1} \rangle \prec x^n \leftrightarrow$$
$$(\langle \ulcorner \phi \urcorner, a^{n-1} \rangle \prec x^n \wedge \langle \ulcorner \psi \urcorner, a^{n-1} \rangle \prec x^n))]\}$$

(Intuitive gloss: $\ulcorner \phi \wedge \psi \urcorner$ *is true in the model relative to assignment* a^{n-1} *just in case* ϕ *and* ψ *are.)*

It is then straightforward to characterize logical consequence for $\mathcal{L}$:

$$\phi \text{ is a logical consequence of } \Gamma \equiv_{df}$$
$$\forall x^n [\text{M}(x^n) \rightarrow$$
$$(\forall \psi (\psi \in \Gamma \supset \forall a^{n-1}(A(a^{n-1}) \supset \langle \psi, a^{n-1} \rangle \prec x^n)) \supset$$
$$\forall a^{n-1}(A(a^{n-1}) \supset \langle \phi, a^{n-1} \rangle \prec x^n))]$$

By using the technique in Rayo and Uzquiano (1999), this *explicit* characterization of logical consequence for a full nth-level language in a basic $(n+1)$*th*-level language can be transformed into an *implicit* characterization of logical consequence for a basic $(n+1)$th-level language in a full $(n+1)$th-level language.

REFERENCES

Andrews, P. B. (1965) *A Transfinite Type Theory with Type Variables.* North-Holland Publishing Company, Amsterdam.

Beall, J., (ed.) (2003) *Liars and Heaps.* Oxford University Press, Oxford.

Bernays, P. (1942) 'A System of Axiomatic Set Theory, IV', *Journal of Symbolic Logic* 7:4, 133–45.

Black, M. (1970) 'The Elusiveness of Sets', *Review of Metaphysics* 24, 614–36.

Boolos, G. (1984) 'To Be is to Be a Value of a Variable (or to be Some Values of Some Variables)', *The Journal of Philosophy*, 81, 430–49. Reprinted in Boolos (1998a).

—— (1985a) 'Nominalist Platonism', *Philosophical Review* 94, 327–44. Reprinted in Boolos (1998a).

—— (1985b) 'Reading the *Begriffsschrift*', *Mind* 94, 331–4. Reprinted in Boolos (1998a).

—— (1998a) *Logic, Logic and Logic.* Harvard, Cambridge, MA.

—— (1998b) 'Reply to Parsons' "Sets and Classes"'. in Boolos (1998a), 30–6.

Burgess, J. and Rosen, G. (1997) *A Subject With No Object.* Oxford University Press, New York.

Cartwright, R. (1994) 'Speaking of Everything', *Noûs* 28, 1–20.

Dales, H. G. and G. Oliveri, (eds.) (1998) *Truth in Mathematics.* Oxford University Press, Oxford.

Dummett, M. (1963) 'The Philosophical Significance of Gödel's Theorem', *Ratio* 5, 140–55. Reprinted in Dummett (1978).

—— (1978) *Truth and Other Enigmas.* Duckworth, London.

—— (1981) *Frege: Philosophy of Language.* Harvard, Cambridge, MA, 2nd edn.

—— (1991) *Frege: Philosophy of Mathematics.* Duckworth, London.

—— (1993a) *The Seas of Language.* Clarendon Press, Oxford.

____ (1993b) 'Wittgenstein on Necessity: Some Reflections', in Dummett (1993a).

Field, H. (1998) 'Which Undecidable Mathematical Sentences have Determinate Truth Values?' In Dales and Oliveri (1998). Reprinted in Field (2001).

____ (2001) *Truth and the Absence of Fact.* Oxford University Press, Oxford.

Glanzberg, M. (2004) 'Quantification and Realism', *Philosophy and Phenomenological Research* 69, 541–72.

Hazen, A. P. (1993) 'Against Pluralism', *Australasian Journal of Philosophy* 71:2, 132–44.

____ (1997) 'Relations in Lewis's Framework Without Atoms', *Analysis* 57, 243–8.

Hossack, K. (2000) 'Plurals and Complexes', *The British Journal for the Philosophy of Science* 513, 411–43.

Jané, I. (2005) 'Higher-Order Logic reconsidered', in Shapiro (2005).

Kreisel, G. (1967) 'Informal Rigour and Completeness Proofs', in Lakatos (1967).

Lakatos, I., (ed.) (1967) *Problems in the Philosophy of Mathematics,* North Holland, Amsterdam.

Lepore, E. and B. Smith, (eds.) (forthcoming) *Handbook of Philosophy of Language.* Oxford University Press, Oxford.

Lewis, D. (1970) 'General Semantics', *Synthese* 22, 18–67. Reprinted in Lewis (1983).

____ (1983) *Philosophical Papers,* Volume I, Oxford University Press, Oxford.

Linnebo, Ø. (2003) 'Plural Quantification Exposed', *Noûs* 37, 71–92.

McGee, V. (1992) 'Two Problems with Tarski's Theory of Consequence', *Proceedings of the Aristotelian Society* 92, 273–92.

____ (1997) 'How We Learn Mathematical Language', *Philosophical Review* 106, 35–68.

____ (2000) "Everything", in Sher and Tieszen (2000).

____ (forthcoming) 'Universal Universal Quantification', in *Liars and Heaps.*

Montague, R. (1970) 'Universal Grammar', *Theoria* 36, 373–98.

Oliver, A. and T. Smiley (2001) 'Strategies for a Logic of Plurals', *Philosophical Quarterly* 51, 289–306.

____ (typescript) 'A Modest Logic of Plurals'.

Parsons, C. (1974a) 'The Liar Paradox', *The Journal of Philosophical Logic* 3, 381–412. Reprinted in Parsons (1983).

____ (1974b) 'Sets and Classes', *Noûs* 8, 1–12. Reprinted in Parsons (1983).

____ (1983) *Mathematics in Philosophy.* Cornell University Press, Ithaca, NY.

____ (1990) 'The Structuralist View of Mathematical Objects', *Synthese* 84, 303–46.

Priest, G. (2003) *Beyond the Limits of Thought.* Oxford University Press, Oxford, 2nd edn.

Quine, W. V. (1986) *Philosophy of Logic, Second Edition.* Harvard, Cambridge, MA.

Rayo, A. (2002) 'Word and Objects', *Noûs* 36, 436–64.

____ (2003) 'When does "Everything" Mean *Everything*?' *Analysis* 63, 100–6.

____ and G. Uzquiano (1999) 'Toward a Theory of Second-Order Consequence', *The Notre Dame Journal of Formal Logic* 40, 315–32.

____ and T. Williamson (2003) 'A Completeness Theorem for Unrestricted First-Order Languages', in Beall (2003).

Rayo, A., and S. Yablo (2001) 'Nominalism Through De-Nominalization', *Noûs* 351, 74–92.

Resnik, M. (1988) 'Second-Order Logic Still Wild', *Journal of Philosophy* 852, 75–87.

Russell, B. (1906) 'On Some Difficulties in the Theory of Transfinite Numbers and Order Types', *Proceedings of the London Mathematical Society* 4, 29–53.

Schein, B. (forthcoming) 'Plurals', in Lepore and Smith (forthcoming).

Shapiro, S. (1991) *Foundations Without Foundationalism: A Case for Second-Order Logic.* Clarendon Press, Oxford.

Shapiro, S. (2003a) 'All Sets Great and Small: And I do Mean All', 467–90. in Hawthorne, J. and D. Zimmerman, (eds.) *Philosophical Perspectives 17: Language and Philosophical Linguistics*. Blackwell, Oxford.

—— (2003b) 'Prolegomenon to Any Future Neo-Logicist Set Theory: Abstraction and Indefinite Extensibility', *British Journal for the Philosophy of Science* 54, 59–91.

—— (ed.) (2005) *The Oxford Handbook for Logic and the Philosophy of Mathematics*. Clarendon Press, Oxford.

Sher, G., and R. Tieszen, (eds.) (2000) *Between Logic and Intuition*. Cambridge University Press, New York and Cambridge.

Simons, P. (1997) 'Higher-Order Quantification and Ontological Commitment', *Dialectica* 51, 255–71.

Williamson, T. (1998) 'Indefinite Extensibility', *Grazer Philosophische Studien* 55, 1–24.

—— (1999) 'Existence and Contingency', *Proceedings of the Aristotelian Society, Supplementary Volume* 73, 181–203. Reprinted with printer's errors corrected in *Proceedings of the Aristotelian Society* 100 (2000), 321–43 (117–39 in unbounded edition).

—— (2003) 'Everything', 415–65. In Hawthorne, J. and D. Zimmerman, (eds.) *Philosophical Perspectives 17: Language and Philosophical Linguistics*. Blackwell, Oxford.

10

All Things Indefinitely Extensible

Stewart Shapiro and Crispin Wright

The direct concern of our chapter is not with unrestricted quantification. Or at least: not *unrestrictedly unrestricted* quantification—quantification over absolutely everything there is. Our direct concern is with whether it is admissible to quantify over *sets* without restriction—whether it is coherent to speak of, and have bound variables ranging over, all pure sets, or all pure set-like totalities (see also Shapiro, 2003). ('Well, but didn't you just do so?') Closely connected questions, also within our focus, are whether it makes sense—and if so, what kind of sense—to speak of all *cardinal numbers*, or all cardinalities, and all *ordinal numbers*, or all order-types of well-orderings?

That such quantification is somehow illicit has of course often been suggested as the principal lesson to be taken from the Russell, Cantor, and Burali-Forti paradoxes. And if quantification over all sets, for example, is indeed illicit, so much the worse, presumably, for the even more ambitious 'absolutely everything'. (Of course even if quantification over all sets is permissible, there could still be residual problems for 'absolutely everything'. But we will not attempt to explore the territory opened by that observation here.)

10.1 INDEFINITE EXTENSIBILITY INTUITIVELY UNDERSTOOD

In a much-discussed letter to Dedekind, Cantor wrote:

> ... it is necessary, as I discovered, to distinguish two kinds of multiplicities ... For a multiplicity can be such that the assumption that *all* of its elements 'are together' leads to a contradiction, so that it is impossible to conceive of the multiplicity as a unity, as 'one finished thing'. Such multiplicities I call *absolutely infinite* or *inconsistent multiplicities.*
>
> As we can readily see, the 'totality of everything thinkable', for example, is such a multiplicity ...
>
> If on the other hand the totality of elements of a multiplicity can be thought of without contradiction as 'being together', so that they can be gathered together into '*one* thing', I call it a *consistent multiplicity* or a 'set'.
>
> (Cantor, 1899, 114)

This connotation of the word 'set' is now standard, and we will stick to it here. Cantor's distinction between sets and 'inconsistent multiplicities' goes back at least to his (1883). Prior to that, he only considered sets of some fixed 'conceptual sphere', such as sets of natural numbers or sets of real numbers (see Tait, 2000). In the 1883 *Grundlagen*, he wrote that 'By a 'manifold' or 'set' I understand any multiplicity which can be thought of as one, i.e., any aggregate of determinate elements which can be unified into a whole by some law'. In defining the transfinite numbers, Cantor invoked two principles. The first is that each number α has an immediate successor $\alpha + 1$. The second is that each set S of numbers which has no largest member has a limit: the smallest number larger than every member of S. It follows immediately that the transfinite numbers cannot compose a set and are thus an inconsistent multitude. As Cantor somewhat obliquely expresses it, the numbers are the result of 'a thoroughly endless process of creation'. His work presupposes that every number is 'generated' from one of these two principles.

A few years later, Russell provided a more nuanced characterization of what appears to be essentially the same idea. His (1906) begins with an examination of the standard paradoxes, and concludes:

> the contradictions result from the fact that ... there are what we may call *self-reproductive* processes and classes. That is, there are some properties such that, given any class of terms all having such a property, we can always define a new term also having the property in question. Hence we can never collect *all* of the terms having the said property into a whole; because, whenever we hope we have them all, the collection which we have immediately proceeds to generate a new term also having the said property.

Citing this passage, Michael Dummett (1993, 441), writes that an

> *indefinitely extensible* concept is one such that, if we can form a definite conception of a totality all of whose members fall under the concept, we can, by reference to that totality, characterize a larger totality all of whose members fall under it
>
> (emphasis ours).

According to Dummett, an indefinitely extensible concept P has a 'principle of extension' that takes any definite totality t of objects each of which has P, and produces an object that also has P, but is not in t (see also Dummett, 1991, 316–19). Let us say that a concept P is *Definite* if it is not indefinitely extensible. Connecting this with Cantor's terminology, we can say that P is Definite if and only if the P's are 'consistent', and thus form a set.

Obviously, Dummett's remarks won't do as a definition, since he uses the complementary 'definite' to characterize what it is for a concept to be indefinitely extensible. And Russell, of course, does no better by speaking unqualifiedly of 'any class of terms all having such a property', since he means us to take it as given that classes, properly so regarded, are 'wholes'—are Definite. But the following familiar material makes salient the pattern that Russell and Dummett both discern:

(1) *The Burali-Forti paradox*. Rather than work with the usual identification of the ordinals with sets in the iterative hierarchy, such as von Neumann ordinals, let us here think of them in an intuitive way simply as order-types of well-orderings: an ordinal

is an object denoted by a nominalization of a predicate for a well-ordering. Let O be any Definite collection of ordinal numbers. Let O' be the collection of all ordinals α such that there is a $\beta \in O$ for which $\alpha \leq \beta$. It is easy to see that O' is well-ordered under the natural ordering of ordinals. Let γ be the order-type of O'. So γ is itself an ordinal. Let γ' be the order-type of $O' \cup \{\gamma\}$. That is γ' is the order-type of the well-ordering obtained from O' by tacking an element on at the end. Then γ' is an ordinal number, and γ' is not a member of O. So *ordinal number* is indefinitely extensible. As Dummett (1991, 316) puts it,

> if we have a clear grasp of any totality of ordinals, we thereby have a conception of what is intuitively an ordinal number greater than any member of that totality. Any [D]efinite totality of ordinals must therefore be so circumscribed as to forswear comprehensiveness, renouncing any claim to cover all that we might intuitively recognise as being an ordinal.

In the next section we will offer an argument that the notion of ordinal number is in fact the central paradigm of an indefinitely extensible concept.

(2) *The Russell Paradox*. Let R be any set of sets that do not contain themselves; so if $r \in R$ then $r \notin r$. Then R does not contain itself. So the concept, *set that does not contain itself*, is indefinitely extensible—any set of such sets omits a set, namely itself. A fortiori, *set* itself is indefinitely extensible, since any Definite collection—set—of sets must omit the set of all of its members that do not contain themselves.

(3) *The Cantor Paradox*. Let C be a collection of cardinal numbers. Let C' be the union of the result of replacing each $\kappa \in C$ with a set of size κ. The collection of subsets of C' is larger than any cardinal in C. So *cardinal number* is indefinitely extensible.

To be sure—though perhaps with the exception of the reasoning leading to Russell's paradox—these examples are not completely uncontentious. One can challenge the set-theoretic principles (Union, Replacement, Power-set, etc.) that are invoked in the constructions. Or else one can tinker with the logic. Nevertheless, we think it reasonable to agree with Russell and Dummett that the concepts in question do have the 'self-reproductive' feature which the notion of indefinitely extensibility gestures at. There remain the questions

(i) Whether the notion can be characterized more satisfactorily, without circularity;
(ii) Which are the indefinitely extensible concepts/totalities when the notion is best understood,

and

(iii) What bearing the notion has on the various issues in the philosophy of mathematics, including

> the proper diagnosis of the paradoxes;
> the legitimacy of unrestricted quantification;
> the content of quantification (if legitimate at all) over indefinitely extensible totalities and the legitimacy of classical logic for such quantifiers;
> the proper conception of the infinite; and
> the possibilities for neo-logicist foundations for set-theory,

on each of which it has been held to have some import. A satisfactory treatment of this agenda would be a task for a substantial book. But each of the listed issues will be touched on, if only modestly, in the discussion to follow.

10.2 INDEFINITE EXTENSIBILITY AND THE ORDINALS: RUSSELL'S CONJECTURE

Russell (1906, 144) wrote that it 'is probable' that if *P* is any concept which demonstrably does not have an extension, then 'we can actually construct a series, ordinally similar to the series of all ordinals, composed entirely of terms having the concept *P*'. Putting the presumably metaphorical talk of construction aside,[1] Russell's conjecture is in effect that if *P* is indefinitely extensible, then there is a one-to-one function from the ordinals into *P*. Russell does not give an argument for this, but here is one:

Let α be an ordinal and assume that we have a one-to-one function f from the ordinals smaller than α to objects that fall under *P*. Consider the collection $\{f\beta \mid \beta<\alpha\}$. This is Definite. Since *P* is indefinitely extensible, there is an object *a* such that *P* holds of *a*, but *a* is not in this set. Set $f\alpha = a$.

Thus for any ordinal α, if all the ordinals smaller than α can be injected into *P*, then the ordinals up to and including α can be injected into *P*. So all the ordinals can be injected into *P*.

This reasoning requires transfinite recursion on ordinals—but that can hardly be doubted. It is part of what it is to be an ordinal that definitions by transfinite recursion and proofs by transfinite induction are valid. (Both points seem to follow from Cantor's two principles noted above together with the assumption that every ordinal is 'constructed' from one or the other of them.) The argument also relies on a version of Replacement: if a totality *t* is equinumerous with an ordinal, then *t* is Definite.[2]

[1] This and cognate metaphors are pervasive in the source literature. Cantor speaks of a process of 'creation' of ever more numbers. Russell notes that indefinitely extensible concepts come with 'processes' which 'seem essentially incapable of terminating', and Dummett speaks of 'principles of extension'. The metaphors are stretched. It is stretching things, for example, to think of the ordinals, classically conceived, as generated by a *process*. Processes take place in time, and time does not have enough structure to carry the 'construction' of ordinals very far into the transfinite (see Parsons, 1977). A major part of the interpretative and analytical project in the vicinity is to provide a satisfactory reading of the intent of these metaphors.

[2] Depending on the exact formulation of the notion of indefinite extensibility, the argument might also invoke a *global choice* principle, or at least a choice function on sub-totalities of the given indefinitely extensible property. Recall the clause from the first passage from Russell: 'there are some properties such that, given any class of terms all having such a property, we can always define a new term also having the property in question'. If this means something like 'given any class of terms all having such a property, there is a new term also having the property in question', Choice is needed in the argument. On the other hand, if Russell's clause is taken (more or less) literally, the ability to 'define' a new term is part of what it is for a notion to be indefinitely extensible. If so, then Choice is not needed in the argument. Similarly, Dummett says that an indefinitely extensible property *P* has a 'principle of extension' that takes any Definite totality *t* of objects each of which has *P*, and produces an object that also has *P*, but is not in *t*. If this principle of extension is a function, then

There is no knowing whether Russell had something like the above argument supporting his conjecture in mind. Whether or not he did, later in the same article, he invokes the conjecture to motivate a 'limitation of size' resolution of the paradoxes. But, as we saw, the above argument invokes Replacement, which itself expresses a limitation of size principle. So for Russell's own purpose, the argument offered him above would beg the question.[3]

The converse of Russell's conjecture seems solid for its part: if there is a one-one function taking the ordinals into the objects satisfying a concept P, then P is indefinitely extensible. For let f be a one-to-one function from the ordinals into the P's, and let C be a Definite collection of P's. Let c be the collection of ordinals α such that $f\alpha$ is in C. By Replacement, c is a Definite collection (and thus a set) of ordinals. Let α' be the smallest ordinal not in c. Then $Pf\alpha'$, but $f\alpha'$ is not in C. If the ordinals can be embedded into the P's, then P inherits the indefinite extensibility of the ordinals.

So both Russell's conjecture and its converse are plausible. Together they imply that a concept is indefinitely extensible if and only if there is an injection of the ordinals into it. This is the reason, foretold in the previous section, to take the ordinals to be the paradigm case of an indefinitely extensible totality, and the mechanics of the Burali–Forti paradox to be the paradigm of indefinite extension.

Historical note: Cantor himself made frequent use of the converse of the Russell conjecture. To show that a given multiplicity is 'inconsistent', he would show how to embed the series of ordinals into it. The aforementioned letter to Dedekind contains a sketch of the series of alephs. Cantor asks whether there is a set whose cardinality is not an aleph:

> This question is to be answered *negatively* . . . If we take a definite multiplicity [i.e., a set] V and assume that *no aleph* corresponds to it *as its cardinal number*, we conclude that V must be *inconsistent*. For we readily see that, on the assumption made, the whole system Ω [of transfinite numbers] is projectible into the multiplicity V, that is, there must exist a submultiplicity V' of V that is equivalent to the system Ω.

Cantor thus provides an argument for what would later be Zermelo's (1904) well-ordering theorem. In his capacity as editor of Cantor's collected works, Zermelo added a long footnote to the published version of Cantor's letter taking him to task for his talk of 'procedures' and the like:[4]

> Cantor apparently thinks that successive and arbitrary elements of V are assigned to members of Ω in such a way that every element of V is used only *once*. *Either* this procedure would come

we do not need Choice in the foregoing argument. The presumed principle of extension does the 'choosing'.

[3] The 'limitation of size' conception is that a given 'totality' forms a set if and only if it is not too 'large'. From this perspective, the sets, the ordinals, and the cardinals do not themselves form sets because there are too many of them. Russell's conjecture fits in well with this conception. If it were the case that the ordinals could be embedded into any indefinitely extensible totality T, then, since there are 'too many' ordinals to form a set, there are also too many T's to form a set. The replacement principle is a contrapositive, of sorts, to this observation. It says that if a collection S is Definite, and there are exactly as many U's as S's, then the U's form a set as well. Thanks to Michael Potter here.

[4] Cantor's letter and Zermelo's note are published in van Heijenoort (1967, 113–17).

to an end once all elements of V had been exhausted, and then V would be mapped onto a *segment* of the number sequence and its cardinality would be an aleph, contrary to the assumption, *or* V would remain inexhaustible, hence contain a constituent part that is equivalent to all of Ω and therefore inconsistent. Thus the intuition of time is applied here to a process that goes beyond all intuition ... Only through the 'axiom of choice', which postulates the possibility of a *simultaneous* choice and which Cantor uses unconsciously and instinctively everywhere but does not formulate explicitly anywhere, could V' be defined as a subset of V. But even then there would still remain a doubt: perhaps the proof involves 'inconsistent' multiplicities, indeed possibly contradictory notions, and is logically inadmissible already because of that. It is precisely doubts of this kind that impelled the editor (Zermelo) a few years later to base his own proof of the well-ordering theorem (1904) purely upon the axiom of choice without using inconsistent multiplicities.

10.3 'SMALL' INDEFINITELY EXTENSIBLE CONCEPTS? CASE STUDY (1): THE BERRY PARADOX

Russell's Conjecture, taken with its converse, makes for an extensional connection between *ordinal* and *indefinite extensibility*: the totality of elements falling under an indefinitely extensible concept contains a system isomorphic to the ordinals. Clearly, though, even if this connection is accepted, we still want for an analysis, or further conceptual elucidation, of the notion: something to provide some leverage on the cluster of issues itemized at the conclusion of Section 10.1—something the connection made with the ordinals, unsupplemented, manifestly fails to do.

But is the connection made by Russell's Conjecture correct in any case? Dummett for one has characteristically taken it that the natural and real numbers are indefinitely extensible totalities in just the same sense that the ordinals and cardinals are, with similar consequences, in his view, for the understanding of quantification over them and the standing of classical logic in the investigation of these domains. And in the article (Dummett, 1963) which contains his earliest published discussion of the notion, he argues that the proper interpretation of Gödel's incompleteness theorems for arithmetic is precisely to teach that *arithmetical truth* and *arithmetical proof* are indefinitely extensible concepts—yet neither presumably has an even more than countably infinite extension, still less an ordinals-sized one. (For the ordinary, finitely based language of second-order arithmetic presumably suffices for the expression of any arithmetical truth.) It is disconcerting to have lost contact with one of the leading friends of indefinite extensibility so early in the discussion. But then where does the argument for Russell's conjecture and its converse go wrong, or betray Dummett's intent?

It is relevant to recall that Russell (1908) himself, in motivating a uniform diagnosis of the paradoxes, included in his list of chosen examples some at least where the 'self-reproductive' process seems bounded by a relatively small cardinal. For instance the Richard paradox concerning the class of decimals that can be defined by means of a finite number of words makes play with a totality which, if indeed indefinitely extensible, is at least no greater than the class of decimals itself, i.e. than $2^{\aleph_0}$. Was

Russell simply unaware of this type of example in 1906, when he proposed the Conjecture discussed above? Or did he not in 1906 regard the Richard paradox and others involving 'small' totalities as genuine examples of the same genre, revising that opinion two years later?

Well, *are* they examples of the same genre? To fix ideas, let us consider in some detail the so-called Berry paradox, the paradox of 'the smallest natural number not denoted by any expression of English of fewer than seventeen words'. This is an English expression which, on plausible assumptions, should denote a natural number—but it contains sixteen words. So its referent—the smallest natural number not denoted by any expression of English of fewer than seventeen words—is denoted by an English expression of sixteen words. Is this a paradox of indefinite extensibility?

Let's try to state the paradox more carefully. Define an expression t to be *numerically determinate* if t denotes a natural number and let C be the set—if there is one—of all numerically determinate expressions of English. Consider the expression b: 'the smallest natural number not denoted by any expression in C of fewer than seventeen words'. Assume: (1) that b is a numerically determinate expression of English (i.e., $b \in C$) and (2) that C indeed exists. Then contradiction follows from (1) and (2) and the empirical datum that b has sixteen words (counting the contained occurrence of 'C' as one word).

Evidently, there are some issues that would need to be addressed in a watertight version of the paradox. Notice, for instance, that assumption (1) presupposes that 'C' is an expression of English. But, of course, you won't find it in any dictionary of the English language. The paradox presumes to take 'English' to include expressions introduced by new explicit abbreviative definitions of English expressions. Assumption (1) also presupposes of course that b—'the smallest natural number not denoted by any expression in C of fewer than seventeen words'—denotes something in English. But what in that case is being assumed about the decimal numerals? Are they part of English? If so, how many words do they contain? If e.g. '1002' ranks as a one-word English expression, then assumption (1) is contradicted and the paradox is stillborn. We could take the view that each occurrence of one of the ten basic decimal numerals within a compound decimal numeral counts as one word. But once we allow English to contain abbreviative definitions, what is to stop us taking an infinite series of—presumably—single-symbol expressions,

T T T T T T

asymptotically approaching a size half that of the first, and then assigning to each nth expression in this series the nth natural number as referent and deeming the whole to be part of English? In that case, b has again no denotation in English.

But suppose we manage to work these issues out and get a rigorous contradiction. Then the diagnostic thought, shared by Russell and Dummett, will be that the paradox is due to the indefinite extensibility of the concept, *numerically determinate expression of English*. The problem, on this proposal, is the assumption that any such set as C—the set of all numerically determinate expressions of English—exists. There is no such set. Rather, any set of such expressions aids and abets the construction of a new such expression, in the kind of way illustrated by the paradox, which it demonstrably cannot contain.

The analogy with the classic paradoxes looks good. But, as emerges if we think the process of 'indefinite extension' through, it is not quite right. Again: take P as the concept, *numerically determinate expression of English*, and let D be any definite, finite collection of P's. Introduce a (one word) name d for D (counting d, as remarked above, as part of 'English'), and consider 'the smallest natural number not denoted by any member of d of fewer than seventeen words'. Call this sixteen-worded expression 'w'. It is clear that w is a P (i.e., a numerically determinate expression of English); for there will be a definite finite subset, D^*, of D comprising exactly those of the members of D with fewer than seventeen words, and—since all these expressions are numerically determinate—a definite greatest number, k, denoted by any member of D^*. So the referent of w is less than or equal to $k + 1$. However w is not in D, since no member of D denoting w has fewer than seventeen words. Clearly we can iterate the process, now taking $D \cup \{w\}$ for D, and giving this set a new one-word English name. Still the process is not *indefinitely* extensible.

To see why, let the initial collection D just consist of the Arabic numerals, '0'-'9'. Do the Berry construction on this to get a w_1—it will denote 10—that is P, but not in D. Let $D1$ be $D \cup \{w_1\}$. Give $D1$ a one-word name. Now do a Berry on $D1$, producing w_2. Let $D2$ be $D1 \cup \{w_2\}$. Give D2 a one-word name. Do the Berry construction again. Keep going ... Now let $D\omega$ be the union of $D, D1, D2, \ldots$ What happens next?—what happens when we apply the Berry construction to $D\omega$?

The answer is that it fails. For reflect that 0 to 9 are all denoted by single-word members of D; 10 is denoted by the sixteen-worded 'the smallest natural number not denoted by any member of [write in the one-word name of D] of fewer than seventeen words'; 11 is denoted by the 'the smallest natural number not denoted by any member of [write in the one-word name of $D1$] of fewer than seventeen words'; 12 is denoted by the 'the smallest natural number not denoted by any member of [write in the one-word name of $D2$] of fewer than seventeen words'; and so on. So the 'the smallest natural number not denoted by any member of [write in the one-word name of $D\omega$] of fewer than seventeen words' has no reference—for *every* natural number is denoted by at least one member of $D\omega$ of fewer than seventeen words.

Of course the construction fails in a more pedestrian way if we do not allow ourselves to include as part of English the countably many one-word abbreviations needed to press the iteration beyond the finite. What it seems fair to say is that, with that idealization—if that is what it is—of what counts as English, there is a *kind* of indefinite extensibility about the concept, *numerically determinate expression of English*. But it is a *bounded* indefinite extensibility, as it were—indefinite extensibility up to a limit (ordinal). If union is a Definiteness preserving operation, there will be, in such bounded cases, a *definite* collection of entities of the kind in question that does not in turn admit of extension by the original operation. So they will not be *indefinitely* extensible, at least not in the spirit of our initial characterization.

10.4 'SMALL' INDEFINITELY EXTENSIBLE CONCEPTS? CASE STUDY (2): ARITHMETICAL TRUTH

As noted earlier, Dummett (1963) argues that Gödel's incompleteness theorem shows that *arithmetical truth* is indefinitely extensible. Given any definite collection C of arithmetical truths, one can construct a truth—the Gödel sentence for C—that is not a member of C.

This is prima facie a puzzling claim. If 'definite collection' means something like *set*, and if the latter concept is understood as in classical mathematics, then it just seems wrong—arithmetical truth is not indefinitely extensible. Following Tarski, one can give a straightforward explicit definition of 'arithmetical truth'. It then follows from the *Aussonderungsaxiom* that there is a set of all arithmetical truths. There is no 'Gödel sentence' for this set. But, of course, Dummett's claim is not offered, presumably, within the context of the classical conception of set.

Fix an effective Gödel numbering of the sentences of arithmetic. It follows from Tarski's theorem that the notion of arithmetical truth is not arithmetic.[5] In other words, there is no formula $T(x)$ in the language of arithmetic, such that for each natural number n, $T(n)$ if and only if n is the Gödel number of a truth of arithmetic.

A generalization of Gödel's theorem does suggest something approximating indefinite extensibility: if C is any *arithmetic* set of (Gödel numbers of) truths of arithmetic, then there is a truth of arithmetic that is not in C. Indeed, let $A(x)$ be a formula in the language of arithmetic that characterizes C. That is, for every natural number n, $A(n)$ if and only if $n \in C$. A fortiori, for each natural number n, if $A(n)$ then n is the Gödel number of a true sentence of arithmetic. Let P be a fixed point for the formula $\neg A(x)$. That is, if p is the Gödel number of P, then

$$P \equiv \neg A(p)$$

is a theorem of arithmetic. It follows that P is true,[6] and thus $\neg A(p)$. So p is not in C.

Given Dummett's general outlook in the philosophy of mathematics, he would surely deny that the 'totality' of arithmetical truths is Definite. It is certainly not decidable. Perhaps it is reasonable to hold that, for Dummett, a 'totality' of natural numbers is Definite only if it is recursively enumerable, or at least arithmetic. If so, the foregoing construction shows that, for Dummett, something in the neighborhood of indefinite extensibility holds for arithmetical truth.

[5] A property (or set) of natural numbers F is *arithmetic* if there is a formula $\Phi(x)$ in the language of arithmetic, with only x free, such that for each natural number n, n is an F (or $n \in F$) if and only if $\Phi(n)$ holds. The general form of Tarski's (1933) theorem is that no sufficiently rich interpreted language can define its own truth predicate. The specific form here is that there is no arithmetic definition of 'truth in arithmetic'.

[6] Assume $A(p)$. Then p is the code of a truth of arithmetic. But p is the code of P. So P is true. But P is equivalent to $\neg A(p)$, which is thus true. Contradiction. So $\neg A(p)$, which (again) is equivalent to P.

More specifically, it is straightforward to initiate something that looks like a process of 'indefinite extension'. Let A_0 be a given Definite set of arithmetical truths—for instance, let A_0 be the theorems of some standard axiomatization of arithmetic. For each natural number n, let A_{n+1} be the collection A_n together with a Gödel sentence for A_n. Presumably, if A_n is Definite, then so is A_{n+1}, and, of course, A_n and A_{n+1} are distinct. Unlike the above situation with the Berry paradox, this 'construction' can be continued into the transfinite. Let A_ω be the union of $A_0, A_1, \ldots$ Arguably, A_ω is Definite. Indeed, if A_0 is recursively enumerable, then so is A_ω; if A_0 is arithmetic, then so is A_ω. Thus, we can define $A_{\omega+1}, A_{\omega+2}, \ldots$ Then we take the union of those to get $A_{2\omega}$, and onward, Gödelising all the way (so to speak).

On the usual, classical construal of the extent of the ordinals, however, the 'construction' does not continue without limit. It 'runs out' well before the first uncountable ordinal. Let λ be an ordinal and let us assume that we have defined A_λ. The foregoing construction will take us on to the next set $A_{\lambda+1}$ only if the collection A_λ has a Gödel sentence. And this is possible only if A_λ is arithmetic. Clearly, it cannot be the case that for every (countable) ordinal λ, A_λ is arithmetic. There are only countably many arithmetic sets (at most one for each formula in the language of arithmetic), but there are uncountably many (countable) ordinals.[7] Let κ be an ordinal such that A_κ is not arithmetic. For a Dummettian, presumably, A_κ is not Definite.

One option, to be sure, is that of accepting the Russell-conjecture but maintaining that there is no such ordinal as κ. The proof, in set theory, that such an ordinal exists relies on excluded middle. But, for the classical mathematician at least, the notion of arithmetical truth is not fully indefinitely extensible; we cannot run on indefinitely through the ordinals in iterating Gödel sentences.

10.5 INDEFINITE EXTENSIBILITY EXPLAINED

Let's take stock. Russell's Conjecture, that indefinitely extensible concepts are marked by the possession of extensions into which the ordinals are injectible, still stands. Apparent exceptions to it, like *numerically determinate expression of English* and *arithmetical truth*, are not really exceptions. For the principles of extension they involve are not truly *indefinitely* extensible but stabilize after some series of iterations isomorphic to a proper initial segment of the ordinals. Or at least they do so if the ordinals are allowed their full classical structure. As we just noted, the friend of small indefinitely extensible concepts has the option of preserving Russell's Conjecture by

[7] We can be a bit sharper. If λ is a limit ordinal, then the contents of A_λ, if it exists, depend on the particular Gödel numbering chosen and, more importantly, on the method for coding countable ordinals as natural numbers (so we can 'axiomatize' A_λ). For any such coding, there are countable ordinals that have no code. Let κ be the smallest such (for a given coding). Then for each $\lambda < \kappa$, A_λ exists and is arithmetic. So we can go on to $A_{\lambda+1}$. We can take the 'union' of all such sets, which is A_κ. But this is the end of the line: A_κ is not arithmetic, and thus has no Gödel sentence. The construction sketched here, of iterating the Gödel construction into the transfinite, is well-studied. For more details, see Turing (1939) and Feferman (1962), (1988).

'cutting back' the ordinals appropriately far. At the limit, when only the finite ordinals are countenanced, there will then be many more indefinitely extensible concepts than otherwise, including *numerically determinate expression of English* and *arithmetical truth*; and all will, indeed, be 'small'.

Any invocation of the notion of ordinal number in the *explanation* of indefinite extensibility may seem to invert the priorities, but actually there is something importantly right about it. Intuitively the indefinite extensibility of *P* has to do with the *P*-conservativeness of some germane principle of extension *no matter how long a series* of iterated applications of it may be made. What one thinks that means will inevitably depend on how one thinks about the structure of the *measures* of such a series of iterated applications—and so will depend on one's preconceptions about ordinal number. More or less generous such preconceptions will consequently factor into the extension of indefinite extensibility. This relativity, we suggest, was inbuilt from the start, and the concept of indefinite extensibility is consequently open to refinement and mutation in tandem with developments, sophisticated or unfortunate, in one's conception of how long such series can in principle be (see Section 10.9 below).

That said, though, Russell's Conjecture, even if extensionally correct, is not the kind of characterization of indefinite extensibility we should like to have. To get a clear sense of the shortfall, reflect that if Russell's Conjecture provided a full account, it would be a *triviality* that the ordinals are indefinitely extensible. Whereas what is wanted is a perspective from which we can explain *why* Russell's Conjecture is good if indeed, as it seems, it is—equivalently, a perspective from which we can explain what it is about *ordinal* that *makes* it the paradigm of an indefinitely extensible concept.

Any indefinitely extensible totality *P* is intuitively unstable, 'restless', or in 'growth'. Whenever you think you have it safely corralled in some well-fenced enclosure, suddenly—hey presto!—another fully *P*-qualified candidate pops up outside the fence. The primary problem in clarifying this figure is to dispense with the metaphors of 'well-fenced enclosure' and 'growth'. Obviously a claim is intended about sub-totalities of *P* and functions on them to (new) members of *P*. Equally obviously, we need to qualify for which type of sub-totalities of *P* the claim of iterative extensibility within *P* is being made. Clearly it cannot be sustained for absolutely *any* sub-totality of *P*: if for example, we continue to take it that *ordinal* is a paradigm of indefinite extensibility, we do not claim that *ordinal* itself picks out a sub-totality of the relevant kind (though of course there are issues, which will occupy us later, about whether one can avoid that claim). Nor would it help to restrict attention to proper sub-totalities: *ordinal other than three* does not pick out the right kind of sub-totality either. If we could take it for granted that the notion of indefinite extensibility is in clear standing and picks out a distinctive type of totality, or concept, then we could characterize the relevant kind of sub-totality exactly as Dummett did—they are the *Definite* sub-totalities. For the indefinite extensibility of a totality, if it consists in anything, precisely consists in the fact that any Definite sub-totality is merely 'proper'. But unless there is some direct route into the intended notion of Definiteness other than via 'not indefinitely extensible' we make no explanatory progress. No doubt circularity in our best explanation of a concept need not—pace Quine (1951)—enforce skepticism about it. Concepts can be explained by giving illustrative instances, for one thing. But the problem in this case is that the intended concept is too sophisticated to allow of explanation only by examples: what the standard examples seem to illustrate—if indeed they genuinely illustrate anything distinctive at all—cannot be a basic resemblance, beyond further articulation, but surely *has* to be something which allows of explicit characterization.

What is the way forward? Here is our suggestion. In order, at least temporarily, to finesse the 'which sub-totalities?' issue, let's start with an explicitly relativized notion. Let P be a concept of items of a certain type τ. Typically, τ will be the (or a) type of individual objects. Let Π be a concept of concepts of type τ items. Let us say that P is *indefinitely extensible with respect to* Π if and only if there is a function F from items of the same type as P to items of type τ such that if X is any sub-concept of P such that ΠX then

(1) FX falls under the concept P,

(2) it is not that case that FX falls under the concept X, and

(3) $\Pi X'$, where X' is the concept instantiated just by FX and every item which instantiates X (i.e., $\forall x[X'x \equiv (Xx \vee x = FX)]$; in set-theoretic terms, X' is $(X \cup \{FX\})$).

Intuitively, the idea is that the sub-concepts of P of which Π holds have no maximal member.[8] For any sub-concept X of P such that ΠX, there is a proper extension X' of X such that $\Pi X'$.

This relativized notion of indefinite extensibility is quite robust, covering a lot of different situations. Below we give twelve examples. (The reader may choose to skip some at first reading.)

1. Px iff x is a finite ordinal (or cardinal) number; ΠX iff there are only finitely many X's; FX is the successor of the largest X. So being a finite ordinal (or cardinal) is indefinitely extensible with respect to 'finite'.
2. Px iff x is a countable ordinal (i.e., countable well-ordering type); ΠX iff there are only countably many X's; FX is the successor of the union of the X's. So being a countable ordinal is indefinitely extensible with respect to 'countable'.
3. In general, let κ be any regular cardinal number,[9] and define Px iff x is an ordinal smaller than κ. ΠX iff there are fewer than κ-many X's; FX is the successor to the

[8] Say that P is *weakly indefinitely extensible with respect to* Π if and only if for each sub-concept X of P such that ΠX, there is an item t of type τ such that

(1) Pt,
(2) it is not that case Xt, and
(3) $\Pi X'$, where X' is the concept which applies to t and to every item to which X applies.

The difference, of course, is that with the stronger notion characterized above, it is required that there be a *function* that gives the extra element t. The strong notion is equivalent to the weak one if we assume a strong choice principle:

$$\forall X \exists x R(X, x) \rightarrow \exists f \forall X R(X, f X),$$

where x is a variable of type τ, X has the type of concepts of type τ items, and f has the appropriate function-type. See note 2 above.

[9] Recall that a cardinal κ is 'regular' if no set of size κ is the union of fewer than κ-many sets each of which is smaller than κ. It follows from the axiom of choice that every infinite successor

union of the X's. So, for each regular cardinal κ, the concept of 'being an ordinal smaller than κ' is indefinitely extensible with respect to 'smaller than κ'.

A converse holds. A cardinal κ is regular if and only if 'being an ordinal smaller than κ' is indefinitely extensible with respect to 'smaller than κ' using the indicated 'successor of union' function.

4. Let κ be any infinite cardinal, and define Px iff x is an ordinal smaller than κ. ΠX iff there are fewer than κ-many X's; FX is the smallest ordinal λ such that $P\lambda$ & $\neg X\lambda$. So, for each infinite cardinal κ, the concept of 'being an ordinal smaller than κ' is indefinitely extensible with respect to 'smaller than κ'.
5. Let κ be a strong inaccessible. Px iff x is an ordinal smaller than κ; ΠX iff there are fewer than κ-many X's. FX is the powerset of the union of the $X's$. So, for each strong inaccessible κ, the concept of 'being an ordinal smaller than κ' is indefinitely extensible with respect to Π via this function. (Here, again, there is a converse.)
6. Px iff x is a real number; ΠX iff there are only countably many X's. Define FX using a Cantorian diagonal construction. So being a real number is indefinitely extensible with respect to 'countable'.
7. Px iff x is (the Gödel number of) a truth of arithmetic; ΠX iff the X's are recursively enumerable. FX is a Gödel sentence generated by the X's, or the straightforward statement that the X's are consistent. Then, if every member of X is true of the natural numbers, then so is the sentence FX. And, of course, FX is not one of the X's. So being (the Gödel number of) a truth of arithmetic is indefinitely extensible with respect to the property of being recursively enumerable.

As noted, Dummett first introduced the terminology of indefinite extensibility in his (1963). The only indefinitely extensible notion discussed there is the preceding, for which the case can be generalized as indicated in the previous section:

8. Px iff x is the Gödel number of a truth of arithmetic; ΠX iff the X's are arithmetic, i.e., iff there is a formula $\Phi(x)$ with only x free such that $\Phi(x)$ iff Xx. FX is a fixed point for $\neg\Phi(x)$: the Gödel number n of a sentence Ψ such that $(\Psi \equiv \neg\Phi(n))$ is provable in ordinary Peano arithmetic (and so true). So being (the Gödel number of) a truth of arithmetic is indefinitely extensible with respect to the property of being arithmetic.

With even more generality, Tarski's theorem is in effect that the notion of truth for any sufficiently rich language is indefinitely extensible with respect to concepts definable in that language. Another generalization is studied in recursive function theory:

9. Let A be a productive set of natural numbers (see Rogers, 1967, 84). Px iff $x \in A$; ΠX iff X is recursively enumerable. So, for each productive set A, the concept

cardinal is regular. Given Choice, the smallest infinite non-regular cardinal is $\aleph_\omega$. It is common nowadays to identify ordinals with von Neumann ordinals and to identify cardinals with alephs, which, in this context, are von Neumann ordinals of minimal cardinality. That is, κ is an aleph if κ is a von Neumann ordinal and the cardinality of each $\lambda \in \kappa$ is less than that of κ. With these identifications, Px iff $x \in \kappa$.

of being a member of A is indefinitely extensible with respect to the property of being recursively enumerable.

Notice that the set of Gödel numbers of arithmetic truths is productive.

Finally—and as they had better—the three notions invoked at the start to introduce the notion of indefinite extensibility also fit the present template:

10. Px iff x is an ordinal (or a von Neumann ordinal); ΠX iff each of the X's is an ordinal and the X's are themselves isomorphic to an ordinal (under the natural ordering). In other words, ΠX iff each X is an ordinal and the X's have (or exemplify) a well-ordering type. (In still other words, ΠX iff the X's are a set of ordinals.) FX is the successor of the union of the X's. So being an ordinal is indefinitely extensible with respect to the property of being isomorphic to an ordinal (or exemplifying a well-ordering type).

This, of course, is just the Burali–Forti construction.

11. Px iff x is a set that does not contain itself; ΠX iff the X's form a set, i.e., $\exists y \forall x(x \in y \equiv Xx)$. FX is just the set of X's: $\{x|Xx\}$. So being a set that does not contain itself is indefinitely extensible with respect to the property of being, or constituting, a set.
12. Px iff x is a cardinal number; ΠX iff the X's form a set (with a cardinal number). Given such an X, take the union of a totality consisting of at least one set whose cardinality is in a set that has X (using Choice and Replacement); FX is the powerset of that. So being a cardinal number is indefinitely extensible with respect to the property of being, or constituting, a set.

Most of these instances of relativized indefinite extensibility are unremarkable. They do not, as far as they go, shed any philosophical light on the paradoxes. Our ultimate goal, of course, remains to define an unrelativized notion of indefinite extensibility, a notion that covers *ordinal*, *cardinal*, and *set* and at least purports to shed some light on the paradoxes, in the sense that the latter should emerge as somehow turning on the indefinite extensibility of the concepts concerned. So what next?

Three further steps are needed. Notice to begin with that the listed examples subdivide into two kinds. There are those where—helping ourselves to the classical ordinals—we can say that some ordinal λ places a lowest limit on the length of the series of Π-preserving applications of F to any X such that ΠX. Intuitively, while each series of extensions whose length is less than λ results in a collection of P's which is still Π, once the series of iterations extends as far as λ the resulting collection of P's is no longer Π, and so the 'process' stabilizes. This was the situation noted with *numerically determinate expression of English* and *arithmetical truth*, as discussed in preceding sections, and it is also the situation of all but examples 10, 11 and 12 listed above. In those three cases, by contrast, there is no ordinal limit to the Π-preserving iterations. With 10, this is obvious, since the higher-order property Π in that case just is the property of having a well-ordering type. Indeed, let λ be an ordinal. Then the first λ ordinals have the order type λ and so they have the property. The 'process' thus does not terminate or stabilize at λ. With 11 and 12, we get the same result if we assume that for each ordinal λ, a totality that has order type λ is a set and has a cardinality. This is just the replacement principle invoked in the argument for the Russell conjecture in Section 10.2 above.

Let's accordingly refine the relativized notion to mark this distinction. So first, for any ordinal λ say that P is *up-to-λ-extensible with respect to* Π just in case P and Π meet the conditions for the relativized notion as originally defined but λ places a limit on the length of the series of Π-preserving applications of F to any sub-concept X of P such that ΠX. Otherwise put, λ iterations of the extension process on any ΠX 'generates' a collection of P's which form the extension of a non-Π sub-concept of P. Next, say that P is *properly indefinitely extensible* with respect to Π just if P meets the conditions for the relativized notion as originally defined and there is no λ such that P is up-to-λ- extensible with respect to Π. Finally, say that P is *indefinitely extensible* (simpliciter) just in case there is a Π such that P is properly indefinitely extensible with respect to Π.

Our suggestion, then, is that the circularity involved in the apparent need to characterize indefinite extensibility by reference to *Definite* sub-concepts/collections of a target concept P can be finessed by appealing instead at the same point to the existence of some species—Π—of sub-concepts of P/collections of P's for which Π-hood is *limitlessly* preserved under iteration of the relevant operation. This notion is, naturally, relative to one's conception of what constitutes a limitless series of iterations of a given operation. No doubt we start out innocent of any conception of serial limitlessness save the one implicit in one's first idea of the infinite, whereby any countable potential infinity is limitless. Under the aegis of this conception, *natural number* is properly indefinitely extensible with respect to *finite* and so, just as Dummett suggests, indefinitely extensible simpliciter. The crucial conceptual innovation which transcends this initial conception of limitlessness and takes us to the ordinals as classically conceived is to add to the idea that every ordinal has a successor the principle that every infinite series of ordinals has a limit, a first ordinal lying beyond all its elements—the resource encapsulated in Cantor's second number principle. If it is granted that this idea is at least partially—as it were, initial-segmentally—acceptable, the indefinite extensibility of *natural number* will be an immediate casualty of it. (Critics of Dummett who cannot see what he is driving at are presumably simply taking for granted the orthodoxy that the idea is at least partially acceptable.)

10.6 INDEFINITE EXTENSIBILITY AND THE PARADOXES

Roughly, then, P is indefinitely extensible just in case, for some Π, any Π sub-concept of P allows of limitless Π-preserving enlargement. There seems to be nothing inherently paradoxical about this idea. So what is the connection with paradox—how is the indefinite extensibility of *set*, *ordinal* and *cardinal* linked with the classic paradoxes that beset those notions? The immediate answer is that in each of these cases there is powerful intuitive reason to regard P itself as having the property Π. For example, in case P is *ordinal*, and ΠX holds just if the X's *exemplify a well-order-type*, it seems irresistible to say that *ordinal* itself falls under Π. After all, the ordinals are well-ordered. But then the relevant principle of extension kicks in and dumps a new object on us that both must and cannot be an ordinal—must because it corresponds, it seems, to a determinate order-type, cannot because the principle of extension always generates a non-instance of the concept to which it is applied. So we have the Burali–Forti paradox.

The question, then, is what leads us to so fix our concepts of *set*, *ordinal*, and *cardinal* so that they seem to be indefinitely extensible with respect to Π's which are, seemingly, characteristic of those very concepts themselves? These remarks of Dummett (1991, 315–16) suggest what we believe is the key insight:

> to someone who has long been used to finite cardinals, and only to [finite cardinals], it seems obvious that there can only be finite cardinals. A cardinal number, for him, is arrived at by counting; and the very definition of an infinite totality is that it is impossible to count it . . . . [But this] prejudice is one that can be overcome: the beginner can be persuaded that it makes sense, after all, to speak of the number of natural numbers. Once his initial prejudice has been overcome, the next stage is to convince the beginner that there are distinct transfinite cardinal numbers: not all infinite totalities have as many members as each other. When he has become accustomed to this idea, he is extremely likely to ask, 'How many transfinite cardinals are there?'. How should he be answered? He is very likely to be answered by being told, 'You must not ask that question'. But why should he not? If it was, after all, all right to ask, 'How many numbers are there?', in the sense in which 'number' meant 'finite cardinal', how can it be wrong to ask the same question when 'number' means 'finite or transfinite cardinal'? A mere prohibition leaves the matter a mystery. It gives no help to say that there are some totalities so large that no number can be assigned to them. We can gain some grasp on the idea of a totality too big to be counted . . . but once we have accepted that totalities too big to be counted may yet have numbers, the idea of one too big even to have a number conveys nothing at all. And merely to say, 'If you persist in talking about the number of all cardinal numbers, you will run into contradiction', is to wield the big stick, but not to offer an explanation.
>
> What the paradoxes revealed was not the existence of concepts with inconsistent extensions, but . . . indefinitely extensible concepts.

We have already noted that indefinite extensibility does not *per se* seem paradoxical, so the insight that Dummett is giving expression to is not well summarized by the last two quoted lines. The insight is rather into the interconnection, in the case in point, between the indefinite extensibility of *cardinal number* and the temptation to say that the concept falls under—*ought* to fall under—the relevant Π. We get the indefinitely extensible series of transfinite cardinals up and running in the first place by insisting on one-one correspondence between concepts as necessary and sufficient for sameness, and hence existence, of cardinal number in general—not just in the finite case—and then, under the aegis of that insistence, by bringing to bear the Axioms of Union and Powerset, and then Cantor's theorem. A conception of cardinal embracing both the finite and the spectacular array of transfinite cases only arises in the first place when it is taken without question that concepts in general—or at least any that sustain determinate relations of one-one correspondence—have cardinal numbers, identified and distinguished in the light of those relations. That is how the intuitive barrier to the question, how many natural numbers are there, is overcome. But then the lid is off Pandora's box: for the intuitive barrier to the question, how many *cardinal* numbers are there is overcome too. *Cardinal*, it seems, has to be both indefinitely extensible with respect to *has a cardinal number* and an instance of it.

It is straightforward to transpose this diagnosis to our paradigm, the ordinals, taken intuitively as the order-types of well-orderings. Consider an imaginary Hero (cf. Wright, 1998) being introduced to the ordinal numbers. Suppose that she has been introduced to the finite ordinals, but not the infinite ones. She wonders about the order-type of the finite ordinals, and realizes that she has no ordinal for this—yet. So she thinks that there is no ordinal of finite ordinals. But we tell her that the finite ordinals do indeed have an ordinal, just not one that she has encountered already. She thus meets ω, and she formulates the notion of 'countable ordinal'. Hero then learns about $\omega + 1, 2\omega, \omega^2, \omega^\omega, \varepsilon_0$, etc. Perhaps she reads Cantor (1883), or a contemporary text in set theory. So now she naturally asks about the order-type of the countable ordinals, and she encounters the same problem. We tell her that the countable ordinals do have an ordinal—just not one that she has encountered already. So she learns about ω_1. Hero is a quick study, and she recognizes the pattern: every initial segment of the ordinals has an order-type—just not one featuring in the segment itself, but rather the next one after all those. But now she notices that the ordinals themselves are well-ordered, and so she inquires after the order-type of *all* ordinals. This time it seems we have the option neither of telling her that the ordinals do indeed have an order-type—just not one among those she has encountered already—nor of denying that they have any order-type. She asked about the order-type of ALL ordinals, and since the ordinals are well-ordered, there ought to be one. But if this order-type exists, it too is an ordinal and must therefore occur among the ordinals whose collective order-type she asked about. *Ordinal* has been so explained to her as to be indefinitely extensible with respect to *has instances which exemplify a well-order-type*—and the nemesis is that there then seems no option but to allow that it is itself an instance of this Π.

We leave it to the reader to construct a narrative for Hero's corresponding experience with the notion of *set* itself.

The three classic paradoxes of the transfinite, then, arise not with indefinite extensibility as such—at least, not if that is characterized as we have proposed—but with a particular twist taken by the examples concerned: cases where we unwittingly load a concept with a principle of indefinite extension whose trigger-concept—the relevant Π—can be denied of the concept in question only by making an arbitrary exception to a connection—e.g. that well-ordered collections have order-types, that concepts which sustain relations of one-one correspondence have cardinals, that well-defined collections comprise sets—which is integral to the operation of the principle in question. Of course it may seem perverse to caption the making of an exception necessary to avoid contradiction as arbitrary. But, as Dummett said, intimidation is one thing, and explanation is another.

The situation we find ourselves in is one in which, in the view of Graham Priest (2002), we bump up against one of a number of 'limits of thought'—effectively, the limit involved in the attempt coherently to conceive of an *absolutely limitless* process of iteration. Abstractly put, the attempt involves successively thinking beyond anything that presents itself as a limit, always being ready to postulate a next element or stage lying beyond what temporarily passes as a barrier—a new element of the same general category as everything that comes before but differing, of course, by virtue of being, in one or another respect, of a new species. (Cantor's second number principle, see Section 10.11 above.) The 'limit of thought' is reached when we attempt to form a conception of the entirety—the whole array—of the elements or stages involved in the absolutely limitless iteration. If we accept that, this time, the array cannot be transcended, then it seems there is a limit after all and accordingly that we have not succeeded in conceiving of genuine iterative limitlessness. But this time we no longer have the option of postulating another instance of the generic category of object in question (ordinal, cardinal, set), because we are supposed to be dealing with ALL of them—or at least trying to.[10]

Priest himself suggests a dialetheic resolution: give up the law of non-contradiction, and allow, for instance, that *ordinal* both does and does not have an order-type. So the ordinals are indeed absolutely limitless and at the same time transcended in thought: there is an ordinal which succeeds all the ordinals (and is itself succeeded in turn by ordinals . . .) For those of a nervous disposition who find this too strong to stomach, it may seem that the only option is to deny that there is an ordinal of all ordinals, a set of all sets, and a cardinal of all cardinalities. There are several options—see Section 10.11 below. That standard set-theory (ZFC) itself sanctions these denials does not of course make them principled.

10.7 A CONFESSION

Sua culpa. From the perspective just arrived at, the notion of 'proper class'—made free use of in Shapiro (1991)—now looks quite illegitimate. Invoking proper classes is an attempt to do the very thing we are intuitively barred from doing—a fudge which attempts to allow both that *set* itself falls under various of the Π's that trigger relevant principles of extension for sub-concepts/collections of it and that a new kind of 'collection' provides the corresponding values. The theorist who invokes proper classes thus confusedly thinks of himself as doing something analogous to Hero's move from finite to countable ordinals. But he has forgotten that *set* is supposed to encompass the *maximally general category* of entities of the relevant kind. The point is trenchantly made by George Boolos, 1998a, 35–6:[11]

> Wait a minute! I thought that set theory was supposed to be a theory about all, 'absolutely' all, the collections that there were and that 'set' was synonymous with 'collection' . . . If one admits that there are proper classes at all, oughtn't one to take seriously the possibility of an

[10] Perhaps Cantor is giving expression to the strain here when he writes (1883, endnote 2): 'we shall never reach a boundary that cannot be crossed; but we shall also never achieve even an approximate conception of the absolute. The absolute can only be acknowledged, but never known, not even approximately.'

[11] Boolos's observation here is the main motivation behind his well-known pluralist reading of (monadic) second-order quantifiers—in effect, an attempt to make sense and secure some of the theoretical advantages of second-order set theory, without admitting special items for the higher-order quantifiers to range over.

iteratively generated hierarchy of collection-theoretic universes in which the sets which ZF recognizes [merely] play the role of ground-floor objects? I can't believe that any such view of the nature of '$\in$' can possibly be correct. Are the reasons for which one believes in [proper] classes really strong enough to make one believe in the possibility of such a hierarchy?

Similar strictures apply to what may be called 'super-ordinals'—which would be well-orderings that are too big to be ordinals—and super-cardinals, which would be the sizes of proper classes. Cantor's 'inconsistent multiplicities'—considered as genuine objects—seem to be the same sort of thing as proper classes, and just as illegitimate. Zermelo was well advised to eschew all reliance on such 'things'.[12]

10.8 NEO-LOGICISM, ANTI-ZERO AND FRIENDS

The first stage in the neo-logicist program is to develop arithmetic from Hume's principle (HP):

$$\forall F \forall G[(\mathrm{N}x : Fx = \mathrm{N}x : Gx) \equiv (F \approx G)],$$

where $F \approx G$ is an abbreviation of the second-order statement that there is a relation mapping the F's one-to-one onto the G's. In both Frege (1884) and Wright (1983), the opening quantifiers are unrestricted. This seems to be well motivated. One insight that underlies both Frege's own treatment and neo-logicism is the universal applicability of arithmetic (Frege, 1884, §14). So long as one has objects, one can count them: arithmetic is applicable to absolutely any objects. So a principle governing identity of cardinal number in general should be formulated in such a way as to embrace (concepts of) objects of absolutely any sort (see Wright, 1998, 356–7).

Well motivated or not, Boolos (1997) launched an intriguing criticism of neo-logicism on the basis of this point. It follows from HP that *self-identical* has a cardinal number. This would be the number of all objects whatsoever—dubbed 'anti-zero' by Wright. Similarly, HP entails that there is a number of all cardinal numbers, a number of all ordinal numbers, and a number of all sets. Boolos observes that prima facie, this presents a conflict with ordinary Zermelo–Fraenkel set theory:

[I]s there such a number as [the number of all objects whatsoever?] According to [ZF] there is no cardinal number that is the number of all the sets there are. The worry is that the theory of number [based on HP] is incompatible with Zermelo–Fraenkel set theory plus standard definitions.

(Boolos, 1997, 260)

A first reaction to the objection is that it involves an illicit commutation. Boolos writes 'According to [ZF] there is no cardinal number that is the number of all the sets there are', but all that is justified is something like the weaker 'It is not the case that according to [ZF] there is a cardinal number that is the number of all the sets there are.' ZF does not countenance proper classes, to be sure, and thus it does not assign

[12] See the passage quoted at the end of Section 10.2 above.

numbers to such items. But ZF does not *deny* the existence of such large 'numbers'. As a first-order theory, it cannot even formulate the question. One would not criticize standard Peano arithmetic for failing to recognize real numbers, so why fault ZF for failing to recognize numbers of some (proper class sized) concepts?

However, as we interpret it, Boolos's criticism of HP runs deeper than this, and is of a piece with his rejection of proper classes. The first-order variables of set-theory are supposed to range over *every* set-like object there is. If proper classes are set-like they should have been included in the range of the variables of set theory. With the axiom of choice, it is plausible to hold that a concept has a size only if it is equinumerous with a cardinal. If we reject proper classes, then cardinals are sets, and only sets have cardinals.

Wright (1999, 12–13) himself gives an independent argument against anti-zero, arguing that the cardinality operator is properly restricted to concepts that are sortal and that *self-identical* is not one of them. That point, however, offers no treatment of Boolos's objection in relation to *ordinal, cardinal,* and *set.* For these cases Wright granted the force of Boolos's objection, allowing 'the plausible principle ... that there is a determinate number of *F*'s just provided that the *F*'s compose a *set*', and observing that 'Zermelo–Fraenkel set theory implies that there is no set of all sets. So it would follow that there is no number of all sets'. On the same count, there is no number of all ordinals and no number of all cardinals—contra the straightforward reading of HP. Wright's response is further to restrict the second-order variables in HP, so that some sortal concepts do not have numbers, and to invoke the notion of indefinite extensibility for this purpose. He writes:

> I do not know how best to sharpen [the notion of indefinite extensibility] ... Dummett could be [wrong about some of his claims concerning the notion but still] ... emphasizing an important insight concerning certain very large totalities—ordinal number, cardinal number, set, and indeed 'absolutely everything'. If there is anything at all in the notion of an indefinitely extensible totality ... one principled restriction on Hume's Principle will surely be that [cardinal numbers] *not* be associated with such totalities.
>
> (Wright, 1999, 13–14)

Thus, Wright suggests that the second-order variables in HP be restricted to sortal concepts that are Definite. Wright's programmatic suggestion provoked Shapiro (2003a). If we can restrict HP in the way Wright suggests—to avoid saying that there is a number of all ordinals, a number of all sets, etc.—then why not restrict Basic Law V similarly, and perhaps resurrect set theory along neo-logicist lines? Indeed, if *P* is a Definite concept, then the extension of *P* is just the set of *P*'s. No danger of contradiction there. Of course, to develop this project, we need a robust articulation of indefinite extensibility. We consider this direction further in Section 10.10 below.

In response to Wright's proposal, Peter Clark (2000) argued that the best candidate for 'not indefinitely extensible' is 'set sized', where 'set' is the notion given by Zermelo–Fraenkel set theory. That is, Clark argues that 'Definite' just means something like 'equinumerous with a member of the iterative hierarchy'. So if the notion of indefinite extensibility is indeed needed for the neo-logicist program, then that program is hopeless. It requires that we articulate the iterative hierarchy before we can give the proper foundation even for arithmetic—before we can even so much as state Hume's Principle in full generality.

If our proposals above about the proper characterization of indefinite extensibility are accepted, Clark's objection has been answered. It may prove to be, as he suggests, that the extension of *Definite* coincides with that of *set-sized*. But that is not the direction in which to seek a proper characterization of *Definite* or its contrary. Rather, to repeat, an indefinitely extensible concept P is one such that, for some Π, any Π sub-concept of the original allows of *limitless* Π-preserving intra-P enlargement. There is no implicit appeal to the notion of set. It is true that, as we stressed above, the conception of limitlessness is parametric in the characterization, and one construction of it will run in harness with the ZF treatment of the ordinals. But that is (one) working out of the notion of indefinite extensibility, rather than something which belongs with the kind of explanation that would have to be given before a restriction of HP—or Basic Law V, for that matter—to Definite concepts could be presumed intelligible. And of course however it works out, finite concepts will pass the test. So at least the neo-logicist treatment of arithmetic is safe.

10.9 INDEFINITE EXTENSIBILITY, LIMITATION OF SIZE AND THE TRUE INFINITE—HOW MANY IS 'TOO MANY'?

The principal thesis of Russell's (1906) limitation of size conception of sets is that 'there [is] (so to speak) a certain limit of size which no [set] can reach; and any supposed [set] which reaches or surpasses this limit is ... improper ... , i.e., is a non-entity'. Someone in sympathy with the tendency of our discussion so far will find it hard to take Russell's expression of his point literally. Those of us trained in set theory will in any case find it natural to think of 'size' as something only sets have, following Cantor, Zermelo, et al. If a 'collection' is not a set, then it is nothing, has no size at all, and so can't be 'too big'. Indeed Russell himself speaks of 'non-entity'. Moreover if Wright's (1999) suggestion just rehearsed is accepted, indefinitely extensible concepts will determine neither sets nor cardinals; so there will be no size(s) for the 'non-entities' to have.

From the present point of view, the solid core to the suggestion that sets are subject to limitation of size is nothing but the thesis that indefinitely extensible concepts do not determine sets. What is striking is that Russell (1906, 153–154), for his part, dismisses the limitation-of-size conception (in favor of the no-class theory) almost as soon as he raises it, and that the reason he gives for doing so is absolutely consistent with and germane to this proposed interpretation of it. He writes:

> A great difficulty of this theory is that it does not tell us how far up the series of ordinals it is legitimate to go. It might happen that ω was already illegitimate: in that case all proper [sets] would be finite .... .. Or it might happen that ω^2 was illegitimate, or ω^ω, or ω_1 or any other [limit] ordinal ... [O]ur general principle does not tell us under what circumstances [a concept is Definite].
>
> It is no doubt intended by those who advocate this theory that all ordinals should be admitted which can be defined, so to speak, from below, i.e., without introducing the notion of the

whole series of ordinals. Thus, they would admit all of Cantor's ordinals, and they would only avoid admitting the maximum ordinal. But it is not easy to state such a limitation precisely: at least I have not succeeded in doing so.

It is obvious, of course, that anyone who wishes to propose a set theory developed in terms of 'limitation of size' must face the conceptual problem of delimiting just how 'many' objects a concept must apply to, in order for it to rank as inadmissibly big. But Russell's objection, re-expressed in the light of the interpretation of size-limitation latterly proposed, comes to the concern that, without some independent and well-motivated grip on the idea of *limitless iteration*, we have no principled characterization of which concepts determine sets. Since limitless iteration is iteration without ordinal limit, it is not too far off the mark to express the point by wondering 'how far up the series of ordinals it is legitimate to go'. But a better expression of the question would be: what structure should we attribute to the series of ordinals?

Dummett (1991, 317) himself writes that the 'principle of extendibility constitutive of an indefinitely extensible concept is independent of how lax or rigorous the requirement for having a [D]efinite conception of a totality is taken to be, although that will of course affect which concepts are acknowledged to be indefinitely extensible'. That is exactly the same concern if we take it that one has such a Definite conception only if the 'construction' of the totality in question has an ordinal limit.

The issue is critical. We can sharpen our feel for it if we consider philosophers and mathematicians at two polar extremes. At the conservative end, Dummett evidently sympathizes with—and in some passages seemingly adopts—Russell's intendedly flippant suggestion that even ω is too big to be Definite. In other words, Dummett claims that the concept of being a *finite* ordinal is already indefinitely extensible—that the finite ordinals have no ordinal limit. The structure of the ordinals—all the Definite ordinals—is that of a (misleadingly termed!) ω-sequence. He notes that it is common for mathematicians to concede that concepts like *set* and *ordinal* (as normally liberally understood) are indefinitely extensible, but most hold that domains like the natural numbers and the real numbers are perfectly Definite. Dummett argues that this last belief is ungrounded:

> We have a strong conviction that we *do* have a clear grasp of the totality of natural numbers; but what we actually grasp with such clarity is the principle of extension by which, given any natural number, we can immediately cite one greater than it by 1. A concept whose extension is intrinsically infinite is thus a particular case of an indefinitely extensible one. Assuming its extension to constitute a [D]efinite totality ... may not lead to inconsistency; but it necessarily leads to our supposing that we have provided definite truth-conditions ... for statements that cannot legitimately be so interpreted.
>
> (Dummett, 1991, 318, see also 1993, 442–3)

The last remark asserts a connection between the indefinite extensibility of a concept and issues concerning determinacy of sense for certain kinds of statements concerning its instances—par excellence, quantified statements; an issue which takes us to the heart of the agenda for the present volume and to which we shall shortly turn. But in its general outline, though not of course in respect of that claimed connection,

Dummett's stance belongs to the tradition initiated by Aristotle and elegantly represented by Leibniz:[13]

It could . . . well be argued that, since among any ten terms there is a last number, which is also the greatest of those numbers, it follows that among all numbers there is a last number, which is also the greatest of all numbers. But I think that such a number implies a contradiction . . . When it is said that there are infinitely many terms, it is not being said that there is some specific number of them, but that there are more than any specific number.

(Letter to Bernoulli, Leibniz 1863, III 566, translated in Levey 1998, 76–7, 87)

. . . we conclude . . . that there is no infinite multitude, from which it will follow that there is not an infinity of things, either. Or [rather] it must be said that an infinity of things is not one whole, or that there is no aggregate of them.

(Leibniz 1980, 6.3, 503, translated in Levey 1998, 86)

Yet M. Descartes and his followers, in making the world out to be indefinite so that we cannot conceive of any end to it, have said that matter has no limits. They have some reason for replacing the term 'infinite' by 'indefinite', for there is never an infinite whole in the world, though there are always wholes greater than others ad infinitum. As I have shown elsewhere, the universe cannot be considered to be a whole.

(Leibniz, 1996, 151)

For Leibniz, the infinite just *is* limitlessness; *no* actual infinities exist. The only intelligible notion of infinity is that of potential infinity—the transcendence of any limit.

For witnesses of the other polar extreme, we turn to the ultra-liberals, Cantor and Zermelo. In a sense, Cantor accepted the conception of the true infinite as pure limitlessness. His achievement, for those who believe in it, was to have discovered the rich 'paradise' of limits beyond the finite: the realm of *transfinite* ordinals and cardinals. Cantor's belief in the actuality of the transfinite is supported by appeal to the alleged instability of the potentialist conception, sometimes in theological terms:

the potential infinite is only an auxiliary or relative (or relational) concept, and always indicates an underlying transfinite without which it can neither be nor be thought.

That an 'infinite creation' must be assumed to exist can be proved in many ways . . . One proof stems from the concept of God. Since God is of the highest perfection one can conclude that it is possible for Him to create a *transfinitum ordinatum*. Therefore, . . . we can conclude that there actually is a created *transfinitum*.

(Cantor, 1887, 391, 400)

Responding to the suggestion that the actual infinite is unintelligible, 'that *we* with our restricted being are not in a position to actually conceive the infinitely many individuals . . . belonging to the set . . . in one intuition', Cantor replies:

But I would like to see that man who, for instance, can form the idea distinctly and precisely in one intuition of all the unities in the *finite* number 'thousand million', or some even smaller numbers. No one alive today has this ability. And yet we have the right to acknowledge the

[13] Thanks to Roy Cook for suggesting these references.

finite numbers, however great, as objects of discursive human knowledge, and to investigate their concepts scientifically. *We have the same right also with respect to the transfinite numbers.*

(Cantor, 1887, 402)

With these remarks, Cantor challenges his opponents to delimit a principled alternative to strict finitism—a finitism going no further than our actual practical limitations of intuition and understanding—that does not also sanction the transfinite.[14] Grasping the notion of a *large finite* set already requires idealization. What reason is there to limit the idealization to the arbitrarily large but still finite?

We are invited to answer 'none'. But if we do, where should we locate the true infinite—as opposed to the merely transfinite? Recall Cantor's definition (from (1883, note 1)): 'By a "manifold" or "set" I understand any multiplicity which can be thought of as one, i.e., any aggregate of determinate elements which can be unified into a whole by some law'. The idea here is that if it is (merely) consistent for some objects to be a 'unity', then it *is* a unity—there is an actual set that contains just those objects. This principle underlies Cantor's entire project. Once we cast off the shackles of potentialism, only consistency is allowed to put a brake on the exhilarating rush beyond.

Almost half a century later, Zermelo (1930) articulates a version of second-order ZFC with *urelements*, in pretty much its contemporary form, and he freely discusses models of the axiomatization. If a model of the theory lacks *urelements*, then it is isomorphic to a rank V_κ in which κ is a strong inaccessible. He proposes (1930, 1233) an axiom stating the existence of 'an unbounded sequence' of such models. Each such model V_κ has subsets (like κ, the collection of ordinals in the model) which are not members of the model.[15] However,

> [w]hat appears as an 'ultra-finite non- or super-set' in one model is, in the succeeding model, a perfectly good, valid set with both a cardinal number and an ordinal type . . . To the unbounded series of Cantor ordinals there corresponds a similarly unbounded . . . series of essentially different set-theoretic models. Scientific reactionaries and anti-mathematicians have so eagerly and lovingly appealed to the 'ultra-finite antinomies' in their struggle against set theory. But these are only apparent 'contradictions', and depend solely on confusing *set theory itself* . . . with individual *models* representing it . . . The two polar opposite tendencies of the thinking spirit, the idea of creative *advance* and that of collection and *completion*, ideas which also lie behind the Kantian 'antinomies', find their symbolic reconciliation in the transfinite number series based on the concept of well-ordering. This series reaches no true completion in its unrestricted advance, but possesses only relative stopping-points, just those [strong inaccessibles] which separate the higher model types from the lower. Thus the set-theoretic 'antinomies', when correctly understood, do not lead to a cramping and mutilation of mathematical science, but rather to an, as yet, unsurveyable unfolding and enriching of that science.

In present terms, then, Zermelo's proposal is that the series of models of second-order ZFC—and so the series of strongly inaccessible cardinals—is *itself* indefinitely

[14] For an extensive, insightful, and compelling account of Cantor's views here, see Hallett (1984), especially §§1.2–1.3.

[15] To get the idea, consider someone, say our friend Hero, whose entire universe is one of these models (a set that we, from the outside, see as a V_κ). For Hero, some of (what we see as) subsets of V_κ, such as κ itself, are indefinitely extensible, non-entities, whatever. But once Hero recognizes the next model after V_κ, she sees see that those totalities are perfectly good sets.

extensible. Each strong inaccessible is a Definite collection, but any set of inaccessibles gives rise to further, larger, strongly inaccessible sets, cardinals, and ordinals. So there is no set of *all* such models or all such cardinals.

Zermelo proposed 'the *existence of an unbounded sequence of* [inaccessible ranks] as a new *axiom* of "meta-set theory".' In effect, the new principle states that for each ordinal α, there is a unique inaccessible cardinal κ_α. This, of course, is what the Russell conjecture (from Section 10.2 above) would predict, concerning the statement that the strong inaccessible cardinals are themselves indefinitely extensible.

It is common for set-theorists to use language like Zermelo's. We are not so bold as to suggest, for even one minute, that we—or they—do not know what they mean. Nevertheless, this is an almost literally breathtaking marginalization of the scope of the Aristotelian infinite. Each inaccessible is an actual infinity; the only potential infinity is the 'collection' of all strong inaccessibles. The 'process' of generating more strong inaccessibles has absolutely no limit, not even an inaccessibly large one. (Of course, this stretches the notion of 'process' even further, well beyond recognition; it also constitutes an exception to Cantor's second number principle.)

As we saw, Russell (1906, 154) suggested that the underlying idea is that the actual infinite extends as far up the iterative hierarchy as it consistently can. Everything infinite in the hierarchy is actually infinite. It is hardly a substantial observation that the perspective of Cantor and Zermelo is ontologically extravagant! (Boolos, 1998b). But the real concern is that it is, au fond, *unprincipled.* 'Keep going until you run into contradiction' is not a principle but a refusal to be disturbed by the lack of one. The statement is intuitively insufficient for just the same reason that it is an intuitively insufficient response to the *semantic* paradoxes to claim simply that it is analytic of the concept of truth that the Equivalence Scheme (P iff it is true that P) holds in all cases save where it leads to contradiction. The fact is that one does run into contradiction unless a brake is put on proceedings somewhere, and one wants a principled account of where—something which marks off the exceptions as an independent species and provides an explanation of why a treatment which overlooks their distinctive character could be expected to lead to trouble. Yet the polar opposite, thoroughgoing conservative, Aristotelian view that *all* infinities are indefinitely extensible seems far too restrictive—it denies us what most will find no cause to doubt to be perfectly clear conceptions of the structures distinguished in at least the 'early' stages of the Cantorian transfinite. But then where, and how, is the line to be drawn? Dummett's (1963) original claim that *arithmetical truth* is indefinitely extensible is perhaps consistent with setting the 'limit' a bit higher than ω. We might admit computable (or recursive) countable ordinals, for example. But Dummett's 'limit' must be well short of ω_1, and thus of the real numbers. We presume that most mathematicians have come to accept at least a few uncountable, Definite infinities—say the collection of all real-valued functions. But how is this issue to be adjudicated? On what grounds?

To summarize: we are proposing that the Aristotelian infinite is to be understood as the indefinitely extensible. The two polar views are then respectively that there is no Definite infinite—the infinite *is* the indefinitely extensible—and that the Definite infinite extends as far as it may consistently be taken to do. The first is 'principled' enough—it amounts to an across-the-board repudiation of Cantor's Second

Principle: *no* collection of numbers, sets or ordinals which has no largest member has a limit: a smallest number, set or ordinal greater than any in the original. Unbridled liberalism, by contrast, which holds that the only exceptions to the principle are those dictated by mere consistency, is open to the charge of casuistry. A natural standpoint—'natural' at least in the anthropological sense that it seems to come naturally to many—is to want something in between: to want to be in position to make principled use of Cantor's second principle, rather than simply reject it, while able to corral and account for the exceptions.

Hitherto we have understood the Definite simply as that which is not indefinitely extensible, that which is not limitless. But the parametric role of the concept of limitlessness in the characterization of indefinite extensibility means that there is no hope of progress past the impasse latterly outlined unless we can infuse Definiteness with some additional independent operational content, sufficient to provide a criterion for which are the Definite infinite totalities. But how is this to be achieved? As noted, Dummett concedes for his part that we can consistently think of ω, ω_1, etc., as Definite, but argues that this simply begs the question. In (1991, 317–8), he seemed resigned to settling for a stand-off:

One reason why the philosophy of mathematics appears at present to be becalmed is that we do not know how to accomplish the task at which Frege so lamentably failed, namely to characterise the domains of the fundamental mathematical theories so as to convey what everyone, without preconceptions, will acknowledge as a definite conception of the totality in question: those who believe themselves already to have a firm grasp of such a totality are satisfied with the available characterizations, while those who are sceptical of claims to have such a grasp reject them as question-begging or unacceptably vague. An impasse is thus reached, and the choice degenerates into one between an act of faith and an avowal of disbelief, or even between expressions of divergent tastes. Moreover, the impasse seems intrinsically impossible of resolution; for fundamental mathematical theories, such as the theory of the natural numbers or the theory of real numbers, are precisely those from which we initially derive our conceptions of different infinite cardinalities, and hence no characterisation of their domains could in principle escape the accusation of circularity

But just a couple of years later, Dummett can be found arguing that the burden of proof lies with his opponent, one who claims that there are Definite infinite totalities:

It might be objected that no contradiction results from taking the real numbers to form a definite totality. There is, however, no ground to suppose that treating an indefinitely extensible concept as a definite one will always lead to inconsistency; it may merely lead to our supposing ourselves to have a definite idea when we do not

The totality of natural numbers contains what, from our perspective, are enormous numbers, and yet others [relative] to which those are minute, and so on indefinitely; do we really have a grasp of such a totality?

A natural response is to claim that the question has been begged. In classing *real number* as an indefinitely extensible concept, we have *assumed* that any totality of which we can have a definite conception is at most denumerable; in classing *natural number* as one, we have assumed that such a totality will be finite. Burden-of-proof controversies are always difficult to resolve; but, in this instance, it is surely clear that it is the other side that has begged the question.

It is claiming to be able to convey a conception of the totality of real numbers, without circularity, to one who does not yet have it ... [The beginner] does not *assume* as a principle that any totality of which it is possible to form a definite conception is at most denumerable: he merely has as yet no conception of any totality of higher cardinality ... The fact is that a concept determining an intrinsically infinite totality—one whose infinity follows from the concept itself—simply *is* an indefinitely extensible one.

(Dummett, 1993, 442–3)

Dummett's stance in this passage is apparently that one should refuse to accept that the natural numbers or the real numbers—let alone the power set of the continuum, or totalities associated with inaccessible, or supercompact cardinals—are Definite until it has been *shown*, without circularity and without begging any questions, that Definite conceptions are possible of such totalities.

But Dummett here sets his opponents a task of which he has provided no adequate characterization. What should count as accomplishing it? We have some idea, perhaps, what is it to possess a Definite conception of a totality *modulo* a given assumption about the extent of the ordinals: it is to possess an (adequately clear?) conception of a totality which is either finite or only up-to-λ extensible for some ordinal λ recognized by that assumption. But how does one show that one has a Definite conception in the more robust sense now demanded—a conception, in particular, that would let one *justify* assumptions about the extent of the ordinals themselves? In general, argument that a burden of proof lies with an opponent is more persuasive when accompanied by the courtesy of an explanation of what exactly is the content of that which has to be proved, and what will be accepted as amounting to proof of it![16]

Fortunately, there is an alternative to a resolute adherence to either of the polar views, even without philosophical progress on the main issue: it is to think of modern arithmetic, analysis, and set theory as exploring the consequences of a *working hypothesis* that the natural numbers, the real numbers, and other very large, infinite totalities allow of coherent conception as Definite. We cannot—yet, and maybe never will be able to—*justify* these hypotheses from first principles in the Philosophical Theory of Understanding, but we do not have to. Since Gödel, we have become used to flying without a safety net. In this way, the mathematician can in good conscience rest content with the theories in question, even without possessing the justification whose want the philosopher laments. *Pro tem,* he may let them stand or fall on the basis of the fruits they bear, wherever these fruits may lie.

In an insightful article on Cantor, Tait (2000, §4) writes in a similar spirit:

It was Cantor's construction of the system of transfinite numbers ... that opened a Pandora's box of foundational problems in mathematics, namely, the question of what cardinal numbers there are. One can, in a way, understand the resistance to Cantor's ideas on the part of the mathematical law-and-order-types—in the same way that one can understand the Church terrorizing the elderly Galileo: in defense of a closed, tidy universe. In that respect, Hilbert's

16 Dummett's claims concerning the burden-of-proof are no doubt consonant with the sometime verificationist and foundationalist elements in his metaphysics; but one might well indeed despair of progress, we submit, if the issue cannot be resolved without entry into the chamber of such vexed debates.

reference to Cantor's 'Paradise' is ironic: it was the Kroneckers who wanted to stay in Paradise and it was Cantor who lost it for us—bless him

there are many mathematicians who will accept the Garden of Eden, that is, the theory of functions as developed in the nineteenth century, but will, if not reject, at least put aside the theory of transfinite numbers, on the grounds that it is not needed for analysis. Of course, on such grounds, one might also ask what analysis is needed for, and if the answer is basic physics, one might then ask what that is needed for. When it comes to putting food in one's mouth, the 'need' for any real mathematics becomes somewhat tenuous. Cantor started us on an intellectual journey. One can peel off at any point, but no one should make a virtue of doing so.

Once again, it seems overly restrictive to follow Dummett and reject any Definite infinite totalities, or even any uncountable infinite totalities. Cantor's paradise is too enticing, and fruitful. It is *ad hoc* to look for a 'boundary' or 'limit' intermediate between the staunch conservative, 'law-and-order' extreme and Cantor's and Zermelo's admission of everything. Any proposed place to stop the expansion of the actual infinite, say at 2ω, ω_1, or the ninth strongly inaccessible, is artificial. Why stop *there*? As Tait (*ibid.*, 284) puts it:

Pandora's box is indeed open: Under what conditions *should* we admit the extension of a property of transfinite numbers to be a set—or equivalently, what transfinite numbers are there? No answer is final, in the sense that, given any criterion for what counts as a set of numbers, we can relativize the definition of Ω to sets satisfying that criterion and obtain a class Ω' of numbers. But there would be no grounds for denying that Ω' is a set: the preceding argument that Ω is not a set merely transforms in the case of Ω' into a proof that Ω' does not satisfy the criterion in question. So ... we can go on. In the foundations of set theory, Plato's dialectician, searching for the first principles, will never go out of business.

Suppose, for example, that someone—a less moderate minimalist—tries to define an ordinal to be a well-ordering-type that is 'accessible' (i.e., not strongly inaccessible). Then she can conclude that all ordinals are accessible, and be done with it. But, in the spirit of Cantor and Zermelo, it seems better to claim that we now have a reason to believe in an inaccessible ordinal: the 'totality' of our friend's ordinals is itself an inaccessible well-ordering type, and thus an inaccessible ordinal.

Nevertheless, we must add the annoying reminder that one must 'peel off' Cantor's journey at some point, to use Tait's metaphor. The laws that drive the journey—Cantor's two principles of generation (Section 10.1 above)—cannot be exceptionless, on pain of paradox. But where do we stop?

10.10 NEO-LOGICIST SET THEORY

We now return briefly to a question deferred from Section 10.8—the question whether the diagnosis of the paradoxes as, in effect, due to a failure to exclude indefinitely extensible concepts from within the range of legitimate set abstraction is in any way helpful when it comes to the attempt to develop a reasonably powerful set-theory along neo-logicist lines. 'Reasonably powerful', we shall take it, should involve provision of resources sufficient not just for the reconstruction of classical arithmetic and analysis but for recovery of at least all the less than inaccessibly infinite sets in the standard iterative hierarchy and their standard mathematical treatment. It would be a significant coup for neo-logicism if such a theory could be based just on second-order logic and otherwise acceptable abstraction principles—in effect, if a neo-logicist reconstruction of ZFC could be accomplished whose epistemological basis was in no interesting way different from that of Frege Arithmetic—arithmetic based on second-order logic and Hume's Principle. The purpose of this section is to indicate why, as we believe, this prospect is no closer.

Specialized to the case where courses-of-values are extensions of concepts—or we may as well say, sets—Frege's inconsistent Basic Law V may be represented thus:

$$(\forall F)(\forall G)(\{x : Fx\} = \{x : Gx\} \equiv (\forall x)(Fx \equiv Gx)),$$

a principle that both encapsulates the extensionality of sets and associates every concept with its own set. Frege's own reaction to the paradox was to qualify extensionality: we can still count it, he suggested, as sufficient but not necessary in order for the set of F's to be identical with the set of G's that F and G be coextensive—rather what is necessary and sufficient is that F and G hold of exactly the same items *save possibly the respective sets themselves*. Frege's proposal is obviously philosophically hopeless from the neo-logicist point of view: its formulation involves not just impredicative quantification on the right hand side of the abstraction over the newly introduced abstracts—something which is epistemologically controversial, of course, but which neo-logicism is anyway committed to arguing can be acceptable—but explicit *mention* of them using the canonical notation which the abstraction is supposed to explain. Worse, it lets us identify a pair of objects in circumstances where one has a property which the other lacks! Worst of all, it is also, as Frege must have rapidly realized, technically hopeless since inconsistent in any domain of more than one object.[17]

If there is to be a progressive neo-logicist modification of Law V, it must come, it would appear, from tweaking not its extensionality component, but the comprehension it affords: not all concepts can be permitted to determine (extensionally individuated) sets. In his (1986), George Boolos put forward one naturally and ingeniously conceived proposal: restrict Law V to concepts which, in keeping with the tradition of limitation of size, are 'small', with the complement of smallness glossed as 'equinumerous with the universe'—a restriction which may be defined using only second-order logical restrictions.

There are two ways one can write in the restriction. One is to have it as antecedent in a universally quantified conditional whose consequent is Law V less its initial higher-order quantifiers:

$$(\forall F)(\forall G)[(\mathit{smallF}\&\mathit{smallG}) \rightarrow (\{x : Fx\} = \{x : Gx\} \equiv (\forall x)(Fx \equiv Gx))],$$

but this has the drawback that one cannot decide whether a set is well-behaved—is individuated extensionally—before one knows how big the universe is. For example,

[17] See Quine (1955) and Geach (1956). The first to remark on this seems to have been Lesniewski (see Sobocinski, 1949). A useful diagnostic discussion is Resnik (1980, 211–20).

even if $x \neq x$ is treated as a small concept as a matter of courtesy, as it were, one will struggle to distinguish $\{x : x \neq x\}$ from $\{x : x = \{x : x \neq x\}\}$ by the proposed principle unless one has it independently that the universe consists of more than one thing.

Hence the direction which Boolos actually took:

New V

$$(\forall F)(\forall G)(\{x : Fx\} = \{x : Gx\} \equiv ((non{-}smallF \;\&\; non{-}smallG) \vee (\forall x)(Fx \equiv Gx)))$$

The right hand side is still an equivalence relation, since co-extensiveness is a congruence for *non-small.* Every concept gets an extension, but those bijectable with the universal concept all get the same extension, whether or not co-extensive. According to New V, $x \neq x$ and $x = \{x : x \neq x\}$ are assigned distinct extensions, just as they should be, since they are not co-extensive and cannot both be non-small.

As Boolos shows, New V encompasses a surprising range of standard set-theoretic axioms. A 'set' is the extension of a small concept. Extensionality, Null Set, Pairs, Choice, Separation (*Aussonderung*), and Replacement hold on all sets; and Union and Foundation hold on so-called 'pure sets', those built up, hereditarily, from the empty set. New V provides for a satisfactory theory of the hereditarily finite pure sets and a foundation for arithmetic. But as Boolos shows, it fails to provide Infinity—to ensure that there is any well-behaved (i.e. small) infinite set—and, even if we collaterally assume that there is such a set, New V fails to ensure that it has a well-behaved power set. So Paradise is postponed.

Shapiro (2003a) launches an investigation of what, in general terms, may be expected foundationally from abstractions of the general pattern that New V exemplifies:

$$(\forall F)(\forall G)(\{x : Fx\} = \{x : Gx\} \equiv ((badF \;\&\; badG) \vee (\forall x)(Fx \equiv Gx))).$$

Obviously the paradoxes entailed by original Law V will now discharge themselves into proofs that the relevant concepts—and in particular, *not-a-member-of-itself*, and (subject to appropriate definitions) *ordinal* and *cardinal*—are all bad, thus harmlessly marginalizing the concepts concerned.

Very well. So here is the salient question: how would matters turn out if—as would have been entirely consonant with our reflections in the early part of the preceding section—Boolos had proposed not *non-smallness* but *indefinite extensibility* as the appropriate reading of *bad*?—if he had proposed what we may dub *Indefinite V*:

$$(\forall F)(\forall G)(\{x : Fx\} = \{x : Gx\} \equiv ((indef.\ extensibleF \;\&\; indef.\ extensibleG) \vee (\forall x)(Fx \equiv Gx))).$$

There is one immediate potential point of improvement over New V. On pain of the Burali–Forti paradox, *ordinal* has to be bad under whatever reading. So if *bad* is *equinumerous with the universe*, as with New V, then there is a bijection between the ordinals and everything that there is, and the universe is consequently well-ordered (see Shapiro and Weir, 1999). So the existence of a global well-ordering is a consequence of New V. It follows that the non-abstracts are well-ordered, and that contravenes Wright's (1997, pp. 230–3) conservativeness requirement for abstraction principles, that—roughly—(a priori) acceptable abstractions should not entail new results about the old ontology. This problem will not affect Indefinite V, however, unless it can be shown that all indefinitely extensible concepts are bijectable with each other. The strongest result we have in the vicinity is Russell's Conjecture, that every indefinitely extensible concept sustains an *injection* of the ordinals, not a bijection.

If indefinite extensibility is a matter of 'size'—that is, if any collection equinumerous to a sub-collection of a Definite collection is itself Definite—then Separation (*Ausserondurung*) and Replacement seem to follow from Indefinite V. If we grant that finite concepts are Definite, we get Null Set and Pairs. If we restrict quantifiers to pure sets, Foundation follows, and perhaps Choice is close to a truth of logic. Nevertheless, there is cause to doubt the suitability of Indefinite V for the neo-logicist purpose. For one thing, it is not clear that any purely logical characterization of indefinite extensibility can be given. As the notion has been explained here, indefinite extensibility proper stands opposed to up-to-λ extensibility and a characterization of the latter will naturally demand, over and above the resources of higher-order logic, the ideology of the theory of the ordinals (which would activate an objection along the lines of Clark (2000), discussed at the close of Section 10.8 above). In this respect, then, Indefinite V, at least on the characterization of indefinite extensibility offered here, marks a step back from New V. (We shall return to this question in Section 10.13.)

Even if that problem can somehow be surmounted, however, the most serious foreseeable difficulty remains, as in the case of New V, with comprehension and, in the first instance, with Infinity. New V had the problem that, unless it is somehow independently given that the universe is more than countable, any infinite concept may consistently be taken to be bad and so not at the service of the abstraction of a well-behaved infinite set. Indefinite V looks certain to be encumbered with an exactly analogous problem: unless it is somehow independently given that some infinite concept is Definite, any infinite concept may consistently be taken to be bad, that is: indefinitely extensible, and so, again, not at the service of the abstraction of a well-behaved infinite set. But that is the issue about the prospects for whose resolution we just, in the previous section, concluded a pessimistic discussion. The idea that a strictly neo-logicist construction of a decently strong set-theory might proceed via second-order logic and Indefinite V comes, in effect, to the thought not merely that Dummett's Aristotelianism might be refuted using just those materials but more, that any position could be similarly refuted which—from a classical standpoint—places indefinite extensibility anywhere short of the inaccessible.

There is a general problem of formulating a restriction of Law V which is both consistent and strong enough to develop a theory as strong as Zermelo–Fraenkel set theory (perhaps together with other abstraction principles). As with other attempts to develop a consistent (or even dialetheic) 'naive' set theory, that is non-trivial and sufficiently powerful, we have to add analogues of certain of the ZF axioms explicitly. In the case of Indefinite V, we seem to require an explicit axiom that there is a Definite infinite concept, to get Infinity. Similarly, we have to explicitly add an axiom that if a concept of sets is Definite, then so is its union and powerset.[18] None of these follow from the general characterization of indefinite extensibility.

[18] In a sense, this is the moral of Shapiro (2003a).

10.11 QUANTIFYING OVER INDEFINITELY EXTENSIBLE TOTALITIES

We at last directly broach the topic of this volume. The question, simply, is whether it is ever appropriate or intelligible to speak of *all* of the items that fall under a given indefinitely extensible concept. Can we talk about all ordinals, or all cardinals, or all sets? The discussion for this and the next section will be organized through three closely related issues, focusing respectively on whether unrestricted quantification over the instances of an indefinitely extensible concept is intelligible, whether it is legitimate, and how—if it is to be both intelligible and legitimate—it requires to be understood.

There can hardly be any question about intelligibility from the extreme liberal point of view of Cantor and Zermelo (assuming that the viewpoint itself is intelligible, of course). If each particular transfinite cardinal, ordinal, and inaccessible rank, exists as an actual infinity, then they all do. Or so it would seem. The talk of the 'potential' infinity of the transfinite numbers (a la Cantor) or the inaccessible ranks (a la Zermelo) is just a picturesque way of saying that there is no *set* of all such numbers or ranks. But they do all actually exist, even if there is no set of them all and, it seems, we have just talked about them—*all* of them. Just in the very act of calling them indefinitely extensible, we somehow quantify over all of them, don't we? What is the problem?

Extreme conservatism, it seems, must surely grant intelligibility too, albeit for quite different reasons. Dummett holds that the natural numbers and certainly the real numbers are indefinitely extensible. Someone who agrees with him but holds that we cannot legitimately have quantifiers ranging over any indefinitely extensible totality, would have to conclude that we can have no theory of arithmetic or analysis involving quantification over all the natural numbers, or all the reals—so no worthwhile arithmetic or analysis at all. That, of course, is not Dummett's view. So he implicitly grants that one *can* intelligibly quantify over at least the natural numbers and the real numbers—so over at least *those* indefinitely extensible totalities. Dummett's view has to be that arithmetic and analysis intelligibly and legitimately quantify over indefinitely extensible totalities.

The picture is more complicated, however. In a well-known passage in the last chapter of his (1991) Dummett suggests that Frege's major 'mistake'—what doomed him to Russell's paradox—consisted in 'his supposing there to be a totality containing the extension of every concept defined over it; more generally [the mistake] lay in his not having the glimmering of a suspicion of the existence of indefinitely extensible concepts' (Dummett, 1991, 317). So now a reader might take it that Dummett thinks that there are at least *some* indefinitely extensible totalities over which one may *not* quantify. At least, she might draw that conclusion if she is also mindful of the many passages in Dummett's writings in which he apparently endorses the idea that objectual quantification, if it is to be determinate in sense, requires the antecedent specification of a *domain*, i.e. a set of objects, over which the bound variables are to range.[19] If quantification of determinate sense requires antecedent specification of a domain; and if a domain is a set; and if indefinitely extensible concepts do not determine sets, then the reader will need no help to see what follows. But then what to make of the apparent concession that the quantifiers in arithmetic and analysis are in good standing? Is it that some legitimate quantification doesn't require a domain? Or that some indefinitely extensible concepts do determine domains? Or what? We'll return to this.

Boolos (1993, 222) takes it that the foregoing *is* Dummett's line of argument:

it would seem that [Dummett] does think that there has to be a—what to call it—totality? collection? domain? containing all of the things we take ourselves at any one time to be talking about. He would seem to believe that whenever there are some things under discussion, being talked about, or being quantified over, for example some or all of the ordinals, there is a set-like item, a 'totality', to which they all belong. That is, he supposes that whenever we quantify, we quantify not over all the (ordinals or) sets that exist but only over some of them . . .

I suspect that Dummett would agree . . . that whenever we use quantifiers, there must be some domain, some totality of objects, over which our variables of quantification range; so if we take ourselves to be quantifying over all classes, then we must assume that there is a totality or domain containing all classes. And it may be thought that it is part of what we mean by 'quantify over' that there must be some such domain. Certain textbooks may reinforce this impression by telling us that to specify an interpretation we must first specify a non-empty set (class, collection, totality), the universe of discourse (or domain) over which our variables range (p. 223)

In arguing for the legitimacy of unrestricted quantification, Richard Cartwright (1994, 7) dubs this presupposition the 'All-in-One Principle'. It is of course a staple of contemporary model theory that each interpretation of a formal language contains a *set* to serve as a domain for the variables. In effect, Cartwright argues that this is only an artifact of the standard kind of model theory we use today, and not a regulative ideal for semantics generally. In present terms, the only conclusion to draw is that quantification over an indefinite extensible 'totality' is not covered by model theory. Boolos agrees:

If we look at the presentation of class theory found in Kelley's *General Topology* (1955), we find that the theory presented there is a full-fledged theory of classes in which variables range over (pure) classes and in which 'set' is defined to mean 'member of a class' . . . Kelley's axiom of extent (extensionality) reads, 'For each x and y it is true that $x = y$ if and only if for each $z, z \in x$ when and only when $z \in y$.' . . . Now, it seems to me that insofar as we have a grip at all on the use of the phrase 'quantify over', we have to say that Kelley, in laying down his axiom of extent, is quantifying over all classes (aggregates, collections). I take it that when

[19] Dummett (1981, 567): 'the one lesson of the set-theoretic paradoxes which seems quite certain is that we cannot interpret individual variables in Frege's way, as ranging simultaneously over the totality of all objects which could meaningfully be referred to or quantified over. That is . . . why modern explanations of the semantics of first-order predicate calculus always require that a domain be *specified* for the individual variables . . . the one thing we may confidently say hardly any modern logician believes in is wholly unrestricted quantification. All modern logicians are agreed that, in order to specify an interpretation of any sentence or formula containing bound variables, it is necessary expressly to stipulate what the range of the variables is to be.'

Kelley says 'each', he means it. How else are we to understand the axiom of extent ... except as saying that *any* classes x and y are identical iff x and y have the same members?

Why should we for a moment think that therefore there must be a collection of all the things that Kelley was using his variables to range over? If one checks the exposition of *General Topology*, at any rate, one will find no suggestion at all that there must exist some sort of super-class, containing all of the classes that the theory talks about ... [W]e can simply say: Our variables range over all classes

Or: over all ('absolutely', if you insist, all) objects there ('really') are. If Frege thought his variables could so range, as of course he did, he was not in error. (pp. 223–4)

Cantor's and Zermelo's texts also seem to presuppose that quantification over indefinitely extensible 'totalities': transfinite numbers or inaccessible ranks, is fully intelligible and fully legitimate. Consider, for example, the language in which Zermelo describes his program and in which his theorems are proved. What are we to make of his talk of 'models', 'normal domains' (i.e., inaccessible ranks), 'order-types', and the like? As noted, he proposed 'the *existence of an unbounded sequence of* [inaccessible ranks] as a new *axiom* of "meta-set theory".' Again, the new principle states that for each ordinal α, there is a unique inaccessible cardinal κ_α. How are we supposed to interpret *that* except as talking about *all* ordinals, and *all* inaccessible ranks? Zermelo's axiom is not meant as an assertion about some particular set-sized model but is surely intended to be taken at face value. The words in the meta-axiom are *used*, and not merely mentioned in a statement of satisfaction.[20]

Characteristically, set-theorists are not content merely to *quantify* in the cases in point. Commonly, they introduce linguistic items that at least look like *singular terms* that stand for indefinitely extensible 'totalities'. Cantor himself used 'Ω' for the transfinite numbers; nowadays this symbol is used for (the von Neumann) ordinals. And 'V' is the accepted term for the pure iterative hierarchy. This much, to be sure, need not be particularly problematic. Typical uses of these literary devices are easily paraphrased away, in terms of predicates. For example, '$\alpha \in \Omega$' is just shorthand for 'α is an ordinal'. The axiom V=L is just the statement that every set is constructible. One can reject the All-in-One principle, allow quantification over indefinitely extensible totalities, and still traffic in such apparent terms, provided they are only apparent—provided, as seems to be so, there is no pressing reason why expressions of the kind just noted should be conceived as standing for 'Ones'.

Boolos and Cartwright seem to be insouciant about rejecting the All-in-One principle. However, as noted in Shapiro (2003), things are far from comfortable for a free-wheeling acceptance of indefinitely extensible quantification. Above, we defined an

[20] Of course, we can profitably ask about the set-theoretic models of Zermelo's meta-axiom. A standard model of the meta-axiom would be a rank V_λ for which λ is a fixed-point in the series of inaccessibles: $\lambda = \kappa_\lambda$. These fixed points are next (after 'inaccessible') in the series of so-called 'small large cardinals'. Zermelo's meta-axiom does not entail the existence of such an inaccessible. The natural next maneuver would be to postulate another axiom asserting the existence of an unbounded sequence of such fixed points. This would be a meta-meta-axiom, stating that the fixed points in question are themselves indefinitely extensible. Then we can inquire into the models of this axiom. The interplay between using principles like this and then studying their models (mentioning the principles) is rich indeed (see Drake, 1974).

'ordinal' to be the order-type of a well-ordering. The problem is that the very definition of a well-ordering seems, like the brooms of the Sorcerer's Apprentice, to give rise to ever more well-orderings. It is, of course, routine to show that the relation of 'less than' on ordinals (or membership on the von Neumann ordinals) is itself a well-ordering: any sub-totality has a least element. But, of course, there is no order-type of the ordinals—no All-in-One in this case—on pain of contradiction. Yet is easy to define a two-place predicate that apparently characterizes a well-ordering that is strictly *longer* than Ω: Let α and β be ordinals. Say that $\alpha \prec_1 \beta$ if $\alpha \neq 0$ and either $\alpha < \beta$ or $\beta = 0$. That is, we make the order longer just by putting 0 at the 'end'. A routine trick. And why stop there? We can also define a relation that intuitively characterizes a well-ordering *twice* as long as Ω: $\alpha \prec_2 \beta$ if either α is a limit ordinal and β is a successor ordinal, or α and β are both limits and $\alpha < \beta$, or α and β are both successors and $\alpha < \beta$. In $\prec_2$, the limit ordinals come before the successors, and the limit ordinals and the successor ordinals are each isomorphic to the ordinals (and are thus each indefinitely extensible), according to ZFC anyway. Finally, here is a well-order that is Ω times as long as Ω (if you can pardon the expression): let $<x,y>$ be the ordered pair of x and y. If $\alpha,\beta,\gamma,\delta$ are ordinals, then let $<\alpha,\beta> \prec_3 <\gamma,\delta>$ if either $\alpha < \gamma$ or both $\alpha = \gamma$ and $\beta < \delta$.

Notice that the constructions here are somewhat independent of how 'many' ordinals one thinks there are. If one goes for a strict Aristotelian account, and maintains that all Definite totalities are finite, then Ω, the property, totality, or whatever, of all ordinals will be what the set-theorist calls 'ω'. The above predicate characterizing $\prec_1$ would thus define $\omega + 1$, which, for the strict Aristotelian, is longer than the ordinals. One can go on to define 2ω, ω^ω, etc. (although the use of limit ordinals will not be available). Similarly, if someone allows the existence of all but only classically countable ordinals, then Ω will be what the classicist calls 'ω_1', the first uncountable ordinal, and it will then be routine to write predicates that characterize well-orderings corresponding to $2\omega_1, \omega_1^2$, etc. In short, whether one is a staunch conservative like Leibniz or Dummett, an ultra liberal like Cantor and Zermelo, or something in between, one will still have his special Ω, the property of being an ordinal. This 'totality'—the ordinals themselves—will be well ordered, and one can seemingly define well-orderings longer than that.

On the surface, it is legitimate to do transfinite recursions and inductions over ordinals and, presumably, only over ordinals. Nevertheless, set theorists occasionally seem to invoke transfinite recursions and inductions whose 'length' is at least that of $\prec_2$, i.e., twice as long as the well-ordering of all ordinals. For example, the concept L of being a constructible set is defined by transfinite recursion over all ordinals (i.e., of length Ω). But set theorists go on to do transfinite recursions on L, which are also of length Ω. So, in effect, we have a transfinite recursion of length 2Ω. But over what objects?

The following appears in a survey article on mouse theory:[21]

[21] Thanks to Tim Bays for drawing our attention to some of the relevant literature here. Mouse theory is a very technical branch of abstract set theory. As just noted, 'L' is the constructible hierarchy, used in Gödel's proof of the consistency of the axiom of choice and the generalized

We begin by constructing L level by level. The first ω levels are exactly the hereditarily finite sets, the next ω_1^L levels are exactly the sets that are hereditarily countable in L, and so on. Now we ask ourselves what comes next.

(Schimmerling, 2001, 486–7)

Of course, this talk of 'construction' is, as usual, only a metaphor. What is literally true is that we *define* the constructible sets (L) by transfinite recursion over all ordinals. And proofs about L invoke transfinite induction over all ordinals. This much is captured in ordinary mathematical language with unrestricted quantification over ordinals. But what is the literal meaning of Schimmerling's question, 'what comes next'? What can possibly come *after* the ordinals? He continues:

For although we have climbed up to the minimal transitive proper class model of ZFC, foundational considerations that fall under the category of *large cardinals* have tempted us to adopt certain theories that extend ZFC. These extensions are not true in L, for they imply that there exists a non-trivial elementary embedding j:L→L, which is known to fail in L. So how do we continue or revise the construction in a way that buys us the existence of such an embedding? One naíve idea is to continue the construction past all the ordinals and throw in the proper class j at stage Ω or beyond, but this approach leads to some obvious metamathematical problems that we find annoying.

What was that?—We are to go *past* all of the ordinals? Metaphor or not, one fears a lapse into nonsense. If there is a 'past all the ordinals' to 'go on to', we have not gone through all of the ordinals—through *all* of the well-ordering types. With 'constructions' like these what we surely *have* gone beyond are the 'limits of thought'!

Typically, the way around the 'annoying' meta-mathematical problems to which Schimmerling refers is to replace the long transfinite recursions with codings. That is, the set theorist works hard to simulate the long transfinite recursion within ordinary, first-order set theory. Nevertheless, it seems to us that this grand transfinite recursion is coherent as it stands, or at least as coherent as anything else in set theory. If we can indeed legitimately and intelligibly talk about all ordinals, then, as we saw above, it is straightforward to define a predicate that characterizes a relation of order-type 2Ω. The pairs of ordinals that satisfy this predicate also satisfy the second-order predicate of being a well-ordering. So why can't we do transfinite recursions and inductions over them? Using variables or schematic letters, we can even do a transfinite recursion along the order-type $\prec_3$ above, of length Ω^2. And of course, this is not as far as we can go. There is a predicate corresponding to the 'order-type' of any polynomial involving Ω, essentially reproducing what Cantor proposed with ω; Ω^Ω is not out of reach.

Of course, one must be careful how things are put, to avoid the obvious contradiction. If we say that the recursion has length 2Ω, as in our informal gloss, then we

continuum hypothesis. The notion is defined by transfinite recursion over ordinals: L_0 is the empty set; for each ordinal α, $L_{\alpha+1}$ is the set consisting of L_α together with all sets definable in terms of L_α. If λ is a limit ordinal, then L_λ is the union of all L_β, with $\beta < \lambda$. A set x is constructible if there is an ordinal α such that $x \in L_\alpha$. See any text for set theory, such as the excellent Jech (2002), for details.

are saying that there *is* a 'past all the ordinals'. As noted, one can define a two-place predicate in the language of (first-order) set theory whose extent is the putative well-ordering in question (so to speak). The recursion and induction is done over that predicate, or over the ordinals (or pairs of ordinals) that satisfy the predicate. The 'pain' of contradiction comes, of course, if we think of this predicate as defining an order-type, a 'length', or any other sort of all-in-one. So the talk of the 'length' of the procedure, (2Ω, Ω^2, etc.), is only a metaphor.[22] The legitimacy of the technique is a working hypothesis.

At this point, one might protest, paraphrasing Boolos (1998a, 35):

> Wait a minute! I thought that set theory was supposed to include a theory about all, 'absolutely' all, the well-orderings and transfinite recursions that there are and that 'well-ordering-type' was synonymous with (or at least coextensive with or isomorphic to) 'ordinal'.

Well, indeed. But the problem, to stress, is that predicates corresponding to these 'order-types' are definable as soon as we make the assumption that we can talk about—have bound variables ranging over—all ordinals.

Once again, the defender of absolutely unrestricted quantification (the 'absolutist') can—and presumably must—claim that there are no 'objects'—no ordinals—that correspond to these explicitly definable long well-ordering predicates. Just as indefinitely extensible concepts determine no 'Ones', so these predicates simply have no associated order-types. The grounds for the Boolosian rejection of proper classes, endorsed earlier, must also preclude order-types Ω, 2Ω, Ω^2, and the like, provided that these are construed as objects.

Shapiro (2003) tentatively proposes what is, admittedly, a thin straw for the absolutist to grasp. The key observation is that the definition of a property (or predicate) being a well-order is second-order (see Shapiro, 1991, §5.1.3). So the absolutist can avoid the issue by demurring from using second-order variables in theories whose first-order variables range over an indefinitely extensible totality. Then the notion of a 'class-sized well-ordering' cannot even be formulated—and there will be no formula that expresses the seemingly patent facts that the ordinals are well-ordered, and that the formula that expresses 2Ω defines a well-ordering. Shapiro's proposal would block the construction of mice in the unrestricted theory of the entire range of sets, ordinals, and models (at least if the text is taken literally).

22 An advocate of the Zermelo program can, of course, think of the definition of mice as restricted to (or as 'taking place within') a fixed arbitrary model M of set theory. The 'totality' of von Neumann ordinals in M is, of course, not a member of M, but the ordinals in M do constitute a set, and thus a von Neumann ordinal, in all later models in the hierarchy (thanks to the 'meta-axiom' above asserting that the models of set theory are themselves indefinitely extensible). In effect, we rely on later models in the series to sanction the long transfinite recursions in M (see note 15 above). We saw above, however, that Zermelo's own text has variables that range over *all* models of set theory, and thus, all ordinals whatsoever. That text is used to describe the hierarchy of models and to prove things about it. We suggest, at least tentatively, that it is legitimate to develop mouse theory on the entire hierarchy. One can write down a formula representing the definition of mice-in-the-hierarchy, and we can do the transfinite induction needed to show that it works.

It is a thin straw, though. Even putting to one side the (in our view) compelling arguments in favor of second-order languages in Shapiro (1991), Boolos's later writings (e.g., 1984, 1985, 1985a), and elsewhere, the general point remains that denying the existence of the long well-orderings Ω, 2Ω, Ω^2 (as objects) merely seems like an ad hoc maneuver. As noted, one can define the long well-orderings (if that is what they are) as soon as the notion of 'ordinal' has been defined.

Boolos himself (e.g., 1984, 1985, 1985a) provides another way out. We can think of the formulas defining the long well-orderings as pluralities. There is no 'thing' that corresponds to, say, 2Ω, but we can talk about the ordinals, in the plural, that satisfy the relevant defining formula. We do the transfinite recursion over *them* (see also Agustín Rayo's contribution to this volume).

But what if we just let them be? What, exactly, is wrong with the long transfinite recursions and inductions? Why can't we just introduce such 'ordinals', or names for them, by suitably expanding our ontology? We just introduce a singular term, like 'Ω', that is to denote the order-type of all ordinals, without intending to paraphrase it away. This gives rise to another singular term for 2Ω, another for Ω^2, and one for Ω^Ω, and off we go. In doing so, we are just giving genuine names to well-orderings that we are capable of understanding and using, and treating those well-orderings as objects. The resulting theory is consistent if standard set theory together with an axiom asserting the existence of an inaccessible cardinal is. The envisioned theory is thus coherent, and, moreover, it seems to be *true* when Ω is interpreted as the order-type of the ordinals of ordinary set theory. So what's wrong?

Well, again, simply that we have contradicted the understanding of Ω with which the process starts. Ω is the series of *all* ordinals—all possible order-types. Not all the ordinals except those that come after, the 'proper' ordinals, or higher-ordinals, or whatever. *All* of them. There may be a consistent formal theory, but it does not sustain the intended interpretation except at the cost of informal paradox—the same old Burali–Forti paradox—and for good measure, some additional variations on the theme—that was there all along.

Let's stop running in circles and step back. So far as we can see, there are exactly five possible positions (at least, for anyone inclined to accept ordinals as objects; nominalism is another response, but cannot be considered in proper detail here).[23] They are as follows:

[23] In his contribution to this volume, Geoffrey Hellman argues that considerations like those broached here point toward nominalism. For Hellman, set theory is understood in terms of what collections, and what well-orderings, are logically possible. For formal details, see Hellman (1989) (and Parsons, 1977). For the usual reasons, there is no largest possible well-ordering: any possible well-ordering can be extended. By refusing to reify possible collections and possible well-orderings, the nominalist avoids temptation, or is at least less tempted, to postulate a (possible) order-type of all possible well-orderings. The situation with constructions like that of mice shows that we can study the properties of a given well-ordering by considering even longer well-orderings. No problem with that. It is analogous to limiting the construction to a single model in Zermelo's hierarchy. In Hellman's system, the definition of long well-orderings—over all possible models—is blocked by a formation rule that does not allow free second-order variables to occur within the scope of a modal operator. This restriction is the analogue of the above proposal, from Shapiro (2003), of not allowing bound higher-order variables when the first-order variables range over an indefinitely extensible

(I) Reject the intelligibility/legitimacy of quantification over all ordinals. In this case, the troublesome predicates, like '$\prec_1$', '$\prec_2$', '$\prec_3$', cannot be defined, and so the issue of whether they have order-types does not get off the ground. *Cost*: we cannot express what seem to be not only perfectly intelligible but *true* thoughts about the ordinals in general. Indeed, presumably we cannot even use plural expressions like 'the ordinals' (for if we could *refer* to them—to them all!—what could possibly prevent legitimate quantification?)

(II) Allow the intelligibility/legitimacy of quantification over all ordinals but deny oneself second-order resources (Shapiro, 2003). The predicates '$\prec_1$', '$\prec_2$', '$\prec_3$', can be defined, but we cannot state, much less prove, that they are well-orderings. *Cost*: abrogation of what are arguably perfectly sound and legitimate expressive resources.

(III) Allow the unrestricted quantifications and the definitions of the troublesome predicates, but deny that they are associated with ordinals (order-types). *Cost*: transfinite inductions and recursions of the relevant 'lengths' then come into question (at least on the assumption that transfinite recursions and inductions require an associated order-type) which are part of expert practice and seemingly quite intelligible. Perhaps more importantly, the resulting stance is open to the objection, stressed in Section 10.9, that it amounts to an unprincipled/casuistic restriction on principles (that every kind of well-ordered series has an order-type, that every initial segment of the ordinals has a limit) without which we don't get the ordinals, liberally conceived, to fly the first place.

(IV) Allow the quantification and the predicates, allow the associated order-types, but deny that they are ordinals as originally understood—rather, they are 'higher-order' ordinals, 'proper' ordinals, 'super-ordinals', or whatever. *Cost*: Hypocrisy. Recall that Ω was supposed to encompass the ordinals in a *maximally general* sense of *ordinal*, common to all types of well-orderings. Also, the option is unstable. If we are now saying that Ω does not encompass a maximally general sense of ordinal, and that we need to distinguish (how many?) successive orders of ordinals, then just consider *all* of these, and the dialectical situation repeats itself, only without this fourth option.

(V) Allow the quantification and the predicates, allow the associated order-types, allow that they are ordinals as originally understood, . . . and just accept that there are ordinals that come later than all the ordinals. *Cost*: none—unless one demurs from the acceptance of contradiction.

Frankly, we do not see a satisfying position here. It seems that every one of the available theoretical options has difficulties which would be justly treated as decisive against it, were it not that the others fare no better. Such situations are not unprecedented in philosophy, but this one seems particularly opaque and frustrating. Since it is impossible to advance any particular response with any degree of conviction, any unqualified profession that unrestricted quantification—or quantification over

'totality'. Perhaps the maneuver is less ad hoc here, since Hellman's restriction is independently motivated.

indefinitely extensible totalities—is perfectly intelligible and legitimate seems to us misplaced. Unrestricted quantification is one component in the aporetic situation latterly reviewed. Like the others, it merits watchfulness.

10.12 DUMMETT'S 'NEW ARGUMENT' AGAINST CLASSICAL QUANTIFICATION

We return to the question of how Dummett's attitude to indefinitely extensible quantification is to be interpreted. As noted, it cannot plausibly be that quantification over indefinitely extensible totalities is simply impermissible, or unintelligible since, as we have several times had cause to observe, Dummett regards even the natural numbers as indefinitely extensible and is nevertheless quite content to endorse intuitionistic arithmetic (which of course treats exactly the same class of sentences as meaningful as classical arithmetic does). In fact, however, there is a reasonably clear position to be extracted from Dummett's remarks (and which is pretty much explicit in his (1994)). The view can be summarized in two claims: first, the Aristotelian claim that infinity is always merely potential (though perhaps with some modest degree of relaxation to allow at least some Definite countably infinite totalities); second, the claim that where quantification over an indefinitely extensible totality takes place, it cannot legitimately be understood *classically*. The relevant aspect of the classical understanding of the quantifiers is that they are in effect conceived as truth-functions, logical product and sum, issuing in statements which are determinate in truth value whenever all their instances are. In Dummett's view, the appropriateness of such a conception of the meaning of quantified statements lapses as soon as their range becomes indefinitely extensible. In such cases, we do better to work with the broad model of the content of quantified statements proposed by the intuitionists—in effect, the inferentialist model pioneered in the work of Gentzen and refined by Prawitz—against a background in which the principle of bivalence is dropped.

Here we shall have nothing more to say about the generally intuitionistic direction which Dummett proposes. Our concern is purely with the first step towards it, the claim that classical quantification misconstrues the legitimate content of quantification where indefinitely extensible totalities are concerned. The matter has received much discussion, and requires more, but we shall here attempt no more than to exclude a natural line of misinterpretation and to offer a suggestion about how, we believe, Dummett's position may be better understood.

Consider the following set-up. We construct a long strip of paper—perhaps as much as twenty meters in length—whose color starts out scarlet at one end but then fades very gradually and seemingly continuously to a yellowish-orange at the other. It is a Sorites strip, if you will. On it are inscribed a series of randomly selected decimal numerals, in Times 10 point font, as close together as they can be consistently with their ready distinguishability one from the next. Consider the statement (A) 'All the numerals on a red background denote multiples of 7.' Each instance of (A) is decidable and determinate in truth-value. But that is, plausibly, totally insufficient for the conclusion that (A) itself has to be determinate in truth-value. It is insufficient for the obvious reason that it is not fully determinate which the instances are. The phrase 'numeral on a red background' is vague.

That this, or something like it, might approximate Dummett's thought is encouraged by his apparent adherence to the All-in-One principle, at least for quantification as classically understood. To require, it might be suggested, that quantification have the back-drop of a specified domain—a specified set of objects to constitute the range of the quantifiers—is tantamount to the requirement that it be Definite to what population of objects the quantified statements in question are to be accountable. If no domain is specified, we run the risk of indeterminacy in the range of admissible witnesses, and thereby indeterminacy in the truth-conditions of what we say. This is what happens in the case of the Sorites strip. 'Numeral on a red background' exactly fails to specify any determinate set of inscribed numerals, with indeterminacy in the truth-conditions of quantifications over them the immediate result.

Dummett does, it is true, sometimes speak of indefinite extensibility as a kind of vagueness (e.g., Dummett, 1963, *passim*). But the foregoing rather simple-minded proposal had better not be the intended argument. What is vague in the Sorites strip is where the numerals-on-red stop and the others begin. The quantified statement (A) is vague because there is no sharp cut-off between the numerals that satisfy its antecedent and those which do not. But nothing like that is true of the ordinals, to stay with our paradigm, however liberal or conservative one may be—not unless we really do think we can attach a sense to the idea of 'going past' all the ordinals. Even then the analogy limps, since there will be a determinate *first element* of whatever other sort of thing we are pleased to postulate—a first 'proper' ordinal, or whatever. The key component in the analogy of the Sorites strip is that the numerals on red are indeterminate in extent within a wider population of numerals on the strip. No counterpart of that features in anyone's conception of the ordinals (even someone tempted by the prospect of 'proper' ordinals)—and in particular not in Dummett's.

Is that feature, though—indeterminacy of extent within a wider population—essential to the intended point? Dummett (1991, p. 316–17) writes:

> Better than describing the intuitive concept of ordinal number as having a hazy extension is to describe it as having an increasing sequence of extensions: what is hazy is the length of the sequence, which vanishes in the indiscernible distance.

It is true that it is indeterminate how far the numerals-on-red extend within the Sorites strip of numerals, and that that is not the way to describe the indeterminacy of the extent of the ordinals—there is no 'larger strip' on which they peter out. But still, it may be suggested, they *are* indeterminate in extent. Hence the stand-off between conservative and liberal positions. It is conceptually open whether to regard them as confined to the finite, or the recursive, or the countable, or the accessible, or . . . , or whether we let them rip, stopping only when the apparatus buckles on Burali–Forti. And if this matter is conceptually open, then there is still going to be potential indeterminacy in the truth-conditions of quantifications over all ordinals, when conceived classically as functions from aggregates of truth-values to truth-values. There will be such indeterminacy because it is indeterminate what goes into the argument pool. All we can legitimately say is that such statements may be counted true provided it is guaranteed they will hold *no matter how far the series is legitimately taken to extend*; and false if exceptions are guaranteed under the same hypothesis.

Yet this interpretation too—however much his own remarks may encourage it—cannot be true to Dummett's intent. It cannot be true to his intent because he himself has a *position* on the issue in question—the position of Aristotelianism (or something close to it). The train of thought outlined is at best impressive for a theorist who lacks a position, who views the extent of the ordinals as open. A theorist who, for good reasons or bad, takes the view that Cantor's second principle fails for the totality of ordinals of such-and-such a kind, has no motive to sympathize with the argument, even though he may allow that the totality in question is indefinitely extensible. So the connection we seek has still to be made out.

We do not suggest that Dummett is confused on the matter. But we do suggest that the comparison between indefinite extensibility and forms of vagueness, or indeterminacy, is badly conceived. More accurately, the comparison is misleading when taken as an invitation to think about the alleged counter-classical implications of indefinite extensibility on the model of (what would be widely accepted as) the counter-classical implications of (one or another form of) vagueness. The right comparison is only in the *effect*: both indefinite extensibility and vagueness may be held to call into question the validity of the principle of bivalence for a relevant range of statements. So the question still remains: *why* (might it be supposed that) indefinite extensibility has that effect?

We have no answer to offer which effectively clarifies whether Dummett is right or wrong, but we think we know where to look. The key to understanding his argument has to be found in the implicit comparison between the operation of set-formation and the operation of universal quantification (for example) as classically conceived. Think of a set as the value of a many-one function that takes exactly the elements of the set as argument. If the objects of some kind are indefinitely extensible, the set-function cannot generate a set of them all—for any value it can give will immediately be at the service of the definition of a new object of the appropriate kind, demonstrably excluded from the set in question. Now think of quantification in similar terms, as a many-one function that yields a truth-value when given a range of instances as argument. If the elements which the instances concern are indefinitely extensible, then no application of the function can embrace them all—for any collection of the instances to which it is applied will immediately be at the service of the definition of a new instance, so far unreckoned with.

The crucial thought is thus that a function requires a *stable* range of arguments if it is to take a determinate value. Any vagueness, then, in the extent of an indefinitely extensible concept is not really the point. The operation of classical quantification on indefinitely extensible totalities is frustrated not because it is vague what the arguments are, but because any attempt to specify them subserves the construction of a new case, potentially generating a new value. The reason why quantification, classically conceived, requires a domain—a Definite totality— to operate over is just that.

As stated, our purpose here is only to try to locate the real issue at stake in Dummett's 'new argument', not to take sides. It certainly is robustly part of the classical, model-theoretic semantics of quantification to see it as a function, standardly set-theoretically conceived, whose argument- and value-ranges are accordingly likewise sets. Since indefinitely extensible concepts do not determine sets, that much of classical semantics is certainly in jeopardy in the present context (as noted already, in Section 10.11 above). But the question whether quantification over the instances of such concepts may legitimately be viewed nonetheless as *determinate* is still open. Whether the last line of argument proposed can be developed strongly enough to force the issue is left for another occasion.

10.13 INDEFINITE EXTENSIBILITY AND REFLECTION

The passage quoted from Tait (2000, 284) at the end of Section 10.9 above captures a widely held conviction that the iterative hierarchy in its entirety is ineffable. Any attempt to characterize it uniquely not only fails, but provides us with the resources to characterize more sets. This suggests a *reflection principle*: for any formula Ψ in the language of set theory, if Ψ is true (in V, so to speak) then there is a *set* that satisfies Ψ—anything true of all the sets is true of the elements of some set. If the variable x does not occur in Ψ, then let $\Psi^{[x]}$ be the result of restricting the first-order variables in Ψ to x, restricting the monadic second-order variables to subsets of x, etc. If Ψ does not contain the variable x, then the following is an instance of the reflection principle:

$$\Psi \rightarrow \exists x \Psi^{[x]}.$$

Each instance of the reflection principle in which Ψ is first-order is already a theorem of ZFC. Instances of the reflection principle in which Ψ is higher-order entail the existence of so-called small large cardinals. For example, we note that the conjunction of the axioms of second-order set theory are true, and so, by reflection, there is a set that satisfies these axioms. The set or ordinals contained in such a set is a strongly inaccessible cardinal. Thus, the principle entails the existence of an inaccessible cardinal (see Lévy (1960 and 1960a); Shapiro (1987 and 1991, Chapter 6)).[24]

So the reflection principle is a substantial set-theoretic thesis. Bernays (1961) shows how many of the axioms of set theory, plus some small large cardinal principles, can themselves be deduced from a strong version of the reflection principle, and hence that it can play a unifying role in axiomatic set theory (see Burgess, 2004).

Now, the reflection principle has impressed a number of theorists as of-a-piece with, or at least implicated in, the indefinite extensibility of the iterative hierarchy, at least intuitively. This suggests a different way in which indefinite extensibility might

[24] Note that this argument presupposes the legitimacy of second-order statements as applied to the entire iterative hierarchy (V), contrary to the tentative proposal in Shapiro (2003) noted above. We have also had occasion to note that ordinary model theory does not allow for interpretations in which the bound variables range over an indefinitely extensible 'totality'. Shapiro (1987) shows that with a reflection principle, the restriction does not change the extension of validity. The idea is that if an indefinitely extensible 'totality' shows an argument to be invalid (i.e., true premises, false conclusion), then, by reflection, there is a set that also shows that argument to be invalid. So, in a sense, a reflection principle is a presupposition of the use of set-theoretic model theory as the semantics of higher-order languages.

have a bearing on the construction of foundations for a strong set-theory. Rather than seek an appropriate abstraction principle, or principles, to reflect the indefinite extensibility of the sets, in the fashion under scrutiny in Section 10.10 above, perhaps one can appeal to indefinite extensibility to ground the reflection principle as a special axiom to be used *alongside* whatever other foundational principles—they can as well be abstraction principles—are motivated by one's theoretical standpoint. This is a strategy explored by John Burgess in his (2005).

However the connection between reflection and indefinite extensibility seems to us fugitive on closer scrutiny. Burgess (2004, 2005) proposes the following heuristic train of inter-connections leading from one to the other:[25]

(1) ... the sets are indeterminately or indefinitely many. (*Indefinite Extensibility*)

(2) ... the sets are indefinably or indescribably many.

(3) ... any statement Φ that holds of them fails to describe how many they are.

(4) ... any statement Φ that holds of them continues to hold if reinterpreted to be not about all of them but just about some of them, fewer than all of them.

(5) ... any statement Φ that holds of them continues to hold if reinterpreted to be not about all of them but just some of them, few enough to form a set. (*Reflection*)

Burgess is, of course, fully aware that these transitions are not immune to challenge. It seems to us that the move from (1) to (2) in particular needs more motivation. The idea that the pure sets or the ordinals are indefinitely extensible does not entail, or even suggest, that they cannot be described distinctively. As above, indefinite extensibility only says that any Definite collection of sets or ordinals can be extended. To make the connection from (1) to (2) one might try to argue for the contrapositive: that if a given sentence is true of the *B*'s, and of no proper sub-collection of them, then the *B*'s are Definite. But, right now, we do not see how to construct a plausible such argument.

The statement (3) seems problematic. As noted above, the very notion of indefinite extensibility, and the statement that the sets are indefinitely extensible, is itself neutral on the matter of how conservative or liberal one is on the question of 'how many' ordinals (etc.) there are, so to speak. It is not part of the meaning of 'ordinal', nor is it part of indefinite extensibility as such that one cannot describe the totality of the ordinals. A staunch Aristotelian or one who thinks that all sets are accessible can hold that the sets are indefinitely extensible, and have no trouble describing 'how many' of them there are. The former gives a second-order formula that is satisfied by all and only countably infinite properties; the latter uses a formula that holds of all and only properties the size of the first inaccessible (see Shapiro, 1991, §5.1.2).

It seems to us that the putative connection with reflection is best made under the aegis of the ultra-liberal view of Cantor, Zermelo, and most practicing set theorists, namely, the view that only inconsistency will be allowed to keep us from going on. In

[25] The reader should be aware that Burgess goes on to state that he, 'like Boolos, [has] no use for Michael Dummett's notion of indefinite extensibility'. The sketch he offers is for those who do have some use for the notion.

keeping with the above passage from Tait (2000, 284), our liberal might claim that any non-trivial criterion C for, say, being an ordinal, would *not* show that all and only ordinals have C. Instead, she takes the criterion to show that there are ordinals that lack C. For example, an opponent might suggest, with the staunch conservative, that being finite is a criterion for being an ordinal. No, says the ultra-liberal. This shows that there are ordinals that are not finite. The semi-conservative suggests that being accessible is a criterion for being an ordinal. After all, every ordinal we have defined so far is accessible. No, says the liberal. This shows that there are ordinals with inaccessibly many predecessors.

It is straightforward to interpret the liberal as appealing to reflection at each attempt of a conservative opponent to corral the ordinals and the sets. When the staunch conservative claims that being finite is a criterion for being an ordinal, the liberal notes that there are infinitely many (finite) ordinals. So, by reflection, there exists an infinite set and thus an infinite ordinal. The semi-conservative concedes this, but then claims that every ordinal is accessible. The liberal notes that there are inaccessibly many ordinals thus conceded. So, by reflection, there is an inaccessible set and thus an ordinal with inaccessibly many predecessors.

The reflection principle itself has an extensibility that is of a piece with the liberal perspective. We noted just above that the reflection principle entails the existence of an inaccessible cardinal. We apply the reflection principle to the statement that there is an inaccessible cardinal. This gives us the existence of a standard model m of set theory that itself satisfies this statement. The set of ordinals in m is an inaccessible that contains an inaccessible as a member. Thus we have the existence of *two* inaccessibles. Similar repeated applications of the reflection principle yield the existence of 2, 3, . . . inaccessibles. Then, repeating in the transfinite (so to speak), we show that there is an ωth inaccessible, a fixed point in the hierarchy of inaccessibles, and so on through small large cardinals (short of the so-called indescribable cardinals, which are the smallest models of the reflection principle, see Shapiro 1987).[26]

As Tait says, one can peel off Cantor's journey at any point. In a sense, the reflection principle expresses our intent to not do so unless consistency demands that we do. Any attempt to 'peel off' too early just gives rise to more, previously unheard of, ordinals. The principle represents another of Priest's (2002) 'limits of thought': the limit of the expressible.

In any case, even if indefinite extensibility (with or without the liberal orientation) neither entails nor is entailed by reflection, there are interesting connections bearing on matters discussed earlier. One concerns the prospects for neo-logicist set-theory based on Indefinite V discussed in Section 10.10. Noting the role of *limitlessness* in the concept of indefinite extensibility, and the seemingly unavoidable need to invoke the ideology of the ordinals in characterizing that, we expressed scepticism about the *logical* definability of indefinite extensibility, prerequisite for the logicism in 'neo-logicism'. But the reflection principle enforces a stronger pessimism: that one cannot characterize the notion of indefinite extensibility even given all the expressive

26 The play with Zermelo-type meta-axioms in note 20 above can also be seen as applications of reflection.

resources provided by set theory. For if we assume that each pure set is Definite and that the sets themselves are indefinitely extensible, then it follows from the reflection principle that there is no formula $\Phi(X)$ in the language of set theory in which all quantifiers of Φ are restricted to X, such that for each concept P, $\Phi(P)$ holds if and only if the P's are indefinitely extensible. Let Ψ be the result of instantiating X with the universal concept in Φ (e.g., replace any subformula of the form Pt with $t = t$). Then Ψ is true of the sets. Thus, by the reflection principle, there is a set v that satisfies Ψ. So $\Phi(P)$ holds when P is the concept of being a member of v. But this concept is Definite.

The reflection principle also gives a surprising alternative resolution to the main matter treated in Section 10.8, concerning Hume's Principle and 'anti-zero'. Recall that in responding to one objection made in Boolos (1997), Wright (1999) accepted 'the plausible principle ... that there is a determinate number of F's just provided that the F's compose a *set*', and so 'there is no number of sets', no number of cardinal numbers and no number of ordinals. Wright's proposal was that the variables in HP be restricted to Definite (sortal) concepts.

But wait. It follows from the reflection principle that there is a global well-ordering of the set-theoretic hierarchy. For suppose that there is no such well-ordering. Then the second-order statement stating the existence of such an ordering (see Shapiro, 1991, ch. 5, §5.1.3) is false. So, by reflection, there is a set that lacks a well-ordering. This contradicts Zermelo's well-ordering theorem. In sum, with the reflection principle, the usual axiom of local choice (the 'C' in 'ZFC') entails Global Choice, and (with Foundation) Global Choice entails the existence of a global well-ordering.

It follows from this that if P is a concept of (pure) sets, then if there is no set that contains all of the P's, then the P's are equinumerous with the von Neumann ordinals. That is, in the presence of the reflection principle, any two indefinitely extensible 'totalities' of sets are equinumerous to each other.[27]

So it follows from the foregoing principles that the unrestricted HP *is* satisfiable on the pure sets. Each set has an aleph as its cardinality, as normal, and there is in addition one (and only one) more cardinality for the indefinitely extensible totalities. Any non-aleph will do. Let's call it '∞'. So, after all, we *can*—correctly and intelligibly—say that there is a cardinal of all cardinals, and a cardinal of all ordinals, and a cardinal of all sets. It is just ∞. And if we can say this, then why shouldn't we? Since all indefinitely extensible concepts of sets are equinumerous (as above), then why shouldn't we associate them with a 'size', a size bigger than any set-size? If it is felt that 'size' should be restricted to sets, we can just use another name. We hereby introduce a new concept: the *schmize* of a set is the aleph that is equinumerous with it; and the *schmize* of an indefinitely extensible collection of sets is ∞. HP is then satisfied if we interpret '$Nx{:}Fx$' as the schmize of the F's.

[27] There is a similarity between the derivation of the existence of a global well-ordering here and that in Section 10.10 above, on neo-logicist set theory. Here the conclusion follows from reflection and the (local) axiom of choice, whereas the previous conclusion follows from New V alone, without local choice. Indeed, local choice also follows from New V, from global choice. So we have no immediate reason to think that the reflection principle runs afoul of Wright's principles of conservation.

But what of the above claim, common to Wright and Boolos, that there is no cardinal of all cardinals? Well, one question, of course, is whether there is indeed compelling philosophical mandate for the reflection principle. Even if there is, there may still also be good philosophical reason—as Wright suggests—why the concept of cardinal number should be restricted to Definite concepts. But if so, the point can be accommodated by regarding HP as characteristic of cardinality only for the Definite case. So regarding it does not require that we limit the application of the N-operator to Definite concepts: we merely cease to regard it as connoting cardinality or 'size' when applied to the indefinitely extensible, secure in the knowledge that, given reflection, Hume's Principle is satisfiable in any case.

Boolos's charge was that HP is false on the pure sets. As we noted earlier, the way he presented the charge left some scope for maneuvering about its force. But Wright's response was concessive, granting that there was philosophical reason to restrict the principle in any case. What we have just seen is that, given reflection, there is a response to the objection that avoids any such concession. Hume's principle, to repeat, *is* satisfiable in the iterative hierarchy if reflection holds. The only philosophical issue is the proper interpretation of the N operator. But we shall take matters no further here.

REFERENCES

Bernays, P. (1961) 'Zur Frage der Unendlichkeitsschemata in der axiomatischen Mengenlehre', *Essays on the Foundation of Mathematics*, (ed.) Y. Bar-Hillel et al., Jerusalem, Magnes Press, 3–49; trans. as 'On the Problem of Schemata of Infinity in Axiomatic Set Theory', by J. Bell and M. Plänitz, in *Sets and Classes: On the Work of Paul Bernays*, (ed.) G. Müller, Amsterdam: North Holland Publishing Company, 1976, 121–72.

Boolos, G. (1984) 'To Be is to Be a Value of a Variable (or to be Some Values of Some Variables)', *Journal of Philosophy 81*, 430–49; reprinted in Boolos (1998), 54–72.

____(1985) 'Nominalist Platonism', *Philosophical Review* 94, 327–44; reprinted in Boolos (1998), 73–87.

____(1985a) 'Reading the *Begriffschrift*', *Mind* 94, 331–44; reprinted in Boolos (1998), 155–70.

____(1986) 'Saving Frege from Contradiction', *Proceedings of the Aristotelian Society* 87, 137–51; reprinted in Boolos (1998), 171–92.

____(1993) 'Whence the Contradiction?', *Aristotelian Society Supplementary Volume* 67, 213–33, reprinted in Boolos (1998), 220–36.

____(1997) 'Is Hume's Principle Analytic?', in Richard Heck, Jr (ed.), *Language, Thought, and Logic*, Oxford: Oxford University Press, 245–61.

____(1998) *Logic, Logic, and Logic*, Cambridge, MA: Harvard University Press.

____(1998a) 'Reply to Charles Parsons' "Sets and Classes"', in Boolos (1998), 30–6.

____(1998b) 'Must we Believe in Set Theory?', in Boolos (1998), 120–32, and Sher and Tieszen (2000), 257–68.

Burgess, J. (2004) '*E Pluribus Unum*: Plural Logic and Set Theory', *Philosophia Mathematica* (3) 12, 193–221.

____(2005) *Fixing Frege*, Princeton: Princeton University Press.

Cantor, G. (1833) *Grundlagen einer allgemeinen Mannigfaltigkeitslehre. Ein mathematisch-philosophischer Versuch in der Lehre des Unendlichen*, Leipzig: Teubner.

—— (1887) 'Mitteilugen zur Lehre vom Transfinitten 1, II, *Zeitschrift für Philosophie und philosophische Kritik* 91, 81–125, 252–70; 92, 250–65; reprinted in G. Cantor, *Gesammelte Abhandlungen mathematischen und philosophischen Inhalts*, (ed.) E. Zermelo, Berlin: Springer, 1932, 378–439.

—— (1899) 'Letter to Dedekind', van Heijenoort (1967), 113–17.

Cartwright, Richard L. (1994) 'Speaking of Everything', *Noûs* 28, 1–20.

Clark, P. (2000) 'Indefinite Extensibility and Set Theory', talk to Arché Workshop on Abstraction, University of St Andrews.

Drake, F. (1974) *Set Theory: An Introduction to Large Cardinals*, Amsterdam: North Holland Publishing Company.

Dummett, M. (1963) 'The Philosophical Significance of Gödel's Theorem', *Ratio*, 5, 140–55.

—— (1981) *Frege: Philosophy of Language*, 2nd edn, Cambridge, MA: Harvard University Press.

—— (1991) *Frege: Philosophy of Mathematics*, Cambridge, MA: Harvard University Press.

—— (1993) *The Seas of Language*, Oxford: Oxford University Press.

—— (1994) 'Chairman's Address: Basic Law V', *Proceedings of the Aristotelian Society* 94, 243–51.

Feferman, S. (1962) 'Transfinite Recursive Progressions of Axiomatic Theories', *Journal of Symbolic Logic* 27, 259–316.

—— (1988) 'Turing in the Land of O(z)', in *The Universal Turing Machine*, (ed.) R. Herken, New York: Oxford University Press, 113–47.

Frege, G. (1884) *Die Grundlagen der Arithmetik*, Breslau, Koebner; *The Foundations of Arithmetic*, trans. by J. Austin, 2nd edn, New York: Harper, 1960.

Geach, P.T. (1956) 'Frege's Way Out', *Mind* 65, 408–9

Hale, Bob, and Crispin Wright (2001) *The Reason's Proper Study*, Oxford: Oxford University Press.

Hallett, M. (1984) *Cantorian Set Theory and the Limitation of Size*, Oxford: Oxford University Press.

Hellman, G. (1989) *Mathematics without Numbers*, Oxford: Oxford University Press.

Jech, T. (2002) *Set Theory: The Third Millennium Edition*, Berlin: Springer Publishing Company.

Kelley, J. L. (1955) *General Topology*, Princeton: van Nostrand.

Leibniz, G. (1863) *Mathematische Scriften von Gottfried Wilhelm Leibniz*, (ed.) C. I. Gerhart, Berlin: A. Asher, H. Halle, W. Schmidt, 1849–63.

—— (1980) *Samtliche Schriften und Briefe: Philosophishce Schriften*. Series 6, Vols. 1–3, Berlin: Akademie-Verlag, 1923–80.

—— (1996) *New Essays on Human Understanding*, Ed. and Trans. by P. Remnant and J. Bennett, New York: Cambridge University Press.

Levey, Samuel (1998) 'Leibniz on Mathematics and the Actually Infinite Division of Matter', *Philosophical Review* 107, 49–96.

Lévy, A. (1960) 'Principles of Reflection in Axiomatic Set Theory', *Fundamenta Mathematicae* 49, 1–10.

—— (1960a) 'Axiom Schemata of Strong Infinity in Axiomatic Set Theory', *Pacific Journal of Mathematics* 10, 223–38.

Parsons, C. (1977) 'What is the Iterative Conception of Set?', *Logic, Foundations of Mathematics and Computability Theory*, (ed.) R. Butts and J. Hintikka, Dordrecht: Holland, D. Reidel, 335–67.

Priest, G. (2002) *Beyond the Limits of Thought*, 2nd edn, Oxford: Oxford University Press.
Quine, W. V. O. (1951) 'Two Dogmas of Empiricism', *Philosophical Review* 60, 20–43.
____(1955) 'Frege's Way Out', *Mind* 64, 145–59.
Resnik, M. (1980) *Frege and the Philosophy of Mathematics*. Ithaca: Cornell University Press.
Rogers, H. (1967) *Theory of Recursive Functions and Effective Computability*, New York: McGraw-Hill.
Russell, B. (1906) 'On some Difficulties in the Theory of Transfinite Numbers and Order Types', *Proceedings of the London Mathematical Society* 4, 29–53.
____(1908) 'Mathematical Logic as Based on the Theory of Types', *American Journal of Mathematics* 30, 222–62.
Schimmerling, E. (2001) 'The ABC's of mice', *Bulletin of Symbolic Logic* 7, 485–503.
Shapiro, S. (1987) 'Principles of Reflection and Second-Order Logic', *Journal of Philosophical Logic* 16, 309–33.
____(1991) *Foundations without Foundationalism: A Case for Second-Order Logic*, Oxford: Oxford University Press.
____(2003) 'All Sets Great and Small: And I do Mean ALL', *Philosophical Perspectives* 17 (2003), 467–90.
____(2003a) 'Prolegomenon to any Future Neo-Logicist Set Theory: Abstraction and Indefinite Extensibility', *British Journal for the Philosophy of Science* 54, 59–91.
____and A. Weir (1999) 'New V, ZF, and Abstraction', *Philosophia Mathematica* (3) 7, 293–321.
Sher, G. and R. Tieszen, (eds.) (2000) *Between Logic and Intuition: Essays in Honor of Charles Parsons*, Cambridge: Cambridge University Press.
Sobocinski, B. (1949) 'L'Analyse de l'antinomie russellienne par Lesniewski: IV. La correction de 'Frege', *Methodos* 1, 220–8.
Tait, W. (2000) 'Cantor's *Grundlagen* and the Paradoxes of Set Theory', in Sher and Tieszen (2000), 269–90.
Tarski, A. (1933) 'Der Warheitsbegriff in dem formalisierten Sprachen', *Studia Philosophica 1*, 261–405; Trans. as 'The Concept of Truth in Formalized Languages', in A. Tarski, *Logic, Semantics and metamathematics*, Oxford: Clarendon Press; 2nd edn, (ed.) John Corcoran, Indianapolis: Hackett Publishing Company, 1983, pp. 152–78.
Turing, A. (1939) 'Systems of Logic Based on Ordinals', *Proceedings of the London Mathematical Society* 45, 161–228; reprinted in M. Davis, M. *The Undecidable*, Hewlett, New York: The Raven Press, 1965, pp. 155–222.
Van Heijenoort, J. (ed.) (1967) *From Frege to Gödel*, Cambridge, MA: Harvard University Press.
Wright, C. (1983) *Frege's Conception of Numbers as Objects*, Aberdeen: Aberdeen University Press.
____(1997) 'On the Philosophical Significance of Frege's Theorem', in R. Heck (ed.), *Language, Thought and Logic; Essays on the Philosophy of Michael Dummett*, Oxford: Oxford University Press, 201–44; reprinted in Hale and Wright (2001), 229–55.
____(1998) 'On the Harmless Impredicativity of N= (Hume's Principle)', in Mathias Schirn (ed.), *The Philosophy of Mathematics Today*, Oxford: Oxford University Press, 339–68; reprinted in Hale and Wright (2001), 229–55.
____(1999) 'Is Hume's Principle Analytic', *Notre Dame Journal of Formal Logic* 40, 6–30; reprinted in Hale and Wright (2001), 307–32.

Zermelo, E. (1904) 'Beweis, dass jede Menge wohlgeordnet werden kann', *Mathematische Annalen* 59, 514–16; trans. as 'Proof that every Set can be Well-Ordered', in van Heijenoort (1967), 139–41.

——(1930) 'Über Grenzzahlen und Mengenbereiche: Neue Untersuchungen über die Grundlagen der Mengenlehre', *Fundamenta Mathematicae* 16, 29–47; Trans. as 'On Boundary Numbers and Domains of Sets: New Investigations in the Foundations of Set Theory', in William Ewald (ed.), *From Kant to Hilbert: A Source Book in the Foundations of Mathematics*, Oxford: Oxford University Press, 1996, Vol. 2, 1219–33.

11

Unrestricted Unrestricted Quantification: The Cardinal Problem of Absolute Generality

Gabriel Uzquiano

Philosophical inquiry abounds with putative examples of absolute generalizations. When a philosopher utters the sentence 'There are no merely possible objects', we generally take the domain of her inquiry to be absolutely unrestricted. And yet, it remains highly controversial whether we should take the appearance of absolute generality of such utterances at face value. Some have casted doubt upon the implicit assumption that there is an all-inclusive domain to begin with. Others have granted the assumption of an all-inclusive domain but have nonetheless questioned that our quantifiers ever manage to unequivocally range over the most comprehensive domain.

It is not my intention to confront this difficult question directly but rather to discuss an internal problem for absolutism, by which I mean the thesis that we should indeed take the appearance of absolute generality of some of our utterances at face value and, more generally, agree that there is no principled obstacle for the formulation of absolutely general statements in our theorizing. When we help ourselves, in addition, to absolutely unrestricted plural or, otherwise, higher-order quantification in the formulation of absolutely general statements we accept, we risk imposing non-trivial constraints on the size of the universe of all objects. The problem I would like to discuss arises when we notice that plausible formulations of absolutely general theories may unexpectedly come into conflict by imposing incompatible constraints on the size of the universe.[1] What makes some of the conflicts particularly unexpected is they involve absolutely general theories with not only different but even disjoint non-logical vocabularies. Specific instances of this phenomenon will raise difficult

This chapter emerged as an attempt to both generalize and explore the implications of a difficulty originally discussed in Uzquiano (2006) for the problem of absolute generality. Many thanks to all who helped me with that paper. In addition, I am grateful to Matti Eklund, Kit Fine, Geoffrey Hellman, Paul Hovda, Vann McGee, Stewart Shapiro, Stephen Yablo, and audiences at MIT's 2005 Meeting of the Minds in Metaphysics, Macalester College and the University of Manitoba.

[1] By an *absolutely general theory*, I mean a theory some of whose statements are absolutely general. The problem may still arise in the presence of more modest resources such as schematic second-order logic. Schematic second-order logic is discussed for example in Shapiro (1991), McGee (1997) and Lavine (1994). I owe this observation to Kit Fine.

methodological questions and suggest to some that there is a potential obstacle for the unrestricted use of absolute generality in our theorizing.

11.1 PRELIMINARIES

I would like to begin by making explicit three background assumptions required to generate the problem. Because I will assume them without argument, some may be tempted to revisit them in the face of the difficulty. I will consider this move in the final section of the paper.

First, I will assume that there is an all-inclusive domain that comprises absolutely all there is. This is the most comprehensive domain. To assume that there is an all-inclusive domain doesn't by itself commit us to one or another answer to the question of whether there are, for example, past and future objects or whether there are merely possible objects in addition to actual ones. The question of whether there are past and future objects, like the question of whether there are merely possible objects in addition to actual ones, should be settled with the help of separate metaphysical considerations. But at least this much is true: If there are past and future objects, then they lie in the most comprehensive domain; likewise, if there are possible objects that are not actual, then they lie in the most comprehensive domain.

Next, I will assume that there is no difficulty in principle for our quantifiers to unequivocally range over an all-inclusive domain. This is an additional assumption; some non-absolutists have no quarrel with the existence of an all-inclusive domain but suggest that other factors stand in the way for our quantifiers to range unrestrictedly over absolutely all there is. Two broad grounds are generally cited against the availability of unrestricted quantification over an all-inclusive domain. One begins with the observation that our quantifiers are generally subject to explicit or contextual restrictions that vary from context to context. Not only is there no reason to think there is a context in which our quantifiers unrestrictedly range over absolutely all there is, familiar Russellian paradoxes suggest our quantifiers could never manage to accomplish this feat.[2] The other broad concern questions the presumption that our quantifiers may unequivocally range over an all-inclusive domain.[3] In contrast, it is suggested that our quantifiers are systematically ambiguous and deny we have the resources to distinguish absolutely unrestricted quantification from quantification over a less-than-all-inclusive domain. For present purposes, I will assume that both concerns are unfounded. There are contexts in which our quantifiers are, in fact, unrestricted and manage unequivocally to range over an all-inclusive domain.

Finally, I will assume that plural quantification or, otherwise, second-order quantification over an all-inclusive domain is available for the formulation of absolutely

[2] This view is discussed, for example, in Parsons (1974), Parsons (1977), Glanzberg (2004), Williamson (2003) and Hellman, Lavine and Glanzberg's contributions to this volume.

[3] What is probably the most influential argument for the semantic indeterminacy of the quantifiers comes originally from Quine (1968) and Putnam (1980). Field (1998) contains another recent discussion of the argument. McGee and Lavine's contributions to this volume discuss similar arguments.

general theories. We have known that the two are closely related since George Boolos taught us in Boolos (1984) that plural quantification is interdefinable with monadic second-order quantification. But the availability of absolutely general plural or, otherwise, second-order quantification is not forced upon us by our adherence to absolutism. One might tolerate absolutely general first-order quantification and yet regard absolutely general plural or, otherwise, second-order quantification as unintelligible. Indeed, such a view has been recently explored in Shapiro (2003) in connection to Ernst Zermelo's open-ended conception of the universe of set theory. In what follows, I would like to suggest that this combination of views is less than optimal.

Once one incurs in the commitment to absolutely general first-order quantification, the model theory for absolutely general languages provides one with a motive to embrace absolutely general plural or, otherwise, second-order quantification. When we indulge in first-order quantification over an all-inclusive domain, we soon find ourselves in a quandary. Orthodoxy tells us that an interpretation for a first-order language is an ordered pair $\langle D, I\rangle$, where D is a non-empty set and I is a function specifying semantic values for all the non-logical terms of the language. Unfortunately, there is, in standard treatments of set theory, no set of all objects, and, in particular, no structured set whose domain consists of all objects there are. Nor will there be interpretations of predicate letters to which no set corresponds. This is unfortunate because it reveals that no model-theoretic interpretation manages to capture the intended interpretation of a first-order language equipped with absolutely unrestricted quantification. As Timothy Williamson has recently reminded us in Williamson (2003), we must increase the expressive resources of first-order languages if we want to expand standard model theory to allow for models of first-order languages with an all-inclusive domain as well as for interpretations of predicates to which no set corresponds. To that purpose, we must either ascent to second-order logic and make use of second-order quantification over predicate position or, alternatively, help ourselves to devices of plural quantification.[4] This suggests that the ascent to absolutely general plural quantification or, otherwise, second-order quantification may be motivated by

[4] In Williamson (2003) Williamson defended the flight to higher-order quantification, but the resources of plural quantification are presumably enough for the purpose of accommodating interpretations where the quantifiers range over an all-inclusive domain in the model theory for first-order languages. We could, for example, conceive of an interpretation as given by some ordered pairs satisfying certain constraints. Some ordered pairs in the interpretation would encode the domain of discourse while others would encode the interpretation of the non-logical symbols of the language. One implementation of the proposal would, for example, code the universe of discourse of the interpretation by the second components of the ordered pairs of the form $\langle \forall, x\rangle$. The interpretation of an n-place predicate letter P^n would likewise be coded by the ordered n-tuples of individuals that figure as a second component in ordered pairs of the form $\langle P, \langle x_1, \ldots, x_n\rangle\rangle$. Finally, the interpretation of an individual constant c would be coded by the unique individual x that figures as a second component in ordered pairs of the form $\langle c, x\rangle$. This model theory has been developed in Rayo and Uzquiano (1999). More recently, in Rayo and Williamson (2003) Agustín Rayo and Timothy Williamson have proved a completeness theorem for first-order logic with genuinely unrestricted quantification based on a similar semantics formulated with the help of second-order quantification.

the needs of a model theory for first-order languages equipped with absolutely general quantifiers.

But once absolutely unrestricted plural quantification or, otherwise, second-order quantification is on board, we may as well use it in the formulation of absolutely general theories. Our problem precisely arises when we notice that, when formulated with the help of plural or, otherwise, second-order quantification over an all-inclusive domain, different absolutely general theories may place incompatible constraints on the size of the universe. How urgent this problem turns out to be will largely depend on whether such a conflict ever arises between two absolutely general theories for which one has independent motivation. The purpose of this paper is threefold. First I would like to suggest that some such conflicts may sometimes arise between independently motivated absolutely general theories. Second, I would like to express some pessimism for the prospects of a unified systematic solution for all such conflicts. Finally, I would like to suggest that in some cases at least, the best solution to such a conflict may involve abandoning the claim to absolute generality for at least one of the purported absolutely general theories.

The plan of the chapter is as follows. In Section 11.2, I will outline two conflicts between absolutely general theories for which philosophers and mathematicians have provided independent motivation. In both cases, one of the parties involved in the conflict will be an absolutely general formulation of set theory with individuals. In Section 11.3, I will suggest that absolutely general set theory with individuals is not to be blamed for the conflicts and that there is no reason to expect a unified solution for the two conflicts. Sections 11.4 and 11.5 will argue that, in some cases, the conflict between two absolutely general theories is best resolved by restricting the scope of at least one of the theories involved. Finally, Section 11.6 will discuss the question of whether our problem gives us reason to ultimately reject one or more of the three background assumptions required to generate the problem.

11.2 CONFLICTS

The purpose of this section is to illustrate the general risk of conflict between absolutely general theories.

Before I do, let me stress that since my present aim is merely to illustrate the risk of conflict between two absolutely general theories, my choice of examples should not automatically be taken to indicate endorsement. How urgent the conflict is, to be sure, will depend to a large extent on whether there is independent reason to accept each absolutely general theory. But all I need for my purposes is to make sure that the two absolutely general theories involved in the conflict may plausibly thought to have exerted a considerably pull on a great variety of philosophers. If you find yourself to have independent reasons to accept each of the absolutely general theories involved in the conflict, then you will face a difficult predicament. But even if you remain unmoved by one or more of the absolutely general theories involved, I hope the conflict will at least provide you with some reason to watch for the possibility of conflict between pairs of absolutely general theories you may be more inclined to accept.

11.2.1 ZFCSU vs Atomistic Extensional Mereology

First, I would like to sketch a conflict between two absolutely general theories concerned with membership and the relation of part to whole, respectively. Not only will the two absolutely general theories differ with respect to their non-logical vocabularies, their vocabularies will not even overlap.

The first contender is an absolutely general formulation of Zermelo–Fraenkel set theory, including choice, with individuals (ZFCU) supplemented with an axiom stating that the individuals form a set.[5] Call this theory ZFCSU. I will assume ZFCSU has been formulated in an absolutely general first-order language supplemented with devices of plural quantification. Its language contains two primitive predicates: $\in$ and *Set*. As I mentioned above, the appeal to plural quantification is not a needless extravagance. As formulated in a first-order language, ZFCSU is an infinitely axiomatized theory, some of whose axioms are instances of the Replacement Axiom Schema:

Replacement Axiom Schema: $\forall x \forall y \forall (z(\phi(x,y) \wedge \phi(x,z)) \rightarrow \forall x(\mathrm{Set}(x) \rightarrow y = z) \rightarrow \exists y(\mathrm{Set}(y) \wedge \forall z(z \in y \leftrightarrow \exists w(w \in x \wedge \phi(w,z)))$

But this is merely a schema that gives partial expression to a perfectly general principle set theorists believe. We improve considerably on the Replacement Axiom Schema when we help ourselves to plural quantification. Call some ordered pairs *functional* if they pair each of their first components with exactly one object. We are now in a position to replace the Replacement Axiom Schema with a single Replacement Axiom which would be the formalization of the following principle into the first-order language of ZFCU supplemented with plural quantifiers;

Replacement Axiom: If some ordered pairs are functional, then if x is a set, then there is a set y such that a set z is a member of x just in case z is paired with a member of x by one of the ordered pairs.[6]

The result is a finitely axiomatized theory whose formulation of replacement gives faithful expression to a perfectly general principle set theorists seem to believe.

While ZFCU doesn't pronounce on whether the individuals form a set, ZFCSU includes an axiom explicitly stating that they do. Two broad lines of motivation have been offered in the literature in support of this axiom. Some have suggested the axiom that the individuals form a set is implicit in the iterative conception of set, which is thought to motivate some of the axioms of ZFCU.[7] This is a view of sets on which sets are formed in stages of a certain cumulative hierarchy. We begin with individuals. Stage 0 consists of all individuals, which are assumed to be given prior to sets. The sets formed at stage 1 are all sets of individuals. Stage 2 consists of individuals

[5] Mathematicians generally prefer formulations of set theory that make no room for individuals that fail to be sets. Nevertheless, philosophers and mathematicians interested in a broad range of applications have preferred ZFCU to more standard formulations of set theory. For some recent examples, consider McGee (1997), Potter (2004) and Burgess (2004).

[6] The other axiom that is sometimes formulated with the help of plural quantification is the axiom of separation, but, in the presence of replacement, the latter is redundant.

[7] Boolos (1989) expresses some doubt about whether the iterative conception is by itself able to motivate the axioms of choice and replacement.

and sets of items available at stages 0 and 1. The sets formed at stage 2 are all sets of individuals, sets of sets of individuals and sets of individuals and sets of individuals. After stage 2 comes stage 3 consisting of all individuals and sets of items available at earlier stages, etc. Immediately after all finite stages 0, 1, 2, . . . , there is a stage, stage ω. The sets formed at stage ω are all sets of items formed at finite stages earlier than ω. After stage ω comes stage $\omega + 1$ where all sets of sets formed at stage ω are formed, etc. In general, stage α consists of individuals and sets of items formed at stages earlier than α.[8]

On this description of the cumulative hierarchy of sets, if given prior to sets, individuals are available at stage 0 in which case a set of them is formed at stage 1.[9] Unfortunately, one might question the assumption that individuals are given prior to sets.[10] Perhaps some individuals are generated in tandem with sets. For a concrete example, consider the view that ordinals, though formed alongside well-order sets of increasingly higher order-type, are themselves not sets. If ordinals are not sets, they will be individuals. Yet, they will never form a set because no stage will be one in which all ordinals have become available.

What may strike one as a better consideration in support of the axiom appeals to the universal applicability of mathematics. Mathematics is generally understood to investigate structures presented with by the other sciences. But it is not uncommon to think of set theory as a foundation for mathematics and to conceive of all mathematical objects as sets. Thus the universal applicability of mathematics would seem to require the universe of sets to be sufficiently rich and varied to be able to represent any structure whatever presented to us by other sciences. But what if the need arises to consider a structure whose domain includes all individuals there are? Modulo ZFCU, the existence of a set-theoretic surrogate for any such structure is guaranteed by the existence of a set of individuals. Not only this, but, in the context of ZFCU, the axiom that the individuals form a set guarantees that the universe of pure sets is, in fact, sufficiently rich and varied to guarantee the existence of isomorphic copies of any structure presented by any other discipline.[11]

Whatever its motivation, I would like to call attention to ZFCSU partly because, when formulated in a first-order language supplemented with devices of plural quantification, ZFCSU places serious constraints on the size of the universe. In particular,

[8] When we begin with a set of individuals, the result is a transfinite sequence of stages, which provides us with a map of the set-theoretic universe. If U is the set of individuals:

$$\begin{aligned} U_0 &= U; \\ U_{\alpha+1} &= U \cup \mathcal{P}(U_\alpha); \\ U_\lambda &= \textstyle\bigcup_{\alpha<\lambda} U_\alpha, \text{ for } \lambda \text{ a limit.} \end{aligned}$$

[9] This consideration has been suggested in McGee (1997) and Uzquiano (2002).

[10] Thanks to Kit Fine for pressing this point.

[11] This consideration has been independently advanced, for example, by Allen Hazen and Vann McGee, respectively, in Hazen (2004) and McGee (1997). As Matti Eklund reminded me, however, it should be noticed that this is not a genuinely mathematical consideration for the axiom but rather one philosophers and mathematicians may entertain when they engage in the philosophy of set theory.

the universe of all objects is the domain of an interpretation satisfying the axioms of ZFCSU only if the size of the entire universe is strongly inaccessible.

Notice that the axiom that the individuals form a set is not crucial for the development of the problem. The problem will arise even for theorists who remain unmoved by the attempts to motivate the axiom that the individuals form a set. At the end of the day, this axiom is not strictly required to make sure the size of the universe is strongly inaccessible. The hypothesis that the pure sets are in $1-1$ correspondence with all there is would have done just as well.[12] If I have chosen ZFCSU for present purposes it is only because it is a particularly simple axiomatization of set theory with individuals whose axioms have generally been accepted by philosophers and mathematicians who have allowed for individuals in the formulation of set theory.[13]

A word of clarification. When I speak of the size of the universe of all objects, it is not my intention to suggest that there is a set-theoretic cardinal that measures its size.[14] Instead, we should understand talk of size of a domain that doesn't form a set in (conveniently pluralized) second-order terms as outlined in Shapiro (1991). Like this: D is *strongly inaccessible* if and only if: (i) D is not denumerable in size; (ii) D cannot be reached from below by taking powers: the power domain of size less than D still has size less than D; (iii) D cannot be reached from below by taking unions: the union of fewer (than the size of D) domains of size less than D still has size less than D.[15] The official plural translation of clauses (ii) and (iii) will have to be devious in order to paraphrase apparent talk of domains of domains, but the details have been carefully developed in Shapiro (1991).

When I say that ZFCSU requires the universe to be strongly inaccessible, I mean that ZFCSU is satisfied in a model whose domain comprises all there is only if the domain of all objects satisfies clauses (i), (ii) and (iii) above. This is because the axioms of ZFCSU guarantee that the domain of pure sets is strongly inaccessible. But it is a deductive consequence of ZFCSU that the pure sets are in $1-1$ correspondence with all there is.[16] It follows that the domain of all objects should be strongly inaccessible.

The second contender is an absolutely general formulation of what I will call *atomistic extensional mereology*. I will take the language of atomistic extensional mereology to be a first-order language supplemented with devices of plural reference and

[12] I have discussed the hypothesis that the pure sets are in $1-1$ correspondence with all the objects there are in Uzquiano (2006). One motivation for it comes from the fact that it is a consequence of von Neumann's limitation of size principle according to which some objects form a set if and only if they are not in $1-1$ correspondence with the universe.

[13] For some examples, consider again Hazen (2004), McGee (1997) and Potter (2004).

[14] A set-theoretic cardinal κ is strongly inaccessible just in case:

(i) κ is not denumerable,
(ii) For any $\lambda < \kappa$, $2^{\lambda} < \kappa$, and
(iii) κ cannot be represented as the supremum of fewer than κ smaller ordinals.

In sum, κ cannot be reached from lower cardinalities through applications of the operations used in (ii) and (iii).

[15] D is a monadic predicate.

[16] This is proved, for example, in McGee (1997).

quantification. David Lewis is the author of a succinct presentation of the classical extensional mereology that has made extensive use of plurals in Lewis (1991). It contains a single primitive non-logical predicate 'overlaps' and standard definitions of 'part', 'discrete', and 'sum'.[17] When formulated with the help of plural quantification, the axioms of atomistic extensional mereology read:

Transitivity: If x is part of some part of y, then x is part of y.

Unrestricted Composition: No matter what some objects are, there is a sum of them.

Uniqueness of Composition: It never happens that the same things have two different sums.

Alfred Tarski observed in Tarski (1935) that the axioms of classical extensional mereology make sure that the part–whole relation has the structure of a complete Boolean algebra without a zero element.[18]

Atomistic extensional mereology is the theory that results when the axioms of classical extensional mereology are supplemented with Atomicity:

Atomicity: There are no objects whose parts all have further proper parts.[19]

One may wonder whether an absolutely general formulation of classical extensional mereology will not do for our purposes. After all, one soon finds oneself in trouble when one couples this absolutely general theory with a simple absolutely general consequence of ZFCU:

Singletons: Every object has a singleton.

Trouble arises when we take singletons to express an absolute generalization. For the combination of singletons with classical extensional mereology is incompatible with a certain attractive hypothesis about the interaction of the part–whole relation and membership:

[17] In particular, I will assume the following definitions:

x is *part* of y iff for every z, if z overlaps x, then z overlaps y.
x and y are *discrete* iff x and y do not overlap.
x is a *sum* of some objects iff x has all of them as parts and has no part discrete from each of them.

This axiomatization of classical extensional mereology traces back to Tarski (1929).

[18] Tarski's formulation of classical extensional mereology in Tarski (1935) included in addition:

Reflexivity: x is part of x
Anti-Symmetry: If x is part of y and y is part of x, then $x = y$
Strong Supplementation: If x is not part of y, then some part of x doesn't overlap y.

But there are straightforward derivations of Reflexivity and Anti-symmetry from Lewis's axioms. What follows is a derivation of Strong Supplementation for which I'm indebted to Paul Hovda. Suppose every part of x overlaps y, i.e., the negation of the consequent of Strong Supplementation. By Unrestricted Composition, there is a sum of x and y, call it z. But z is a sum of y: y is part of z, and every part of z overlaps either x or y—since z is a sum of x and y. Therefore z is a sum of y. Since, by Reflexivity and the definition of 'sum', y is a sum of y, by Uniqueness of Composition, we have that $y = z$. But since x is part of z, we conclude that x is part of y.

[19] Notice the use of plural quantification in the formulation of the axiom.

Unique Decomposition: A singleton is part of a sum of singletons if and only if it is one of them.

A Cantorian argument will do for our purposes.[20] Singletons being an absolute generalization makes sure the singleton operation provides us with a 1–1 map between the singletons and all the objects there are. Unfortunately, the operation taking a sum of singletons to its singleton provides us, in effect, with a 1–1 map of the domain of all sums of singletons into the domain of all singletons. But a generalization of Cantor's theorem shows that no such map exists on pain of contradiction. This is because classical extensional mereology entails that (i) no matter what some singletons the *xx*s may be, there is a unique sum of them. By Unique Decomposition, (ii) the sum of some singletons *xx*s is identical with the sum of some singletons *yy*s just in case the *xx*s are the *yy*s. The relevant generalization of Cantor's theorem entails that (i) and (ii) hold only if there are strictly more sums of singletons than there are singletons.

Philosophers have generally been disturbed by this conflict, and, in response, one might suggest that we take ZFCSU to be concerned with a restricted domain that leaves out arbitrary sums of sets, some of which are to be thought of as proper classes.[21] Yet, as plausible as it may seem, Unique Decomposition is primarily concerned with the interaction of the part–whole relation and membership. So one may still try to attack the present difficulty not by questioning absolutely general formulations of ZFCSU or classical extensional mereology but rather by denying Unique Decomposition and suggesting that the interaction between the part–whole relation and membership is subtler than one might have initially thought. Unfortunately, this move would do nothing to assuage a conflict between absolutely general formulations of ZFCSU and atomistic extensional mereology.

Atomicity is a thesis many philosophers have found congenial. But when formulated as an absolutely general theory formulated with the help of plurals, atomistic extensional mereology places serious constraints on the size of the universe. Since atomistic extensional mereology ensures the universe exemplifies the structure of a complete atomic Boolean algebra, it requires the size of the universe to be identical to the size of the power domain of the domain of mereological atoms.

Atomicity almost immediately spells trouble for theorists who take sets to enter into the part–whole relation. One difficulty, though not the one I want to raise, has to do again with the interaction of the part–whole relation and membership and is motivated by the thought that atomistic extensional mereology is concerned with all objects in general and with all sets in particular. This problem doesn't, however, require us to suppose set theory is concerned with all there is. Four theses are incompatible:

(a) All sets are parts.

20 I have discussed other ways in which the conflict may be manifested in Uzquiano (2006).

21 David Lewis has suggested a similar view in Lewis (1991) in response to a different, but related problem.

(b) The domain of all sets is closed under the part–whole relation.[22]
(c) When formulated with the help of plural quantification, the axioms of ZFCSU are true of membership.
(d) When formulated with the help of plural quantification, the axioms of atomistic extensional mereology are true of the part–whole relation.

The combination of (a), (b), and (d) requires the universe of pure sets to be a model of atomistic extensional mereology. But we know that a model of atomistic extensional mereology is a complete atomic Boolean algebra (without a zero element). Now, the domain of a complete atomic Boolean algebra must be in 1–1 correspondence with the power domain of the domain of mereological atoms. Unfortunately, (c) ensures that the universe of pure sets is strongly inaccessible in size, which tells us that it is not of the size of a power domain.

This conflict still requires us to move beyond classical extensional mereology because there are models of classical extensional mereology of strongly inaccessible size. This is because a model of classical extensional mereology is a complete Boolean algebra and we know there are complete Boolean algebras of strongly inaccessible size.[23] This tells us that there are formal models of classical extensional mereology whose domain is the universe of pure sets. The trouble with such models is that the relation that interprets the part–whole predicate is by no means one we would ordinarily recognize as the part–whole relation on pure sets.

One may well be tempted to fault (b) for the problem. Why think the universe of sets should be closed under the part–whole relation? Why think, in particular, that a mereological sum of sets must itself be a set? To be sure, each of (a), (c) and (d) rest on much firmer ground than (b). (a) is an immediate consequence of the assumption that the axioms of atomistic extensional mereology are absolutely general principles concerned with all the objects there are. And it would be highly revisionary to question (c), which still remains neutral with respect to the question of whether the individuals form a set. A similar consideration applies to (d). In fact, for the rejection of (d) to help with our puzzle, it would have to be accompanied by an account of how sets enter into the part–whole relation on which some pure sets qualify themselves as composed of atomless gunk. Unfortunately, no such account seems forthcoming. In view of this, one may be led to infer that perhaps the lesson to be learned from this conflict is just that the universe of pure sets is not closed under mereological composition and hence not a model of atomistic extensional mereology.

Unfortunately, the problem persists even when we surrender the thesis that the domain of all sets are closed under the part–whole relation, which is admittedly a 'mixed' principle concerned with the interaction of the part–whole relation and membership, provided, that is, that we insist that ZFCSU is an absolutely general theory. This is in fact the problem I want to raise. Unlike the conflict between (a),

[22] This amounts to the conjunction of two claims: (i) Sets have only sets as parts, and (ii) sets are only parts of sets, whence a mereological sum of sets must itself a set.

[23] More precisely, we know there are complete Boolean algebras of *infinite* cardinality κ if and only if $\kappa^{\aleph_0} = \kappa$ as shown in Koppelberg (1981).

(b), (c) and (d), our final predicament will not prejudge the interaction between the part–whole relation and membership. The final problem arises when we notice that four theses are incompatible:

(1) When formulated with the help of plural quantification, the axioms of ZFCSU are true of membership.
(2) The quantifiers of ZFCSU range over an all-inclusive domain.[24]
(3) When formulated with the help of plural quantification, the axioms of atomistic extensional mereology are true of the part–whole relation.
(4) The quantifiers of atomistic extensional mereology range over an all-inclusive domain.[25]

The problem is this.[26] The combination of (1) and (2) requires the universe of all objects to be strongly inaccessible. But the combination of (3) and (4) requires the universe of all objects to have the structure of a complete atomic Boolean algebra (without a zero element). But the domain of a complete atomic Boolean algebra must be in 1–1 correspondence with the power domain of the domain of mereological atoms. Therefore the size of the universe of all objects can indeed be reached from below by taking powers and is thus not strongly inaccessible.[27]

The predicament doesn't quite require the full strength of Atomicity; all that is required is some guarantee that whatever atomless sums there exist, they are not strongly inaccessible in number.[28] I have chosen Atomicity over the weaker thesis

[24] To make (2) perfectly explicit, notice that it amounts to the conjunction of two theses:

(2a) The singular quantifiers of ZFCSU range over an all-inclusive domain.
(2b) No matter what some objects are, they lie in the range of the plural quantifiers of ZFCSU.

Notice that (2b) is not a trivial thesis. Just as some have suggested our singular quantifiers are hopelessly ambiguous and denied we have the resources to distinguish genuinely unrestricted quantification from quantification over a less than all-inclusive domain, one might object to the present thesis that our plural quantifiers are themselves ambiguous and deny that we are in a position to distinguish between the situation described by (2b) and one in which at least some objects fail to lie in the range of our plural quantifiers. Both concerns have recently been discussed in Rayo (2003).

[25] This again amounts to the conjunction of two different but related theses:

(4a) The singular quantifiers of atomistic extensional mereology range over an all-inclusive domain.
(4b) No matter what some objects are, they lie in the range of the plural quantifiers of atomistic extensional mereology.

[26] Thanks to Agustín Rayo for first calling this kind of problem to my attention.

[27] The conveniently pluralized official translation of all these claims should be kept in mind.

[28] Thanks to Daniel Nolan here. The main reason for this is that it takes a strongly inaccessible number of atomless sums to make sure that the entire domain of a model of classical extensional mereology is strongly inaccessible. If there is atomless gunk, then there are at least continuum-many atomless sums. This is because if there is an atomless sum, then there is an infinite set A of pairwise distinct atomless sums. And any two subsets of A give rise to distinct atomless sums by the axioms of classical extensional mereology.

There are three cases: (i) the number of mereological atoms is strictly less than the number of atomless objects. Distinguish two subcases: (ia) the power domain of the domain of atoms is strictly larger than the domain of atomless sums, in which case the universe will be of the size of the former; (ib) the power domain of the domain of atoms has less or equal size to the domain of atomless sums,

because it seems difficult to think of principled reasons why one should believe that there may be atomless sums in great abundance, just not a strongly inaccessible number of them. Atomicity, by contrast, is a thesis with a distinguished history and whose acceptance is both relatively widespread and based on reasons of principle.

Unless one is prepared to question one or more of the background assumptions used in generating the problem, one has a limited range of options:

- reject (1) and make radical changes in the axioms of ZFCSU.
- reject (2) and restrict the quantifiers of ZFCSU to range over a less-than-all-inclusive domain.
- reject (3) and make radical changes in the axioms of atomistic extensional mereology.
- reject (4) and restrict the quantifiers of atomistic extensional mereology to range over a less-than-all-inclusive domain.

Of the four, the first two may be particularly tempting in view of the fact that absolutely general formulations of ZFCSU are in conflict with other absolutely general theories as well.

11.2.2 ZFCSU vs The General Theory of Abstraction

Far from being an isolated phenomenon, the conflict between ZFCSU and atomistic extensional mereology is an instance of a more general problem. This time the conflict will arise between an absolutely general version of ZFCSU as formulated either in language equipped with plural quantifiers or, otherwise, in a second-order language and an absolutely general theory of abstraction naturally formulated in a third-order language or, with axiom schemata, in a second-order language with quantification over polyadic relations. This will eventually raise the question of whether the role of absolutely general formulations of ZFCSU in more than one conflict provides us with cumulative evidence against such formulations of ZFCSU.

The general theory of abstraction I would like to consider has recently been developed by Kit Fine in Fine (2002). In his study, Fine is concerned with abstraction principles of the form:

$$\forall F \forall G(\S F = \S G \leftrightarrow \Phi(F, G)),$$

where F and G are monadic second-order variables, § denotes a function from the values of second-order variables to objects, and Φ is a formula with two free variables of the given type which gives expression to some binary equivalence relation. For a

which, we have assumed, is not inaccessible. In either case, the universe will not be inaccessible; (ii) the number of atoms equals the number of atomless sums. In this case, the universe will have the size of the power domain of the joint domain of atoms and sums objects and will not have inaccessible size; (iii) the number of mereological atoms is strictly larger than the number of atomless sums. In this case, the universe will have the size of the power domain of the domain of atoms and will not have inaccessible size either.

typical example of a binary equivalence relation on the values of second-order variables, consider the relation of equinumerosity. Hume's principle is the abstraction principle correlated to this equivalence relation:

$$\forall F \forall G(\text{NUMBER}(F) = \text{NUMBER}(G) \leftrightarrow F \sim G)$$

But not all abstraction principles are acceptable. Some are inconsistent like Frege's Axiom V:

$$\forall F \forall G(\text{EXT}(F) = \text{EXT}(G) \leftrightarrow \forall x(Fx \leftrightarrow Gx))$$

Other abstraction principles are not inconsistent when considered in isolation but they are jointly incompatible with other abstraction principles. The goal of Fine's general theory of abstraction is to provide a general criterion that might help us show, once and for all, what principles of abstraction are acceptable.

One necessary condition for the acceptability of an abstraction principle is that the relevant equivalence relation should not give rise to more equivalence classes than there are objects in the domain of the first-order variables. An equivalence relation that satisfies this condition is called *non-inflationary*. This is precisely the problem with Frege's Axiom V. No matter what the size of the first-order domain is, Axiom V requires more extensions than there are objects in that domain.

A criterion for the acceptability of abstraction principles should deal with the question of how to combine into different systems of abstraction principles. Fine's general theory of abstraction first assumes that two abstracts from different abstraction principles are identical only if they correspond to the same equivalence classes. But the concern remains that there might be a system of abstraction principles such that each of them is non-inflationary but such that they are jointly inflationary. That is, they jointly entail the existence of more abstracts than there are objects in the first-order domain. This is called *hyperinflation*. In response to this threat, Fine considers the requirement that each equivalence relation expressed by Φ be *predominantly logical* which he formally defines in terms of the invariance of the relation expressed by Φ under certain permutations. He then proves that systems of abstraction principles whose equivalence relations are predominantly logical and non-inflationary are immune to hyper-inflation provided the size of the domain is unsurpassable. For each cardinal κ, let $cp(\kappa)$ be the number of cardinals less than κ. A cardinal κ is *unsurpassable* if $2^{cp(\kappa)} \leq \kappa$.

Very roughly, as developed in Fine (2002), the general theory of abstraction contains two basic principles:

Identity Principle: Abstracts from different abstraction principles are identical only if the associated equivalence classes are the same.

Existence Principle: If an equivalence relation on concepts is non-inflationary and predominantly logical, then the corresponding abstraction principle will give rise to abstracts.

But not surprisingly, the general theory of abstraction turns out to place serious constraints on the size of the first-order domain. When we assume second-order definitions of 'predominantly logical', 'non-inflationary', and 'unsurpassable', we infer that the general theory of abstraction is true in a model if and only if its domain is unsurpassable.[29] Unfortunately, no strongly inaccessible domain is unsurpassable. Indeed, if a domain is strongly inaccessible, then its cofinality is the size of the domain itself. By (a suitable generalization of) Cantor's theorem, the power domain of a domain must be strictly larger than the initial domain.

Trouble arises for a theorist who accepts (1§) and (2§) below, yet takes the principles of Identity and Existence to be absolutely generalizations that provide us with an accurate account of the true abstraction principles. For the following are incompatible:

(1§) The axioms of second-order ZFCSU are true of membership.
(2§) The quantifiers of second-order ZFCSU range over an all-inclusive domain.
(3§) The axioms of the general theory of abstraction are true of abstraction operations.
(4§) The quantifiers of the general theory of abstraction range over an all-inclusive domain.[30]

The problem should be familiar by now. For reasons completely analogous to the case of (1) and (2), the combination of (1§) and (2§) requires the universe to be strongly inaccessible. But the combination of (3§) and (4§) makes sure that the universe has unsurpassable size. Unfortunately, no unsurpassable domain is inaccessible.[31]

At this point, it is very tempting to take subsections 11.2.1 and 11.2.2 to provide us with cumulative evidence against the combination (1) and (2). The rejection of (1) or (2) or both we would seem to solve both conflicts at once. Surely the prospect of a systematic and unified solution of the two conflicts will appeal to many.

11.3 A UNIFIED SOLUTION?

But what reason is there to expect a systematic and unified solution of all potential conflict between absolutely general theories? What we found is that two absolutely general theories with disjoint non-logical vocabularies sometimes impose incompatible constraints on the size of the universe of all objects. For all we know, different conflicts call for different measures.

But we should nevertheless look at the prospects of solving the two conflicts presented above by questioning (1) or (2) or both. I would like to suggest there is a

[29] Shapiro (1991) has a discussion of the techniques necessary for such formulations.

[30] Since the general theory of abstraction is a second-order theory, (4§) becomes again the conjunction of two theses:

(4§a) The first-order quantifiers of the general theory of abstraction range over an all-inclusive domain.
(4§b) The higher-order quantifiers of the general theory of abstraction take absolutely unrestricted range.

[31] See Fine (2002) for a thorough discussion of this problem.

high cost associated to the rejection of each (1) and (2), a cost that is better avoided in the presence of a better solution.[32] Let me begin with (1). There is no question that to reject one or more of the axioms of ZFCU would be highly revisionary. ZFCU is an incredibly successful mathematical theory with an impressive track record. The apparent incompatibility between ZFCSU and either atomistic extensional mereology or the general theory of abstraction will (and should) not move mathematicians to amend their ways and give up one or more of the axioms of ZFCU.

At this point one might suggest that what we learn from the conflicts is that we should not assume that the individuals form a set. This is precisely Kit Fine's response to the conflict between ZFCSU and the general theory of abstraction in Fine (2002). After all, the suggestion the individuals fail to form a set is far less revisionary than the rejection of one or more of the axioms of ZFCU. However, whatever its merits and drawbacks, one would have thought that the fate of the axiom that the individuals form a set should be decided primarily on the basis of considerations internal to mathematical practice and not on the basis of the apparent incompatibility between an absolutely general formulation of ZFCSU and other absolutely general theories.

Alas, a friend of ZFCSU might reply that the universal applicability of mathematics provides independent support for the addition of the axiom to ZFCU. And, regardless, for the retreat from ZFCSU to ZFCU to be effective, it would have to be accompanied with the hypothesis that there are far more individuals than there are pure sets. But this is not a very plausible hypothesis, or at least not very plausible in the absence of independent considerations.[33]

It might seem more promising to reject (2) and, in particular, the assumption that absolutely all objects enter into the membership relation. It is not that all objects there are are in fact sets, but rather that the truth of singletons, whose quantifiers had been thought to range over absolutely all objects, requires that absolutely every object have a singleton. To question this assumption would be to suggest that at least some objects are not members themselves; they lie outside the scope of the singleton operation. David Lewis has made a similar point in Lewis (1991). According to Lewis there are, in addition to individuals and sets, proper classes that are not sets. Sets are some but not all of the classes there are. The distinction is this. Whereas sets are classes that are members of some classes, proper classes never are members. Not only are proper classes not sets, they are not individuals either. And they lie outside of the domain of ZFCSU, which, despites appearances to the contrary, turns out not be the most comprehensive theory of collections after all.

The main problem with this move is that it saddles us with a mysterious distinction between individuals and sets, which are all members of other sets and thus lie in the

32 I have looked at the question of whether the conflict between set theory and atomistic extensional mereology provides us with a reason to abandon (1) or (2) in Uzquiano (2006).

33 One view of sets often cited in support of some of the axioms of ZFC is the limitation of size doctrine according to which some objects form a set if and only if they are not in 1–1 correspondence with all the objects there are. One immediate consequence of this principle is that there is only one size a domain that fail to form a set may be. It follows, in particular, that if the individuals fail to form a set, then they must be in correspondence with the pure sets, which also fail to form a set.

domain of membership, and other items (classes, presumably), which for some utterly mysterious reason fail to be members, not even members of a singleton set. Perhaps we should not be surprised by the mystery on account of the fact that, as David Lewis has claimed in Lewis (1991), the making of singletons is ill-understood to begin with. But that would do little, it seems to me, to alleviate our perplexity.

Perhaps we should look elsewhere for a resolution of the conflicts outlined above. The purpose of the next two sections is to look at other options and to argue that, at least in some cases, the proper response to a conflict between two absolutely general theories might require us to give up the claim to absolute generality for one of them.

11.4 THE GENERAL THEORY OF ABSTRACTION

It may be that some conflicts between absolutely general theories will move us to take back the claim to absolute generality for one of them, but, unfortunately, the conflict between (1§) and (2§) and (3§) and (4§) is hardly an example. To appreciate this, notice that when we fix (1§) and (2§), two options remain as responses to the conflict between (1§) and (2§) and (3§) and (4§):

- reject (3§) and make radical changes in the axioms of the general theory of abstraction.
- reject (4§) and restrict the quantifiers of the general theory of abstraction to range over a less-than-all-inclusive domain.

Without adjudicating the question of how to best to respond to the conflict, we can presumably discard a restriction of the first-order quantifiers of the general theory of abstraction as a plausible response to the conflict. The general theory of abstraction had been advanced as a perfectly general answer to the question of what equivalence relations, whatever their field, give rise to abstraction operations on the values of the second-order variables. To restrict the range of the first-order quantifiers of the general theory of abstraction would be to renounce to this goal in exchange for an answer to the less interesting question of what equivalence relations on a certain restricted domain give rise to abstraction operations on that domain.

Two options remain. To restrict the range of the second-order quantifiers of the general theory of abstraction or to make radical changes in the axioms of the general theory of abstraction. The restriction of the second-order quantifiers of the general theory of abstraction would still fall under the rejection of (4§) and has been suggested by Stewart Shapiro in Shapiro (2005). The restriction of the second-order quantifiers of the general theory of abstraction to range over set-sized concepts would make sure that the generated abstracts in each case amount to equivalence classes that are themselves sets and fall under the scope of ZFCSU. Notice, however, that the motivation for this had better not be that absolutely unrestricted higher-order quantification over an all-inclusive domain is unintelligible, for we have seen that the combination of this claim with the claim that absolutely unrestricted first-order quantification over an all-inclusive domain is fine is unstable. But it is doubtful that some independent motivation for the restriction is available that doesn't compromise the goals of the general theory of abstraction.[34] And, relatedly, it is unclear whether this move would have much to recommend over explicit modifications of the theory to the effect that only set-sized equivalence relations, for example, give rise to abstracts.

This is in fact the other alternative to consider, which would fall under the rejection of (3§). This move has recently been hinted by Kit Fine in Fine (2005) and amounts to making explicit changes in the axioms of the general theory of abstraction to make sure that only set-sized equivalence relations generate abstracts. The challenge again is to provide some motivation for this changes, which, ideally, would have to be independent from the conflict with absolutely general ZFCSU. If no independent reasons are forthcoming, then the conflict between ZFCSU and the general theory of abstraction has a remarkable moral. We should watch for potential conflicts between absolutely general theories we endorse even if their non-logical vocabularies have nothing in common. For such conflicts may require us to revise commitments for which we thought we had independent motivation.

11.5 ATOMISTIC EXTENSIONAL MEREOLOGY

The situation strikes me as different in the case of the conflict between (1) and (2) and (3) and (4). If we leave (1) and (2) fixed again, two options remain:

- reject (3) and make radical changes in the axioms of atomistic extensional mereology.
- reject (4) and restrict the quantifiers of atomistic extensional mereology to range over an less-than-all-inclusive domain.

There is a cost associated with each of the two options, but I would like to suggest we would do better to take the second route and give up the claim to absolute generality for atomistic extensional mereology. If this is indeed the case, then there is no hope for a unified solution to all conflicts between absolutely general theories.

11.5.1 Reforming Atomistic Extensional Mereology

It is time to look at the cost associated with the rejection of (3) above. Although this option doesn't by itself adjudicate the issue of what axiom to question, two axioms of atomistic extensional mereology immediately stand out as salient candidates for eviction: Atomicity and Unrestricted Composition.[35]

Unfortunately, the rejection of Atomicity will not suit present purposes. Although philosophers have sometimes contemplated violations of Atomicity in the domain of material objects, no one has suggested that there may be atomless sums in the

[34] Shapiro (2005) mentions some reasons for pessimism.

[35] There are other axioms one might abandon in order to evade the problem. I make no claim to offer an exhaustive list of options under (3); instead, I have chosen to focus on two of the most salient alternatives.

extravagant abundance that is required to circumvent our problem.[36] The problem is that fewer than a strongly inaccessible number of atomless sums will do nothing to alleviate the conflict.[37] But the prospects for an independent motivation of this claim are not too bright.

One might perhaps try to overcome this problem by claiming that sets themselves lack a decomposition into mereological atoms and provide us with sufficient atomless sums to fit the bill. The problem with this move is that unless it is accompanied with an account of how sets enter into the part–whole relation on which they all lack a decomposition into atoms, it will remain largely ad hoc and unmotivated. But if there is a contender to play the role of the part–whole relation on sets, this is the subset relation.[38] Unfortunately, this account will not justify the claim that sets provide us with a widespread violation of Atomicity.[39]

Unrestricted Composition now comes to the fore as the prime candidate for eviction. But this move will only be plausible if it is supplemented by some independent rationale.[40] Maybe one is not difficult to come by when we assume sets themselves enter into the part–whole relation. For a little thought on this assumption might lead us to rethink the justification for Unrestricted Composition. Kit Fine has recently made just this sort of suggestion in Fine (2005).[41] Much of what follows is inspired by his discussion.

One might perhaps take a cue from standard presentations of the iterative conception of set as a view on which sets are *formed* in stages of a certain cumulative hierarchy. Typical presentations of the iterative conception are often accompanied with the disclaimer that talk of set formation is metaphorical and should not be taken seriously. We should not think of sets as being literally formed or constructed in stages of the hierarchy. But this of course only raises the question of what lies behind the metaphor. It is not uncommon to explain the metaphor in terms of the ontological priority of members to the set.[42] The crucial difference between individuals and sets of individuals, the suggestion continues, is that while individuals need not depend for their existence on the prior existence of another individual, sets of individuals depend for their existence on the existence of the individuals that are their members. More generally, sets depend for their existence on the existence of their members.

Now ask whether the parts of a mereological sum are likewise ontologically prior to the sum. If they are, then we should presumably conceive of sums as similarly

[36] Zimmerman (1996) develops an argument for the thesis that material objects are made of atomless gunk.

[37] As explained in footnote 29.

[38] There is a qualification often made to restrict the subset relation to non-empty sets.

[39] This point is made in more detail in Uzquiano (2006).

[40] Otherwise, the following principle would do fine for our purposes: '**Limitation of Composition**: Some objects have a mereological sum if and only if their atomic parts are not in 1–1 correspondence with all the objects there are.'

David Lewis and Gideon Rosen have considered this principle in Lewis (1991) and Rosen (1995), respectively, in response to a similar problem. The problem with this principle is that it too seems largely ad hoc and unmotivated.

[41] I learned of this suggestion only after I had completed Uzquiano (2006). What follows is meant to address it.

[42] Michael Potter, for example, does this in Potter (2004).

formed in stages of a certain cumulative hierarchy. This observation, by itself, doesn't yet provide a reason to doubt Unrestricted Composition. When considered in isolation, we may have reason to think that there will be some stage at which all sums will have been generated. It is not that we could not proceed further to a new stage, if we wanted to, but rather that there is no point since no more sums would thereby be generated.[43]

The situation changes drastically when we allow sets to enter into the part–whole relation. For in that case, we have little choice but to consider the formation of mereological sums in tandem with the formation of sets in the cumulative hierarchy. The picture that emerges is this. We begin with atoms. Stage 0 consists of atoms, which are the objects that exist independently. At stage 1 all sets and sums of atoms are formed. That is, stage 1 consists of all sets and sums which presuppose items available at stage 0. Stage 2 consists of atoms, sets of items available at stage 0 and 1, and sums of items available at stages 0 and 1.[44] After stage 2 comes stage 3 consisting of all atoms, sets, and sums of items available at earlier stages, etc.

Immediately after all stages 0, 1, 2, . . . , there is a stage, stage ω. The sets formed at stage ω are all sets of items formed at finite stages earlier than ω. The sums formed at stage ω are all sums of items formed at finite stages earlier than ω. After stage ω comes stage $\omega + 1$ where all sets and sums of items formed at stage ω are formed, etc. In general, stage α consists of atoms, sets, and sums of items formed at stages earlier than α.

Because there is no last stage at which all sets become available, there is no terminal stage at which all mereological sums have been formed. Each stage of the cumulative hierarchy will provide new sets, which, in turn, will generate new mereological sums at the next stage. The problem with Unrestricted Composition is this. Some objects may not be available at any stage of the cumulative hierarchy, in which case there would be a real obstacle for the formation of their mereological sum. There is, for example, no stage at which all sets have been formed, and hence there will not be a mereological sum of all sets.[45]

Our discussion suggests the following restriction on composition:

> **Iterative Composition**. Some objects have a mereological sum if and only there is some stage of the cumulative hierarchy in which they all appear.

What should a proponent of ZFCSU make of the present proposal? Unless sets are themselves sums, Iterative Composition is incompatible with the axiom that the

[43] If we started with some atoms at stage 0, we would obtain all mereological sums of atoms at stage 1. We could then proceed to stage 2 if we wanted to in which case we would obtain sums of sums available at stage 1. But nothing in the picture provided thus far guarantees the formation of new mereological sums not formed in the preceding stage. Or, in other words, for all we have said, it may well be that every mereological sum of sums of atoms is already a mereological sum of atoms and thus available in the preceding stage.

[44] For example, if a and b are atoms available at stage 0, then both their set, $\{a, b\}$, and their sum, $a + b$, are formed at stage 1. But neither the set $\{\{a\}, \{b\}\}$ nor the sum $\{a\} + \{b\}$ become available before stage 2.

[45] This cuts both ways. Because there is no stage at which all mereological sums have been formed, there is no set whose members include all mereological sums. But we now know better than to expect the existence of such a set.

individuals form a set, and, a fortiori, with ZFCSU. Since there is no stage at which all mereological sums are available, and all mereological sums are individuals, there is no stage at which all individuals are available. Therefore, there is never an opportunity to form a set of all individuals.[46] It might be tempting to turn this into an argument against the axiom that the individuals form a set, in which case the proper response to our problem would combine the rejection of Unrestricted Composition with the retreat from ZFCSU to ZFCU. Unfortunately, there are two other reasons for concern with the present strategy.

There is first the presumption that the iterative conception of set requires us to understand the members of a set as ontologically prior to the set. While the fact that some sets are cited before others in the description of the iterative conception might be (mistakenly) assumed to turn on the ontological priority of individuals and sets over sets thereof, it may be better explained merely by appeal to a certain narrative convention. This is a convention that requires to mention first items that appear earlier in a certain salient ordering. As George Boolos explained in Boolos (1989), the iterative conception is primarily a picture of the universe of all sets as ordered by the relation *having lower rank than*. This relation is a salient partial ordering of the universe, and the description supplied by the iterative conception respects a certain narrative convention by mentioning first sets that come earlier in the order. But then the iterative conception need not turn on the ontological priority of the members to the set.

The other line of opposition has to do with the view that the parts are ontologically prior to their sum. This, as it happens, is in tension with an attractive and influential picture of mereological composition as akin to identity. It is not uncommon to hear that the mereological sum of some parts is nothing 'over and above' the parts. Or that once you are committed to the parts, you are committed to the sum. Or that a sum is 'exhausted' by the parts. What lies behind all these suggestive (albeit obscure) slogans is the doctrine of composition as identity.[47] The doctrine comes in at least two versions. On a stronger version, the parts of a sum are strictly speaking identical with the sum. On a weaker, the relation between a sum and its parts is merely analogous to identity in various respects. Only the weaker version of composition as identity is compatible with the view that identity is a one-one relation. The problem is that this picture of composition is oftentimes taken to underlie the plausibility of the axioms of classical extensional mereology. So a friend of atomistic extensional mereology tempted by the ontological priority of the parts to their sum may be forced to abandon the very picture of composition that motivates her acceptance of the axioms.[48]

[46] We avoid this conclusion if we follow David Lewis in identifying sets with mereological sums of singletons. For then there is no guarantee that an individual that is not a set is ever formed after the first stage of the cumulative hierarchy.

[47] The doctrine of composition as identity has been discussed, for example, in Lewis (1991) and Sider (forthcoming).

[48] It is an interesting question whether Composition as Identity may be used to provide a more direct motivation of Unrestricted Composition. Ted Sider discusses this question in Sider (forthcoming).

Not all versions of composition as identity are equally viable, but the success of modest versions of composition as identity would seem to undermine the thought that the parts are ontologically prior to the sum they compose. The point of weak composition as identity is to capture the special intimacy of the part–whole relation, which would seem to place it at variance with membership. Unlike sets, which are formed in stages of the cumulative hierarchy, sums emerge from the hierarchy without having been formed at any stage. To repeat some of the slogans, the sum of all sets would be nothing 'over and above' them. Once you are committed to the sets, you are committed to their sum, regardless of whether the sets occur together at some stage of the hierarchy. This is probably not the place to assess the prospects of weak composition as identity.[49] Suffice it to say that composition as identity has motivated some of the axioms of atomistic extensional mereology and its rejection would presumably come at a cost.

11.5.2 Restricting the Domain of Atomistic Extensional Mereology

The last option in the menu is the restriction of the quantifiers of atomistic extensional mereology. We have a choice at this point. We may restrict the range of the singular quantifiers to range over a less-than-all-inclusive domain or, alternatively, we may restrict the range of the plural quantifiers by insisting, for example, that some objects lie in the range of our plural quantifiers if and only if they form a set. Of the two, the first move is more radical since it requires us to deny that some objects are not in the field of the part–whole relation and thus are not part of themselves.

Unrestricted Composition would have a dramatically different effect if we insisted that some objects lie in the range of the plural quantifiers if and only if they form a set. Some objects (on the unrestricted interpretation) would have a mereological sum if and only if they formed a set, in which case atomistic extensional mereology would indeed be satisfied in strongly inaccessible models. The trouble with this move is that it is largely ad hoc and unmotivated. What is more important, this move has nothing to recommend over more explicit restrictions on mereological composition of the kind considered above.

What I would like to suggest now is that we would do better to restrict the singular quantifiers of atomistic extensional mereology to range over a less-than-all-inclusive domain. This move is not unmotivated. If there is a lesson to be learned from our predicament is that absolutely general inquiry is an audacious enterprise. We have learned that absolutely general theories sometimes impose serious demands on the size of the universe. This consideration alone suggests we take a risk when we present atomistic extensional mereology as an absolutely general theory. Perhaps we should limit the subject matter of atomistic extensional mereology to a less-than-all-inclusive domain.

For this move not to be ad hoc and unmotivated, we should provide some independent reason to restrict the subject matter of atomistic extensional mereology.

[49] Ted Sider has offered an optimistic assessment of such prospects in Sider (forthcoming).

Most proponents of atomistic extensional mereology think that material objects enter into the part–whole relation. Often they think this because they think there is a relation over the domain of material objects that obeys the axioms of classical extensional mereology: If *x* and *y* are material objects, *x* is part of *y* just in case every spacetime point occupied by *x* is a spacetime point occupied by *y*. So they have an account of how material objects enter into the part–whole relation and think that all of the axioms are true when we restrict the domain to include all and only material objects. This is how it should be. It is fine to suggest that material objects stand into the part–whole relation to other sorts of objects. Or to suggest that other sorts of objects enter into the part–whole relation as well. But each suggestion, it seems to me, must be accompanied by an account of how the relevant objects enter into the part–whole relation.

I would like to suggest that in considering the question of whether objects of a certain sort enter into the part–whole relation, the burden of argument should be on whoever thinks they must. Unless they provide an account of how the relevant objects enter into the part–whole relation, our presumption should be that they do not. From this stance, there may be a real obstacle for objects of a certain sort to enter into the part–whole relation. This will happen, in particular, when we find ourselves incapable to identify a suitable relation suitable to play the role of the part–whole relation on the relevant objects. When this happens, I would like to suggest, we should be reluctant to grant that the objects in question lie within the scope of atomistic extensional mereology. For it is unclear what would entitle us to assume that they do.

Sets illustrate this difficulty exemplarily. If one thinks that sets enter into the part–whole relation, then one must explain what it is for a set to be part of another. One attractive hypothesis at this point is that at least when restricted to non-empty sets, the part–whole relation coincides with the subset relation. One may perhaps motivate the restriction to non-empty sets by treating the empty set as an individual on the grounds that, like the rest of individuals, the empty set has no members.[50] What is important is that, on the present suggestion, sets have their subsets as parts:

Main Thesis: The parts of a set are all and only its subsets.[51]

The Main Thesis seems to conform well with ordinary speech. For as David Lewis reminds us in Lewis (1991) we often speak of the set of even integers, for example, as part of the set of integers. Or the set of women as part of the set of human beings. And in fact a cursory look at the history of the subject shows it is not uncommon for Georg Cantor, Ernst Zermelo and others to talk of sets as composed of parts and refer to the subsets of a set as parts of the set. Indeed, German still translates 'subset' as 'Teil' or 'Teilmenge', which are literal translations for 'part' and 'set part', respectively.[52] Unfortunately, this leads to violations of Unrestricted Composition. This is partly

[50] This is just David Lewis's treatment of the empty set in Lewis (1991).

[51] This is parallel to the Main Thesis stated in Lewis (1991), but, unlike Lewis, we need not make room for classes that are not sets. The restriction to non-empty sets is important because it helps Lewis block the consequence that singletons have parts.

[52] Thanks to Ignacio Jané here. Georg Cantor writes in Cantor (1955): 'By a 'part' or 'partial set' of a set M we mean any other set M_1 whose elements are also elements of M.' And, perhaps

because no set is the sum of all singletons. It is, after all, a theorem of ZFCSU that there is no universal set. One may reply that all this shows is that some singletons fail to have a set as their mereological sum. No matter, they still have a proper class, i.e., a class that fails to form a set, as their sum. Some sets, e.g., all singleton sets, have proper classes as their mereological sum. But the singletons are subclasses of the class of all singletons. Hence we should have phrased the Main Thesis in terms not of the subset relation but rather of the subclass relation, which is the relevant relation over the domain of classes, whether proper or improper.

The singletons are of course not alone in their failure to compose a set. If there are proper classes of the sort required to vindicate Unrestricted Composition, then they are of the size of the power domain of all sets. Unfortunately, orthodoxy tells us that there are no proper classes, and, ZFCSU, in particular, certainly makes no room for objects to play the role of the mereological sum of some singletons, which, in turn, fail to form a set.

There is a real obstacle to take sets to enter into the part–whole relation. But what should be made of our ordinary talk of some sets as part of other sets? It seems to me we speak metaphorically when we speak of subsets of a set as parts of the set. Even if the subset relation fails to satisfy all of the axioms of atomistic extensional mereology, the fact remains that there is a close analogy between its structure and the structure of the part–whole relation as governed by the axioms of mereology. This analogy is presumably what guides the metaphor. But we should not read too much into a mere analogy between the two relations, no matter how suggestive it may seem.

An important disanalogy between the part–whole relation and identity has now emerged. While all objects are self-identical and thus lie in the field of identity, not all objects lie in the field of the part–whole relation. I have suggested that sets, in particular, have no parts. Nor are they parts of themselves. So sets lie outside the field of the part–whole relation. Be as it may, this acknowledgment is no reason to discount all the other respects in which the part–whole relation may be analogous to identity, and, in particular, no reason to abandon moderate versions of Composition as Identity.

11.6 LAST RESORT OPTIONS

There is no denying that all of the options we have discussed are very costly. One might be tempted to avoid those costs by questioning one or more of the three background assumptions highlighted at the outset. One might (i) deny that there is an all-inclusive domain of all objects to begin with. Or one might (ii) deny that unrestricted quantification over an all-inclusive domain is ever available for purposes of absolutely general inquiry. Or, alternatively, one might (iii) question the legitimacy of plural or, otherwise, second-order quantification over an all-inclusive domain. The

more interestingly, Ernst Zermelo writes in Zermelo (1908): 'A subset of M that differs from 0 and M is called a *part* of M. The sets 0 and $\{a\}$ do not have parts.'

purpose of this section is to make explicit what would be required of such a response and to suggest it would be far more costly that the options considered above.

Let me begin with the first option. One might (i) deny that there is an all-inclusive domain of all objects to begin with. Without this assumption, the problem never gets off the ground. The difficulty with this move of course is that in the absence of independent support for the skeptical claim, the move will remain ad hoc and unmotivated.

There are in the literature two familiar motivations for the thought that there is no all-inclusive domain of all objects. One claims that the question of what objects there are and how they are individuated is relative to a conceptual scheme. One who asks what exactly is the cardinality of the universe is often under the spell of 'metaphysical realism' and thinks that the question makes sense even from an 'external' vantage point from which to assess her own conceptual scheme. Once one realizes the error, one is supposed to acknowledge that the question of what exactly is the cardinality of the universe is relative to a conceptual scheme. The answer 'a strongly inaccessible cardinal' is perfectly fine relative to the conceptual scheme of a proponent of ZFCSU; likewise, the answer 'a power-of-some cardinal κ' is fine relative to the conceptual scheme of a proponent of atomistic extensional mereology. From the fact that the two answers are incompatible, we might perhaps infer that the two conceptual schemes provide rival descriptions of the world. But since there is no conceptual-scheme-independent answer to the question of what exactly is the cardinality of the universe, none of them have more claim to be true than the other. And the existence of rival descriptions of the world is not, the suggestion ends, much of a reason to be alarmed.

Unfortunately, this will not do as a general response to our problem. For the difficulty arises only for a theorist who is tempted to adopt atomistic extensional mereology and ZFCSU. In the scenario under consideration, atomistic extensional mereology has as much right to be considered part of the theorist's conceptual scheme as ZFCSU. When she assesses the claim implied by ZFCSU that the universe is strongly inaccessible in size, she is not evaluating the answer to the question of what is the cardinality of the universe from an 'external' vantage point but rather from a conflicting theory which happens to be part of her conceptual scheme. Perhaps one will want to conclude that the combination of the two packages, atomistic extensional mereology and ZFCSU, is incoherent and may never be part of a legitimate conceptual framework. The realization of the incompatibility of the two still calls for a decision as to which package to abandon. But it is doubtful that one would then be better off than the 'metaphysical realist'.

The other line of response appeals to considerations of indefinite extensibility. The existence of an all-inclusive domain is now questioned on the grounds that some concepts are indefinitely extensible and thus yield a hierarchy of ever more inclusive extensions. The concept of set, in particular, is supposed to be a case in point. Because there is no maximal extension of the concept *set*, we are, the suggestion continues, not entitled to the claim that the cardinality of the universe of set theory is strongly inaccessible. Talk of the cardinality of the universe of set theory is misguided at best and, according to some friends of indefinite extensibility, outright incoherent.

If sets enter into the part–whole relation, the universe of atomistic extensional mereology, if it exists, will encompass the universe of set theory. Hence if we have reason to think there is no universe of set theory, we will have reason to think that there is no universe of atomistic extensional mereology and the question of what exactly is its cardinality will again be dismissed as incoherent.

But this will not help one unless one already has a use for indefinite extensibility, and it would seem unwarranted to take our problem to show, by itself, that there are indefinite extensible concepts. It seems to me that the question of whether there are indefinitely extensible concepts should be settled by independent considerations. But unless such considerations are in place, indefinite extensibility will not be of much help for present purposes.

Alternatively, one may choose to question either the assumption that (ii) unrestricted quantification is ever available for purposes of absolutely general inquiry or (iii) the legitimacy of plural or, otherwise, second-order quantification over an all-inclusive domain. But if it comes down to a choice between (ii) or (iii), one should probably prefer the first over the second. One had better, I think, to question the availability of unrestricted quantification over an all-inclusive domain. Since the development of a complete semantics for unrestricted quantification requires the flight into plural or, otherwise, second-order quantification, to question the availability of such resources without thereby questioning the availability of unrestricted quantification over an all-inclusive domain would place one into a very uncomfortable position. A philosopher in this position would acknowledge the phenomenon of unrestricted quantification without the benefit of semantic reflection on our language.

We are left with (ii) or the rejection of the availability of unrestricted quantification over an all-inclusive domain. This availability could be questioned on at least two different grounds. One might suggest that our quantifiers are invariably subject to subtle contextual restrictions which prevent them from ranging over an all-inclusive domain of all objects. Or, alternatively, one might hold that our quantifiers are semantically ambiguous and thus subject to some sort of systematic ambiguity akin to Russell's typical ambiguity. Unfortunately, by itself, (ii) will not do as a response to our conflicts.[53] What we learn from the argument used to establish the incompatibility of (1) and (2) and (3) and (4) is that there is no single domain over which the quantifiers used in the formulation of ZFCSU and atomistic extensional mereology range. For such a domain would have to be both strongly inaccessible and power-of-and-strongly inaccessible, which is impossible. This will remain the case even if all our quantifiers are systematically restricted by context or otherwise. And the point will remain even if our quantifiers happen to be systematically ambiguous. So for the strategy under consideration to succeed it must be accompanied by some guarantee that the quantifiers used in the formulation of each package never range over one and the same domain.

But how is such a guarantee to be provided? Perhaps one might argue that, by some very subtle mechanism, context invariably manages to enforce different restrictions

[53] I am indebted to Daniel Nolan and Stephen Yablo here.

on the quantifiers used in the formulation of each package. But unless some account of the relevant mechanism is provided, the present response will be incomplete at best. Moreover, one would in addition face very difficult questions when pressed on the question of what to make of contexts or sentences in which our quantifiers are explicitly required to range over both sets and parts as with the sentence 'All sets have sets as parts.'

More promising, it seems to me, would be to suggest that, despite appearances to the contrary, the quantifiers used in each case are hopelessly ambiguous. We might begin with Zermelo's observation in Zermelo (1930) that there is a well-ordered sequence of universes of ZFCSU, where each universe is strictly more inclusive than its predecessor. But no matter how much we insist on the absence of explicit or otherwise contextual restrictions, we find that nothing in the semantic value of our quantifiers permits us to single out one universe over the others as the intended universe of set theory. A similar suggestion might be made on behalf of atomistic extensional mereology. We know this. No model of ZFCSU is a model of atomistic extensional mereology. But we may take advantage of the fact that the models of ZFCSU are lined up in a well-ordered progression of ever more inclusive universes in order to specify a procedure that will take us from certain models of ZFCSU to models of atomistic extensional mereology. The result will be a progression of ever more inclusive models of atomistic extensional mereology. Our procedure will begin with a model of ZFCSU whose individuals make up a model of atomistic extensional mereology and leave the interpretation of the part–whole relation on individuals unchanged. Then extend the universe of ZFCSU to include all proper classes of items in the initial universe. The proper classes in question are, in fact, sets in the next model in the progression of models of ZFCSU. To obtain a model of atomistic extensional mereology, we will now have to interpret the part–whole relation on sets to apply to a pair of non-empty sets just in case the first is a subset of the second. We may, if we want, follow David Lewis in Lewis (1991) and treat the empty set as the mereological sum of all individuals. The result will be a model of atomistic extensional mereology, albeit not of ZFCSU. We are left with a progression of models of atomistic extensional mereology that mirrors the progression of models of ZFCSU whose individuals make up a model of atomistic extensional mereology. But the suggestion continues, that nothing in the semantic value of our quantifier allows us to single out one universe over the others as the intended universe of atomistic extensional mereology. All we know for sure is that the quantifiers used in the formulation of each package may not simultaneously range over a single domain. That, however, should not be a reason for concern.

But much like before, by itself, the present conflict is not enough to motivate the view that our quantifiers are hopelessly ambiguous. It seems to me that the question of whether they are should be settled by independent considerations. But unless such considerations are in place, typical ambiguity will not be of much help for present purposes.

There is one additional respect on which the responses discussed in this last section are very costly. For they all force us to deny that absolute generality is ever attainable.

But most philosophical inquiry and ontology, in particular, would seem to aim for absolute generality. If our quantifiers are semantically ambiguous, for example, then we will never in a position to unequivocally state an ontological hypothesis such as the view that there are no merely possible objects. One would have expected the truth value of this hypothesis to be settled once and for all. But to declare unrestricted quantification semantically indeterminate undermines this expectation.

Other responses mentioned in this section undermine the prospects of absolute generality in other ways. But my own inclination is to pay some of the costs incurred in by other solutions to our problem in exchange for absolute generality. I am inclined, in particular, to take the conflicts discussed in this paper to show that we must proceed with caution in the formulation of absolutely general theories. We should be aware of the fact that they may impose serious constraints on the size of the universe and, when a conflict arises, be prepared to either modify some of the absolutely general theories we are tempted to accept or, in some cases, abandon the presumption of absolute generality for some of them.

REFERENCES

Beall, J., (ed.) (2003) *Liars and Heaps*, Oxford University Press, Oxford.

Boolos, G. (1984) 'To Be is to Be a Value of a Variable (or to be Some Values of Some Variables)', *The Journal of Philosophy* 81, 430–49. Reprinted in Boolos (1998).

____ (1989) 'Iteration Again', *Philosophical Topics* 17, 5–21. Reprinted in Boolos (1998).

____ (1998) *Logic, Logic and Logic*, Harvard University Press, Cambridge, MA.

Burgess, J. (2004) 'E Pluribus Unum: Plural Logic and Set Theory', *Philosophia Mathematica* (3) 12, 193–221.

Butts, R. E., and J. Hintikka, (eds.) (1977) *Logic, Foundations of Mathematics, and Computability Theory*, Reidel, Dordrecht.

Cantor, G. (1955) *Contributions to the Founding of the Theory of Transfinite Numbers*, Dover, New York, NY.

Dales, H. G., and G. Oliveri, (eds.) (1998) *Truth in Mathematics*, Oxford University Press, Oxford.

Field, H. (1998) 'Which Undecidable Mathematical Sentences have Determinate Truth Values?' In Dales and Oliveri (1998). Reprinted in Field (2001).

____ (2001) *Truth and the Absence of Fact*, Oxford University Press, Oxford.

Fine, K. (1995) 'Ontological Dependence', *Proceedings of the Aristotelian Society* 95, 267–290.

____ (2002) *The Limits of Abstraction*, Oxford University Press, Oxford.

____ (2005) 'Replies', *Philosophical Studies* 122, 367–95. 'Symposium Discussion: Kit Fine. *The Limits of Abstraction*.

Glanzberg, M. (2004) 'Quantification and Realism', *Philosophy and Phenomenological Research* 69, 541–572.

Hazen, A. P. (2004) 'Hypergunk', *The Monist* 87:3, 322–38.

Koppelberg, S. (1981) 'General Theory of Boolean Algebras', in Monk (1989).

Lavine, S. (1994) *Understanding the Infinite*, Harvard University Press, Cambridge, MA.

Lewis, D. (1991) *Parts of Classes*, Blackwell, Oxford.

McGee, V. (1997) 'How We Learn Mathematical Language', *Philosophical Review* 106, 35–68.

Monk, D. (1989) *Handbook of Boolean Algebras*, vol. 1, North Holland, Amsterdam.

Parsons, C. (1974) 'Sets and Classes', Noûs 8, 1–12. Reprinted in Parsons (1983).

—— (1977) 'What Is the Iterative Conception of Set?', in Butts and Hintikka (1977). Reprinted in Parsons (1983).

—— (1983) *Mathematics in Philosophy*, Cornell University Press, Ithaca, NY.

Potter, M. (2004) *Set Theory and Its Philosophy*, Oxford University Press, Oxford.

Putnam, H. (1980) 'Models and Reality', *The Journal of Symbolic Logic* 45:3, 464–82.

Quine, W. V. (1968) 'Ontological Relativity', *Journal of Philosophy* 65, 185–212. Reprinted in Quine (1969).

—— (1969) *Ontological Relativity and Other Essays*, Columbia University Press, NY.

Rayo, A. (2003) 'When Does "Everything" Mean Everything?' Analysis 63, 100–6.

—— and G. Uzquiano (1999) 'Toward a Theory of Second-Order Consequence', *The Notre Dame Journal of Formal Logic* 40, 315–25.

—— and T. Williamson (2003) 'A Completeness Theorem for Unrestricted First-Order Languages', 331–356, in Beall (2003).

Rosen, G. (1995) 'Armstrong on Classes as States of Affairs', *Australasian Journal of Philosophy* 73:4, 613–25.

Shapiro, S. (1991) *Foundations Without Foundationalism: A Case for Second-Order Logic*, Clarendon Press, Oxford.

—— (2003) 'All Sets Great and Small: And I Do Mean ALL', *Philosophical Perspectives* 17:1, 467–90.

—— (2005) 'Sets and Abstracts', *Philosophical Studies* 122:3, 315–32, in Symposium Discussion: Kit Fine *The Limits of Abstraction.*

Sider, T. (forthcoming) 'Parthood', *The Philosophical Review.*

Tarski, A. (1929) 'Foundations of the Geometry of Solids', 24–9, in Alfred Tarski, *Logic, Semantics and Meta-Mathematics.*

—— (1935) 'On the Foundations of the Boolean Algebra', 320–41, in Alfred Tarski, *Logic, Semantics and Meta-Mathematics.*

Uzquiano, G. (2002) 'Categoricity Theorems and Conceptions of Set', *The Journal of Philosophical Logic* 31:2, 181–96.

—— (2006) 'The Price of Universality', *Philosophical Studies* 129, 137–69.

Van Heijenoort, J., (ed.) (1967) *From Frege to Gödel*, Harvard University Press, Cambridge, MA.

Williamson, T. (2003) 'Everything,' *Philosophical Perspectives* 17:1, 415–65.

Zermelo, E. (1908) 'Untersuchungen über die Grundlagen der Mengenlehre I,' *Mathematische Annalen* 65, 261–81. English translation by Stefan Bauer-Mengelberg, 'Investigations in the Foundations of Set Theory I', in Van Heijenoort (1967).

—— (1930) 'Über Grenzzahlen und Mengenbereiche: Neue Untersuchungen über die Grundlagen der Mengenlehre', *Fundamenta Mathematicae* 16, 29–47.

Zimmerman, D. (1996) 'Could Extended Objects Be Made of Simple Parts? An Argument for Atomless Gunk', *Philosophy and Phenomenological Research* 56, 1–29.

12

Is it too much to Ask, to Ask for Everything?

Alan Weir

Most of the time our quantifications generalize over a restricted domain. Thus in the last sentence, 'most of the time' is arguably not a generalization over all times in the history of the universe but is restricted to a sub-group of times, those at which humans exist and utter quantified phrases and sentences, say. Indeed the example illustrates the point that quantificational phrases often carry an explicit restriction with them: 'some people', 'all dogs'. Even then, context usually restricts to a sub-domain of the class specified by the count noun. Although teenagers like to have fun by being, they mistakenly think, overly literal—'Everyone is tired, let's get to bed': 'everyone: you mean every person in the entire universe?'—competent language users have to be sensitive to context virtually all the time.

But is it *always* the case that generalization is over a restricted domain? On the face of it, to claim this is paradoxical. If we say:

(1) For every generalization and every domain D, if D is a domain over which the generalization ranges, D is restricted; that is, there are some things x which do not belong to D.

what do the quantifiers in (1) range over? Not everything, if (1) is correct. But if 'every generalization' does not include in its scope all generalizations then (1) is compatible with some generalizations being unrestricted. If the variable D does not range over all domains, then perhaps some domains are unrestricted, notwithstanding what (1) says. If these two quantifiers range over all generalizations and all domains, respectively, consider the union of the domain range which, by assumption, contains all the domains. This certainly seems to be a totality we can consider. If we substitute this totality, call it $\bigcup$D, for D then we get 'there are some things x which do not belong to $\bigcup$D' which is false because the quantifier 'there are some things x' ranges over items in $\bigcup$D and there is nothing in $\bigcup$D which does not belong to it.[1]

Like others in this debate, I will call the proponent of the problematic sentence (1) the 'relativist', because she believes *all* generalization is relative to a non-universal domain or context, and I will call her opponent the absolutist. The most popular response by relativists to the problem just adumbrated (indeed it is hard to think

Thanks for advice and comments on an earlier draft to the editors, to Kit Fine, Christopher McKnight, and Stewart Shapiro, with especial thanks for detailed comments which forced some needed clarification to Agustín Rayo.

[1] Cf. David Lewis (1991), p. 20, Vann McGee (1997), p. 48, Timothy Williamson (2003).

of any other plausible alternatives) is to appeal to some sort of schematic generality or systematic ambiguity.[2] How does this help? If, in a sentence such as $\varphi x \rightarrow \psi x$, the variable x is interpreted schematically then, so 'schemers' tell us, it must not be thought of as elliptical for a generalization of the form $\forall x(\varphi x \rightarrow \psi x)$ read as, [all φs are ψs]. The sentence on its own cannot be used to make any assertion but should be thought of as essentially gappy. A notation such as $\varphi(\,) \rightarrow \psi(\,)$ perhaps brings out the point better. We interpret a schema by specifying a class of substitution instances for a language L for which we have already given a full interpretation. The schema is correct in a given interpretation of L iff all sentences of the form $\varphi(\mathbf{t}) \rightarrow \psi(\mathbf{t})$ are true in L, where **t** belongs to the appropriate substitution class. Thus the axiom schema of separation (or subsets schema) of set theory:

$$\forall x \exists y \forall z (z \in y \leftrightarrow (z \in x \,\&\, (\,)z))$$

is correct just in case for all one-place formulae with free variable z in our set-theoretic language, the result of substituting any such formula for $(\,)z$ in the above is true in L.

The idea then is that we interpret D in (1) as a schematic variable. But if we imagine our informal metalanguage has been formalized as a language ML we run back into the same problems. To claim that (1) is correct is to claim that every appropriate substitution for D in (1) is true in ML. But when the relativist steps back and interprets the metalanguage ML in which she makes her claims, the range R of its variables will include all domains, including R itself, and when we substitute R for D we get the claim that

there are some things x which do not belong to R

which is false in ML.

The relativist is well aware that it is a fatal mistake to try to interpret schematic readings of claims such as (1) in a non-schematic metalanguage: we must go schematic 'all the way up'. When we take the scare-quotes away and try to be more literal, appeal will be made to some hierarchies: an 'open-ended sequence' of substitution classes and a hierarchy of metalanguages generated by the expansion of the class of substitution terms for the schematic variable. What manner of beasts are the 'sequence' of substitution classes and the 'hierarchy'? Are they set-theoretic animals? Surely not, else it seems inevitable we could give a non-schematic account of them which would yield a non-schematic generalization over all domains. But if not, we need to know more about them. Moreover if the relativist really does go schematic 'all the way up' then she will never say anything assessable as true or false. She will be in the position of someone always making utterances like $\varphi(\,) \rightarrow \psi(\,)$ but counselling us never to take these as elliptical for [every φ is a ψ].

[2] Cf. Geoffrey Hellman, 'Against "Absolutely Everything"!' and Shaughan Lavine, 'Something about Everything', both in this volume. This tradition goes back to Charles Parsons (1974) and a similar line is also pursued re. semantic paradoxes by Tyler Burge (1979). However a very different and original relativist response is developed by Kit Fine in this volume; in my view, his response presupposes a radically anti-realist interpretation of the ontology of mathematics but I cannot expand on this here.

But I will not follow the dialectic with the relativist any further. In my view, Timothy Williamson in his 'Everything' (2003) has already given us a very detailed and powerful critique of relativism. If nothing else, Williamson shows us that it is a highly problematic and paradoxical, if not downright incoherent, position. Why on earth, then, would any philosopher want to adopt it? Why make such a paradoxical claim? As so often, philosophers have been driven from one paradox into the arms of another. Because of its great simplicity and power, set theory has been the preferred way to do formal semantics. The idealized languages which some theorists investigate with a view to shedding light on natural languages are interpreted by set-theoretic *models* in which generalization is over a domain (or domains) and each such domain is in turn a set. Thus we might interpret a formalized version of set theory itself, say first-order ZFC, by taking its variables to range over a domain which consists of inaccessibly many objects which are, or are to play the role of, the sets. But it is a theorem of ZFC and related set theories that there is no universal set. If there were a set **u** with $\forall y(y \in \mathbf{u})$ then by the following instantiation of the subsets axiom scheme:

$$\exists y \forall z(z \in y \leftrightarrow (z \in \mathbf{u} \,\&\, z \notin z))$$

we would quickly prove the existence of the Russell set **r** with $\mathbf{r} \in \mathbf{r} \leftrightarrow \mathbf{r} \notin \mathbf{r}$ and just as quickly prove, in classical and many other logics, a contradiction.[3] So there cannot be a universal domain, if domains are sets.

Although one might not adopt set-theory as a framework for formal semantics—category theory or a theory of properties might be pressed into service instead, among other alternatives—the problem seems quite general. There is no universal *domain*, no *object* which can play the role of a range for quantifiers in a systematic semantic theory and to which everything belongs, including the universal domain itself.[4]

We seem to be in Kantian territory here: we have highly plausible arguments in favour, on the one hand, of the proposition that there can be no unrestricted quantification and, on the other, of the proposition that there must be such quantification. Perhaps a presupposition common to both opposing sides is false; abandon it and a solution to the antinomy will emerge. I am going to suggest that something along those lines might indeed be what is going on. In the next two sections I look at some extant forms of absolutism, first what I will call 'domain-free' absolutism, next domain-based absolutism. I reject both but come down in favour of a heterodox domain-based absolutism; the remaining sections sketch the main elements of it.

12.1 ABSOLUTISM: DOMAIN-FREE SEMANTICS

There is a strong and well-argued tradition—Richard Cartwright's 'Speaking of Everything' (1994) provides an early and influential statement—which argues that

[3] So quickly that many writers treat a biconditional of the form $p \leftrightarrow\sim p$ as itself a contradiction.

[4] See Williamson's generalization (2003, p. 426) of Russell's paradox which makes no appeal to set theory but rests mainly on the assumption that interpretations are objects.

interpretations, including interpretations of quantificational languages with unrestricted quantification, need not be based on domains. I will understand, in what follows, 'domains' to be objects, indeed objects which satisfy a principle of comprehension. That is, for each domain D there is some predicate φ of current English (or 'scientific English') such that something belongs to D iff it satisfies the predicate φ. In Cartwright's view, there need be no 'domain', no 'range', no 'totality' over which the variables generalize. How can this be? Do we not need domains in order to achieve the goals for which the formalization of language is a means?

What goals are these? One aim is to give a rigorous account of logical consequence so that we can investigate its properties (and, as it happens, turn up interesting and surprising facts about expressibility, computability and so on). Our informal notion of consequence is that premises Δ entail a conclusion C just in case there is no possibility of all the premises being true but C false; in any possible situation in which all the premises are true, the conclusion is. In pursuit of rigor, we replace the murky notion of possibility with that of a model and say that in all models in which all of Δ are true, C is true (equivalently, in classical bivalent semantics, in any model in which C is false, one of Δ is false). But models are set-theoretic entities containing domains and so, in generalizing over models, we generalize over domains.

Another goal is to give a systematic account of the meaning of important logical notions such as 'every'. We semi-formalize some mathematical English into a sentence such as 'for every number x there is some number y with $x < y$'. Our account of truth for generalizations entails that this universal generalization is true relative to an assignment σ to variables just in case for every x-variant assignment $\sigma(x/\alpha)$ like σ except, at most, that it assigns α from the domain D to x, the open sentence ⌜there is some number y such that $x < y$⌝ is true relative to $\sigma(x/\alpha)$. How can we give such an account unless the definition of truth generalizes to truth relative to all variant assignments? Can we do this without domains?

The answer seems to be yes. George Boolos (1985) developed an ingenious alternative.[5] A slight variant of his idea is that of an *interpretative relation* R. This relates predicate and variable terms to objects subject to the requirement that the relation must be a function when restricted to singular terms. For a singular term **t**, we never have R(**t**, α) and R(**t**,β) holding with $\alpha \neq \beta$. Boolos showed how to define a notion of truth for a sentence P relative to the relation R–True(R, P)–without any substantive use of set-theory. For particular sub-languages we can reinstate our old set-theoretic ways of looking at things: the range of the relation R is just the domain of the model, the set $\{x\text{: R}(\text{F},x)\}$ is just the extension of the predicate term F. But there is no reason to think we can, or need to, do this in general. In particular, when we interpret a language with unrestricted quantification, the interpretative relation R will have no range. There is no domain. Yet we can still define consequence, e.g. by something like

$$\forall \text{R}(\forall s(s \in \Delta \rightarrow \text{True}(\text{R}, s)) \rightarrow \text{True}(\text{R, C})).$$

[5] For further elaboration see e.g. Rayo and Uzquiano (1999), Rayo and Williamson (2003), and Williamson (2003).

An obvious problem arises. Thus far I have been assuming languages are first-order but now we are utilizing higher-order quantification to give a semantics for first-order language. Yet higher-order logic is still under a cloud in some quarters; and even if we accept it we have now incurred an obligation to explain its semantics.[6]

Two different types of worry about higher-order quantification must be distinguished. One concerns the expressive power of second-order languages. On 'standard' interpretations, second-order logical consequence, semantically defined, is not recursively axiomatizable; no program will churn out all and only the sequents in which the antecedent set logically entails the conclusion. But I have no worries about this recursive unmanageability, which after all is shared by many systems other than second-order logic. The distinctive worry, relevant to our current concerns, is as follows. A natural way to explain what

$$\forall R(\forall s(s \in \Delta \rightarrow \text{True}(R, s)) \rightarrow \text{True}(R, C))$$

means is that it means that for all relations R, if all sentences s in Δ are such that True(R,s) then True(R, C). Similarly second-order mathematical induction:

$$\forall X \forall x((X0 \;\&\; \forall y(Xy \rightarrow X(Sy))) \rightarrow Xx)$$

might be glossed, in the context of a first-order domain of numbers as: for all properties P, if zero has P and the successor of any number which has P also instantiates P then every number instantiates P. But a generalization of the form

all properties P such that . . . P . . . are such that _P_

is grammatically of the same type as

all numbers *n* such that . . . *n* . . . are such that _*n*_.

Higher-order quantification seems to be just quantification over a restricted subdomain, a subset of a universal domain of 'entities'; this universal domain includes relations, properties and objects (that is, particulars–entities which have no instances). The denial that this all-inclusive, cross-categorical domain exists would seem to be just a special case of the relativist denial of unrestricted quantification, with the same paradoxical consequences. Thus:

[6] Boolos interpreted the higher-order quantification as plural quantification (1984). It may be contested whether plural quantification really is higher-order but all that really matters for current purposes is that it is not first-order quantification and that, in the hierarchy of metalanguages to be considered below, plural quantification has to be explicated in turn by locutions which cannot be glossed as English plural quantification. For more on the limitations of plural quantification see Weir (1998*a*), §6 and Williamson (2003), §9, pp. 455ff. My own view is that ordinary English plural quantification—'some dogs are black'—is a pre-theoretical, vague version of 'at least *n* dogs are black' where the lower-bound cut-off point for *n* which turns the plural generalization from false to borderline true varies with context but is always greater than one. The readings which do the work for Boolos—'some critics admire only each other' etc.—seem to me most naturally read as quantification over 'Aristotelian' properties, i.e. instantiated properties. But nothing hinges on whether I am right on this point.

A property like having mass one gram and an object like the moon stand in no relation *Rxy* whatsoever; thus they do not both belong to the same domain which variables *x* and *y* range over.

seems to be a self-stultifying claim in much the same way that the claim that all quantification is restricted is.[7]

If we accept, however, that higher-order quantification is just one sort in a multi-sorted system of quantification, one sub-domain of a wider overall domain, then, however construed, it is not going to enable us to interpret languages as having unrestricted quantification. Not unless we make some highly unorthodox moves in logic and set theory, at any rate. For Cantor's theorem, which is provable in pure second-order logic,[8] shows us that if, for every subset of the domain of individuals U, there corresponds an element in the range of the second-order quantifiers (and no two subsets of U correspond to the same element of the quantifier range) then U cannot be the entire universe. This assumption about the range of the second-order quantifiers is standard, for 'standard' second-order logic. Hence our individual quantifiers do not range over absolutely everything; at least some of the 'properties' cannot also be in the first-order domain so it does not cover all the entities one can generalize over.

Williamson's answer is not to cling to the anchor in a shipwreck but rather to hold his higher-order nerve (2003, p. 455). He does not seek to explicate higher-order quantification metalinguistically by using first-order quantification but instead treats it as *sui generis*. Or rather he treats it as belonging to a hierarchy of kinds, second-order quantification interpreted by third-order, third-order by fourth-order and so on. I have raised qualms about the conceptual framework in terms of which one develops this hierarchy elsewhere (1998*a*, §8).

But suppose we rest content for the moment with a broadly hierarchical position. Williamson still has the problem of explaining what higher-order quantification means, if we are not to gloss it as first-order multi-sorted quantification over sub-domains of the domain of individuals. His answer[9] is firstly to adopt a fragmented Fregean ontology, with mutually exclusive categories of property and object[10] and then to argue that

It is quite within the spirit of Frege's philosophy to insist that one can state matters perspicuously only in a formal language such as his *begriffsschrift*. In that notation (without Basic Law V), quantification into predicate position is simply incommensurable with quantification into name position; (p. 458)

continuing (p. 459):

[7] Frege's notorious troubles with 'the concept horse' spring to mind here but bring in additional issues, concerning whether the property/object distinction can be given a purely syntactic formulation, which I do not intend to address.

[8] Shapiro (1991), pp. 103–4.

[9] For a similar answer, see also Rayo (this volume), especially Section 9.5.

[10] Frege's division was actually between functions and objects; the semantic value of predicates being special functions which map objects to truth values. The choice of *Begriff*, 'concept', as the term for such functions is unfortunate for anyone who is a realist about properties, that is, who sharply distinguishes mind-independent properties from linguistic and psycho-semantic items such as predicates and concepts.

Perhaps no reading in a natural language of quantification into predicate position is wholly satisfactory. If so, that does not show that something is wrong with quantification into predicate position, for it may reflect an expressive inadequacy in natural languages. We may have to learn second-order languages by the direct method, not by translating them into a language with which we are already familiar.

Now it is certainly true that we can expand natural language by the incorporation of concepts and locutions which had been deliberately introduced into artificial languages. If one looks at proofs in mathematics books, for example, (as opposed to print-outs of computer-generated proofs) they are very rarely fully formal but are written in natural language with a sprinkling not only of logical symbols but also of logical syntax:

$$\forall x,\ \text{if } x \text{ is such that } \exists y, x \in y \text{ then } \ldots$$

and so on. Proofs are written in 'Loglish', as Montague put it; the formal ideas augment English.

Of course when introducing tyros to notions such as the universal quantifier, we explain its meaning in a natural language such as English or some other. We might, for example, explain the role of bound variables by noting the functional similarities with anaphoric pronouns and have a stab at explaining multiple quantification using those more unnatural parts of English (e.g. lawyers' English, spoken as it is by unnatural people) where something like it is needed.[11] But even in this case the formal symbols are no mere codes or abbreviations for pre-existing natural language locutions.

But although Williamson is clearly right on this in the general case, we do, nonetheless, gloss a sentence such as $\forall x(x \in \omega \rightarrow \exists y(y \in \omega \ \& \ x \in y))$ by ⌜for all sets x, if x belongs to ω then there is a set y in ω to which x belongs⌝ or something similar. It is essential to the role which $\forall$ plays when it is used in informal natural language proofs that it gets that gloss.[12] The conceptual innovation Frege, Peirce and Schröder made was to extract from arbitrary sentences multiple-gap open sentences; to see in $(\mathbf{m} \in \omega \ \& \ \mathbf{n} \in \mathbf{m})$ a pattern which would come to be represented in lambda notation as $\lambda xy(y \in \omega \ \& \ x \in y)$, thus as a closed relational predicate; or by $\lambda y(y \in \omega \ \& \ x \in y)$ hence as an open one-place predicate to which a quantifier such as $\exists$ can be applied to yield $\exists[\lambda y(y \in \omega \ \& \ x \in y)]$.

But if we are not to interpret higher-order quantification by glosses such as 'for all properties P', can they play the role we wish them to play in semantics? If, for example:

$$\Pi R(\forall s(s \in \Delta \rightarrow \mathrm{True}(R, s)) \rightarrow \mathrm{True}(R, C))$$

is offered as a formal surrogate for 'in any possible situation in which all of Δ are true, C is true', how can it play this role if we are explicitly warned not to construe ΠR as [for any relation R] or anything along those lines. One might look to analogy,

[11] Cf. George Boolos (1985), pp. 165–6.

[12] Some may reject the gloss of $\forall$ as 'for all' and $\exists$ as 'for some' on free logic grounds; if so, assume the rules which govern the quantifiers are amended in your favoured free logic fashion.

as theists often do when they tell us that 'good' is correctly applicable to God not in a univocal way, as applied to a good human, nor in an equivocal way, as a pun in bad taste, but rather analogically. The formal analogies, however, between the proof theory for Π and the proof theory for first-order ∀ are not sufficient. We often teach the meaning of ∀ by exploiting the formal analogies between, on the one hand, ∀I and ∀E and, on the other, *n*-ary &I and &E for multiple conjunction (P_1 & P_2 . . . & P_n) but these analogies do not mean that finite conjunction can play the role of the universal quantifier in formalising ideas like 'all numbers have a unique prime factorization'. The matter does not admit of conclusive adjudication but I submit that if higher-order quantification is definitely not to be construed along the lines of 'for all properties P' and so on then it is very unclear how it can play a role in explicating logical consequence and the semantics for ordinary quantification in which we generalize over interpretative relations.

12.2 ABSOLUTISM: DOMAIN-BASED SEMANTICS

What has motivated domain-free semantics is surely the feeling that the set-theoretic paradoxes render impossible a domain-based account of unrestricted quantification. True, there are set theories which admit a universal set: Quine's NF and ML, the theories of Church, Mitchell and Oberschelp (1973),[13] for example—all theories which can be developed within classical logic. But they block paradox by restricting the subsets axiom. As Williamson points out (2003, pp. 425–6), thus crippled the theories seem incapable of providing an adequate account of ordinary restricted quantification which can be over domains specified by any arbitrary condition expressible in our language, or of logical consequence interpreted as truth under arbitrary substitutions of meaningful terms for simple terms. One could reply that the subsets axioms itself is incoherent or mathematically impossible but this is hugely implausible.

Perhaps the only domain-based picture which has been taken seriously as a foundation for a semantics of unrestricted quantification is the Dummettian notion, developed from ideas of Russell, of indefinite extensibility.[14] An interpreted predicate—'set', 'ordinal', 'object', as used in English, say—is indefinitely extensible iff given any *definite* totality of items satisfying the predicate, a new object not in that totality but satisfying the predicate can be generated. Clearly the theory of sets presupposed here is not naïve set theory, for according to naïve set theory, for any predicate P there is a set $S = \{x\colon Px\}$ whose members are all and only the individuals which satisfy the predicate.

I have expressed the doctrine in terms of *definite* totalities but Dummett often talks also of *indefinite ones*.[15] It seems that to every predicate P (including indefinitely extensible ones) there corresponds a unique indefinite totality. For indefinitely

[13] For Church and Mitchell, see T. E. Forster (1992), especially chapter 4.

[14] For indefinite extensibility see Dummett (1991), p. 317 especially footnote 5. See also 'The Philosophical Significance of Gödel's Theorem', in Dummett (1978) especially pp. 194–7 and Dummett (1981), pp. 531–3; (1993), pp. 441–3, 454–5.

[15] Dummett (1981), p. 516; (1991), p. 316.

extensible P, we may associate a growing sequence of definite totalities, each a more accurate approximation to the predicate's extension but none fully adequate; the limit point of this sequence, the extension itself, is an indefinite totality. According to Dummett, intuitionist, not classical logic is the right logic to use when quantifying over such domains.

What, though, are such limits of the sequence of ever more closely approximating partial extensions but naïve sets, or perhaps naïve properties, satisfying naïve comprehension: x belongs to the indefinite totality corresponding to property P iff x is a P? If so, then a move merely to intuitionist logic is not radical enough since naïve comprehension is inconsistent in intuitionist as well as in classical logic. Alternatively when Dummett describes indefinite totalities as 'illegitimate totalities' (1981, p. 529) he may mean that there is no such totality, no such object at all; what is indefinitely extensible is the concept or interpreted predicate and the only extensions which are assigned to it are 'definite' sets, albeit in a sequence of 'hazy' length (cf. 1991, pp. 316–17, see also 1994, p. 248). Leaving aside worries about what the singular term 'length' can refer to here, other than a naïve, universe-sized ordinal,[16] development of Dummett's idea in this direction would seem to involve eschewing domain-based semantics for the domain-free version we have just been discussing.

12.3 RESOLUTION: GOING NAÏVE

Relativist and absolutist approaches to quantification, whether domain-free or else based on domains seem each and all to run into contradictions or become self-stultifying. The only approach scouted which has not done so is a domain-based approach in which domains are naïve or 'indefinite' totalities. An assumption underlying virtually all the recent discussions, however, is that this approach is definitely ruled out since it, most clearly of all, runs into contradiction; doesn't the Russell paradox show this? This is the assumption which I believe must be challenged. Of course the package of classical logic, which we can divide into classical operational rules and classical structural rules, taken together with naïve set theory is, as Russell (and Zermelo) showed, inconsistent and trivial. To be more precise, then, the assumption which should be challenged is that the fault lies with the set theory rather than with the logic. Given the intuitive plausibility of the classical operational rules, the most likely other culprit is the classical structural rules. [17]

This radical line has thus far only been developed to any significant extent by Graham Priest (1987), and other dialetheists. Priest believes that some

[16] For this point see my (1998*b*), §IIIi.

[17] It is true that the distinction between operational and structural rules is not clear-cut and can be effected in different ways in different proof architectures but it is, I would argue, clear enough for the purposes to which I wish to put it here. Thus in Gentzen–Prawitz natural deduction systems, one-step moves such as &I and &E are operational rules; by contrast, Cut or Transitivity, is a structural rule. This is a rule which says, for example, that a structure which consists of proof of A from Δ and one B from Γ and finishes with an extension to A&B by &I is itself also a proof from premises $\Delta \cup \Gamma$.

contradictions are true and in some cases is prepared to embrace contradictory theories, such as he believes naïve set theory to be. He has, of course, to work with a paraconsistent logic in which contradictions do not trivialise the theory. Dialetheists seek to gain converts by speaking to the unconverted in a gentile tongue, for example ZFC in a background of classical logic, showing from within that background that naïve set theory in a paraconsistent logic such as LP is not trivial. But despite rising interest in dialetheism most philosophers remain unconverted, refusing to accept that there can be true contradictions. Now I too am of that number, though I think dialetheism is a thought-provoking position which deserves serious consideration.[18] Given the choice between the difficulties which relativism, domain-free absolutism and 'non-naïve' domain-based absolutism run into on the one hand, and embracing true contradictions on the other, most philosophers, myself included, would settle for one of the former three options. What I will attempt to do in the remainder of this piece is sketch a different way to 'go naïve', a way which does not involve embracing true contradictions.

How should we compare the different approaches in this area, for example domain-free with domain-based absolutism? Among the desiderata for a comprehensive semantics of quantification for a language L, I would include the following:

(i) an account of logical consequence for L inside L;

(ii) a naïve satisfaction predicate L expressible within L;

(iii) a soundness proof for L from within L;

(iv) a recursive explication of how the semantic value of complex expressions, such as quantifications, depends on those of their parts;

(v) a conditional, in terms of which key equivalences can be expressed, which satisfies the deduction theorem: if Δ, A $\models$ B then $\Delta \models$ A $\rightarrow$ B;

(vi) accommodation of a universal domain—this being an *object* in the universal domain to which all members of the domain, including itself, belong to;

(vii) a reassuring validation that the whole package is coherent via the provision of a model from within some comfortable, familiar theory such as ZFC.

The main motivation for the first three criteria is idea that hierarchical approaches to the paradoxes merely engender super-paradoxes at a different level (see Weir, 1998a, Priest, 1987). Clause (iv) is what we would expect from any compositional semantics whilst (v), in my view, has strong independent motivation. The sixth clause is motivated by the severe problems I have urged attend both relativism and domain-free absolutism whilst the seventh seems to speak for itself.

But perhaps not. Certainly it is too much to ask, if we ask for all of (i) to (vii). Moreover I would target (vii) as first to be thrown out the balloon. If one is convinced by the anti-hierarchical considerations and thinks there is something rotten in the foundations of ZF-type theories, why expect them to cohere with a proposed alternative? But if that is right, the only fully satisfactory way to go is to adopt the

[18] See my 'There are no true contradictions' (2004).

proposed non-classical logic and naïve set theory in the informal metatheory. Since, however, that would be a task way beyond the confines of this paper I will also try to speak to the Gentiles. I will develop an approximation to a fully satisfactory position, working with a naïve theory of properties to play the role of domains, rather than full naïve set theory, and show it consistent from within a conventional classical background.

As one ought to expect, this 'naïve recapture', this attempt to get at a naïve perspective from within the jaded classical framework, will not in the final result give us all of (i) to (vi). I will return at the end to consideration of how much we have achieved, how it compares with rival perspectives, especially domain-free absolutism, and what this all says about the Kantian predicament we seem to find ourselves in.

12.4 SYNTAX AND SOME SEMANTICS

The obvious direction to look, if one is wanting to approximate naïve semantics in a framework of standard set theory and classical logic, is towards inductive theories of truth as found in Kripke (1975) and in Martin and Woodruff (1975). The first task is to develop a naïve theory of properties.[19] Probably the most natural approach for an anti-hierarchical, domain-based absolutism is multi-sorted first-order logic in which properties are a sub-category of the domain of individuals. However I will work here in second-order logic in order to facilitate comparison with what I take to be the most promising extant absolutism, the domain-free approach of theorists such as Rayo, Uzquiano, and Williamson.[20]

I will develop this approach starting from a second-order base language L_0 which has countably many singular and first-order relational constants and countably many first and second-order variables. L_0 is to have the usual bivalent semantics with the second-order variables ranging over what I will call the 'attributes' of the individuals. I will, for convenience only, identify them with sets of individuals. For reasons which will become clear, I will adopt a Henkin semantics: that is the class of attributes in a model need not be the full power set of the set of individuals; models will, however, be 'faithful' that is satisfy the second-order Axiom of Comprehension.[21]

It will be convenient to assume that theories in L_0 all contain a standard set theory; I will choose second-order ZFCU, that is second-order ZFC amended to allow for atoms or urelements in the object language.[22] L_0 contains, then, the membership predicate $\in$ and the identity predicate $=$ and also a distinguished predicate S to pick out the sets. Since we can model sequences of elements, including urelements, in ZFCU we can dispense with n-ary relational variables for $n > 1$ and simulate them

[19] Hartry Field (2003*a*, 2003*b*, 2004) has developed a naïve theory of properties but using a different conditional from my own. I am indebted to Field for some points made in conversation and correspondence which saved me from going down a blind alley.

[20] Rayo and Uzquiano (1999), Rayo and Williamson (2003), and Williamson (2003), Rayo this volume and Uzquiano this volume.

[21] Cf. the slightly different definition in Shapiro (1991), p. 89.

[22] So I assume a stronger set theory in the informal metatheory.

by attributes true of *n*-ary sequences.[23] For future use I will distinguish also another predicate NP which is to pick out, among the urelements, the naïve properties.

A model for language L_0 is, therefore, a pair $\langle D, I\rangle$ with the domain D divided firstly into a domain of individuals in turn divided into two infinite, exclusive and exhaustive sub-domains, the Sets and the Urelements, and secondly into a domain of attributes each a subset of the individuals. The interpretation *I* assigns to the distinguished predicate constant S the members of Sets as its extension and assigns to the binary predicate $\in$ a relation with Sets as its range (identity is interpreted standardly). For any individual α in Sets, the diagram of $I(\in)$ determines the 'members' of α, all those members β of D such that $\langle\beta, \alpha\rangle$ belongs to $I(\in)$. Given an adequate set-theoretic definition of ordered pairs, this in turn determines which members of Sets are functions, that is satisfy the usual definition of function, which members are in the domain of a particular function, what the image of the function is for a particular individual as argument and so on. *I* assigns to each constant an item of the appropriate type: an element of the domain for singular constants, attributes—subsets of the domain—for predicate constants.

Now it will be useful proof-theoretically to have a two-place function term, which I will write $x\langle y\rangle$. The intended interpretation here is that if, in a meta-theoretic assignment μ, we assign to x a function and to y an item in the domain of that function, then $\mu(x\langle y\rangle)$ is the image of $\mu(y)$ under $\mu(x)$. In all other cases we choose some dummy object as the referent. What we want, in particular, is that the following rule be sound:

$$\frac{\exists! z\langle y, z\rangle \in x}{x\langle y\rangle = z}$$

Hence we stipulate that *I* interprets the application operator $x\langle y\rangle$ so that the application rule above is sound:–if α is a function with β in its domain and γ the image of β under α, the application function maps $\langle\alpha, \beta\rangle$ to γ.

It will also simplify proofs if we admit class brackets $\{x : \varphi x\}$ and λ terms $\lambda x\varphi x$; for future use we also add property terms $[x : \varphi x]$. To do this, recursively define a countable hierarchy of languages by expanding the singular terms of L_{n+1} to include those of L_n augmented by terms $\{x : \varphi x\}$ and $[x : \varphi x]$, with φ a one-place open sentence of L_n and expand the atomic predicates so that L_{n+1} includes $\lambda x\varphi x$; inductively define the rest of the wffs of L_{n+1} as normal. The language L is the union of all the languages of this hierarchy.

Semantically, the intended interpretation of $\{x : \varphi x\}$ is that it stands for the set of all those objects which satisfy φ, if such a set exists in the domain. That is, if there is an element of the domain to which all and only the objects which satisfy φ bear the relation we assign to '$\in$' then this is the referent of the class term. What if there is no such object? Empty terms do not gel well with inductive semantics so I will work with a non-free logic and stipulate that in this case the class term picks out an urelement. This ensures that all instances of the schema:

$$\sim \exists x\forall y(y \in x \equiv \varphi y) \supset\sim S\{x \colon \varphi x\}$$

[23] See Shapiro (1991), §9.1.1.

are true. The logical constant $\supset$ is a defined constant, defined by $A \supset B =_{df.} \sim A \vee B$ with $A \equiv B =_{df.} (A \supset B) \; \& \; (B \supset A)$. We also distinguish one special individual among the individuals with no members as the empty set, the sole member-less object which is a set:

$$S\{x\colon x \neq x\}.^{24}$$

Thus at L_{n+1} the semantic clauses for the term-forming operators are that the referent of $\{x : \varphi x\}$, relative to an assignment μ to free variables, is the item α in Sets such that the class of all β such that $\langle \beta, \alpha \rangle$ belongs to $I(\in)$ is just the extension of φ in L_n relative to μ, if, that is, there is such an α. If not, the referent is some designated dummy item in Urelements. For λ terms, the attribute assigned to $\lambda x \varphi x$ in L_{n+1} is simply the extension of φx in L_n. Hence λ conversion is sound for our semantics: from the formula $\varphi x/\mathbf{t}$ we can conclude to the atomic predication $\lambda x(\varphi x)\mathbf{t}$ and vice versa. For our second-order quantifier rules, then, we can specify $\forall$I and $\exists$E as in standard first-order natural deduction with the appropriate restrictions on free variables whereas generalization in second-order $\exists$I and instantiation in second-order $\forall$E only allows replacement of the quantified variable for atomic predicates, a category which includes λ terms.[25]

A proof by induction shows us that the semantic value of an expression remains constant in every language L_i to which it belongs so that $L = \bigcup_{i \in \omega} L_i$ has a well-defined semantics. What of the semantics for property terms? Referents for these terms are defined outright independently of the hierarchy of languages, in a way I will specify below, and exhaust the sub-domain NP.

The admissible models of L are those models which satisfy the axioms and rules, that is the axioms and rules of second-order logic (including comprehension) the axioms of second-order ZFCU and the application rule (call this system $ZFCU^+$). With set brackets in play, our axioms can take such forms as

$$\forall x S(\{y\colon \forall z(z \in y \supset z \in x)\});$$

this is the power set axiom, saying that for any individual the subsets of that individual form a set. Sets, non-urelements, then satisfy the comprehension axiom:

$$\forall Y(S(\{x\colon Yx\}) \supset \forall x(x \in \{x\colon Yx\} \equiv Yx))$$

Since we want to be able to carry out formal syntax inside our object language, we assume that arithmetic is developed inside ZFCU in a way which allows for that. In this development, certain set-theoretic terms will be designated standard numerals of the numbers and one term will be the canonical name **S** of the successor function. Given a coding of the simple expressions of syntax as numbers (or an identification of them with numbers), expression strings, construed as sequences of numbers, are part of the ontology of our theory. Using Gödelian techniques, we can further code

24 In ZFCU, of course, the extensionality axiom has to be weakened to $(Sx \; \& \; Sy) \supset (\forall z(z \in x \equiv z \in y) \supset x = y)$.

25 I assume standard classical first-order proof theory for L.

these strings as numbers, and show that key syntactic and proof-theoretic categories are definable as recursive sets of numbers. In particular, we can prove the representability of the provability relation and prove Gödel's diagonalization lemma: for any one-place predicate φx of L there is a sentence δ such that

$$\mathrm{ZFCU}^{+} \models \delta \equiv \varphi|\delta|$$

Here $|\varphi|$ is a metalinguistic parameter whose interpretation is as follows: if metalinguistic parameter φ is assigned as referent an object language expression with Gödel code n, $|\varphi|$ is assigned the object language numeral $\mathbf{S}^n\mathbf{0}$ (i.e. $\mathbf{0}$ preceded by n occurrences of S), that is, it is assigned the canonical name of that expression (under the coding). The arithmetization of syntax in our precise language L means that we have all the formal mechanisms in place to develop a semantical theory in ZFCU^{+} itself.

12.5 NAÏVE PROPERTIES

But to do this we need to loosen up a little and get a bit fuzzy by expanding from L to a language L^{+} for which bivalence fails and for which we will provide an inductive semantics. We add to the vocabulary of L a new relational predication which is to express instantiation. I will use a different style of epsilon—ε—for this. We can also add countably many new predicate constants. As is common, I will approximate indeterminacy, in this classical framework, by introducing a third truth value $1/2$ in addition to truth (1) and falsity (0). I will interpret the logical operators by the strong Kleene rules; that is, negation flips 1 and 0 and maps 1/2 to itself whilst conjunctions are true only if both conjuncts are true, false if one conjunct is and otherwise take value 1/2. The clause for disjunction is dual to the conjunction clause while the quantifiers simply generalize the conjunction and disjunction rules. That is, keeping a fixed domain D implicit and letting $\mu[x/\alpha]$ be the assignment function which agrees with μ except, at most, on variable x to which it assigns $\alpha \in \mathrm{D}$, an existential generalization $\exists x\varphi x$ is true according to μ (write this as $\mu(\exists x\varphi x) = 1$) if there is an $\alpha \in \mathrm{D}$ such that $\mu[x/\alpha](\varphi x) = 1$, $\mu(\exists x\varphi x) = 0$ if for every $\alpha \in \mathrm{D}$, $\mu[x/\alpha](\varphi x) = 0$, otherwise $\mu(\exists x\varphi x) = 1/2$. The clause for $\forall$ is dual and the second-order clauses are the same except that second-order X is assigned an attribute from the domain of attributes. For L^{+} this is a set of pairs, each pair e consisting of two mutually exclusive subsets of D, positive e^{+} and negative e^{-} extensions. Predicate constants belonging to L are always assigned a pair whose terms exhaust D.

The atomic clause in the definition of satisfaction is the obvious one:

$Y(x_1, \ldots x_n)$ takes value 1 relative to μ if $\langle\mu(x_1), \ldots \mu(x_n)\rangle \in \mu(Y)^{+}$, takes value 0 if $\langle\mu(x_1), \ldots \mu(x_n)\rangle \in \mu(Y)-$, otherwise takes value 1/2. (Where one of the terms in the atom is a constant, it receives in every assignment the value assigned by I.)

L^{+} is formed by accumulating a hierarchy of languages L^{+}_{n+1} just as with L with the same recursive clauses for class and λ terms but with the proviso that $\{x : \varphi x\}$ is assigned the dummy non-set individual if the extension of φ in L^{+}_{n} is not bivalent. The λ terms are assigned the same extensions as the embedded open formulae, as before, only this time the extensions are positive and negative pairs, not always exhaustive. An inductive proof shows that no sentence of the sub-language L of L^+ has an indeterminate value.

The central idea in inductive theories is that we start from the valuation v_0 given by model $\langle D, I\rangle$ and proceed to generate a hierarchy of richer valuations $v_1, v_2, \ldots, v_\omega, v_{\omega+1}, \ldots$. with earlier and later valuations related by $v \ll v'$, which is to be read: if $v(P) = 1$ then $v'(P) = 1$ and if $v(P) = 0$ then $v'(P) = 0$. That is v' may render determinate a sentence indeterminate in v but never change the value of a sentence determinate in v. We then add a 'jump operator' $J(x)$. This is what takes us from one valuation to its successor–v_1 is $J(v_0)$–(plus a further rule for limit ordinals). The crucial property required of the jump operator is *monotonicity*, the preservation of the $\ll$ relation, that is if $v \ll v'$ then $J(v) \ll J(v')$. Not every semantics for the logical operators is compatible with monotonicity, but the Kleene semantics is. Under this semantics, a complex sentence never 'loses' determinate value, when the value of an immediate constituent changes, so long as the change in the constituent is merely from indeterminate to determinate.

Now as Kripke noted in his account of truth (Kripke, 1975, p. 70), he could have given an inductive theory of a satisfaction relation, a relation holding between assignments and open formulae, rather than a truth predicate applied to sentences. But the technique which works for $\ulcorner\sigma(x)$ satisfies $|\varphi x|\urcorner$ will also work for $\mathbf{t}\ \varepsilon\ [x : \varphi x]$.

First of all we need to define the reference relation for property terms. Consider 'unrestricted' inductive models $\langle D, I\rangle$ in which referents may be assigned completely freely to property terms: though syntactically complex they are treated in such models as semantically unstructured. Define $\varphi \cong \psi$ by: in every unrestricted model, and for every assignment to free variables, the value of φ is the same as the value of ψ. Partition the class of predicate terms by the relation $\cong$. Expand the notion of a model to that of a triple $\langle D, I, N\rangle$ where N bijects the partition onto NP. The referent of $[x : \varphi x]$ is then $N(\|[x : \varphi x]\|)$ where $\|[x : \varphi x]\|$ is the equivalence class to which φx belongs.

Having fixed the reference of each property term, we must now characterize inductively the extension of ε. We stipulate that every admissible model assigns a completely empty extension to ε, i.e. $\langle\emptyset, \emptyset\rangle$. The J rule is very simple: at $J(v)$ the value of $\mathbf{t}\ \varepsilon y$, relative to an assignment μ to free variables, is exactly the value at v of $\varphi x/\mathbf{t}$, relative to the same assignment μ where $\mu(y) \in$ NP and $N^{-1}(\mu(y))$ is $\|[x : \varphi x]\|$, 0 where $\mu(y) \notin$ NP. For this definition to be sound, $\psi x/\mathbf{t}$ and $\theta x/\mathbf{t}$ must take exactly the same value at v, where both ψx and θx belong to $\|[x : \varphi x]\|$. But this follows since $\psi x \cong \theta x$ and v is a special case of an unrestricted inductive model.

At limit stages of the sequence of valuations generated from v_0 by the jump rule we set the positive extension of ε, the set of all pairs on which ε takes value 1, to be the union of the positive extensions at each earlier valuation. Similarly, the negative extension at v_λ is the union of the negative extensions at all earlier valuations v_α, $\alpha < \lambda$.

The jump operator is indeed monotonic, under this interpretation of ε.[26] The proof is by induction on formulae complexity. The key clause is the atomic clause for ε:

[26] I leave the relativity to an assignment μ implicit.

Suppose $v \ll u$ but it is not the case that $J(v) \ll J(u)$, in particular

(i) $J(v)(\mathbf{t}\ \varepsilon\ [x : \varphi x]) = 1$ but

(ii) $J(u)(\mathbf{t}\ \varepsilon\ [x : \varphi x]) = 0$. (The case with 1 and 0 reversed is symmetrical, the extrapolation to cases in which the right-hand term of the relation is not a property term being straightforward).

From (i) and (ii), the jump rule gives us $v(\varphi x/\mathbf{t}) = 1$ and $u(\varphi x/\mathbf{t}) = 0$. But this contradicts $v \ll u$.

A similar proof for limit ordinals shows that, in our hierarchy of valuations, for $\alpha < \beta$, $v_\alpha \ll v_\beta$. The positive and negative extension of ε 'grow' as we ascend the hierarchy, nothing ever drops out of one or other. But simple cardinality considerations show that, just as in the natural and economic worlds, this growth cannot go on for ever. Let the domain D of individuals of our base model be of cardinality $\aleph_\alpha$. Then the maximum size of the positive extension of ε is $(\aleph_\alpha \times \aleph_0) =$ (granted the axiom of choice) $\aleph_\alpha$, likewise for the negative extension. Hence the hierarchy must reach a fixed point v_κ, with $v_{\kappa+1} = J(v_\kappa) = v_\kappa$, for some ordinal κ of cardinality $\leq \aleph_\alpha$. It cannot extend, adding new pairs at each stage, into larger ordinals for there are not enough pairs to provide fuel for the growth.

It follows that

$$v_\kappa(\mathbf{t}\ \varepsilon[x\colon \varphi x]) = v_{\kappa+1}(\mathbf{t}\ \varepsilon[x\colon \varphi x]) = v_\kappa(\varphi x/\mathbf{t}).$$

At the fixed points of the construction, in other words, we 'equalize' the two sentences $\mathbf{t}\ \varepsilon\ [x : \varphi x]$ and $\varphi x/\mathbf{t}$–they must take the same value, 1, 1/2 or 0. The semantic value of a wff of L^+ for a model $M = \langle D, I\rangle$ can therefore be defined as its value at the fixed point generated from its base valuation v_0 which starts from the empty extension assigned to ε.

Thus the following two rules:

X	(1) $\varphi x/\mathbf{t}$	Given	X	$\mathbf{t}\ \varepsilon\ [x : \varphi x]$	Given
X	(2) $\mathbf{t}\ \varepsilon\ [x : \varphi x]$	1, εI	X	$\varphi x/\mathbf{t}$	1, εE

are sound under any sane definition of soundness. When $\varphi x/\mathbf{t}$ is true so is $\mathbf{t}\ \varepsilon[x : \varphi x]$ and vice versa, when one is false so is the other.

What are the relations between attributes and properties in this theory?[27] Well, for every attribute there is a unique corresponding property:

$$|\forall X \exists! y(y = [x\colon Xx])$$

For every assignment of an attribute, a subset of the domain, to X, the assignment of the referent of $[x\colon Xx]$ to y, and of it alone, renders $y = [x\colon Xx]$ true. Oddly, though, it is not the case that to every property there corresponds an attribute; thus $\exists Y([x\colon x \neq x] = [z\colon Yz])$) is false in every model since $[x\colon x \neq x] = [z\colon Yz]$ is false in every model

[27] I have chosen these two expressions simply to reflect the categorical distinction between the two–second-order versus first-order–in the system, with no thought at all to traditional metaphysical usages of the terms.

relative to every assignment to Y, the two predicate terms belong to distinct equivalence classes under $\cong$ (the introduction of substitutional quantifiers would get round this problem). Moreover although:

$$\forall X\ \forall y(Xy \equiv y\ \varepsilon[x\colon Xx])$$

is never false, the vagaries of the material bi-conditional $\equiv$ mean that it is not true either: no instance in which we assign a non-bivalent extension to X is true (see ahead Section 12.9). Nonetheless, in the special case of the ε rules in which φ is a predicate variable X we have the interderivability of $X\mathbf{t}$ with $\mathbf{t}\ \varepsilon\ [x\colon Xx]$ *no matter what attribute we assign to* X (or what object we assign to **t**). This is true, moreover, in all models including full standard models in which the attribute domain is the power set of the domain of individuals, which itself may be of any cardinality we like.

How can that be since we know 'from the outside' that there are only countably many properties? What turns the trick is the coordinated flexibility, via the inductive clause for ε, of the free variable sentences $X\mathbf{t}$ and $\mathbf{t}\ \varepsilon\ [x\colon Xx]$ which can do duty simultaneously for any and every claim concerning which members of D belong to which subsets of D. Moreover when we come to one-place open sentences, with only one individual variable free, there are only as many of those as the size of the language.

Nonetheless, because the informal metatheory is standard model theory, familiar limitations re-surface. Our domain D contains as one among the other objects a universal property $[x\colon x = x]$ which is to serve as a universal domain. But it is not *really* a universal domain. Though every member of D bears the instantiation relation of the model to $[x\colon x = x]$, we know 'from the outside' that D is only a mere (representation of a) set, not a universal domain. Does this not represent capitulation to the relativists? Compare the domain-free absolutist who can give a metatheoretic semantics for object theories L without, it seems, any ontological contraction: the variables of L are interpreted as ranging over everything.[28]

The difference with relativism is this: convinced, as I hope everyone will be, by the coherence of the naïve theory of properties (and the 'naïve' account of interpretations I will base on it) we can expand the resources of our informal metatheory to include the naïve theory and carry out the semantics not using Kripkean inductive methods but the naïve theory of interpretation. Having promoted naïve properties to our actual language, we take them at face value. The property of being self-identical really is universal: everything instantiates it, and since it is an 'it', it is an object which can function as a universal domain.

One obvious objection is that no one in their right mind will be convinced of the coherence of the naïve theory of properties. Even without extensionality, the theory falls to a version of Russell's paradox, namely the heterologicality paradox. Here we make trouble with the property **h**: $[x\colon \sim(x\ \varepsilon\ x)]$, the property of not instantiating oneself:

[28] But if the argument of Section 12.1 is right, this is an illusion. The domain-free absolutists apparent generalization over everything contains an explicit restriction to a sub-domain of particulars thus excluding some entities, namely properties.

1	(1) $[x: \sim (x \varepsilon x)] \varepsilon [x: \sim (x \varepsilon x)]$	H[29]
1	(2) $\sim([x: \sim (x \varepsilon x)] \varepsilon [x: \sim (x \varepsilon x)]$	1εE
1	(3) $\perp$	1,2, ~E
—	(4) $\sim([x: \sim (x \varepsilon x)] \varepsilon [x: \sim (x \varepsilon x)]$	3,~I
—	(5) $[x: \sim (x \varepsilon x)] \varepsilon [x: \sim (x \varepsilon x)]$	4 εI
—	(6) C	4,5 ~E

where C is any sentence whatsoever. (I take the ~E rule to have as its conclusion any sentence one likes, including the absurdity constant $\perp$ which features in the (classical and intuitionist) ~I reductio rules.) Line (6) thus shows us that C is a theorem, whatever C is, of classical logic augmented by the ε rules. Clearly we cannot work in classical logic.

12.6 LOGIC

This illustrates the important moral that giving a definition of truth in a model is only one part of formal semantics. We also need a non-classical definition of logical consequence. In (1998b), I developed a 'neo-classical' restriction, one which I claimed achieved a pleasing 'classical recapture', that is validated full classical logic in the special case of sub-languages (such as L) where every sentence has a determinate truth value. The idea is to retain classical operational rules but to hold that the structural principles of classical logic which we use to build longer proofs out of individual inference steps are technical artefacts which are not embedded in the very meanings of the logical operators. These structural principles are entirely sensible in the contexts for which classical logic was developed, namely the formalization of standard mathematics, but it is very rash to suppose that they hold sway for reasoning in general, in vague contexts, for example, or in semantics.

The Sorites perhaps illustrates this most clearly. We are faced with a series of steps each of which is intuitively compelling leading us from premises which seem obviously true to a conclusion which seems obviously false. There is a clash between classical operational rules, classical structural rules, the assumption that all the sentences have determinate truth values, and the evident non-falsity of the premises and non-truth of the conclusion. A natural pre-theoretical response is to say that the argument as a whole is not valid even though each step seems acceptable. A further natural intuition is that the vague predicates in Sorites arguments have many instances intermediate, in obvious senses, between the true premise and false conclusion, instances which are neither determinately true nor false. To hold that it is this intuition, that some of the sentences lack a determinate truth value, which must go in order to preserve principles of proof architecture devised by mathematical logicians for use in the precise and determinate world of standard mathematics seems to me bizarre.

Now it is incontestable that for singular arguments—one premise, one conclusion—P entails Q only if the transition is truth-preserving. Cashing this out in formal

[29] This is the rule of hypothesis or rule of assumptions reflecting the reflexivity of $\vdash$.

semantics means that in no admissible model is P true and Q not true. But it is equally essential that a valid singular inference be upwards falsity-preserving: in no model is Q false but P not false. This direction is often forgotten about in classical bivalent contexts, where it follows directly from the truth-preservation clause, but in non-bivalent frameworks in which it does not follow this clause should be added on; the refutation of hypotheses by valid derivation of false consequences is as much part of logic as teasing out of (potentially) new truths by valid derivation from a true premise.

But how do we generalize this twin, bi-directional notion of entailment to multiple premise arguments? In 1998*b* I argued for the following 'neo-classical' definition of entailment:
a set of wffs X neo-classically entails a set Y (from now on I will use $\models$ to represent neo-classical entailment) iff:

(a) For any wff C in Y, in any model M in which all wffs in X are true[30] but all in Y but C are false, C is true in M.
(b) For any wff P in X, in any model M in which all wffs in Y are false but all in X but P are true, P is false in M.

For single conclusion logics, and I will largely neglect multiple conclusion logics in what follows, this amounts to:

> $X \models C$ iff in all models M if all of X are true in M then C is true and if C is false and all of X but P are true, then P is false.

There are two stronger, more classical notions of entailment. One requires a true conclusion, if all premises are true and also a false premise if all premises are false. The second merely rules out having all premises true but all conclusions false. But the first rules out the highly intuitive (at least to those uncorrupted by relevantism) rule of disjunctive syllogism $P, \sim P \vee Q \vdash Q$ whilst the second would permit one to move from a clear logical truth to a necessarily indeterminate sentence, the Liar say, and also from the latter to a clear logical falsehood, thus blocking the most simple form of transitivity of entailment: if $P \models Q$ and $Q \models R$ then $P \models R$.

The neo-classical account, I argued, matches our linguistic behaviour towards multiple premise inferences such as &I: $A, B \vdash A\&B$. If we accept A but reject A&B, we will also reject B. Generalizing this idea, if one rejects the conclusion of an inference but accepts all premises but P, it is incumbent on one to reject P, mere agnosticism is insufficient. The neo-classical account of entailment matches this nicely.

On the neo-classical account of entailment, $X \models Y$ if, in every model, the minimum value of X is no greater than the maximum value of Y–call this the minimax condition. In the single conclusion case (in propositional logic) this means that any

30 When discussing 'true' and 'false' in connection with model-theoretic semantics I am talking of truth-in-a-model or valuation and likewise falsity (that is truth of negation) in a valuation or model, and not ordinary disquotational truth. The notion of 'truth in a model' is closer to 'determinate truth', a notion which certainly comes apart from that of truth. But rather than write 'true in model M' each time, I will leave this relativization implicit.

rule allowing us to go from the sequent X:A to X:B, where A minimax entails B, preserves neo-classical correctness. We can give a complete set of rules for this minimax transition—de Morgan rules, associativity, commutativity, distributivity, double negation rules plus the rule allowing us to go from A of the form (C & ~C) to B of the form (D ∨ ~D). But there are non-minimax rules which are sound as single inference steps yet chaining them together by the usual structural principles of (generalized) transitivity leads to unsoundness. Thus ~E:

$$\frac{P \qquad {\sim}P}{C}$$

is neo-classically correct. The truth-preservation direction is standard; in the other direction if C is false in a model but one premise true then, by the semantics for negation, the other is false. Yet a couple of quick steps applying ~E to the minimax correct &E can lead us to neo-classical incorrectness, from P&~P to C, where P and so P&~P is gappy and C false:

$$\frac{\dfrac{P \,\&\, {\sim} P}{P} \qquad \dfrac{P \,\&\, {\sim} P}{{\sim} P}}{C}$$

Neo-classically, then we can have A, B $\models$ C but not A&B $\models$ C. How can we implement this proof-theoretically? We need to add a determinacy restriction to the ~E rule requiring that any assumption on which both major and minor premise of the rule are based has to be determinate, that is have a value 0 or 1. Where Det P expresses the claim that P is determinate the restriction, in Gentzen-Prawitz proof architecture[31] is:

$$\begin{array}{ccccc} X & Y & Z_1 & \ldots & Z_n \\ \ldots & \ldots & \ldots & & \ldots \\ P & {\sim}P & \mathit{Det}\ Q_1 & \text{—} & \mathit{Det}\ Q_n \\ \hline \multicolumn{2}{c}{C} & & & \end{array}$$

(the line under $\mathit{Det}\ Q_1 \ldots \mathit{Det}\ Q_n$ is dashed)

where the italicized premises are required for any $Q_i \in X \cap Y$.

This format makes it clear that the restriction is a global, structural one and that the basic inference step, from P, ~P to C is legitimate. For reasons of convenience in presenting proofs I will use, instead of this natural deduction format, the sequent version in the familiar Lemmon format, though this obscures somewhat the fact that the restrictions are on the structural not operational rules:

X	(1) P	Given
Y	(2) ~P	Given
$Z_i, i \in I$	(3.*i*) Det Q	Given, $\forall Q \in X \cap Y$
$X, Y, \bigcup_{i \in I} Z_i$	(3) C	1,2, [3.*i*, $i \in I$], ~E

[31] For a very clear presentation of Gentzen's system as developed by Prawitz, see Tennant (1978).

where it is required that $\bigcup_{i \in I} Z_i \cap (X \cup Y) = \emptyset$. In general I will omit the index set I where it is clear from the context what it is and bracket the determinacy premise line numbers (i.e. in this example the premises 3.*i*) by '[' and ']' as above.

The only other neo-classical restrictions, on the language with operators &, ∨, ~, ∀ and ∃, are restrictions on ∨E–any assumption on which both the major premise P ∨ Q depends and on which also one or other of the minor premise depends must be determinate–with an analogous restriction for first and second-order ∃E.[32]

But there is a problem in the inductive framework. How do we define determinacy, Det P? Surely we should want, for *determinate* determinacy, that Det P takes value 0 if P takes value ½, 1 otherwise.[33] But we cannot incorporate such a determinacy operator in a monotonic framework. For if P went from value ½ in valuation v to value 1 in J(v) Det P would flip from 0 to 1, contrary to monotonicity. The next best thing is to use instances of the law of excluded middle (LEM) as surrogates for determinacy. So Det Q, in the above, is just Q ∨ ~Q which at least has the advantage of being true when Q takes value 0 or 1, even though it is only gappy, not false, when Q is gappy. The rules, with the determinacy restrictions expressed in this way, are still sound.

We augment the logic with axioms of the form Det P for every sentence P which is determinate in every admissible model. Thus Det **t** = **u** is an axiom for every pair of singular terms since we have chosen to interpret the identity relation as determinate. Similarly, since every sentence of L is determinate in every admissible model, Det P, for P ∈ L, is an axiom. This gives us our classical recapture. We can reason in wholly classical fashion inside L since the extra determinacy clauses required in applications of ~E, ∨E and ∃E are axiomatic.

Since the system is sound, paradox cannot emerge in it. For example, the proof of the heterologicality paradox is blocked in the following way (**h**, remember, is [x: ~ (x ε x)]):

1	(1) **h** ε **h**	H
1	(2) ~(**h** ε **h**)	1 ε E
3	(3) **h** ε **h** ∨ ~(**h** ε **h**)	H
1,3	(4) ⊥	1,2, ~E [3]
3	(5) ~(**h** ε **h**)	4, ~I
3	(6) **h** ε **h**	5 ε I
7	(7) (**h** ε **h** ∨ ~(**h** ε **h**)) ∨ ~((**h** ε **h** ∨ ~(**h** ε **h**)))	H
3,7	(8) ⊥	5,6 ~E [7]

We can go on from here to discharge line (3) and prove ~(**h** ε **h** ∨ ~(**h** ε **h**)), a sentence which entails by minimax moves **h** ε **h** & ~(**h** ε **h**). But we can only prove it from line (7) as assumption. We have 7⊢ ~ 3 and, indeed, 3⊢ ~ 7 but this is

[32] For soundness see Weir (1998*c*).

[33] We also need some Det P sentences to be themselves indeterminate if we want to incorporate higher-order indeterminacy as, in fact, we need to if we want to handle paradoxes such as the Curry paradox; but I will leave this complication out. See Weir (1999).

unproblematic as the succeedent formulae at lines 3 and 7 both take value $1/2$ in every admissible model.

12.7 HOW TO GET SATISFACTION

Now to move to interpretations in domains, including our universal domain $[x\colon x = x]$. For this we need a satisfaction predicate. Let us assume, then, that L^+, as well as adding the instantiation relation ε to L, also adds a three-place predicate Sat(x, y, z). Our goal is to validate these rules:

X	(1) $\{\psi(\sigma\langle|v_i|\rangle, \ldots, \lambda x(x\, \varepsilon\sigma\langle|V_j|\rangle), \ldots)\}^{[x:\, \varphi x]}$	Given
Y	(2) NA(σ)	Given
X,Y	(3) Sat$([x\colon \varphi x], \sigma, |\psi(v_i, \ldots, V_j, \ldots)|)$	1,2 SatI

X	(1) Sat$([x\colon \varphi x], \sigma, |\psi(v_i, \ldots, V_j, \ldots)|)$	Given
X	(2) $\{\psi(\sigma\langle|v_i|\rangle, \ldots, \lambda x(x\, \varepsilon\, \sigma\langle|V_j|\rangle), \ldots)\}^{[x:\, \varphi x]}$	1, SatE$_1$

X	(1) Sat$([x\colon \varphi x], \sigma, |\psi(v_i, \ldots, V_j, \ldots)|)$	Given
X	(2) NA(σ)	1 SatE$_2$

Some explanation is in order. In the application of the rules, the three terms of the predicate Sat must be filled appropriately. In the first argument place there must occur a property expression $[x\colon \varphi x]$. The second argument place can contain any term, but we shall stipulate shortly that for the predication to be true in a model the term must stand for a 'naïve assignment'. This is a function from the variables of L (and hence L^+) which maps all second-order variables into the *properties*, the members of the extension of NP. Thus the notion of a naïve assignment function can be defined in L in ZFCU, NA abbreviates this definition. The final argument place is to be filled with a numeral whose referent codes for an n-place predicate.

In the introduction rule SatI, then, the second premise requires that the second argument place name a naïve assignment to the variables. In the first premise

$$\{\psi(\sigma\langle|v_i|\rangle, \ldots, \lambda x(x\, \varepsilon\sigma\langle|V_j|\rangle), \ldots)\}^{[x:\, \varphi x]}$$

is the open sentence which results from $\psi(v_i, \ldots, V_j, \ldots)$ (where the v_i are the free individual variables and the V_j the free predicate variables) by replacing each individual free variable v_k by $\sigma\langle|v_k|\rangle$ and each free predicate variable V_m by $\lambda x(x\, \varepsilon\, \sigma\langle|V_m|\rangle)$ and finally by restricting all quantified variables to the property $[x\colon \varphi x]$ by the usual sort of relativization operation *:

$^*\forall v\theta v$ is $\forall v(v\, \varepsilon\, [x\colon \varphi x] \supset {}^*\theta v)$;

$^*\exists v\theta v$ is $\exists v(v\, \varepsilon\, [x\colon \varphi x]\ \&\ {}^*\theta v)$;

$^*\forall V\varphi V$is $\forall V(\forall v(Vv \supset v\, \varepsilon\, [x\colon \varphi x]) \supset {}^*\theta v)$ and

$^*\exists V\theta V$ is $\exists V(\forall v(Vv \supset v\, \varepsilon\, [x\colon \varphi x])\ \&\ {}^*\theta v)$;

How does the inductive semantics validate these rules? We start at the base valuation v_0 (with ε assigned the empty extension as before). Sat($\mathbf{t}_1$, $\mathbf{t}_2$, $\mathbf{t}_3$) is false at v_0 (generated by underlying model $M = \langle D, I, N \rangle$) relative to a (meta-theoretic) assignment μ if either of these conditions holds:

(a) $\mu(\mathbf{t}_1)$ is not a member of the extension of NP in M;

(b) $\mu(\mathbf{t}_2)$ is not a naïve assignment function in D (whether it is or not is determined by the bivalent classical sub-model of M for L);

(c) $\mu(\mathbf{t}_3)$ is not the code of an n-place open sentence;

and we add

(d) in all other cases, the sentence has value $1/2$.

Now we must expand the rule for the jump operator J to cater for Sat. We take over the same clauses (a) to (c) above but change (d) to:

Otherwise Sat($\mathbf{t}_1$, $\mathbf{t}_2$, $\mathbf{t}_3$) takes the same value in $J(v)$ as

$$\{\psi(\sigma\langle|v_i|\rangle, \ldots, \lambda x(x \,\varepsilon\, \sigma\langle|V_j|\rangle), \ldots)\}^{[x:\ \varphi x]} \text{ has in } v.$$

where the equivalence class to which φx belongs is mapped to $\mu(\mathbf{t}_1)$ by N, where $\mu(\sigma) = \mu(\mathbf{t}_2)$, and where $\mu(\mathbf{t}_3)$ codes for $\psi(v_i, \ldots, V_j, \ldots)$.

For this definition to be sound it has to be the case that

$\{\psi(\sigma\langle|v_i|\rangle, \ldots, \lambda x(x \,\varepsilon\, \sigma\langle|V_j|\rangle), \ldots)\}^{[x:\ \varphi x]}$ has the same value in v as

$\{\psi(\sigma\langle|v_i|\rangle, \ldots, \lambda x(x \,\varepsilon\, \sigma\langle|V_j|\rangle), \ldots)\}^{[x:\ \psi x]}$

where $\varphi x \cong \psi x$, but this is easily seen.

These clauses determine the valuation $v_{\alpha+1} = J(v_\alpha)$ given v_α. For valuations v_λ, λ a limit ordinal, the rule is that the positive extension of Sat, the set of all triples under which Sat takes value 1 when the ith component of the triple is assigned to the ith term of the relation, is the union of the positive extensions at each earlier valuation. Similarly, the negative extension at v_λ is the union of the negative extensions at all earlier valuations v_α, $\alpha < \lambda$.

Monotonicity still holds for the augmented jump operation. The argument in the key atomic case now goes:

Suppose $v \ll u$ but it is not the case that $J(v) \ll J(u)$, in particular[34]
$J(v)(\text{Sat}([x\colon \varphi x], \sigma, |\psi(v_i, \ldots, V_j, \ldots)|)) = 1$ but
$J(u)(\text{Sat}([x\colon \varphi x], \sigma, |\psi(v_i, \ldots, V_j, \ldots)|)) = 0$. (The case with 1 and 0 reversed is symmetrical).

Given Sat has value 1 in J (v), neither of clauses a) to c) is satisfied. Hence
$v(\{\psi(\sigma\langle|v_i|\rangle, \ldots, \lambda x(x \,\varepsilon\, \sigma\langle|V_j|\rangle), \ldots)\}^{[x:\ \varphi x]}) = 1$ and $u(\{\psi(\sigma\langle|v_i|\rangle, \ldots,$
$\lambda x(x \,\varepsilon\, \sigma\langle|V_j|\rangle), \ldots)\}^{[x:\ \varphi x]}) = 0$. But this contradicts $v \ll u.\theta$ □

and proceeds as before in limit cases and in showing the existence of fixed points. The fixed point generated from the base interpretation of ε and Sat and with Sat and

34 Again the cases where the terms in Sat are not of the displayed forms are easily extrapolated from this one.

ε characterized by their respective inductive clauses provides the semantic valuation of all wffs in the model M from which it is generated.

The Sat rules are neo-classically sound. It is a condition of correct application of the rules that clauses (a) and (c) in the semantics for Sat are met. Thus if it is true in model M that σ stands for a naïve assignment then the truth values of

$$\text{Sat}([x\colon \varphi x], \sigma, |\psi(v_i, \ldots, V_j, \ldots)|) \text{ and}$$

$$\{\psi(\sigma\langle|v_i|\rangle, \ldots, \lambda x(x \,\varepsilon\, \sigma\langle|V_j|\rangle), \ldots)\}^{[x\colon \varphi x]}$$

are the same. If all the antecedent wffs of the conclusion sequent of SatI are true in M then, by the correctness of the premises, both premise succeedents $\{\psi(\sigma\langle|v_i|\rangle, \ldots, \lambda x(x \,\varepsilon\, \sigma\langle|V_j|\rangle), \ldots)\}^{[x\colon \varphi x]}$ and NA(σ) are true hence Sat($[x\colon \varphi x], \sigma, |\psi(v_i, \ldots, V_j, \ldots)|$) is true in M. Suppose, in the other direction, the latter is false and all members of X, Y but P are true. It may be that NA(σ) is false in M in which case P $\in$ Y, and is false by the correctness of the second premise. If NA(σ) is not false in M, hence true then $\{\psi(\sigma\langle|v_i|\rangle, \ldots, \lambda x(x \,\varepsilon\, \sigma\langle|V_j|\rangle), \ldots)\}^{[x\colon \varphi x]}$ must be false in M, so P $\in$ X and is false. The soundness of the two Sat elimination rules is also straightforward.

12.8 UNRESTRICTED QUANTIFICATION IN THE NEO-CLASSICAL FRAMEWORK

How do naïve properties and naïve satisfaction help us provide a domain-based semantics for unrestricted quantification? We let our domains be naïve properties, so that we do indeed have a universal domain, namely $[x\colon x = x]$. The combination of naïve comprehension for domains together with the characteristics of the satisfaction predicate enables us to get a great deal of what we want, semantically speaking, even given the determinacy restrictions placed on the logic. We have a naïve satisfaction predicate for our language expressible in that language itself. We have a universal domain which includes every member of the domain and thereby every property of members of the domain; moreover to every attribute there corresponds a property in the domain of individuals, as explained above. Hence interpreting second-order variables by naïve assignments, as is done 'inside' L^+, rather than by subsets of the domain, as is done 'from the outside', is perfectly reasonable. In our semantic theory as given by the Sat predicate, we can interpret an arbitrary predicate variable by any property we like, since for arbitrary σ and property P, $\sigma(X/|[x\colon \varphi x]|)$ is also a naïve assignment, where $N(|[x\colon \varphi x]|) = \text{P}$. Any condition stateable in the language determines a property which can function as a domain of interpretation.

Furthermore, we can give, inside L^+, what is arguably a complete recursive account of the meaning of quantification in L^+, at least insofar as the quantification is over determinate domains. By a determinate domain I mean a property $[x\colon \varphi x]$ such that $\varphi x/\mathbf{a} \vee \sim \varphi x/\mathbf{a}$ is an axiom, where $\mathbf{a}$ is any singular term. That is, in every admissible model and for every assignment μ to $\varphi x/\mathbf{a}$, $\mu(\varphi x/\mathbf{a})$ takes value 1 or 0. There are determinate domains: any predicate ψ of L yields one as does the universal domain $[x\colon x = x]$ (so determinate domains do not correspond to sets of ZFCU). A complete account should tell us that, granted a universal generalization $\forall v\varphi v$ is true, relative to such a domain and an assignment σ to its free variables, it follows that every assignment $\sigma(v/\alpha)$ like σ except that it assigns a member of the domain α to v is true. Likewise from the latter assumption we should be able to prove (neo-classically) that $\forall v\varphi v$ is true, relative to σ. Similar proofs should be given for existential generalization and for (almost all) second-order quantifications. (Appendix.)

In particular, upon assuming that a universal generalization $\forall x\varphi x$ (or $\forall X\varphi X$) is absolutely true, true relative to $[x\colon x = x]$, it follows that if we take absolutely anything we like in the entire universe (or, more narrowly, any property in the universe), it satisfies $\varphi x(\varphi X)$; similarly if we assume everything whatsoever (or just every property) satisfies $\varphi x(\varphi X)$ then it follows that the respective generalizations are true. The noun phrase 'the universe' in this explanation looks, walks and quacks like a singular term and that is exactly what its formalized version $[x\colon x = x]$ is: another item in the universe, for of course $[x\colon x = x]\ \varepsilon\ [x\colon x = x]$.

Now, as already acknowledged, our semantics for $[x\colon x = x]$ does not really assign it the *real* universe, the entire shebang, in our formal models. The extension of $[x\colon x = x]$, in the sense of the class of all those items in D which bear to $N(|[x\colon x = x]|)$ the relation assigned to 'ε', is just the domain D itself and this, in the metatheory, is a ZFCU set. But, as I emphasized in Section 12.5, this does not represent a betrayal of absolutism. L^+ is a mathematical construct, a formal system designed to shed light on, and perhaps extend or modify, the conceptual and logical resources of natural language. If we are confident that the modelling of naïve properties and the Satisfaction relation in the formal language shows the coherence of those notions then we can add those notions to our metatheoretic repertoire and reason with them providing we are prepared to abide by the determinacy restrictions on $\sim$E, $\vee$E and $\exists$E. Thus (if our confidence is reasonable) we are justified, in the metatheory, in generalizing over interpretations and domains, in saying that a universal domain exists and in concluding that, for example, 'everything has spatio-temporal location' is true granted that every object in the universal domain, every object whatsoever that is, has spatio-temporal location.

Hence of the desiderata set out in Section 12.3, (vi)—accommodation of a universal domain, (iv)—a recursive explication of how the semantic value of a quantifier depends on that of its parts and (ii) a naïve satisfaction predication for the L^+ inside L^+ have all been met. What of goal (i), an account of logical consequence for L^+ inside L^+?

We already have relativization of satisfaction to different 'models', that is domains.[35] We can go further if we appeal Bolzano-style to substitution functions. A substitution function is a finite function, thus a finite set of ordered pairs, the first constituent in each being a code for a simple singular or predicate constant whilst the second codes a

[35] We could further complicate the Sat rules by requiring, of each constant in the quoted sentence, that φt, in the singular case, and that $\forall x(Fx \rightarrow \varphi x)$ for a predicate constant F, furthermore that the range of the naïve assignment be a subset of the extension of φ in the model. That way, the relativization of satisfaction to the domain of φ is essentially a relativization to a sub-model. Since our main interest, however, is in the utterly unrestricted universal domain I will eschew such further complication.

well-formed expression (with no free variables) of the same category as the first, simple or complex. Since admissible models are each to contain a model of ZFCU we exclude $\in$ from the domain of substitution functions, we treat it as a logical constant. We can define each substitution function in ZFCU and, using Gödelian techniques, code each such substitution function by a number. We can define, in turn, a four-place satisfaction predicate $\text{Sat}^+(x, y, s, z)$ by $\exists w \text{Sb}(z, w, s)$ & $\text{Sat}(x, y, w)$, where $\text{Sb}(z, w, s)$ is a ZFCU expression which is true in a model just in case the value σ of s is a substitution function and the value of w is the image of the value of z under σ.

Granted this, logical consequence can be defined as truth and falsity preservation under all substitution functions. Specifically, neo-classical logical consequence is definable in L^+ by:

$$\text{C}(X, P) \equiv_{\text{df.}} \forall x \forall y \forall z((\text{NP}(x) \,\&\, \text{NA}(y) \,\&\, \text{Sub}\,(z) \,\&\, \text{Wff}(\text{X}, \text{P})) \supset$$

$$(\sim(\forall Q(Q \in X \supset \text{Sat}^+(x, y, z, Q))\& \sim \text{Sat}^+(x, y, z, P)) \,\&\, \sim (\text{Sat}^+(x, y, z,$$

$$\sim P)\&\exists Q \in X(\sim\text{Sat}^+(x, y, z, Q) \,\&\, \forall R((R \in X \,\&\, R \neq Q) \supset \text{Sat}^+(x, y, z, R)))))).$$

Here Sub(z) is the ZFCU expression representing $\ulcorner z$ is a substitution function$\urcorner$. Thus the definition says that where X is a set of codes of formulae, and P a code of a formula (formalized by Wff(X, P)), the Xs entail P just in case for every property as domain, every naïve assignment to variables and every substitution function, (a) if all the substitution instances of the Xs are true relativized to the domain and assignment in question, the substitution instance of P is true and (b) if the latter is false and all other premises but Q are true then Q is false.

This definition is adequate in the following sense. If the metatheoretic claim that Δ neo-classically entails θ ($\Delta \models \theta$) is untrue (and hence false) then it can be shown that $\text{C}(X, P)$ is not true in any model, with X assigned, (under the interpretation of $\in$ in N) the set of codes of the Δ sentences and P the code of θ. Conversely if $\text{C}(X, P)$ is not true, in some model M and on those assignments, then $\Delta \models \theta$ is not true, and thus false.

While untruth matches untruth, we do not get the 'internal' falsity of $\text{C}(X, P)$ matching external falsity of $\Delta \models \theta$. This is because while $\models$ is bivalent, $\text{C}(X, P)$ is not. For example, if $\sim\text{Sat}(x, y, z, P)$ takes value $1/2$ in N but $\forall Q(Q \in X \supset \text{Sat}(x, y, z, Q))$ takes value 1 then the truth-preservation direction of $\text{C}(X, P)$ is itself gappy. That an entailment claim can be indeterminate is not, in my view, objectionable. If one accepts genuine indeterminacy of truth it is not clear on what grounds one can exclude lack of truth value for entailment claims. The problem is that the internal entailment claim is gappy when it should not be: when we have all premises determinately true and the conclusion determinately gappy, for example.

One response would be to introduce a determinate satisfaction predicate. Set aside a three-place monadic predicate of L^+ to play this role, call it DetSat. Let the language $L^\pm$ be the language whose primitives are those of L^+ minus DetSat and consider an arbitrary model M of L^+. Starting with the same domains and interpretation as M, modify the jump rule for Sat by changing clause (d) from

(c) $\mu(t_3)$ is not the code of an n-place open sentence to

(c) $\mu(t_3)$ is not the code of an *n*-place open sentence of $L^{\pm}$

so that we treat sentences of $L^{+} - L^{\pm}$ as, in effect, non-sentences. On the new jump rule Sat is false of all sentences of $L^{+} - L^{\pm}$, relative to all assignments to variables, from v_0 on. Expand to a fixed point as before to get a variant M*. In this variant we get equalization between a sentence θ and the application of Sat to (a code for) a relativized substitution instance of θ only when θ is in $L^{\pm}$. Now construct from M a further variant M** which differs only in that the positive extension of DetSat consists of all sentences of $L^{\pm}$ which are true in M* (relative to the given domain and assignment) and whose negative extension is the rest of D. DetSat is thus a bivalent predicate. Expand to a fixed point using the usual jump rule so that we get equalization across all of L^{+} for Sat in M**; an inductive proof shows that M**, M*, and M agree on $L^{\pm}$.

DetSat(*x*) therefore gives us a determinate truth predicate for the proper sublanguage $L^{\pm}$, DetSat(neg*x*) a determinate falsity predicate, where 'neg' expresses the syntactic negation-forming operator. If a sentence $P \in L^{\pm}$ is true in M** hence in M* and M, DetSat(|P|) is true in M**; if P is not true in M**, DetSat(|P|) is false there. Thus the analogues of $SatE_1$ and $SatE_2$ hold for DetSat restricted to $L^{\pm}$ but the analogue of SatI does not hold for DetSat, even thus restricted. We cannot conclude DetSat(|P|) from P since if the latter is gappy, the former is false; falsity-preservation upwards fails.

DetSat does indeed enable us to express determinate truth and determinate falsity, and to regiment inside L^{+} the metatheoretic proof of soundness; ZFCU gives us all the resources we need for carrying out the usual inductive proof. But only determinate truth and soundness for the proper sublanguage $L^{\pm}$. Similarly, changing 'Sat' to 'DetSat' in the definition of C(*X*,*P*) gives us a bivalent, determinate and accurate definition of neo-classical entailment inside L^{+}: but only for the proper sub-language $L^{\pm}$. The ghosts of metalanguages have not been exorcised and clearly not all the desiderata can be met.

12.9 PROBLEMS

So close—but no cigar. Which desiderata are not met? Certainly goal (v), incorporating a conditional which satisfies the Deduction Theorem, cannot be met. For the deduction theorem for ⊃ fails neo-classically because ⊃I is not unrestrictedly sound. We do have the special case where the antecedent is axiomatically determinate:

Δ, A	(1) B	Given
—	(2) $A \vee \sim A$	Given
Δ, A	(3) $A \supset B$	1, ∨I
4	(4) $\sim A$	H
4	(5) $A \supset B$	4, ∨I
Δ	(6) $A \supset B$	2,3,5∨E

But for indeterminate A we can have Δ, A $\models$ B, all of Δ true yet A $\supset$ B gappy (e.g. where $\Delta = \emptyset$ and A and B both take value ½ in every model; this will be the case when A = B = the Liar, for example).

This is not great news. For example, if we assume, for closed P, $\forall\sigma\,(\mathrm{Sat}([x\colon x = x], \sigma, |P|))$,—abbreviate the formula as True |P|—then we can conclude from this P and vice versa. Therefore it is very natural to put this the following way: if True |P| then P and if P then True |P|. But that cannot be done in L^{+}. If we had the Deduction Theorem, for $\supset$ in L^{+} then from the interderivability of the truth claim and the disquoted sentence itself we could, indeed conclude:

$$\models \text{True } |P| \equiv P.$$

But this we cannot do; similarly we cannot prove $\mathbf{t}\;\varepsilon\;[x\colon \varphi x] \equiv \varphi x/\mathbf{t}$.

It is possible to introduce a conditional $\rightarrow$ for which the Deduction Theorem holds neo-classically but if the conditional is extensional, it must have the Lukasiewiczian property that A $\rightarrow$ B is true when both A and B take value ½ so that A $\leftrightarrow\sim$A is true when A is gappy. See Weir (1998*c*) where I take $\sim$(A $\leftrightarrow\sim$A) to define determinacy. This is a more adequate definition of determinacy than A $\vee$ $\sim$A but for that very reason such a conditional cannot feature in inductive semantics. Monotonicity fails just as with any attempt to give a fully adequate expression of determinacy in the inductive framework because if A and B are gappy in valuation v but A is true, B false in $J(v)$ then A $\rightarrow$ B flips from value 1 to 0. Similarly it would be natural, when attempting to formalize domain-restricted quantification, to consider non-standard formalizations such as binary quantification: $\forall x(\varphi x, \psi x)$ read as [all φs are ψs]. But we would want $\forall x(\varphi x, \varphi x)$ always to be true: all bald men are bald men. Again such an operator would violate monotonicity, indeed we could define $\rightarrow$ by it:

$$A \rightarrow B \equiv_{\text{df.}} \forall x(x = x \;\&\; A, x = x \;\&\; B) \;(x \text{ not in A or B}).$$

This problem is not insuperable. In Weir (2005) I show how to introduce a non-extensional conditional into inductive semantics in such a way that A $\rightarrow$ B and so A $\leftrightarrow\sim$A comes out true when A and B are gappy and where, indeed, all Tarskian biconditionals for a semantically closed notion of truth come out as true. Moreover, unlike Hartry Field's conditional,[36] which also validates unrestricted Tarskian biconditionals, the rule $\rightarrow$I, in the form

A	(1) B	Given
—	(2) A $\rightarrow$ B	1 $\rightarrow$I

holds for my conditional.

The structural rules for the resulting logic are more restricted and convoluted than for the neo-classical logic for non-inductive, as it were, $\rightarrow$ but this is no serious problem, if I am right in thinking that we have no reason to suppose that classical proof-architecture should hold sway in the realm of the indeterminate. But the restricted logic of this framework just exacerbates a deep problem with the current

[36] See again the references in footnote 19.

one. Although we can do a lot of semantics for L^+ inside L^+, thus far we have only sketched how to demonstrate soundness for the proper sub-fragment $L^{\pm}$.

Can we do any better? For some limited cases this can be done: thus for 'minimax' rules such as $\sim$I we can show in L^+ that this rule, as applied to arbitrary arguments in L^+, is truth-preserving. But we cannot hope to carry this rule for all steps. There are a number of problems, such as extending mathematical induction to the full non-bivalent language and handling falsity-preservation upwards and, most critically, the fact that the determinacy restrictions in the rules $\vee$E, $\sim$E and $\exists$E (and in the $\rightarrow$ rules), when they recur metatheoretically, block a boot-strapping proof of soundness of those very rules (see Weir, 1999).

So goal (iii)—a semantically closed soundness proof—is not available either; and since not all of the package is available, the final goal, validation of the whole set inside a familiar theory, fails too.

12.10 COMPARISONS AND CONCLUSIONS

What is the upshot then? It has been shown, from within a standard, classical meta-theoretic framework, that there are coherent object languages L^+ which contain a naïve satisfaction predicate together with a theory of naïve properties and can thereby express a good deal of their own semantics. Specifically, our L^+ theory T, that is $ZFCU^+$ together with naïve property theory, can explicate, at least in rule form, the recursive determination of the truth-conditions of first and second-order quantifiers as relativised to arbitrary domains including a universal domain, a domain whose instances are all the members of the individual domain of L. Moreover, it is provable inside the theory that to every attribute, every member of the range of the second-order quantifiers, there corresponds a property in the domain of individuals.

I suggested that the coherence of an object language theory with these properties makes it reasonable to assume that the metalanguage in which we carry out these systematic philosophical reflections has these characteristics too, though of course we can never have an absolute guarantee of freedom from contradiction. That is, we can assume a naïve satisfaction theory and naïve theory of properties in the metatheory, providing we are willing to accept the neo-classical determinacy restrictions. If so then in the context of the background framework the universal domain, the property of self-identity, really is universal. Everything belongs to the universal domain, including every property. In this framework, there is no real need to distinguish attributes from properties or to think of second-order quantification as categorically different from first-order. We can take over from L^+ the semantic account of the truth-conditions of generalizations relativized to contexts; when the context is the universal domain, we have an intuitive account of a truly unrestricted generalization.

On the negative side, we have seen that though a notion of logical consequence can also be expressed inside L^+ it does not correspond exactly with the meta-theoretic notion. This last difficulty is one of a number of less than optimal features, including the absence of a conditional answering to the Deduction Theorem and the inability to prove soundness for the language as a whole, though a few special cases are possible.

How does this compare with domain-free absolutism? In the latter framework, there is no need to restrict the familiar classical logic. Moreover we seem to get a pleasing ontological stability; we can interpret an object language L in such a way that its ontology is exactly the same as that of the informal metalanguage, which is assumed to be utterly unrestricted; there is no ontological contraction as there is in inductive semantics where the 'universal domain' of our formal object language L^+ is merely a (non-naïve) set.

However it is noteworthy that domain-free theorists in fact find it very difficult to avoid ontological expansion, Rayo and Williamson use second-order predicates, predicates taking first-order predicates as arguments, in order to provide a semantics for ordinary second-order logic which generalizes over 'collections' of individuals. But

> the semantic value of a second-order predicate might consist of any 'supercollection' of collections of individuals . . . there are 'more' supercollections of individuals than there are collections of individuals . . . So there are semantic values a second-level predicate might take which are not captured by any S[econd]O[rder]-interpretation. Again, this informal explanation is strictly nonsense, since 'is a collection' and 'is a supercollection' take the position of first-level predicates in sentences of natural language, even though they are intended to capture higher-order notions; nonetheless, it draws attention to a helpful analogy between first and higher-order notions.
>
> Rayo and Williamson (2003, p. 353).

What does it mean to say that such locutions are nonsensical ladders to be thrown away? If this is read in a very resolute sense—the domain-free theory contains an essential core of absolute nonsense—then I see no reason why we should spend any time considering the theory further. But the last comments indicate something different is meant: the phrases in current English are nonsense but they point to a conceptual expansion of the language in which analogous claims make determinate and illuminating sense.

This returns us to the argument in Section 12.5: it is not at all clear that the domain-free theorist really does achieve ontological stability. Specifically, the need to ascend to higher-order logic, in particular the need to interpret first-order languages using second-order (or plural) quantification prima facie shows that the supposedly unrestricted quantification being read into the object language L is in fact restricted: to non-properties. If the arguments of Rayo and Williamson in favor of a non-ontological reading of higher-order quantification (which nonetheless suffices for its applications in e.g. expressing logical consequence) fail, ascent to higher-order languages involves ontological as well as ideological expansion.

Moreover the ideological expansion to stronger semantic notions in the non-naïve case means that the soundness of the rules of the language is not even supposed to be *thinkable*, far less provable, even in special cases. True we can conceive of, and prove, soundness for e.g. $\sim$I, for restricted sub-languages, say for the language of arithmetic. But in the application of metatheoretic $\sim$I or similar rules in that proof, we are supposed to pretend that we cannot even conceive of what it means for the rules on which our demonstration of soundness is based to be themselves sound—we lack the requisite semantic notions. We should smell a rat here.[37]

Standing back from the specific contrast between domain-based and domain-free absolutism, what of the claim that the paradoxical elements here point to a Kantian antinomy? What is the presupposition which generates antinomy? I suggest it is the rejection of naïve comprehension and more generally the rejection of naïve, closed semantics. It is true that the issue of unrestricted quantification is relatively independent of that of the coherence of naïve semantics. One could, for example, espouse unrestricted quantification and be sceptical of the very existence of a systematic semantic theory, naïve or 'jaded'.

Nonetheless there are structural connections. A naïve semantics for language L, a systematic theory in L of the workings of L, seems to be blocked by the Liar, by Tarski's undefinability result on truth. Unrestricted quantification over a domain, conceived of as an object, seems to be blocked by Russell's paradox, or Williamson's variant. Though the connection between the semantic and the set-theoretic paradoxes is controversial there are certainly parallels in the standard proofs of antinomy in each case (and in the ways these are blocked in the neo-classical system). Moreover when we consider in particular a naïve semantics for a language with a universal domain the connection seems even closer; Cantor's powerset theorem and the theorem on the non-existence of a universal set, both with close connections to Russell's paradox, seem to block the possibility of a naïve semantics.

Thus my suggestion that we abandon the view that naïve semantics and universal domains are impossible and look to revision of the structural rules of logic to block contradiction. Clearly, given the partial nature of the results in this paper, I cannot do much more than raise the standard for the naïve approach. What I have tried to establish, however, is, firstly, that the costs of adopting a naïve absolutist approach are nothing like as high as ordinarily supposed; less, I would argue, than the costs of persevering with classical logic and being driven through all the minefields which await relativist and conventional absolutist theories. Secondly that, whatever the final prospects for naïve semantics, the idea of a universal domain is perfectly coherent and should be taken seriously by absolutists. As for relativism, insofar as it is primarily motivated by fear, if not loathing, of a universal domain, it lacks rational grounds.

It's not too much to ask for everything; not too much at all.

[37] I am not suggesting that we should doubt $\sim$I as applied to arithmetic. The function of a genuine soundness proof is similar to that of a demonstration within naturalized epistemology of the reliability of, say, our perceptual belief in the table in front of us. If successful, the demonstration does not strengthen our belief in the table, if unsuccessful it threatens not our belief in the table but our belief in the psychological and philosophical theories we used in an attempt to account for that belief. Similar remarks apply to semantic and philosophical theories of the nature of logical particles and the workings of our language.

APPENDIX

A recursive account of the dependence of the semantic value of an individual universal quantifier on those of all its instances can be given in the following rule form, as restricted to any determinate domain. These proofs are schematic: the terms φ, σ, and ψ can be replaced by any expressions of appropriate category in L^+ and the result will be proofs. I will simplify, though, in one respect, namely by considering the case of a generalization with one free variable, an individual free variable v_1:

1	(1) $\text{Sat}([x\colon \varphi x], \sigma, \vert\forall v_0 \psi(v_0, v_1)\vert)$	H
1	(2) $\{\forall v_0 \psi(v_0, \sigma\langle\vert v_1\vert\rangle)\}^{[x\colon \varphi x]})$	1 SatE_1
1	(3) $\forall v_0(v_0 \varepsilon\ [x\colon \varphi x] \supset \{\psi(v_0, \sigma\langle\vert v_1\vert\rangle)\}^{[x\colon \varphi x]})$	2 Def
1	(4) $(\mathbf{a}\ \varepsilon\ [x\colon \varphi x] \supset \{\psi(\mathbf{a}, \sigma\langle\vert v_1\vert\rangle)\}^{[x\colon \varphi x]}$	3 $\forall$E
5	(5) $\sim(\mathbf{a}\ \varepsilon\ [x\colon \varphi x])$	H
6	(6) $\mathbf{a}\ \varepsilon\ [x\colon \varphi x]$	H
5,6	(7) $\{\psi(\mathbf{a}, \sigma\langle\vert v_1\vert\rangle)\}^{[x\colon \varphi x]}$	5,6 $\sim$E
8	(8) $\{\psi(\mathbf{a}, \sigma\langle\vert v_1\vert\rangle)\}^{[x\colon \varphi x]}$	H
1,6	(9) $\{\psi(\mathbf{a}, \sigma\langle\vert v_1\vert\rangle)\}^{[x\colon \varphi x]}$	4,7, 8$\vee$E
1	(10) $\text{NA}(\sigma)$	1 SatE_2
1,6	(11) $\{\psi(\sigma(v_0/\mathbf{a})\langle\vert v_o\vert\rangle, \sigma(v_0/\mathbf{a})\langle\vert v_1\vert\rangle)\}^{[x\colon \varphi x]}$	9, 10 ZFCU^+
1,6	(12) $\text{NA}(\sigma)(v_0/\mathbf{a})$	10 ZFCU^+
1,6	(13) $\text{Sat}([x\colon \varphi x], \sigma(v_0/\mathbf{a}), \vert\psi(v_0, v_1)\vert)$	10,12 SatI
1,6	(14) $\mathbf{a}\ \varepsilon\ [x\colon \varphi x] \supset \text{Sat}([x\colon \varphi x], \sigma(v_0/\mathbf{a}), \vert\psi(v_0, v_1)\vert)$	13 $\vee$I
5	(15) $\mathbf{a}\ \varepsilon\ [x\colon \varphi x] \supset \text{Sat}([x\colon \varphi x], \sigma(v_0/\mathbf{a}), \vert\psi(v_0, v_1)\vert)$	5 $\vee$I
—	(16) $\mathbf{a}\ \varepsilon\ [x\colon \varphi x] \vee \sim\mathbf{a}\ \varepsilon\ [x\colon \varphi x]$	Axiom
1	(17) $\mathbf{a}\ \varepsilon\ [x\colon \varphi x] \supset \text{Sat}([x\colon \varphi x], \sigma(v_0/\mathbf{a}), \vert\psi(v_0, v_1)\vert)$	16, 14, 15, $\vee$E
1	(18) $\forall x(x\varepsilon\ [x\colon \varphi x] \supset \text{Sat}([x\colon \varphi x], \sigma(v_0/x), \vert\psi(v_0, v_1)\vert))$	17 $\forall$I

Lines 4:9 illustrate how disjunctive syllogism (DS), i.e. modus ponens for $\supset$, is neo-classically derivable in the form [from C:A and D: $\sim$A $\vee$ B conclude C,D: B] where C and D are two distinct sentences. Similarly ZFCU^+ at lines 11 and 12 indicates that we can derive these intermediate conclusions from their premises by purely classical reasoning from ZFCU^+ because all determinacy clauses are axiomatically true; we are reasoning about determinate set-theoretic objects, namely assignment functions. Here

$$\sigma(v_0/a) =_{\text{df.}} \{\langle x, y\rangle : (\langle x, y\rangle \in \sigma \ \&\ x \neq v_0) \vee (x = v_0 \ \&\ y = a)\}$$

In the other direction we have:

1	(1) $\forall x(x\varepsilon\ [x\colon \varphi x] \supset \text{Sat}([x\colon \varphi x], \sigma(v_0/x), \vert\psi(v_0, v_1)\vert))$	H
2	(2) $\mathbf{a}\ \varepsilon\ [x\colon \varphi x]$	H
1	(3) $\mathbf{a}\ \varepsilon\ [x\colon \varphi x] \supset \text{Sat}([x\colon \varphi x], \sigma(v_0/\mathbf{a}), \vert\psi(v_0, v_1)\vert)$	1 $\forall$E
1,2	(4) $\text{Sat}([x\colon \varphi x], \sigma(v_0/\mathbf{a}), \vert\psi(v_0, v_1)\vert)$	2,3 DS
1,2	(5) $\{\psi(\sigma(v_0/\mathbf{a})\langle\vert v_0\vert\rangle, \sigma(v_0/\mathbf{a})\langle\vert v_1\vert\rangle)\}^{[x\colon \varphi x]}$	4 SatE_1
1,2	(6) $\text{NA}(\sigma)$	4, SatE_2
1,2	(7) $\{\psi(\mathbf{a}, \sigma\ \langle\vert v_1\vert\rangle)\}^{[x\colon \varphi x]}$	5,6 ZFCU^+

—	(8) $\mathbf{a}\ \varepsilon\ [x\colon \varphi x] \vee \sim(\mathbf{a}\ \varepsilon\ [x\colon {}^{\varphi}x])$	Given
1	(9) $\mathbf{a}\ \varepsilon\ [x\colon \varphi x] \supset \psi(\mathbf{a}, \sigma\ \langle\lvert v_1\rvert\rangle\ \}^{[x\colon {}^{\varphi}x]}$	7 [8] ⊃I
1	(10) $\forall v_0(v_0\ \varepsilon\ [x\colon {}^{\varphi}x] \supset \{\psi(v_0, \sigma\ \langle\lvert v_1\rvert\rangle)\}^{[x\colon {}^{\varphi}x]})$	9∀I
1	(11) $\{\forall v_0 \psi(v_0, \sigma\ \langle\lvert v_1\rvert\rangle)\}^{[x\colon {}^{\varphi}x]}$	10 Def.
12	(12) $\mathrm{NA}(\sigma)$	H
1, 12	(12) $\mathrm{Sat}([x\colon \varphi x], \sigma, \lvert\forall v_0 \psi(v_0, v_1)\rvert)$	11,12 SatI

Here the disjunctive syllogism or modus ponens at line 4 is provable in the same way as in the previous proof. At line (6) the reasoning is again purely classical reasoning inside ZFCU$^+$ where we show that the result of applying the assignment which assigns **a** to v_0 to v_0 is indeed **a** and the result of applying $\sigma(v_0/\mathbf{a})$, which is like σ except on v_0, to the distinct variable v_1 is just $\sigma\langle v_1\rangle$. The ⊃I at line 8 is legitimate because the antecedent is determinate: see the discussion at the beginning of Section 12.9.

A recursive account of the truth conditions of individual existential quantification can be given in similar fashion. What about second-order quantification? We can give a nearly complete account, in rule form. The qualification is that we cannot give a recursive semantics, using properties instead of attributes, for second-order quantification into property terms $[x\colon \theta x]$. The proofs in the existential case are as follows (again I exemplify, for simplicity, a case with two free variables, an individual variable v_1 and a predicate variable V_1 each provably distinct from V_0 not in the scope of $[x\colon \theta x]$):

1	(1) $\mathrm{Sat}([x\colon \varphi x], \sigma, \lvert\exists V_0 \psi(V_0, v_1, V_1)\rvert)$	H
—	(2) $\mathrm{NA}(\sigma) \vee \sim \mathrm{NA}(\sigma)$	Axiom[38]
3	(3) $\mathrm{NA}(\sigma)$	H
1	(4) $\{\exists V_0 \psi(V_0, \sigma\langle\lvert v_1\rvert\rangle, \lambda x(x\ \varepsilon\ \sigma\langle\lvert V_1\rvert\rangle))\}^{[x\colon {}^{\varphi}x]})$	1 SatE_1
1	(5) $\exists V_0(\forall v_2(V_0(v_2) \supset v_2\varepsilon\ [x\colon \varphi x])\ \&$ $\{\psi(V_0, \sigma\langle\lvert v_1\rvert\rangle, \lambda x(x\ \varepsilon\ \sigma\langle\lvert V_1\rvert\rangle))\}^{[x\colon {}^{\varphi}x]})$	4 Def
6	(6) $\forall v_2(\mathbf{A}(v_2) \supset v_2\varepsilon\ [x\colon \varphi x])\ \&$ $\{\psi(\mathbf{A}, \sigma\langle\lvert v_1\rvert\rangle, \lambda x(x\ \varepsilon\ \sigma\langle\lvert V_1\rvert\rangle))\}^{[x\colon {}^{\varphi}x]}$	H
6	(7) $\{\psi(\mathbf{A}, \sigma\langle\lvert v_1\rvert\rangle, \lambda x(x\ \varepsilon\ \sigma\langle\lvert V_1\rvert\rangle))\}^{[x\colon {}^{\varphi}x]}$	6 &E
6	(8) $\psi;(\mathbf{A}, \sigma)$	7 Def.[39]
6	(9) $\psi;(\mathbf{A}, \sigma(V_0/[x\colon \mathbf{A}x])$	8 ZFCU$^+$
6	(10) $\psi;(\lambda x(x\ \varepsilon\ [x\colon \mathbf{A}x]), \sigma(V_0/[x\colon \mathbf{A}x])$	9 Lemma[40]
6	(11) $\psi;(\lambda x(x\ \varepsilon\ \sigma(V_0/[x\colon \mathbf{A}x])\langle\lvert V_0\rvert\rangle)\ , \sigma(V_0/[x\colon \mathbf{A}x])$	10 ZFCU$^+$
6	(12) $\forall v_2(\mathbf{A}(v_2) \supset v_2\varepsilon\ [x\colon \varphi x])$	6 &E
3,6	(13) $\mathrm{Sat}([x\colon \varphi x], \sigma(V_0/[x\colon \mathbf{A}x]), \lvert\psi(V_0, v_1, V_1)\rvert)$	3,11 SatI

38 Since $\mathrm{NA}(\sigma)$ is a wff in L.

39 I introduce this as a definitional abbreviation for the formula on line 7; substitutions henceforth on formulae containing ';' are to be understood as abbreviations for the results of substitutions corresponding to those on line 7.

40 Here we need the substitution lemma, provable by induction, that $x\ \varepsilon\ [x\colon \varphi x]$ is intersubstitutable with φx everywhere except in the scope of $[x\colon \theta x]$.

3,6 (14) $\forall v_2(\mathbf{A}(v_2) \supset v_2\varepsilon\, [x\colon \varphi x])\ \&$ 12,13 &I
$\mathrm{Sat}([x\colon \varphi x], \sigma(V_0/[x\colon \mathbf{A}x]), |\psi(V_0, v_1, V_1)|)$

3,6 (15) $\exists X(\forall v_2(X(v_2) \supset v_2\varepsilon\, [x\colon \varphi x])\ \&$ 14 ∃I
$\mathrm{Sat}([x\colon \varphi x], \sigma(V_0/[x\colon Xx]), |\psi(V_0, v_1, V_1)|))$

1,3 (16) $\exists X(\forall v_2(X(v_2) \supset v_2\varepsilon\, [x\colon \varphi x])\ \&$ 5,15, ∃E
$\mathrm{Sat}([x\colon \varphi x], \sigma(V_0/[x\colon Xx]), |\psi(V_0, v_1, V_1)|))$

17 (17) $\sim\mathrm{NA}(\sigma)$ H

1 (18) $\mathrm{NA}(\sigma)$ 1 SatE_2

1,17 (19) $\exists X(\forall v_2(X(v_2) \supset v_2\varepsilon\, [x\colon \varphi x])\ \&$ 17, 18,∼E
$\mathrm{Sat}([x\colon \varphi x], \sigma(V_0/[x\colon Xx]), |\psi(V_0, v_1, V_1)|))$

1 (20) $\exists X(\forall v_2(X(v_2) \supset v_2\varepsilon\, [x\colon \varphi x])\ \&$ 2, 16, 19∨E
$\mathrm{Sat}([x\colon \varphi x], \sigma(V_0/[x\colon Xx]), |\psi(V_0, v_1, V_1)|))$

In the other direction we have:

1 (1) $\exists X(\forall v_2(X(v_2) \supset v_2\varepsilon\, [x\colon \varphi x])\ \&$ H
$\mathrm{Sat}([x\colon \varphi x], \sigma(V_0/[x\colon Xx]), |\psi(V_0, v_1, V_1)|))$

2 (2) $\forall v_2(\mathbf{A}(v_2) \supset v_2\varepsilon\, [x\colon \varphi x])\ \&$ H
$\mathrm{Sat}([x\colon \varphi x], \sigma(V_0/[x\colon \mathbf{A}x]), |\psi(V_0, v_1, V_1)|)$

2 (3) $\mathrm{Sat}([x\colon \varphi x], \sigma(V_0/[x\colon \mathbf{A}x]), |\psi(V_0, v_1, V_1)|)$ 2 &E

2 (4) $\forall v_2(\mathbf{A}(v_2) \supset v_2\varepsilon\, [x\colon \varphi x])$ 2 &E

2 (5) $\{\psi(\lambda x(x\, \varepsilon\, \sigma(V_0/[x\colon \mathbf{A}x])\langle|V_0|\rangle)\, , \sigma(V_0/[x\colon \mathbf{A}x])\langle|v_1|\rangle,$
$\lambda x(x\, \varepsilon\, \sigma(V_0/[x\colon \mathbf{A}x]\langle|V_1|\rangle)))\}^{[x\colon \varphi x]})$ 3 SatE_1

2 (6) $\mathrm{NA}(\sigma(V_0/[x\colon \mathbf{A}x]))$ 3 SatE_2

2 (7) $\{\psi(\mathbf{A}, \sigma\langle|v_1|\rangle, \lambda x(x\, \varepsilon\, \sigma\langle|V_1|\rangle)))\}^{[x\colon \varphi x]}$ 5, 6[41]ZFCU$^+$

2 (8) $\forall v_2(\mathbf{A}(v_2) \supset v_2\varepsilon\, [x\colon \varphi x])\ \&$ 4, 7 &I
$\{\psi(\mathbf{A}, \sigma\langle|v_1|\rangle, \lambda x(x\, \varepsilon\, \sigma\langle|V_1|\rangle)))\}^{[x\colon \varphi x]}$

2 (9) $\exists X(\forall v_2(X(v_2) \supset v_2\varepsilon\, [x\colon \varphi x])\ \&$ 8∃I
$\{\psi(X, \sigma\langle|v_1|\rangle, \lambda x(x\, \varepsilon\, \sigma\langle|V_1|\rangle)))\}^{[x\colon \varphi x]})$

2 (10) $\{\exists X\psi(X, \sigma\langle|v_1|\rangle, \lambda x(x\, \varepsilon\, \sigma\langle|V_1|\rangle)))\}^{[x\colon \varphi x]})$ 9 Def.

2 (11) $\mathrm{NA}(\sigma)$ 10 ZFCU$^+$

2 (12) $\mathrm{Sat}([x\colon \varphi x], \sigma, |\exists V_0\psi(V_0, v_1, V_1)|)$ 9,11, SatI

1 (13) $\mathrm{Sat}([x\colon \varphi x], \sigma, |\exists V_0\psi(V_0, v_1, V_1)|)$ 1,2, 12∃E

REFERENCES

Boolos, George (1984) 'To be is to be the Value of a Bound Variable (or to be some Values of some Variables)', *The Journal of Philosophy*, 81, pp. 430–49. Reprinted Boolos (1998) p. 54–72.

—— (1985) 'Nominalist Platonism', *The Philosophical Review*, 94, pp. 327–44. Page references are to the version in Boolos (1998), pp. 73–87.

—— (1998) *Logic, Logic and Logic*. Cambridge, MA. Harvard University Press.

[41] Here we need the Lemma cited in the previous proof and the ZFCU$^+$ proofs that $\sigma\langle|v_1|\rangle = \sigma(V_0/[x\colon \mathbf{A}x])\langle|v_1|\rangle$ and that $\sigma(V_0/[x\colon \mathbf{A}x]\langle|V_1|\rangle = \sigma\langle|V_1|\rangle$.

Burge, Tyler (1979) 'Semantical Paradox', in Martin 1984, pp. 83–117. Originally published in 1979 in *The Journal of Philosophy*, 76.

Cartwright, Richard (1994) 'Speaking of Everything', *Noûs*, 28, pp. 1–20.

Dummett, Michael (1963) 'The Philosophical Significance of Gödel's Theorem', in his *Truth and Other Enigmas*, London: Duckworth, 1978, pp. 186–201. Originally published in 1963 in *Ratio*, V.

——(1981) *Frege: Philosophy of Language*. London: Duckworth, 2nd edn.

——(1991) *Frege: Philosophy of Mathematics*. London: Duckworth.

——(1993) 'What is Mathematics about?', in his *The Seas of Language*, Oxford: Clarendon, 1993, pp. 429–45. Also published in 1994 in Alexander George (ed.) *Mathematics and Mind*, Oxford: Oxford University Press.

——1994: 'Chairman's Address: Basic Law V', *Proceedings of the Aristotelian Society*, New Series 94, pp. 243–51.

Field, Hartry (2003*a*) 'A Revenge-Immune Solution to the Semantic Paradoxes', *Journal of Philosophical Logic* 32.

——(2003*b*) 'The Consistency of the Naïve(?) Theory of Properties', in Godehard Link (ed.) *One Hundred Years of Russell's Paradox- Logical Philosophy Then and Now* (Walter de Gruyter).

——(2004) 'The Consistency of the Naïve Theory of Properties', *The Philosophical Quarterly* pp. 78–104.

Forster, T. E. (1992) *Set Theory with a Universal Set*. Oxford: Clarendon Press.

Kripke, Saul (1975) 'Outline of a Theory of Truth', in Martin (1984) pp. 53–82. Originally published in 1975 in the *Journal of Philosophy*, 72.

Lewis, David (1991) *Parts of Classes*. Oxford: Blackwell.

Martin, R. L. (ed.), (1984) *Recent Essays on Truth and the Liar Paradox*. Oxford: Clarendon Press.

Martin, R. L. and Woodruff, P. W. (1975) 'On Representing "True-in-L" in L', in Martin, 1984, pp. 47–52. Originally published in 1975 in *Philosophia* 5.

McGee, Vann (1997) 'How We Learn Mathematical Language', *The Philosophical Review*, 106, pp. 35–68.

——(2003) 'Universal Universal Quantification', in J. C. Beall (ed.), *Liars and Heaps*, Oxford: Clarendon Press, pp. 357–64.

Oberschelp, Arnold (1973) *Set Theory Over Classes*, in *Dissertationies Mathematicae*, CVI, Warsaw: Panstwowe Wydawnictwo Naukowe.

Parsons, Charles (1974) 'Sets and Classes', in his *Mathematics in Philosophy: Selected Essays* Ithaca: Cornell University Press, 1983 pp. 209–21. Originally published in 1974 in *Noûs*, 8.

Priest, Graham (1987) *In Contradiction*. Dordrecht: Nijhoff.

Quine, W. V. (1970) *Philosophy of Logic*. Englewood Cliffs NJ: Prentice Hall.

Rayo, A., 'Beyond Plurals', *this volume*.

——and Uzquiano, G. (1999) 'Toward a Theory of Second-Order Consequence', *Notre Dame Journal of Formal Logic* 40 (1999) pp. 315–325.

——and Williamson, T. (2003) 'A Completeness Theorem for Unrestricted First-Order Languages', in J. C. Beall, (ed.), *Liars and Heaps*. Oxford: Oxford University Press, 2003.

Shapiro, Stewart (1991) *Foundations without Foundationalism: A Case for Second-Order Logic*. Oxford: Clarendon.

Tennant, Neil (1978) *Natural Logic*. Edinburgh: Edinburgh University Press.

Uzquiano, G., 'Unrestricted Unrestricted Quantification', *this volume*.

Weir, Alan (1998*a*) 'Naïve Set Theory is Innocent!' *Mind* 107, 1998, pp. 763–98.

Weir, Alan (1998*b*) 'Dummett on Impredicativity', *Grazer Philosophische Studien* 55, 1998, pp. 65–101.

——(1998*c*) 'Naïve Set Theory, Paraconsistency and Indeterminacy I'. *Logique et Analyse* 161–3, 1998, pp. 219–66.

——(1999) 'Naïve Set Theory, Paraconsistency and Indeterminacy II, *Logique et Analyse,* 167–8, 1999, pp. 283–340.

——(2004) 'There are no True Contradictions', in G. Priest, J. C. Beall, B. Armour-Garb (eds.), *The Law of Non-Contradiction; New Philosophical Essays*, Oxford: Oxford University Press, 2004 Ch. 22, pp. 385–417.

——(2005) 'Naïve Truth and Sophisticated Logic', in B. Armour-Garb, J. C. Beall, (eds.), *Deflationism and Paradox,* Oxford: Oxford University Press, pp. 218–49.

Williamson, Timothy (2003) 'Everything', in J. Hawthorne and D. Zimmerman (eds.), *Philosophical Perspectives* 17, *Language and Philosophical Linguistics*, Blackwell, Malden, 2003, pp. 414–66.

13

Absolute Identity and Absolute Generality

Timothy Williamson

The aim of this chapter is to tighten our grip on some issues about quantification by analogy with corresponding issues about identity on which our grip is tighter. We start with the issues about identity.

13.1

In conversations between native speakers, words such as 'same' and 'identical' do not usually cause much difficulty. We take it for granted that others use them with the same sense as we do. If it is unclear whether numerical or qualitative identity is intended, a brief gloss such as 'one thing not two' for the former or 'exactly alike' for the latter removes the unclarity. In this paper, numerical identity is intended. A particularly conscientious and logically aware speaker might explain what 'identical' means in her mouth by saying: 'Everything is identical with itself. If something is identical with something, then whatever applies to the former also applies to the latter.' It seems perverse to continue doubting whether 'identical' in her mouth means *identical* (in our sense). Yet other interpretations are conceivable. For instance, she might have been speaking an odd idiolect in which 'identical' means *in love*, under the misapprehension that everything is in love with itself and with nothing else (narcissism as a universal theory).

Let us stick to interpretations on which she spoke truly. Let us also assume for the time being that we can interpret her use of the other words homophonically. We will make no assumption at this stage as to whether 'everything' and 'something' are restricted to a domain of contextually relevant objects. We can argue that 'identical' in her mouth is coextensive with 'identical' in ours. For suppose that an object x is identical in her sense with an object y. By our interpretative hypotheses, if something is identical in her sense with something, then whatever applies to the former also applies to the latter. Thus whatever applies to x also applies to y. By the logic of identity in our sense (in particular, reflexivity), everything is identical in our sense

Thanks to Kit Fine, Øystein Linnebo, Agustín Rayo, and Gabriel Uzquiano for helpful comments on a draft of this chapter. A version of the material was presented at the conference at the Central European University in Budapert; thanks also to the audience there, especially the commentator Katalin Forkas, for useful discussion.

with itself, so x is identical in our sense with x. Thus being such that x is identical in our sense with it applies to x. Consequently, being such that x is identical in our sense with it applies to y. Therefore, x is identical in our sense with y. Generalizing: whatever things are identical in her sense are identical in ours. Conversely, suppose that x is identical in our sense with y. By the logic of identity in our sense (in particular, Leibniz's Law), if something is identical in our sense with something, then whatever applies to the former also applies to the latter. Thus whatever applies to x also applies to y. By our interpretative hypotheses, everything is identical in her sense with itself, so x is identical in her sense with x. Thus being such that x is identical in her sense with it applies to x. Consequently, being such that x is identical in her sense with it applies to y. Therefore, x is identical in her sense with y. Generalizing: whatever things are identical in our sense are identical in hers. Conclusion: identity in her sense is coextensive with identity in our sense.[1]

Of course, coextensiveness does not imply synonymy or even necessary coextensiveness. Thus we have not yet ruled out finer-grained differences in meaning between her use of 'identical' and ours. If we can interpret her explanation as consisting of logical truths, then, given that the argument invoked about identity in our sense (reflexivity and Leibniz's Law) are also logical truths, we can show that the universally quantified biconditional linking identity in her sense with identity in ours is a logical truth, so that coextensiveness is logically guaranteed. If the relevant kind of logical truth is closed under the rule of necessitation from modal logic, then the necessitated universally quantified biconditional too is a logical truth, so that necessary coextensiveness is also logically guaranteed.[2] But not even a logical guarantee of necessary coextensiveness suffices for synonymy: we have such a guarantee for 'cat who licks all and only those cats who do not lick themselves' and 'mouse who is not a mouse', but they are not synonymous. Nevertheless, even simple coextensiveness excludes by far the worst forms of misunderstanding.

But now we must reconsider our homophonic interpretation of all our speaker's other words. In her second claim, 'If something is identical with something, then whatever applies to the former also applies to the latter', how much did 'whatever' cover? We can regiment her utterance as the schema (2) of first-order logic (for the record, we also formalize her first claim as (1)):

$$(1)\quad \forall x\, xIx$$

$$(2)\quad \forall x\, \forall y\, (xIy \rightarrow (A(x) \rightarrow A(y)))$$

Here 'I' symbolizes identity in her sense; $A(y)$ differs from $A(x)$ at most in having the variable y in some or all places where $A(x)$ has the variable x. Our speaker will instantiate (2) only by formulas $A(x)$ and $A(y)$ of her language. But our argument for coextensiveness in effect involved the inference from xIy and $x = x$ to $x = y$, where '=' symbolizes identity in our sense. To use (2) for that purpose, we must take $A(x)$ and $A(y)$ to be $x = x$ and $x = y$ respectively. By what right did we treat $x = x$ and $x = y$ as formulas of her language, not merely of ours? Perhaps her language has no

[1] The argument goes back to Quine (1961); see the reprinted version in Quine (1966) at 178.

[2] The logic of indexicals is arguably not closed under the rule of necessitation (Kaplan 1989). Such problems do not seem to arise for (1) and (2).

equivalent formulas, and both (1) and all instances of (2) in her language are true even though '*I*' does not have the extension of identity in our sense.

We can be more precise. Let M be an ordinary model with a nonempty domain D for a first-order language L. Define a new model M* for L as follows. The domain D* of M* contains all and only ordered pairs $\langle d, j\rangle$, where d is a member of D and j is a member of some fixed index set J of finite cardinality | J| greater than one; pick a member # of J. If R is an n-adic atomic predicate of L, the extension of R in M* contains the n-tuple $\langle\langle d_1, j_1\rangle, \ldots, \langle d_n, j_n\rangle\rangle$ if and only if the extension of R in M contains the n-tuple $\langle d_1, \ldots, d_n\rangle$. If the constant c denotes d in M, c denotes $\langle d, \#\rangle$ in M*. More generally, if the n-place function symbol f of L denotes a function φ in M, f denotes the function φ^* in M*, where $\varphi^*(\langle d_1, j_1\rangle, \ldots, \langle d_n, j_n\rangle)$ is $\langle \varphi(d_1, \ldots, d_n), \#\rangle$. Given this definition of M*, it is routine to prove that exactly the same formulas of L are true in M* as in M.[3] Now suppose that the dyadic atomic predicate I of L is interpreted by identity in M; its extension there consists of all pairs $\langle d, d\rangle$, where d is in D. Thus (1) and all instances of (2) are true in M. Consequently, (1) and all instances of (2) are true in M*. Nevertheless, I is not interpreted by identity in M*, for the extension of I in M* contains the pair $\langle\langle d, j\rangle, \langle d, k\rangle\rangle$ for any member d of D and members j and k of J. Thus in M* everything has the relation for which I stands to |J| things, and therefore to |J|−1 things distinct from itself, although one cannot express that fact in L. Nor does any formula, simple or complex, of L express identity in M*, whether or not identity is expressed in M by some formula.[4] We cannot rule out M*

[3] Sketch of proof: Let a be any assignment of values in D* to variables. Let $a^\wedge$ be the assignment of values in D to variables such that for any variable v, if $a(v)$ is $\langle d, j\rangle$ then $a^\wedge(v)$ is d. It is routine to prove that for any term t, if t denotes $\langle d, j\rangle$ in M* relative to a then t denotes d in M under $a^\wedge$ (by induction on the complexity of t). Thus any atomic formula $Rt_1 \ldots, t_n$ is true in M* under an assignment a if and only if it is true in M under $a^\wedge$, by definition of the extension of R in M*. We show that any formula A of L is true in M* under an assignment a if and only if it is true in M under $a^\wedge$ by induction on the complexity of A. The induction step for the truth-functors is trivial. For the universal quantifier, the induction hypothesis is this: for every assignment b of values in D*, A is true in M* under b if and only if it is true in M under $b^\wedge$. Suppose that $\forall x A$ is not true in M* under an assignment a. Then, under some assignment b of values in D* that differs from a at most over x, A is not true in M*. By the induction hypothesis, A is not true in M under $b^\wedge$. By construction, $b^\wedge$ differs from $a^\wedge$ at most over x. Thus $\forall x A$ is not true in M under $a^\wedge$. Conversely, suppose that $\forall x A$ is not true in M under $a^\wedge$. Then, under some assignment $a^\wedge!$ of values in D that differs from $a^\wedge$ at most over x, A is not true in M. Let b be the assignment of values in D* like a except that $b(x)$ is $\langle a^\wedge!(x), \#\rangle$. Thus $b^\wedge$ is $a^\wedge!$, so A is not true in M under $b^\wedge$. By induction hypothesis, A is not true in M* under b. Since b differs from a at most over x, $\forall x A$ is not true in M* under a. Thus any formula A is true in M* under an assignment a if and only if it is true in M under $a^\wedge$. Finally, we show that a formula is true in M* iff it is true in M. If A is not true in M*, then, under some assignment a of values in D*, A is not true in M*, so A is not true in M under $a^\wedge$, so A is not true in M. Conversely, if A is not true in M, then, under some assignment \$ of values in D, A is not true in M; but \$ is $a^\wedge$ for some assignment a of values in D* (since we can set $a(v)$ to be $\langle \$(v), \#\rangle$), so A is not true in M* under a, so A is not true under a. The whole construction is adapted from the standard proof of the upward Löwenheim–Skolem theorem for first-order logic without identity. All it really requires is a homomorphism in a suitable sense from M* onto M; thus it is inessential that an equal and finite number of members of D* are mapped to each member of D.

[4] Proof: Suppose that $A(x,y)$ expresses identity in M*: for every assignment a of values in D*, $A(x,y)$ is true in M* under a if and only if $a(x)$ is $a(y)$. For some member d of D, let a be an assignment of values in D* such that both $a(x)$ and $a(y)$ are $\langle d, \#\rangle$. By hypothesis, $A(x,y)$ is true in

by adding a sentence of L that is false in M* to our theory of identity ((1) and (2)), for any such sentence will also be false in M, the 'intended' model.

We may object that M* is not a model for a first-order language with identity, precisely because it does not interpret any atomic predicate of the language by identity. What distinguishes first-order logic with identity from first-order logic without identity is that the former treats an atomic identity predicate as a logical constant. In standard first-order logic with identity, logical consequence is defined as truth-preservation in all models, and all models are stipulated to interpret that predicate by identity. Unintended interpretations of some basic mathematical terms can be excluded in first-order logic with identity but not in first-order logic without identity.

An example is the concept of linear (total) ordering. In first-order logic with identity, we standardly axiomatize the theory of (reflexive) linear orders (such as $\leq$ on the real numbers) by (3), (4) and (5):

(3) $\forall x \forall y \forall z((xRy \& yRz) \rightarrow xRz)$ (transitivity)
(4) $\forall x \forall y (xRy \vee yRx)$ (connectedness)
(5) $\forall x \forall y ((xRy \& yRx) \rightarrow x = y)$ (anti-symmetry)

The models of this little theory are exactly those in which *R* is interpreted by a reflexive linear order (over the relevant domain). The use of the identity predicate in the anti-symmetry axiom (5) is essential. For if *R* is interpreted by a reflexive linear order, then the open formula *Rxy* & *Ryx* must express identity (over the relevant domain). But we have seen that in first-order logic without identity any theory with a model M has a model M* as above in which no formula expresses identity, therefore in which *R* is not interpreted by a reflexive linear order. Consequently, no theory in first-order logic without identity has as models exactly those in which *R* is interpreted by a reflexive linear order. Since the models of first-oder logic with and without identity differ only over the interpretation of the identity predicate, even in first-order logic with identity no theory axiomated purely by sentences without the identity predicate has as models exactly those in which *R* is interpreted by a reflexive linear order.

The position is substantially the same for irreflexive linear orders. To axiomatize the theory of irreflexive linear orders (such as $<$ on the real numbers), we standardly retain axiom (3) but replace (4) and (5) by (6) and (7):

(6) $\forall x \forall y (xRy \vee yRx \vee x = y)$ (linearity)
(7) $\forall x \forall y (xRy \rightarrow \sim yRx)$ (asymmetry)

The use of the identity predicate in the linearity axiom (6) is essential. For if *R* is interpreted by an irreflexive linear order, then the open formula $\sim xRy$ & $\sim yRx$ must express identity (over the relevant domain). In first-order logic without identity, any theory with a model has a model in which no formula expresses identity, therefore

M* under *a*. Let *b* be an assignment of values like *a* except that $b(y)$ is $\langle d, \#\# \rangle$ for some member ## of J distinct from #. By hypothesis, $A(x, y)$ is not true in M* under *b*, since $b(x)$ is not $b(y)$. By the argument of the previous footnote and in its notation: $A(x, y)$ is true in M* under *a* if and only if it is true in M under $a^\wedge$; $A(x, y)$ is true in M* under *b* if and only if it is true in M under $b^\wedge$. But $a^\wedge$ is $b^\wedge$. Thus $A(x, y)$ is true in M* under *a* if and only if it is true in M* under *b*. Contradiction.

in which R is not interpreted by an irreflexive linear order. Consequently, no theory in first-order logic without identity has as models exactly those in which R is interpreted by an irreflexive linear order. Even in first-order logic with identity, no theory axiomatized purely by sentences without the identity predicate has as models exactly those in which R is interpreted by an irreflexive linear order.

First-order logic with identity is superior in expressive power to first-order logic without identity in mathematically central ways.[5]

Nevertheless, the appeal to first-order logic with identity may not resolve the doubts of those who take the problem of interpretation seriously. Indeed, it may strike them as cheating. For how do we know that the speaker whom we are trying to interpret is using a first-order language with identity at all? For example, how do we know that she is trying to talk about linear ordering? To pose the problem in less epistemic terms: what makes it the case that the speaker is using a first-order language with identity?

Quine has a short way with bloated models such as M*. He excludes them by his methodology of interpretation, which requires us to interpret the language in such a way that the strongest indiscernibility relation expressible in it is identity. Roughly speaking, he applies *a priori* the inverse of the operation that took M to M*. As he says, we thereby 'impose a certain identification of indiscernibles', adding 'but only in a mild way' (1960, 230). The 'mildness' consists in this: indiscernibility in the relevant sense is the negation of weak discernibility, not of strong discernibility. Objects d and d^* in the domain of the interpretation are strongly discernible if and only if, for some open formula $A(x)$ of L with one free variable (x) and assignments a and a^* to variables of values in the domain, a^* is like a except that $a(x)$ is d while $a^*(x)$ is d^*, and the truth-value of $A(x)$ under a differs from its truth-value under a^*. The definition of weak discernibility is the same except that variables other than x are allowed to occur free in $A(x)$. For example, consider a language with just one atomic predicate, a dyadic one I, without constants or function symbols, and an interpretation with an infinite domain, over which I is interpreted by identity. Let d and d^* be distinct members of the domain. Then d and d^* are not strongly discernible, but they are weakly discernible by the formula xIy and assignments a and a^*, where $a(x)$ is d, $a(y)$ is d^* and a^* is like a except that $a(x)$ is d^*. In this case, Quine's methodology does not erase distinctions between members of the domain: doing so here would involve collapsing the domain to a single object and so switching the formula $\forall x \forall y\ (xIx \rightarrow xIy)$ from false to true. The identification of indiscernibles as he apparently intends it has the hermeneutically appealing feature that it does not alter the truth-value of any formula.[6]

[5] For the view that identity is not a logical constant, which puts first-order logic with identity in an anomalous position, see Peacocke (1976).

[6] The text does not follow Quine in inessential details. He speaks of the satisfaction of a formula with a given number of free variables by that number of objects in a given order, rather than of the truth of a formula under an assignment of objects to all variables. Quine (1960, 230) incorrectly claims that the relevant kind of discernibility is relative discernibility: satisfaction of an open formula with two free variables by the objects in only one order. Quine (1976) implicitly corrects the mistake. In the example in the text (taken from that article), no two objects are even relatively discernible.

In other examples, Quine's methodology has more radical effects on the model. For instance, consider another language with just two atomic predicates, the monadic F and G, without constants or function symbols, and an interpretation on which 1,000 members of the domain are in the intersection of the extensions of F and G, just one is in the extension of F but not of G, 1,000,000 are in the extension of G but not of F, and just one in the extension of neither. Objects are weakly discernible if and only if either one is in the extension of F while the other is not or one is in the extension of G while the other is not. Thus Quine's 'mild' identification of indiscernibles collapses the 1,000 objects in the intersection of the extensions of F and G into a single object, and the 1,000,000 objects in the extension of G but not F into another single object.[7]

Moreover, Quine's methodology does not preserve the truth-values of all formulas once we add generalized quantifiers to the language. For instance, let us add a binary quantifier M for 'most' to the language in the last example, where Mx ($A(x)$; $B(x)$) is true under an assignment a if and only if most (more than half) of the members d of the domain such that $A(x)$ is true under $a[d/x]$ are such that $B(x)$ is true under $a[d/x]$, where the assignment $a[d/x]$ is like a except that $a[d/x](x)$ is d. The addition of M to the language makes no difference to weak discernibility. On the original interpretation, the sentence Mx (Fx; Gx) is true, because 1,000 of the 1,001 objects in the extension of F are in the extension of G, while Mx (Gx; Fx) is false, because only 1,000 of the 1,001,000 objects in the extension of G are in the extension of F. By contrast, after the identification of indiscernibles, both sentences are false, because exactly one of the two objects in the extension of F is in the extension of G and exactly one of the two objects in the extension of G is in the extension of F. Moreover, no attempt to reinterpret 'M' as a logical quantifier other than 'most' in line with the identification of indiscernibles would preserve the truth-values of all formulas. For the collapsed model is symmetrical between F and G: each applies to exactly one thing to which the other does not. Thus on any interpretation of 'M' as a logical quantifier Mx (Fx; Gx) and Mx (Gx; Fx) will receive the same truth-value in the collapsed model, whereas they have different truth-values in the new model (see Westerstähl (1989) for logical quantifiers).

Thus the ability of Quine's identification of indiscernibles to preserve the truth-values of all formulas depends on an unwarranted restriction of the language to the usual quantifiers $\forall$ and $\exists$.[8] In the presence of other quantifiers, his identification of indiscernibles does not preserve truth-values, and so is hermeneutically unappealing. Of course, the example was a toy one; the expressive resources of the language were radically impoverished by comparison with any natural human language.

The text attributes a domain to the interpretation, perhaps contrary to Quine's intentions, in order to make it clear that the argument here does not rely on contentious premises about unrestricted quantification.

[7] See Wiggins (2001, 185) for discussion of a related example, attributed to Wallace (1964).

[8] The addition of generalized quantifiers impacts on the 'bloated' model M*. No problem arises for 'most', since the construction preserves the ratios between the cardinalities of the extensions of predicates (for the index set J was stipulated to be finite), but numerical quantifiers must be reinterpreted in order to give all formulas the same truth-values as in M: 'at least m' is interpreted as 'at least $m|J|$'.

Nevertheless, it shows that Quine's methodology does not provide an adequate solution to the problem of interpreting an identity predicate. For if independent considerations have not eliminated interpretations of a natural language on which its domain contains distinct indiscernibles, the use of Quine's methodology to do so risks imposing on the language an interpretation far less charitable to its speakers than some of the 'bloated' interpretations are.

An alternative, anti-Quinean, proposal is to move from first-order to second-order logic. We could then replace the first-order schema (2) with a single second-order axiom:

$$(2+)\quad \forall x\, \forall y(xIy \rightarrow \forall P\,(Px \rightarrow Py))$$

In the usual models for higher-order logic, the second-order quantifier $\forall P$ is required to range in effect over all subsets of the first-order domain. Given any two objects d and d^*, some subset of the domain (for example, $\{d\}$) contains d but not d^*. Similarly, if one interprets $\forall P$ as a plural quantifier, there are some objects of which d is one and of which d^* is not one. Thus (2+), conjoined with (1), forces the predicate I to have the extension of identity over the domain. For practical purposes, one could even use the open formula $\forall P\,(Px \rightarrow Py)$ simply to *define* identity, although it is unlikely that second-order quantification is conceptually more basic than identity in any deep sense.[9] But the appeal to second-order quantification may not satisfy those who are seriously worried about the problem of interpreting the identity predicate. For how do we know, or what makes it the case, that the second-order quantifier $\forall P$ should be interpreted in the standard way? Consider an interpretation of the first-order fragment of the language (with I as an atomic predicate) on which not all pairs of distinct members of the domain are weakly discernible, and the extension of I contains exactly those pairs of members of the domain that are not weakly discernible. We can now construct a non-standard interpretation of the full second-order language by stipulating that the range of the second-order quantifiers is to be restricted to those subsets of the domain with the property that if d is a member and d^* is not weakly discernible from d with respect to the first-order fragment then d^* is also a member (a similar stipulation is available for the plural interpretation).[10] It can then be shown that, on this interpretation, objects are weakly discernible with respect to the full second-order language if and only if they are weakly discernible with respect to the first-order fragment. Consequently, not all distinct pairs of members of the first-order domain are weakly discernible with respect to the full second-order language. Nevertheless, (1) and (2+) come out true on such an interpretation even though I is not interpreted by identity over the domain. Thus invoking second-order logic only pushes the problem back to that of interpreting higher-order languages.[11]

[9] See also Shapiro (1991, 63). Since the values over which the second-order quantifier ranges are closed under complementation relative to the individual domain, strengthening the conditional in the *definiens* to a biconditional would make no difference.

[10] The construction can be generalized to polyadic predicate variables and to orders greater than two, if desired.

[11] Such non-standard models are models in the sense of the non-standard semantics with respect to which Henkin (1950) proves the completeness of higher-order logic. As Shapiro (1991, 76)

If we conceive the hermeneutic problem as purely epistemic—how do we know whether another means *identical*?—then we may suppose that it does not arise in the first-person case: how can I be mistaken in thinking that by 'identical' I mean *identical*? But if the problem is constitutive—in virtue of what does another mean *identical* by 'identical'?—then it presumably arises just as much in the first-person case: in virtue of what do I mean *identical* by 'identical'? Despairing of an answer, someone might doubt the very conception of identity that underlies the question. One might even become a relativist about identity in the manner of Peter Geach, with a conception of a predicate's playing the role of *I* relative to a given language, by verifying (1) and all instances of (2) in that language, but reject any conception of its playing the role absolutely, by verifying (1) and all instances of (2) in all possible extensions of the language.[12]

Such a reaction would be grossly premature, resting on no properly worked out, plausible account of interpretation. Questions of the form 'In virtue of what do we mean *X* by "X"?' are notoriously hard to answer satisfactorily, no matter what is substituted for 'X' (Kripke 1982). It is therefore methodologically misguided to treat a particular expression (for instance, 'identical') as problematic merely on the grounds that the question is hard to answer satisfactorily for it.[13] Of course, the details of the alternative interpretations and surrounding arguments depend on the nature of the expression at issue, but that should not cause us to overlook the generality of the underlying problem. It is extremely doubtful that the skeptical reaction yields anything coherent when generalized. In the particular case of identity, few have found Geach's arguments for his local skepticism convincing or his relativism plausible. In any case, let us suppose that we do use 'identical' in an absolute way, and ask in virtue of what we do so. Given what has just been said, we should not expect more than a sketchy answer.

Somehow or other, 'identical' means what it does because we use it in the way that we do. A central part of that use concerns our inferential practice with the term, as summarized by (1) and (2) or (2+). What is crucial in our use of the first-order schema (2) (or a corresponding first-order inference rule) is that we do not treat it as exhausted by its instances in our current language. Rather, we have a general disposition to accept instances of (2) in extensions of our current language. That is not to say that in all circumstances in which we are or could be presented with an instance

remarks, 'Henkin semantics and first-order semantics are pretty much the same'. It is therefore no surprise that, once Henkin models are allowed, higher-order logic is no advance on first-order logic in solving the interpretation problem. Similarly, the substitution of Henkin semantics for the standard semantics throws away the advantages of second-order logic over first-order logic as a setting for mathematical theories. For example, the result that all models of second-order arithmetic are mutually isomorphic holds only for the standard semantics; non-standard models of first-order arithmetic can be simulated by appropriate Henkin models of second-order arithmetic.

[12] Geach gives his views on identity in his (1967), (1972), (1980), (1991) and elsewhere. For critical discussion of them see Dummett (1981, 547–83) and (1993), Noonan (1997) and Hawthorne (2003, 111–23). See also Wiggins (2001, 21–54).

[13] Geach can allow that in a suitable context 'identical' may means *same F*, understood as identity relative to the informative sortal expression *F*; the question concerns the use of 'identical' in contexts that supply no such sortal.

of (2) in an extension of our current language, we accept it. Obviously, we may reject it as a result of computational error, or die of shock at the sight of it, or roll our eyes as a protest against pedantry; some instances may be too long or complex to be presented to us at all. But the existence of a large gap of that kind between the disposition and the conditionals is the normal case for dispositions, including ordinary physical dispositions such as fragility and toxicity: external factors of all sorts (such as antidotes) can intervene between them and their manifestations. The link between the disposition to D if C and conditionals of the form 'If C, it Ds' is of a much looser sort. The failure of some of the associated conditionals does not show the absence of the disposition.[14] We have the general disposition because we respond, when we do, to the general form of the schema (2) (or of a corresponding inference rule) rather than treating each of its instances as an independent problem. Our non-intentionally described behaviour alone does not explain why we count as responding to the actual form of (2) and not to some gerrymandered variant on it with *ad hoc* restrictions for cases beyond our ken: it is also relevant that the actual form is more natural than the gerrymandered one in a way that fits it for being meant (it is a 'reference magnet').[15]

Our understanding of (2) as transcending the bounds of our current language is already suggested by our use of the phrase 'Leibniz's Law' for a single principle. We do not usually think of the phrase as ambiguously denoting lots of different principles, one for each language.

In the case of the second-order axiom (2+), what is crucial is that we do not treat the rule of universal instantiation for the second-order quantifier as exhausted by its instances in our current language. Rather, we have a general disposition to accept instances of universal instantiation for the second-order quantifier in extensions of our current language. Again, the presence of the disposition is consistent with the failure of some of the associated conditionals. We have the general disposition because we respond to the general form of universal instantiation rather than treating each of its instances as a separate problem.

The sort of open-ended commitment just described is typical of our commitment to rules of inference. For example, my commitment to reasoning by disjunctive syllogism is not exhausted by my commitment to its instances in my current language; when I learn a new word, I am not faced with an open question concerning whether to apply disjunctive syllogism to sentences in which it occurs. Indeed, open-ended commitment may well be the default sort of commitment: one's commitment is open-ended unless one does something special to restrict it.

Open-ended commitment is just what is needed to reinstate the argument given at the beginning for a homophonic interpretation of another's use of the word

[14] On the relation between dispositions and conditionals see Martin (1994), Lewis (1997), Bird (1998), and Mumford (1998). For the specific application to rule-following see Martin and Heil (1998).

[15] On the role of naturalness in the constitution of meaning see Lewis (1983). Of course, we may have to check putative instances of (2) to ensure that they really have the form that they appear to have and do not involve intensional or quotational contexts, shifts of reference in indexicals and so on. But such problems are not at the heart of the dispute between absolutists and relativists about identity.

'identical', given her commitment to (in effect) (1) and (2). We reason as follows. Let agents S and S* speak distinct first-order languages L and L* respectively. For simplicity, assume that S and S* coincide in their logical vocabulary, with the possible exception of an identity predicate. Their interpretation of the other logical vocabulary is assumed to be standard; although the present style of argument can be extended to the other logical vocabulary, that is not our present concern. Let I be a predicate of L but not of L* and I^* a predicate of L* but not of L. Suppose that S has an open-ended commitment to (1) and (2), while S* has an open-ended commitment to (1*) and (2*), the results of substituting I^* for I in (1) and (2):

(1*) $\forall x\, xI^*x$

(2*) $\forall x \forall y\, (xI^*y \rightarrow (A(x) \rightarrow A(y))$

Now merge L and L* into a single first-order language L+L* whose primitive vocabulary is the union of the primitive vocabularies of L and L*. Thus we can treat (1) and (1*) as sentences of L+L* and (2) and (2*) as schemas of L+L*. The interpretation of the logical vocabulary of L+L* is assumed to be standard, like that of L and L*, again with the possible exception of an identity predicate. The quantifiers of L+L* are interpreted as ranging over the intersection of the domains of the quantifiers of L and of L*, for our present question is in effect whether I and I^* can diverge for objects over which both are defined. By the open-endedness of their commitments, S is committed to (1) as a sentence of L+L* and to all instances of (2) in L+L*, while S* is committed to (1*) as a sentence of L+L* and to all instances of (2*) in L+L*. Here are instances of (2) and (2*) respectively in L+L*:

(8) $\forall x \forall y(xIy \rightarrow (xI^*x \rightarrow xI^*y)$

(8*) $\forall x \forall y(xI^*y \rightarrow (xIx \rightarrow xIy)$

Reasoning in L+L*, we deduce (9) from (1*) and (8) and (9*) from (1) and (8*):

(9) $\forall x \forall y(xIy \rightarrow xI^*y)$

(9*) $\forall x \forall y(xI^*y \rightarrow xIy)$

Thus, given the pooled commitments of S and S*, I and I^* are coextensive over the common domain. The result should not be interpreted as concerning only the extensions of I and I^* in a new context created by the fusion of L and L*. For the open-ended commitments in play were incurred by S and S* in using I and I^* in the original contexts for L and L* respectively; that is the nature of open-endedness. Thus the result concerns the extensions of I and I^* in the original contexts for L and L* too.

In the way just seen, (1) and the open-ended schema uniquely characterize identity (recall that the other logical vocabulary in (9) and (9*) is being given its standard interpretation). A similar argument can be given for the second-order analogue of (2). The arguments are in fact a special case of a more general pattern of reasoning that shows all the usual logical constants to be uniquely characterized by the classical principles of logic for them.[16]

[16] For further discussion and references see Harris (1982), Williamson (1987/8) and McGee (2000).

Of course, these remarks fall far short of a fully satisfying account of what makes 'identical' mean *identical*. The connection between which logical principles a speaker *accepts* for a given expression and which logical principles are *correct* (true or truth-preserving) for that expression is quite loose; no reasonable principle of charity in interpretation guarantees freedom from logical error. Misguided philosophers who reject standard logical principles for 'identical' probably still mean *identical* by the word, because they continue to use it as a word of the common language.[17] It is a fallacy to reason from the premise that someone has a wildly deviant theory to the conclusion that they speak a deviant language. Perhaps even more misguided philosophers could argue themselves into the view that the logic of the phrase 'in love' comprises analogues of the standard logical principles for 'identical', while still meaning *in love* rather than *identical* by the phrase, because they continue to use it as a phrase of the common language. Nevertheless, such examples do not suggest that the account above of how 'identical' means *identical* does not at least point in the right direction, for they may still be parasitic on a loose underlying connection between inferential practice and meaning.

Naturally, the account will not help if it is incoherent, as Geach would claim it to be. According to him, generalizing over all predicates in all possible extensions of the language generates semantic paradoxes (1972, 240; 1991, 297). Now the foregoing account does not assume that speakers who reason with (1) and (2) or (2+) must themselves have a conception of all predicates in all possible extensions of the language. For the sentences involved in such reasoning need not be metalinguistic. If speakers already have metalinguistic vocabulary in the language, they can use it in what they substitute for $A(x)$ and $A(y)$ in (2), but that does not imply that the schema itself is distinctively metalinguistic. Agents may lack the conceptual apparatus necessary to give a reflective account of their own practices. However, the foregoing theoretical account does deploy something reminiscent of the conception of all predicates in all possible extensions of the language on its own behalf, in explaining the nature of speakers' open-ended commitments. Thus Geach's charge is at least relevant.

Unfortunately, Geach does not bother to argue in detail that the theorist of absolute identity really requires conceptual resources powerful enough to generate semantic paradoxes. In fact, when we consider identity over a given set domain, we need only generalize over all subsets of that domain, or over all subsets of the Cartesian product of the domain with itself.[18] For the unique characterization argument above, we need merely consider expansions of the language by a single dyadic atomic predicate I^*, whose extension is a subset of the Cartesian product of the original domain with itself. Similarly, schema (2) forces I to have the extension of identity over the domain as soon as we consider its instances in expansions of the language by a single monadic atomic predicate, whose extension is a subset of the original domain. In standard (Zermelo–Fraenkel) set theory, sets are closed under the power set operation and the formation of Cartesian products. Thus quantification

[17] See Williamson (2003b) for arguments of this type.

[18] The Cartesian product of sets X and Y is the set of all ordered pairs whose first member belongs to X and second member belongs to Y.

over subsets of the original set domain or of its Cartesian product with itself is quantification over another set domain. Consequently, the kind of generalization required for the theorist of absolute identity over a given set domain is of a quite harmless sort. It poses no serious threat of semantic or set-theoretic paradox. Some mysteries about the power set operation remain unsolved, notably Cantor's continuum problem (how many subsets has the set of natural numbers?), but they are not paradoxes. In any case, they are largely independent of the application to identity, for they concern the size of the whole power set, whereas in order to characterize identity it suffices to have just the singleton sets of members of the original domain; there are no more singletons of members than members. Geach's argument for the incoherence of absolute identity theory does not withstand attention.

Suppose that the foregoing account of our grasp of absolute identity is correct, as far as it goes. What does it suggest about our grasp of absolute generality, generality over absolutely everything, without any explicit or implicit restrictions whatsoever?

13.2

Sympathetic readers will have felt little difficulty in understanding the words 'absolute generality, generality over absolutely everything, without any explicit or implicit restrictions whatsoever': but in principle those words are open to alternative interpretations. 'Absolute' might be read as itself relative to a background contextually supplied standard, and the quantifiers 'any' and 'whatsoever' over restrictions as themselves contextually restricted. One can find oneself saying 'By "everything" I mean *everything*' with the same desperate intensity with which one may say 'By "identical" I mean *identical*'. How deep does the similarity of the interpretative challenges go?

Let us start with the question of unique characterization. Here are standard rules for a (first-order) universal quantifier:[19]

$\forall$-Introduction	Given a deduction of A from some premises, one may deduce $\forall vA(v/t)$ from the same premises, where $A(v/t)$ is the result of replacing all occurences of the individual constant t in the formula A by the individual variable v, provided that no such occurence of v is bound in $A(v/t)$ and that t occurs in none of the premises.
$\forall$-Elimination	From $\forall vA$ one may deduce $A(t/v)$, where $A(t/v)$ is the result of replacing all free occurences of the individual variable v in the formula A by the individual constant t.

Consider a universal quantifier $\forall$ in a language L governed by those rules, and another universal quantifier $\forall^*$ in a language L* governed by exactly parallel rules, $\forall^*$-Introduction and $\forall^*$-Elimination. Suppose that the commitment of speakers of L and L* to their principles is open-ended in the way discussed above for the case of the identity rules. Merge L and L* into a single language L+L*, whose primitive vocabulary is the union of the primitive vocabularies of L and L*. Let A be a formula

[19] For simplicity, functional terms are ignored. To qualify a variable or constant as 'individual' is just to say that it occupies singular term position.

of L+L* in which the individual constant t does not occur and no variable except v occurs free. We reason in L+L*. From $\forall vA$ we can deduce $A(t/v)$ by ∀-Elimination. Therefore, since t does not occur in the premise and A is the result of replacing all occurences of t in $A(t/v)$ by v, and no such occurrence of v thereby becomes bound in A, from $\forall vA$ we can deduce $\forall^* vA$ by ∀*-Introduction. Conversely, from $\forall^* vA$ we can deduce $A(t/v)$ by ∀*-Elimination, and therefore $\forall vA$ by ∀-Introduction. Thus, given the pooled commitments of speakers of L and L*, the two quantifiers are logically equivalent.[20]

The result should not be interpreted as concerning only the reference of ∀ and ∀* in a new context created by the fusion of L and L*. For the open-ended commitments in play were incurred by S and S* in using ∀ and ∀* in the original contexts for L and L* respectively; that is the nature of open-endedness. Thus the result concerns the reference of ∀ and ∀* in the original contexts for L and L* too.

Observe that the argument for unique characterization did not proceed by semantic analysis of the quantifier. It did not invoke the idea of unrestricted generality. In particular, the argument was not that only an unrestricted interpretation of ∀ validates ∀-Introduction and ∀-Elimination. Rather, it was a syntactic argument for interderivability. Thus it is not circular to use the unique characterization result to support the claim that we have an idea of unrestricted generality.

Nevertheless, it is tempting to suspect the argument for unique characterization of sophistry. For ∀-Introduction and ∀-Elimination are standard rules for a universal quantifier in standard first-order logic, for which the standard model theory interprets the quantifier as restricted to the domain of a model. It may therefore look as though the argument must prove too much, since ∀-Introduction and ∀-Elimination are valid if ∀ is interpreted over a domain D, while ∀*-Introduction and ∀*-Elimination are valid even if ∀* is interpreted over a distinct domain D*.

In that form, the objection is unthreatening, for it neglects the stipulation that the commitment of speakers of L and of L* to the respective quantifier rules is open-ended in the sense explained in Section 13.1. If ∀ is restricted to a domain D, then speakers of L do not have an open-ended commitment to ∀-Elimination, even if the latter has no counter-instance in L, since it has the potential for a counter-instance with a new term t that denotes something outside D in a language such as L+L*. In the setting of L+L*, ∀-Elimination would require an extra premise involving t to the effect, concerning what t denotes, that it belongs to D. Then t would occur in one of the premises from which $A(t/v)$ was deduced, so the condition for the application of ∀*-Introduction would not be met. Of course, if ∀* were restricted too, to a domain D*, then one might modify ∀*-Introduction accordingly, by allowing t to occur in one extra premise of the envisaged deduction of A to the effect, concerning what t denotes, that it belongs to D*. With no guarantee that D includes D*, however, the deduction of $\forall^* vA$ from $\forall vA$ could not be carried through. The converse deduction faces an exactly analogous problem. It may sometimes be hard to know whether a given speaker's commitment is open-ended, but the considerations

20 See McGee (2000) and Rayo (2003) for related discussion. For opposed views see Dummett (1981) and Glanzberg (2004).

of Section 13.1 indicated that open-ended commitment to a rule is a genuine, recognizable phenomenon, and no reason has emerged to view the quantifier rules as exceptional in that respect. Indeed, as before, open-ended commitment may be the default sort of commitment to ∀-Introduction and ∀-Elimination; it would be implausible to suggest that all speakers are always doing something special to override the default.

The pertinent objection is not to the argument for unique characterization from the open-ended understanding of the quantifier rules. Rather, it is to the open-ended understanding of the quantifier rules itself. More precisely: it is not straightforward that the open-ended versions ∀-Introduction and ∀-Elimination are really valid on the unrestricted reading of the quantifier.

Let us take ∀-Elimination first. Free logicians will object to it that, even if ∀ is supposed to be unrestricted, the rule is too strong because the individual constant t may be an empty name. For example, ∀-Elimination enables us to derive from the logically true premise $\forall y \exists x\, x = y$ the conclusion $\exists x\, x = t$, which is false on the unrestricted reading of the quantifier if t denotes nothing whatsoever.

One response to that objection to ∀-Elimination is that the only role of t in the unique characterization argument is as an arbitrary name, which functions like a free variable. The success of any empirical or conceptual process of reference-fixing for t is irrelevant to the argument. Thus, if one shares the free logicians' qualms, one can replace 'individual constant' by 'arbitrary name' or 'free variable' throughout ∀-Introduction and ∀-Elimination, and envisage t as denoting merely relative to an assignment.

A less concessive response can also be made. In assessing validity, our concern is with truth-preservation only when the relevant formulas are fully interpreted. For a sentence to be fully interpreted, it is not enough that it is a meaningful formula of the language; it must also express a proposition as used in the relevant context. For example, although 'This is that' is a meaningful sentence of English, it fails to express a proposition in a context in which no reference has been assigned to the demonstratives 'this' and 'that'. It would be foolish to object to the usual introduction rule for disjunction (deduce a disjunction from any of its disjuncts) that it takes one from the true premise '$2 + 2 = 4$' to the conclusion '$2 + 2 = 4$ or this is that', which is not true when no reference has been assigned to 'this' and 'that' because it expresses no proposition (plausibly, a disjunction expresses a proposition only if each of its disjuncts does). Truth-preservation is required only once any singular terms in the argument have been assigned a reference. Consequently, the free-logical objection to ∀-Elimination fails. Let us adopt this conception of validity and therefore leave ∀-Elimination unmodified.

'Inclusive' logicians object to ∀-Elimination because it does not allow for the empty domain: given axiom (1) for identity, one can prove $\exists x\, x = x$ (as an abbreviation of $\sim\forall x \sim x = x$), which is false in that domain.[21] But once the language contains unbound singular terms, as ours does, then it cannot be fully interpreted in the sense just sketched over the empty domain. For such languages, our notion of validity

[21] Logic for the empty domain is somewhat trickier than the remark in the text indicates; see Williamson (1999b).

excludes the empty domain. More controversially, one can argue that $\exists x\, x = x$ is a logical truth on the unrestricted interpretation of the quantifiers, by appeal to Tarski's model-theoretic account of logical truth: it is true on all models (interpretations) that preserve the intended interpretations of the logical constants in it, for it is true and it contains no nonlogical constituents.[22] Since Tarski (1936) understood a model as an assignment of reference to the nonlogical atoms of the language (more exactly, as an assignment of values to variables, which replace those atoms), his treatment of interpretation is consistent with the notion above of a fully interpreted formula. The relevance of Tarski's conception of logical truth and logical consequence to the logic of unrestricted quantification will be discussed more fully below.

Given an appropriate notion of validity, open-ended ∀-Elimination is valid on the unrestricted reading of the quantifier. What of ∀-Introduction? The obvious worry is this. Suppose that ∀ is unrestricted while ∀* is restricted to a domain D*, and that the term t is constrained by a 'meaning postulate' to be in D*. Thus from $\forall^* x\, x \in D^*$ alone we can infer $t \in D^*$ by the restricted elimination rule for ∀*; since t does not occur in the premise, ∀-Introduction therefore permits us to infer $\forall x\, x \in D^*$, which is false because D* does not contain absolutely everything, from the true $\forall^* x\, x \in D^*$. What has gone wrong here is that $t \in D^*$ was not *freely* deduced from $\forall^* x\, x \in D^*$, in a sense of 'free' that has nothing to do with free logic. The deduction was unfree in the sense that it invoked special rules that required t to satisfy constraints beyond simply being a singular term that occurs in none of the premises. That is still a syntactic feature of the deduction. Let us therefore read 'deduction' in ∀-Introduction as 'free deduction', and 'deduced' in both ∀-Introduction and ∀-Elimination as 'freely deduced'. With that understanding, both ∀-Introduction and ∀-Elimination are valid on the unrestricted reading of the quantifier.

Given that the two rules are materially valid on the unrestricted reading, someone might still worry that they are not strictly logically valid, because the unrestricted reading of the quantifier is not part of its logic. The discussion so far has been framed in terms of the background assumption that the unrestricted universal quantifier as such should be classified as a logical constant, subject to rules of inference that exploit its unrestrictedness. For those who admit the coherence of unrestricted quantification, the salient alternative is to have as a logical constant a universal quantifier such that, for any things whatsoever, for purposes of defining logical truth and logical consequence the quantifier can be interpreted as ranging over those things and nothing else (interpretations here play the role of models). It does not matter whether there are too many of those things to form a set or set-like domain. The quantifier can be legitimately interpreted as ranging over all things whatsoever, or over all sets whatsoever, but it can also be legitimately interpreted as ranging over just the books on my shelves. A conclusion is a logical consequence of some premises only if, however they are legitimately interpreted, the conclusion is true if the premises are.[23] On this view,

[22] See Williamson (1999a) and Rayo and Williamson (2003) for this approach to the logic of unrestricted quantification. For reasons explained in the latter, the first-order quantification over interpretations in the text is a loose rendering of the higher-order quantification that is needed for an accurate metalogic of unrestricted quantification.

[23] Cartwright (1994) takes this view.

open-ended $\forall$-Elimination is invalid, since in a language such as L+L* with different sorts of quantifier a term *t* may denote something in the domain of one of those other quantifiers that is not in the domain of $\forall$ on some unintended interpretation. Let the *constant account* be that on which the quantifier is mandatorily interpreted as unrestricted and the *variable account* be that on which, for any things, it can legitimately be interpreted as ranging over just those things. Both accounts are framed within a broadly Tarskian approach to the concept of logical consequence.

The difference between the two accounts has dramatic implications for first-order logic. Let $\exists n$ be the usual first-order formalization of the claim that there are at least *n* things, where $n > 1$. On the variable account, $\exists n$ is not a logical truth, because the quantifier can legitimately be interpreted as ranging over fewer than *n* things. On the constant account, $\exists n$ is a logical truth, because the quantifier must be interpreted as ranging over absolutely everything and there are in fact at least *n* things: for example, at least *n* symbols occur in $\exists n$ itself. The sentences $\exists n$ for all natural numbers *n* turn out to exhaust the extra logical consequences generated by the constant account, in the sense that the result of adding them as extra axioms to first-order logic can be proved complete as well as sound on the constant account.[24] By contrast, the variable account is logically conservative: it delivers exactly the same logical consequence relation for first-order logic as does the standard model theory with set domains.[25]

The difference between the two accounts is robust. Even if we relativize interpretations to various parameters for the context of utterance or circumstance of evaluation, the sentences $\exists n$ still all come out as logical truths on the constant account, because the unrestricted reading of the quantifier forbids us to interpret it as ranging only over a domain associated with the context of utterance or circumstance. Someone

[24] See Friedman (1999), Williamson (1999a) and Rayo and Williamson (2003) . The result depends on a global choice assumption; Friedman discusses non-theorems of this logic that are logically true on some anti-choice assumptions. As an alternative to axioms of the form $\exists n$, the proponent of the constant account can use the following structural *Rule of Atomic Freedom*. Let $\Gamma\cup\{\gamma\}$ be a set of sentences, and $\Delta\cup\{\delta\}$ ($\delta \notin \Delta$) a set of atomic sentences each consisting of a non-logical predicate that does not occur in Γ and individual non-logical constants that do not occur in Γ such that $\Gamma, \Delta \vdash \delta$; then $\Gamma \vdash \gamma$ (Γ is inconsistent; it entails everything). To see why this rule preserves validity on the constant account, suppose that all members of Γ are true on some interpretation. Then all members of $\Gamma \cup \Delta\cup\{\sim \delta\}$ are also true on some interpretation, for we can stipulate that each constant in $\Delta\cup\{\sim \delta\}$ denotes itself and that the extension of each *n*-place predicate in $\Delta\cup\{\sim \delta\}$ is the set of *n*-tuples of singular terms with which it is concatenated in Δ; thus every member of Δ is true, and δ is false because $\delta \notin \Delta$ (a simplified Henkin construction, which does not itself assume the existence of infinitely many things). Since the vocabulary of Γ is disjoint from that of $\Delta\cup\{\sim \delta\}$, it can be interpreted as originally; thus every member of Γ is true on the new interpretation too (this part of the argument would not work on the variable account, since there may be more constants in $\Delta\cup\{\sim \delta\}$ than things quantified over on the original interpretation). By contraposition, Atomic Freedom preserves validity. To see how to use Atomic Freedom to derive all sentences of the form $\exists n$, it suffices to look at the case $n = 3$. Let *R* be a triadic predicate, *a*, *b* and *c* distinct constants, $\Gamma = \{\sim \exists 3\}$, $\Delta = \{Raac, Raba, Rabb\}$ and $\delta = Rabc$. By ordinary first-order reasoning, $\sim \exists 3, Raac, Raba, Rabb \vdash Rabc$ (unless there are at least three things, the three constants cannot all have distinct denotations); therefore, by Atomic Freedom, $\sim \exists 3 \vdash \bot$, so $\vdash \exists 3$. Note that the rule of Atomic Freedom is formulated without reference to any particular logical constant (contrast axioms of the form $\exists n$). Another way to think of the constant account is therefore as freeing up the interpretation of atomic formulas.

[25] See Cartwright (1994); the argument goes back to Kreisel (1967).

might reply that if the domain contains everything that exists in the relevant possible world then the restriction is merely apparent, because in that world there is nothing else to quantify over. But that objection in effect treats the semantic clause for ∀ as though it were a misleading approximate translation of a more fundamental semantic clause in which an unrestricted universal quantifier of a more fundamental modal meta-language occurs within the scope of a modal operator. But the Tarskian framework for the theory of logical consequence is not a modal one. It defines logical consequence without using modal operators, interpreted metaphysically or epistemically. The non-modal meta-language should therefore be taken at face value: a semantic clause according to which ∀ ranges only over the domain of some world is inconsistent with the unrestricted reading, just as it appears to be. Indeed, it is part of Tarski's great achievement to have cleanly separated the concept of logical consequence from metaphysical and epistemic clutter. Not that there is anything wrong with metaphysical and epistemic modalities in their place: but it is methodologically wrong-headed to mix them up with the simple but powerful non-modal concept of logical consequence that Tarski painstakingly isolated, which compels and rewards investigation in its own right. This chapter works within the Tarskian paradigm.

The dispute between the variable and constant accounts raises deep questions about the metaphysical and epistemological status of logic that we cannot hope to answer here. But the analogy with identity does help us to see what is wrong with one argument against the constant account. It is sometimes urged that the variable account is preferable because it has greater generality, since every legitimate interpretation on the constant account is also legitimate on the variable account (for it allows us to interpret the quantifier as ranging over absolutely everything), but not *vice versa*. However, there is an analogous argument against first-order logic with identity, according to which first-order logic without identity is preferable because it has greater generality, since every legitimate interpretation in first-order logic with identity is also legitimate in first-order logic without identity (for it allows us to interpret a dyadic predicate by identity), but not *vice versa*. The latter argument clearly fails, because the point of making identity a logical constant is to capture its distinctive logic by excluding unintended interpretations. No significant generality is thereby lost, because all the other interpretations can be shifted to other dyadic predicates. The former argument against the constant account fails similarly, because the point of making the unrestricted universal quantifier a logical constant is to capture its distinctive logic by excluding unintended interpretations. No significant generality is thereby lost, because all the other interpretations can be captured by complex restricted quantifiers consisting of the simple unrestricted quantifier and a restricting predicate.

Of course, we have some sense of which expressions deserve to be treated as logical constants: very roughly, those whose meaning is 'purely structural'.[26] By that standard, the unrestricted universal quantifier is at least as good a candidate as identity is. Moreover, like identity, the unrestricted quantifier has the kind of stark simplicity in

[26] Tarski (1986) proposes the more precise criterion of invariance under all permutations of individuals in this spirit.

meaning that we seek in a logical constant that is to be treated as basic (some purely structural meanings are very complicated). Although unrestricted quantification is less central to mathematical reasoning than identity is, it does enable us to capture the generality that principles of a set theory with ur-elements (non-sets) such as ZFU need if mathematics is to have its full range of applications: for absolutely *any* objects x and y, there is a set of which x and y are members, for example.

In using absolute identity to support absolute generality, we must be careful to check that the latter does not squash the former. For Geach's arguments against the coherence of absolute identity look superficially more formidable in the context of absolute generality. The previous section considered absolute identity over a set-sized domain; despite Geach's threats, no danger of paradox arises in characterizing it by quantifying over subsets of the domain, or plurally over members of the domain, or the like.[27] But if our first-order quantifiers are absolutely unrestricted, then the interpretation of the corresponding second-order quantifiers is a much trickier business. There is no set domain over whose subsets they could range. Indeed, any attempt to interpret them in terms of values of the second-order variables will generate a version of Russell's paradox, given an adequately strong comprehension principle concerning the existence of such values, since an absolutely unrestricted first-order quantifier must range over them too. But not even considerations of this kind can rescue the charge of incoherence against absolute identity. First, the paradox results from the attempt to interpret the second-order quantifiers of the object-language in a first-order meta-language, by first-order quantification over sets. If one interprets the second-order quantifiers more faithfully, in a second-order meta-language, by second-order quantification read plurally or in some other non-first-order way, then no paradox results. Second, even if one interprets the second-order quantifiers as ranging over 'small' sets, with an appropriately qualified comprehension principle, that suffices for characterizing identity, although not for all other purposes. Third, if absolute identity is coherent for each set-sized domain, then it is simply coherent: for any objects o and o^*, absolute identity is coherent over the set-sized domain $\{o, o^*\}$ by hypothesis, which is all that we need coherently to ask whether o and o^* are absolutely identical.

If there is a threat of paradox, it comes from the idea of absolute generality, not from that of absolute identity. A 'paradox' here is a proof of an explicit contradiction from premises to which generality absolutists are committed by rules of inference to which they are also committed, something like the Russell or Burali–Forti paradox. The greatest strength of generality relativism is the suspicion that generality absolutism is ultimately inconsistent because it leads to such a paradox.

Generality relativists also tend to use a second sort of argument: that generality absolutism is inarticulate, in the sense that whatever utterances generality absolutists assent to or dissent from in trying to articulate their position, on some generality relativist interpretations all the assents were to truths and all the dissents from falsehoods

[27] For the plural interpretation see several of the essays in Boolos (1998) (and 48–9 and 54 for brief remarks on the logic of identity). Williamson (2003a) argues in favor of an interpretation that takes more seriously the idea of quantification into predicate position.

(according to the generality relativist). In that sense, absolutism about identity is also inarticulate: whatever utterances identity absolutists assent to or dissent from in trying to articulate their position, on some identity relativist interpretations all the assents were to truths and all the dissents from falsehoods (according to the identity relativist). It does not follow that absolute identity is inexpressible, for all those interpretations were incorrect: as explained in Section 13.1, they misidentified our dispositions to make inferences using the identity predicate. Similarly, if generality absolutism is inarticulate, it does not follow that absolute generality is inexpressible, for the generality absolutist can argue that all the generality relativist interpretations were incorrect, because they misidentified our dispositions to make inferences using the universal quantifier. The generality absolutist may endorse a reflection principle to the effect that any quantified sentence true on the intended unrestricted interpretation of the quantifier is also true on some unintended restricted interpretation of the quantifier. Nevertheless, such a result does make the generality absolutism and its negation somewhat elusive for purposes of theoretical dispute.

It may be less widely appreciated than it should be that the generality relativist cannot combine the two objections to generality absolutism, by charging that it is *both* inconsistent *and* inarticulate. For suppose that generality absolutism is both inconsistent and inarticulate. Since it is inconsistent, there is a proof of an explicit contradiction from premises to which generality absolutists are committed by rules of inference to which they are committed. By hypothesis, generality absolutism is also inarticulate, so on some generality relativist interpretation the premises of the proof are true (according to the generality relativist) and the rules of inference are truth-preserving (according to the generality relativist). Thus the generality relativist is committed to the truth of the conclusion of the proof on the generality relativist interpretation. But the conclusion is a contradiction, and so is not true even on that interpretation (according to the generality relativism). Thus generality relativism is inconsistent. To sum up: if generality absolutism is inarticulate, then it is inconsistent only if generality relativism is also inconsistent. Therefore, the generality relativist is ill-advised to accuse generality absolutism of being both inconsistent and inarticulate. In effect, the assumption that generality absolutism is inarticulate yields a consistency proof for generality absolutism relative to generality relativism.

Perhaps we can generalize the result. Given any argument against generality absolutism, why can't it be reinterpreted as an argument against something that the generality relativist accepts, if generality absolutism really is inarticulate?

Generality relativists seem to be faced with a choice. They can drop the charge of inarticulacy, try to explain why it seemed compelling, and then, treating generality absolutism as an articulated theory, try to prove a contradiction in it. If they succeed in that, they win (dialetheism is a fate worse than death). But if they cannot produce such a proof, then they had better drop the charge of inconsistency: put up or shut up. Alternatively, they can drop the charge of inconsistency right away, and press the charge of inarticulacy. But that charge is hardly damaging to absolutism about generality, for it applies equally to absolutism about identity.

REFERENCES

Bird, A. (1998) 'Dispositions and Antidotes', *Philosophical Quarterly* 48: 227–34.

Boolos, G. (1998) *Logic, Logic, and Logic*. Cambridge, MA: Harvard University Press.

Cartwright, R. (1994) 'Speaking of Everything', *Noûs* 28: 1–20.

Dummett, M.A.E. (1981) *Frege: Philosophy of Language*, 2nd edn. London: Duckworth.

——(1993) 'Does Quantification Involve Identity?', in Dummett, *The Seas of Language*. Oxford: Clarendon Press.

Friedman, H. (1999) 'A Complete Theory of Everything: Validity in the Universal Domain', www.math.ohio-state.edu/~friedman/.

Geach, P.T. (1967) 'Identity', *Review of Metaphysics* 21: 3–12.

——(1972) *Logic Matters*. Oxford: Blackwell.

——(1980) *Reference and Generality*, 3rd edn. Ithaca, NY: Cornell University Press.

——(1991) 'Replies', in H.A. Lewis (ed.), *Peter Geach: Philosophical Encounters*. Dordrecht: Kluwer.

Glanzberg, M. (2004) 'Quantification and Realism', *Philosophy and Phenomenological Research* 69: 541–72.

Harris, J. H. (1982) 'What's so Logical about the "Logical" Axioms?', *Studia Logica* 41: 159–71.

Hawthorne, J. (2003) 'Identity', in M. Loux and D. Zimmerman (eds.), *The Oxford Handbook of Metaphysics*. Oxford: Oxford University Press.

Henkin, L. (1950) 'Completeness in the Theory of Types', *Journal of Symbolic Logic* 15: 81–91.

Kaplan, D. (1989) 'Demonstratives: An Essay on the Semantics, Logic, Metaphysics and Epistemology of Demonstratives and other Indexicals', in J. Almog, J. Perry and H. Wettstein (eds.), *Themes from Kaplan*. Oxford: Oxford University Press.

Kreisel, G. (1967) 'Informal Rigour and Completeness Proofs', in I. Lakatos (ed.), *Problems in the Philosophy of Mathematics*. Amsterdam: North-Holland.

Kripke, S. (1982) *Wittgenstein on Rules and Private Language*. Oxford: Blackwell.

Lewis, D. (1983) 'New Work for a Theory of Universals', *The Australasian Journal of Philosophy* 61: 343–77.

——(1997) 'Finkish Dispositions', *Philosophical Quarterly* 47: 143–58.

Martin, C.B. (1994) 'Dispositions and Conditionals', *Philosophical Quarterly* 44: 1–8.

——and Heil, J. (1998) 'Rules and Powers', *Philosophical Perspectives* 12: 283–312.

McGee, V. (2000) '"Everything"', in G. Sher and R. Tieszen (eds.), *Between Logic and Intuition*. Cambridge: Cambridge University Press.

Mumford, S. (1998) *Dispositions*. Oxford: Oxford University Press.

Noonan, H. (1997) 'Relative Identity', in R. Hale and C. Wright (eds.), *A Companion to the Philosophy of Language*. Oxford: Blackwell.

Peacocke, C. (1976) 'What is a Logical Constant?', *Journal of Philosophy* 73: 221–40.

Quine, W.V. (1960) *Word and Object*. Cambridge, MA: MIT.

——(1961) 'Reply to Professor Marcus' 'Modalities and Intensional Languages', *Synthese* 13: 323–30.

——(1966) *The Ways of Paradox and Other Essays*. New York: Random House.

——(1976) 'Grades of Discriminability', *Journal of Philosophy* 73: 113–16.

Rayo, A. (2003) 'When does "Everything" mean *Everything*?', *Analysis* 63: 100–6.

——and Williamson, T. (2003) 'A Completeness Theorem for Unrestricted First-Order Languages', in J. C. Beall (ed.), *Liars and Heaps*. Oxford: Clarendon Press.

Shapiro, S. (1991) *Foundations without Foundationalism: A Case for Second-Order Logic.* Oxford: Clarendon Press.

Tarski, A. (1936) 'O pojciu wynikania logicznego', *Przegląd Filozoficzny* 39: 58–68. English trans. by J. H. Woodger, 'On the concept of logical consequence', in Tarski, *Logic, Semantics, Metamathematics*, Indianapolis: Hackett, 2nd edn. 1983.

____ (1986) 'What are Logical Notions?', *History and Philosophy of Logic* 7: 143–54.

Wallace, J. (1964) *Philosophical Grammar.* Stanford University Ph.D. Published by University Microfilms Ltd, Ann Arbor, Michigan, 1969.

Wiggins, D. (2001) *Sameness and Substance Renewed.* Cambridge: Cambridge University Press.

Williamson, T. (1987/88) 'Equivocation and Existence', *Proceedings of the Aristotelian Society* 87: 109–27.

____ (1999a) 'Existence and Contingency', *Proceedings of the Aristotelian Society*, supp. vol. 73: 181–203; reprinted with printer's errors corrected, 100: 321–43.

____ (1999b) 'A Note on Truth, Satisfaction and the Empty Domain', *Analysis* 59: 3–8.

____ (2003a) 'Everything', *Philosophical Perspectives* 17: 415–65.

____ (2003b) 'Understanding and Inference', *Aristotelian Society* supp. vol. 77: 249–93.

Index